38.95
T
4/88

CAREER DEVELOPMENT FOR ENGINEERS AND SCIENTISTS

Organizational Programs and Individual Choices

ROBERT F. MORRISON, Ph.D.
RICHARD M. VOSBURGH, Ph.D.

Van Nostrand Reinhold Series in Managerial Skills in Engineering and Science

VNR VAN NOSTRAND REINHOLD COMPANY
——— New York

Copyright © 1987 by Robert F. Morrison and Richard M. Vosburgh
Library of Congress Catalog Card Number 86-32543
ISBN 0-442-26351-1

All rights reserved. No part of this work covered by the copyright
hereon may be reproduced or used in any form or by any means—
graphic, electronic, or mechanical, including photocopying,
recording, taping, or information storage and retrieval systems—
without written permission of the publisher.

Printed in the United States of America

Designed by Beth Tondreau

Van Nostrand Reinhold Company Inc.
115 Fifth Avenue
New York, New York 10003

Van Nostrand Reinhold Company Limited
Molly Millars Lane
Wokingham, Berkshire RG11 2PY, England

Van Nostrand Reinhold
480 La Trobe Street
Melbourne, Victoria 3000, Australia

Macmillan of Canada
Division of Canada Publishing Corporation
164 Commander Boulevard
Agincourt, Ontario M1S 3C7, Canada

16 15 14 13 12 11 10 9 8 7 6 5 4 3 2 1

Library of Congress Cataloging-in-Publication Data

Morrison, Robert F.
  Career development for engineers and scientists.

  Bibliography: p.
  Includes index.
  1. Engineering—Vocational guidance. 2. Science—
Vocational guidance. I. Vosburgh, Richard M.
II. Title.
TA157.M623 1987   502'.3   86-32543
ISBN 0-442-26351-1

To three men who have made lasting contributions to the field of industrial/organizational psychology and to our own lives—Williams A. Owens, Ben J. Winer, and Herbert H. Meyer—and to two wonderful people who are our constant companions—Anne and Kay.

Van Nostrand Reinhold Series in Managerial Skills in Engineering and Science

M. K. Badawy, Series Editor
Virginia Polytechnic Institute and State University

Developing Managerial Skills in Engineers and Scientists: Succeeding as a Technical Manager by M. K. Badawy

Modern Management Techniques in Engineering and R&D by J. Balderston, P. Birnbaum, R. Goodman, and M. Stahl

Improving Office Operations: A Primer for Professionals by Jack Balderston

Managing the Engineering Design Function by Raymond J. Bronikowski

Applied Finance and Economic Analysis for Scientists and Engineers by James R. Couper and William H. Rader

Career Development for Engineers and Scientists: Organizational Programs and Individual Choices by Robert F. Morrison and Richard M. Vosburgh

Series Introduction

Career Development for Engineers and Scientists is the sixth volume in the Van Nostrand Reinhold Series in Managerial Skills in Engineering and Science. The series will embody concise and practical treatments of specific topics within the broad area of engineering and R&D management. The primary aim of the series is to provide a set of principles, concepts, tools, and practical techniques for those wishing to enhance their managerial skills and potential.

The series will provide both practitioners and students with the information they must know and the skills they must acquire in order to sharpen their managerial performance and advance their careers. Authors contributing to the series are carefully selected for their experience and expertise. While series books will vary in subject matter as well as approach, one major feature will be common to all volumes: a blend of practical applications and hands-on techniques supported by sound research and relevant theory.

The target audience for the series includes engineers and scientists making the transition to management, technical managers and supervisors, upper-level executives and directors of engineering and R&D, corporate technical development managers and executives, continuing management education specialists, and students in technical management programs and related fields.

We hope that this dynamic series will help readers to become better managers and to lead most rewarding professional careers.

M. K. BADAWY
Series Editor

Preface

Career Development for Engineers and Scientists: Organizational Programs and Individual Choices is addressed to all levels of professionals, their managers, and their supporting staff who wish to become better at managing their careers. It is a book that views the careers of professionals from the perspectives of both the organization and the individual. Individual professionals, from the student facing graduation to the senior person looking at retirement, are introduced to their career questions and potential solutions. Organizations, from the small consulting firm to very large, complex ones, are provided with a systematic approach to career management. This book provides a means to place the two different viewpoints and sets of requirements into an integrated context.

The book seeks to provide practical applications that both the organization and its members can use. These program examples are placed within a systems model. Research and practice are referenced to allow the reader to determine how far the state of the art has progressed for each program and how effective that program might be in resolving a specific problem. To aid the practitioner, implementation problems are identified and solutions presented. Our aim is to provide: practical guidance and examples for managers of professionals and their human resource staff to use in the evaluation of current career development programs and the design of new ones, and, with further references, for professionals to use in the resolution of their own career questions; a professional-school text for courses on the career development of professionals; and a state-of-the-art reference that can serve as a point of departure for research and innovation within the field of career development.

Why use such a complex approach? Most available books on career development cover either the organization's career management programs or career planning for individuals. Our premise is that the two components need to be integrated so that they can build upon each other. Career development requires both points of view. Career management cannot work unless individuals actively participate in a knowledgeable, congruent way via their career decision making and activities. Career planning becomes very difficult without the support of the organization because of the dearth of information about career opportunities and the absence of developmental opportunities and any rewards for participation.

Unlike any other source book, *Career Development for Engineers and Scientists* blends application, research, and theory. Most of the chapters describe state-of-the-art career management or career-planning programs that are in current use. However, many of these programs, designed without using research or theory about adult careers, are in fact huge, uncontrolled "experiments" or pilot programs. While they may be the best that are available today, they may not be nearly as effective as they should be. Therefore, we have attempted to point out appropriate theories, available research, and voids in our knowledge that need to be filled. The field of research in adult career development is embryonic. Very little is available regarding the career management portion of the puzzle and the unique problems of professionals.

The third factor that makes this book different from others is its concentration on professionals who are ready to leave or have left the academic environment. Most texts in career development are really about the development of the organization's managers or students' decisions on career choices. This book helps professionals who are approaching the end of their long academic training look at their career development over the rest of their working lives.

The book is organized into an introduction and three complementary parts. The introduction (chapter 1) provides a careful description of a profession and the characteristics of professionals. A contrast between professionals and nonprofessionals is made. Career development and each of its components, career management and career planning, are defined.

The development and practice of an organization's career management system is covered in part 1. The components of a career management system, contributing human resource systems, and supporting programs are presented in chapter 2, along with many organizational practices. Programs that bring professionals into an organization and move them through it are discussed in chapter 3. An organizational human resource review process (chapter 4) and techniques for managing professionals from their point of entry until their departure are provided (chapter 5), including the continuous development of professional knowledge and skills (chapter 6). Issues surrounding the implementation of career management programs are then reviewed (chapter 7).

Part 2 addresses individual career decision making and planning as it pertains to the practicing professional. An overview (chapter 8) is followed by a description of steps to be taken when deciding about an organization, type of job, or a move from professional to manager (chapter 9). Next, the process of personal development is presented, along with what needs to be done when the professional leaves the organization or job (chapter 10). In chapter 11, specific programs that a professional can use are introduced.

The state of the art of career development is covered in part 3 (chapter 12). The strengths, weaknesses, and voids in present practices and research are outlined.

Writing this book has been a long, tortuous process. Our deepest appreciation goes to Anne Morrison and Kay Vosburgh for their understanding throughout the many years it has taken to complete *Career Development for Engineers and Scientists*. Many colleagues, too numerous to mention without slighting someone, have contributed insights, anecdotes, and practices that have been incorporated. Many of these instances have been unconsciously included as they became part and parcel of our own thinking. A special note of thanks goes to Victoria Feldmann for her careful typing and frequent corrections of much of the manuscript.

As this book's writing drew to a close, so did a chapter in the life of one author. This book must also be dedicated to the memory of Richard's father, Stephen E. Vosburgh, Sr., who unselfishly gave of himself to make life better for his family.

We hope that this volume will prove to be a rich source of questions, ideas, information, and activities for all who read it. While we cannot provide pat answers to specific problems, we have tried to present a blend of theory, research, questions, and examples that can guide each professional to a personal solution. This book can serve as a ready reference while learning about career development, designing a career management system or program, resolving career questions, or even developing a program of career research.

R. F. MORRISON

R. M. VOSBURGH

Contents

Preface	ix

Chapter 1. An Introduction to Professional and Career Development — 1
- What Is a Professional? — 2
- What Is Career Management and Development? — 6
- Organization of the Book — 7
- Summary — 7
- References — 8

PART 1. ORGANIZATIONAL PROGRAMS: WHAT THE ORGANIZATION CAN DO — 11

Chapter 2. Career Management Systems — 13
- General Systems Model — 13
- Career Management System Model — 13
- Contributing Systems — 16
- Supporting Programs — 18
- Career Management Practices — 21
- Summary — 28
- References — 28

Chapter 3. Entering and Moving in the Organization — 31
- Recruiting and Orientation Systems — 31
- Organizational Information Requirements — 38
- Internal Selection and Placement Systems — 40
- Case Study — 47
- Assessment Systems — 51
- Summary — 64
- References — 68

Chapter 4. Human Resource Review Systems — 67
- The Case for Review Systems — 68
- The Organizational Review of Human Resources — 69
- The Business-Plan-based Review — 74
- The Tactical Work-Group Review — 83
- Alternative Review System Components — 87
- Summary — 93
- References — 94

Chapter 5. Career Assessment: Processes and Outputs — 95
- Performance Assessment and Feedback Systems — 95
- Career Management Programs — 99
- Career Paths and Patterns — 114
- Outplacement — 116
- Retirement — 118
- Summary — 119
- References — 119

Chapter 6. Professional Development on the Job — 123
- Learning from the Job Itself — 123
- Job Design — 126
- Avoiding Obsolescence — 129
- Training and Education Systems — 130
- Individual Development Planning — 135
- Summary — 138
- References — 138

Chapter 7. Career Program Implementation Issues — 141
- Implementing a Career Management System — 141
- Implementing a Human Resource Review — 146
- Barriers to Implementation — 149
- Gateways for Implementation — 155
- Policy Implications — 159
- Summary — 163
- References — 163

PART 2. INDIVIDUAL CHOICES: WHAT YOU CAN DO — 165

Chapter 8. The Individual's Career Transitions — 167
- Major Career Decisions of a Professional — 168
- Making Career Decisions — 169
- The Reasons Why You Make Decisions the Way That You Do — 171
- Does Development Mean Change throughout Life? — 177

Social Learning Theory of Career Decision
   Making   181
Summary   184
References   185

Chapter 9. Establishing a Career   187
Choosing the Organization   187
Choosing the Job   191
The Job Search   194
Moving into Management   202
Summary   206
References   206

Chapter 10. Individual Career Processes and Outputs   209
Learning about the Organization   209
Leaving the Function or the Organization   212
Changing Professional Areas   213
Avoiding Obsolescence   213
Losing Your Job   215
Planning for Retirement   219
Summary   220
References   220

Chapter 11. Programs the Individual Can Implement   223
Individual Career Planning   223
Career Management by Objectives (MBO)   224
A Paired-Comparison Approach
   to Establishing Priorities   226
Life Planning   227
Supervisory Skills Training   228
Handling the Career-Planning Discussion   232
Workshop/Career-Counseling Approaches   234
Summary   236
References   236

PART 3. CONCLUSIONS   239

Chapter 12. Delving into the Unknown   241
Career Management: The Organizational
   Perspective   241
Career Planning: The Individual Perspective   248
Career Development: The Integration
   of Management and Planning   254
Special Issues in Career Research   255
Summary   256
References   257

Appendix 1. A Comparison of Training Methods   261
Appendix 2. A Career-Planning Workbook   267

Index   289

CAREER DEVELOPMENT FOR ENGINEERS AND SCIENTISTS

Chapter 1

An Introduction to Professional and Career Development

Career management and development has become increasingly interesting to both organizations and their employees. Many books and articles have been published, policies developed, and programs initiated, with most based on current fads, some derived from thoughtful analysis or theory, and a few emanating from thorough research and evaluation. The latter two categories are limited because of the dearth of research on *adult* career development. This field encompasses the growth of an individual over a major portion of life, up to fifty years or more, within many different career situations. Therefore, adequate research becomes time consuming, complex, and expensive, and it demands the patience of sponsors, participants, and the researchers themselves. Final answers to the problems of initiating and conducting adequate career management and development within an organization are not presently available.

This book can be distinguished from others by four characteristics. The first is an attempt to update the reader on the current status of theory, research, and application of the art and science of managing the careers of professional employees.

Second, application will be the primary thrust of the book, with theory and research providing a base for the material. In the emphasis on application, alternate approaches to meeting the requirements of a career management and development program will be provided. The pros and cons of those alternatives will be noted.

A third characteristic of this book will be its emphasis on the professional who is already employed. There will be minimal coverage of recruiting, preemployment selection, and initial assignment. Outplacement as a result of reduction in force (lay-offs), firings, or retirement will also be given limited coverage so that the internal career process can be adequately handled.

The fourth major characteristic of this work will be its concentration on the professional, scientific, and technical employee. As Labor Department statistics demonstrate, "knowledge workers" (professionals) constitute an increasing proportion of the American work force. In 1940, one employee in twenty-two was a college graduate. In 1981, it was one in four. Between 1960 and 1980, the number of white-collar workers employed in the United States increased from 28.5 to 49 million (72 percent) while the blue-collar work force increased only 30 percent (from 24 to 31.2 million). Professional and technical workers led the increase by more than doubling in size with computer specialists, accountants, social scientists, and quality control experts leading the way (13). This growth may not stop as our economy continues its transition from a manufacturing to a service orientation.

The characteristics of a profession and its members are very different from the characteristics of nonprofessionals and the groups with which they associate. For example, the allegiance of professionals to the organization will be much less than their nonprofessional counterparts, and their need for continuous complex, specialized education will be very high. As a result, the career management of professionals from both the organization's and individual's perspectives must be approached differently from typical recruiting, management development, and production employee training programs. If it is not, the danger is that professionals will either not enter the organization, leave very quickly after they do, or cease to function as professionals. Any of these three results will tend to minimize the technical knowledge and skill that are available to the organization to apply to the development of new products, processes, services, and other technical requirements (1,26,36,40).

The organization can use the material in this book to determine if it is willing to accept the idiosyncrasies and career management needs of professionals and, if so, to adopt personnel policies and programs that will attract high-quality professionals to enter, remain, and produce throughout their careers (36). If this is not done, the organization will be cut off from new knowledge and technologies such as changes in tax law, new products, unique computer applications, and the like, and its ability to adapt to changing environmental demands will be limited. To reach its goals, the organization must manage the careers of its professionals (41).

Likewise, individuals must plan their own careers to ensure that their personal aspirations for success are achieved to the greatest possible extent. The material in this book can be used by professionals to help them in making career decisions, planning their careers, and evaluating the organizations in which they are employed. The material presented should help them determine if they should be a manager or a professional, should try to transfer to other parts of their own organization, or make another choice altogether.

Our assumption is that the organization is responsible for providing the interface between its management of the professional work force and individuals' management of their personal careers. Unless this interface is developed, the individual and organizational career systems will be in conflict, resulting in questionable achievement of either organizational or personal goals.

WHAT IS A PROFESSIONAL?

Books on management, organization behavior, and personnel seldom consider the unique case of professionals in organizations. In 1970, only one of many management texts introduced this area of unique concern (27), but later editions of that one de-emphasized the topic by dropping specialized chapters. This may be because of the reduced emphasis on research and development during the 1970s or because the term *professional* is difficult to define. To enhance the status of their occupations, many groups classify themselves as "professional" as soon as they demonstrate any characteristic of a profession. To add to the dilemma, even the traditional professional occupations of medicine and law include many members who do not meet all of the criteria of a professional.

Ideally, the essential characteristics of a profession (10,27,28) are:

1. *Unique Body of Knowledge.* Professions have a sympathetic, unique body of abstract knowledge. Skill is normally acquired from prolonged, specialized training. Preparation involves both intellectual and applied experience.
2. *Expert Power.* Members of a profession have authority derived from a highly superior level of knowledge. This expertise is acknowledged by the professional's clientele, and the authority conferred extends only as far as the boundaries of the professional's specialized field of competence. The acceptance of expertise by the clientele confers autonomy on the part of the professional to make choices concerning both the means by which their work is done and the end products they produce.
3. *Societal Recognition.* Society has sanctioned via laws and regulatory bodies the expert authority and uniqueness of the profession by giving the profession certain powers and privileges. Controlled entry into the profession, maintenance of standards by colleagues, and confidentiality of communications between the professional and client are examples of these.
4. *Ethics.* There is a self-imposed obligation on the part of members of a profession to provide service without regard to self-interest and without becoming emotionally involved with the client.
5. *Identification.* Members of a profession identify with the profession and fellow professionals, thereby increasing their commitment to the work and the profession. Thus, a professional culture results, ignoring geographical and organizational boundaries.

There are few pure examples of professionals, even within a widely recognized profession such as medicine (10). To approach the career management, development, and planning of professionals without constant caveats and repetitive wordy clarification, we will use a comparison between two extremes: the "pure" professional and the "pure" nonprofessional. It should be kept in mind throughout the book that the distribution of people in an organization may be heavily concentrated in the category of part professional and part nonprofessional.

The following example illustrates the problem of comparing professionals and nonprofessionals when the differences are not all black or white. A characteristic that discriminates between the two extreme groups is how closely the individual group members identify with their field of work or occupation in contrast to the employing organization. Most professionallike employees fit into a central category in which the organizational goals and the rewards are valued, but the individuals might leave the organization rather than change their chosen field. In the sciences, fitting into this central category (mixed orientation) is a typical engineer, while research scientists with their extreme commitment to their work serve as an example of the "pure" professional shown in figure 1-1 (25,49). Administrators serve as examples of the nonprofessionals who owe their allegiance to their organizations.

Professionals demonstrate several additional characteristics that make them difficult and costly to manage. These include the following:

1. They may not demonstrate loyalty to the organization or their supervisor. Instead their loyalty may be to their professional colleagues whether they are part of the same organization or not. The turnover of such individuals may be high without

1-1. Professional versus organizational orientation.

Professional orientation	Mixed orientation	Organizational orientation
Values the field of work above all else	Values organizational goals and rewards but would leave if required to change chosen field	Values the organization regardless of the job assignment

Adapted from Hutcheson, P., and Chalofsky, N. 1981. Careers in human resource development. *Training and Development Journal* 35 (7): 12–15.

the presence of continuing professional challenge and some autonomy.
2. Professionals desire to share information with their colleagues—even if they are members of a competing organization. They expect to be provided with the opportunity to exchange such information.
3. In some roles, the professional may invoke ethical standards that seem restrictive to the organization. For example, a company psychologist may not ethically share information about an employee when such information is the result of a privileged counseling relationship.
4. A professional may set a higher standard of excellence than that deemed appropriate by management. Such a conflict in values may be costly.

To add to the problem, these characteristics are even more likely to be exhibited by the most talented and valued of professionals. For example, their competence and expertise is so great that their peers/colleagues from outside the organization in the professional societies and informal groups acknowledge their contributions. These external groups reward them with a level of prestige that cannot be obtained within the organization. Such factors require the organization to be more flexible than it typically desires to be. If it is not willing to put forth the required effort, it will have to purchase professional services from outside.

What Occupational Groups are Professions?

The classic examples of professions are law, medicine, and the clergy. American society has acknowledged them as such by helping them control access to the fields via limiting educational opportunities and administering licensing procedures (15). All three groups have been provided the opportunity to define the boundaries of their professional tasks and to police their members' behavior, including their competence and ethics. Nearly the same status has been provided more recently for certified public accountants (CPAs), dentists, civil engineers, pharmacists, and a few others (27). Nursing, psychology, and other fields have many characteristics of the professions but still must fend off the challenges of other occupational groups for a piece of their territory. Some groups, such as personnel administrators, have set up societies and even self-certification as initial steps to becoming acknowledged ultimately as professions.

Although they will be referred to as such in this book, scientists are a group that have many but not all of the characteristics of a profession. Like other professionals, they do not have clients but tend to serve other scientists. Therefore, they are not required to become licensed to protect a less knowledgeable public from incompetence or unethical behavior (27).

Much of the research about professionals has involved engineers and scientists. Unfortunately, these groups were often combined as though they were homogeneous (28). During the last decade, it has become clear that we must separate the two groups using the same differences that distinguish professionals from nonprofessionals (2,3,4,28).

Characteristics of Professionals

There has been considerable research comparing professionals and scientists to nonprofessionals. Psychologists, sociologists, organization behaviorists, economists, and physical and life scientists have tackled this area from different perspectives but with similar results.

Background. Sociologists concentrate on background differences between professionals and nonprofessionals more than other researchers do. Consistent with the definition of a professional, they are more highly educated than nonprofessionals. Their income increases in concert with increased education at the same rate as it does for nonprofessionals (managers). However, although socioeconomic status, organizational tenure, and the presence of a wife who is not employed outside the home predict the level of income for managers, they do not for professionals (43).

Personality Characteristics. As individuals become less and less professional, they become more interpersonally oriented in contrast to an *orientation toward knowledge and objects* (5,8,29–31). Managers have higher scores in interpersonal orientation (dominance, capacity for status, and social presence) than development engineers, and development engineers score higher than research scientists (22,39,49). Computer specialists demonstrate the same relationship to computer users that research scientists do to their managers (8). However, lawyers and CPAs, who must interact with clients, express more interest in social activities than professionals who do not have to interact (49).

In comparison with the people in successful manufacturing organizations, more professionallike people in successful research organizations do not show as much *deference to authority* and the formal organization's policies and procedures (31). When computer specialists are contrasted with computer users, the results are similar: specialists show less deference to the organization than users (8).

Scientists characterize themselves as more *tolerant of ambiguity* (the ability to deal with ambiguous situations in contrast to the need for clear, structured circumstances) than their managers view themselves (38). Similarly, computer specialists and research personnel are more tolerant of ambiguity than computer users and manufacturing personnel are (8,31). Similarly, development engineers react in a more dogmatic (inflexible) manner than do research scientists (22,39).

While development engineers prefer applied activities and managers describe themselves as pragmatic, scientists (researchers) reflect more interest in scholarly activities and teaching. They characterize themselves as inquisitive with a professional orientation (38,39).

Professional employees in a successful research organization have shown superior ability to integrate information and develop a complex set of alternative solutions to problems when contrasted with those in less successful research organizations and successful manufacturing organizations (31). This is referred to as cognitive or integrative complexity and has resulted in the proposition that individuals' cognitive styles are related to the styles that are used in thinking about careers (12). For example, the highly complex, integrative decision style of the professional would be consistent with a highly adaptive career style, or "spiral," in which one changes field or major direction every five to ten years. However, many professionals appear to choose a "steady-state" career concept in which they concentrate in a specialized area to hone their competence to the ultimate degree. The theory proposes that the individual with a steady-state career concept has a "decisive" decision style in which very little information is sought and a single alternative generated from it. It does not appear logical that professionals such as pathologists or criminal lawyers who research large quantities of information in their daily activities using a complex cognitive style would switch dramatically under different circumstances, that is, when making career decisions. We must assume that such a theory has not provided the final answer to how professionals think about their careers.

Even with many distinctions, the bottom line is that professionals do not differ from nonprofessionals in a large number of personality traits. Not surprisingly, the differences *within* the professional or nonprofessional group turn out to be greater than the differences *between* the two groups. Some generalized distinctions can and will be drawn as long as we remember that there are always unique individual differences within each group. One of the major career theories proposes that people can be slotted into six different personality types or combinations thereof that can be related to various occupations (23). However, this theory does not separate professionals from nonprofessionals because each personality type is represented by at least one profession. For example, the "enterprising" type includes lawyers, the "conventional" type includes certified public accountants, the "social" type includes clergymen, the "artistic" occupations include the architect, the "investigative" includes physicians and physicists, and the civil engineer is considered a "realistic" type.

Attitudes, Values, and Needs. The attitudes, values, and needs of professionals have been of as much interest to researchers as those of nonprofessionals have been. Much of this work has been summarized elsewhere (36) but will be modified and updated here using six categories—autonomy, level of risk, personal development, sense of competence, standards of excellence, and interaction with colleagues.

Autonomy. A greater degree of personal autonomy than is available in most work is a factor that is highly valued by professionals (8,27,29,31,32,35,42). Research scientists report that they enjoy their work because there is less pressure on a daily basis and much less "bureaucratic hassle" in the form of progress reports and project justification than engineers face when they work on applications for sponsors of the work (36). Medical personnel reveal that they leave their organization to have more control over their own destinies (47). Such values are consistent with the personality characteristics of low deference to authority and the desire to work with ideas and objects rather than people. The need for autonomy is typically expressed as a desire to establish their own means of achieving goals but not necessarily to define the goals (6,9,52). Junior personnel in a research-and-development laboratory desire this level of autonomy while senior personnel also want to define the goals.

Level of Risk. Scientists reveal that they are attracted to research because the technological risk (challenge) involved is higher than the "practical engineering solutions" required by development program sponsors (36).

This result is consistent with descriptions of high-performance scientists who value challenge and ambiguity of task very highly, because the more ambiguous task has a greater probability of failure, making success an achievement (14,31,45,51).

Personal Development. Scientists have reported that involvement in new research is a major contributor to their development of an area of specialization. It helps them maintain state-of-the-art knowledge in their fields and allows them to broaden their knowledge into other, related fields (20,36,40,45). This is a highly valued need among professionals (28,35). There are many examples demonstrating that the nature of varying research projects requires scientists to learn new fields so that they can complete their work (36). Thus, the challenge of new research assignments results in a meaningful growth of new technical knowledge (14,34). Such a value system is consistent with the level of intellectual inquisitiveness that was described as a personality characteristic.

Sense of Competence. Professionals place a high value on expertise as reflected in feelings of competence and of worth to the organization and their colleagues (28,31,32). Scientists from eight laboratories commented on how important the contribution of challenging research was to their feelings of competence. Several respondents had attained national—and even worldwide—reputations for their work (36). They were recognized by the laboratories' top management for their technical expertise via the opportunity to research some of their own ideas (14). Their peers and management within the laboratories acknowledged their competence by seeking their advice. Interacting with colleagues, along with the opportunity to publish, contributes to the professional's ethic of serving society as well as enhancing a sense of competence.

Standards of Excellence. Highly competent professionals have high standards of excellence (20,28,31,35) and emphasize the quality of their work rather than quantity (30). Research entails less time pressure than applied engineering. As a consequence, the research scientist has a legitimate, sanctioned opportunity to identify more alternative approaches to work than is available in direct problem-solving applications. Such work requires the development and maintenance of high standards of excellence.

Interaction with Colleagues. The satisfaction of professionals—and partially their performance—is heavily dependent upon interaction with external colleagues (11,14,28,51). High-quality, challenging work is required to provide the basis for such interaction, which occurs during professional meetings and conferences, site visits, correspondence, workshops, papers and presentations, and telephone conversations (36). Such contacts involve a colleagual recognition of competence (32), the acquisition of new knowledge and techniques, and some social interaction.

Scientists in the forefront of their fields in the past were intensely competitive and strove to achieve, present their work, and be acknowledged as first (33). Although such competitiveness is still present, it is not as extreme as in the past. The struggle to be first—possibly perceived as vanity—is really the inner need for assurance that one's work really matters and that one has measured up to the hard standards maintained by at least some members of the community of scientists. This is the need for recognition. The unending exchange of critical appraisal, praise, and punishment is highly developed. Only after significant others have attested to the originality and the consequence of the work can a scientist feel reasonably confident about it. Praise is important.

The above set of values, interests, and needs indicates that the goal orientation of different groups of professionals is similar; they all emphasize maintaining a high level of expertise (competence), producing quality work (standards of excellence), and changing things (levels of risk). In contrast, nonprofessionals focus on their present employer, achieving results quickly and simply, and resisting change (5,8,25,29,31).

Schein's career theory combines these concepts by using career anchors that are composites of needs, values, attitudes, and abilities that tie individuals to certain kinds of careers as a base (46). Each person has facets of all career anchors but one dominates the others. Career anchors stabilize after individuals are five to ten years into their careers and are vocationally mature. Not all professionals have the same career anchor. For example, scientists may have a technical career anchor indicating that they are concerned with constantly increasing their proficiency and expertise. In contrast, a clergyman's career anchor may be based on the need to reach out and be helpful to others.

However, such orientations may change over time (21). Economic factors intervene to increase or decrease the need for security (50). Organizational opportunities can alter the relationship among orientations. For example, in many organizations professional commitment is considered to be antithetical to commitment to organizational goals. However, if the goals of the organization reflect the goals of the profession, a professional can develop high commitment to both organization and profession.

Whereas the professional's emphasis on knowledge as a source of authority and control is imposed by self and colleagues, conflict with the organization occurs when hierarchical forms of authority are imposed along with bureaucratic rules as controls. Adaptation by the organization to minimize such conflict appears to be possible, as reflected in the success of Bell Labs (52).

With these unique characteristics, professionals face special career concerns. A major career issue is how to acquire up-to-date technical and professional knowledge, thereby maintaining the authority of professional and colleagual acceptance and continuing to contribute effectively at work. Another major career issue is the decision concerning whether to remain a professional or to make the transition into management with its very different role demands. The new role requires adaptations in behaviors, value systems, and reward priorities. Career planning and development can be used to help resolve these career concerns for the individual. The management of professional careers by managers can be combined with the resolution of individual career concerns so that both individual and organizational goals can be achieved. The key is to focus on the goals that are reasonably compatible.

WHAT IS CAREER MANAGEMENT AND DEVELOPMENT?

As a result of the growth in adult career research since the mid-1960s and of employers' experimentation with new career policies and programs, common terminology has been evolving. People associate the term *career* not only with their occupation or field of work, but also with their organization (37). The linkage is shown in figure 1-2. The term *career* is nearly synonymous with occupation or field of work. However, both terms—especially *career*—are strongly associated with the organization as well. Any consideration about location is essentially independent of the other three. We assume that the term *career* is not a static idea but is very dynamic, connoting work-related experiences over a relatively long period of time. It seems impossible to make sense of a person's growth and development unless progress over time is taken into account; "without paying attention to the temporal framework against which a human life progresses, it is never possible to be knowledgeable about cumulative aspects of learning and development" (24).

Pulling together these facets, the term *career* will be defined operationally as a sequence of work roles that are related to each other in a rational way so that some of the critical knowledge and experience acquired in one role is used in the next (16). Making the transition from engineering to engineering management would not be considered a change in career, but moving from engineering to the ministry would be. This definition is not constrained by factors such as geography, organizational boundaries, or promotion opportunities (48).

Career Management. Career management will be defined as a "process whereby organizations endeavor to match individual interests and capabilities with organizational opportunities through a planned program encompassing such activities as the design of effective internal career systems, employee career counseling, job rotation opportunities, and a blend of positional experiences with on- and off-the-job training assignments" (17).

An effective career management subsystem not only must translate the organization's immediate and long-term requirements into action programs designed to meet those needs but also must be flexible enough to respond to individual career plans. It should be recognized that the organization's career management system will be heavily influenced by external factors such as competition, government, and the economy.

There is an entire set of career management activities required to combine the career needs of individuals with the long-term needs of the organization (17,44,46). The organization is responsible for the effectiveness with which these activities are performed.

Career decision making and planning are two concepts that are difficult to separate operationally. *Career decision making* is composed of an accumulation of decisions that are made in sequence. This stream of decisions is represented by a career plan. Much of the research literature on adult careers emphasizes two early career choices: what field to enter and for which organization to work. These are major decisions, but many more lie ahead for the individual. A scientist at various times may need to consider learning new technologies, moving into management, spending time in operations, becoming active in a professional organization, spending personal time preparing publications, requesting a departmental change, changing careers, moving back to the "bench" from administration, and so on.

If a sequence of decisions is formulated to identify the career steps that one will follow in the future, the individual is involved in explicit *career planning*. Thus, the individual's analog to the organization's career management is career planning or self-management with

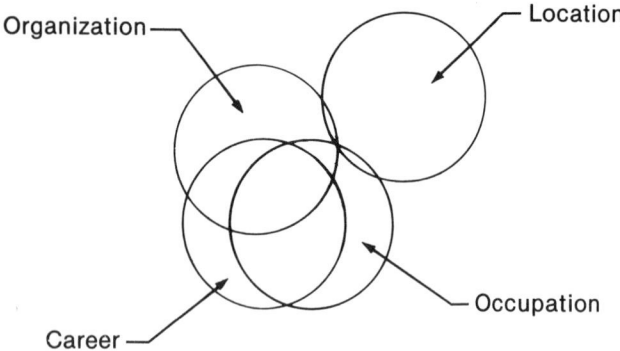

1-2. The relationship between career and other decisions.

This section is adapted from Morrison, R. F., and Holzbach, R. L. 1980. The career manager role. In *Work, family, and the career,* ed. C. B. Derr, pp. 75-93. New York: Praeger.

individuals exerting personal control over their own careers (19). This personal process includes the establishment of career goals and the planning of routes one will follow to obtain these goals through career, geographical, and organizational decisions, job assignments, work activities, and developmental programs. The individual's career-planning system is heavily influenced by factors such as family, economy, and profession, in addition to the organization and its career management system.

Career Development. Career development will be used to characterize the change occurring within the individual as a result of the dynamic relationship between the individual and the work environment and tasks over time (17,19,44,46). It is important to note that traditional career development programs that are composed primarily of education and training contain only two elements contributing to individual career development. Here, the major emphasis will be on career development via different experiences and assignments, with only secondary reference to education and training.

With the stage set by describing the purpose of the book, identifying the people involved, and defining the terminology as summarized in figure 1-3, the next step is to establish how the task will be approached.

ORGANIZATION OF THE BOOK

The basic ingredients that separate career management and development from historical personnel and management development programs are: constant change of the career plans and programs over time; continuous information flow between the individual and the organization; and integration of the various component programs in the career system. Usually the social science disciplines treat individual and organizational concerns separately. Individual career choice and career planning are handled by counselors and guidance experts, usually in high school or college. Organizational selection and recruitment are handled by personnel and industrial psychologists within work organizations. Given the lack of contact between professionals (academics and practitioners alike) in these two fields, it is not surprising that career management and development are so poorly integrated (18). We will attempt to consider the dynamic nature of careers and integrate the individual and the organization throughout the book.

Part 1 describes the organization programs that should be considered when designing the career management system. Chapter 2 provides a generic introduction to the career management system, its component programs, and its requirements for supporting elements. Chapters 3, 4, 5, and 6 present specific applied program examples with their implementation discussed in chapter 7. Organization programs are discussed before individual planning and development because the organization provides the primary framework within which the individual functions. Reference is made in part 1 to the specific requirements for exchanging information with individuals and the support that will be provided to the individual.

Part 2 is oriented toward individual career planning within the organization, beginning in chapter 8 with a generic introduction to the person and process used in career decision making, planning, and development. Chapters 9 and 10 describe specific information on designing a career strategy and Chapter 11 is an introduction to how it can be implemented.

In chapter 12, the previous chapters are put into perspective by pointing out the voids in career research that should be filled. There is an attempt to predict where the practice of career management development may go in the next twenty years.

SUMMARY

This chapter has covered three principal topics: professionals and their characteristics, the function of career development, and the organization of the book. The professionals are acknowledged by society as having a unique, high level of knowledge and skill in a specific

1-3. The human resource system.

HUMAN RESOURCE MANAGEMENT (ORGANIZATION)	Career Development	
	CAREER MANAGEMENT (INTERFACE)	CAREER PLANNING (INDIVIDUAL)
The set of policies, procedures, and activities required to manage the total organizational work-force so that the short- and long-term requirements of the organization are met	A process whereby organizations endeavor to match individual interests and capabilities with organizational opportunities through a planned program	Self-management of the career by establishing career goals, planning out the routes to achieve the goals, and implementing the plan

Adapted from Morrison, R. F., and Holzbach, R. L. 1980. The career manager role. In *Work, family, and the career*, ed. C. B. Derr, pp. 75-93. New York: Praeger.

field. Their key characteristics are their commitment to their field rather than the organization, high standards of quality, and independence.

Career development is defined as a combination of career management (the organizational perspective) and career planning (the individual view). The book is organized to cover the former in part 1 and the latter in part 2.

REFERENCES

1. Ackoff, R. L. 1981. *Creating the corporate future.* New York: John Wiley & Sons.
2. Badawy, M. K. 1970. Selected research on scientists and engineers in industry: a review and assessment. *Academy of Management Journal* 10:210–12.
3. ———. 1971. Understanding the role orientation of scientists and engineers. *Personnel Journal* 50 (6):449–54, 485.
4. ———. 1973. Industrial scientists and engineers: motivational style differences. *California Management Review* 14 (1):11–16.
5. ———. 1973. The myth of the "professional" employee. *Personnel Journal* 52 (1):41–45.
6. Bailyn, L. 1982. *Inner contradictions in technical careers.* MIT Sloan School of Management Working Paper 1281-82.
7. ———. 1984. *Autonomy in the industrial research and development lab* (TR-ONR-30). Cambridge, MA: Sloan School of Management, Massachusetts Institute of Technology, AD-A148075.
8. Carroll, A. B. 1982. Behavioral aspects of developing computer-based information systems. *Business Horizons* 25 (1):42–51.
9. Chuben, D. E. 1983. Career patterns of scientists and engineers. In *Scientists, engineers, and organizations,* edited by T. Connolly, pp. 310–27. Monterey, CA: Brooks/Cole.
10. Cullen, J. B. 1983. An occupational taxonomy by professional characteristics: implications for research. *Journal of Vocational Behavior* 22:257–67.
11. Dewhirst, H. D., Arvey, R. D., and Brown, E. M. 1978. Satisfaction and performance in research and development tasks as related to information accessibility. *IEEE Transactions in Engineering Management,* EM-25 (3):58–63.
12. Driver, M. J. 1980. Career concepts and organizational change. In *Work, family, and the career,* edited by C. B. Derr, pp. 5–17. New York: Praeger.
13. Ewing, D. W. 1981. Professionals and managers: the knowledge worker. *The San Diego Union,* Oct. 4:C-4, C-6.
14. Farris, G. F. 1975. Motivating R&D performance in a stable organization. In *Career management: a guide to combating obsolescence,* edited by H. G. Kaufman, pp. 101–6. New York: IEEE Press.
15. Gieryn, T. F., Bevins, G. M., and Zehr, S. C. 1985. Professionalization of American scientists: public science in the creation/evolution trails. *American Sociological Review* 50 (June):392–409.
16. Gutteridge, T. G. 1976. Some theoretical perspectives on career development. Paper presented at symposium, Organizational Career Development: State of the Practice. Annual meeting of the Academy of Management, Kansas City, August.
17. ———. 1976. Commentary: a comparison of perspectives. In *Careers in organizations,* edited by L. Dyer, pp. 37–46. Ithaca, NY: NYSSILR, Cornell University.
18. Hall, D. T. 1976. *Careers in organizations.* Pacific Palisades, CA: Goodyear.
19. Hall, D. T., and Hall, F. S. 1976. Career development: how organizations put their fingerprints on people. In *Careers in organizations,* edited by L. Dyer, pp. 1–15. Ithaca, NY: NYSSILR, Cornell University.
20. Hall, D. T., and Lawler, E. E., III. 1971. Job pressures and research performance. *American Scientist* 59:64–73.
21. Hall, D. T., and Mansfield, R. 1975. Relationships of age and seniority with career variables of engineers and scientists. *Journal of Applied Psychology* 60:201–10.
22. Hansen, J., and Johansson, C. B. 1974. Strong vocational interest blank and dogmatism. *Journal of Counseling Psychology* 21:197–201.
23. Holland, J. L. 1985. *Making vocational choices* (2nd ed.). Englewood Cliffs, NJ: Prentice-Hall.
24. Howe, M. J. A. 1982. Biographical evidence and the development of outstanding individuals. *American Psychologist* 37:1071–81.
25. Hutcheson, P., and Chalofsky, N. 1981. Careers in human resource development. *Training and Development Journal* 35 (7):12–15.
26. Jewkes, G., Thompson, P., and Dalton, G. 1979. How to stifle a technical organization in ten easy steps. *Research Management* 22 (1):12–16.
27. Kast, F. E., and Rosenzweig, J. E. 1970. *Organization and management: a systems approach.* New York: McGraw-Hill.
28. Kerr, S., Von Glinow, M. A., and Schriesheim, J. 1977. Issues in the study of "professionals" in organization: the case of scientists and engineers. *Organization Behavior and Human Performance* 18:329–45.
29. Lawrence, P. R., and Lorsch, J. W. 1967. *Organization and environment.* Boston: Harvard University.
30. Levinson, H. 1965. What an executive should know about scientists. *Think Magazine,* Sept.–Oct.
31. Lorsch, J. W., and Morse, J. J. 1974. *Organizations and their members: a contingency approach.* New York: Harper & Row.
32. McCall, M. W., Jr. 1983. Leadership and the professional. In *Scientists, engineers, and organizations,* edited by T. Connolly, pp. 328–45. Monterey, CA: Brooks/Cole.
33. Merton, R. K. 1969. Behavior patterns of scientists. *American Scientist* 57 (1):1–23.
34. Miller, D. B. 1975. Changing job requirements: a stimulant for technical vitality. In *Career management: a guide to combating obsolescence,* edited by H. G. Kaufman, pp. 62–74. New York: IEEE Press.
35. Miner, J. B. 1980. The role of managerial and professional motivation in the career success of management professors. *Academy of Management Journal* 23:487–508.
36. Morrison, R. F. 1981. Utilizing discretionary research funds to support an applied laboratory's goal: a preliminary investigation. Paper presented at symposium, The Management of Research and Development. Annual meeting of the Academy of Management, San Diego, August 2–5.
37. Morrison, R. F., and Cook, T. M. 1985. *Military officer career development and decision making: a multiple-cohort longitudinal analysis of the first twenty-four years,* MPL TN85-4. San Diego: Navy Personnel Research and Development Center.
38. Morrison, R. F., et al. 1962. Factored life history antecedents of industrial research performance. *Journal of Applied Psychology* 46:281–84.
39. Mossholder, K. W., Dewhirst, H. D., and Arvey, R. D. 1981. Vocational interest and personality differences between de-

velopment and research personnel: a field study. *Journal of Vocational Behavior* 19:233-43.
40. Mosteller, F. 1981. Innovation and evaluation. *Science* 211:881-86.
41. Northrup, H. R., and Malin, M. E. 1985. *Personnel policies for engineers and scientists.* Philadelphia, PA: Industrial Research Unit, The Wharton School, University of Pennsylvania.
42. Pelz, D. C., and Andrews, F. M. 1976. *Scientists in organizations: productive climates for research and development.* Rev. ed. Ann Arbor, MI: Institute for Social Research, Univ. of Michigan.
43. Pfeffer, J., and Ross, J. 1982. The effects of marriage and a working wife on occupational and wage attainment. *Administrative Science Quarterly* 27:66-80.
44. Pinto, P. R. 1976. Commentary: neglected issues, unanswered questions. In *Careers in organizations,* edited by L. Dyer, pp. 47-51. Ithaca, NY: NYSSILR, Cornell University.
45. Ranftl, R. M., ed. 1978. *R&D productivity: study report.* 2nd ed. Culver City, CA: Hughes Aircraft Co.
46. Schein, E. H. 1978. *Career dynamics: matching individual and organizational needs.* Reading, MA: Addison-Wesley.
47. Smith, M. S. 1979. The Naval officer/medical officer quandary. *Proceedings* 105 (9):42-45.
48. Spilerman, S. 1978. Work during the middle and late years. *The future and the past: essays on programs.* New York: Russell Sage.
49. Terman, L. M. 1955. Are scientists different? *Scientific American*, January:25-29.
50. Tuma, N. B., and Grimes, A. J. 1981. A comparison of models of role-orientations of professionals in a research-oriented university. *Administrative Science Quarterly* 26:187-206.
51. Wolff, M. F. 1979. How to find—and keep—creative people. *Research Management* 22 (5):43-45.
52. ———. 1982. Managing large egos. *Research Management* 25 (4):7-9.

PART 1

ORGANIZATIONAL PROGRAMS: WHAT THE ORGANIZATION CAN DO

Chapter 2

Career Management Systems

The philosophy that the personnel of the organization are a long-term resource (asset) rather than a short-term cost item requires that a systems approach be taken to the management of the resource. This chapter will provide a broad outline of such a system and introduce its unique characteristics applied to the management of professionals. Career management is a long-term process (twenty to fifty years for the individual) and must be considered within such a context or the system will not be successful in its contribution to the organization's goals.

GENERAL SYSTEMS MODEL

The general outline of a system is provided in figure 2-1. It will be assumed that the direct flow of the human resource in such a system is from *input* (products and people from inside or outside the organization) through *process* to the *output* (products or people moving within the organization or outside it). A feedback loop is present to indicate that the output of one activity (process) may be an input to the next activity (process) or remain an output and leave the organization. The *contributing systems* are what make each input, processing action, and output work and progress in the intended direction.

Starting a section with an abstract outline may be somewhat disconcerting to the reader who is looking for applications to use in solving problems. However, this overview is essential to a quick understanding of the interrelationships present in a career management system and provides a framework for this and the five chapters that follow.

CAREER MANAGEMENT SYSTEM MODEL

The general systems model has been translated into a specific career management system model in figure 2-2. The components within the input, process, output, and contributing modules of the career management system must now be reviewed according to general corporate practices and formed into a model by delineating relationships among them (21).

Career Management System Inputs

External Inputs. The primary method for acquiring new professional resources from outside the organization is via the employment of permanent personnel. Other potential external sources are consultants and temporary employees, but by their nature, they are not relevant inputs to a career management system. Such a system is useful only for the long term and does not provide short-term resources efficiently.

Internal Inputs. While it would appear that the inputs for an organizational system would come only from outside, in a career management system model, many inputs are actually personnel already employed. In fact, the majority of the professionals that serve as inputs to career management programs never leave their present jobs even when they become outputs of the program; the minority become inputs to new jobs or job situations.

For example, a scientist who is an effective researcher (output) on a research project (process) becomes a candidate (input) for a corporate-sponsored educational program (process) to increase the technical capability (output) of the organization. Thus, the most common

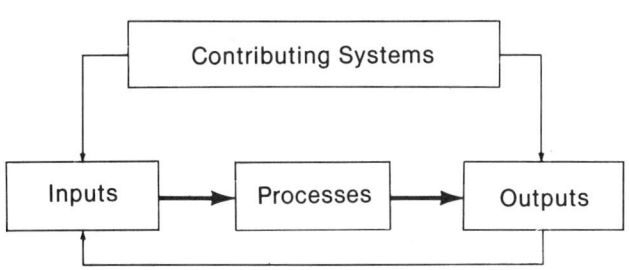

2-1. A general systems model.

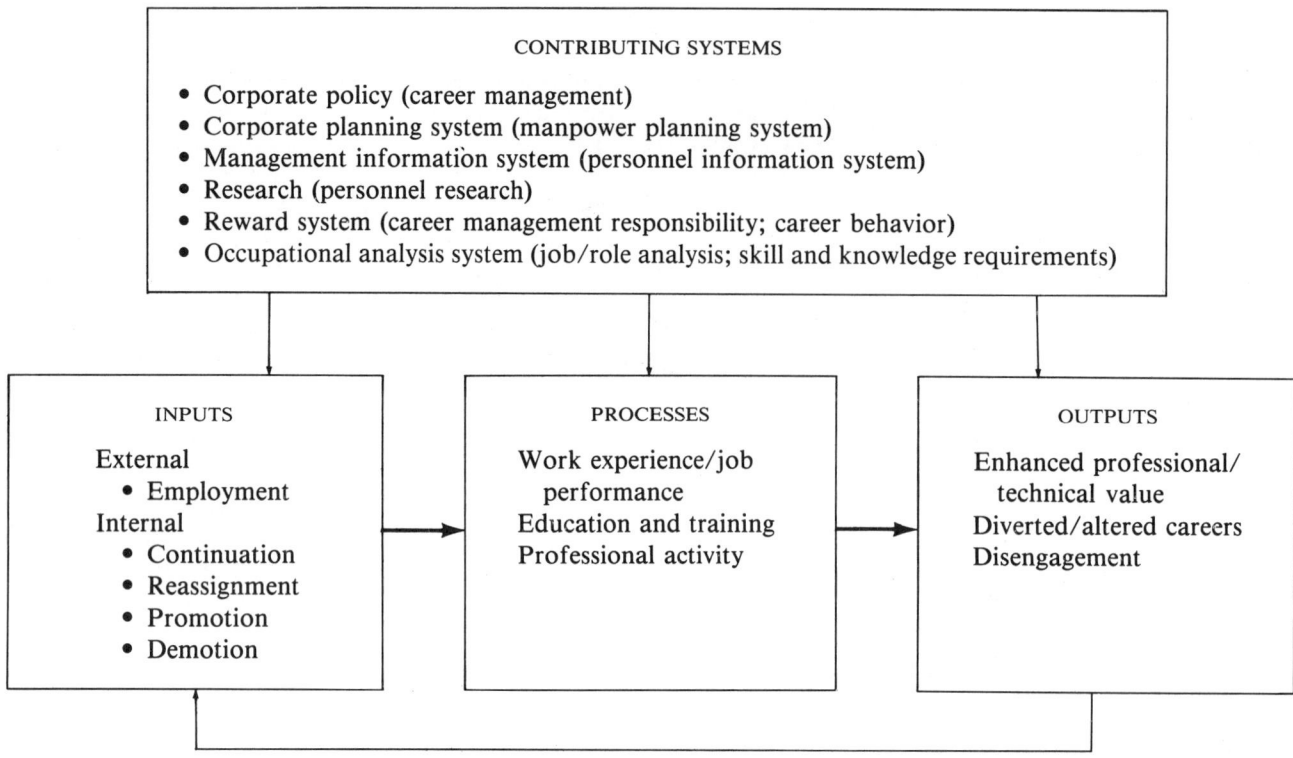

2-2. A career management system.

outputs of the career management process are professionals with increased knowledge or skill who continue in their present position.

The next largest source of internal inputs are transfers—or reassignments. Reassignment occurs for three primary reasons: to use an employee's unique abilities in a new way; to further overall employee development; and to solve employee or organization problems. Only the first two are relevant in the career management system.

The third major internal input source is through promotion. The fourth source is temporary assignments or loans and the fifth is demotions. In contrast to the naive new employee, internal personnel are more aware of the effect such actions have on their careers. As a result, such actions, especially reassignment, may be open for negotiation between the individual and the organization. In fact, the individual may seek reassignment to a project or job that appears to be especially attractive.

A major factor that must be kept in mind is that internal human resource inputs are already organization members. This requires that their needs and desires be considered within each input element, and feedback about the process and decisions must be provided quickly and clearly. The honesty, accuracy, and availability of such information will have a direct impact on the career satisfaction and organizational commitment of the personnel.

System inputs and input programs are described in more detail in chapter 3.

Career Management System Processes

The processes used in a career management system evolved initially from education and training, and the effort of most organizations has been focused mostly on those two activities. More recently it has become apparent that focused work experience is more critical than either education or training (6). As a result, the development process using focused work experience will be emphasized over education and training both here and in more detail in chapter 6.

Work Experience and Job Performance. In the initial assignment, the newly employed professional not only applies the technical expertise learned in the past, but also learns the norms and practices of the organization and work group (11). While organizations and research have focused recently on the need for careful initial assignments for new employees who are fresh out of college, an early socialization-orientation program and time period is also relevant for experienced people who are hired from outside or reassigned internally. It appears that the employee who gets off to a fast start in a new assignment does better, not only in that job but also in later positions and promotions (2). In addition, the new professional brings a high level of academic training and possibly intern-style experience to the initial assignment and expects the organization to make immediate use of that ability. Although the level of such expectations may be unrealistic, they need to be understood, clarified, and partially met, or else the individual may leave.

For professionals, a change in assignment periodically is required to aid individuals to develop not only in their field of specialization, but also in their ability to learn and adapt (51). Research-and-development organizations use discretionary funds to aid not only the organization to produce new products but also the individual to learn new technology (43). Special project assignments can do the same for other professionals. In apprentice and managerial positions, career paths have been laid out formally or informally to identify which assignment sequence provides the experience and knowledge required to perform effectively in some target position. This is very difficult to do for professionals since the position that is a target twenty-five years after the individual enters the organization will require expertise in an area that is not known at the time of entry. The scientific portion of a dual ladder (scientific/managerial) can be identified early, but not necessarily the technological content of the most senior position(s) on it. Therefore, the ability to learn new technology must be constantly encouraged in professionals. Since they expressed not only their ability but also their interest in their field very early by participating in an extensive preemployment educational process (typically at least two years of postgraduate work), such encouragement is not difficult if the organization works at it. Technical—and professional—knowledge is acquired by mature scientists—and professionals—primarily through challenging, responsible work and only secondarily via education (28).

For the professional who desires to test whether a move to management should be made, special project assignments that include managerial functions should be provided. Such assignments need to be of sufficient duration to allow management skills and requirements to surface without being masked or substituted by professional knowledge or competence.

An often overlooked developmental process is the organization's emphasis on the individual producing a high level of professional-quality output within a reasonable amount of time. To do this requires that the organization set professional-quality results as more important than quick results and provide the support the professional needs to accomplish such results. The professional who must spend a large proportion of time in administrative matters or must place such matters ahead of professional activities soon recognizes the organization's lack of interest in professional output and either leaves or channels efforts into nonprofessional pursuits. By emphasizing the professional quality of results, the organization channels developmental efforts of the individual in the direction of achieving professional excellence.

Education and Training. Because of the advanced level of knowledge most professionals bring to their first jobs, training in the specific area of expertise required in the initial assignment is not always appropriate. The new professional needs to develop skill in using the knowledge that was acquired in academia by performing in an appropriate job. Orienting a new employee to the organization's administrative procedures and requirements, available administrative and technician support, reporting relationships, products, and processes is essential to his/her effective application of technology or professional knowledge.

When professionals have not completed advanced education, the completion of a professional graduate degree aids in the development and maintenance of job performance many years into their careers (10,26,31). Specific technical training or long-term education are most valuable when the material is presented outside the organization and the participants will immediately apply the new knowledge on the job (23). In-house education programs have not been improving the performance of scientists as expected (25), although they appear to be effective in aiding the instructor (28). Weak in-house programs may be the result of the lack of accountability required from participants by the organization or instructor. Making pay increases or reimbursement for course fees contingent upon grades or program completion appears to have degraded the quality of evening education at most universities. Linking pay raises, assignments, or promotions to performance based on the acquisition of new knowledge via education would increase the level of professional expertise available to the organization.

Brief introductory lectures on new technology, new expertise, and new applications help to keep the professional aware of developments in the field, but they may be handled better by a professional society than through an in-house program.

Professional Activity. Professionals are avid readers and require access to periodicals, journals, books, microfiche, computer research, and other written sources to acquire new technology for use in their work and self-development. However, a major source of learning for adults who are a few years beyond school is social interchange (43). Applications, theories, tests, and new technical knowledge are exchanged at conferences, meetings, and workshops; during visits and presentations; through correspondence and publications; and by participation in professional societies. These contacts should be encouraged to aid the developmental process as long as the content is related to the professional's role in the organization. Without access to the most current knowledge in the field and to the opportunity to test self-developed technology, ideas, and uses in dialogue with others in the field, the professional will become isolated from peers. The organization gains the reputation of being supportive of such professional interaction or antagonistic toward it.

In several research laboratories, top management has discretionary money available to fund independent research in new technology or products that are proposed by the researcher. Such resources not only produce new products and solve esoteric technical problems, but also aid researchers in broadening or deepening their area of expertise (43). In a similar vein, academia provides sabbaticals (paid leaves of absence) and seed money for small new research projects to aid its faculty to renew and develop themselves.

Career Management System Outputs

For the purpose of this text, the system outputs will be restricted to those that directly affect personnel and will omit indirect, nonpersonnel outcomes such as recruiting image and new products (43).

Enhanced Professional/Technical Value. The outcome that is most commonly considered in the career management of professionals is the acquisition of technology that maintains or enhances knowledge and ability within the individual's present area of expertise. In many cases, this is referred to as overcoming technical obsolescence. While increased depth or maintenance of knowledge and ability is one outcome, another is broadening the area of knowledge or introducing a new one. Examples of the broadening of ability are the addition of tax accounting to expertise in cost accounting or the accretion of a new capability, such as patent law for a research engineer. Each alternative enhances the individual's value to the organization.

Individuals who move from technical work to the supervision of others can attribute most of their initial influence to the respect that subordinates have for their technical expertise rather than their positions in the organization. The value of such individuals in the research environment has been described (12), but it appears that the same roles are relevant for other organizations of professionals such as accounting, medical, and legal firms.

Diverted or Altered Careers. Throughout the professional career literature, two topics are dominant. First is professional obsolescence that was referred to under "enhanced professional/technical value." Second is professional management that can also be considered as a "career diversion." Entry levels in technical management require a significant level of professional competence. The importance of this work element decreases as professionals move higher into management and modify their behavior and central interests in accordance with the job and organization requirements.

While other professionals emphasize the application of their knowledge for the use of others, scientists tend to believe that the only relevant application of their knowledge is research. When such individuals change their emphasis to applying the results of research, the technical demands of the work are partially supplanted by the need to understand and serve the customer or client. This new emphasis on application can be thought of as diversion in the career of a scientist.

A third career diversion is typical of the obsolete professional who is demoted to the level of a technician. Such a position does not require the level of knowledge and ability required of a professional.

As a result of a change in career interest and/or gradual technical obsolescence, many professionals alter their careers into other fields of work (such as administration in personnel or training) within the same organization. Their knowledge and experience allow them to contribute to the organization by recruiting professional personnel or administering professional training programs.

Disengagement. To maintain current effectiveness and long-term viability, an organization provides for the involuntary disengagement of personnel by lay-off, firing, and "forced" retirement, or voluntary disengagement by retirement or resignation. An extreme failure of a career management system would be to require the early retirement or lay-off of a professional during economic downturns because of marginal technical abilities. Even more drastic would be discharge as a result of professional obsolescence and limited ability to apply the expertise of the profession. The euphemism for this is often "outplacement."

CONTRIBUTING SYSTEMS

The management of careers is based on the premise that the organization can maintain and nurture the human resource competencies it requires over the entire career span of its employees. This process can be greatly facilitated if there is a human resource plan that specifies both the number of personnel required in the future and their quality as expressed in the occupational groups they represent and the professional and technical fields of expertise required (69). Such a human resource plan is a subsystem within the corporate planning system. An important output of the planning system is the new technical or professional requirements that the organization must fulfill to become or remain successful over the long term. Many human resource planning models do not provide the technical or professional information required for the career management of professionals. A typical planning technique models the flow of personnel in the hierarchy on the organization as it exists, considering only increases or decreases in quantity rather than changes in skill mix or the inclusion of new fields (35).

The corporate management information system should include several subsystems to support various personnel systems such as compensation and career management. A personnel information subsystem can provide data on the skills, past performance, assessment, education, training history, and other career-related attributes of individual employees.

The occupational classification system provides data on individual jobs, clusters of jobs, and career patterns composed of job sequences that comprise career ladders. Job analysis provides the skill, knowledge, and experience requirements that are so important to effective career management. This system produces the data necessary to establish career paths that provide the work experience and to design education and training programs required to prepare professionals for target, senior positions.

Reward systems should consider not only job performance (1), but the long-term potential and technical competence of professionals (14) and the management of professionals' careers by supervision. The reward system must provide the incentives that make the career management system function effectively (8). The following example illustrates how important it is for the reward system to be consistent with the career management system by making rewards contingent upon the career behavior desired by the organization:

> A military organization wants its line officers to become proficient not only in their area of warfare expertise, but also in a second field such as financial management. The secondary field is most critical to the organization at a senior grade, when the individual has over twenty-three years of service and is needed to manage a major staff activity such as a regional finance center. If the early development of a secondary skill is not acknowledged and rewarded via promotion during the first ten to twenty years of the career, the astute, top individuals will concentrate on performance in warfare line jobs and will stay away from the secondary field. Such a strategy may maximize the individual's opportunity for promotion for the first twenty years but leaves the organization with a dearth of senior managers with the correct skills for top staff assignments later.

The executive guidance for the career management system should be reflected in organization policy. The introduction of a career management system will require new policy even if no written policy previously existed. For an existing organization, tradition may have established an unwritten policy. Any change must be shown in written policy to signal the new direction prescribed by management. A typical example of a required change would be to shift the control of individual careers from a supervisor or department head to the corporate level of the organization. In this way, the individual becomes an asset or resource to the entire organization. It is also essential that the organization establish policy regarding who has access to career data on individuals, publishing, participation in professional activities, support for technical updating, and the like (14,43).

The final corporate system that can provide a major contribution to the career management system is research. Research on the career management system can provide the creative ideas and technology that keep the system operating at peak effectiveness, making its contribution to both individual professionals and the organization optimal over a long period of time.

The career management system shown in figure 2-2 is based on the general systems model in figure 2-1. However, the systems model cannot work effectively unless it is provided with a supporting cast of programs. The supporting programs are outlined in figure 2-3 and described on the following pages.

2-3. Career management system: supporting programs.

INPUT		PROCESS	OUTPUT
External	*Internal*	*Organization*	• Outplacement assistance
• Recruiting	*Organization*	• Assignment procedures	• Retirement planning
• Selection	• Inventory and assessment	• Special projects	
• Placement	• Succession planning and career patterns	• Performance appraisal	
• Job preview		• In-house training	
• Orientation	*Individual*	• Continuing education	
	• Personal assessment	• Long-term training	
	• Career decision aids	*Individual*	
	• Career planning	• Professional association activities	
	• Life planning	• Publishing	

SUPPORTING PROGRAMS

Inputs

Recruiting/Selection/Placement. Three primary programs are required to support the external input into the system via employment. Recruiting describes the effort used to identify appropriate outside sources of personnel. The quality and quantity of input is determined by the adequacy of financial and human resources used in the recruiting effort, the quality of sources contacted, the efficiency with which the program is conducted, and the continuity with which the effort is maintained over time. A competent recruiting program sets the stage for effective performance later in the organization (73).

Selection determines who does or does not gain entry to the organization. Along with recruiting, it controls the quantity and quality of the input by establishing and administering employment requirements concerning level and type of education, previous work experience, life experience, and personal characteristics. For professionals, selection standards communicate the value that the organization places on the factors that are important to them. Such standards must be valid requirements of the work and organization, or morale and turnover problems will develop later (73), and equal employment opportunity statutes will be violated.

Initial placement requires an effective match between the attributes individuals bring with them and the demands of the position and organization. If the new engineer has the characteristics and background of a scientist and is placed in production engineering rather than research and development, performance, morale, and turnover problems can be expected to develop in the future (36).

Job Preview and Orientation. A preview of the organization, its work, and career opportunities is the fourth program that may be used to support external inputs during both recruiting and selection. Professionals have unique opportunities to provide realistic insight into the organization. Internships for six months to a year as part of graduate education are similar to cooperative programs for undergraduates. Summer employment of students according to professional merit can also provide a preview of organization activities, standards, and expectations. The temporary summer employment of faculty members provides an indirect preview as they convey their experience to students involved in employment decisions. When organization members serve as guest lecturers at a university, the students become familiar with the organization and its work. When scientists interact with faculty members by cooperative research, correspondence, or professional meetings, the faculty members become familiar with the organization and pass this on to students.

The preview continues and becomes more specific as orientation to the initial placement situation occurs. For the highly educated professional, the orientation period should be different than for the less educated generalist or technical individual who requires considerable training. The professional will need to go to work immediately as a respite from extensive schooling, with an orientation program spread over the first six months to one year in the new job.

Inventory and Assessment. The programs that support the internal inputs to the career management system are directly parallel to the programs that support external inputs. The analog to external recruiting/selecting/placement is the internal posting of job openings, assessment of performance, and assignment of individuals. Planning for this sequence of activities is expressed in the inventorying and review of the internal supply of human resources. In contrast to the typical inventory and review of management resources, the same function applied to professionals is more complex because of the very specific interests, education, training, and job experience such people have. For example, production cost accountants will need to be distinguished from tax accountants, and electronics engineers from mechanical engineers. Because of their specialization, they are not as interchangeable as managers who perform similar functions. The inventory must be broken down into the many classes of skills that represent the skills of the human resource and the requirements of the organization over several years. The inventory establishes the position of current individuals whom the organization has identified as eligible for reassignment, promotion, or demotion. Job posting allows self-identification by those who feel that they are qualified for openings but have not necessarily been identified by the organization.

Assessing the potential and promotability of the professional provides a parallel to the selection of applicants from external sources of labor. This function has a major advantage over selection because the organization has the opportunity to develop an extensive portfolio of information about its employees. Professionals in the organization have had the opportunity to express their interests, demonstrate their ability to acquire new knowledge and skills, and show their adaptability to new situations. Although it is often difficult to assess the practicing specialist's potential for an effective shift into management, it is still possible to acquire information about the individual's ability to make such a career shift if managerially oriented opportunities in special projects and other situations are provided. Assessment information has been used for company succession planning, identification for management and professional openings, selection of employees for job rotation or other development opportunities, planning for training needs, and personal career planning (65).

Succession Planning and Career Patterns. If employees are to be treated as an asset rather than an operating cost—as assumed in career management—they need to be managed as a continuing resource. However, professionals do not fit a traditional set of back-up charts as used in the career management of managers. It is more appropriate to establish groupings of professionals within occupational areas according to their level of experience, skill, and knowledge. Strengthening or broadening an individual's professional abilities provides alternate career strategies for increasing the value of technical groups.

The occupational groupings can be considered steps within career patterns for professionals. The career patterns present logical sequences of groupings that lead toward a target position—or positions—such as senior scientist. Each assignment or grouping in the pattern is designed to provide the unique experience required for effective performance in the target position or some required step en route (45).

If the organization is to manage its professionals effectively, it must provide positions in their career patterns that are equivalent to those of top management. Such a career ladder provides a major reward to a high-achieving professional. The organization will also need professionals in management, and a clear career pattern for professionals as managers should be developed. Work experience can be programmed to provide individuals with the opportunity to obtain a taste of management without commiting themselves to that switch in career.

The programs briefly described above and in more detail in chapters 3 through 6 are primarily aimed at assisting the organization to manage the careers of its professional employees. Other programs are required to aid individuals to manage their own careers as well as help the organization. A brief description of these follows and more detail is provided in chapters 9 through 11.

Personal Assessment. The assessment of psychological needs, abilities, interests, and developmental requirements can be accomplished by various methods, from self-help workbooks to professional counseling to assessment centers. The information is essential to the effective management of the individual's career by the organization and to effective career planning by the professional employee. Such an assessment establishes the current developmental status of the individual, the direction that the person's career should take, and the developmental voids that should be filled to achieve desired career goals.

Career Decision Aids. To participate effectively in an organization's career management system and to obtain the optimum benefit for themselves, individuals will be involved in many career choices. These are primarily centered on determining where they will work within the organization but may include consideration of the location in which they will work. Professionals will not usually be engrossed in occupational choices because those decisions were made at the time they entered and continued through their long academic education. However, this type of decision becomes salient when the individuals face the choice of leaving their professional field and entering management. It may also become relevant for those who become dissatisfied with their earlier decision and want to move into something different. The fourth category of career decisions considers job choices, especially sequences of jobs. The individual considers not only whether the job/work will be enjoyable but also whether it will be advantageous in the achievement of career goals. A series of career decisions becomes a career plan.

Career Planning. The organization can aid the individual in the development of a career plan by providing information about organizational career requirements and developmental opportunities. The most common source of such information is the immediate supervisor, followed by peers, personnel specialists, organization publications, and counseling specialists.

The first set of supporting programs (inputs) has as its goal to assist the organization to manage its employees' careers; the second group is designed to aid individuals to manage their own careers as well as help the organization; and a third group is aimed at helping individuals relate and meld their career decisions with the more overriding concern of personal life management. The programs provide an indirect aid to the organization by enhancing employee motivation and satisfaction through their participation in career and life management.

Life Planning. A program to assist individuals in planning their lives can help to put career aspirations into perspective and aid in the formation of a career plan that fits in with the whole person—the life context—and the organization's demands and opportunities.

Processes

The career management system processes also need strong supporting programs.

Assignment Procedures. Work experience provides the greatest amount of developmental experience. Therefore, the match between the job requirements and the individual's current performance level and developmental need is crucial. The individual should not be assigned to a job that is so tough that a high level of performance is not achievable within a reasonable period of time—such as two years—or the developmental process will not occur. The corollary of this is assignment to a job that is so easy that top performance is achieved immediately and no development occurs. There does not appear to be any research to provide guidance on the length of an individual's stay in a job to achieve an optimum combination of development and productivity goals. Development is required to maintain learning skills and to enhance future value to the self and organization over the long term, while a reasonable return on the organization's investment in selecting, transferring, and developing the individual and disrupting the flow of the work group is essential in the short term. If the individual has to learn both new technology and new organization or group operations to cope with a new task, it will take a long time to reach optimum performance. Such performance must be maintained for a considerable period to make a reassignment cost-effective. As the complexity of the new assignment demands drops, so does the amount of time required for the organization to obtain an adequate return on its investment and maintain effective operations. If the technology and organization are the same in both old and new assignments, only the work group will be new, and an optimum level of performance can be achieved in a few months. However, very little development occurs and the long-range needs of the individual and organization are not being met unless the organization requires constant adaptability from its members, as is required in consulting or large project construction.

Special Projects. Several research laboratories use discretionary funds not only to develop new products or technology but also to deepen or broaden the skills of scientists (43). The scientists have the opportunity to delve into new areas by proposing their own research.

Within jobs, supervisors can assign professionals to ad hoc tasks or special projects that provide the opportunity to search out answers to a problem by probing deeper into their area of expertise or by seeking answers in adjacent or new areas. Such projects allow the professional to try out new occupations such as management or purchasing without developing a stigma of failure if the individual does not choose to pursue that field in the future.

Appraisal. An appraisal program that considers both productive efforts and developmental progress is important in making work experience effective as a developmental tool. Such a program will not produce the desired results unless the individual's developmental status and needs prior to entering the job are identified, and developmental behaviors and goals are planned, monitored, and measured.

In-house Training. A considerable amount of the training done within organizations is not very effective for professionals (28). The training that is specific and can be used immediately on the job appears to work best.

Continuing Education. Many organizations support continuing education programs in job-related fields via tuition reimbursement, time off from work, and other procedures. Although such programs are widespread, they may not be effective (28). The instructor may get the most out of such programs.

Long-term Training. In a few instances, when the organization needs new technology and has a current employee who could learn it in a relatively short time, the individual—and family—are sent to work in another organization, teach in a graduate program, or engage in a similar activity. Such a program is a long-term immersion in a learning situation without any job performance required. A few programs are laissez-faire without a developmental focus, similar to the academic sabbatical.

Publishing. The opportunity to publish establishes a network for the professional dialogue (37). Such a dialogue provides feedback about developmental growth and excellence in the field plus expert critique of the work. Time, secretarial services, and a library are necessary for professionals who publish.

Outputs

There are not many supporting programs required on the output side of the career management system because most employees are continued, transferred, or the like, and thus recycled as inputs to the system. However, programs are required to support those personnel who are faced with leaving the organization.

Outplacement Assistance. When employees are laid off or fired or when they resign at the request of the organization prior to eligibility for retirement, many organizations help the employee adjust to the circumstances and find a new position elsewhere. For professionals, occupational retraining is not common, but training in job-finding skills is. Such training along with aid in finding a new position is often contracted out to consulting firms that specialize in this work. An alternative for the organization is to sponsor the ex-employee in a self-help firm such as Forty-Plus for a specific period of time.

Retirement Planning. Most employees face retirement at some time in their career. It is not uncommon for scientists to go through phased retirement by working part-time for awhile. Others continue to work in their field by consulting, teaching, publishing, or doing private research on an ad hoc basis for the rest of their lives.

Implementation

While figure 2-3 summarizes the programs that support the career management system, the system is still not complete. There are other mechanisms that are required to implement the system. These activities are the glue that holds it all together, the oil that makes it run smoothly.

Organization Structure. Establishing relevant "dual career" paths is not sufficient. The roles of immediate supervisors, individuals, managers, executives, personnel administrators, and career systems specialists must be clearly—and realistically—defined along with their responsibilities.

Communication Mechanisms. Newsletters, job posting, reference materials, computer-assisted counseling, and the like are techniques that can make it feasible for the individual and supervisor to participate effectively within the system. Generally, the organization equates communication with written materials. It appears that adults communicate more effectively verbally and face to face. Field trips by career specialists and personnel administrators and telephone conferences can enhance communication dramatically. Computer systems may play a large role in the future.

Training to Participate. Establishing an organization's structure with its role descriptions and accountabilities in writing or through diagrams is not sufficient. Training, consultation, and control mechanisms are also required. Individual participants, supervisors, and other personnel must all be trained in what to do and how to do it. Such training should not take place only at the start-up of a career management system but should be continued to prepare new employees, retrain employees who change roles, and periodically upgrade the system performance of all participants.

System Control and Audit. A control system should be developed and implemented to ensure that the career development system is operating as it was designed and is producing the intended results. An internal review of the system's implementation can assess its performance in the short term. Because of its nature, the effectiveness of career management can be evaluated only on a long-term basis. In contrast with the accounting system, a career management system is not traditionally audited on an annual basis, but a review of the system's effectiveness in contributing to the organization's goals should be done periodically. An audit should be conducted every three to five years by an external agency such as a professional consulting firm or team of knowledgeable academics.

CAREER MANAGEMENT PRACTICES

Trends and Influential Factors

A fundamental challenge of the 1980s is to elevate career management activities to a full partnership status with the more traditional functions of personnel departments (34). "In time it will become increasingly evident that career management programs are cost justified in the same terms as staffing programs; that is, each approach contributes to improved utilization of employees and overall organizational effectiveness, not to mention improved productivity and innovation levels" (34, p. 32). The need for career management in the 1980s has accumulated as a result of many historical factors. The post–World War II baby boom, equal employment opportunity legislation, the economy, and technological advances have all influenced career management needs.

The "age bulge" created by the baby boom has exerted effects for twenty years and will continue to influence organizations' career programs for the next thirty or forty years. The 1950s saw the labor force in the United States expand from 62.8 to 72.1 million, at the rate of about 1.25 percent per year (53, p. 559). In the 1960s, this rate accelerated to 1.65 percent per year, and the 1970s (the "sizzling seventies") saw a 2.3 percent per year rise. Projections are that the 1980–85 rate will be about 1.9 percent and the 1985–90 rate, 1.1 percent. The 1990–2000 rate of 1.0 percent per year would be 61 percent below the average rate of the 1970s. The history of research-and-development funding shows similar extremes, with the 1950s and 1960s being growth years, the 1970s and, more dramatically, the 1980s showing steep declines in government-sponsored funding. "Most engineering managers have had years of experience with managing growth and rarely with managing stability or decline" (40, p. 63).

The large influx of women into the work force during the 1970s has helped to exaggerate the impact of the age bulge. As the baby-boomers reach middle management positions, these grown-ups will clog the desirable positions from promising same-age and younger employees. This becomes a concern for the organization. Under these conditions, career aspirations are frustrated and loss of productivity or increased turnover results.

Similar extremes can be traced in the economy: the boom of the 1950s when anything was possible; the Great Society in the 1960s; the reawakening to economic frailties in the 1970s when our country struggled with the oil embargo and the post-Vietnam economic shock wave; and the severe cutbacks in the 1980s' quest for the balanced budget. None of these things occurs in a vacuum; each is woven into the fabric of organization life. The economic climate affects the number of jobs available and the amount of voluntary turnover that occurs.

As the age bulge moves through the system, as women become incorporated as a natural part of the human resources supply, and as the economy stabilizes, certain human resource supply-and-demand equations will become obvious and will squarely affect organizations. As the *supply* of available talent shrinks in comparison to the *demand* for that talent, the worth of the talent will increase. Simply stated, this means that the shrinking labor-force expansion and a stabilizing economy will result in a greater probability of turnover as employers compete for the limited labor. Inevitably, this spells higher costs for the organization and a greater need for the effective implementation of well-planned career management programs.

These issues strike organizations with scientists, engineers, and professionals especially hard because technological obsolescence compounds the effects of all the previous issues. The matching of organization and individual needs and goals and the retention of valued talent becomes even more critical when the definition of talent changes so swiftly. "There was a time when a person who went to school and graduated as a mechanical engineer could count on a forty-year professional life built on that educational base—it was all one career. By the later 1950s it became evident that life for the professional engineer should probably be made up of several careers. In fact, this was happening and the time had come for both the individual and management to organize and direct the change" (40, p. 75).

Along this line, career management programs encompass any programs or efforts to improve the quality of working life, thereby facilitating the ability of the organization to retain valued contributors. Resignations can be very damaging to an organization: having spent years learning the job and the workings of the organization, the person usually leaves after two weeks notice, usually quite unexpectedly. Even in the troubled economic times of the 1970s, about 10 million people changed jobs every year, and executive searches quadrupled (68). However, projections suggest that the organization will also take a stronger lead in determining which employees will stay and which will go. Outplacement efforts were expected to grow ten times over in the 1980s (68).

Members of the American Society of Personnel Administration expect that the major effect on their roles as the 1980s draw to a close will be the use of "computer systems for personnel forecasting and planning" (68). The importance of information generated from career management systems is also highlighted in other work (58). In contacts with 2,000 chief executives, 825 stated that the most important personnel information they received was on manpower planning and development.

Elsewhere, the major issue of the 1980s was identified as employee loyalty and commitment levels (34). These are really two sides of the same coin. Career management occurs at the interface of the organization's human resource needs and the individual's career-planning needs. Therefore, both the organization and the individual have strongly vested interests in protecting their "investments" and furthering their "profit." Career management and the implementation issues identified herein become critical to both running a business and building a career.

The first part of this chapter has described the elements that could be expected to be present in a complete, formal career development system. Is this the way it is in the real world? The answer is yes! And no! All of the elements are present in every organization informally, if not formally. Human resource planning may be done "by guess and by god" rather than in a systematic, formal fashion but each decision-maker thinks about it for at least an instant or so. The same is true for everything else from recruiting to retirement. In the following section, the career management practices of organizations will be described and some of the reasons for the formal establishment of such practices will be pointed out. An attempt has been made to concentrate on current systems and components that focus on the career management of professionals, but there is a dearth of information in that area. Therefore, most of the material that follows has been derived from surveys of managerial career development programs. It will be grouped into four categories:

1. An overview of present practices
2. External labor market input practices
3. Internal labor market input practices
4. Career management system process practices

An Overview of Present Practices

It appears that no organization has a complete operational career development system as described earlier in this chapter, but a few like General Foods come close (9,20). Typically, management puts an ad hoc program in place to solve a specific, immediate problem, although once in a while it will be done because it is a socially acceptable thing to do or is part of corporate stewardship over its resources. Some of the current, external forces that influence interest in career development are technological change (rapid obsolescence of processes, products, and the like, and the presence of career development technology), legal (such as equal employment opportunity and voluntary retirement), economic (such as inflation and competition), social (such as dual-career families and lifestyle changes), and demographics (such as an aging work force and the availability of educated personnel) (64). For example, the presence of government contracts was a major factor in the introduction of career development activities in Delaware Valley firms (30).

Internal forces have even more influence (64). Some of these forces are financial (such as profitability and cost), technical (such as change in process, products, or services), human resources (such as the supply of professional and managerial talent), organizational (such as growth, diversification, and reorganization), and political (employee requests or the personal interest of a powerful individual, for example).

In a major AMA study of 225 companies, the factors shown in figure 2-4 were identified as influencing the organization to develop career management programs (73). A quick review of the list of factors indicates that organizations do not respond to humanitarian concerns but simply reflect pragmatic personnel issues that inevitably accompany business concerns. Career management systems do not exist in isolation; in most cases they are linked to established personnel programs. Ostensibly, the traditional personnel programs benefit from the added interest, motivation, and information from individuals, brought about by career management programs. Based on the AMA study (73), companies with career planning programs and the personnel programs shown in figure 2-5 linked the two together in a large percentage of cases. These programs were identified as either central to a career management system or important to supporting it. Therefore, linking them together is necessary for the implementation of any career management program, and these statistics show that many organizations directly address that requirement. Surprisingly, however, many organizations do not attempt to establish such linkages. The personnel programs in figure 2-5 have been the bread-and-butter of the traditional personnel function. Career management program implementation cannot succeed without consideration of the interplay among these traditional programs.

To keep pace with the changing times, career management programs will have to be less "tacked on" and more integral to the traditional personnel functions of selection, assessment, training, and the like. Already it can be seen that the most successful career management programs tend to be linked to other basic personnel systems. The challenge is to continue making those connections and making good use of the information for organization development and individual development.

An organization puts in place a career development program designed for professionals primarily to provide the talent required to manage such personnel and to ensure that the technical or professional knowledge and skill required by the organization are available. Individuals desire such programs so that they can increase or maintain their sense of personal worth to themselves and the organization that is associated with their work.

Aggregate information is not available to describe the

2-4. Factors influential in program development.

FACTOR	% MAJOR FACTOR	% MINOR FACTOR	% NOT A FACTOR
Desire to develop from within	88%	12%	0%
Shortage of promotable talent	63	29	8
Desire to aid career planning	56	35	9
Strong expression of employee interest	30	52	18
Desire to improve worker productivity	40	46	14
Affirmative action program commitments	38	49	13
Concern about turnover	31	46	23
Personal interest of unit managers	26	53	21
Desire for positive recruiting image	25	53	22
Attitude-survey findings	17	32	51
Personnel staff research or experimentation	15	42	43
Desire to motivate employees under limited growth conditions	18	29	53
Desire to avoid unionization	20	25	55
Desire to encourage early retirement	0	14	86

From Walker, J. W., and Gutteridge, T. G. 1979 *Career planning practices: an AMA survey report.* New York: AMACOM.

2-5. Corporate practices linking traditional personnel programs and career management systems.

PERSONNEL PROGRAM	% WITH LINKED PERSONNEL/CAREER-PLANNING SYSTEMS
Special rotational programs	87%
Management succession and replacement	87
Promotion and transfer practices	80
External training and development	80
Performance appraisal	79
Affirmative action goals	77
Skills inventory	76
Designed training programs	71
Job posting/job matching	67
Manpower forecasting	67
Scheduling existing programs	65
Recruitment practices	59
Personnel information system	59
Job description/job evaluation	52
Outplacement service	47
Compensation administration	43

Adapted from Leach, J. J. 1980 (October). Career development: some questions and tentative answers. *The Personnel Administrator* 25 (10): 31-34.

practices of organizations in the United States in a total career development system or its many components. Local surveys are available along with one major survey of career planning (individual approach). These will be described in the next three sections.

External Labor Market Input Practices

The external input side of the career development system has unique programs available to minimize errors in recruiting and selecting from the external professional/scientific labor markets and adapting the new employees to the organization (74). Cooperative programs, such as IBM's Federal Systems Division with North Carolina State University, have provided the opportunity for the organization to evaluate the performance of a student very carefully as well as to develop realistic employment expectations in the new employee prior to making an offer of permanent employment. In such programs, undergraduate students work approximately half-time with an organization during their junior and senior years and go to school the remaining time. At Martin Marietta, the engineers from a cooperative program that was developed with Drexel University and the University of Cincinnati accepted job offers in a higher ratio, remained with the company longer, and moved up in the technical hierarchy faster than a similar group of engineers who joined the company after graduation. At the Mead Corporation, a comparison of summer hiring programs in two plants indicated that technically trained college juniors who were assigned responsibilities for technical tasks and projects accepted employment at a much higher rate than those assigned laborer and other miscellaneous duties. To achieve similar results with more senior personnel, both private and government employers have developed intern programs for scientists who are approaching the end of their academic preparation and desire research experience and/or data for a dissertation (43).

For professionals to maintain their viability over a full career, advanced education appears to be important (10,26). Advanced-degree personnel are acquired primarily through recruitment although internal programs can be used to upgrade current employees and obtain improved performance (31). In a survey of twenty-one large laboratories, it was found that temporary postdoctoral positions were used to employ some new graduates so that their competence could be assessed prior to permanent employment (70). Research-and-development engineers who complete a graduate degree have exhibited high performance well beyond midcareer, while those who attain only a bachelor's degree tend to have low performance ratings after reaching the half-life period in their careers (10). Therefore, advanced-degree people or those who express interest in obtaining an advanced degree should be recruited if they are expected to maintain or increase their professional or technical expertise.

Academic achievement, interview results, and references appear to be the primary measures organizations use to aid them in the selection of new professional employees. If a sample of performance is available via a cooperative, intern, or postdoctoral program, that information is used, but standardized techniques such as assessment centers or personnel tests are very seldom employed.

The initial introduction of new professionals to the organization is handled more often perfunctorily than it is designed to present a realistic picture of the organization's nature and goals and to initiate individual career development. It is not uncommon for new professional employees to go through plant tours, attend lectures on products and processes, read publications on benefit programs and administrative procedures, and be given an overview presentation by corporate officers within the first couple of weeks. This approach inundates new employees with a horrendous amount of irrelevant information at a stage in the career where the desire is to get to work and demonstrate competence in a field that has been studied for a long period of time. Such a program should be deferred for six months to a year until the employees have sufficient knowledge of the organization and its terminology to absorb the new information and place their jobs and desires in perspective. Some organizations use a simple checklist to force new employees to meet some personnel within the administrative network and become familiar with the location of facilities that will be used. However, this approach provides little orientation outside of facilities and no introduction to the policies and practices of the organization.

The initial job assignment appears to be critical to later performance and career achievement for the individual (2). A two-year, four-assignment rotational program for new technical employees, such as the one at General Electric (76), may provide a general orientation for the individual and an opportunity for the organization to assess the individual's potential. However, it does not provide the individual with the chance to demonstrate competence quickly. The organization needs to determine which expectations should be established in the mind of the new employee.

An extreme example of effective early assimilation into the organization—or function—is the federal personnel career program. This takes employees with or without any education or training in personnel and introduces them to the federal personnel system and its rules, regulations, policies, and procedures in a very specific job rotation program similar to an apprentice program for technicians (24). A highly structured program such as this can produce an undesired emphasis on "ticket punching" in which the goal is to move through the required positions without stumbling rather than to attain top-notch performance and to try new things (44). The results of an explicit set of career steps for personnel without a required entry level of specialized education appears to be employees who are wedded to the organization (locals) because their knowledge and skills are not transferable. Because such individuals do not enter with any external contacts, it is also difficult for them to develop contacts to give the organization an infusion of new ideas. Without new ideas, job performance can be concentrated on the administration of those technologies, practices, rules, and regulations that are already present rather than on any improvements that are needed to help the organization.

Internal Labor Market Input Practices

The assessment and inventorying of scientific and professional employees for knowledge-oriented careers in an organization does not appear to be done as systematically in most organizations as it is for managerial candidates (7). In a survey of twenty-one large laboratories, it was reported that evaluations were often made by immediate and second-level supervisors to identify exceptional talent and performance declines (70). The managers of research bias the results of their appraisal of subordinate job performance toward managerial behaviors even when they are specifically instructed to evaluate only creative output, using a form designed for that purpose (46). In an attempt to reduce this type of perceptual bias, Florida Power and Light uses a unique multiple rater process and form (65). The employees choose five to nine co-workers, including the supervisor, that they have worked with during the past eighteen months to rate their performance. From these data, comparisons are made among the other participants. The format includes specially developed scaled behaviors for each of eleven criteria (33). Seven criteria are common to managers and professionals but four are not. Professionals are rated on their technical/job knowledge and ability to learn, but not the managerial scales of leadership and ability to delegate. This system is used for personal career planning, company succession planning, planning for training needs, selecting employees for development opportunities, and identifying people for promotion.

The use of supplements such as performance tests or assessment centers to complement supervisory appraisals is extremely rare (67). The Canadian Civil Service has studied the use of the in-basket technique to predict the advancement of scientists and found that it may be predictive of future managerial performance (49). Such techniques appear to have been implemented to predict managerial success, but job performance assessed by supervisory judgments remains the method to assess future technical performance. The inventorying of professionals appears to be most commonly done by broad classes of knowledge and skill, typically represented by initial or source academic fields such as tax law, chemical engineering, astrophysics, social psychology, or orthopedics.

Although relatively common in managerial programs (7), the establishment of target positions and succession plans for the professional/scientific side of the dual-career ladder appears to be uncommon. This may be because the forecasting of technical manpower requirements is difficult and seldom done (48,59). When a forecast is made, it is done at such an aggregate level that it has little value to career management or planning (35). Promotions on a scientific/professional career ladder appear to be conducted on an ad hoc, earned basis as determined by management or a scientific advisory group as at Imperial Chemical Industries (42), rather than on a structured replacement basis.

Career patterns in the form of the parallel or dual-ladder concept are relatively common in larger organizations (56,70). In such an organization structure, there will be an equivalent number of steps or positions in the scientific/professional career hierarchy as there is in the managerial hierarchy except for the very top one. The top position is restricted to the managerial side and encompasses the authority over both organization hierarchies (38). There are many variations on the theme. At Rohm and Haas Company, research is separated from development (13). Union Carbide provides an administrative ladder for support activities such as personnel and accounting (60).

The remaining system input program categories are aimed at aiding the individual to participate effectively in career development through career planning (see chapter 8).

Career Management System Process Practices

A career pattern consists of a sequence of jobs that progress from an initial position to a target one. Using progressively complex and comprehensive work experiences to develop required knowledge and experience as planned for line executives at Sears, Roebuck (66) is seldom done for professionals. Such a systematic approach to experience-based development requires a clear career structure for a limited number of stable jobs or levels of technical knowledge, as designed for one data-processing department (52). This may be difficult to provide when the technology within the critical tasks of an assignment is constantly changing as it does for professionals. However, generalized career paths may provide sufficient guidance to managers who are identifying personnel for reassignment and for individuals who desire or are being considered for it. If the career paths are too broad and the technologies are not clearly associated, professionals will not have the feeling that they are developing an area of expertise. If the paths are too narrow, people become too specialized and face technological obsolescence (56). Most large laboratories rotate their scientists and engineers among assignments for developmental purposes (56,70).

Ranftl's fifty-nine technically oriented respondent organizations indicated that the best technique for avoiding obsolescence was daily stimulating work (56). The individuals who appeared to be in the best situation to develop or retain technical expertise were scientists engaged in basic research. Another group, one hundred engineers in several organizations, indicated that the best aids to updating their technical knowledge and skills were immersion in state-of-the-art technology in their work and having free time available to work on new ideas (14). The primary inhibitors to updating were nonchallenging assignments and lots of nontechnical work.

While job assignment may be the single most important method or factor in career development, it can be detrimental (12). The federal personnel career system (24) and line military officer career patterns are examples of rotation programs that are too structured. If the amount of time in a position and the requirement to have been in each specific assignment are prescribed, individuals trade their desire to perform well in their work for getting their career requirements checked off so they can be eligible for promotion. Such career "ticket-punching" behavior appears to be dysfunctional to the organization because performance standards are not high and to the individual because risky challenges are avoided and learning is minimized.

Ranftl's survey of fifty-nine technical organizations indicated that most had company-sponsored education and training programs (56). They observed that the programs that helped the scientists and engineers to help themselves were the best, especially graduate program courses. Their experience indicated that their top performers were the best instructors of their in-house training programs, not the volunteers who liked to teach. Van Atta's survey of twenty-one large laboratories indicated that only a few of the staff participated in continuing education (70). The dominant source was fee reimbursement for external programs taken on their own and for short courses. The predominant feeling in these labs was that retraining within the individual's field was sometimes useful, and continuing education, tailored for application and the older student, should take over at the graduate level. Monsanto has implemented a small but significant effort to alleviate technical obsolescence and to assist in the reassignment of people. These individuals are looking for jobs as a result of plant closings and product discontinuance or a desire to return to engineering from managerial positions (50). A one-year program in process control was developed in conjunction with Washington University. Ten to twenty participants, typically forty to fifty years old with over twenty years of service, are thoroughly screened and admitted. The company pays salary, tuition, and relocation costs. Nearly ninety-five percent of the participants have completed the course work and returned to jobs in which significant contributions have been made.

Several professions such as medicine and psychology require the participation of their members in periodic continuing education programs. Although ninety-three of one hundred large corporations surveyed had a tuition aid program, only 3 percent of the employees participated (8). Iowa and a few other states require professional engineers to update their skills, and the idea is spreading. Typically, members of professional groups do not update their knowledge of their fields unless the organization or society provides rewards or punishments for their participation and achievement.

It appears that the benefits of continuing education to either the laboratory or the personnel are not evaluated (25). One reason may be that the results would be embarrassing since engineers in twelve companies reported that their jobs required little technical expertise (32). If technical *adequacy* rather than *competence* is the norm, skill training should be emphasized rather than professional education. However, in research and development the graduate degree recipients exhibit high performance well beyond midcareer, while those who attain only the B.S. degree level have low performance ratings on the average after their half-life period (10).

A few large, high-technology organizations offer educational leaves of absence with pay, typically for a year (25). Fourteen percent of the research-and-development professionals participate, the same proportion that is eligible. Government employees or "elite" scientists are the highly selected participants. No evaluations of the effectiveness of such programs are offered. Possibly such programs are administered as much for rewards for superior performance as they are for technical updating.

The development of effective forms for evaluating the performance of professionals has not been easy. Examples of excellence in this area of organization practices are not readily available. For scientists, creativity and its resultant outcomes—new technology, processes, or products—have been very difficult to define and measure because of the inability to distinguish between effective and ineffective behaviors and the long period of time between the initiation of work and the production of a result. As the time factor becomes critical, the outcome of the work may be interfered with by factors that are outside of the control of the scientist, such as cost and lack of corporate interest. Professionals work primarily with their minds, and it is very difficult to associate observable behaviors with the desired outcomes.

When this is done via a difficult, time-consuming procedure, the complexity of the program and the cost of its maintenance and upgrading can cause it to fall into disuse, as occurred with systems designed to appraise the performance of nurses (61). The controversy over the appraisal of elementary and secondary teachers is indicative of the problem, as are the results of research conducted in the 1970s regarding the performance of university faculty members. It became apparent that students could not evaluate the faculty members' ability to teach, but only how much they were affectively impressed by the conduct of a class. Therefore, many diverse sources of information are required to appraise the performance of a faculty member, and different outcomes should be considered according to the capability of the individual and the requirements of the organization.

Weyerhaueser uses a Behavioral Observation Scales (BOS) form as part of a goal-setting program to increase the productivity of its research-and-development personnel. Observable behaviors, in contrast to the trait approach in traditional appraisal techniques, were provided by scientists, engineers, and their managers. The effective behaviors were grouped into scales entitled planning, problem solving, interacting with others, communicating, and maintaining objectivity. Examples of ineffective behaviors that were identified were: getting involved in tangential issues or personal interests at the expense of the assignment; not keeping others informed of their activities; insisting on doing everything themselves; verbally offending others by pointing out shortcomings rather than solutions; being unconcerned with the economic feasibility of a project; and accepting more assignments and responsibilities than one person can handle (33). If professional/technical updating is going to be important to the organization and its personnel, the appropriate behaviors should be included as part of the performance appraisal process and rewarded along with work output (14).

Some organizational practices are heavily dependent upon the initiative of the individual; these include participation in professional association activities and publishing (see chapter 8).

Output Program Practices

Outplacement (lay-off, firing, or forced resignation) is a traumatic process for both the employee and the supervisor. The practices of organizations vary widely from providing generous severance pay and outplacement assistance to ignoring both areas, from providing a year's notice to a few hours'. Outplacement assistance is provided in some organizations by human resource department personnel but is more frequently contracted out to consultants who specialize in the work. The latter may provide personal counseling to alleviate the anger of the terminated professional and rebuild self-esteem. The individual is then coached in how to prepare a résumé, develop contacts, identify job possibilities, and exploit openings by interviews, telephone follow-ups, and letter writing, as well as how to conduct an interview and negotiate salary. Many personnel have been out of the job market for years and do not have the knowledge and skills required to find a new, appropriate position.

A successful, low-cost approach has been the job club, a kind of self-help firm. Such an organization provides the jobless individual with a place to work and the social support of peers who are in a similar situation. Organizations typically sponsor such groups, providing some contacts for openings. The environment is highly structured with the members required to contribute a significant portion of personal time to assist others who are also jobless. The success rate of such organizations has been very good, with new jobs located in an average of less than six months.

Another major outplacement activity is retirement. Out of 118 of the nation's largest corporations responding to a recent survey, 56 percent claimed to have a retirement-planning program (18). This is in stark contrast to earlier surveys (47,54). The purpose of such programs is to prepare employees for an experience they have never previously faced. Comprehensive programs start as early as five years prior to retirement and may include the following topics:

1. Development of a healthy outlook toward retirement—using societal support systems, keeping active, for example
2. Effective use of leisure time
3. Community and government programs that are available, including senior citizen discounts, continuing education, and Medicare
4. Housing and living arrangements and possible relocation
5. Sources of funds and personal budgeting—should the individual work or not?—revenue-producing hobbies and activities
6. Programs and assistance available through the employer such as recreational activities, newsletters, and meetings
7. Miscellaneous topics such as the preparation of wills, the health problems of older people, and marital adjustment

In some organizations the work load of the employee is reduced so that retirement does not mean an abrupt change. This can be done by extending vacations, reducing the work week, or shortening the work day. A factor that should be included in the transition to retirement is the spouse, on whom the impact of retirement may be as great as it is on the employee.

SUMMARY

This chapter has provided an overview designed to place part 1 of the book in perspective. The general systems model serves as an introduction to the inputs, processes, and outputs required to make a system function. The general systems model is made more explicit by defining it in terms of a career management system model. In this instance, the input programs are employment (external) and continuation, reassignment, promotion, or demotion (internal). The process programs include work experience and job performance, education and training, and professional activity. The output programs consist of enhanced professional/technical value, diverted or altered careers, and disengagement.

The career management system cannot stand alone but requires contributing systems and support programs. Contributing systems, such as corporate policy and the reward system, provide the guidance that gives the career management system direction and structure. The supporting programs such as recruiting (input), assignment procedures (process), and retirement planning (output) provide implementing mechanisms for the system.

After reading this chapter, you should be able to answer the following questions:

What is a career management system and what elements are present in it?
What systems contribute to the effective operation of a career management system?
What programs are required to support the operation of a career management system?
What are some examples of good—and bad—career management practices?

REFERENCES

1. Abbey, A., and Dickson, J. W. 1983. R&D work climate and innovation in semiconductors. *Academy of Management Journal* 26 (2):362–68.
2. Berlew, D. E., and Hall, D. T. 1966. The socialization of managers: effects of expectations on performance. *Administrative Science Quarterly* 11:207–23.
3. Burack, E. H. 1972. *Strategies for manpower planning and programming.* Morristown, NJ: General Learning.
4. Burack, E. H., and Mathys, N. J. 1980. *Career management in organizations: a practical human resources management approach.* Lake Forest, IL: Brace-Park.
5. Burack, E., and Walker, J. W., eds. 1972. *Manpower planning and programming.* Boston: Allyn & Bacon.
6. Campbell, S. 1985. Personal communication with author, 14 January.
7. Carnazza, J. P. 1982. *Succession/replacement planning: programs and practices.* New York: Center for Research in Career Development (Columbia Univ.).
8. (Continuing education) = (.05) (career management). 1978. *New Engineer* Aug./Sept.:31–39.
9. Courtney, R. S. 1986. A human resources program that helps management and employees prepare for the future. *Personnel,* 63 (May):32–40.
10. Dalton, G. W., and Thompson, P. H. 1971. Accelerating obsolescence of older engineers. *Harvard Business Review* 49 (5):57–67.
11. ———. 1986. *Novations: strategies for career management.* Glenview, IL: Scott, Foresman.
12. Dalton, G. W., Thompson, P. H., and Price, R. L. 1977. The four stages of professional careers—a new look at performance by professionals. *Organizational Dynamics* 6 (1):19–42.
13. Emmons, W. D. 1977. The dual ladder—the pioneering research approach. *International Journal of Research Management* 20 (4):27–29.
14. Farr, J. L., et al. 1979. The measurement of organizational factors affecting the technical updating of engineers. Paper presented at the annual meeting of the Academy of Management. Atlanta, GA, August.
15. Ferdinand, T. N. 1966. On the obsolescence of scientists and engineers. *American Scientist* 54 (1):46–56.
16. Ferguson, L. L. 1966. Better management of managers' careers. *Harvard Business Review* 44 (Mar./Apr.), 139–52.
17. Glueck, W. F. 1974. *Personnel: a diagnostic approach.* Dallas, TX: Business Publications.
18. Griffith, A. R. 1980. A survey of career development in corporations. *Personnel and Guidance Journal* 58 (April):537–42.
19. Gutteridge, T. G. 1977. Career planning: state of the practice. Paper presented at symposium, Experiential Approaches to Career Assessment and Planning. Annual meeting of the Academy of Management, Orlando, August.
20. ———. 1981. Personal communication, 5 August.
21. ———. 1986. Organizational career development systems: the state of the practice. In *Career development in organizations,* edited by D. T. Hall and Associates, pp. 50–94. San Francisco, CA: Jossey-Bass.
22. Hard, A., and Erickson, C. 1976. Career development at the Naval Weapons Center. Paper presented at symposium, Organizational Career Development: State of the Practice. Annual Academy of Management meeting, Kansas City, MO, August.
23. Jewkes, G., Thompson, P. H., and Dalton, G. W. 1979. How to stifle a technical organization in ten easy steps. *Research Management* 22 (1):12–16.
24. Junker, M., and Crane, D. P. 1976. The federal personnel career program: a case study. Paper presented at symposium, Organizational Career Development: State of the Practice. Annual Academy of Management meeting, Kansas City, MO, August.
25. Kaufman, H. G. 1977. Factors affecting the relationship between continuing education and performance: a state-of-the-art review. In *Continuing education in science and engineering.* Washington, DC: National Science Foundation, Dec.
26. ———. 1978. Continuing education and job performance: a longitudinal study. *Journal of Applied Psychology* 63:248–51.

27. ———. 1978. Technical obsolescence: an empirical analysis of its causes and how professionals cope with it. *ASEE Annual Conference Proceedings:* 194-206.
28. ———. 1980. Personal communication, 24 Sept.
29. Kellogg, M. S. 1972. *Career management.* New York: American Management Association.
30. Kleiman, M. P. 1982. An exploratory investigation of career development activities within selected organizations in the Delaware Valley. *The Career Development Bulletin* 3 (2):12-13.
31. Kopelman, R. E. 1977. Career hurdles and how to clear them. *IEEE Spectrum* 14 (2):66-69.
32. Landis, F. 1975. Continuing engineering education: who really needs it? In *Career management: a guide to combating obsolescence,* ed. H. G. Kaufman, pp. 201-20. New York: IEEE Press.
33. Latham, G. P., and Wexley, K. N. 1981. *Increasing productivity through performance appraisal.* Reading, MA: Addison-Wesley.
34. Leach, J. J. 1980. Career development: some questions and tentative answers. *The Personnel Administrator* (Oct.):31-34.
35. Liang, T. T. 1983. *Civilian manpower planning model for scientific and engineering personnel in the Navy R&D Center,* Technical report no. 83-12. San Diego, CA: Navy Personnel Research and Development Center, Feb.
36. Lorsch, J. W., and Morse, J. J. 1974. *Organizations and their members: a contingency approach.* New York: Harper & Row.
37. McBride, R. P. 1984. *Continuing education for scientists: suggestions for integrating learning and research.* Ottawa, Canada: Science Council of Canada, Oct.
38. Meisel, S. L. 1977. The dual ladder—the rungs and promotion criteria. *International Journal of Research Management* 20 (4):24-26.
39. Miller, D. B. 1975. Changing job requirements: a stimulant for technical vitality. In *Career management: a guide to combating obsolescence,* ed. H. G. Kaufman, p. 62. New York: IEEE Press.
40. ———. 1977. How to improve the performance and productivity of the knowledge worker. *Organizational Dynamics* (Winter):63-75.
41. Moment, D. 1967. Career development. *Personnel Administration* 30 (July/Aug.):6-11.
42. Moore, D. C., and Davies, D. S. 1977. The dual ladder—establishing and operating it. *International Journal of Research Management* 20 (4):14-19.
43. Morrison, R. F. 1981. Utilizing discretionary research funds to support an applied laboratory's goal: an exploratory investigation. Paper presented at the annual meeting of the Academy of Management, San Diego, Aug. 2-5.
44. ———. 1983. *Officer career development: surface warfare interviews,* NPRDC TN 83-11. San Diego, CA: Navy Research and Development Center, July.
45. Morrison, R. F., and Hoch, R. R. 1986. Career building: learning from cumulative work experience. In *Career development in organizations,* edited by D. T. Hall and Associates, pp. 236-73. San Francisco, CA: Jossey-Bass.
46. Morrison, R. F., et al. 1962. Factored life history antecedents of industrial research performance. *Journal of Applied Psychology* 46:281-84.
47. Most firms neglect retirement counseling. 1971. *Administrative Management* 32 (Oct.):44-45.
48. Naval Weapons Center and Naval Ocean Systems Center. 1978. *Implications of applying SHORSTAMPS to Director of Naval Laboratories research, development, test and evaluation efforts.* 1978. China Lake and San Diego, CA: Authors, August.
49. Pederson, L. 1980. Managerial success for a group of professionals via the in-basket. Paper read at the 9th International Congress on the Assessment Center Method. Toronto, Canada, Apr.
50. Perry, N. J. 1982. 'Recycled' engineers provide talent and technical experts at Monsanto. *World of Work Report* 7 (6):41, 43-44.
51. Pinder, C. C., and Walter, G. A. 1984. Personnel transfers and employee development. *Research in Personnel and Human Resources Management* 2:187-218.
52. Proske, A., and LaBelle, C. D. 1976. Human resource matrixing. *Administrative Management* 37 (1):22-25.
53. Pursell, D. E. 1981. Planning for tomorrow's personnel problems. *Personnel Journal* (July).
54. Pyron, H. C. 1969. Preparing employees for retirement. *Personnel Journal* 98:722-27.
55. Randolph, A. B. 1981. Managerial career coaching. *Training and Development Journal* 35 (7):54-55.
56. Ranftl, R. M. 1978. *R&D productivity: study report.* 2nd ed. Culver City, CA: Hughes Aircraft Co.
57. Roth, M. R. 1982. *A critical examination of the dual ladder approach to career advancement.* New York: Center for Research in Career Development, Graduate School of Business, Columbia Univ.
58. Russ, C. F., Jr. 1982. Manpower planning systems: part 1. *Personnel Journal* (Jan.):40-45.
59. Schubert, W., et al. 1979. *Methodology for developing manpower requirements for direct R&D Navy functions,* final report NWRC-TR-23. Menlo Park, CA: Naval Warfare Research Center, SRI International, May.
60. Smith, J. J., and Szabo, T. T. 1977. The dual ladder—importance of flexibility, job content and individual temperament. *International Journal of Research Management* 20 (4):20-23.
61. Smith, P. C., and Kendall, L. M. 1963. Retranslation of expectations: an approach to the construction of unambiguous anchors for rating scales. *Journal of Applied Psychology* 47:149-55.
62. Spangenberg, D. N. 1978. Career-path classification for professional scientific and engineering personnel. M.S. thesis, Naval Postgraduate School, Sept.
63. Stockard, J. G. 1970. *Career development and job training.* New York: AMACOM.
64. Storey, W. D., ed. 1978. *A guide for career development inquiry,* research paper no. 2. Madison, WI: American Society for Training and Development.
65. Tapping management and professional talent at FPL. 1982. *Career Development Bulletin* 3 (3):4-5.
66. Thompson, P. H., and Dalton, G. W. 1976. Are our engineering organizations obsolete? Unpublished paper, 6 May.
67. Thornton, G. C., III, and Byham, W. C. 1982. *Assessment centers and managerial performance.* New York: Academic Press.
68. Toedtman, J. C. 1980. A decade of rapid change: the outlook for human resources management in the '80's. *Personnel Journal* (Jan.):29-35.
69. Ulrich, D. 1986. Human resource planning as a competitive edge. *Human Resource Planning* 9 (2):41-50.
70. Van Atta, C. M., Decker, W. D., and Wilson, T. 1975. Professional personnel policies and practices of R&D organizations. In *Career management: a guide to combating ob-*

solescence, edited by H. G. Kaufman, pp. 122–92. New York: IEEE Press.
71. Von Glinow, M. A., et al. 1983. The design of a career-oriented human resource system. *Academy of Management Review* 8:23–32.
72. Walker, J. W. 1973. Individual career planning: managerial help for subordinates. *Business Horizons* 16 (1):65–72.
73. Walker, J. W., and Gutteridge, T. G. (1979). *Career planning practices: an AMA survey report.* New York: AMACOM.
74. Wanous, J. P. 1977. Organizational entry: newcomers moving from outside to inside. *Psychological Bulletin* 84:601–18.
75. Wellbank, H. L., et al. 1978. Planning job progression for effective career development and human resources management. *Personnel* 55 (2):54–64.
76. Wheat, D. 1982. Career development for operations managers at General Electric. *Career Development Bulletin* 3 (3):3–4.
77. *Workload definition project.* 1975. Final technical report under contract #N00123-74-C-0281. San Diego, CA: Space and Military Applications Division, Boeing Computer Services, 8 Aug.

Chapter 3

Entering and Moving in the Organization

As our first two chapters have indicated, people have different needs and career aspirations. While the organization cannot assume that everyone is motivated by the same values and goals, there are some common characteristics and factors that can be useful. Professionals, for example, share a concern for professionalism, competence, and credibility. For the pure research scientist, there is a clear quest for scientific excellence in pursuit of truth. Answers come only after detailed, meticulous study and endless repetitions and replications. For the pragmatic manager, there is a practicality and willingness to negotiate. Answers come without all the facts based on the best available information, and decisions are made to handle the exception rather than establish the unyielding rule. The laws of physics are impermeable and constant; the policies and procedures of management require somewhat greater flexibility.

The types of people who are interested and successful in these two types of jobs also differ. Professional education is a socialization process as well as an academic one. Very intelligent youngsters entering the pure science fields are not aspiring toward a management job, yet almost all will have supervisory experience in their careers, and a good proportion will leave science behind to enter management. All too often these transitions are made with no preparation and little training or ongoing support. Too often people are called into management more because they are available (being between major projects) than because they have readied themselves for the move.

A clear organizational need exists to preplan at least the next logical step in a successful person's career. An organizationwide review mechanism is needed to establish direct comparisons between people and to meet the organization's need for technical and managerial people. In many high-technology businesses, people are the only asset. Their experience and expertise are the real products of the firm. The organization's challenge is to assess accurately the current performance and future potential (technical, managerial, or both) of these "knowledge workers" and to provide the support necessary to maximize the person's contribution.

As chapter 2 described, career management entails much more than succession planning. Rather, it covers the broader scope of both individual and organizational concerns throughout the life of the person and the "life" of the organization. Figure 3-1 outlines these concerns—the first column identifying the *individual's* concern, and the second column, the *organization's* concern. The third column, which identifies an organizational program that can be leveraged against both concerns, becomes the "plan" for the next four chapters.

RECRUITING AND ORIENTATION SYSTEMS

There is a big difference between talent, promotability, and bench strength, yet employment planning significantly affects all three. Talent in a given position or at a given level is what is necessary now, today, to perform a given function up to the standards of performance that are determined by the organization. It represents a static picture of what is necessary to be a fully functioning, effective organization. However, organizations change and standards of performance can also change. Over time people move in, through, and out of positions and the organization changes. Therefore, talent is not a sufficient condition for success. An organization must also look upward from a given level and inquire about promotability; likewise a downward view to inspect one's bench strength is equally advisable. This represents a dynamic viewpoint which more accurately mirrors reality. As should be obvious by now, we are differentiating:

Talent: ability at the current level (performance)
Promotability: expected ability at a higher level (potential)
Bench strength: promotable talent at lower levels

3-1. Career management systems.

INDIVIDUAL CAREER PLANNING CONCERN	ORGANIZATIONAL CAREER MANAGEMENT CONCERN	RELEVANT ORGANIZATIONAL PROGRAM
GETTING IN AND PROGRESSING		
• What organization should I work for? Which will I really feel a part of?	• What people should work for us? How can we get them committed quickly?	• Recruiting/Orientation Systems
• What type of work and organizational position is really best for me?	• What person is really best for each type of work and position?	• Selection and Placement Systems
• What, realistically, are my development needs and future potential?	• What, realistically, is each person's development needs and future potential?	• Assessment Systems
• Will this organization meet my individual needs?	• Will these people meet our organizational business needs?	• Human Resource Review Systems
CAREER PROCESSES AND OUTPUT		
• Where do I stand in my current job?	• How is each person performing in his or her current job?	• Performance Assessment and Feedback Systems
• How can I plan for future positions within the organization?	• How can we help our people plan future positions to meet our business needs? How do we retain the people we want?	• Career Planning Programs
• How can I avoid becoming technically and professionally obsolete?	• How can we ensure that we do not end up with a group of obsolete professional/scientific people?	• Learning from the Job Itself
• How can I educate myself for future opportunities?	• How can we train our people to meet future demands?	• Training and Education Systems
• Should I stay within this organization or is it time to leave?	• How do we manage people who are not contributing as we would like?	• Termination, Outplacement, and Retirement Systems

Given a promotion-from-within policy, any one move sets up a series of interrelated moves until an external candidate is hired, usually at an entry-level position, whether in a professional or management career track. Given an external recruiting policy, constantly filling key upper-level positions with new people might negatively affect the forward movement of the organization. To some extent, position openings will always come as a surprise, but it is our conviction that these surprises can be minimized through a planned-employment process. Rather than react to each move as a crisis situation, planned backups can be developed ahead of time and a specific strategy for filling different types of positions can be formulated.

Entry-level Positions. More often than not, the only definition for entry level is an operational definition devoid of theoretical or system-specific meaning. In short, entry level usually means simply hiring from the outside, and little, if anything, more. Yet more should be expected from a systems perspective.

The act of bringing a person into an organization entails a complex social/political enculturation process that should not be blithely ignored. The entry-level position should exhibit certain characteristics in order to maximize the productivity and organizational commitment of the newcomer. In particular, an entry-level job should:

- Challenge the individual
- Have clearly defined performance standards
- Be supervised by an effective role model
- Provide a greater than normal degree of feedback
- Provide numerous different types of opportunities to develop friendly on-the-job relationships with others
- Have clearly defined career paths
- Help define and shape personal career goals
- Provide the forum for exploring personal expectations and internal conflicts
- Give some high-visibility opportunities

The message to the organization should be clear—plan entry-level positions, rather than just letting them happen. The new person, upon initial entry into the organization, is more open to change and enculturation to organizational norms than at any other time in his or her career and will later define the organization's talent, promotability, and bench strength. Berlew and Hall eloquently apply Lewin's field theory to describe this situation as it applies to the new manager; the new professional has similar concerns:

> . . . when the new manager first enters an organization, that portion of his life-space corresponding to the organization is blank. He will feel a strong need to define this area and develop constructs relating himself to it. As a new member, he is standing at the boundary of the organization, a very stressful location, and he is motivated to reduce this stress by becoming incorporated into the "interior" of the company. Being thus motivated to be accepted by this new social system and to make sense of the ambiguity surrounding him, he is more receptive to cues from his environment than he will ever be again, and what he learns at the beginning will become the core of his organizational identity. In terms of Lewin's model of attitude change, the new manager is unfrozen and is searching for information and identification models on the basis of which he can change in the direction he feels the organization expects him to change (4, p. 210).

In a more recent work (21, pp. 122–23), Hall describes potentially unexpected outcomes that he observed in some companies that upgraded initial jobs:

1. Supervisors must be carefully chosen and trained because they largely define the job.
2. Upgrading initial jobs should entail a commitment to upgrade jobs throughout the organizational structure. Otherwise, the person advances from an "enriched" job to a "regular" job and might become disillusioned and leave the organization.

Unless jobs are enriched at the second level and so on up the line, the organization is simply postponing the individual's turnover decision.

Developmental Positions. What does it mean to be "moved on a developmental assignment"? Is it a backhanded way of shuffling an incompetent employee aside, or is it used only for top performers and favorites? What does a developmental position have to do with employment planning?

Regardless of position, level, organization, or tenure, individuals all have some specific development needs relevant to current or future positions. Different people might require different experiences to pull out their talents and motivations. At the same time, certain common needs exist that are differentially represented in current positions. To some extent it might be possible to designate generic "developmental positions" that will most likely be special project assignments or staff, support, or "assistant-to" positions.

In many cases a position will be designated developmental because it meets the specific short-term need of an individual. Some of the characteristics of such a position would be:

- A "safe" environment in which to try out new and more effective behavior
- A clear, behaviorally documented set of goals and a specific plan
- A supervisor who facilitates the development plan by providing a role model and the necessary experiences and feedback
- A time commitment such that the person is assured of the "pass through" nature of the position
- Individualized and group training

A developmental position that follows the enriched job should build on initial gains. The next position should then give the individual an opportunity to extend the learnings and characteristics of the enriched job into a new area of the organization. This is a very important way of transmitting new technological knowledge and skills through the use of assignments, a key process in career development.

People should not be assigned to developmental positions on the basis of weaknesses alone. Building on current strengths is equally or more important. Most organizations would not want to place a poor decision-maker in a key decision-making role simply to develop the person at the expense of the organization. There may, however, be transition-type positions that will improve the person's skills without dramatically exposing the organization. In some situations developmental moves should be made to encourage and improve an individual's already strong points. For example, an interpersonally effective scientist might be asked to spend six months to a year as a public relations coordinator, which would broaden his or her perspective on the organization and its interface with the general public.

Technical/Managerial Positions. To some extent employment plans will differ depending on the technical or managerial makeup of the job because the talent pool and recruiting sources will differ. Every position in the organization can be characterized by some mixture of technical and managerial skill requirements along with personal/motivational requirements.

Technical and managerial skill criteria concern ability; personal/motivational criteria concern desire. Some positions might be relatively low in managerial skill requirements, perhaps needing only organizing, planning, or oral communication skills. Others may lack a strong technical skill base, requiring only general functional knowledge while stressing leadership and project management skills. Personal or motivational requirements include a concern for the degree to which there is a match between organizational objectives and individual career goals.

Different tracks should differentiate purely technical, purely managerial, and mixed technical/managerial career alternatives. A determination of the numbers of positions needed and a decision on recruiting sources would be the next likely step. A revealing exercise is to prepare a historical review of each position in terms of the highest probability "feeder" positions; and the most likely next step. In some cases this analysis will highlight what can be considered as failures in the transition from a highly technical to a highly managerial position. An intervening mixed technical/managerial position is much more likely to ensure later success than if that step were bypassed.

Recruiting

Internal versus External Search. What is your organization's commitment to promotions from within? What are the internal search procedures, if any? In what positions would "new blood" be preferable? Some positions clearly require a knowledge of the organization, making internal search the requisite process. Other positions might be so highly technical that a recognized specialist or newly trained graduate is required from outside. In most cases, the question of internal versus external search is less clearly answered. Wherever possible, positions should be predefined as generally fillable through internal or external channels. Internally filled positions then become the legitimate target of people who are career planning within the organization. It makes no sense for current employees to spend a lot of time and effort preparing for a position, to be told after it opens that only external candidates are being considered.

Internal search processes have a direct impact on individual career-planning efforts. How does a person place his or her name up for consideration? Or, how does the organization generate an effective selection list? Whatever the answer, the process should be well-defined to allow a fair, open, equitable process to occur.

Filling the Pipeline. Once entry-level positions are identified, what will be the strategy for filling them? As one opens, will one be recruited? Similarly, positions that are filled internally also require a staffing plan. "Filling the pipeline" refers to the practice of generating pools of qualified candidates prior to the availability of a given position. When the position becomes available, the staffing plan is triggered and the selection is handled quickly. The alternative is a repeated scurry of activity each time a position opens up, somewhat akin to the crisis-management style of decision making.

Specialized recruiting efforts are often used in the professional area. Often, contacts are made at professional meetings, or professionals will recruit in their former schools where they have colleagues. They learn to use the informal system in a formal manner. Trial periods and temporary jobs have been a highly successful method of developing realistic job expectations and aiding the selection process by allowing both the individual and the organization to assess each other. Readily used programs include:

- Internships
- Postdoctoral assignments
- Co-op programs
- Summer programs

Internal/External Mix. Due to the specialized nature of many scientific and engineering positions, filling the pipeline may be difficult. Part of the organization's task will necessarily be to identify those positions requiring replacement from the outside, and their most likely source. For example, sometimes the source will be college recruiting efforts, in which close relationships with appropriate universities are made ahead of time for success in filling the pipeline. For particularly sensitive positions, "trainee" positions could be created to bring new talent on board.

Organizations must mix internal and external candidates for positions for a variety of reasons. Loyalty and organizational knowledge and commitment can accrue from internal promotions, while new ideas, current education, and motivation come from external hiring. Too much of the former and the risk is stagnation; too much of the latter and the risk is a debilitating lack of continuity. The internal/external mix is a critical quantity that must be monitored and managed.

"Person-Position" Match. Essentially the person-position match means developing a profile of the type of person who will best match the position. Some jobs may call for a candidate who is independent and strong on theory; others may require someone with a particular technical skill. The job itself may fit within an entire career track. Aiming high can result in hiring a long-time valuable contributor. A more limited view will probably net someone who can do the job that is open and perhaps little else.

If turnover in scientific and engineering ranks is a problem, three elements should be examined: characteristics of the situation; characteristics of the people; and the fit between the two. Often turnover is not the critical issue; rather, the issue is often one of the most suitable placement and use of the resource available. In either case, the "person-position match" can help guide searches.

First Job Placement. Recruiters are usually careful to screen and select candidates based on technical qualifications. The question they ask is, "Does this candidate have the requisite training, education, and experience to perform the functions of this job?" There are other questions that might also be asked at this point: "Will the individual's career aspirations be served by our organization, that is, can we retain this person?" or, "How many levels is this person likely to achieve in the next five-to-ten years?" These questions address not just immediate organizational needs to fill a position, but long-range needs for people to rise from within the organization.

Some jobs will be highly technical in nature, yet may be the main "feeder position" for a project leader's job. Does the candidate have managerial skill? As long as the majority of workers move into a particular type of position within a reasonable period of time (approximately five years), then use of those positions' requirements as selection criteria are legally defensible. As an organization, is this a strategy which you wish to follow?

A more difficult assessment is the question of the degree to which an individual's personal value system is consistent with the organization's culture. This is bound to be a much grayer area with regard to legally defensible selection criteria, even though specific programs have been developed which do just this (25). The more acceptable system is to provide a realistic picture of the organization and let the candidate determine if that is the kind of place he or she would want to work. In this way, personal choice takes the place of organizational rejection of candidates. Too often, jobs are oversold or overglamorized, leading to disillusionment and turnover.

Recruiters must be especially sensitive to this issue. For example, some years ago, Marcson found that recruiters unwittingly distorted important facts in their zeal to bring talented young scientists aboard (33). Scientists expected to do basic research, and the laboratories expected them to produce devices that could be manufactured and sold. Likewise, French states, "Attempts to assess the value orientation of the candidate also seem useful. A scientist who has a strong need for the approval of fellow scientists in other organizations might appropriately be employed in a laboratory doing basic research, but that person might be grossly misassigned as a technical assistant in a pilot plant, or in manufacturing, or in administration" (20).

Figgins has recently advanced a system that allows a person to decide on a job by breaking that "large" decision down into a series of "smaller" decisions (17). He calls this the Decision Analysis Chart (DAC) method, and it involves the person determining the personal importance of various job factors and the degree to which the job meets these needs. It is presented from the individual perspective, yet the organization has cause to be concerned about this type of matching process as well. Some organizations, such as Citibank's "Jobmatch," have developed elaborate computerized systems to handle job matches (47).

Maximizing the First Job. Early in their careers, scientists and engineers stress certain factors that hiring organizations should address:

- Need for self-fulfillment, autonomy, and involvement in the job (23)
- Job challenge (9)
- Opportunity to do important and interesting work in an environment characterized by freedom and individual responsibility (1)
- Recognition from the scientific community or from top management (20)

These factors are not very different from what any employee wants and expects from the first job. Newly graduated scientists and engineers, having never worked within an organization, may be quite naive with regard to the realities of business. Even if the business is "pure research," the bureaucratic need to provide some linkage to a useful product will consistently produce conflict. The realities of the processes of goal setting, decision making, feedback, salary review, and the like will undoubtedly convince the person that the pure research laboratory is, after all, part of a political organization.

One journal has outlined a number of steps that the organization should take to maximize the positive impact of the first job (22). Judging by the aforementioned concerns of young scientists and engineers, the following steps are even more meaningful:

- Offer a challenging first job, which includes some tasks with a reasonable probability of failure. If these are achieved, the exhilarating feeling of psychological success motivates the person for even more difficult tasks.
- Provide job enrichment, by adding responsibility and authority or by giving the person a more whole, complete job to accomplish.
- Assign the new recruit to demanding bosses who are also supportive and will express confidence. The new employee will gain tremendously by being "stretched" early.
- Give realistic job previews. Show the negative part of the job. Talk about why previous employees have left. Relay the most likely problems or frustrations.

The new professional is confronted with numerous challenges upon entering an organization.* In particular, a balance needs to be struck between a willingness

---

*This discussion was inspired by an article in *Organizational Dynamics* (14).

to accept and carry out routine, detailed work and an aggressive searching out of new and more challenging tasks. The brightest and best college seniors may expect to enter the organization as an "independent contributor," rather than serve time as an "apprentice," thereby skipping one career stage. Consider the following quote attributed to a physicist in a highly respected laboratory:

> My first year here was frustrating. I had a good record in graduate school. I was ready to go to work and make a contribution. But for a year, no one paid much attention to my suggestions. I almost left. It took me a year to realize that I didn't yet understand the complexity of the problems we were working on. Now I try to take enough time with people to help them understand the dilemma of that first year (14, p. 25).

A little sensitivity by the organization and its management to these types of issues can go a long way toward maximizing the individual contributor's first job.

Orientation Systems

Bringing a new person on board is an important and often overlooked process. In the first few days and weeks simple experiences become critical incidents in forming that person's view of the organization. The process can be thought of as similar to the *imprinting* phenomenon that is observed in its most obvious form among newly hatched chicks. The chick will follow the first moving object it sees, "imprint" upon it, and become dependent on it as a maternal figure. In a similar manner, a new employee is open to cues within the workplace. The organization can actively manage this process and allow the person to "imprint" upon it. Since people differ in what they are looking for in the workplace, orientation programs should entail a "core" that everyone experiences followed by individually tailored experiences designed to ease the person's transition into the organization.

A recurring special problem that organizations have with new professional/scientific hirees should be addressed in the design of orientation programs. These new employees have gone through years of extensive education and are anxious to use it right away. Immediate formal orientation by the organization should be kept to a minimum. The new employee should be allowed to settle into the job for a while. Then, they can be oriented to the overall organization and more complex companywide programs. If the formal orientation program is given three to six months after the start of the job, the professional tends to be much more receptive. Recall of the material will be better because the language is more familiar and "information overload" less of a problem.

The first step in designing an orientation program is to specify its objectives. Such a program might aim to:

- Develop a feeling within the employee of being committed to the organization and its goals
- Provide a historical overview of the organization
- Provide an opportunity to meet key decision-makers, supervisors, and peers
- Introduce the person to his or her work group and provide an "ice-breaking" experience
- Familiarize the person with the physical facility, supplies, and equipment
- Ensure that the person understands company policies, overtime policies, company norms, tradition, and other aspects of the "corporate culture"
- Familiarize the person with the job, how it relates to other jobs, how it fits into the "big picture," performance standards, and similar topics
- Help integrate the new employee's family into the community

Naturally, the program's structure will be based on its objectives. Actions to address each objective can be summarized according to whose responsibility it is—personnel department, hiring department, or employee.

The personnel department will generally be responsible for the basic activities that encompass organization-level information and, perhaps, for overseeing the departmental orientation activities. One researcher (46) has suggested content outlines, on which this one is based, for personnel:

ORGANIZATION OVERVIEW
- CEO welcome
- History and goals
- Traditions and customs
- Organizational structure and functions
- Products/services
- Scope/impact of organizational activities
- Key people
- Community involvement
- Key policies and procedures

COMPENSATION
- Salary ranges
- Performance evaluation procedures
- Salary increase policies
- Required and optional deductions
- Credit union
- Business expense reimbursement policy

BENEFITS
- Insurance
- Medical/dental
- Holidays/vacations
- Leave policy
- Retirement plans

- Recreational/social activities
- Cafeteria
- Other services/benefits

SAFETY
- Safety policies and procedures
- Fire prevention and control
- Accident procedures
- First-aid equipment/facilities
- OSHA requirements
- Alcohol/drug use

EMPLOYEE RELATIONS
- Grievance procedures
- Disciplinary procedures
- Termination policies and procedures
- Personnel records
- Communications (suggestion plans, postings, and so on)
- Employee rights and responsibilities
- Union/contract provisions

STAFFING
- Selection and placement systems
- Career management systems
- Job posting and self-nomination procedures

PHYSICAL FACILITIES
- Tour of facilities
- Food services/cafeterias
- Break areas
- Employee entrances
- Restricted areas
- Parking
- Restrooms
- Supplies/equipment
- Exercise/fitness centers

The hiring department also has certain critical responsibilities when it comes to orientation. By its nature, the personnel department's topics will be general, whereas the hiring department can be specific and provide more personal orientation opportunities. Some topics would include:

DEPARTMENTAL OVERVIEW
- Strategic plans and business issues
- Departmental structure and functions
- Interrelationship of jobs and sections
- Departmental goals and priorities

POSITION ACCOUNTABILITIES
- Job description and accountabilities
- Performance expectations
- Common problems/possible solutions

KEY PEOPLE
- Interviews with key members of the department—section heads, interfacing departments, and others.

The individual must also be made responsible for his or her own orientation. This can be done through special project assignments of limited duration. These should be determined on an individual basis as part of that person's development plan. They must not be pointless assignments; they should contribute to the person's understanding of the organization and ability to perform the job effectively. For professionals, such assignments can provide an entry into the professional groups that operate within the organization.

The informal orientation that occurs in unplanned, unofficial ways, usually by co-workers, will have a big impact on the new employee's feeling about the organization. A "lunch program" in which current employees lunch with new employees to talk about their jobs and the organization can be helpful. Invitation for involvement in company sports or special interest groups may also facilitate the informal process.

According to St. John, there are sixteen cautions to observe when setting up an orientation program (46):

1. Tailor topics to fit the organization
2. Fix orientation responsibilities and ensure that roles are understood
3. Include a cross-section of employees to plan the program without relying solely on managers, supervisors, or the personnel department
4. Keep an orientation file containing new ideas, other organizations' programs, employee feedback, and program evaluation forms
5. Avoid overwhelming employees with too much information too fast
6. Anticipate employees' potential problems and needs for information
7. Identify both company and job-level informational needs and divide into personnel department or local supervisory responsibility
8. Use a checklist system to ensure everything necessary is covered
9. Insist that the employee sign the checklist as proof of receiving the information or material
10. Impart the most important information in writing *and* verbally
11. Use a loose-leaf notebook for maintaining written materials to permit easy updating
12. Show the employee how his or her job relates to other jobs and affects the organization's final results
13. Identify job expectations, performance standards, departmental goals, and the like clearly, preferably in a give-and-take, question-and-answer discussion
14. Choose only effective, respected, well-informed employees with realistic, positive attitudes as "buddies" if a "buddy system" is used

15. Seek ongoing new employee feedback to provide a means of revising the program to fit needs
16. Include the spouse at one session to help develop a family understanding of and commitment to the job and the organization

In particular, it must be remembered that orientation to the job and organization is essentially a socialization process. Not only must informational requirements be met, but effective interpersonal and working relationships with others must also be established. This can be especially tricky with new graduates who have limited experience in relating to peers, subordinates, and superiors in a working environment. Professionally trained employees have been socialized to certain ethical standards and state-of-the-art theoretical models, which must then be put under fire and potentially compromised by the demands of the organization. As Joan M. Pearson of Honeywell states the issue:

> ... a newcomer's difficulty in attaining career goals was the best predictor of how much thought the newcomer was giving to leaving the new job. This relationship underscores the importance that professional level employees place on career opportunities, and implies that companies concerned about retaining these employees need to structure career-planning and development programs that meet the company's manpower needs as well as satisfy the career aspirations of employees (45).

ORGANIZATIONAL INFORMATION REQUIREMENTS

In career management activities the organization and the individual need information about each other. This chapter is concerned with the organization's side of the process; in part 2 the individual's self-analysis and communication of individual information to the organization are discussed.

What do individuals want to know about the organization? The answer, succinctly, is everything that they see as relevant to them. The organization, then, needs to make a realistic determination of what information can be made available and what will remain confidential. For example, it would certainly help a person to know the strategic business plans of the organization to understand where tomorrow's "hot" areas and personal opportunities will be. And to know how the business is changing, what new products are planned, what government grants or contracts are being sought or new acquisitions planned, and what areas are being phased out. For a variety of reasons, some of these questions may not be answered by the organization. The point here is that organizational decision-makers need to think through the extent to which information will be made generally available to employees.

The informal, organization-initiated career management system has always been run to some extent according to how information is used by people "in the know." The question the organization must address is the degree to which it is willing to move to a formal, "public," individual-initiated career management system. The more formalized and "open" the system, the greater the burden on the organization to make relevant business-related information available.

Annual Report to Employees. Even in the absence of formal career planning programs, some companies generally make organizational information available through an annual report to the employees. Similar in style to the annual report to stockholders, this publication might address the following topics:

- Our business—yesterday, today, and tomorrow
- General human resource policy statement
- Charts: how we are organized
- Major departmental programs and projects
- What's new—this year and next

To the degree that such a publication is personalized rather than general and increases a person's knowledge about the business and its objectives, it will be useful. To the degree that it is linked to a career management approach that seeks to gain the understanding, involvement, and commitment of its members, it will be invaluable.

Departmental Meetings. Annual reports may provide a broad overview of the large organization, but the individual likely also wonders about specific plans unique to his or her section or department. Managers and department heads, left to their own systems, will differ greatly in the degree to which information of this sort is made available. If the organization wants to ensure that local questions and issues are raised and discussed, departmental meetings could be planned by section or department, coinciding with the publication of the employee report. Astonishingly, in many cases, people within the same unit do not understand the jobs of others in the unit. An employee meeting might have an agenda such as this:

- Introduction (by department head)
- Section program overview (by section heads to describe the objectives and activities of their sections)
- Position and project descriptions (by incumbents)
- Technical/professional support (by respected employees to describe proposed roles and relationships with professional societies and with others they need to interact with to get the immediate job

done, for example, technical editors, computer support, purchasing, or travel)
- Questions and answers (fielded by section/department heads)

In reference to the position and project descriptions by individuals, consider the following approach. First, limit the number of positions and projects described based on multiple incumbency, degree of specialization, likelihood of movement, and other similar factors. Second, use this as an opportunity to challenge the presentation skills of people who may need development in this area. Third, have a structured system for imparting position information. The person would then provide the "color commentary" with examples, anecdotes, critical incidents, and the like that are related to the job. At a minimum the following should be presented:

- Position title: major function of the position (two sentences, top line)
- How it fits in the organization: department and section, supervisor's title and name, subordinates' titles (if any), close working relationships with specific other departments/sections
- Major program responsibilities (including typical projects)
- Major position activities (beginning with action verbs such as *provide, check, calculate, ensure, monitor, administer*)
- Major position knowledges (describe what you need to *know* in the job—theories, practices, procedures, standards, systems, principles)
- Position demands and restrictions (the downside of the job—what you have to put up with)
- Position characteristics (anything else that characterizes the job)
- Position requirements: technical skills needed, managerial skills needed, educational/experience requirements
- Career considerations: typical source/feeder positions, typical lateral/promotional opportunities

Some may scoff at this type of presentation as an amateur show-and-tell contest, but it can be much more than that. It brings the sharing of organizational information down to the department, section, and *individual* level. People *like* to talk about what they do, and this approach provides that opportunity. In fact, the individual who must make the presentation is likely to do a serious job of putting the information on his or her position together in a meaningful and descriptive way. When all such information is compiled, the organization will have developed its own position profile book with important information on departments, sections, and positions.

A departmental meeting of this nature and content is likely to have much more meaning to the individuals than most canned "career planning seminars." The issue as always is to achieve the prior commitment of that department head to the meeting—the department should feel ownership, it should not be seen as a personnel department program.

Depending on the individual development needs of the department's people, the meeting could be held in varying ways. For example, if the department head recognized that several people were having difficulty working with other sections, those people might be given a special project requiring them to present the positions in that other area rather than their own position. This would get the two sections working closely together and perhaps enable them to gain a better understanding of each other's priorities, pressures, competing requests, and other factors.

The format of the meeting personalizes the approach and allows face-to-face discussion regarding the functions of other areas and how they relate to one's own job. Even in the absence of career management objectives, other purposes are served by such departmental meetings. Simply understanding how a job "fits in" gives an employee the "big picture," often improving performance as a result. Feeling part of an organization that has these values and does things like this strengthens a person's commitment to the organization. The risk is that the person will determine that the organization is unsuitable, perhaps without opportunities for him or her; the next day, résumés are sent out. The organization must weigh that risk against the benefits.

Many organizations have attempted to group jobs that are alike in key respects into so-called job families. The idea behind this is that movement within a job family is most likely—so people know which other jobs to plan toward and the organization knows which jobs to tap for talent pools when a position opens. In most organizations there are no formal, published job families, but there are commonly shared, implicit assumptions and beliefs about which jobs seem to "hang together." A departmental meeting allows the local determination of what movement is likely from each job in that function. Groupings will most likely be based on the technology or knowledge content of the job. The compensation people may call one level "Scientist 1," but that does not mean anything from a career-planning perspective (astronomer or agronomist?). This should be brought out in the meeting under the "career considerations" topic for each position.

Although concern for "information overload" must always be considered, the departmental meeting could be expanded in another way. Information giving by various personnel representatives could be added as needed to address specific employee concerns. Employees often want to know about the existing management systems that partially control their fate within the organization. These include, but are not necessarily limited to:

COMPENSATION DEPARTMENT
- How are levels determined?
- When do jobs need to be reevaluated?
- What are the salary increase guidelines?
- What are the compensation structures for a professional career ladder?

SELECTION/STAFFING DEPARTMENT
- What is the internal selection system?
- What information is used for internal selections?
- What information is in an employee's file?
- What other information is available on that person's abilities, experience, or interests?
- How can an employee self-nominate for a particular position?

PROFESSIONAL AND MANAGEMENT DEVELOPMENT
- What professional or management development courses are available?
- What is the educational reimbursement policy?
- How can a person get opportunities on the job to grow and develop?
- What human resource planning information is available?
- Are there any individual career-planning workbooks or information available?

This type of information could also be assembled as part of a career-planning workbook for general distribution or as a handout during a departmental meeting. The written format tends to be less alive, more impersonal, and more likely to make the program be perceived as a personnel staff function rather than a departmental initiative. Used *alone,* it is less likely to be useful.

A more detailed description of an example career planning workbook is given in Appendix 2. The message of this section is simply that information about the organization is a critical factor in career management. That information can be collected and imparted in numerous ways. It will happen in an inconsistent and potentially inaccurate way if done informally. Benefits can be achieved by systematizing the information process whether or not an entire career-planning program is formalized.

INTERNAL SELECTION AND PLACEMENT SYSTEMS

Once the person is in the organization, the organization needs an ongoing system to ensure proper placement and use of employees. The organization, however, can never be omniscient with regard to the knowledge, abilities, and motivation of employees. Organizational systems, therefore, require some individual input to work effectively. Throughout this section, "interface" ideas that connect the individual and the organization are presented. Neither the organizational nor the individual perspective is alone sufficient. Effective career management occurs when the two perspectives can be merged successfully so that the myopic viewpoint of each is supplemented and expanded. Both sides need to use a variety of methods to learn about each other. In this section we will describe informational systems that the organization can make available to involve the individual in making person-to-position matching considerations.

Skill Classifications

Positions vary a great deal in their managerial and technical skill requirements. Taxonomies or classifications abound with regard to the appropriate listing, categorization, and hierarchy of managerial and technical skills. None can be considered at this time to be uniformly correct. One taxonomy of managerial skill dimensions and skills is summarized in figure 3-2. The importance of each skill listed there will vary depending on the specific position being discussed. For example, a supervisory job would more likely include leadership, people development, and interpersonal skills as critical whereas a staff scientist position might require analytical, quantitative, and organizing and planning skills. Neither the overall list nor the determination of which are the critical skills for a job should be determined by armchair fiat. Rather, a rigorous empirical process known as a job analysis must be conducted.

Job Analysis

Reliable information regarding jobs in the organization, collected in a standardized and planned manner, will be the cornerstone of every piece which follows. (In this regard, the *Handbook for Analyzing Jobs* should be consulted [24].) Since the job analysis comes first, it is recommended that it be constructed to produce all the necessary information for every phase of the career management program. Job analysis information (including for example, the identification of managerial activities and technical skills) can be used to contribute to a variety of outcomes such as:

- Position profiles
- Career planning and counseling
- Performance standards/evaluations
- Targeted selection interviews
- Training programs
- Qualifications and standards development
- Test development and validation
- Job restructuring
- Job evaluation/position leveling

3-2. Managerial dimensions and skills abilities.

ADMINISTRATIVE

ORGANIZING AND PLANNING

- Handle several projects at one time
- Be punctual for meetings, appointments, and other occasions
- Plan and organize activities to meet a goal
- Coordinate resources to reach goal
- Organize work for self
- Organize work as part of a group effort
- Complete assignments in a time-efficient manner
- Classify and categorize related information
- Organize data or facts provided by others
- Be well-prepared for meetings and presentations
- Have needed information readily accessible
- Set realistic goals within time constraints
- Establish appropriate priorities
- Systematically structure information and activities in meeting task requirements
- Schedule "things to do"
- Allocate time and activities to meet priorities
- Avoid crisis management through proper planning

RESULTS ORIENTATION

- Press for completion and closure
- Express sense of urgency
- Work for speed as well as accuracy
- Show initiative
- Have a high energy and activity level
- Put in long hours when necessary
- Be goal-oriented and strive for success
- Take pride in evidence of effectiveness
- Persist at tasks until completed
- Set challenging but attainable goals
- Overcome obstacles
- View problems as opportunities
- Operate with a minimum of direction
- Reach out for more responsibility
- Persist until successful
- Demonstrate confidence in ability to succeed
- Do a very thorough job
- Take some risks to achieve maximum benefits
- Make personal sacrifices to meet company goals
- Strive for high goals, a drive to excel
- Patiently and relentlessly persevere

WRITTEN COMMUNICATION

- Write clear, concise reports
- Express ideas clearly in writing
- Present a persuasive, attention-holding case
- Use proper grammatical forms
- Write memos and reports that are easy to follow and understand
- Make effective use of outlines, headings, and subheadings when presenting reports
- Provide clear, concise instructions to others via memos or other written correspondence
- Use correct sentence structure, paragraphs, and punctuation

DECISION MAKING

ANALYTICAL

- Emphasize detail and completeness
- Produce highly accurate reports
- Catch all typos, incorrect numbers, and other errors
- Define parameters of and objectives for a task
- Test assumptions
- Develop hypotheses
- Analyze results
- Grasp new concepts, approaches, or systems quickly
- Reorganize information in unique ways
- Recognize problems
- Comprehend, identify, and assimilate the critical elements of a situation
- Separate a large task into component parts
- Attend to details of a problem
- Cut to the heart of an issue
- Interpret implications of various courses of action
- Perceive how information relates or is related
- Recognize priority issues
- Draw accurate conclusions from data
- Extract the most relevant information
- Logically proceed from individual cases to general principles
- Apply a general principle to a particular case

QUANTITATIVE

- Perform mathematical calculations correctly
- Prepare accurate numerical reports
- Conduct statistical analyses
- Interpret numerical/statistical reports
- Describe numerical trends
- Develop or apply pricing or financial plans
- Formulate measurement systems
- Identify and correct mathematical errors
- Forecast, budget, and/or report quantitative data

JUDGMENT

- Make high-quality decisions
- Base decisions on facts
- Present logical rationale for decisions
- Explore alternatives
- Examine pros and cons
- Remain objective—not allowing personal opinions to bias decisions
- Gather as much relevant information from as many sources as possible

(continued)

3-2. (Continued)

- Approach situations realistically, with common sense
- Discriminate ideal from practical and realistic
- Set sensible time frames and goals
- Generate creative solutions
- Use innovative techniques
- Anticipate problems
- Identify critical factors
- Solve problems the first time to prevent their return
- Balance short- and long-term effects
- Foresee accurately impact of decisions
- Make and execute decisions compatible with company goals
- Validate the truth or accuracy of information before using it
- Show good judgment
- Decide when to make or to postpone a decision

DECISIVENESS

- Make all the decisions necessary in a given situation
- Strongly defend decisions
- Make decisions in ambiguous situations or when all the information is not available
- Stick with the decided course of action
- Promptly and firmly take action when required
- Demonstrate courage to act
- Take a firm stand when challenged
- Take action in the face of conflicting or contradictory information
- Make unpopular but necessary decisions
- Set up new procedures or routines
- Take action necessary in the interim
- Strongly commit to a decision
- Tenaciously stick with a problem or line of thought
- Stand alone

FLEXIBILITY

- Take a problem-solving approach to disruptions
- Adapt to interruptions, changes, or disorder without losing composure or efficiency
- Handle repetitive as well as unique tasks willingly
- Maintain composure and effectiveness under pressure
- Change approaches to problems or tasks with the presentation of new information
- Be receptive and adaptive to changes in the situation
- Acknowledge and incorporate alternative points of view
- Reconsider and modify approach based on progress made on the task
- Modify behavioral or management style as necessary to be effective
- Resist or tolerate stress

SUPERVISORY

LEADERSHIP

- Provide clear direction to peers and subordinates
- Delegate appropriately and effectively
- Take charge and initiate action
- Maximize use of resources
- Minimize dissension among people
- Create a healthy atmosphere
- Involve others in task completion
- Give credit where credit is due
- Effectively differentiate roles
- Accept responsibility
- Thrive on competition with peers
- Encourage flow of information
- Coordinate the activities of others
- Influence decision making in groups
- Deal effectively with subordinates, regardless of competence
- Inspire and stimulate the best effort of others
- Direct and persuade others
- Comment on the contributions of others
- Use subordinates effectively
- Command attention and respect
- Achieve personal recognition
- Control events in the environment
- Manage the time and activities of others

CONTROL AND FOLLOW-UP

- Monitor activities against plans
- Establish specific schedules, deadlines, or quotas
- Track and summarize progress
- Set up systems to check, test, or verify that assigned actions are carried out
- Take steps to determine the impact of decisions
- Schedule specific date, time, and place for follow-up meetings
- Evaluate the results of delegated assignments

PEOPLE DEVELOPMENT

- Appraise and develop others
- Define current job performance of others
- Develop specific, attainable, measurable goals
- Provide day-to-day information feedback
- Conduct performance reviews effectively
- Discuss promotional opportunities
- Contribute to the planning and execution of a development plan
- Describe the developmental opportunities of subordinates
- Provide positive reinforcement
- Set goals in measurable terms
- Constructively correct subordinates so they learn from mistakes
- Work with a person on *how* to improve
- Communicate clear standards of performance

3-2. (*Continued*)

- Provide negative feedback to the *task,* not the person's self-worth
- Choose and assign tasks according to the development needs of subordinates
- Leverage accountabilities to challenge subordinates
- Use participative management when appropriate

INTERPERSONAL

- Effectively work with people
- Establish personal likability and credibility
- Show an interest in people and their work
- Deal with people tactfully
- Show concern for people's job satisfaction
- Be easily approachable
- Read other people accurately
- Make a good "first impression"
- See both strengths and weaknesses in others
- Be sensitive to and concerned about the needs and feelings of others
- Be accepting rather than critical
- Exhibit a good sense of humor
- Influence others on an informal basis
- Perceive impact of self on others
- Be a team player
- Gain the respect of peers and subordinates
- Make friends easily
- Work effectively with many constituents (customers, the public, co-workers)
- Gain the confidence and trust of others
- Establish and maintain harmonious relations with others
- Create and maintain a congenial, supportive work environment
- Be receptive to and accepting of individual differences
- Reconcile differences of opinion effectively
- Deal effectively with others regardless of level, status, or background
- Remain pleasant and even-tempered
- Adopt a self-effacing style; express humility
- Deal with people politely and helpfully

SELF-MANAGEMENT

- Act in a professional manner
- Show behavior appropriate to a wide range of situations
- Exercise personal control
- Avoid impulsive comments or actions
- Control strong feelings or temper
- Deal diplomatically with tense situations
- React in a positive manner to constructive criticism
- Maintain appropriate appearance
- Actively engage in self-development
- Work effectively within company guidelines
- Relate own goals to that of the company
- Follow professional ethical standards of behavior
- Recognize and act in accordance with organizational norms
- Put good of the company above selfish desires

ORAL COMMUNICATION

- Express self well in informal communications
- Express self well in formal presentations
- Project well; use a clear, strong voice
- Maintain good eye contact
- Speak to audience level
- Use appropriate gestures
- Use vocal inflection to emphasize points
- Listen effectively
- Respond to questions clearly and directly
- Use vocabulary and style appropriate to the situation
- Describe complicated concepts or information
- Persuade, influence, or argue convincingly
- Use correct grammar
- Be interesting and articulate
- Understand the communications of others
- Take actions based on convictions

The managerial and technical skill identification process describes the overall organization's behavioral requirements and isolates individual position requirements. A managerial skill taxonomy has already been presented in figure 3-2. A focus on more technically oriented skills is best exemplified by McCormick's development of the position analysis questionnaire over the past two decades (36,37). An overall analysis was conducted on data for 3,700 jobs and 182 job elements (34), resulting in the taxonomy presented in figure 3-3.

Several items have been deleted on this list because they overlap with the managerial dimensions and skills previously presented. Also, the technical dimensions identified in figure 3-3 are conceptualized as characteristics of the job, whereas the managerial dimensions identified in figure 3-2 are conceptualized as characteristics of the person. This is an important comparison because the next step will be to compare the person's skills with the position's skill demands. The two approaches (position-to-person match or person-to-position match) are not really opposite because the matching process is the same. Any given program should take a consistent approach to the way these are defined. This might mean having parallel lists of job characteristics and individual skills that correspond. In part, this is a semantic issue since the job characteristic, "required to

3-3. Technical dimensions and skills.

INFORMATION INPUT

- Perceptual interpretation
- Evaluation of sensory input
- Visual input from devices/materials
- Input from representational sources
- Environmental awareness

MENTAL PROCESSES

- Use of job-related knowledge
- Information processing

WORK OUTPUT

- Manual/control activities
- Physical coordination
- General body activity
- Manipulating/handling activity
- Adjusting/operating machines or equipment

---

perform complex multivariate statistical analyses" would correspond to an individual skill of "ability to perform complex multivariate statistical analyses."

Figure 3-4 is an example of the kind of form into which job analysis information can be sorted. The managerial and technical skill dimensions will vary from organization to organization, but for each position, major skill requirements can be identified using a common rating system. Details on each position would then be used to write a position profile. A word of caution: design the job analysis questionnaire only after clearly defining the objectives and outcomes desired.

The position information in figure 3-4 can help an employee form realistic career aspirations. It identifies areas in which a person would need to develop to become a competitive candidate and, through the "position fill requirements" column (which must be forecast based on historical trends and future business plans), allows a person to decide whether it would be desirable to plan toward that position.

The power of this type of information is indisputable. In some cases, employees feel for the first time as though they can take an active part in preparing themselves for positions that have clear skill requirements. Position skill requirements then become the job-related basis for personal career self-analysis and planning-type workbooks. The requirements may also become the basis for individual feedback and development programs and for group training sessions.

Given position requirements, the next logical step is to construct a human resources inventory that parallels the managerial and technical skill dimensions. In figure

3-4. Managerial and technical skills: position requirements.

POSITION TITLE AND NUMBER	Managerial Dimensions				Technical Dimensions				Position Fill Requirements	
	ADMINIS- TRATIVE	DECISION MAKING	SUPER- VISORY	PER- SONAL	INFORMA- TION INPUT	MENTAL PROCESSES	WORK OUTPUT	JOB CONTEXT & CHARACTER- ISTICS	WITHIN 1 YEAR	1-3 YEARS

Rating Scale:
- 5 = heavily required by the position
- 4 = required by the position
- 3 = helpful in the position
- 2 = somewhat helpful in the position
- 1 = not required by the position
- 0 = not applicable to the position

3-5. Managerial and technical skills: human resources inventory.

EMPLOYEE NAME AND NUMBER	Managerial Dimensions				Technical Dimensions				Promotability	
	ADMINIS-TRATIVE	DECISION MAKING	SUPER-VISORY	PER-SONAL	INFORMA-TION INPUT	MENTAL PROCESSES	WORK OUTPUT	JOB CONTEXT & CHARACTER-ISTICS	WITHIN 1 YEAR/ POSI-TION	1–3 YEARS/ POSI-TION

Rating Scale:
5 = well above satisfactory
4 = above satisfactory
3 = satisfactory
2 = below satisfactory
1 = well below satisfactory
0 = not applicable/can't rate

3-5 employees are rated on these dimensions by their supervisors; ratings are reviewed up the line to ensure accuracy. The information contained in figures 3-4 and 3-5 can be matched through sophisticated computer technology or through a simple person-to-position matrix. The human resources game is to have the right people in the right number at the right place and time to perform the right tasks that lead to the right objectives (and so on). This approach to inventorying people and positions and forecasting needs for the same can help an organization keep up with personnel changes.

For the department head or individual manager, is all this useless unless the organization adopts the whole program? Certainly not, because the same logic applies in the individual case. Simply touching all the bases previously outlined can help ensure proper human resource utilization within your function. Your own program may not look as nice or be printed on forms, but the logic of matching position requirements and human resource skills remains unarguable. Even an individual contributor with no supervisory responsibility would benefit by analyzing jobs of interest, determining their probable availability, and matching his or her own skills and likelihood of promotion against that knowledge base. At the very least, this can result in a constructive and detail-oriented career-planning discussion between supervisor and individual rather than the somewhat selfish and shallow discussion predictably beginning with the individual saying, "I think I deserve a promotion—what are you going to do for me?"

Use of Position Information

The individual professional generally has a very limited knowledge of organizational opportunities, and his or her immediate supervisor often has only a slightly better perspective. If the individual is indeed urged to take responsibility for career planning, the organization has a corresponding responsibility to make information about positions available to individuals. Both professional and managerial positions should be described so that the individual can choose his or her preferred route, rather than have management *assume* that everyone wants to get into management.

Often some dimensions of the other positions are met through job-related interactions, leading some individuals to conclude that the position is an easy one. Yet there may be much more to it: knowledge requirements, managerial skills, and unseen demands. Some professionals may wish to remain individual technical contributors and would like to identify other positions of that nature that would be challenging and might require learning new technologies that counteract overspecialization. Other professionals may be interested in management careers, and will be seeking information about positions of greater scope and responsibility than their present ones that will ease the transition into management.

A "job description" alone does not fully summarize the position. The job description usually deals with bottom-line accountabilities and defines the scope or dimensions of a job in order to properly define salary levels. A career-planning position profile, in contrast, must include those things that lead to a person fulfilling the responsibilities effectively. In the career management section of chapter 5, there is an example position profile in terms of the specific characteristics, and associated concerns for the professional, that are shown in figure 3-6. The questions asked under each heading are addressed to both the individual and the organization.

Person-to-Position Matching. The matching process between the individual's qualifications and the position's requirements can now be conducted in ways that vary widely in sophistication. Some of the more sophisticated systems use a computerized matching process. Citibank uses a task-based matching system (47). That is, if a position requires task A, and the individual has experience with completing task A, then a match occurs on that task. Each position has tasks identified, and presumably, so too does each individual. General Telephone Company of Florida (GTF, part of the GTE system) set up a similar automated search system to support the selection system component of GTF's integrated personnel system while Richard Vosburgh was on staff. Searches could be made based on career choices, previous positions, geographical locations, and the like. Both of these approaches demand: considerable "up-front" time-generating information about each position; considerable maintenance time updating old information or adding new information; and enough position openings to support the investment in an automated system.

Less sophisticated programs that meet the basic informational requirements can be used. For example, the individual can be made responsible for researching positions of interest and creating his or her *own* "position profile" for the job through observation, interviews, and the like. General direction on what to look for or ask about could be provided by career-planning facilitators who are trained in each functional area to help employees manage the organization's career systems. People are generally quite pleased to talk about their jobs; the matching process simply objectifies and standardizes some of the categories by which we describe positions. The simpler approach has a few spin-off benefits: the exploring employee meets some of the people who may later make employment decisions about him or her; the process reveals a level of motivation that has ramifications for advancement; the process fosters an environment of communication and discussion about

---

3-6. Position profile characteristics and professional concerns.

MAJOR FUNCTIONS

- What is the overall mission of the job?
- Is this likely to be a source of professional pride?
- Will there be opportunities to publish journal articles or to present papers?
- Is the mission something to which I can personally and ethically or morally contribute?

POSITION ACTIVITIES

- On a day-to-day basis, what activities does a person in this position perform?
- Is this something I would be interested in, or is it more of the same?
- What level of control, or discretion, do I have over these activities?
- Are the activities those of a technician or a respected professional?

POSITION KNOWLEDGE

- What technical/scientific areas do I need to know?
- Is this a position that demands that I stay current?
- Is this a "short-run" technology that may be outdated in two years?
- Are these things I need to know ahead of time, or can I learn them on the job?

POSITION DEMANDS AND RESTRICTIONS

- What are the demanding aspects of the job?
- How will the position affect my family and off-the-job interests?
- Will the position provide the rewards and recognition I need?
- Is this really something I want to do?

POSITION CHARACTERISTICS

- What else does the position involve?
- What degree of specialization is involved?
- What discretionary authority goes with the position?
- What is the technical, managerial, and financial scope of the position?

MANAGERIAL SKILLS

- Independent of supervisory skills, what other skills are demanded?
- Is the job heavily oriented toward project management, requiring skills such as organizing and planning?
- Is the job heavily "hands-on," requiring perceptual and analytical skills?
- Is the job heavily "people-oriented," requiring skills such as flexibility and oral communication?

positions and how they interrelate; and all these things are accomplished cheaply and on an "as needed" basis.

There are similar matching processes for less objectively job-related items than those discussed thus far. In one, for example, a decision/analysis chart was designed to aid an employee in weighing the job situation against personal goals, thereby minimizing "job misalliance and turnover" (17). In another program, performance alignment was aimed at improving the match between an individual and his or her job (8,15). At least one program has been warned against as a less well defined matching process whereby selectors tend to select based on the values they hold rather than the degree to which the person matches the values required by the position (25). In all of these cases, the organization bears a legal as well as fiduciary responsibility to ensure that selection decisions are based on objective, job-related qualifications rather than individual characteristics unrelated to job performance.

It is the individual's responsibility to identify the positions that reflect his or her personal goals. Likewise, the organization needs to consider the "career fit" of a position with prospective candidates. In professional positions, the issues of stagnation and technical obsolescence must be addressed. The questions become two-parted: short range, can the person perform the job?; and long range, what are the career implications of this move?

Internal Résumé. Suppose through some process an individual identifies two jobs of extreme interest. How is this fact relayed to management? One of the simplest procedures is to submit an internal résumé with either the group having the position or with the personnel department, depending on the method by which positions are actually filled. Such a résumé would outline the usual education and experience items, but would also detail the individual's qualifications for the position's required activities, knowledge, managerial skills, and other facets (see figure 4–13). If a position profile exists, the person would simply outline his or her qualifications for each specific item. Otherwise, the candidate would have to take the initiative and search out the information, reporting it in a similar position profile fashion.

The organization might also have an interest in generating a different type of internal résumé for its key people. Above a certain level of management or professional classification, an internal résumé would outline education and experience, as well as short- and long-range career potential, strengths, and development plans. In this way, the future availability of talent can be considered from a "career fit" point of view.

Job Posting/Bidding. Organizations often post lower level positions and allow employees to bid on them. To what degree would this process be applicable to higher level professional employees? Knowledge of position openings is powerful information. If these higher level professional employees want this information, the organization should closely examine its reasons for not making it available previously. Lack of a formal system certainly does not negate the influence of the informal system. Quite the opposite. Those in the work group with the opening and others working with that group may know about it, but there might be twenty other employees who would be interested in the position if they knew about it. Unless we falsely assume total omniscience by the organization, it is unlikely each person will be considered.

If the position opening is announced in some way and a bidding process is made available, it opens up the system and generates larger candidate pools. On the positive side, this means that a larger talent pool is identified; on the negative side, many more people will have to be disappointed by not getting the job. The previous sections have described means by which an objective, realistic bid can be assured. Therefore, a bidding process might make the most sense in conjunction with a viable self-matching process, as described earlier.

The Selector's Task. Throughout this book, the focus on career management is clearly objective and job-related. Similarly, the selection decision must be anchored in job-specific requirements rather than personal characteristics unrelated to a person's ability to perform the job. The information contained on the position profiles was an indication of that orientation. The decision-making process inherent in a selection decision must be anchored in job-related specifics if it is to be a quality decision and if it is to be legally defensible in terms of equal employment opportunity.

A CASE STUDY

General Telephone Company of Florida (GTF) has developed a new selection system as part of their Integrated Personnel System.* It is supported by three other components of the integrated system: a career-planning program; an assessment center; and an annual career- and organizational planning review.

The GTF selection system uses information generated from the other components of the Integrated Personnel System. Five selection categories are identified:

- Job-related activities
- Job-related knowledge
- Managerial skills
- Past accomplishments
- Career-planning information

*The selection system component described in this section was designed by Dennis Archambeau, Ph.D., under the supervision of Dennis Whipple at General Telephone Company of Florida in Tampa. The section draws heavily on the company booklet *Identification, Selection, Development: Procedures and Guidelines.*

The first three categories are directly from the position profiles described earlier in this chapter. The selector works with the selection worksheets. Worksheet 1 (fig. 3–7) is used to identify the specific activities, knowledges, and skills required to show how much weight is given to each of the five categories in making the final decision. This is done *before* the selector is given a candidate list. Worksheet 2 (fig. 3–8) is then used by the selector to rate each candidate's level of experience and ability with the job requirements previously identified. The information from Worksheet 1 serves as the guide for the individual analysis in Worksheet 2.

Worksheet 3 (fig. 3–9) is the third step; in it the selector makes direct comparisons between candidates. Using the "percent of decision based on this category" from Worksheet 1, candidates are then ranked with respect to each selection category. The "top" candidate for each category is identified in the far right column. In this way, the candidate with the best qualifications for the job is identified, and the selection is supported with job-relevant information.

Finally, GTF's concern for effective career planning is mirrored in an important feedback loop that is established following the selection decision. A selection and placement summary (fig. 3–10) specifies job-related reasons why the candidate was selected *and* job-related reasons why the other candidates were not.

This information is made available to individuals and their supervisors as immediate feedback to career-planning discussions. In addition, position profiles are updated to mirror the realities of the selection decision factors. The summary is used as an informal assessment of training needs. Areas in which many employees need development can become clear through analyzing the reasons for the candidates' rejection.

A detailed program such as this requires quite a bit of time from the selector. Generally, the rewards will support the program if implemented on an organiza-

---

3–7. Selection worksheet 1: selection factors.

Job Title (Selection): _____

SELECTION FACTORS

PERCENT OF DECISION BASED ON THIS CATEGORY

1. Job-related Activities Required:

_____ %

2. Job-related Knowledge Required:

_____ %

3. Managerial Skills Required (Rank Order):

_____ %

- _____ Leadership
- _____ Control & follow-up
- _____ Organizing & planning
- _____ Decision making
- _____ Decisiveness
- _____ Perceptual & analytical
- _____ Interpersonal
- _____ Flexibility
- _____ Oral communication
- _____ Written communication

_____ _____ _____ _____

4. Past Accomplishments (information to be evaluated by selector)   _____ %

5. Career Planning Information (information to be evaluated by selector)   _____ %

3-8. Selection worksheet 2: individual match with selection factors.

Candidate: _____   **Present Job Title:** _____

Job Title (Selection): _____   **Date:** _____

1. Job-related Activity Analysis (Sources of information to evaluate these activities include: previous job experience, formal education and training, technical training courses)

ACTIVITY	CANDIDATE'S LEVEL OF EXPERIENCE	BASIS FOR RATING ASSIGNED
No. 1		
No. 2		
No. 3		
No. 4		
No. 5		
Overall Rating		

2. Job-related Knowledge Analysis (Sources of information to evaluate these knowledges are identical to those for job-related activity analysis, *above.*)

KNOWLEDGE	LEVEL POSSESSED BY CANDIDATE	BASIS FOR RATING ASSIGNED
No. 1		
No. 2		
No. 3		
No. 4		
No. 5		
No. 6		
No. 7		
No. 8		
Overall Rating		

3. Managerial Skills Analysis (Sources of information to evaluate these managerial skills include: assessment center results, previous job experience, formal education and training)

MANAGERIAL SKILL	LEVEL POSSESSED BY CANDIDATE	BASIS FOR RATING ASSIGNED
No. 1		
No. 2		
No. 3		
No. 4		
No. 5		
No. 6		
No. 7		
No. 8		
No. 9		
No. 10		
Overall Rating		

4. Past Accomplishment Analysis (Sources of information to evaluate past performance include: salary review, performance appraisal, special assignments)

	LEVEL POSSESSED BY CANDIDATE	BASIS FOR RATING ASSIGNED
Overall Rating		

(*continued*)

3-8. (*Continued*)

5. Career Planning Information Analysis (Sources of information to evaluate career planning information include: career action plan, developmental activities)

CREDIT ASSIGNED
TO CANDIDATE   BASIS FOR RATING ASSIGNED

Overall Rating _____   _____

Rating Key:
- 0 = Unknown or does not apply.
- 1 = The candidate's qualifications are weak with respect to this area. He/she would not be expected to meet the requirements of the job.
- 2 = The candidate's qualifications are below satisfactory in this area. He/she could be expected to be successful in this job only if additional time were spent in developing this area.
- 3 = The candidate's qualifications are average or satisfactory in this area. He/she would be expected to meet the requirements of the job fully.
- 4 = The candidate's qualifications are above satisfactory in this area. He/she would be expected to exceed the basic requirements of the job.
- 5 = The candidate's qualifications are outstanding with respect to this area. He/she would be expected to far exceed the basic requirements of the job.

3-9. Selection worksheet 3: direct comparison between candidates.

Job Title (Selection): _____

FACTOR	PERCENT OF DECISION BASED ON THIS FACTOR	CANDI-DATE NO. 1	CANDI-DATE NO. 2	CANDI-DATE NO. 3	CANDI-DATE NO. 4	CANDI-DATE NO. 5	TOP CAN-DIDATE
1. Job-related activities analysis							No.
2. Job-related knowledge analysis							No.
3. Managerial skills analysis							No.
4. Past accomplishments analysis							No.
5. Career planning information							No.

100%   Candidate selected, No. _____

Notes:

3-10. Selection and placement summary.

Selecting Manager: _____ **Title:** _____ **Date:** __/__/__

Candidate selected: _____

Primary reason for selection:

Candidates not selected:

Name: _____
Primary reason for decision:

Name: _____
Primary reason for decision:

Name: _____
Primary reason for decision:

Name: _____
Primary reason for decision:

---

tionwide basis. In fact, the individual selector who is concerned about the quality of his or her decision could also independently walk through the same type of system as that described here. It need not be formalized or be a function of a centralized personnel department to be an effective addition to the selection decision-making process.

In many organizations, it is simply much too easy for individual selectors to make selection decisions. From an organization's point of view, some type of challenge process should be built into the decision. This need not be the elaborate system just described, but rather a simple requirement for a two-level hiring decision, with job-related support and "career fit" implications considered. The message is simple: develop a mechanism to challenge the job-related and career-related criteria in selection decisions.

ASSESSMENT SYSTEMS

Potential versus Performance Assessment. What, exactly, do we mean by *potential* assessment and how does that differ from *performance* assessment (see chapter 4)? Performance would be defined fairly narrowly in terms of a person's ability to meet the expectations and standards of a specific job. The responsibilities and accountabilities of that job define the expectations, and measurements of meeting those job objectives become the measure of performance. Potential assessment covers a far broader territory and cannot be so narrowly defined. The dictionary definition of potential uses words such as latent, unrealized, undeveloped. To measure something that under normal circumstances is latent, therefore unseen, is a challenge, but one that it is necessary for organizations to address.

Potential is essentially a measure of *future* worth to the organization. It is not so much that a person has or does not have "potential." Rather, the worth of a person to the organization will be a result of the interactive effect of what the organization requires for success and what the people within the organization have to offer. When potential is assessed, development needs are identified as well as data relating to back-up or succession planning.

An important differentiation is between current performance (in a given, well-defined role) and future potential (in numerous, alternative, ill-defined roles). An organization may have people who are meeting its current needs, but what about future needs? In this context, and consistent with our model, assessment of potential is really the assessment of the internal input to the development process.

The Assessment Center

Many methods are used by organizations to assess potential. In general management, supervisory evaluations and managerial nominations are fairly common practices. Within the professional and scientific community, peer review and committee methods are fairly common. Perhaps the least common yet most precise is the assessment center method, a program in which several trained assessors observe the behavior of the participants in many standardized situational simulations and reach consensus on the effectiveness of each person in specific, well-defined skill areas.

Assessment centers have been historically designed to measure *managerial* skills, not technical/professional/scientific knowledge. It can be used for selection purposes and/or for defining the development needs of the person. Simply because managerial skill dimensions are the classic areas in which assessment centers operate, there are no compelling reasons why an assessment center could not be developed which is weighted on the "technical management" side. Dimensions which are critical to effective performance in a purely technical, mixed technical/managerial, and purely managerial position would have to be determined through a job analysis.

The table in figure 3–11 shows a smorgasbord of managerial and technical skills which could potentially be assessed in an assessment center. Skills would be chosen which correspond (according to the job analysis) to those needed for successful performance of a target job or target-level job. For example, there might be a need for scientific project managers. This is a key position which is viewed as a possible stepping stone into higher levels of management. Because of the emphasis on developing people and managing a highly technical project, the following skills might emerge:

- Project management
- People development
- Results orientation
- Judgment
- Quantitative
- Technical writing
- Managerial writing
- Organizing and planning

In this case, people development might be partially defined by client/customer/supplier relations and the ability to translate highly technical data into "lay" language with useful recommendations for applications. A scientific project manager's position might also be defined in terms of the person's ability to predict organizational needs and to take the appropriate steps to develop the data needed for decision making. For example, it would be relevant to ask, "What product will be obsolete, when, and what do we do to replace it?"

The situations or exercises used in skill assessment would also be tailored to reflect the critical types of activities likely to differentiate a good from a poor project manager. An assessment center such as this might be used to decide who will receive special recognition via

3–11. Technical and managerial characteristics.

	MOSTLY TECHNICAL	MIXED TECHNICAL/ MANAGERIAL	MOSTLY MANAGERIAL
Technical curiosity	X		
Technical reading	X		
Technical writing	X		
Inductive reasoning	X		
Deductive reasoning	X		
Detail orientation		X	
Analytical		X	
Quantitative		X	
Judgment		X	
Organizing and planning		X	
Project management		X	
Oral communication		X	
Decisiveness			X
Flexibility			X
Results orientation			X
Managerial writing			X
Leadership			X
Control and follow-up			X
People development			X
Interpersonal			X
Self-management			X

the allocation of special project funds. Particularly novel or interesting research ideas would be investigated by the *best* people, who would understand the honor it was to have been chosen. The organization then gets a special project team of the highest caliber, and its members get recognition and a chance to develop their technical and managerial skills further.

It might be argued, and convincingly so, that many of the "technical skills" described would be better assessed through an on-the-job evaluation of competencies. Professional and technical knowledge may well be better evaluated through other means (see performance assessment, chapter 5). In fact, the classical design of assessment centers is to make use of situations with low demands for technical ability and high demands for managerial skill ability. Realistically organizations are interested in identifying people with both the technical and the managerial skill to fill key interface positions. For this reason, organizational nomination procedures based on a person's technical skills and current performance would be followed by an assessment-center procedure to assess the person's managerial skills and future potential.

One problem often experienced in professional organizations is that highly specialized and technical functions may suffer from a lack of supervisory or managerial skill. The best performer (based on technical skills as an individual contributor) may get promoted into a project leadership or managerial position that requires very different skills from those the individual has. Both the organization and the individual can avoid a good deal of unnecessary trauma by giving the person an opportunity to "try out" under the simulated situational conditions of an assessment center. If used in conjunction with an assessment of technical ability, the assessment center can be a valuable tool for identifying and developing people with the managerial skills to make a real difference.

Assessment centers reflect a history of use unrelated to the intrinsic validity or utility of the methodology. Originally developed by the Office of Strategic Services (O.S.S.) during World War II for the selection of U.S. secret service military men (44) and by the British War Office Selection Board (40) for similar purposes, the technique gradually found its way into the industrial sector. Early success by the American Telephone and Telegraph organization (AT&T) in the late 1950s and 1960s (5) led to the institution of similar programs in the 1960s (and concomitant validation studies) at such organizations as Standard Oil of Ohio (49), IBM (26), General Electric (38,39), and Sears Roebuck (3).

By 1970 it was almost as though "the word was out" and everyone wanted an assessment center. The flurry of activity resulted in well over a hundred companies involved in such centers by 1973 (27) and over a dozen countries by 1975 (31) to nearly two thousand organizations by 1980 (53). In the Bell system alone, over 200,000 candidates have been evaluated in seventy centers in the past twenty-five years (53). Why the popularity of the method? Why does there also appear to be a decline in the popularity of what some would characterize as a dangerous fad? These questions will be addressed by outlining the concept of the assessment center, the center's validity, and utility in career management.

Concept. Assessment centers for the evaluation of managerial skills and potential have important similarities and variations. According to the Task Force on Assessment Center Standards (48), the following are essential elements which must be present in an assessment center:

1. Multiple assessment techniques are used, at least one of which is a simulation.
2. Multiple assessors are used, all of whom have been thoroughly trained.
3. Overall judgments are made, based on pooled information from assessors and techniques.
4. Observation of behavior and evaluation of its effectiveness occur at different points in time.
5. Simulation exercises are used which are job-related and pretested for objectivity and relevance to the organization.
6. An analysis of relevant job behavior is conducted to identify the dimensions, attributes, characteristics, qualities, skills, abilities, or knowledge evaluated.
7. The techniques which are used are designed to elicit information on the dimensions which were previously determined.

Many of the "failed-assessment-center" stories we have heard can be traced to a failure to measure up to these standards. The rapid rise in the popularity of the assessment center evidently led some individuals and companies to take shortcuts in their development, which turned out to be a fatal flaw. What is seen on the surface—multiple assessees in multiple techniques reflecting multiple situations with multiple assessors—is simple and easily replicated. What is not seen is the extensive background work (job analysis in particular) required to design an effective program.

Other program failures can be attributed to the lack of a clear policy statement and role for the assessment center. The same task force (48) argued the need to operate as a part of an integrated human resource system and to have a policy statement covering:

1. Program objectives
2. Assessees and their selection
3. Assessors and their selection, training, and certification

4. Data use, availability, confidentiality, file time, and the like
5. Professional qualifications of the developer of the center
6. Validation model being used and report availability

Probably the most damaging indictment of the assessment center is that some overzealous enthusiasts consider it the end-all answer to their selection needs, when they run it as little more than a fraternity initiation or standardized cocktail party. There is no "magic" in an assessment center—the objectivity of its results can be assured only when professionally and ethically developed, implemented, and administered.

The concept sports many advantages, outlined by Finkle (18). The technique can be extraordinarily thorough in its assessment of valued behavioral traits. It will generally have good face validity and acceptance in that it appears to measure what it does measure, and in realistic situations. Content validity arguments tend to survive court tests. Assessment centers provide additional information, such as training needs analyses, and are very helpful as a basis for a career-planning program. The content of the center can be geared to specific jobs or job classes. Assessors benefit by the experience and become better managers. Assessees develop more realistic job expectations. Coaching does not appear to help—people's real skills show through, performance cannot be faked. It can be an excellent tool for making sound affirmative action advances, and it enhances the organization's reputation for being up-to-date.

Assessment centers also have many potential disadvantages (18). Employees generally experience it as a one-shot all-or-nothing chance for success and stardom, or failure and obscurity. There is something patently unfair about that situation. The process by which assessment-center participants are chosen is sometimes held suspect. In some simulations, the ethics of deception must be faced. The value is reduced by the degree to which you already know about people's strengths and weaknesses through their on-the-job performance. The assessment center may simply be an expensive means of organizational self-prophecy, that is, the people already believed to be high potential show as "stars" and the people already believed to be at their highest level show as "plateaued."

Pros and cons notwithstanding, the concept of the assessment center does effectively address many of the problems of traditional testing or performance rating techniques. The overlap between the "test" and the actual on-the-job situation is increased dramatically through the use of situational simulations which reflect job demands and provide the opportunity to exhibit valued managerial skills. Within organizations where supervisors rate managerial skills and potential, nothing is controlled or standardized—that is, different supervisors with different standards evaluate subordinates in different jobs based on different conceptions of what a given managerial skill really is or "how it looks" in a behavioral sense. The assessment center objectifies and standardizes these variables: Each participant is given the opportunity to handle the same situation given the same temporal and informational constraints. Every participant is evaluated against well-defined behavioral criteria, and overall ratings are assigned based on the convergence of evidence from independent observations.

This degree of standardization is the first task of the assessment center's administrator. It is the only point at which comparative evaluations can be made between people. Even though the assessment is made to the demands of the target-level job, the point comes after the evaluation when two people may need to be compared. Ratings by the assessment center may be the only direct comparison possible. Managerial skill ratings are independent assessments and are not additive in the sense of deriving a meaningful "score" of "overall potential" upon which both can be compared. Rather, the strengths and weaknesses of each candidate should be evaluated relative to the demands of the job.

Assessment centers can be used for two main purposes: the *selection* of employees for positions or projects; and the *identification* of employees' development needs in the areas assessed by the center. With regard to selection, the program results in skill ratings, which can be used in a number of different ways:

- As evidence of ability for a given level of management
- As evidence of qualifications for a specific job or assignment
- As a description of the person's short- and long-range potential
- As input into succession staffing plans

With regard to employee development, an assessment center can provide very useful and revealing data for numerous purposes:

- As specific, objective, detailed feedback to the individual on strengths and weaknesses
- As a method to define situations in which additional practice may be needed following the assessment
- As the leverage to force critical self-analysis and the "unfreezing" which is needed to support behavior change
- As a general management development tool
- As an integral part of a career-planning program for the individual

It is important to decide ahead of time whether your organization's assessment center will be for selection, development, or both purposes. This basic decision will directly affect subsequent decisions on the design, development, implementation, and administration of the center.

Validity. A good deal of research has been conducted on the reliability and validity of the assessment center. Reliability is essentially the degree to which the assessment center is consistently and accurately measuring something, and is inferred from measures of the internal consistency, stability, and dependability of scores. Validity is essentially the degree to which the assessment center is measuring what it purports to measure, and is inferred from studies which relate assessment center scores with other measures of the same construct or with actual advancement to the levels of potential which were predicted.

AT&T's Management Progress Study is undoubtedly the most noteworthy of all the studies (8). Between 1956 and 1960, the company assessed the performance of 125 college and 144 noncollege men, then subsequently tracked their progress in management. The assessment center's results were not made available to anyone so as not to affect future decisions. The table in figure 3-12 shows the results. The prediction of management advancement was highly accurate for both groups: In the college sample, 50 percent of the group predicted to reach middle management actually did, whereas only 11 percent of those predicted not to reach middle management actually achieved that level. The same comparison in the noncollege sample shows 37 percent making it when predicted versus only 5 percent making it when the prediction was that they would not make it. It is important to realize that with this entire group, none of the assessment center's results were fed back to management such that none of the ensuing personnel decisions (promotions, for example) could be based on the prediction. Performance in the assessment center also showed a highly significant correlation with salary progression, and was more predictive than any other single technique (such as ratings or test scores).

Standard Oil of Ohio (SOHIO) validity studies later established the assessment center's ratings as moderately predictive of managerial performance and highly predictive of management potential and progress (10, 19). Validation studies at numerous other companies support the predictive validity of the assessment center. Other companies contributing such research include IBM (16,32,52), General Electric (37,38), the FBI (43), Sears (31), and GTE (51). Excellent reviews of these and other validity studies have also been published (12,27).

Numerous studies have examined the impact of assessment centers on minority groups, essentially to determine whether there is an adverse impact. The results are quite favorable, for example:

- Disadvantaged and minority employees respond favorably to the assessment center, and a higher percentage scored well compared to more traditional, written tests (30).
- The assessment center shows no discrimination against minorities (50).
- Assessment center's ratings are predictive of job performance and potential for advancement for both black and white employees (29).
- The assessment center provides an early identification of female talent (6).
- The future performance of women is predicted as accurately as that of men (42).
- Blacks and females are not assessed differently (35, 41).

This lengthy track record builds an impressive case for the validity of the assessment center's methodology. It must be remembered, however, that validity evidence is always relative to a particular program within a particular organization. An organization cannot buy a "valid assessment center"; it must construct the program using procedures that generate the supportive data necessary to establish the validity of that specific program. The Task Force on Assessment Center Standards cautions:

> The historical record of the validity of this process cannot be taken as a guarantee that a given assessment program will or will not be valid in a given setting. Ascertaining the validity of an assessment center program is a complicated technical process, and it is important that validation research meet both professional and legal standards (48).

Overall, we can conclude along with Badawy that the assessment center's method of identifying management

3-12. AT&T Management Progress Study.

PREDICTIONS BY THE ASSESSMENT CENTER: *WILL* OR *WILL NOT* REACH MIDDLE MANAGEMENT

ACTUAL MANAGEMENT LEVEL ACHIEVED	College Sample		Noncollege Sample	
	WILL NOT	WILL	WILL NOT	WILL
First-level supervision	11%	2%	59%	7%
Second-level supervision	78	48	36	56
Middle management	11	50	5	37
N =	63	62	103	41

potential "is a sounder and fairer method than those traditionally used by management" (2, p. 56).

Utility. Even though the assessment center method is valid (in the sense that it predicts managerial advancement), the question of utility remains: how useful is the assessment center; what *value* does it *add* to existing selection or development systems?

The cost of an assessment center is often raised as a negative point. Costs are highly variable but are generally no greater than the cost of management development programs of similar length and professionalism. The more important question relates to the *value added* concept. As Kraut points out:

> Costs are relative to the value of the information and the use to which such information is put. They must be weighed against the consequences of a poor decision. The information from an assessment center will be relatively more valuable when the performance of the person in a particular job really makes a big difference, and if an ample number of candidates for such a job are available (31).

Critical, multi-incumbent jobs therefore seem the best areas in which to develop assessment centers. The technical-to-management transition is perhaps the best area in which to use the assessment center. The managerial competence of the person already in a managerial position can be assessed to some degree based on his or her current job performance—the assessment center can add additional independent objective evidence on top of this base. However, the person in the technical position is simply not given opportunities on the job to exhibit a full range of managerial skills. Evaluation is based on technical competence, and often promotion is based on this same criterion. The classic problem is then that the best technical person may make a poor supervisor. Neither the organization nor the person is happy with this—everyone loses and the costs are high. The assessment center is the best method available for providing a structured opportunity to exhibit the managerial skills which are critical for successful performance in a supervisory or managerial position.

Although cost/benefit ratios will vary and are not directly available in the professional/scientific area, Cheek provided some estimates of the hard dollar savings experienced by Xerox in their sales-manager assessment program (11). For a cost of $340,000 the company netted benefits in excess of $4.9 million.

Huck made some interesting and informative comparisons of the "value added" aspect of the assessment center vis-à-vis more traditional methods (28). If individuals are chosen at random, the probability of selecting an above-average performer is 15 percent. Traditional management nomination procedures raise this probability to 35 percent. Adding the assessment center's ratings raises the probability to 76 percent. If monetary figures are attached to this process, it can be shown clearly that the value added by an assessment center can be great. Regardless of the absolute cost of the program, the assessment center can be shown to be a cost-effective system in these terms. The proof is more impressive to the degree that the individual's success or failure in the job is critical to the success of the organization. For highly knowledgeable workers in specialized areas of expertise, the impact can be enormous.

Based on their survey (13), Cohen and Cascio presented the cost/benefit issue in a slightly different way, using the following logic:

1. A typical assessment center costs $25,000 to develop and $89,000 annually to execute.
2. The savings to the organization of not putting a "failure" into a managerial job is $54,000 per person.
3. Based on an estimated annual number of participants (147) and the incremental prediction capability of a center, the typical assessment center can show a yearly savings of $371,000.

Cohen and Cascio also showed the utility of instituting an effective screening mechanism for the assessment center. By increasing the success rate from 44 to 68 percent, the cost per participant for each "success" drops from $3,425 to $2,190. On a different note, Vosburgh presents some technical cautions on the development of effective screening mechanisms in his report of the validity of a battery of screening tests, but agrees on the utility of such a device (51).

The fact that assessment centers can result in numerous auxiliary benefits tends to support its usefulness. Perhaps the most striking benefits accrue to the internal assessors who are trained in key areas:

- Interviewing skills
- Behavioral observation skills
- Analytical skills
- Employee feedback skills

As a result of this training, employees who serve as assessors often show a broadened repertory of behavior, improved managerial skills, and a greater appreciation for normative standards of performance.

The first step in the development of an assessment center is a job analysis, which can have important benefits of its own; for example, it can be used:

- To write position profiles that accurately describe the job
- To identify the skills that are critical for performance in each position
- To identify training needs

The utility of an assessment center is also enhanced to the degree that it is used as a tool to force organizational consensus on a "success profile." That is, exactly what *is* required for success in specific positions or functions? How can we measure those things behaviorally? To the extent these questions are answered, the results can be a cornerstone for a career development program.

Example Program

It is contingent upon each organization to develop and validate an assessment center that meets its own specific needs. The following material is intended as an example, not the one correct method.

Development of Dimensions and Skills. Job analysis is the first step in the development of an assessment center. The main purposes are: to identify the skills required for successful performance in the job or job level to which the assessment center is to predict; and to describe classic situations that are critical to successful performance in the job or job level. Sideline benefits include the opportunity to develop position profiles which differ from job specifications or position descriptions in their emphasis on career planning–related information. A central benefit of the job analysis is the establishment of content validity for the assessment center. Content validity refers to the degree to which the content of the assessment center accurately represents the content of the job or level at which the assessment is pitched.

Situational Exercises. What are some of the critical situations which occur in a target-level job? Which ones really force the difference between a good and poor performer? Although there are some variations, five "core" managerial situations are often represented in an assessment center: handling unfinished business; analyzing problems; scheduling; employee counseling; and participating in leaderless group discussion.

Unfinished Business. The participant assumes the role of a newly appointed manager and is confronted with a large volume of written materials (such as memos, letters, and reports) left in the in-basket of his or her predecessor requiring some sort of action. The participant is given a specific amount of time (often one and a half hours) to respond to the items by making notes, outlining planned telephone calls, setting up meetings, writing memos and letters, delegating tasks to subordinates. Usually the only resources that the participant may use are the actual in-basket items, which often include a calendar, organizational charts, and the like. After the participant works independently on the in-basket items, he or she is usually interviewed by an assessor to clarify the actions taken.

Problem Analysis. The participant could be given information about numerous alternative technologies or products, that vary widely in the degree to which they meet organizational needs. A specified time period is allocated for the participant to analyze the information and prepare a recommendation in written form. After this the participant meets with "company officials" (played by assessors) to present the recommendation formally. In this exercise, therefore, the participant analyzes requirements and alternatives, reaches a decision, and supports that decision under challenge.

Scheduling. In this exercise, the participant assumes the role of a project manager who must make numerous, detailed, interrelated scheduling decisions. The setting can be that of a major research, engineering, product-development, or takeover project. The information is both quantitative (budget figures, predicted needs) and qualitative (requests from people within the organization). The participant must review the information, determine allocation of resources, make the necessary scheduling decisions, and inform those affected. Following completion of the task or the specified time period, the participant is interviewed by the assessor to clarify the actions that were taken.

Employee Counseling. The participant is placed in a supervisory position and given information from several sources about problems being experienced by a subordinate. After reviewing the material the participant meets with the "subordinate" (played by an assessor) to discuss the problems and may be required to write a synopsis of what occurred in the meeting.

Leaderless Group Discussion. In this exercise the participants assume the roles of members of a task force or special project. Common and unique information is given to each participant, usually such that each represents a different group or area. The group is given a common goal requiring group decision making. In some cases, new information is interjected into the situation.

Having multiple independent situations provides a different view of each of the skills which are assessed. For example, "leadership" in the employee-counseling situation (one-on-one with a subordinate) would be characterized differently from "leadership" in the leaderless group discussion (peers with no formal authority structure). Both situations would provide different views of the general skill of leadership. The fact that there are multiple measures by multiple judges in multiple situations serves to increase the reliability and validity of the measurement dramatically.

Combining Skill and Situation Data. As part of the content validation of an assessment center, the job analysis information should be combined in a meaningful way to support both the skills and the situational exercises chosen for the assessment center. Interview statements of importance for the position or level being assessed should be classified under both a skill and at least one exercise.

Documenting Observational Evidence. One of the real strengths of an assessment center is its grounding in observed behaviors. Whereas a participant might become very defensive if given general trait-related feedback ("Your leadership was below satisfactory"), this is less likely when given specific observable evidence ("You provided no direction to three of your subordinates who specifically requested guidance"). The specificity of the feedback also aids efforts to improve because it tells the person what to do to be more effective. How, then, are these behaviors documented?

Generally, a two-stage method is used. Within the situation the assessor writes copious notes on the participant's performance. Everything is happening too fast to do much more than record behavior. As an additional aid for assessors, behavior is often videotaped so that observations can be double-checked and refined. Videotapes also help the participant in managerial skill development.

After behavior is recorded the assessor then categorizes behaviors into the managerial skills being assessed, generally grouping similar observations. An assessor's observational report for a participant describes specific behavior grouped under the relevant managerial skill.

Administrators of some assessment centers have moved toward a checklist approach to behavioral documentation. What this approach loses in specificity and adequacy of developmental feedback, it gains in assessor time reduction and associated costs. The approach is more acceptable for exercises where the range of possible behaviors is limited, as in handling unfinished business, but unacceptable when a greater stylistic range is likely, as in employee counseling.

Assessor Team Meeting. After all observational reports are written for each participant in each exercise, the assessors meet to review each participant in detail. Beginning with the first participant's first exercise, the assessor observing that performance reports on one managerial skill at a time. Performance in the next exercise is then reviewed, usually by a different assessor, and ratings are assigned to each skill in each exercise using a matrix or worksheet (fig. 3-13).

As each assessor presents evidence, the others must listen attentively and challenge the presenting assessor with regard to miscategorized behaviors, need for additional behavioral evidence, or appropriateness of the assigned ratings. In turn, each assessor presents the ratings and behavioral evidence for the participant in the exercises observed. Consensus is then reached on an *overall* skill rating for each managerial skill. After all the exercises are reviewed, each assessor independently assigns an overall skill rating for each skill. These are then compared and where there is a lack of agreement, further discussion ensues to clarify competing points of view. This is accomplished by going back to the observational reports or the exercises themselves to produce more direct evidence for one rating or another. The interchange of challenge and behavioral support contrib-

3-13. Assessment center performance matrix.

Participant: _____   Assessors: _____
                                         Date reviewed: _____

MANAGERIAL SKILL	UNFINISHED BUSINESS	PROBLEM SOLVING	SCHEDULING	EMPLOYEE COUNSELING	LEADERLESS GROUP DISCUSSION	OVERALL
Leadership						
Technical curiosity						
Organizing and planning						
Decision making						
Technical writing						
Oral communication						
Decisiveness						
Analytical						
Detail orientation						

utes to the fairness and objectivity of the assessment process.

Participant Report Preparation. A final report is often prepared summarizing the person's performance either by exercise or by managerial skill. This report can be used for several purposes, such as:

- The basis for detailed feedback to the participant
- A review document for the participant's supervisor
- A reference document as part of the selection process
- The basis for an individualized training program

The detail of the report will vary as a function of its purpose.

Participant Feedback. Participants should be given detailed verbal feedback on their performance as soon after participation as possible. For example, the schedule in figure 3-14 might be used to fit a one-week period. Assessors should be trained to deliver this feedback; for them, this is the point of the whole process. It is not always an easy task, because often many participants will not perform well.

The feedback meeting must be well-structured, perhaps by following these guidelines:

OPENING
1. Set participant at ease.
   - Social amenities.
   - "The purpose is to provide you with information regarding both the center and your performance."
   - "I want you to understand so feel free to ask questions and take notes."

3-14. Assessment center schedule.

	PARTICIPANT	ASSESSOR
Monday A.M.	Exercises	Exercises
P.M.	↓	↓
Tuesday A.M.		
P.M.	Behavior	Observational
Wednesday	Modeling	Reports
A.M.	Skills	
P.M.	Development	
Thursday		
A.M.	↓	Team
P.M.	Feedback	Meeting
Friday	Preparation	↓
A.M.	↓	
P.M.	Feedback	Feedback

2. Describe center development.
   - Description of skills (based on job analysis; required for effective management).
   - Development of exercises (job analysis; representative of management positions).
   - Assessor training (prior successful performance in another assessment center as a participant and completion of a lengthy, intensive training course).
3. Describe assessment process.
   - Observers take detailed notes on behavior in all the situations.
   - Behavior summarized and categorized under the managerial skills.
   - Everything documented.
   - Observers meet as a team and reach consensus (so ratings are not based on just one assessor's observations).
   - Process based on observable behavior *not* inferences regarding psychological traits.
   - Highly reliable and valid process (consensus by assessors, standardized conditions, same evaluation standards, research).
4. Describe rating scale.
   - Seven-point scale.
   - Entire range of scale used (not just upper end).
   - "Satisfactory" does not equal *C*—it means that this skill needs no further development for acceptable performance in a management-level position.
5. Describe how results will be used.
   - To work with your supervisor to write a development plan.
   - To help you compare against job demands of positions for which you are interested.
   - As input into the selection system for the following jobs.
6. Lay ground rules.
   - Feel free to ask questions and take notes.
   - Ratings are not open to debate—will *not* be changed.
   - Assessors will be as direct and honest as possible.
   - Purpose is helpfulness, development, information-sharing.

FEEDBACK
1. Define the managerial skill.
2. Summarize performance.
   - "One example of an effective analytical (or other) skill was . . ."
   - "However, to give you an example of ineffective deductive reasoning, when you . . ."
3. Provide rating.
   - "Considering all the situations your technical writing skill rating was highest."

4. Repeat for each skill.
   - Begin and end with fairly good performance.
5. Summarize situational patterns.
   - Effective in which situations.
   - Ineffective in which situations.

CLOSING

1. Answer all questions.
2. Stress confidentiality of final report, ratings, and so on.
   - "You have a responsibility to the center to maintain the confidentiality of exercises, so no other participant has an unfair advantage."
   - "Also maintain the confidentiality of the ratings because patterns differ, can't just sum across ratings—each skill is independently evaluated."
3. Respond to defensiveness (if necessary).
   - Assessors relied on observable actions, cannot read a participant's mind or intentions, but must rely on physical evidence.
4. Conclude supportively.
   - Empathize as a past participant of the assessment center.
   - Emphasize strengths and possibility of overcoming weaknesses.
   - Appreciate how hard the participants worked, how seriously they approached the task, and the like.

In the rare case when a participant protests vehemently, the program administrator should be asked by the assessor to intervene. This is not a common occurrence because the weight of the behavioral evidence will overwhelm most participants in a very convincing manner.

Supervisory Review. The performance of participants may also be reviewed with the participant's supervisor. This is usually done a short time after participation in the assessment center to allow preparation of a final report. This report is then reviewed with the supervisor and the participant, usually by a member of the assessment center's staff. Before reviewing the employee's performance, the supervisor must be given a good deal of background information on the assessment center and its objectives. In summary, the sequence for feedback is: the assessors' verbal feedback to participant; assessors' write-up of final report; and the assessment center's staff administrator's review of the written report with the participant and his or her supervisor.

Preparation for Questions. The assessment center's staff, assessors, and sponsors need to be well-versed in the rationale and procedure of the center. The following are examples of frequently asked questions and one company's response to them:

Q. What is the name of this program?
A. The Assessment and Development Program of our company's Professional Development Center.

Q. How was I selected to attend?
A. A step-by-step nomination procedure was followed. Your supervisor recommended you for promotion to Project Leader, your department/division as a whole nominated you, and we were able to schedule you to attend. Other considerations, both individual (your expressed interests and background) and organizational (the type of job to be filled), also entered into the final decision to invite you to participate.

Q. Will I be promoted to Project Leader?
A. We cannot definitely say at this time. Promotions depend not only on managerial skills, but also on other factors, including your mobility, the job's location, your interests, job-related knowledge and training, technical ability, and previous work experience. We *can* say definitely that when choices are made in the future, the center ratings will be strongly considered.

Q. Will the ratings I receive here affect my present job?
A. No. They will only be used for promotional decisions when a position at the target level for this program is available and your mobility, interests, background, and skills suggest that you should be a viable candidate. The selecting manager will make this final determination.

Q. How did I compare to other participants?
A. We don't make comparisons among people; in every situation we were observing behaviors which reflected specific skills. In the past, participants at the center have varied widely in their skills, but comparisons are never made among people. The standard against which people are compared is the skill demands of the target level job, *not* other people.

Q. What can I do about the weaknesses you have identified?
A. There are several possibilities. Now that you have a clearer indication of weak areas, you can involve yourself in outside training programs, university courses, company training courses, special assignments, or even community activities—depending, of course, on the skills you wish to develop.

Q. When can I be reevaluated in another assessment center?
A. We presently have no plans to reassess people who have been through the program. Since this is a new program and there are many employees whom we would like to schedule to attend, we expect to have a large pool of people anxious to attend for the first time.

Q. Did I do poorly just because I'm the quiet type and didn't speak up?

A. Not necessarily. You probably noticed that each exercise was different and required a different approach. In one situation you worked alone and wrote several memos. Whether you are outgoing or not would not affect your performance in this task. However, in another situation, your level of participation would determine your impact on the group. Where evaluation is based on observed behavior and very little behavior is manifested, there is little information to go on. Assumptions about what you "might have done" or "thought about doing" cannot be made.

Q. Did I do poorly just because this is "play-acting" and some people are better actors than others?
A. The assessment center does not really represent a "play-acting" situation. Each exercise reflects specific job requirements, and your performance in these situations also reflects how you would perform on the job at this level, if given the opportunity. The situations and the critical skills were identified from a thorough analysis of the Project Leader job. In a sense, this is a try-out for that level of position, but it is far from a contrived, play-acting situation. You should keep in mind that even in "real life" we are all called upon to play certain roles (husband, wife, father, mother, employee, manager), yet we rarely consider this to be play-acting.

Q. What do you mean when you say you assess "potential"? How does that differ from performance?
A. We think it is important to differentiate present on-the-job performance from potential to perform effectively in a position that might be quite different. To the degree that your present job and a target-level position differ, your present performance cannot be used as a valid indicator of potential for effectiveness in that different job. Individuals presently in some job classifications have little opportunity to exhibit the types of skills required in management positions. Potential for different jobs, therefore, must be defined in terms of performance in situations which reflect these jobs, and not in terms of present job performance.

Q. Why is an assessment center used?
A. It is the most accurate means of assessing potential for different jobs short of actually putting the person in the job. The exercises simulate actual conditions (demands, requirements) found in the jobs. It is a reliable and objective means of measurement because three assessors observe your behavior in five different situations, and they must agree on your final ratings. Each participant is exposed to standardized situations, receives the same treatment, and is evaluated by the same standards. This is hardly ever the case in on-the-job performance evaluations. In addition, all three assessors must agree on the ratings which are made. The focus is on behavior rather than things you can't really see, such as psychological traits.

Q. What are the qualifications of the assessors?
A. First, they have all been assessed in a higher-level program and have demonstrated their abilities to serve as an assessor. Second, they have all been through an eight-day intensive training program. They were trained in behavioral observation and classification, learned the exercises completely, and were trained to use objective standards in evaluating performance.

Q. What do the assessors do?
A. The assessors observe and take notes on your actions in each situation. In some cases, they play a role in order to create a standard situation; in other cases they interviewed you to find out why certain actions were taken. These notes are categorized under the skills for each exercise. The assessors meet as a team and review all of the behavioral evidence for each skill across all the situations and agree on a final rating. Assessors are also responsible for providing participants with feedback and providing the program coordinator with the information necessary to complete a staffing recommendation.

Q. Is a written report prepared?
A. Yes, a final written report covers much of the same material reviewed with you in the feedback session, but in less detail. You will have the opportunity to review this report if you like. However, it does not contain anything which was not reviewed with you during feedback.

Q. Where will the report be stored and who has access to it? Can I see it? Can I keep a copy? For how long is it active?
A. Obviously a lot of concerns here. First, the report is stored here at the center in a file totally separate from your formal personnel file. Both you and your supervisor will review the report and take notes on developmental needs. We do not give you a copy because the descriptions would help other participants who have not yet attended, and we want to ensure that everyone has the same chance at the center. A selecting manager would have the opportunity to review your report with a staff member here. The report is actively used for a period of three years, after which time it goes to an inactive file and would not be made available for personnel-related decisions.

Selection versus Development. Assessment centers are used for selection or development or both. The organization must clearly define the purpose of the assessment center. Subsequent development of the center's program and communication about it will be strongly affected by this decision. Ideally nonsupervisory technical groups should attend at least a selection program whereas higher level, technically oriented professional groups with some supervisory responsibility in their current jobs should attend a joint selection/development program. The reasoning is simple—it would be a waste of valuable time developing management skills in people who are not currently in positions requiring those skills and who may be unlikely to assume such a position in the foreseeable future. The supervisory-level professional groups are more likely to benefit from the management development efforts regardless of whether they move up the management ladder or not.

Use in Selection. From the organization's perspective valuable information is lost if *not* used for selection purposes. The role that the assessment center's ratings play in promotional decisions must be clearly stated and the policy consistently enforced. Although overall ratings of something as general as an individual's "potential" can be generated by an assessment center, the most valuable ratings are those of the specific, behaviorally defined skills, which are independently assessed.

Everyone shows a different pattern of strengths and weaknesses. Consider also that different positions require different critical skills; these are the conceptual rudiments of a sophisticated selection system. The task is simply to match the skill requirements of the job with the strengths of the individual. Given prescreening on technical competence, the individual selected for the job would have both the technical *and* managerial skills to be successful.

Use in Development. Even those organizations that use assessment centers for developmental purposes will often communicate particularly impressive or abysmal performances to the personnel staffing section. It is naive to believe that an assessment center which is billed as developmental will not be perceived as influential in one's own career. If the program is to be truly and solely developmental, strong confidentiality policies must be drafted and tight procedural restrictions enacted. Programs such as assessment centers tend to raise anxiety in some quarters *anyway;* nothing will damage the integrity of a developmental program more than having results leak out and be used for selection decisions. It is far preferable to design a controlled access system for integration with the selection system. Please note that if any assessment center results are used for employment-related decisions, then the center is a selection instrument in the eyes of the law and must be validated as such.

Regarding the development issue, there is some question about the degree to which the skills measured in the assessment center can be developed, if at all. Skills *vary* in the degree to which they can be developed. For example, "control and follow-up" might easily benefit by training in systems for planning, tracking, and taking corrective actions. Conversely, weaknesses in a skill such as "flexibility" may be much more deeply ingrained in the habit patterns and behavioral repertoire of the individual. Development would then require a lengthy process of behavioral assessment, feedback, and behavior change which might not be sustained back on the job.

The most incontrovertible data on skill change comes from AT&T (7). Eight years after their initial assessment, managers were again assessed, and there was evidence of stability in some, but not all, of the characteristics measured. This is to be expected. Managerial skill development is not a magic process or one which occurs with the simple provision of *information*. Skills must be enacted in behavior in order to improve, and that is exactly why the assessment center can be a key factor in skill development.

If performance in the assessment center is videotaped, this can be used as a very effective developmental aid. It establishes a base line of performance, which the individual participant can assess in depth much as an assessor would (with the aid of the assessment center staff). The relevance, being one's own performance, is dramatic and unarguable. Another videotape could be used to show examples of highly effective, behaviorally enacted skills in that *same* situation. It is not the "*right* answer," but it *is* a model performance which extends the potential repertory of behaviors available to the person. The person then *practices* the new behavior, receives feedback, and practices again. This, essentially, is the behavior-modeling approach to skill development that is described in more detail in chapter 6. It has been shown to be a very effective technique, and the assessment center naturally leads into it. Through this type of self-appraisal and development process, both short- and long-range development plans can be written to address areas of opportunity. This can be particularly critical when planning the transition from a technically oriented "hands-on" job to a managerially oriented generalist position.

From a cost-effectiveness viewpoint, it is most beneficial to use the results of an assessment center operation within a controlled selection procedure *and* to contribute to a process for development purposes. Relative emphasis on selection or development may vary as a function of the level of technical or managerial position being addressed.

Ethical Issues and Assessment Centers. One of the most damaging indictments of the administration of some assessment centers is that they allow the development of a "Success or Failure" syndrome to occur. An individual who performs well may be touted as though he or she can do no wrong. Another individual, perhaps an equally valued employee, who does not perform well may (rightly or wrongly) perceive their career to be ruined. What can be more unfair than to struggle for years on the job, only to be told in what some might consider a "play-acting school" that his or her skills are "well below satisfactory" for project leadership or the next level of management? What could be worse for the technical whiz-kid than to see promotion blocked by a poor rating at the assessment center? One thing *could* be worse for both the person and the organization: the ill-timed promotion that results in failure.

Assessment centers are not omniscient, nor are their administrators perfect. The method should add evidence to the decision-making arena, but not be the "make-it-or-break-it" final screening mechanism. Many factors might affect performance on a given day—these should not affect the assessor rating process but should be considered within the final report or recommendations. For example, in one case, a participant ran over and killed a cat on her way to the assessment center. Fond of cats, she was shaken by the incident but insisted on continuing in the center. Her performance took a beating.

From a more formal validation point of view, all statistical techniques of validation are based on group results, with findings given in terms of group averages. It makes no sense to speak of the validity of any one person's scores; they may be reliable (based on the convergence of independent observations), but they are not necessarily accurate. There is always error in any process. According to the psychometric model, the error is spread evenly across the group and any given prediction is within a "plus or minus percentage point" of accuracy. For whatever reason, assessment centers may from time to time be way off in their prediction of managerial ability and potential for advancement. This is bound to be a more rare occurrence than for traditional testing and performance appraisal "misses" in prediction, but is also bound to be much more highly visible. At some point, the system is likely to be challenged by a star performer who fails miserably in the assessment center and either tries to negotiate higher ratings or attempts to demean the value of the center.

One thing is certain: assessment center ratings are important to participants. They want to perform well, are motivated to perform up to their potential, and take the feedback very seriously. It is difficult to argue with ratings when they are supported by behavioral evidence that was observed by several different assessors. The results are much more than just one person's opinion.

If a participant does not perform well, he or she will want to know if the ratings can be changed, what they mean to his or her career, how the skills can be improved, and finally when a reassessment can be scheduled. The organization must establish a formal policy on reassessment before the first person is assessed for the first time. In most cases, reassessment is prohibited. This is because the validity of an assessment center is well-established for the first-time participant but questionable for repeat participants in the same exercises, and organizational resources are usually stretched to handle the volume of first-time participants. Repeat participants do not represent a cost-effective use of the assessment center. Instead, the dissatisfied person should be given the opportunity to draw up a development plan to address weak areas, and the results of this plan should later be attached to the assessment center results. If nothing more, this is evidence of individual motivation and personal initiative to change.

The impact of assessment center results on an individual can be great. The program administrator certainly needs to think through the issues raised in this section and plan appropriate positions prior to implementing the center. Professional ethical practices must not be sacrificed in the interest of organizational expediency.

Alternative Assessment Systems

The full-fledged assessment center and its systems, as described in this chapter, are not necessarily the most relevant or applicable for *all* organizations. There is no *one* cure-all appropriate for every organizational ailment. The assessment center is but one tool that can be used to assess the potential and development needs of professionals and scientists. The assessment center will generally be most appropriate within larger organizations with numerous multi-incumbent positions. However, even within the smallest or most highly diversified organization, the lessons of what works in the assessment center process can be generalized so that we can define the critical attributes of alternative systems.

A real workable alternative that incorporates elements of the assessment center is the peer review or committee method. This is a common approach in the scientific and professional community. It can be very effective in a variety of situations, for example:

- Group review of published works as evidence of technical and written skills—for tenure review
- A written test of highly complex knowledge—for certification
- A "live" oral defense or standup test of conceptual, integrative abilities and response to pressure and challenge—a dissertation defense
- A lecture on presentation of material in one's area of expertise—for scientific or academic selection consideration

The assessment center methodology would make the following recommendations for improving the accuracy of review in these situations:

- Use multiple "assessors"—this helps ensure a more objective view of performance.
- Use multiple situations—no single situational test is likely to give complete information on a person's potential and development needs. Mix and match. Consider the inferences that can be drawn about a person's ability given evidence from a particular type of situation.
- Match the situation to the requirements of the job, position, or level to which you are comparing the person. Standup defense is not the best test for a laboratory scientist but might be for the project manager that has to "sell" a certain application to management in committee meetings.
- Standardize the situational nature of the test. If a presentation is used, make sure that each person has the same opportunity to prepare; that the audience size and characteristics are similar; that the level and type of challenge aimed at the person is similar between people.
- Define ahead of time the characteristics being tested in each situation. The situation would then be defined to draw out those characteristics. Leadership ability is not best assessed through a written test!
- Define a well-structured system of pooling the perceptions of the peer group or committee. (See "Assessor Team Meeting" above and decide the most workable method to ensure pooled judgment based on observed behavior.)
- Determine ahead of time what decisions will be based on the review and ensure that the situations produce the data which will lead to those decisions. Just as the assessment center can be used for selection purposes, so too can the peer review/committee method. If this is the focus, the job-relatedness of the situational "tests" must be as clearly documented and validated as a written selection test. Just as the assessment center can be used to identify potential and development needs, so too can the peer review/committee method. In this latter case, the need for clearly specified behavioral feedback with developmental recommendations is paramount. The process should be structured to capture this feedback data.
- Determine ahead of time whether the focus of the assessment will be on *technical* or *managerial* skills. The design of the situations and the process will be directly affected by the focus chosen. Both technical *and* managerial might be a focus. For example, if the job requires a person to understand detailed research data, assessment should include how well they can translate highly technical jargon into "lay" language with useful recommendations for applications to a group of managers. Once the need is directly described like this, the challenge is to create a situation which mirrors these requirements.
- Not every situational test need be given in the same day or two in rapid succession. Individualized committee review plans might be defined to ensure relevant observations in meaningful situations over the course of a six-month period.
- As much as possible, make use of naturally occurring situations as opportunities to assess technical or managerial skills. Try to ensure the comparability of the situation across different people being reviewed.

The point to be made here is that there is no reason to be scared away by the complexity or cost of a formalized assessment center. Any organization could gain by translating the structured, disciplined methodology of the assessment center into the ongoing opportunities to assess talent within the organization.

SUMMARY

Chapter 3 has dealt in some detail with the process of getting into the organization, becoming oriented to the place, moving within the organization, and the assessment of potential for further movement in the organization. It was presented very much from the organization's point of view—that is, how can the management of an organization composed largely of professionals or scientists attract the best people and keep them moving at a rate consistent with their abilities?

The reader should now be able to answer the following questions:

What should the entry-level jobs be?
When should I consider internal, and when external, candidates?
What "job match" factors should I consider when bringing a new person on board?
Should I focus on a few positions as being developmental and force additional feedback through those positions?
How can I make the first job very challenging?
What can I do during that early "imprinting" phase to create organizational identification?
What information must I make available to the professionals in my organization?
How can I define the technical and managerial skill dimensions for my key positions?
What does job analysis do for me?
What information is required for career-planning purposes?
How can I use information about people and the position in the internal selection and placement process?

What is the difference between performance and potential?

What is an assessment center and how can it be useful in a career management program?

Should the assessment center be used for selection of employees or for their development?

What alternatives are there to a formal, full-fledged assessment center?

REFERENCES

1. Ahlberg, C. D., and Honey, J. C. 1950. *Attitudes of scientists and engineers about their government employment.* Syracuse, NY: Syracuse Univ.
2. Badawy, M. K. 1983. *Developing managerial skills in engineers and scientists.* New York: Van Nostrand Reinhold.
3. Bentz, V. J. 1967. The Sears experience in the investigation, description, and prediction of executive behavior. In *Measuring executive effectiveness,* ed. F. R. Wickert and D. E. McFarland, pp. 147-205. New York: Appleton-Century-Crofts.
4. Berlew, D. E., and Hall, D. T. 1966. The socialization of managers: effects of expectations on performance. *Administrative Science Quarterly* 11.
5. Bray, D. W. 1964. The management progress study. *American Psychologist* 19:419-20.
6. ———. 1971. The assessment center: opportunities for women. *Personnel* (September):30-34.
7. Bray, D. W., Campbell, R. J., and Grant, D. L. 1973. *The management recruit: formative years in business.* New York: Wiley-Interscience.
8. Bray, D. W., and Grant, D. L. 1966. The assessment center in the measurement of potential for business management. *Psychology Monographs* 80: 1-29.
9. Campbell, A., Converse, P. E., and Rodgers, W. L. 1976. *The quality of American life.* New York: Russell Sage Foundation.
10. Carlton, F. O. 1970. Relationship between follow-up evaluations and information developed in a management assessment center. Paper presented at the meeting of the American Psychological Association, September, Miami Beach.
11. Cheek, L. M. 1973. Cost effectiveness comes to the personnel function. *Harvard Business Review* 51 (3):96-105.
12. Cohen, B. M., Moses, J. L., and Byham, W. C. 1977. *A literature review: the validity of assessment centers.* Pittsburgh, PA: DDI Monograph.
13. Cohen, S. L., and Cascio, W. 1979. Estimating the cost/benefit ratio of assessment center operations. Paper presented at the Seventh International Congress on the Assessment Center Method, July, New Orleans.
14. Dalton, G. W., Thompson, P. H., and Price, R. L. 1977. The four stages of professional careers: a new look at performance by professionals. *Organizational Dynamics* 6 (1): 19-42.
15. Delamontagne, R. P., and Weitzul, J. B. 1980. Performance alignment: the fine art of the perfect fit. *Personnel Journal* (February):115-17, 131.
16. Dodd, W. E. 1971. Validity studies at IBM. In W. C. Byham (Chair), Validity of assessment centers. Symposium presented at the meeting of the American Psychological Association, September, Washington, DC.
17. Figgins, R. 1978. How to see if a job is right. *Personnel Journal* (December):691-96, 699.
18. Finkle, R. B. 1976. Managerial assessment centers. In *Handbook of Industrial and Organizational Psychology,* ed. M. D. Dunnette, pp. 861-88. Chicago: Rand McNally.
19. Finley, R. J. 1970. An evaluation of behavior predictions from projective tests given in a management assessment center. Paper presented at the meeting of the American Psychological Association, September, Miami Beach.
20. French, W. L. 1982. *The personnel management process.* Boston: Houghton Mifflin.
21. Hall, D. T. 1976. *Careers in organizations.* Pacific Palisades, CA: Goodyear Publishing Co.
22. Hall, D. T., and Hall, F. S. 1976. What's new in career management? *Organizational Dynamics* 5 (1):17-33.
23. Hall, D. T., and Mansfield, R. 1975. Relationships of age and seniority with career variables of engineers and scientists. *Journal of Applied Psychology* 60:201-10.
24. *Handbook for analyzing jobs.* 1972. Manpower Administration, U.S. Department of Labor. Washington, DC: Superintendant of Documents, Stock Number 2900-0131.
25. Heflich, D. L. 1981. Matching people and jobs: value systems and employee selection. *Personnel Administrator* (March): 77-85.
26. Hinricks, J. R. 1969. Comparison of "real life" assessments of management potential with situational exercises, paper and pencil ability tests, and personality inventories. *Journal of Applied Psychology* 53:425-33.
27. Huck, J. R. 1973a. Assessment centers: a review of the external and internal validities. *Personnel Psychology* 26: 191-212.
28. ———. 1973b. The assessment process: yesterday, today, and tomorrow. Paper presented at the First Annual Industrial and Organizational Psychology Conference, Ohio State University.
29. Huck, J. R. and Bray, D. W. 1976. Management assessment center evaluations and subsequent job performance of white and black females. *Personnel Psychology* 29:13-30.
30. Jaffee, C. L., Cohen, S. L., and Cherry, R. 1972. Supervisory selection program for disadvantaged or minority employees. *Training and Development Journal* 26 (1):22-27.
31. Kraut, A. I. The use of assessment centers. 1975. Paper read at the Midwest Academy of Management Meeting, August, Ann Arbor, Mich.
32. Kraut, A. I., and Scott, G. J. 1972. Validity of an operational management assessment program. *Journal of Applied Psychology* 56:124-29.
33. Marcson, S. 1960. Role adaptations of scientists in industrial research. *IEEE Transactions on Engineering Management* (December), EM-7:159-66.
34. Marquardt, L. D. and McCormick, E. J. 1974. *The job dimensions underlying the job elements of the Position Analysis Questionnaire (PAQ), form B,* report no. 4. Lafayette, IN: Occupational Research Center, Dept. of Psychological Sciences, Purdue Univ.
35. McConnell, J. H. 1971. The assessment center: a flexible program for supervisors. *Personnel Journal* (Sept./Oct.):35-40.
36. McCormick, E. J. 1959. The development of processes for indirect or synthetic validity. *Personnel Psychology* 12: 402-13.
37. ———. 1976. Job and task analysis. In *Handbook of industrial and organizational psychology,* ed. M. D. Dunnette, pp. 651-96. Chicago: Rand McNally.
38. Meyer, H. H. 1970. The validity of the in-basket test as a

measure of managerial performance. *Personnel Psychology* 23:297–307.

39. ———. 1972. Assessment centers at General Electric. Paper read at the meeting of Development Dimensions, San Francisco, CA.

40. Morris, B. S. 1949. Officer selection in the British Army: 1942-1945. *Occupational Psychology* 23:219–34.

41. Moses, J. L. 1973. The development of an assessment center for the early identification of supervisory potential. *Personnel Psychology* 26:569–80.

42. Moses, J. L., and Boehm, V. R. 1975. Relationship of assessment center performance to management progress of women. *Journal of Applied Psychology* 60 (4):527–29.

43. Neidig, R. D., Martin, J. C., and Yates, R. E. 1978. *The FBI's management aptitude program assessment center: research report no. 1.* Washington, DC: Personnel Research and Development Center.

44. OSS Assessment Staff. 1948. *Assessment of men.* New York: Rinehart.

45. Pearson, J. M. 1982. The transitions into a new job: tasks, problems and outcomes. *Personnel Journal* (April):286–90.

46. St. John, W. D. 1980. The complete employee orientation program. *Personnel Journal* (May):373–78.

47. Sheibar, P. 1979. A simple selection system called "Jobmatch." *Personnel Journal* (January):26–29, 53.

48. Task Force on Assessment Center Standards. 1979. Standards and ethical considerations for assessment center operations. Endorsed by the Seventh International Congress of the Assessment Center Method, New Orleans, June.

49. Thomson, H. A. 1970. Comparison of predictor and criterion judgments of managerial performance using the multitrait-multimethod approach. *Journal of Applied Psychology* 54:496–502.

50. Thorenson, J. D., and Jaffee, C. L. 1973. A unique assessment center application with some unexpected by-products. *Human Resource Management* (Spring):3–7.

51. Vosburgh, R. M. 1982. Supervisory experience, reading ability, demographic variables and assessment center performance. *Journal of Assessment Center Technology* 5 (3):1–5.

52. Wollowick, H. B., and McNamara, W. J. 1969. Relationship of the components of an assessment center to management success. *Journal of Applied Psychology* 53:348–52.

53. Zemke, R. 1980. Using assessment centers to measure management potential. *Training* (March):23–27.

Chapter 4
Human Resource Review Systems

While the form of a professional and scientific human resource review depends on the needs of the organization, it always involves merging two closely related functions. The first is individual career planning, or the specific strategy and tactics developed by the individual employee to serve his or her vocational self-interest. The organization may facilitate this through procedures or diagnostic exercises designed to focus an individual's attention on actual abilities, skills, and desires in relation to his or her potential for future advancement. Individual career planning, discussed in chapter 1, involves self-inquiry into career history and aspirations as a prelude to the development of a more realistic career plan.

The second function is reciprocal: organizational career management involving management-generated programs of career planning to meet organizational needs. This includes not only the identification of future "people needs" and the specification of developmental career progressions, but also the assessment of individual performance and potential. Historically, this function has been referred to as "manpower planning," and the way it fits into our model was described in chapter 1 of this book.

Both functions are particularly critical in organizations with engineers, scientists, and professionals. Certain assumptions about the motives and career aspirations of these groups are likely to be made incorrectly by generalist managers. As Badawy has succinctly stated, the value systems and role expectations of scientists and engineers are quite different from each other and from the typical candidate for middle or upper level management (1). Essentially, scientists identify with and orient toward professional rather than bureaucratic or organizational goals. Engineers are more likely to orient toward a "local" organizational perspective and be more concerned about the goals of the organization. From a career management perspective, these differences create the need for more dialogue and a greater understanding of professional versus organizational goals. Grass argues that "technical professionals will be more productive when management pays more attention to their career development [as evidenced by] a periodic human resource review wherein managers are required to assess the career status of each professional and identify appropriate future assignments" (5, pp. 227, 231).

Similarly, Medcof presents substantial research data to support his view that engineers and scientists are more interested in things than in people and that their values, thought process, and style differ substantially from that of managers (8). Therefore, the organization must make programs available that aid in the transition from technical expert to management professional (3,4), and back again if needed (6). Often, these programs are specifically designed for professionals, such as data-processing personnel (2,9) or others (7).

A human resource review is a coordinated approach designed to merge the reciprocal functions of career planning at the individual employee's level and career management or human resources planning at the organization's level. The review forces an intensive evaluation of the current status of an organization's human resources, areas of strength or weakness, and anticipated future needs. It is designed to contribute to the effectiveness of the organization through more systematic and efficient planning of the use of the organization's "brain trust," its professional and scientific employees. The individual's need for professional involvement and recognition, and the organization's need to build a bridge to business goals are both served.

The review is conducted at the top levels of an organization and represents the top-level commitment to matching employee talent and aspirations to career progression possibilities. The review is a process that is much more than a once-a-year meeting to review the progress of the system. It should be a continuous, dynamic process which simplifies needed information and presents it in a usable form. As with other career management systems, the human resource review requires a system, but it must not become an overly mechanical process in which the real people are lost in a paper trail. A review as detailed as the one presented here may not be necessary every year—the timing should be based on the organization's needs. If the organization is at the crossroads of several new projects or contracts, potential reorganization, new technologies, or the like, then the program should be planned to provide input into those decisions. It is important to note that the review is a planning tool that identifies "talent pools" from which qualified lateral and/or promotional candidates can be generated for any position opening up. The review thus serves in a planning and "sorting" capacity. This is especially critical when the plan to bring a talented professional into management might require years and the right set of assignments to ease the transition; or when the plan to staff a new high-technology applications group requires a special blend of professional, scientific, and managerial skills, that may need to be developed internally. The responsibility and authority for internal selection and placement decisions still remains with the selection program of the organization and is unaffected by the review. What *should be* affected is the quality and completeness of the candidate slate, as well as the search time required to generate such a list. The review process can be used to objectify and clarify the criteria used for identifying and referring internal candidates for job openings.

THE CASE FOR REVIEW SYSTEMS

Organizational Needs

"Back of the envelope" manpower planning and career management no longer fit the reality of many organizations' needs today and will be even more out of place tomorrow. Organizations experiencing growth, expansion, or reorganization must develop some type of strategic plan for the use of their human resources. The alternative is reliance on a piecemeal approach to selection and placement, without any unified plan for advancing the goals of the organization through personnel changes. The correct balance of professional and managerial staff must be planned. In times of change, the emphasis shifts from a need to *react* to external influences to a need to *act* through the better planning and development of internal human resources. Active, dynamic planning is more necessary to the degree that external conditions are rapidly changing internal needs. A change in corporate direction is more likely to affect technical/professional/scientific skill needs than it will managerial skill needs, which tend to be more generic.

Periods of slow growth also frequently occur. When they do, there is a reduction in the natural movement of people. The review provides an opportunity to develop strategies for moving people so that everyone benefits. This is often critical for professional people who need to avoid stagnation and obsolescence.

The human resource review provides the organization with the needed integration and coordination of individual employees' career plans and the organization's human resources needs. Simply providing the vehicle by which this process can occur communicates a genuine interest in human resources management. It tells everyone within the organization that the development and maximum use of employees is an important part of the organization's job. It also provides the forum in which to discuss openly professional/management career issues.

Since the process generally involves several levels of review and concurrence, it creates greater familiarity with general organizational issues, problems, and plans. A planned approach to human resources management helps prevent "surprises" when a position opens up, especially when this creates a "domino effect" and many positions must be filled. Rather than being a tremendous headache for the personnel department or the selecting managers, a job opening creates the opportunity to fulfill planned lateral and promotional goals. In fact, the review can even result in a planned "slate" of moves whereby everybody gains without having to wait for a vacancy to create movement. This is an especially important feature in small or very stable organizations in which the opportunity for movement is minimal, and the need for movement, visibility, or "mentoring" for professional purposes is great.

In addition, the review provides the forum in which to monitor a great variety of critical managerial functions. For example, an individual and "bottom-line" salary and performance review would produce greater management familiarity with the performance and potential of all employees. A review of progress on previously approved career plans provides a method by which high-performance personnel can be tracked. A level-by-level review of new career plans ensures that each plan is realistic and all "fit together" to cover organizational needs. The review provides a systematic means by which future short- and long-range human resources needs of the organization can be estimated and plans made to meet these needs. These plans would include individual development plans for identified people, which are monitored closely on a short-term basis. Essentially, the review is designed to ensure that qualified people are available to meet the needs of the organization—in the right numbers, at the needed time, and with the appropriate skills.

Individual Needs

The human resource review meets the individual's need for recognition at the highest level in the organization and for personal control over his or her own development. Especially in this era of advanced technology, broad professional and managerial competence can often more adequately be developed through a planned series of job experiences and training than through a semirandom progression or the unimaginative adherence to a routine set of career moves. Top-level review and approval of individual career plans lets *all* employees know that importance is placed on them by the organization. This may be especially true for the most talented people who may tend to be more aggressive and demanding of immediate challenges and responsibility than other people.

If the review includes feedback to the employee, several individual needs are met. A more realistic view of career alternatives occurs in the analysis of positions that were and were not approved. This type of feedback creates fewer false expectations and lessens the ambiguity with regard to career possibilities. Rarely does anyone receive feedback on performance and potential from top-level management and professional staff. This can be a very sobering experience if the views are other than expected or hoped for. In either case, the individual knows where he or she stands and can proceed accordingly.

Three different approaches to human resource review systems have been constructed to serve different but overlapping purposes:

- The organizational review of human resources, focusing on organizational planning (unit performance, movement, and staffing needs) and individual career planning (career plan review and approval, and assessment center nominations)*
- The business-plan–based human resource review focusing heavily on the degree to which the characteristics of the people and the logic of their groupings contribute to the bottom-line business goals of the organization
- The tactical work-group review matching the competency requirements of positions and projects with the competencies of employees in order to make staffing, recruiting, and training plans

Within each of these three programs is represented a real smorgasbord of human resource review *ideas*. Any section could "stand alone" to meet a given objective. The challenge for the organization is to identify basic needs clearly and to choose accordingly from these detailed yet integrated programs.

THE ORGANIZATIONAL REVIEW OF HUMAN RESOURCES

The organizational review of human resources is an ongoing process, integrating many critical managerial functions and often culminating in a yearly meeting or annual review, although the timing of this will vary with the need. The information that follows will provide some background on the method and give detailed instructions regarding what to prepare for the meeting, what to discuss in the meeting, and what will be generated from the meeting. The review process is designed to meet the needs of both the organization (through the organizational planning component) and its management and professional employees (through the career planning component).

The review is based on the philosophy that a coordinated approach to both career and organizational planning is required. This particular method was developed for two main reasons: to contribute to the effectiveness of the organization through more systematic and efficient planning for the use of management and professional employees; and to provide the final approval point for career action plans and the nomination procedure for the assessment center. The review represents an organization's commitment to matching professional and managerial talent and aspirations to objective job requirements and organizational needs.

The review is directly related to the selection and placement system. Essentially, employees with approved career action plans constitute the "talent pool" from which a slate of candidates can be drawn for any position or project that is available. The review serves in a planning and "sorting" capacity; it does not affect the responsibility or authority for the internal selection or placement decision. The process makes it easier to identify candidates who are both qualified for and interested in specific positions or projects. It also provides management and professional employees with helpful feedback regarding what they must do developmentally in order to be seriously considered for positions or projects in which they are interested.

The review meeting is chaired by the vice-president of each area and is attended by those who report directly to him or her. It is usually held in early November to coincide with salary planning. Under discussion at the meeting will be topics relating to organizational planning and to individual planning. The information presented here should be used to prepare for the review meeting, as a discussion guide during the meeting, and after the meeting to check that the necessary output documents were prepared.

Organizational Planning

Departmental Performance Review. The review begins with a general departmental overview of the year's activities—not only the activities of the past year but also those expected in the coming year. This comparison should identify changing technologies or priorities that would affect staffing requirements. For example,

---

*This is structured after a program which has been used by General Telephone Company of Florida, entitled Career and Organizational Planning Annual Review (COPAR), which was developed by Vosburgh when serving as a consultant to GTE.

planned automation might shift needs from very technical positions to clerks' positions (to handle data entry). This would influence approval of the career action plans later in the review since the plans should cover the needs identified here.

The departmental performance review form is prepared ahead of time and summarized in the meeting (fig. 4-1). The form identifies the significant accomplishments of the unit and the human resources required to achieve them. Specific technical knowledge areas required by the unit are defined with an emphasis on new professional knowledge areas that might be required based on the review. In particular, participants should consider events that might block goal achievement and how these might be avoided through planning.

In discussing the review, each member at the meeting should, in turn, briefly review his/her department's achievements, goals, and potential obstacles to achieving those goals. They should identify the new directions and new knowledge areas needed. Can anything be done now to avoid obstacles to goal achievement? If so, this can be made a specific assignment of one person, with task and follow-up date clearly determined. The vice-president should then present his or her view of departmental performance and future requirements.

The output from this section of the meeting would be the vice-president's acceptance of the "departmental performance review" forms (which may include additional or revised goals) and a general acceptance of performance improvement plans (only if necessary or to avoid obstacles to goal achievement).

Actual and Projected Movement. Both short- and long-range human resource planning occurs at this stage. Actual movement over the past year is used as a "benchmark" to calibrate projections over the next year, the next two to three years, and the next four to five years. Actual movement consists of promotions, lateral moves, retirements, terminations, resignations, demotions, new hirings, and the like, within, into, or out of a department or division. Projected movement might be due to normal turnover, addition to force, or reorganization. Project staffing is also reviewed here in order to better meet future project needs.

The actual movement summary and the projected movement summary forms (figs. 4-2, 4-3) are completed in preparation for this section. As part of the discussion in the review meeting, each member should review briefly both actual and projected movement within his or her department or division. The group must decide whether the projections appear logical and accurate and what might affect the projections. For example, are there new technologies, systems, or organizational directions which might affect them? If possible, the discussion should include a comparison of last year's projected and this year's actual movement to better calibrate future projections. Have there been moves from the technical/professional/scientific track to a management track and is more such movement likely in the future? For specific project staffing, the members should review the status of staff members. From where were people drawn to fill project needs, and where will they go when the projects are completed?

The output from this part of the review includes the completed actual movement summary and projected movement summary as well as a recap of project staffing plans.

Succession Staffing. Since it is not always possible to predict where vacancies will occur, a planning perspective would suggest the need to identify "ready replacements" for all key positions. This portion of the review serves that need.

The succession staffing form (fig. 4-4) is prepared for this section. This form serves to identify:

- "Ready replacements" for everyone reporting directly to a department head or division manager
- "Key positions" below this level but critical enough to require succession staffing, and the corresponding "ready replacements"
- Critical project staff—the key professional/scientific support on key projects and the ready replacements for these people.

4-1. Departmental performance review.

Department/Division: _____   **Section:** _____   **Section Head:** _____   **Date:** _____

Briefly outline your section's achievements over the past year and goals for the coming year where these clearly relate to human resources or staffing requirements. Specifically identify technical knowledge areas required by your section.

4-2. Actual movement summary.

Department/Division: _____   **Dept. Head/Div. Manager:** _____

Dates of Movement: _/ / _ to _/ / _   **Review Date:** _/ /_

		Position			
MOVEMENT	NAME	FROM	TO	DATE	COMMENTS
Within department					
Left the department					
Entered the department					
Professional to management					

4-3. Projected movement summary.

Department/Division: _____   **Dept. Head/Div. Manager:** _____

Dept. Head Signature: _____   **Review Date:** _/ /_

1 YEAR AHEAD: POSITION TITLE	NUMBER NEEDED	DATE (MONTH)	TYPE	"FEEDER" POSITION	COMMENTS
2-3 YEARS AHEAD: POSITION TITLE	NUMBER NEEDED	DATE (QTR.)	TYPE	BACKGROUND NEEDED	COMMENTS
4-5 YEARS AHEAD: FUNCTIONAL AREA AND LEVEL	NUMBER NEEDED	DATE (YEAR)	TYPE	GENERAL BACKGROUND NEEDED	COMMENTS

Type:
  P = professional to management
  T = normal turnover
  A = addition
  R = reorganization
  O = other (specify in comments section)

4-4. Succession staffing.

Vice-Presidential Area: _____   **Vice-President:** _____

Vice-President's Signature: _____   **Review Date:** __/__/__

POSITION TITLE	LEVEL	"READY REPLACEMENT" EMPLOYEES' NAMES	CURRENT POSITION	LEVEL
Department head				
Direct reports				
Key positions				
Critical project staff				

The discussion in the review would tackle the following questions:

- What justification is there for designating the key positions or critical project staff?
- What rationale is there for the identified successors? How are they best suited for the positions?
- Does the list reflect the actual ability and potential of the employees on it?
- What training or development might be made available to the employees listed as ready replacements in preparation for possible new assignments?
- If there is no ready replacement for a given position, is there anyone who could be developed?
- In what areas is there a lack of technical knowledge backup?

The output from this section would include the vice-presidential acceptance of the succession staffing list, a consensus on key positions and critical project staff, and possibly, developmental plans for employees listed.

Staffing Plans. The purpose of this portion of the review meeting is to develop a strategy for filling positions in a way that will most effectively increase the quality of the work force. There are numerous alternatives to be considered, for example, lateral moves, promotional moves, technical-to-management moves, outside recruitment, or management trainee programs. The focus is on positions and projects, not on people. For example, some positions require technical skills or specific company knowledge which can only be gained through experience in a specific job, so that job would be identified as a "feeder" position. In other cases, a particular educational background might be more important, and external hire would be the most reasonable course to pursue. In neither case would specific people be identified.

The form (fig. 4-5) prepared for this section summarizes the information required in making staffing plans. Preparation of this form requires a review of the organization's strategic business plan and the unit's objectives to determine if they have implications for future staffing needs.

The discussion would attempt to isolate the best sources of talent from which to draw, to determine the optimum mixture of alternatives for filling first-level management and technical project positions, and to identify the internal jobs that would normally fill these positions ("feeder" jobs). This might be the time to have the people in these internal jobs assessed as to their managerial or technical skills. It might also provide an opportunity to make affirmative action advances. All these topics must be discussed for a more complete and accurate staffing plan.

4-5. Staffing plans.

Originating Department/Division: ──────────── **Review Date:** __/__/__

POSITION	# NEEDED IN NEXT YEAR	ACCEPTABLE ALTERNATIVES FOR FILLING POSITIONS	# FROM EACH ALTERNATIVE	"FEEDER" JOBS FROM THE ORGANIZATION
Management				
Professional/ scientific				

Individual Planning

Career Plan Review and Approval. This is the final phase of the review meeting—approval of all career plans. It is the stage at which the organization's human resources needs (as identified earlier in the review) and the career aspirations of the organization's high-performance professional and management employees are integrated and coordinated. Final approval signifies a careful process of "prescreening" whereby the career choices of each employee are certified as both realistic and attainable. If possible, key positions identified earlier should coincide with career plans of qualified employees. New input to the plans may well occur due to the varied representation, wider perspective, and higher level of the people making up the review. Recommendations or revisions (via the career plan approval form) which would improve the plan should be encouraged.

Completed career plans from eligible employees should be ready for this section of the review meeting. These will already have been reviewed and approved by the first- and second-level supervisor as well as a senior professional (when applicable). The actual worksheet format of the career plan is not critical to understanding the process behind this section, so none is presented here. Organizations vary greatly in the details included on the career plan form, and that is not the point which is important now.

The review meeting discussion of career plans should address specific questions:

- Is each career plan realistic in terms of the employee's background, performance, and potential?
- Is each career plan attainable in terms of the organization's needs, as identified during the organizational-planning part of the review?
- Could suggestions be made on the approval form that would make the career plan more realistic or more attainable? For example, could additional developmental opportunities be provided?
- Can anything be done to facilitate movement on career plans?
- Do the approved career plans assure that key positions will be filled along with positions that are likely to become available within two years, as identified in the organizational planning component of the review?

The output from this section would be a completed career plan approval form for each newly submitted career plan.

Assessment Center Nominations. The purpose of this portion of the review is to identify people to attend the assessment and development programs of the organization's assessment center. By virtue of their involvement in career planning, these people have already been prescreened based on performance and motivation. In setting priorities for nomination, the question at this point is whether there is an organizational *need* for this person to be assessed in either the professional track, supervisory level, or middle management program. The following three points appear on the career plan approval form:

Priority: This employee has at least one position or project choice listed for the next year that requires attendance at the assessment center in order to assess the employee's professional or managerial skills relative to the demands and activities of that position or project.

Nominee: For whatever reason, it is the considered opinion of the department or division head that this employee be scheduled to attend the assessment center.

Not a Nominee: This employee should not be considered at this time for attendance at the assessment center (including any employee who has already participated in the program).

Participants should come prepared to defend their priority call, which is tentatively set in the second-level review meeting where the two levels immediately above the candidate meet to review the career plan.

The discussion in the review should answer these questions:

- Which employee, based on the needs identified in the organizational planning component of the review, should have his or her professional or managerial skills assessed relative to the demands of a requested position or project?
- Has this person's evidence of leadership been based on *technical* or *managerial* skills?
- Does the employee list a key position on his or her career plan? Are there others who are developing themselves for these positions?
- Is this a professional employee who has expressed a desire to move into management?
- Does the employee list a promotional move to a target-level position within the next year?

The output of this section of the meeting is agreement on who has priority to attend the assessment center, and this decision is noted on the career plan approval form.

THE BUSINESS-PLAN-BASED REVIEW

Because the human resource management systems must support the real business needs of the organization, there must be a review system built around the organization's strategic business plans. Such a business-plan-based (BPB) review system is designed to "roll up" through the organization, culminating in a presentation by each functional vice-president to the chief executive officer. The BPB review has three objectives: to communicate the state of the organization; to provide a forum for identifying human resource plans and progress relative to business and strategic plans; and to reinforce human resource management responsibility within each function. The BPB review integrates information about the organization's structure and business plan with information about the people who must carry out these plans. The review, graphically summarized in figure 4-6, results in:

1. *An employee inventory* showing who is promotable, borderline, or a performance problem—suitable for use in internal searches
2. *Individual development plans* that address individual needs (and the basis for a tracking system to ensure these plans are realized)
3. *Work group/special project development plans* that address total group issues—where are the strengths and weaknesses as they relate to business plans? What knowledge is needed to perform the group's mission successfully?

4-6. A business-plan-based human resource review system.

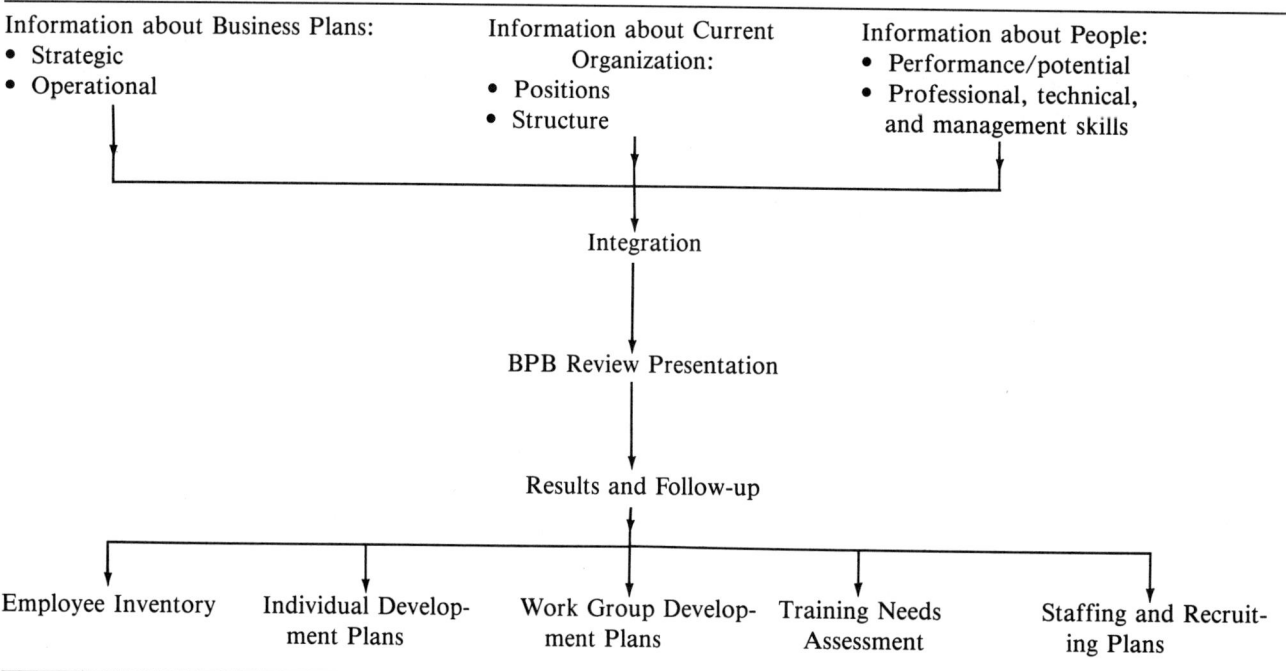

4. *A training needs assessment* summarizing development needs of individuals and groups
5. *Staffing and recruiting plans* that address obvious needs that surfaced in the business plan review

Such a review might follow the agenda summarized below. It covers a lot of ground:

CURRENT YEAR IN REVIEW
- Organizational structure
- Business issues and personnel actions
- Personnel moves

PEOPLE REVIEW
- Technologies covered
- Promotability mix summaries
- Individual reviews
- Demographic mix profile

FUTURE PLANS
- Business issues and personnel actions
- Functional excellence

Current Year in Review

The review of the past year should be kept as brief as possible. This section should provide the highlights rather than a complete review. It is meant to establish the setting against which the people reviews and next year's plan can be better understood and evaluated.

Organization Structure. If there have been structural changes, a before-and-after approach should be used. Use standardized organizational charts for this part of the presentation—and *color code* the chart to show the changes which occurred:

> Green = Eliminated Position
> Yellow = Changed or Moved Position
> Red = Added Position

The focus here is not on people, nor should they be discussed at this point. The discussion centers on *why* changes were made and what resulted from them.

If there have been no structural changes, the current organizational chart should be presented without color coding.

Business Issues and Personnel Actions. A format such as that presented in figure 4–7 should be used to present this portion. Discussion should center on the *results* column. Did the plans work? What impact did they have? Were there deviations from the plan? Why?

Personnel Moves. Here the presenter summarizes key moves, hirings, and losses. An effective method of presenting this information is through the color coding of

---

4–7. Business issues and personnel actions.

BUSINESS ISSUE	PERSONNEL ACTION	RESULT
	HIRING PROGRAMS	
• Company growth and new business contracts dictate that we *upgrade* and *build bench*	• Continue an active college recruiting program • Continue the company's "fast-track" professional and management designate program	• Recruited 82 people, increasing the percentage with advanced engineering degrees to 73% in target jobs • Hired 15 new designates in each category; moved 18 previous designates into target jobs
	DEVELOPMENT PROGRAMS	

	• Provide professional continuing education
	• Develop a "scientist exchange program" with co-contractors
	• Execute management development plans
		• Spent $61,000 on accredited continuing education for professional employees
		• 3 scientists have completed cross-training
		• 4 new courses developed:
		  1. Introduction to management
		  2. Communication and active listening
		  3. Performance counseling and appraisal
		  4. Project management

organizational charts—one chart to show *movement out*, one to show *movement in*:

COLOR	MOVEMENT OUT	MOVEMENT IN
Green	Promoted Out	Promoted In
Yellow	Lateraled Out	Lateraled In
Blue	Left Company	Outside Hire
Red	Open Position	Open Position

This section gives the audience a feel for the flow into and out of positions and targets currently open positions for planning later.

People Review

Once the stage has been set by the overview, the key review of personnel occurs. The entire group is presented using grids and matrices, and individuals are selected for more detailed attention through one-page résumés. Promotability is a major focus. Stability, age, education, and minority status are also reported.

Technologies Covered. Each functional vice-president's area must carry out specific areas of expertise. These areas of technology vary greatly depending on the organization, functional area, and work or project group. The objective of this portion of the BPB review is to ensure that each of these technologies is "covered" in terms of *quantity* (do we have the correct number of people?) and *quality* (do we have the level of expertise needed over the next two to three years?). Figure 4-8 shows an example matrix that can be used to present this information. Current employees (by category such as level or work group) are simply slotted into each box and color coded as to level of expertise in that specific technological area, for example:

Green = Expert Knowledge (can teach it)
Yellow = Working Knowledge (can do it)
Red — Talking Knowledge (knows the terms)

Promotability Mix Summaries. A series of promotability matrices can be used to present the people within the presenter's organization. Up to four different, sequential matrices are appropriate although the first gives most of the information. Figures 4-9 through 4-12 show example blank forms (surnames are simply inserted in the appropriate box). The "current category" refers to the person's current salary level or work group, whichever would be most descriptive in the particular organization.

Obviously, this part of the presentation requires considerable preparation. It allows for identification of promotable people and consideration of the "mix." Is it correct for the organization? Is the percentage of promotable too many, just right, or too few? Are they promotable into those areas that need to be filled?

Another color-coded chart is very useful here. A geographical or functional chart can be used to show the mix of promotability *or* technical ability within a given area. The columns across the top would still be labeled "current category," but the names down the side would be broken out by geography (East, Central, West divisions) or function (equipment and process R&D, product R&D, patent law). Within the boxes of the matrix, the last names of the incumbents would be color coded according to an accepted convention, for example:

Green = Promotable *or* excellent technically
Yellow = Hold *or* acceptable technically
Red = Other *or* technical deficiencies

Again, the discussion here would focus on the appropriateness of the mix given the business issues previously described.

Individual Reviews. Key people and those above a certain level would be reviewed in some depth through the use of an internal résumé. The information contained on the résumé should include:

- Name
- Title
- Current performance and performance trend (decreasing, constant, increasing)
- Short-term promotability
- Long-term promotability
- Strengths
- Development needs
- Development plans
- Demographic background information: age, years in title, years with the organization, salary grade or level, current salary, date of current salary, compensation ratio (salary to midpoint)
- Previous positions within the organization
- Previous positions prior to the organization
- Education: degree and date; school and major
- Date prepared

A great deal of information can fit nicely on a one-page résumé using this "bullet-point" format, as figure 4-13 shows.

The discussion would not be a reiteration of the résumé. Since it is there for participants in the review to read, the presenter should liven it up and personalize it with relevant examples or anecdotes supporting the conclusions of the résumé. The manner in which the person's talents prepare him or her to handle the demands of the business should also be addressed. Finally, "next-step" moves for the person should be described—when and where do you see this person moving next? If there is training or development planned to prepare the person for the next step, that would be the last item covered.

4-8. Technology review.

TECHNOLOGY REQUIRED	Current Category			
	DEPARTMENT HEADS	PROJECT MANAGERS	SCIENTISTS	ENGINEERS

4-9. People mix summary.

	Current Category			
	DEPARTMENT HEADS	PROJECT MANAGERS	SCIENTISTS	ENGINEERS
Promotable				
Level Expandable/Hold in Position				
Other Action				

4-10. Promotable breakout by level.

PROMOTABLE TO:	Current Category			
	DEPARTMENT HEADS	PROJECT MANAGERS	SCIENTISTS	ENGINEERS

4-11. Hold breakout.

HOLD CATEGORY	Current Category			
	DEPT. HEADS	PROJECT MGRS.	SCIENTISTS	ENGINEERS
Irreplaceable				
Expandable in Position or within Category				
Most Suitable Placement				
Too New—Cannot Call				
Performs Acceptably, Replacement Would be an Upgrade				

4-10. Promotable breakout by level.

PROMOTABLE TO:	Current Category			
	DEPARTMENT HEADS	PROJECT MANAGERS	SCIENTISTS	ENGINEERS

4-11. Hold breakout.

HOLD CATEGORY	Current Category			
	DEPT. HEADS	PROJECT MGRS.	SCIENTISTS	ENGINEERS
Irreplaceable				
Expandable in Position or within Category				
Most Suitable Placement				
Too New—Cannot Call				
Performs Acceptably, Replacement Would be an Upgrade				

4-12. Other action breakout.

OTHER ACTION	Current Category			
	DEPT. HEADS	PROJECT MGRS.	SCIENTISTS	ENGINEERS
Lateral due to Performance: Find More Suitable Assignment within Category				
Demote: Find More Suitable Assignment in Lower Category				
Outplace				

4-13. Sample résumé.

> *(First, last name)*
> *(Title)—(MM/YY)*
>
> Performance: (Rating)
>   Future: • (How long in current position)
>   • (Next step move)
>   • (Optional—interim step move)
>   • (Long-term move—5 to 7 years)
>
>   STRENGTHS   NEEDS
>
> • (Short, 1–10 words, to be expanded in the script   • (Also short)
> • presentation)   •
> •   •
> •   •
>
> Key questions: • (What are the *real issues* for this person?
>   • Is there a "career stopper"? May be positive!)
>
>   Age: (Years)   Salary level: (XX)
>   Hire date: (MM/YY)   Years service: (Years/Months)
>   Salary/date: ($XX,000—MM/YY)   Compa-ratio: (.XX)
>   Languages: (Only if applicable)
>
>   History:
> Company: (Year began) (Title) (Begin with most recent)
>
> Prior: (Year began) (Title) (Company) (Begin with most recent)
>
> Education: (Year-degree) (Degree) (Major) (University) (Begin with highest degree)
>
> DATE PREPARED: (XX/XX/XX)

Demographic Mix Profile. Numerous color-coded organizational charts (showing the last names of incumbents and the function) can be used here also. For example, *stability* could be addressed by looking at time in title or time with the organization:

    Green = More than three years
    Yellow = One to three years
    Red = Less than one year

This may show different things—but the discussion should always be oriented toward what it says about the organization's ability to meet its business goals. With *every* mix profile in this section, the following questions should be addressed in the discussion:

1. What is my mix distribution? Am I happy with these percentages? Is it what my unit needs? Does this represent a change over last year? Do I need to do anything about it?
2. How does the mix distribution affect my unit *organizationally*? How do the levels compare? Do I have the mix distribution my unit needs at each level? Do I need to do anything to change the mix at any level?
3. How does the mix distribution affect my unit *functionally*? How do the functional groups compare? Are there any key blocks? Do I need to take any action to change the mix in any function?
4. How does the mix distribution affect my unit *geographically*? How do the groups compare geographically? Do I need to take any action to change the mix in any geographic location?

The focus in this section is *not* on individuals but on the group as a whole—looking at it in horizontal and vertical slices on numerous variables. Other variables which might be of interest, and a simple color-coding scheme for each, might be the following:

MINORITY/FEMALE STATUS:

    Green = Minority
    Yellow = Female

EDUCATIONAL DEGREE

   Green = MBA or Ph.D.
  Yellow = BA/BS
    Blue = AA
     Red = H.S.

YEAR OF EDUCATIONAL DEGREE

   Green = 0–5 years
  Yellow = 6–10 years
     Red = 10+ years

AGE

   Green = 20–30
  Yellow = 31–40
     Red = 41+

Future Plans

Although not lengthy in the time it takes to present, this section is key and should be precise and analytically strong. It wraps up everything that has been said with an action plan to move the organization forward. This section presents conclusions in two ways: personnel actions deriving from strategic business plans are identified; and an overall analysis of the unit's functional excellence is given, along with plans to address key deficits and maximize key opportunities.

Business Issues and Personnel Actions. Figure 4-14 provides an example of the format and content for this section. The presenter summarizes the relevant business issues facing his or her unit and for each issue presents the corresponding personnel action that will support the business goals. These business issues and personnel actions then become the basis for the first section of the review in next year's presentation. In this way, commitments are followed up and monitored for results.

Functional Excellence. The organization must establish for itself the key ingredients for success. What does it take to be successful in today's business environment? Andrall Pearson, past president and CEO of PepsiCo, Inc., now with the Harvard Business School, has clearly identified four main features which help ensure functional excellence:

1. *Leadership at the Top.* Outstanding leaders provide outstanding thoughts and results. They move the business forward. To be successful an organization needs such leaders at least two levels deep at the top.
2. *Talent Throughout.* Talent refers to the technical/functional skills of the person in the current level. Talent requires that your people be well trained and well disciplined at all levels.
3. *A Strong Bench.* This is the ability to close ranks if someone is promoted or leaves the organization. It means having more than just enough people to go around. It is *depth* within each functional area.
4. *A Renewal Process.* These are the programs and policies that support the processes which consistently renew and upgrade the organization in both technical and management areas. This process should be focused mainly at the lower levels.

Once the key requirements of functional excellence are defined, the presenter rates each item on a scale and briefly describes why each rating appears as it does on a form such as figure 4-15, referring to previously presented issues to support the rating. The presenter closes with a statement reflecting their degree of optimism in being able to meet the business goals of the unit.

THE TACTICAL WORK-GROUP REVIEW

The business-plan-based review addresses only one portion of a total human resource management system—the "inventory" of your people relative to business needs. By itself this serves some useful needs and can

4-14. Business issues and planned personnel actions.

BUSINESS ISSUE	PLANNED PERSONNEL ACTION
• Upgrading and building professional depth	• Require professional development plans for all level-one scientists, and track progress quarterly • Support the Ph.D. recruiting program—bring in 20 new Ph.D.'s in targeted technologies
• Competitive intrusion into our most profitable line	• Develop a program to "blunt" competitive intrusion, involve R&D and marketing
• The need for a "winner" product for the next decade	• Upgrade product R&D by adding two new positions and filling with creative and talented engineers • Work with the professional development department to identify a "creativity" workshop for our professional staff

4-15. Functional excellence.

Organizational Unit: _____

```
Leadership at the Top    /_____/_____/
Talent Throughout        /_____/_____/
A Strong Bench           /_____/_____/
A Renewal Process        /_____/_____/
                       Poor                    Adequate                Exceptional
```

Poor = Real opportunity for incremental gains
Adequate = Meets business standards
Exceptional = A strikingly visible asset of the unit

---

contribute to effective use of such traditional personnel systems as selection or training. However, there is also a "next step" which should not be overlooked; it provides a very clear and marketable benefit to your professional staff and functional managers. Departments may have spent a good deal of time preparing the human resource review, yet may not see the direct benefit or payback to them.

In this section we will describe a program known as the tactical work-group review, which serves strategic human resource planning purposes. It is designed to be a two to three hour meeting between a human resource professional (for example, a respected external consultant or internal industrial/organizational psychologist), two functional managers (the direct supervisor/manager over the group to be discussed and his or her boss), and two senior professional people. In some cases, the professionals will take the place of the functional managers. This will depend on specific circumstances. Within the meeting individual performance and promotability is reviewed and plans are made to address the human resource implications of that group's planned operational objectives. The tactical work-group review overlaps other human resource systems (career planning; skills required for success; career paths; compensation; equal employment opportunities; staffing; recruiting) and serves as the point at which all systems can be integrated. Functional managers and senior professionals alike react favorably to the tactical work-group review meeting for two main reasons. First, the human resources professional is responsible for summarizing the data prior to the meeting; the others are required simply to be prepared to talk about their business and their people. Second, the meeting addresses their real concerns; within a structured agenda the discussion can be rather freewheeling such that critical issues unique to that area are sure to surface. The result is a true "tactical plan" addressing numerous operational needs, including contingency plans to deal with possible future situations. A typical tactical work-group review meeting follows this agenda:

- Introduction and objectives
- Business goal summary
- Competency requirements
- Career path issues
- People calls
- Staffing plans
- Issue identification
- Closing and summary

Introduction and Objectives. Here the specific program objectives are identified, the agenda is summarized, and the time available is identified.

Business Goal Summary. The objective of this section is to orient participants' thinking toward the integration of personnel needs and business objectives. It places the review in the context of ongoing business needs. This should not require anything more than the summary of existing business plans that relate to the specific work group being reviewed.

Competency Requirements. The objective of this section is to identify the competencies which are most critical for success within the function. For selection and training concerns, these competencies are then divided into those that a person *must have* coming into the position and those that could be *developed after* being in the position. Competencies include:

- Technical expertise—the professional knowledge needed for success within the function
- Managerial expertise—the management skills required to effectively manage people or projects
- Personal skills—any other "personal package" traits it takes to be successful within the work group

This information can be presented in a form (fig. 4-16); the boxes are simply filled in based on locally developed characteristics required for success.

4-16. Competency requirements.

Work group/position: _____

	REQUIRED	CAN BE DEVELOPED
Technical Expertise		
Managerial Expertise		
Personal Skills		

Career Path Issues. The objective of this section is to orient thinking toward the career implications of the staffing moves that follow. Historical knowledge of where people have "come from" and "gone" can be very helpful. A form, such as that shown in figure 4-17, can be used to identify both internal and external positions that either *lead to* or *follow after* the positions being addressed. Special attention should be given to the possibility of interface between professional and managerial positions.

People Calls. The objective of this section is to ensure timely and accurate information for the staffing plans that follow and to review progress on development plans. Each person is represented in the review by a 5-by-7-inch index card.

All cards are arranged by work group, preferably on a board with Velcro binding (or magnetic card holders and board) so that cards can be moved easily from one position to another. Each card is color coded according to promotability and contains the following information:

- Employee's name and title
- Length of time in position and with the organization
- Expert knowledge competencies
- Expert managerial competencies
- Outstanding personal characteristics

Note that the board would also contain overlapping position *or project* information on each area, that is:

- Position or project name
- Knowledge of organization required
- Expert knowledge needed
- Expert managerial skills needed
- Personal characteristics required

Because all this information is prepared prior to the meeting, this section of the meeting is used to review the accuracy of the data and the organizational groupings. Progress on individual development plans can be reviewed at this time. This must be done for anyone who might require a reassignment of position or project in order to continue development.

Staffing Plans. The objective of this section is to identify staffing and recruiting plans to meet known, probable, and "what if" contingencies. This process begins by looking at *known* moves, identifying, for example:

- Someone who is retiring
- Someone who is leaving the organization
- Someone who is going back to school
- A new position that is being added
- A new project that is being started

4-17. Career path issues.

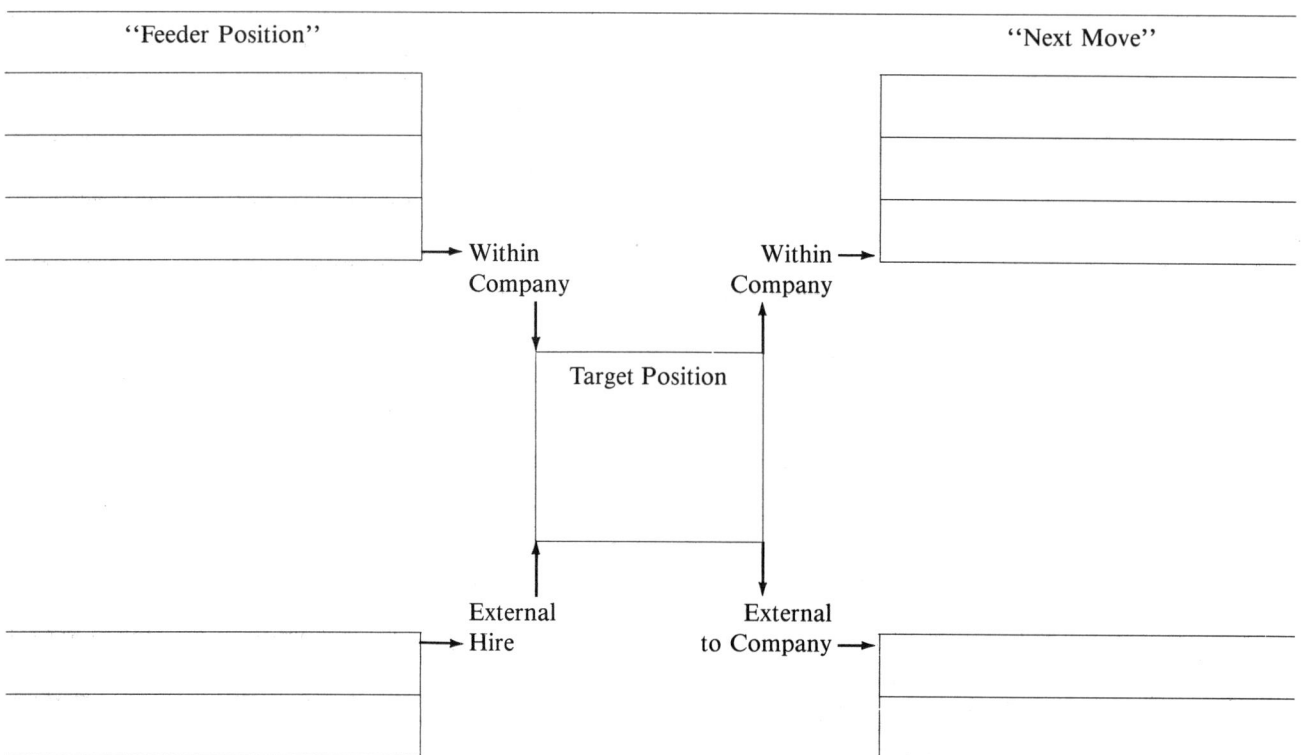

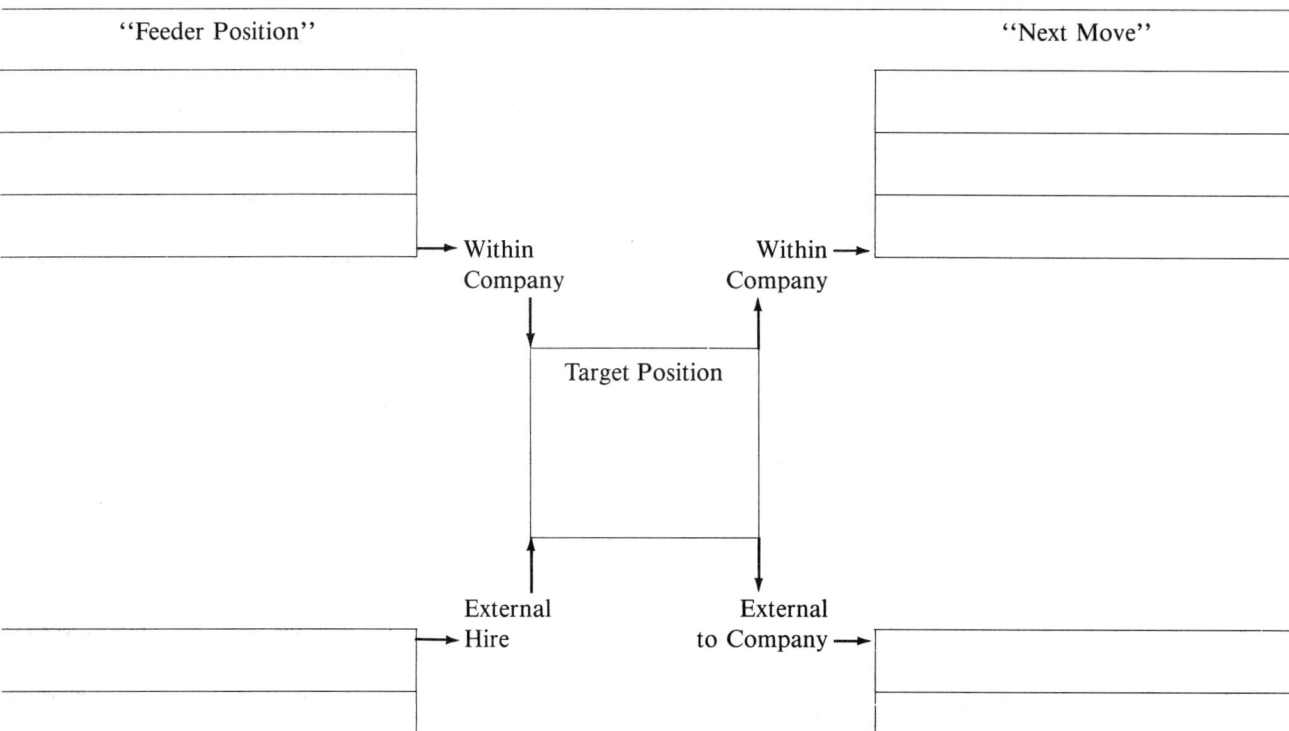

Starting with the open position, the functional manager or the senior professional traces the series of moves that he or she would recommend, all the way through to the point at which an outside hire is made. This is done by physically moving the people cards on the board. The human resource professional documents the thinking by using a form such as that in figure 4-18. Following preparation of the individual moves, a summary of recruiting needs would be made and communicated to the group in charge of that function.

This series of reasoning would be repeated with *probable* and *"what if"* moves. The "what if" move consideration can be particularly useful for the human resource professional to pose in order to challenge the strategic thinking of the functional manager or senior professional. For example:

- *What if* you lost Jones and there does not seem to be anyone else in your organization with expert knowledge in chemical hydrogenation?
- *What if* you are required to set up a catalytic chemical unit as your business plan suggests—how do you plan on staffing that unit?
- *What if* that project leader gets hit by a beer truck tomorrow morning?

Issue Identification. Concurrent with the staffing plan section, issue identification will occur. The objective of this section is to ensure that issues are addressed and actions taken as identified in the staffing plans. Both the needs of the organization and the reasonable expectations or concerns of individuals should be identified here. Categories include:

- Strategic retention needs—are we likely to lose someone whom we cannot afford to lose? If so, how do we convince that person to stay?
- Professional or managerial education needs—based on staffing needs, who requires attention in these areas? Identify specific plans for specific people.
- Career feedback needs—do our people expect something other than they will realistically get? If so, some feedback to them needs to be structured.

Closing and Summary. At this point much has been discussed, a lot of excitement will have been generated, and the human resource professional must wrap up the meeting adequately. The objective of the closing statement is to ensure a common understanding and agreement on the necessary follow-up steps and to achieve commitment to the actions discussed. The human resource function would generally be responsible for summarizing the results of the meeting and the actions agreed to, while the functional manager and senior professional would be responsible for carrying out the plan.

ALTERNATIVE REVIEW SYSTEM COMPONENTS

The programs presented here are but a sample of those that review internal human resources; many others of varying complexity can be designed to meet specific business needs. The "calls" that are made on people and the review used should certainly be tailored to the *specific* needs of the organization. One generic set of "calls" is shown in figure 4-19. Since this is meant to be an organizational evaluation of employees, the supervisor's review of an employee should be challenged at successively higher levels in the organization. As figure 4-19 shows, the "calls" must culminate in a professional development plan if the individual *and* the organization are to benefit from the exercise.

Figure 4-20 reflects a program that is geared toward the technical/scientific career path versus the supervisory/managerial path. As can be seen, organizational review mechanisms such as these serve a dual purpose of telling the organization where its people *are now* and where they *should be* to meet organizational needs. That is, the "calls" made on individuals should be in reference to the organization's strategic business plan. For example, a product line receives a government contract and five new project teams are needed—where will these people come from? What blend of technical and managerial skill will make that project team work? The other apparent requirement evident in figure 4-20 is the need for input from the individual. What are the person's career aspirations? Does the individual have an interest in a technical, managerial, or administrative role? Does he or she understand the concept of a dual-career ladder and the issues raised by it?

Individual development clearly must be patterned after individual *and* organizational needs. In some cases the two are one: "Tell me where the company's going and where the opportunity will be in the next one to five years, *then* I'll tell you what I'm interested in doing." The pure scientist may want nothing to do with the bureaucracy, yet needs to know in what specific field he or she should stay current. Strategic plans must filter down to and become a part of the human resource review process. This serves to reorient all members of the organization toward a shared perspective on goals.

In every business, there are stated or implicit business plans by which the organization orients and moves toward its objectives. The strategic business plan requires effective planning of financial, technical, physical, and human resources. The focus is on the use of human resources through examining a departmental status report or inventory of personnel actions against

4–18. Staffing and recruiting plan.

Function: _____ **Unit:** _____

Event type: Known _____ Probable _____ What if _____

If **this position is open:** (*Date* _____ *Location* _____ *Why Open* _____)

Then **what series of moves occurs as a result?**

OPTION A	OPTION B	OPTION C
	OUTSIDE HIRE: WHERE?	
COMMENTS/ASSUMPTIONS	COMMENTS/ASSUMPTIONS	COMMENTS/ASSUMPTIONS

4-19. Generic internal review "calls."

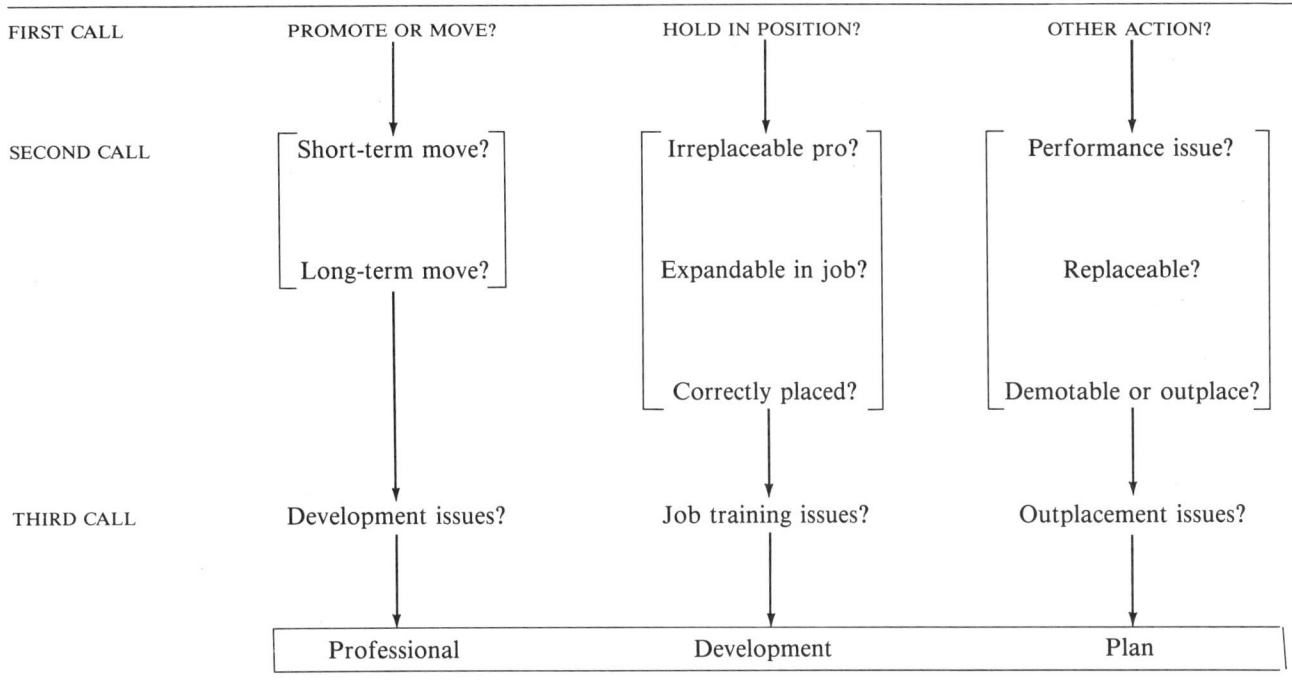

4-20. Career path "calls."

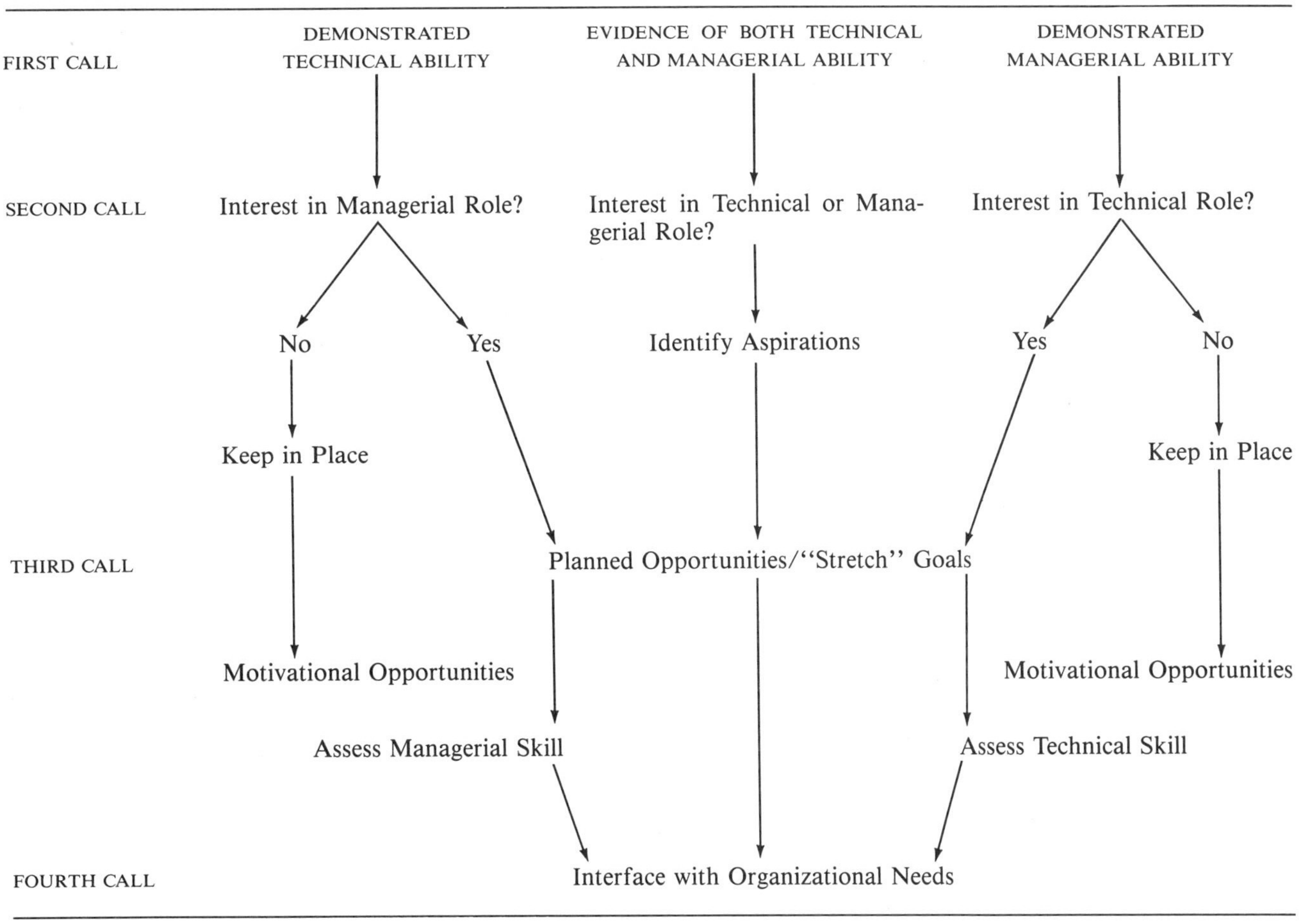

	DEMONSTRATED TECHNICAL ABILITY	EVIDENCE OF BOTH TECHNICAL AND MANAGERIAL ABILITY	DEMONSTRATED MANAGERIAL ABILITY
FIRST CALL			
SECOND CALL	Interest in Managerial Role?	Interest in Technical or Managerial Role?	Interest in Technical Role?
	No → Keep in Place; Yes → Planned Opportunities/"Stretch" Goals	Identify Aspirations → Planned Opportunities/"Stretch" Goals	Yes → Planned Opportunities/"Stretch" Goals; No → Keep in Place
THIRD CALL	Motivational Opportunities		Motivational Opportunities
	Assess Managerial Skill		Assess Technical Skill
FOURTH CALL		Interface with Organizational Needs	

business plans. Business strategies "roll down" from the top; one level's strategy becomes the next level's goals, which are further divided into objectives, tasks, and activities. The level at which this review should occur is no lower than the objectives phase. This first step assumes that in order to forecast future human resource needs, we must first share a common perception of where we are and where we are planning to go from an organizational point of view. The following is an exercise designed to aid this process.

Figures 4-21 and 4-22 summarize information which can be compiled on any business unit. If there is not enough information to do this, the process should "roll up" one more level until the data are available on the overall business plans and strategies, and the personnel actions designed to meet them. Figure 4-21 is a review of the previous year's goals and related personnel actions. Figure 4-22 looks ahead to the next year's business goals and planned personnel actions.

The process that can be built around these forms can be very effective in clarifying issues and forcing important personnel actions. An upward review-and-challenge procedure ensures that everyone understands the issues and makes plans to meet them. These are short-range plans, those that can be accomplished within the next year. As such, they translate easily into a management-by-objectives framework—that is, the personnel actions become the objectives that were rigorously derived from the longer range business strategies of the unit and the organization.

This type of review process can force some tough personnel decisions. The business might be moving in new directions demanding new talent while the contributions of the current professional staff are not great enough to

4-21. Business plan review of 19—.

SYSTEMS R&D BUSINESS-PLAN REVIEW: 19— IN REVIEW

BUSINESS ISSUES	PERSONNEL ACTIONS
• Continuing department wide upgrade of scientific and engineering talent	• Hired George Strathers, Harry Sullivan, and Marty McCracken • Began college recruiting program locally
• Improving coordination between developer and user departments	• Sponsored an interdepartmental conference of professionals • Began a monthly newsletter to keep user departments informed
• Providing professional enrichment opportunities in the scientific/engineering positions	• Offered team-building/job enrichment courses through the professional development department • Ensured professional conference money stayed in the budget
• Maintaining project team continuity	• Six new project teams maintained a personnel overlap of 65% compared to last year's 25%

4-22. Business plan review: 19—.

SYSTEMS R&D BUSINESS-PLAN REVIEW: 19— PLANS

BUSINESS ISSUES	PLANNED PERSONNEL ACTIONS
• Continuing the departmentwide upgrade of scientific and engineering talent	• Hire five engineers and three scientists, half of which will have more than five years' experience
• Continuing to improve coordination between developer and user departments	• Run at least two projects using a matrix management approach which involves the user department from the beginning
• Improving project management capabilities	• Contract with the professional development department for supervisory skill and project management courses
• Supporting the new contract for guidance system components	• Hire one notable authority, train three current scientists to state of the art

4-23. Position-to-person matrix.

Identify current (*o*), previous (*x*), and planned (***) positions.

	Person																									
Position	A	B	C	D	E	F	G	H	I	J	K	L	M	N	O	P	Q	R	S	T	U	V	W	X	Y	Z
A																										
B																										
C																										
D																										
E																										
F																										
G																										
H																										
I																										
J																										
K																										
L																										
M																										
N																										
O																										
P																										
Q																										
R																										
S																										
T																										
U																										
V																										
W																										
X																										
Y																										
Z																										

keep pace with the business. Important placement strategies can be planned by this process. For example, a respected elder professional might become a coordinator or be moved into a matrix management role to allow younger scientists with more relevant education to make stronger individual contributions to several projects and to gain from the elder professional's greater perspective. In other cases, current employees may simply need to upgrade their technical knowledge or alternatively to be sent to the organization's branches that still use older technologies. With other people, outplacement or transfer may be required in order to keep step with new business plans. Preplanning such issues can facilitate the positive steps necessary in carrying out such decisions.

The critical issue is following an approach that puts the organization in a proactive position and keeps it focused forward. Without a strategic-planning approach to human resources, the organization will remain in a reactive position and will forever be fighting fires. To some extent, this approach requires an openness of communication within an organization. This can be threatening in some organizations where knowledge of business plans and strategies are considered a legitimate source of power, not to be shared with others. Organizational sanctions on such behavior will result in the uneven accumulation of individual power and will limit the much greater potential power of commitment to shared organizational goals. This review process is an inexpensive, simple, yet powerful method that can be very helpful in opening communication channels and developing a shared perception of the organization's past achievements, future goals, and the personnel actions that will help to attain those goals.

These exercises are not a personnel department prerogative. Personnel may *coordinate* an organization-wide review, but each functional area will know more about its own plans than the personnel department. It is each department's responsibility to define the key business issues and personnel actions. These should fit into the organization's overall strategic business plan and give the personnel department enough information to plan its own role in meeting those objectives.

Another system that is more workable in a small organization is a simple position-to-person matrix, as in figure 4–23. Critical positions could be highlighted to ensure that sufficient talent was being planned and developed to cover critical business needs. Again, the linkage to development systems must be established and monitored. Another alternative is to use this as a "knowledge-area"-by-person matrix.

4-24. Person/project planning.

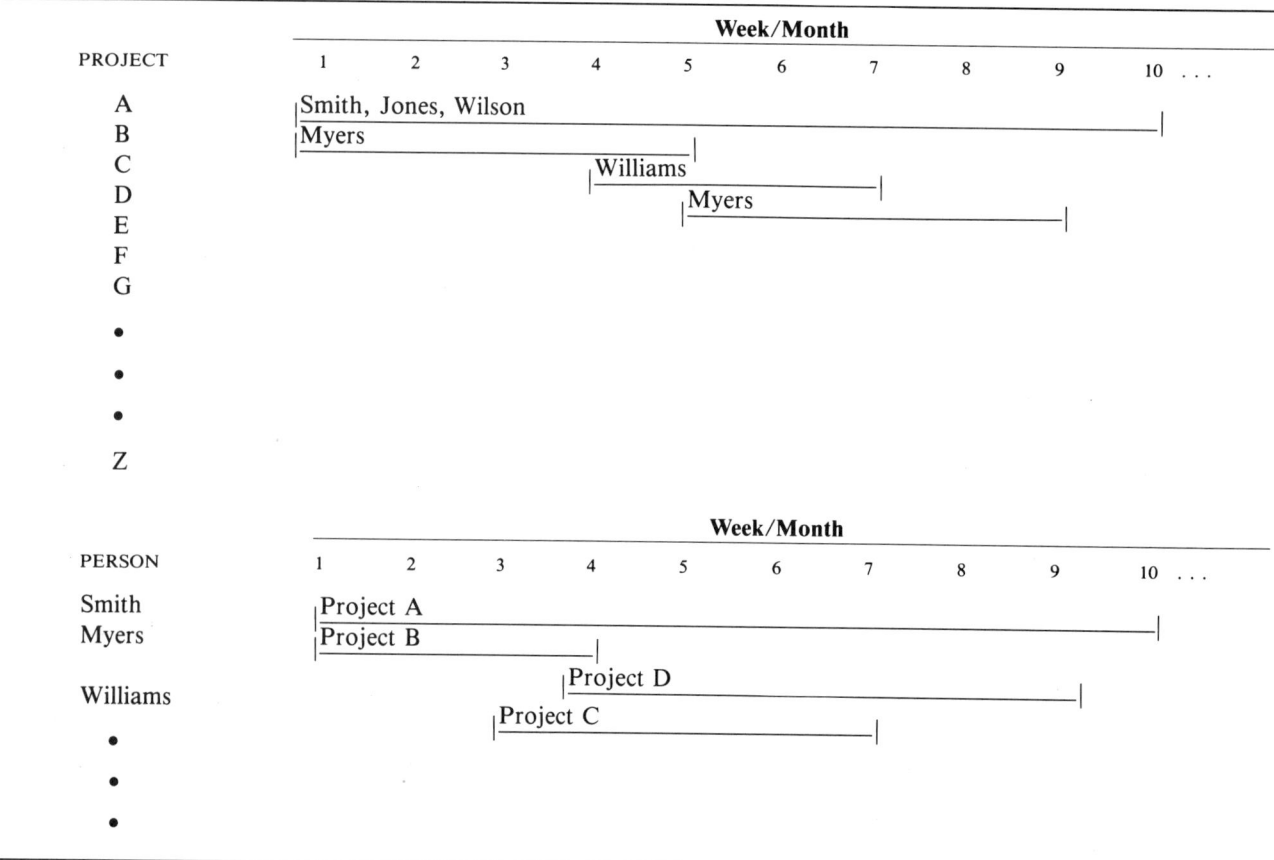

Project teams may require a different type of planning system since they differ in composition and duration. Figures 4-24 and 4-25 represent simple methods to deal with the purposeful planning of human resources talent to meet specific organizational objectives. This is done on a time continuum, to provide planned start and stop points for a given project. Project assignments can be a very valuable tool for the development of employees. Planned projects should be used within the organizational review as key areas in which to set "stretch goals" for upwardly mobile employees. The project can break a person in slowly to the managerial and supervisory skills needed to coordinate an overall project. It gives the individual a chance to determine whether he or she really likes that role and gives the organization a chance to preview that person's capabilities in a variety of situations. The project team can also allow a professional who is *not* interested in management to strengthen an area of application, broaden a technological base, or learn a new technology.

Human resource review systems need not be super-sophisticated or time consuming. Quite the opposite is true—they should be as simple as possible to meet the objective. Paperwork should be minimal. The key is to balance the variety of human resource potential available with the variety of organizational tasks required so that both individual *and* organizational needs are met.

SUMMARY

Chapter 4 has dealt in detail with organizational career-management programs through a treatment of human resource review systems. Several approaches were presented, addressing the use of performance, skills, and promotability information in a planned way to meet organizational needs. Specific forms and review formats were defined to describe the *process* that occurs when organizational decision-makers make use of this type of data. Not all organizations will need every program and form included in this chapter. No one program will meet all needs; the program must be tailored to the specific needs of the organization. The learning focus should be on the *process* and the *thinking* that the program forces within the organization.

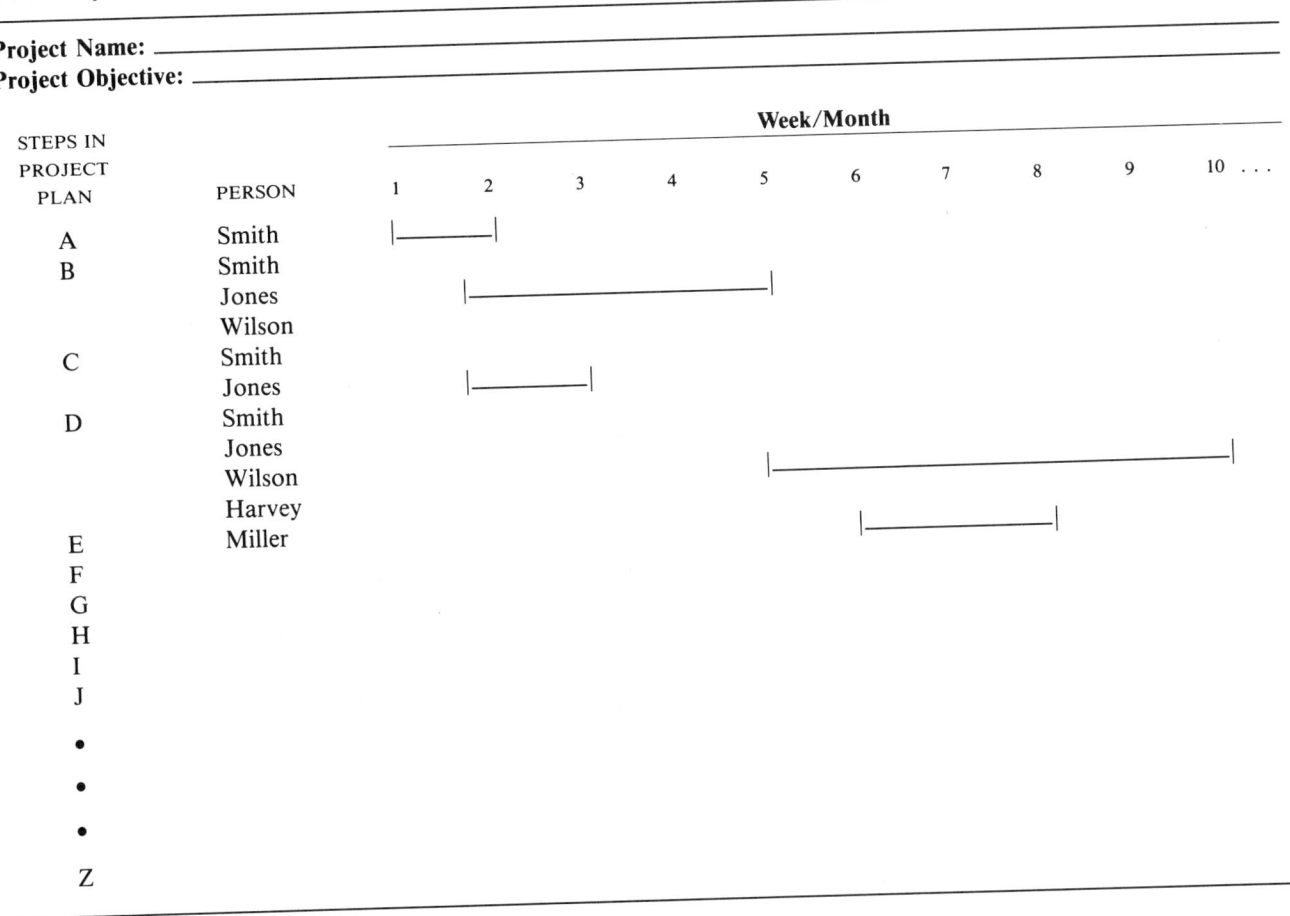

4-25. Project Team Planning.

Completion of this chapter means the reader is able to answer the following questions:

How would I go about making the case for investing in the development of a human resource review process in my organization?

What are the organizational-planning and the individual-planning elements of a human resource review?

How can I tie human resource planning to the organization's strategic business plan?

How do I move from a strategic, long-range plan, to a tactical, short-term plan?

How can I use human resource information to accomplish project management goals?

REFERENCES

1. Badawy, M. K. 1975. Organizational designs for scientists and engineers: some research findings and their implications for managers. *IEEE Transactions on Engineering Management* 22 (4):134–38.
2. Career planning cycle creates a sensible successful strategy. 1985. *Data Management* (October):16.
3. Dougherty, D. E. 1985. *From technical professional to corporate manager: A guide to career transition.* New York: John Wiley and Sons.
4. Given, W. B. 1955. The engineer goes into management. *Harvard Business Review* 33 (1):120–23.
5. Grass, D. 1979. A guide to R&D career pathing. *Personnel Journal* (April):227–31.
6. Koplow, R. A. 1967. From engineer to manager and back again. *IEEE Transactions on Engineering Management.* EM-14 (2):88–92.
7. Levine, H. Z. 1985. Consensus on . . . career planning. *Personnel* (March):67–72.
8. Medcof, J. W. 1985. Training technologists to become managers. *Research Management* 28 (1):18–21.
9. Spiegel, B. I. 1985. Career development and the data processing professional. *Human Resource Planning* 8 (1):49.

Chapter 5
Career Assessment: Processes and Outputs

At this point, the organization has defined programs to bring professional and scientific talent into the organization and to ensure that there are opportunities for advancement. The programs that were covered in chapters 3 and 4 supported the "getting-in-and-progressing" goal and are the *input* pieces of the career management system described in chapter 2 (fig. 2–2). The career management *processes* and *outputs* are: performance assessment and feedback, career management programs, career paths and patterns, outplacement, and retirement.

The organization must address these processes in order to maximize the contribution of professionals. These are not "personnel" programs; quite the contrary, they are processes that address the real concerns of professionals.

PERFORMANCE ASSESSMENT AND FEEDBACK SYSTEMS

Focus on the performance assessment and feedback process has increased in recent years as the need for better management of human resources and the push for increased productivity have been emphasized. Some of the factors contributing to this renewed emphasis include:

- Declining worker productivity
- Changing employee work values and needs
- Management's reluctance to establish and communicate job objectives and performance expectations
- Management's inability to provide constructive, performance-based feedback
- Management's inability to observe and document job-related performance accurately
- Equal employment opportunity demands for fairness and accuracy in performance evaluation systems

All employees need performance feedback and, if it is not freely offered, will find ways to ask the question, "How am I doing, boss?" With professionally educated and oriented employees, the need is even greater. They look for feedback not only from their "boss," but from their respected colleagues and peers within the profession. An informal feedback system provides peer review through responses to journal article submissions, presentations, symposia, reports, white papers, and the like. This will often stimulate a point/counterpoint debate that sharpens issues and pushes knowledge and awareness forward. As important as such peer feedback may be, the official performance review can have a very powerful impact on the professional.

Organizational Appraisal

Within the organizational context, there is the formal, usually annual process in which the performance of employees is officially reviewed. This process always presents certain generic problems.

The first issue that must be squarely addressed in the design of an effective performance appraisal system is to ask that first key question: What are the objectives? For the organization the most obvious ones are:

- Merit salary increase
- Promotional opportunity
- Employee development

The first problem is that these objectives are not always compatible—that is, the approach used in a merit salary review is going to be quite different from the approach that will be effective for promotional considerations or employee development. In a salary review, a one-way judgmental communication with appropriate rationale and support may be sufficient. However, if the intent is to contribute to promotional or personal development, then the need to get commitment from the person on an action plan will require a totally different approach to the discussion. Different approaches may have to be taken to achieve other objectives, for example:

- To let employees know where they stand and to document this for organizational decision making
- To give recognition for good work
- To identify areas needing improvement
- To fix performance of the person in the current job
- To develop the person for higher-level jobs
- To provide information on career paths
- To provide a record for administrative purposes
- To put marginal employees "on notice"
- To find out how employees view their jobs
- To create better understanding between the supervisor and subordinate

Although there may be a laundry list of objectives which vary considerably, typical performance appraisals in most organizations are surprisingly similar and can be characterized as generally ineffective for several reasons:

- Communication tends to be all one-way and authoritarian (boss to subordinate).
- "Raw" feedback that is given threatens the self-esteem of the subordinate and results in defensive reactions.
- The subordinate tends to deprecate the boss; rather than becoming closer, the two are further estranged.
- Feedback is of poor quality—it is not immediate, specific, and behavioral.

A good deal of research has been devoted to the clarification and elucidation of the characteristics of effective performance appraisal discussions, often in the context of career development (36). A review of the literature (15) and subsequent research allows us to draw certain conclusions:

1. *Participation by the employee* in the discussion results in much higher acceptance of the supervisor's observations and greater satisfaction with the appraisal process.
2. *Support from the supervisor* results in greater acceptance and satisfaction by the employee.
3. *Setting specific goals* results in much greater performance improvement than does a discussion of general goals.
4. *Discussing problems and solutions* that might improve performance can have an immediate impact on productivity.
5. *More criticism results in more defensiveness,* and the areas of performance that are most criticized are the areas least likely to be improved; criticism does not result in behavior change.
6. *Opinions presented by the employee* and allowed or encouraged by the supervisor result in greater satisfaction with the appraisal.
7. *The amount of thought and preparation* by the employee is related to positive performance improvement (for example, involvement by analyzing job responsibilities, problems encountered, and the quality of their work).

Bassett and Meyer's classic study of professional and administrative-level employees at General Electric is particularly relevant (5). They examined the effects of making the subordinate responsible for the performance review and for taking the initiative in the appraisal discussion. Higher satisfaction and improved performance resulted from this participatory method. Intangible benefits also included:

- Improved upward flow of information—that is, the supervisor learns about how the person views his or her job accountabilities, performance, and obstacles
- More systematic thinking by the employee about his or her own performance, resulting in a more self-critical, insightful look at performance
- Opportunity to identify and clarify differences of opinion regarding job requirements and job performance.

The implications of these findings for the design of performance appraisals is apparent. Recommendations would have to include:

- Structured preparation work by the subordinate requiring an analysis of his or her own work and of barriers to a higher level of performance, resulting in recommendations for specific job goals
- Structure for a two-way discussion of job problems and solutions with clear participation by the subordinate
- Guidelines that limit the number of negatives communicated to the "vital few" that can be addressed, and the mutual setting of specific goals to address each
- Supervisory training to increase awareness of appropriate performance appraisal approaches

The structure of a successful meeting would best be characterized as a problem-solving approach using the following steps:

PRIOR TO THE MEETING
- Supervisor completes forms and documentation, identifies the "vital few" issues that need to be addressed, and drafts specific job goal statements.
- Supervisor tells the employee when the meeting will occur and asks the employee to give some thought

to his or her job responsibilities and performance and to write down recommendations for specific job goals.

OPENING THE MEETING
- Supervisor explains the purpose of the meeting—to recognize areas in which job accountabilities are being met and to discuss areas which could or should be improved.
- Supervisor asks whether there are any other objectives which the employee would like to address in the meeting.

DISCUSS THE POSITIVE
- Supervisor gives recognition for the two or three "vital" things that the employee has done exceptionally well.
- Supervisor asks the employee if there are other job results that he or she is particularly pleased with or proud of, and reinforces them.

DISCUSS AREAS OF OPPORTUNITY
- Supervisor asks employee to identify areas needing improvement. This might be presented as: "We all have areas in which we can or should improve. What do you see as your areas of opportunity for development in this job?"
- Supervisor listens, draws out the employee's thinking, asking such questions as: "How can I help?" "What should you be doing differently?" "What are your performance goals?"
- Supervisor inserts his or her own evaluative comments into the context of the employee's discussion.
- Supervisor *adds* any other issues which the employee may not have addressed.

AGREE ON SPECIFIC GOALS AND ACTION STEPS
- Supervisor summarizes issues and defines specific goals and action steps. As much as possible, the employee should define these. This may have to be accomplished in a separate meeting.

CLOSING THE MEETING
- Supervisor summarizes and asks if the employee's objectives have been met or if there are additional issues he or she would like to discuss.
- Supervisor expresses confidence in the employee and his or her ability to achieve the goals.
- Supervisor notes, "Remember, I don't want these discussions to happen just once a year—anytime we need to talk about job goals or barriers to achieving them, let's get together."

In summary, the critical discussion steps in reviewing an employee's performance are:

1. Put the employee at ease
2. State the purpose of the discussion
3. Review performance objectives and expectations
4. Ask employee to describe his or her own performance against these objectives
5. Give your evaluation
6. Discuss and reach agreement on the evaluation
7. Express confidence in the employee
8. Establish new objectives or set a date to do so

These are essential steps necessary to meet specific key objectives for a performance appraisal discussion. In this case, these objectives are: to provide formal feedback on a person's performance against the accountabilities or objectives of the position; to motivate by gaining the involvement of the employee in analyzing his or her strengths and weaknesses and making plans to address areas of opportunity; to contribute to ongoing open, clear, nondefensive communication between the supervisor and subordinate.

When the supervisor identifies areas of concern that might be considered performance problems, several questions can be asked to clarify the appropriate strategy for addressing the problem (fig. 5-1).

5-1. Performance analysis.

QUESTION (IF "YES," CONTINUE DOWN THE LIST)	IF "NO"
• Is the problem critical to the job?	• Do not bother with it.
• Are objectives and expectations clear and understood?	• Clarify expectations and objectives
• Have all obstacles beyond the subordinate's control which contribute to the problem been removed?	• Recognize obstacles and remove them, or find alternatives around them
• Does the subordinate know how to perform the task?	• Provide training and practice opportunities
• Are rewards contingent upon satisfactory performance in this area?	• Identify and provide meaningful performance consequences
• Does the subordinate have the basic knowledge, skills, and ability to perform?	• Consider transfer or termination
• Is the subordinate aware that a problem exists?	• Coach subordinate, identify specific issues

The Individual Development Discussion

If all these recommendations cannot be accomplished within the formal performance appraisal system of the organization, it is strongly recommended that *another* program be developed to supplement it. The formal performance appraisal system is often used for salary administration purposes, an objective that is different from and in many ways in conflict with other objectives that a supervisor might have. If the formal salary review puts the supervisor in the role of a judge, it is going to be impossible for the supervisor to double as an impartial counselor during the same meeting. That means that objectives related to two-way communication, the open discussion of areas for improvement, and the writing of an individual development plan would have to be served by a different process that occurs at a different time. A separate process allows the supervisor to avoid much of the negative influence of a person's natural defensiveness during the formal performance review. A separate process also means that the supervisor need not feel constrained by a narrow review of specific behavioral actions and performance against accountabilities, looking only at *results*. A separate development discussion would allow a more freewheeling discussion of the *process* by which those *results* were achieved—or were *not* achieved! That moves the discussion into the area of managerial skills and abilities and ideas on development needs and plans.

Before the development discussion both the supervisor and subordinate must prepare for the meeting. First, the two need to discuss the objectives for the program, the definitions of the managerial skills or categories to be rated, and the standards for the rating scale. Next, each independently uses a rating scale to evaluate the person's main strengths and development needs. This process can be structured somewhat through a formal listing of managerial skills, such as those in chapter 3 described as relevant to the assessment center.

The discussion itself will succeed more readily if the supervisor structures it. First, the supervisor introduces the topic for the meeting, sets the tone to put the employee at ease, then moves quickly to the objective for the meeting—for example, "to have a two-way discussion of managerial skills so I can better learn how you see your performance, then to target a couple of areas for improvement where you will write a development plan." If numerical ratings were made on a structured form, the supervisor must make it clear that it is not critical that they agree on each rating—that it is critical that they work together to target two or three areas for improvement. At this point, it can also help to express confidence in the process by saying, for example, "this program is one that really helps us both—I personally believe it can be a very effective method for developing people on the job." Before getting started the supervisor should also express confidence in the person: "I have looked forward to this meeting because I have great confidence in you and your abilities," or "I am really looking forward to working with you on this process because you are the kind of person who really cares about your performance and wants to be the best you can be."

As quickly as possible, involve the subordinate in the meeting, to draw out his or her views. The supervisor might say, "Now let me ask you to walk me through your thinking and summarize your thoughts—what do you see as your two or three main strengths and your two or three main development opportunities?" This approach is one way to minimize the degree to which the subordinate is likely to feel threatened. The supervisor must sit back at this point and ask short clarifying questions to clarify the person's thinking. This is not the time for the supervisor to offer evaluative comments; before stating any personal views, it is imperative to learn how the employee views the situation.

The supervisor should only begin to offer an assessment of the person *after* gaining an understanding of the employee's perception of his or her own performance. At that point, by being alert, the supervisor can fit management's issues into the context of the subordinate's own views. This will *greatly* increase the chances that the employee will listen, understand, and accept a supervisor's comments. The discussion should focus on specific behavior and example situations and not appear to attack the person or address personality traits. There must be a real interest in changing behavior, not basic personality characteristics. So, for example, instead of stating, "You lack initiative," the supervisor might say, "You often seem to hesitate before going ahead on your own without specific directions from me. For example, last month you completed phase one of a special study, then waited three weeks for my approval before beginning phase two. In situations like that, I would prefer you to use your best judgment and proceed without me." In this way, the supervisor's standards and expectations, which may have been the source of the problem, are also clarified. The wording in this example is also constructive: it was not a personal attack.

In another example, instead of saying, "Your reports are really lousy; I can't even follow what you're trying to say," the supervisor says, "Your reports would be easier to follow if you started with a short introduction stating the purpose of the report and what it will cover. Then, in the body of the report, you should deal with one topic at a time, including all the information the reader should know on the topic before moving on to the next. Then a summary and concluding section highlighting the important points, their implications, and your recommendations, if any. You might also try writing something, putting it away overnight, then looking at it for clarity the next day. Can you see how this approach might improve the quality of your reports?" This type of coaching may mean a little more work for the supervisor because it forces him or her to think through and succinctly express standards and expectations. Conducting the discussion in this manner makes it very difficult for the employee to become defensive. Another way to avoid the defensive response is to concentrate on a reasonable number of things. Limit the suggestions for improvement to a manageable few. This is true of the discussion *and* the development plan. Research and experience shows that it is extremely difficult to change human behavior, especially ingrained habit patterns. It may take a great deal of concentrated effort to change even a single habit pattern. It is much better to have a few successes than to begin with a grand plan and get nothing accomplished. By targeting a few specific areas for improvement and supporting them with real on-the-job examples, the supervisor is much less likely to spark a defensive reaction than if he or she bombarded that person with loads of negatives.

In sharing views with the employee, the supervisor should also recognize the employee's strengths and efforts. It is helpful to point to those areas in which the person has already had a success experience and to identify this as evidence of the employee's ability and willingness to continue development. Developmental changes occur most easily through recognition and reinforcement in those areas. This is one way of telling the person, "This is important to me and to the company, and we recognize your efforts."

A primary objective for the discussion is to identify opportunities for development. The worst thing the supervisor can do is to back the employee into a corner and attempt to extract a confession of guilt or incompetence. The odds of skill development are much greater if the employee participates in defining the issues and formulating the corrective plans. The supervisor asks, "Do you see an area for improvement in this skill?" If the person responds in line with the supervisor's thinking—fine, the purpose is accomplished, and the supervisor can then simply offer to help or to make opportunities available on the job. If on the other hand the employee thinks there is no issue or avoids an issue which has been identified as necessary to discuss, then it is the supervisor's responsibility to raise that issue anyway. Taking a participative approach is *not* a sign of weakness. The supervisor is still responsible for raising relevant issues, while keeping in mind that he or she should talk less than half the time.

During the discussion, both the supervisor and subordinate must take notes on issues and specific activities that were agreed on and summarize them at the end of the discussion. The next step is for the employee to write up a development plan for the supervisor's review. The development plan could be of the following form:

DEVELOPMENT NEED (IS)	DESIRED OUTCOME (SHOULD BE)	DEVELOPMENT PLAN	TIMETABLE (START) (END)

Another meeting will be required to finalize the development plan. Once the plan is written, it is critical for the supervisor to follow up on actions that were committed.

CAREER MANAGEMENT PROGRAMS

The mix and fit between individual aspirations and the organizational availability of positions is a central concern. Some career management systems function more effectively in a dynamic, fast-moving organization whereas other systems may be more effective in more stable organizations. The general economy may also intervene to affect decisions on career management systems. A "fat" organization may be forced to go "lean" for some time, then rebuild. The planning of human resources will have to respond to both sets of exigencies if it is to fulfill its mission to the organization.

Individuals are also sensitive to these changing conditions and are likely to revise their implicit career plan in response. Involvement in formal career-planning programs during lean times may lessen dramatically due to the accurate observation that "there just are not positions or opportunities available." In fact, a time-honored method of cutting back in lean times is simply by not filling positions as natural attrition occurs. With little movement or opportunity for advancement, why should an employee undertake a time-consuming, potentially risky career-planning process? Especially if the perception is that promotion is going to come through a boss's say-so rather than a career-planning program? The slant of these personalized issues represents a situation where the *disincentives* for participation in a formal career-planning process outweigh the *incentives*. The outcome is perfectly predictable—little or no participation by employees.

The employee is making the connection that the organization must also attempt to make. The employee is matching his or her career aspirations with his or her best subjective estimate of the likelihood of a desired, available position. It is likewise contingent upon the organization to identify its own likely position availability, then take steps to estimate employees' interest and the most appropriate method of career management. Incentives for participation must outweigh disincentives.

Because of the varying needs of people and organizations, the best career management systems are simple, flexible, and need-driven (74). They respond to the varying conditions and fill the needs of both the individual and the organization. *Informal* systems respond to changing circumstances and persist; *formal* systems must show similar responsivity and resilience.

The Case for a Career Management System

Movement through jobs is probably the best tool available for the development of employees. As Dalton and his collaborators state: "All our research indicates that the job assignment is the single most important variable in career development; . . . a change of job assignments is no panacea, but it can be pivotal in helping people to develop in their careers" (21, p. 41). Here we will look at the career development process from the organization's viewpoint (career management), with some reference to the individual perspective (career planning).

The following list identifies organizational needs that are served by career management. Organizational programs are generally instituted based on a defined need. Some problem areas are inherent to *any* organization, for example, problems with:

- Turnover
- Performance and productivity
- Identifying promotability and potential
- Development of employees
- Determining training needs
- Affirmative action advances
- Employee motivation and commitment
- Human resource utilization
- Obsolescence or burn-out
- Meeting personal development needs
- Matching business goals and personnel actions
- The organization's image
- Recruiting
- Labor costs
- New employee orientation and training costs

An effective career management program might specifically address any of these issues. However, the organization must initially determine the goals of the career management program. These should be in line with key business goals and should determine the scope of the program.

Professionals within organizations have special problems that a career management program can address. One critical factor emphasized by numerous authorities is the basic incompatibility of bureaucratic and scientific/professional goals (2,30,31). Most organizations strive to instill a loyalty to the organization and heap lavish rewards upon the team player. Scientists or professionals are more likely to be individual contributors and to orient their loyalty and commitment toward their profession and reference groups outside the organization. The bureaucratic value system demands certain things that the scientist or professional value system would reject, and vice versa.

Awareness, communication, and accommodation are keys to dealing with this thorny issue. A career management program facilitates all three. With regard to awareness, the program could provide the forum in which to discuss the different perspectives. Rather than being an undercurrent, never addressed, the issue can be sanctioned and dealt with as part of self-awareness booklets, workshops, and the like. Communication is facilitated by a career management program that involves all levels within the organization. Accommodation is the necessary third step. Unless the organization is ready to come to terms with the needs, motives, and value systems of its employees, then the pot has been stirred for no constructive purpose. This is reflected in several researchers' points of view:

- Within another ten years [we may] become far less concerned with manager development as a means of adapting the individual to the demands of the organization and far more with management development to adapt the organization to the needs, aspirations and potential of the individual (30, p. 52).
- Accommodation requires the organization to take the individual's goals into account in determining its own goals. The organization must be structured and must function so that organizational goals are intrinsically rewarding and provide a means for the individual to achieve his or her own goals at the same time (30, p. 52).
- [Policies and procedures are often designed and adopted] without any special attitude toward distinct groups of R&D manpower on the part of management (2, p. 134).
- If we agree with the premise that success is based on accumulated segments of expertise, then we must agree with the concept of more porous organizational boundaries. The successful firm must have the porosity to allow new concepts to enter and must then have the organizational adaptability to utilize the innovation (29, p. 62).
- Organizational procedures and practices should be sufficiently flexible to prevent the evolution of conformity, . . . goal-setting by R&D management must be done with realism and clarity (31, p. 229).

In one form or another, all of these suggestions reveal the necessity for a collaborative effort toward accommodation. The professional and the bureaucracy are different, but they are very important to each other.

A career management program helps ensure organizational responsiveness to individual needs. It builds into the selection and placement process the vehicle to plan nontraditional developmental moves, revised position responsibilities, task force participation, and other practices. It provides the vehicle by which awareness, communication, and accommodation can occur, and it challenges the organization to respond to identified individual needs.

Organizational Needs. Any organization must necessarily be concerned about the maximum use of its internal resources and the proper administration of its fiscal assets. The loaded labor costs in any budget will confirm the conclusion that effective deployment of human resources is critical to success. Consider the initial cost to recruit, hire, orient, and train a new employee and weigh that against the worth of an experienced professional employee and the same conclusion is reached. Consider the impact on the smooth functioning within and between departments when unplanned turnover in key positions occurs. Again, the conclusion is inescapable: proper use of human resources is critical to success.

The degree to which a person is involved in their job can be a key ingredient in performance, productivity, and turnover. Job satisfaction may also affect performance and propensity to stay. However, more and more research shows that a person's decision to leave an organization is more a function of his or her subjective estimate of future potential with the organization than it is a function of current job satisfaction (45,53,79). Whether or not there is a formal mechanism by which employees receive feedback on organizational judgments of their potential, people make subjective estimates of their chances to "get ahead." Through observation, models of likely career progress are created, and the person develops expectations that may or may not mirror the organization's view. The possibility of misperceptions based on a lack of a formal system is great, and the ramifications can be severe in terms of performance, productivity, promotability, and turnover.

A properly planned and executed career management program can be a very cost-effective tool. One study cited a bank's career management program that saved it $1.95 million in a single year (57). This estimate was based on:

65% turnover reduction
85% performance improvement
75% promotability increase
25% productivity increase

Cohen and Meyer argue that "a successful organization must have well-organized and well-administered human resource and career planning programs" (19). In support of this contention, they present areas where cost savings will result:

- Efficient use of human resources
- Improved performance of incumbents
- Decreased turnover
- Better achievement of affirmative action goals
- Development of internal career-planning expertise—that is, a trained staff
- Development of performance appraisal and counseling skills throughout the organization

To these lists can be added several spin-off benefits:

- Organizational social accountability (career planning is noble and valued in our society)
- Excellent recruiting tool (people with high potential are attracted to places that facilitate career movement)
- Professional and community image (a concerned and responsive organization)
- Obsolescence reduction (through planned development efforts)
- Matching of personnel actions with business strategies (ensuring talent needed down the road)
- Increased lateral movement (minimizing short-run costs and maximizing employee breadth)

If the professional organization fails to engage in career management and development, time and events do not stop—careers continue to "happen." They happen out of an ongoing, discrete chain of responses in which each selection decision prompts a pragmatic reaction—in terms of what is best and most workable *now*. The scenario is too often one of crisis management—over and over again. This will happen *even if* the organization does traditional manpower forecasts based on previous staffing needs. Vosburgh previously summed up the situation:

> From the organization's perspective, human resources planning has traditionally been a concern. However, what happens when the people needs of the organization are identified, yet there is no method of planning employees' career progression to cover those needs? The company is forced into a reactive rather than a planning posture, and often no one will have been appropriately developed for positions that open up. Since many times a promotion in middle or upper management sets up a domino effect of moves, it is especially important to ensure that key positions are covered by realistic career plans (75, p. 830).

The opposite may also be the case with equally damaging results. That is, a career management program may be linked to neither manpower forecasts nor the selection system. Vosburgh also describes the problems inherent in this situation:

> Since it is not formally tied into the needs of the organization or the selection and placement system, the career plan amounts to little more than a dream sheet.

In the long run, rather than developing more positive attitudes on the part of employees (e.g., by getting them involved or providing an outlet for aspirations), this situation is more likely to engender negative attitudes due to the fact that career plans are not being realized (75, p. 830).

The bottom line is this: numerous organizational needs can be filled by an effectively planned and executed career management program. The many barriers to successful implementation will be described in chapter 7. For now, we can conclude with a corollary to our initial conclusion. Proper use of human resources is critical to success—an effective career management program contributes to this objective.

Individual Needs. Ask anyone to describe themselves and within the first few responses will be a reference to their job or profession. It is human nature to identify with one's work. A great deal of research shows that for most people, work is a prime determinant of the quality of one's life (14,58,63,70). Work is the stage upon which the full range of the human drama is played out—our aspirations, fears, needs, and abilities all show through in every combination conceivable. Indeed, it seems unnecessary even to build a case for the personal importance of one's career, especially for the scientist or professional who orients so strongly toward a professional reference group.

If the career is so important to one's life and well-being, why do people adapt such a passive stance with regard to career planning? Some evidence indicates that people tend to let others initiate career decisions for them (62). Social norms have moved in the direction of greater personal involvement, but organizational norms are often surprisingly Victorian in their reliance on the passive receptivity of the employee to move when their number is called. Perhaps this is an overly strong indictment of organizations that lack career management systems. Many organizations have not only survived but thrived under a paternalistic regime where each employee knows that when it is their time, they will move. This approach assumes a level of organizational omniscience and individual malleability that is hard to imagine in today's world.

A basic human need, traced all the way from infancy, is that of efficacy—the need to act upon the environment and to have an observable effect (65,82). Yet oddly enough in the career, the most central area of importance in one's life, many people rely on *others* to affect the environment favorably for them. The surge of popular books in the area of personal career planning attests to the fact that the trend toward passivity in career movement is being reversed—people are taking control of their own destiny. Clearly, an organizational career management program meets some basic human needs for its people.

Program Parameters

Complexity and Formality. Different organizations have different needs. One "generic" model of a career management system will be outlined here. It is not the only solution. The complexity and formality of the program must be matched with the corresponding values of the organization. In some organizations, a simple discussion with the personnel staffing person, expressing a desire to be considered for a handwritten list of positions, might be sufficient. Care must be taken to make even this benefit available equally to all, lest charges of inequity or discrimination appear. This should be a key concern in establishing a minimal level of formality to ensure equal access. The federal government's references to "career paths," "upward mobility," and the "elimination of barriers to promotion" (Executive Order 1246 and Revised Orders 4 and 14 of the Office of Federal Contract Compliance) make it clear that career planning fits under the purview of equal employment opportunity.

Part of the complexity of a career management system will arise naturally from the need to tie it to the selection system and the training and education system. Approval of individual career plans should also be considered in light of predicted available openings, meaning some form of human resources planning is needed (see chapter 4). In many cases, existing systems are in place and a "modular" career management program can be "plugged in" with a few connections. In *most* cases, other systems will need to be developed or modified to support the organization's career management needs.

Given this analysis, it appears that a certain level of complexity and formality is required to satisfy realistic and legal considerations. Beyond that, there is a great deal of latitude in the preparation of materials, training, and systems.

Cost. No special facilities or additional staff are necessary to the development of a career management program. Depending on the size and economic condition of the organization, it may be cost-effective to institute a career development center to administer the program, provide professional career counseling services, or even establish assessment centers and new program designs. More sophisticated human resource systems may wish to take this route, but this level of fiscal commitment is not necessary.

Most costs will relate to program development, material production, and time costs associated with the process. It might be worthwhile to track these costs against expected benefits in order to justify the expenditures on the program—as in the case of the bank that saved $1.95 million in the first year (57).

Short-/Long-Term Needs. Both short- and long-term needs are met by a career management system. For the short term, individual needs to have the organization care and to control one's own destiny are met. Lateral and promotional positions that employees are ready for *now* are identified, which helps the organization in the short run. Long-term individual needs are met because the process brings the employee through a detailed self-analysis that asks him or her to look many years down the road and clarify career aspirations. Long-term organizational needs are met because the individual career plans identify target positions many years down the road, thereby allowing the organization to match these plans with business needs and assure that the right people are being developed for the right job at the right time.

Vertical/Horizontal Emphasis. A career management program provides the opportunity to begin changing attitudes about lateral movement. In the absence of planned moves, the norm develops that the only good move is a promotional move. This is certainly not the case because one of the best ways to ensure success at higher levels is to work in the different positions that report to the higher level position. Promotion through the organization in a shoelace rather than a ladder pattern can be especially beneficial when moving from a highly technical to a more people-management position.

Many people may also express a desire to move into a totally different department in order to gain a well-rounded organizational perspective. A developmental lateral move would be warranted, perhaps ensured by a "buy-back" agreement whereby the originating department agrees to take the person back based on performance or temporal criteria.

Voluntary/Involuntary. A prime issue with regard to participation is whether the program should be voluntary or involuntary. Although there are trade-offs on this question, the decision is fairly obvious—of course the program should be voluntary! If the organization requires data on everyone (such as "potential" ratings), there are easier ways of generating it. A career management program should have an individual career-planning component that can be offered as an employee benefit and can be used or not as necessary. However, employees who are motivated enough to go through the process should receive first consideration on jobs that become available.

Another question relates to whether an employee would have to meet certain criteria before entering the program. Although Vosburgh previously urged that "career planning be a reward for good job performance and that this be made very clear to all employees" (75, p. 837), he now considers this solution appropriate for some but not all goals. Screens for entry into the program will necessarily vary with the goals of the program.

Who bears the primary responsibility for the career development process? The general consensus among professionals is the employee, but the organization and supervisor must support such efforts (21,33,75). Responsibility within the organization should have a central control point but be decentralized through the use of career-planning facilitators. These facilitators should be chosen within each department and be trained to administer the program and train functional supervisors. This effectively transfers "ownership" of the program from the personnel department to each and every other department. The facilitator role can be a key developmental experience.

In all these decisions, the program must be tailored to the organization's needs. As Moravec points out, "Because there is no one 'right' system for all companies, senior management must choose the best combination of counseling and training components, linking mechanisms, accountability systems, and decision-making processes for the organization" (57, p. 32). He suggests considering three issues when tailoring the career management program to the organization:

1. Design to meet *minimum* requirements in a cost-effective manner
2. Fit the personality of the organization to the program (level of formality, openness)
3. Consider the competition and how the program will help to attract, develop, and retain the best people

Participants. Another key question relates to the groups of employees who will be covered. An AMA study identified several special interest groups as targets of career management systems in the 225 companies surveyed (fig. 5-2; 77, p. 8).

An essential part of laying the framework for and designing a career management program rests on the decision of who participates. If any employees are excluded, for whatever reason, there may be some resentment about the program and informal, social pressures for members of the "special group" not to

Fig. 5-2. Candidates for career management systems.

% OF COMPANIES	GROUP
66%	Management trainees
62	Fast-track management candidates
38	Women
36	Minorities
27	Preretirees
19	Midcareer employees
5	Handicapped employees
4	Older workers
9	Other (professional trainees, senior managers)

participate. In most cases, the organization would be better served by allowing entry by any employee. A subprogram could then address the special concerns of certain target groups.

Pros/Cons. There are many favorable points of a career development process from both the individual's (career planning) and the organization's (career management) perspective. The most critical design issue is that of linking career management and career planning and integrating the two with established personnel systems to develop professionals over time. A career development system will not be successful *unless* a systems approach is taken. Vosburgh has succinctly stated some of the benefits of a systems approach:

> At this point, it should be clear that a systems approach to career planning has numerous beneficial effects. From the individual employee's perspective, career planning enhances general job satisfaction by providing an opportunity to actively develop one's own career. Since career plans are developed in conjunction with the employee's own supervisor and then followed up by a level-by-level review, a more realistic view of career potential and alternatives occurs via important organizational feedback. Because of the systems approach to career planning, fewer false expectations are created, and there is less ambiguity with regard to career possibilities. An ancillary benefit which can accrue from the accumulation of career information is the fact that new recruits can be provided with a much clearer and more realistic picture of career opportunities and career progression lines.
>
> Moreover, the systems approach reflects a human resources management policy which sanctions the creation of opportunities for employees to develop broader capabilities through planned developmental moves. By encouraging lateral movement, interfunctional movement and temporary project assignments, the organization's system can provide the opportunity for employees to discover hidden talents and realize untapped potential through exposure to new situations and tasks. This approach also allows the identification of specific developmental needs which the individual might easily overlook if not involved in the career-planning program (75, p. 836).

Potential negative results may occur when the design or execution of the program is not tailored to the organization's needs. The failure of career management systems to live up to expectations is a more common occurrence than many would care to admit. In the AMA study reported earlier, 68 percent of the 225 companies reported only partial effectiveness or complete ineffectiveness of the career management program. The same study showed the vast majority of supervisors were not equipped to carry out the program objectives, did not feel that career counseling was a part of their job, and perceived it as an increased burden for them. The picture is clear—a major drawback of many programs is the failure to:

1. Involve supervisors in defining career-planning needs.
2. Involve supervisors in designing a program to meet those needs.
3. Train supervisors to carry out their part of the program and provide supporting materials and guides.
4. Orient supervisors toward the different social role of the career counselor.
5. Make employee development and career facilitation a part of the supervisor's job, that is, make the supervisor accountable by including a review of their departmental career development activities as part of the supervisor's own performance appraisal.

These steps take time, detailed planning, follow-up, and top-level commitment to the process. If career planning is viewed as a quick and simple "fix," the organization will be disappointed. Moravec, in his article (57, p. 31), argues that a method of measurement, a reward system, and accountability procedures should be used:

1. Set goals regarding the number of employees participating and require supervisors to report the number of their employees involved.
2. Set specific timetables for holding career discussions with employees.
3. Schedule periodic meetings at department-head level to review results.
4. Evaluate and reward managers based on their ability to meet targets and goals.

Many benefits can accrue from an effective career management system, but there are many pitfalls in putting together such a program. If the issues addressed in this section are squarely faced in the design and execution of the program, its chances for success are considerably heightened.

Review and Approval Procedures. Supervisory approval provides one additional level of perspective but should only be the first stage in the review and approval process. The plan should continue up through the reporting levels. A level-by-level review opens communication channels and helps ensure that career plans are realistic and attainable. Employees have many opportunities to observe their supervisor's evaluation of their performance or potential. It is rare to have the opportunity to receive feedback from higher levels regarding how the organization evaluates potential, but that is the key element in tying together the organization's career-management system and the individual's career-planning system.

Additional reasons for a level-by-level review were previously described by Vosburgh:

The interest and involvement of all levels will contribute to the success of the [review]. The upper levels are able to systematically communicate downward their overall company plans and goals, which are taken into account in the human resources planning, while the desires and aspirations of the lower levels reach successively higher levels in the organization. This combination of commitment will contribute greatly to the usefulness and relevance of the [review] (75, p. 837).

Final approval of an individual career plan should also be based on a consideration of the degree to which each plan contributes to the business plans and strategies and fits with the staffing level forecasts (see chapter 4). Approval of career plans in a vacuum or without consideration of organizational realities results in plans which are little more than "dream sheets."

Finally, the approved plans must be tied directly to the formal selection and placement system. If the plans are to serve any real purpose, there must be a clear-cut method by which information can be used and career plans brought to fruition. If there is no definite connection, then it is not likely that interest in or support for career management activities will continue. Vosburgh elaborates:

For example, if the personnel department develops selection lists when a position becomes available, then anyone listing the vacant position on their career plan should automatically be considered (provided they possess the minimum qualifications). Ideally, the approved plans identify the relevant talent pool for any position which opens up, because one function of earlier reviews should have been to match a person's qualifications to the requirements of the jobs listed on the career plan (thus the critical importance of job-analysis information in the development and review of career plans).

An organization's career-planning program need not drastically affect the selection system, but there must be an effective interface early in the process. What can be favorably affected is the quality and completeness of a selection list, as well as the search time required to generate such a list (75, p. 832).

The organization can be considerably enriched by the inclusion on selection lists of professional-to-managerial individuals who have thoroughly explored and prepared for the transition. Certain positions that help ease this transition could be targeted, and the career management system can provide the talent pool from which to draw.

Example Program

Essential Features. Organizational career management systems can vary tremendously but certain key ingredients must be present:

- Information about jobs in the organization
- Corresponding information about people in the organization
- A method of matching the two
- A review and approval procedure which ensures use of results

To provide a structure to this section, a specific career management system paradigm is outlined in figure 5–3. There are obviously many approaches possible when it comes to designing a program such as this. The program outlined in figure 5–3 nonetheless illustrates some key concerns and decision points.

Job Information. Information about jobs in the organization can be gleaned in many ways. Most positions will have job specifications or descriptions that will suffice but are certainly not ideal. These documents tend to vary in content to such a degree that the matching process may be difficult. They tend to be structured around responsibilities or accountabilities rather than categories such as activities and knowledge. They do not tell the whole story in that they leave out demands of the job which may make it unattractive (excessive travel, forty hours at a desk, excessive record keeping). They are also not as amenable to change with the changing needs of either the individual or the organization.

A more complex developmental scheme would involve some level of a job analysis designed to create a career development position profile for each unique position in the company. This profile might be constructed to show:

1. *Major functions:* a brief description of the most important reason(s) for the existence of the job. This is typically one or two sentences in length and reflects the overall mission of the job.
2. *Position activities:* a list of the major activities a person is required to perform as part of the job.
3. *Position knowledge:* a list of the specific kinds of technical knowledge or expertise required to perform the major activities associated with the job.
4. *Position demands and restrictions:* a list of items that reflect the limits, obligations, or requirements placed upon a person in the job.
5. *Position characteristics:* a list of the unique qualities or features of the job not contained in the above sections.
6. *Critical managerial skills:* the critical managerial skills required of the job-holder to successfully perform the major activities associated with the job.

A one-time effort could produce a valuable Career Development Position Guide that contains these profiles. (One warning—compile the guide in a looseleaf binder, and build in systems to update old and add new positions.) Consistency would be greatly improved if a standard list of activities, knowledge, and the like, were

5–3. A career-planning program paradigm.

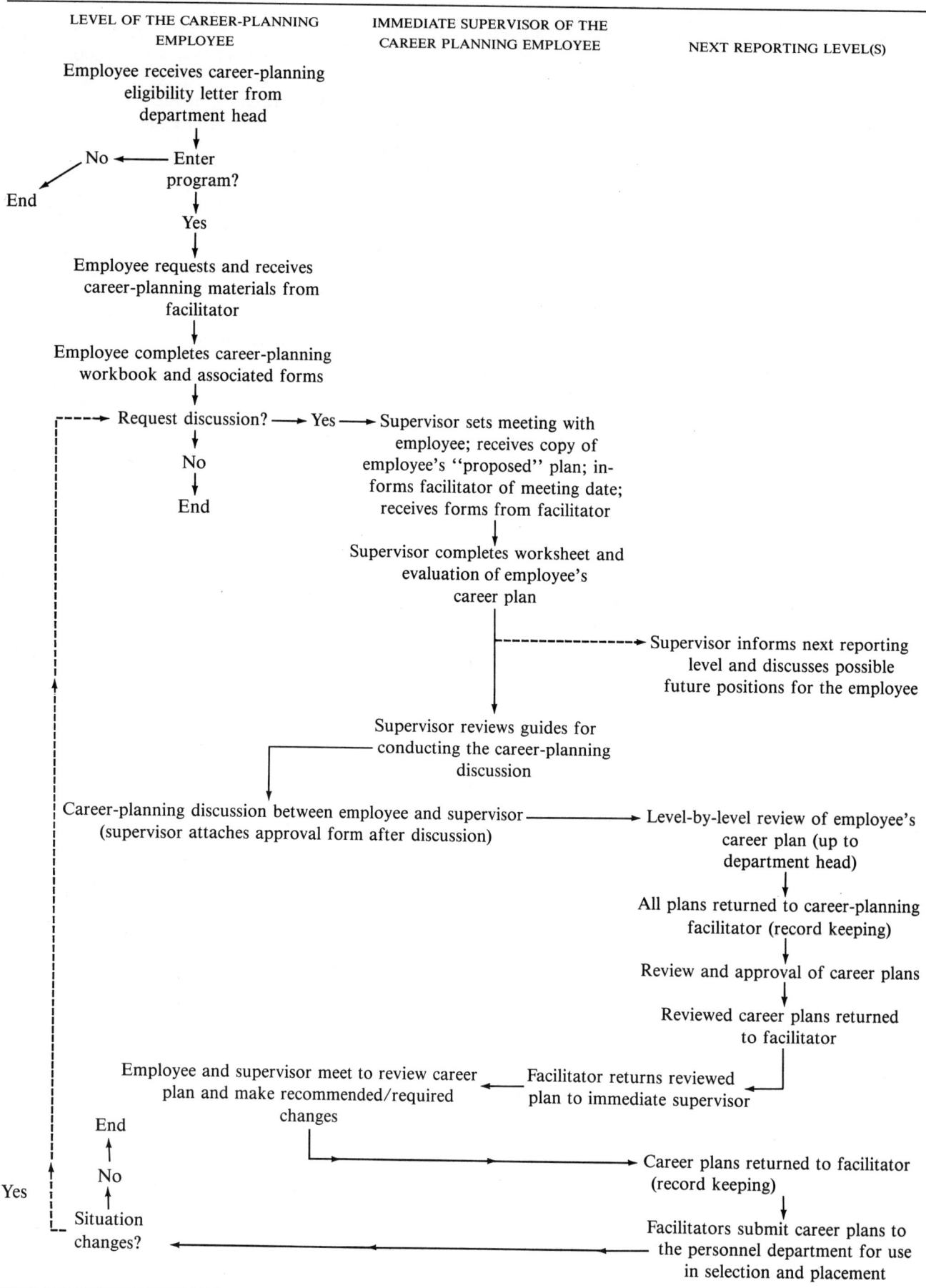

The interest and involvement of all levels will contribute to the success of the [review]. The upper levels are able to systematically communicate downward their overall company plans and goals, which are taken into account in the human resources planning, while the desires and aspirations of the lower levels reach successively higher levels in the organization. This combination of commitment will contribute greatly to the usefulness and relevance of the [review] (75, p. 837).

Final approval of an individual career plan should also be based on a consideration of the degree to which each plan contributes to the business plans and strategies and fits with the staffing level forecasts (see chapter 4). Approval of career plans in a vacuum or without consideration of organizational realities results in plans which are little more than "dream sheets."

Finally, the approved plans must be tied directly to the formal selection and placement system. If the plans are to serve any real purpose, there must be a clear-cut method by which information can be used and career plans brought to fruition. If there is no definite connection, then it is not likely that interest in or support for career management activities will continue. Vosburgh elaborates:

For example, if the personnel department develops selection lists when a position becomes available, then anyone listing the vacant position on their career plan should automatically be considered (provided they possess the minimum qualifications). Ideally, the approved plans identify the relevant talent pool for any position which opens up, because one function of earlier reviews should have been to match a person's qualifications to the requirements of the jobs listed on the career plan (thus the critical importance of job-analysis information in the development and review of career plans).

An organization's career-planning program need not drastically affect the selection system, but there must be an effective interface early in the process. What can be favorably affected is the quality and completeness of a selection list, as well as the search time required to generate such a list (75, p. 832).

The organization can be considerably enriched by the inclusion on selection lists of professional-to-managerial individuals who have thoroughly explored and prepared for the transition. Certain positions that help ease this transition could be targeted, and the career management system can provide the talent pool from which to draw.

Example Program

Essential Features. Organizational career management systems can vary tremendously but certain key ingredients must be present:

- Information about jobs in the organization
- Corresponding information about people in the organization
- A method of matching the two
- A review and approval procedure which ensures use of results

To provide a structure to this section, a specific career management system paradigm is outlined in figure 5–3. There are obviously many approaches possible when it comes to designing a program such as this. The program outlined in figure 5–3 nonetheless illustrates some key concerns and decision points.

Job Information. Information about jobs in the organization can be gleaned in many ways. Most positions will have job specifications or descriptions that will suffice but are certainly not ideal. These documents tend to vary in content to such a degree that the matching process may be difficult. They tend to be structured around responsibilities or accountabilities rather than categories such as activities and knowledge. They do not tell the whole story in that they leave out demands of the job which may make it unattractive (excessive travel, forty hours at a desk, excessive record keeping). They are also not as amenable to change with the changing needs of either the individual or the organization.

A more complex developmental scheme would involve some level of a job analysis designed to create a career development position profile for each unique position in the company. This profile might be constructed to show:

1. *Major functions:* a brief description of the most important reason(s) for the existence of the job. This is typically one or two sentences in length and reflects the overall mission of the job.
2. *Position activities:* a list of the major activities a person is required to perform as part of the job.
3. *Position knowledge:* a list of the specific kinds of technical knowledge or expertise required to perform the major activities associated with the job.
4. *Position demands and restrictions:* a list of items that reflect the limits, obligations, or requirements placed upon a person in the job.
5. *Position characteristics:* a list of the unique qualities or features of the job not contained in the above sections.
6. *Critical managerial skills:* the critical managerial skills required of the job-holder to successfully perform the major activities associated with the job.

A one-time effort could produce a valuable Career Development Position Guide that contains these profiles. (One warning—compile the guide in a looseleaf binder, and build in systems to update old and add new positions.) Consistency would be greatly improved if a standard list of activities, knowledge, and the like, were

5-3. A career-planning program paradigm.

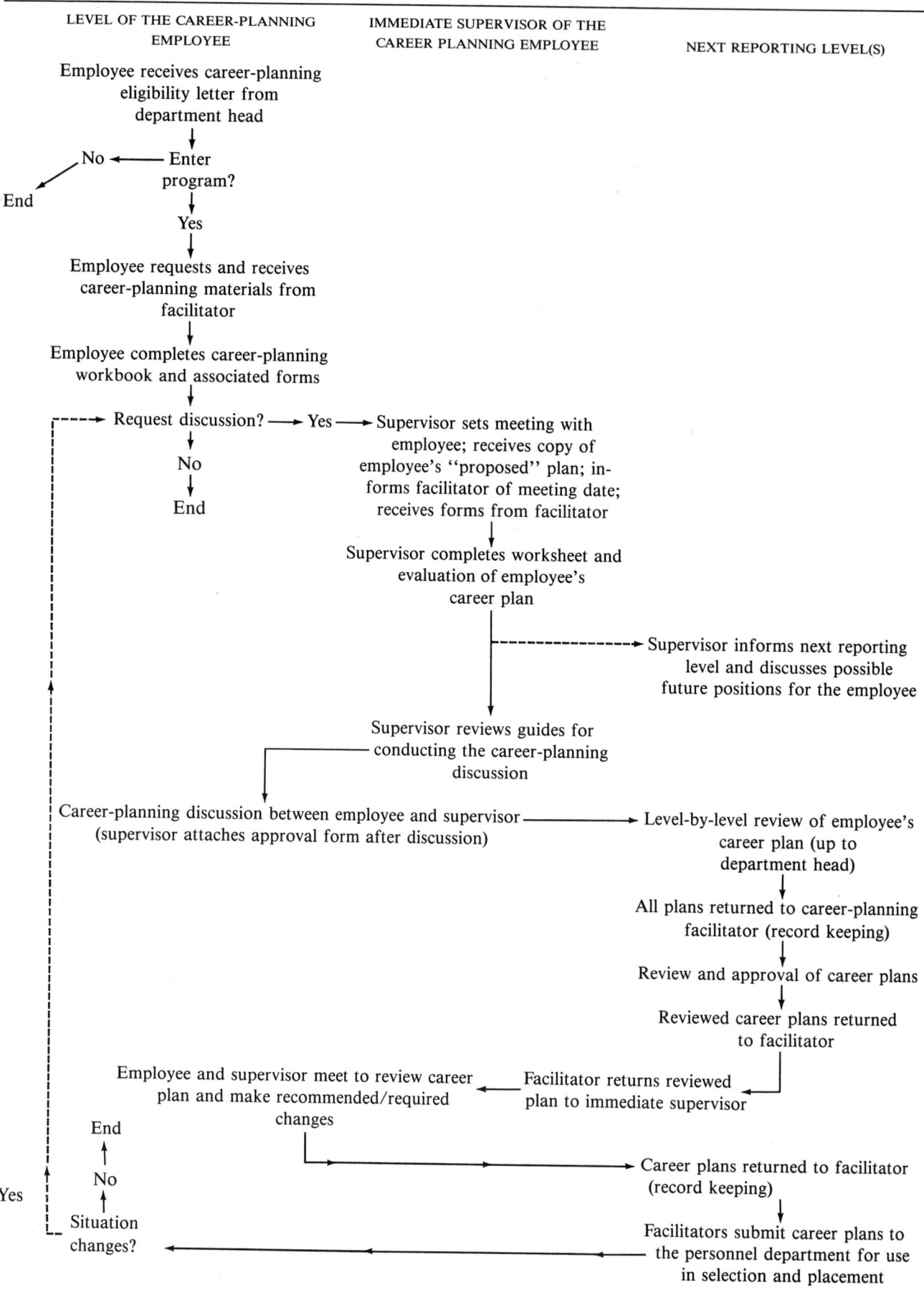

106

compiled ahead of time. These could be coded if the organization was ready to move up to the next level of sophistication—an automated matching process. The process should result in position profiles similar to that in figure 5-4.

These profiles form the basis for the individual's search and the supervisor-to-subordinate discussion. By comparing the knowledge, activities, and so on of past and present positions to those of possible lateral or promotional alternatives, the employee will be able objectively to evaluate his or her chances of being favorably considered for the listed positions. The overlap be-

---

5-4. Example position profile: industrial engineer.

MAJOR FUNCTIONS

The industrial engineer (IE) is responsible for a variety of assignments that help ensure the productivity of the organization. These involve plant layout, manufacturing specifications for operations' processes and packaging assembly, time studies, balancing of work loads, materials flow, and cost improvement.

POSITION ACTIVITIES

- Calculate machine loads
- Prepare justification for new facilities requirements
- Estimate labor requirements for different processes
- Conduct manufacturability studies on new products
- Conduct value engineering studies on products to ensure maximum cost reduction and product flow
- Assemble pilot model units to validate engineering documentation
- Facilitate transition to automated processes
- Ensure quality control
- Analyze and correct process failures and defects

POSITION KNOWLEDGE

- IE methods and standards
- Plant layout
- Project analysis
- Troubleshooting/problem solving
- Inventory evaluation
- Time and motion studies
- Cost analysis
- Critical path method
- Program evaluation review techniques

POSITION DEMANDS AND RESTRICTIONS

- Requires long, tedious hours measuring repetitive motions
- Requires working "in the field" in some of the dirtiest parts of the plant
- Involves working against tough deadlines
- Must deal with emergency situations at irregular hours
- Must often intervene in production disputes
- Requires very close attention to minute detail

POSITION CHARACTERISTICS

- Handles ongoing accountabilities
- Takes on numerous short- and long-term projects
- Interfaces with all levels in the organization
- Requires diplomacy and tact in "selling" improvements
- Involves teamwork with other departments

MOST CRITICAL MANAGERIAL SKILLS

- Problem solving
- Organizing and planning
- Control and follow-up
- Interpersonal

tween positions held previously and positions aspired to should be moderate, with some indication (through developmental activities) of steps to be taken to overcome any deficits. Too great an overlap would suggest that the employee was not being broadened or developed, whereas no overlap would almost surely forewarn either inability to be selected or failure once selected.

Individual Information. Individual information can be generated in many ways. If a complete list of all job requirements exists, the person could check off those that apply to him or her; if an automated system exists, the matching process can be accomplished quickly. An overly mechanical method is not recommended because much of the value of career management systems is in the *process* required to support it. Communication between the supervisor and the subordinate should be facilitated by the program. One method of achieving this is through a career-planning discussion in which the supervisor's goal is to assist the employee in formulating a realistic and attainable career plan.

Prior to requesting a career-planning discussion, the individual should be required to complete self-analysis exercises and identify tentative career tracks. This component will be described in much more detail in chapter 11. One method of accomplishing this in a limited time period is by having both the supervisor and the subordinate complete certain statements:

1. The things (I have/or this employee appears to have) *liked* about current and past jobs are:
2. The things this employee appears to have *disliked* about current and past jobs are:
3. The major *assets* or strengths this employee has brought to the job are:
4. The major *liabilities* or shortcomings this employee has brought to the job are:
5. Some of this employee's major *accomplishments,* or significant achievements, are:
6. Some of this employee's major disappointments, or failures, are:
7. The types of tasks, or *activities,* this employee performs *best* are:
8. The types of tasks, or *activities,* this employee performs *least well* are:
9. The *developmental activities* this employee could perform to become better qualified are:
10. The five *most knowledgeable* areas this employee has are:
11. *Other knowledge* this employee has is:
12. The knowledge this employee *most needs* is:
13. The *developmental activities* this employee could perform to learn these knowledge areas are:
14. The four managerial skills in which this employee is *strongest* are:
15. The managerial skills in which this employee is *weakest* are:
16. The *developmental activities* this employee could perform to practice and develop managerial skills are (the supervisor should consider what *opportunities* he or she could provide):
17. The *personal barriers* (commitment, motivation, ability, style) that might hold this employee back are:
18. The *organizational barriers* (departmental size, structure, or norms for entering; perceptions of others; availability of positions) that might hold this employee back are:

These completed statements would then form the basis for a career-planning discussion, and later the completion of a career plan such as that in figure 5–5. Detailed self-analysis workbooks are already available (8,18,20, 34) or could be developed internally to better match the company's needs. One such example is provided in chapter 11.

Supervisory Involvement and the "Job Match." Within the recommended career development system paradigm, supervisor/subordinate career-planning discussions would occur next. The supervisory role is critical to the process since this is the pivotal point for reality testing and organizational feedback. This discussion can be highly beneficial but will require the training of supervisors. Supervisors are often very uncomfortable in taking this role and conducting this discussion—but it requires the precise people-management skills that supervisors *should* develop. As figure 5–6 shows, the career-planning discussion differs in critical ways from other formal on-the-job discussions. Supervisors need to understand these differences and be sensitive to their varying roles. Training in supervisory skills is discussed in chapter 11; it can be very helpful.

Alternative Programs

This chapter has presented the rudiments of but one model for a career management system. Others can be designed that are either less or more complex. Career management must be more than a once-a-year paper exercise. It must be an ongoing process that embodies a developmental philosophy, reflects an organizational norm, and sets a standard or expectation of supervisors. Career management must be made an important part of the supervisor's job by incorporating it into the supervisor's performance appraisal. Development plans for subordinates should be reviewed on at least a quarterly basis. Unless human resource development is a result against which performance is measured, it will always tend to slip to the end of the list as something optional rather than essential. Detailed implementation issues for career management systems are described in chapter 7.

5-5. Sample career plan.

Employee Name: _____ **Social Security Number:** _____

Position: _____ **Department:** _____

SECTION 1. JOB HISTORY (BEGIN WITH MOST RECENT PREVIOUS POSITION)

JOB TITLE	DEPT./CO.	BEGIN/END DATE

SECTION 2. TRAINING AND EDUCATION

SCHOOL	DEGREE & YEAR	MAJOR

PROFESSIONAL CERTIFICATES/LICENSES

OTHER JOB-RELATED TRAINING

SECTION 3. JOB-RELATED KNOWLEDGE

EXPERT KNOWLEDGE	WORKING/TALKING KNOWLEDGE

SECTION 4. MOBILITY

State any restrictions (provide rationale and time constraints)

SECTION 5. CAREER PLAN

LATERAL CHOICES	DEVELOPMENT PLAN

PROMOTIONAL CHOICES

LONG-RANGE GOALS (3–5 YEARS)

EMPLOYEE COMMENTS

SUPERVISOR'S COMMENTS

SECTION 6. REVIEW AND APPROVAL (SIGNATURES)

Employee _____ Date _____

Immediate Supervisor _____ Date _____

2nd-Level Supervisor _____ Date _____

Professional Development Dept. _____ Date _____

5-6. Differences in supervisory discussions.

	SALARY REVIEW	PERFORMANCE APPRAISAL	CAREER-PLANNING DISCUSSION
Time focus	Present	Past	Future
Outcome	Information	Agreement/objectives	Individual/organizational matching
Issues	Equity	Defensiveness/self-worth	Career perception
Performance focus:	Varies	Performance	Potential

Professionally educated employees face some tough decisions at numerous points in their career, not the least of which is the big jump into management. Figure 5-7 summarizes six individual career decisions that organizations need to manage successfully. Each decision carries with it many issues for both the individual and the organization. In particular, the technical to managerial move should be planned and supported by the organization. Technical and managerial positions vary in numerous ways; some of the dimensions are identified in

5-7. Career decision points.

LATERAL MOVEMENT INTO A NEW ROLE

- Is this really what I want?
- Does this broaden or limit future movement?
- Can I do the job?
- Am I being shuffled aside or developed?
- Should I remain a professional or go into management?

PROMOTIONAL MOVEMENT

- Can I do the job?
- Am I sure of this career path?
- Will I have the opportunity to do the things I do best?
- Am I really ready for this move?
- Should I remain a professional or go into management?

LACK OF MOVEMENT

- Am I being "passed over"?
- Has the organization decided I will never move?
- Should I resign myself to the fact I will never move?
- Am I really where I want to be?
- Am I valued in my current job?
- Why am I not moving?
- Did I really want to go into management?

LOSS OF A JOB

- Was it my own inability? Am I really no good?
- Was it totally situational, due to the economy or reorganization?
- Do I want to stay in this line of work?
- Could I use this as an opportunity to go back to school or change career areas?

SPECIAL OPPORTUNITIES (PROJECT TEAM ASSIGNMENT, TASK FORCE SPECIALIZATION, EDUCATION)

- Is this worth my time?
- Is the additional effort worth the benefits?
- What do I have to give up?

TECHNICAL-TO-MANAGERIAL MOVEMENT

- Should I risk giving up what I am good at and like for uncertainty?
- If I do not succeed, can I come back to my old job?

5-8. Contrasting technical and managerial position.

TECHNICAL	MANAGERIAL
• Technical skill emphasis	• Managerial skill emphasis
• Individual effort and product	• Completing work through others
• Success judged on own work	• Success judged on work of group
• Decisions do not have widespread impact	• Decisions can affect many people
• Decisions made based on detailed data	• Decisions made without all facts
• Well-defined "hard" decision-making criteria	• Ill-defined, "soft" decision-making criteria
• Recognition through professional contributions	• Recognition through hierarchical advancement
• Information as the source of power	• Organizational structure as the source of power
• Political and interpersonal skills minimally needed	• Political and interpersonal skills required
• Bottom line is individual mastery	• Bottom line is profit

figure 5-8. The manager of professionals will necessarily require a stronger set of technical skills than the list in figure 5-8 might imply.

A viable career management system requires attention to these considerations *and* a method of soliciting and receiving position nominations from the pool of all available employees. At the least disciplined extreme, job posting and bidding could be considered career management. At its most formal level, prescreening and development for that unique position are prerequisites for consideration for a position move.

Job posting is useful in some situations and has been most successful in lower level nonexempt positions. The paperwork it generates is sometimes monumental. Since each position opening generates numerous bids and any one individual may bid on numerous jobs, the combinations and permutations of possible comparisons escalates dramatically with each new position. Job bidding is essentially a reactive posture. Career management, in contrast, is proactive. The organization would generally request employees' job selections before any position is actually open. That person's choices would then be screened for realism and adequacy ahead of time. When a position became available, the prescreened pool of available candidates would already be generated. This allows the organization to plan development to meet its human resource needs.

It is clear from a cursory examination of figure 5-9 that the essential features of career management systems are very few, whereas the recommended features are more plentiful. Naturally, as more features are added the program becomes more expensive and potentially more bureaucratic. The simplest career management program would contain only the essential features, and with proper management would work well.

One additional career management system deserves to be considered, based on its simplicity and ease of administration. Essentially it involves making the person responsible for his or her own career development and delineating the supervisor's role in a very structured way. One of the classic issues facing career-planning programs is the fact that most supervisors are not and never will be (regardless of training) effective career counselors. Their past experience and current role demands simply preclude the development of effective diagnostic or counseling expertise. This is especially true of technically oriented employees who have moved into managerial positions. Given this discomfort level, the

5-9. Career management system characteristics.

ESSENTIAL

- Information about positions and career paths
- Procedure for advanced self-nominations (such as bidding on a position before it is open)
- Linkage to the selection system

RECOMMENDED

- Orientation to instruct employees in the process
- Training to support the supervisory role
- Nonthreatening person (perhaps within personnel) available to address special issues
- Workshops to generate enthusiasm
- Linkage to training and development systems
- Level-by-level review to ensure realism of plan and build shared commitment

entire procedure tends to be shunned aside and, if done at all, completed in a haphazard manner. Additionally, the plans that assume everyone can benefit from career-planning discussions and require it of every supervisor are doomed to failure due to supervisory inability, lack of commitment from managers, and an often overly cumbersome administrative/paperwork jungle.

A workable alternative is an employee-initiated program that involves the supervisor in a circumscribed and structured way *at the request of the employee*. The first step in the program would be employee participation in a career-planning workshop, or completion of a career-planning workbook (these are dealt with separately in chapter 11). In either case, the employee does all the work prior to the supervisory discussion. Either the workshop or workbook is used to conduct a detailed self-analysis. The individual then summarizes this analysis in a memo to the supervisor who requests a meeting to discuss the summary and the person's proposed plan. The organizational part of the program would consist of a highly structured memo from an employee to his or her supervisor, for example:

INTRODUCTION

As you are aware, I recently attended the company's career development workshop. During the workshop I examined my strengths, weaknesses, goals, and sources of job satisfaction. In the workshop I also examined the similarities in our work styles so that we could work most effectively together. Based on this thinking I have written some ideas for my career action plan.

The purpose of this memo is to request a conference with you to discuss these ideas. I have scheduled some time on _____ for this purpose. The workshop leader suggested we follow a specific agenda:

1. Performance goals
2. Work styles
3. Skill development
4. Satisfying work elements

PERFORMANCE GOALS

Based on my knowledge of what our department needs to accomplish in the next 3–12 months, I identified the following performance goal for myself:

This is my action plan on how to achieve that goal:

ACTION   DATE

Given that I follow through on this plan, I think you and the organization will benefit in the following ways:

And I will benefit in the following ways:

WORK STYLES

In the workshops we used a series of questionnaires that helped me think through how you approach work and how I approach work. I noted the following similarities:

I also noted some differences in our approaches, that is:

(continued)

I thought through some ideas that may help us work together more effectively. Would it help you if I:

If acceptable to you, it would help me if you would:

SKILL DEVELOPMENT

I had the opportunity to assess my management skills and these are what I see as my major strengths:

I also identified some areas in which I would like to improve:

Do you agree with this assessment?

In order to address the development needs I have constructed the following action plan:

DEVELOPMENT NEED	GOAL	ACTION STEP	DATE

I am interested in your reaction to these plans, and any suggestions for improvement that you might have.

SATISFYING WORK ELEMENTS

I analyzed the work elements inherent in my job and identified the following sources of personal satisfaction that I currently have in my job (and would like to maintain):

There are other things I would like to have as part of the job, and realistically I think the following things would improve my job satisfaction:

I constructed an action plan to increase my job satisfaction and would like to get your ideas and suggestions on it:

GOAL	ACTION STEP	DATE

FOLLOW-UP

Since follow-up on these action plans is the key to success, I have already scheduled myself on your calendar at one-, four-, and seven-month intervals. This will give us an opportunity to monitor progress and talk about our successes on these plans.

This memo to the supervisor is quite descriptive of what the employee got out of the workshop. It is one example of the kind of content that might be appropriate to the process. Note that the focus is on individual development, with career implications relevant throughout. At no point is there a list of positions the employee would like to be considered for; rather, personal self-analysis and a personal self-development plan precedes such issues. Progress on the plan then prepares the person while maintaining maximum flexibility in career movement choices.

CAREER PATHS AND PATTERNS

Realistic career path information is a necessary precondition for the development of good professional/career development plans. In the organization, is such information available to professional employees? Are all the possible options for movement identified? It is very important not to limit the career path to one hierarchically ascending *ladder* within the technical function. All possible moves should be identified within a *matrix* configuration to show visually the variety of alternatives available. Others have done more complete treatises on the development of career path information (12,77), so the details of collecting data from job analysis will not be covered here. However, it is necessary to address the specific concerns of our professional/scientific audience.

Much has been written on key transitions in the career (3,47), and on how quickly one should move (4). The professional is more likely to consider career progression routes that support development within the overall profession rather than within any one organization. There is increasing realization that "up is not the only way" (40,71) for the career advancement of engineers and scientists, and there are specific times to "say no" to a promotional opportunity when it is technical-to-managerial (67). Through the extended years of education and enculturation to the profession, the profession tends to develop norms and expectations regarding the variety of alternatives within the profession. Often the alternatives involve specific career choices:

- Technical contributor within an organization
- Management/administration of professionals within an organization
- Teaching at the college level
- Independent, private practice or consulting

Most organizations do not have the detailed position information that is useful for career choices. Given that professionals have other clearly present viable alternatives to the organization, it is contingent upon the organization to define and "market" its opportunities in order to improve the probability of attracting and retaining the most valued professional contributors. The professional within the organization is unlikely to view his or her career options in a traditional one-rung-at-a-time hierarchical ladder. More likely, he or she will have the more accurate perception of a "matrix" or "shoestring" or "lattice" set of options. This is a direct challenge to the traditional *management ladder* career path concept and suggests that the organization needs to take a close look at the availability and packaging of career and position information.

Parallel and Dual Career Ladders

The most obvious approach to the management of professionals' careers within organizations is through the dual career ladder concept. The dual career ladder model provides a technical career path as an alternative to the management career path. The goal is to provide the technical contributor an opportunity to reach personal financial and status goals while remaining in the technical specialty. The types of organizations using the dual career ladder approach can be divided into two categories. The first type involves the scientific laboratories or product research and development departments in organizations where breakthroughs are a key to the organization's future (electronics, computers, pharmaceuticals, chemicals). In the second type small professional departments (legal, marketing, employee relations) exist within a larger organization.

The dual ladder is not new; it was described in 1958 as a program to reward professionals for their scientific or technically oriented performance without removing them from that work by promoting them to management (69). An example dual career ladder is presented in figure 5-10, relevant to a scientific research-and-development laboratory function.

The research of a number of people identifies many shortcomings of this approach (38,44,64,69), for example:

1. The organization may incorrectly assume that the individual contributor does not want to influence the organizational decision making which eventually affects the scientific work.
2. The two ladders may be inequal, such that the managerial ladder continues to be the route of greater financial reward. For example, in the Department of the Navy, increases in the total budget spent for salaries cannot be controlled by competitive economic factors so the total number of promotions in the laboratories from junior to senior professional/scientist and supervision to management are restricted at key, upper-level transition points. To preserve the organizational structure and hierarchy, all promotions on the professional/scientific side of the parallel ladder are stopped. Promotions to management continue

5-10. Example dual ladder.

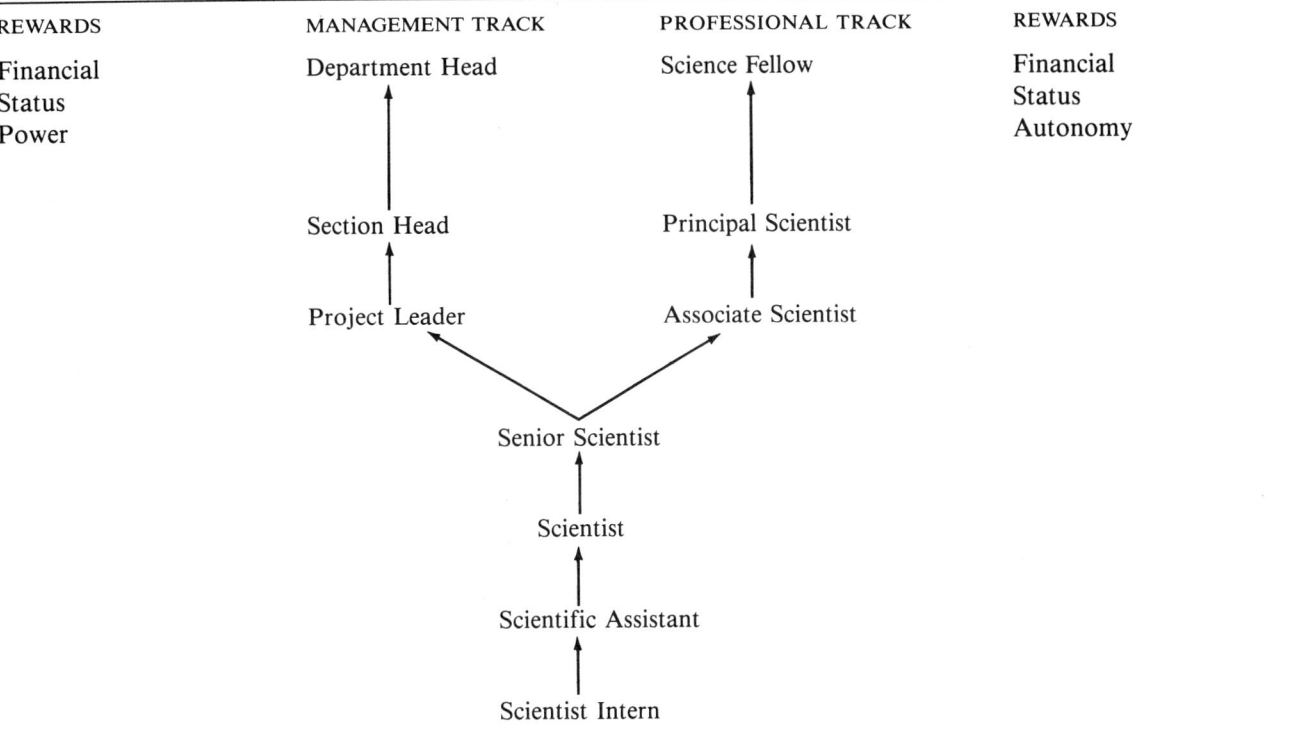

to take place although the frequency is less. Liang has found that this policy causes an 80 percent increase in the attrition of upper-level professionals two years after it is implemented if other factors such as labor market conditions remain constant (50). The effect is repeated to a significant but lesser extent as the policy is felt by scientific and technical employees lower in the hierarchy.

3. There may be a tendency to use the professional side as a place to shelve senior employees who lack management skills.
4. The professional ladder may not carry the same status (either within the organization or within the profession) as the managerial ladder.
5. Assignment to the professional ladder may be taken as evidence that the person does not have the talent to succeed in the mainstream organization. Accepting the position may be perceived as an admission of a lack of leadership or managerial skill.
6. It is difficult to set up the appropriate supervisory relationship with the people on the professional ladder. This can become a problem for both the person and the organization.
7. If the professional ladder is poorly publicized or negatively valued, or the rewards are perceived ambiguously, the sharp professional will be unlikely to choose this option.
8. The dual ladder is more often than not poorly planned and poorly designed. This tends to result in an arbitrary system which may not be administered consistently or fairly.
9. On the professional ladder side it is often very difficult to define the levels of work that would correspond to a higher level on the ladder. On the managerial side, this is done quite easily through the hierarchical nature of the management structure.

Based on the aforementioned problems, several recommendations, particularly those by Roth (64), can be made regarding the effective development and execution of a dual ladder program:

1. Jobs on the technical side must represent distinguishable levels of real work, with formal accountabilities and performance standards. Based on this, formal qualification and advancement criteria must be defined.
2. The highest levels of the professional ladder must be *attainable* if the rewards available are to motivate others to excel. At each level, the jobs must be challenging but achievable.
3. Rewards should be evenly distributed between the two paths. Specifically, the compensation package for equivalent rungs on the dual ladder must be

identical. In addition, the status and noncash rewards should be equalized by finding ways to enhance the prestige of the professional track. A few well-publicized "success stories" of organizationally well-respected individuals can go a long way here.
4. The performance appraisal system must be specifically designed to assess the skills of individual contributors, thereby providing clear criteria for advancement up the technical ladder. Consideration for advancement should involve some form of an objective peer review committee which focuses on technical contributions and potential.
5. Those people at the highest levels of the professional track need to be actively involved in top management decision making. This is another way of increasing the status of the professional ladder and will also tend to create more balanced decision making for the organization.
6. The execution of a dual career ladder system cannot be expected to occur all at once. That is, it requires continuous attention and monitoring to ensure its survival and success.

The dual career ladder concept can be alluringly simple in concept but deceptively difficult in design and execution. It will work only when the issues raised in this section are seriously addressed. The often unspoken truth is that the political decision making within the organization continues to veer away from the professional whose interests may not be well-served by a dual career ladder. The potential pitfalls of the dual structure can be overcome if the organization is responsive to the issues raised in this section.

OUTPLACEMENT

It sometimes becomes necessary for organizations to release professionals in response to changing external conditions. The booms and busts in the engineering profession related to the space program and military contracts is perhaps the best and most well-known example of changing conditions. How can organizations ensure fair treatment of employees in such an unsure, unstable environment? This is a complex issue, especially considering the stress and psychological impact of job loss (6, 13,27,48,78,83) and the fact that there is no consensus on what "fair treatment" is for a terminated employee (56).

Effective outplacement can help cushion the impact of termination and help maintain positive attitudes toward the releasing organization (10). For example, the program at TRW involved: an up-to-date listing of job openings; counseling; and assistance in preparing résumés. Three-fourths of those who found enjoyable new jobs said they would return to TRW if the opportunity arose (49). In organizations operating under such cyclical conditions, the goodwill generated in the human resource marketplace may make any such program worthwhile in the long run. This consideration is becoming even more critical as professionals are now likely to fight for retention of their jobs and their benefits (35,46).

There is some evidence that participants in outplacement programs are able to find work more quickly or at higher salaries (25, p. 4; 55, p. 13; 66, p. 44), although there have also been criticisms that outplacement programs simply assuage the organization's guilt and have little effect (80). Kaufman's review of outplacement programs led him to conclude in 1982 that "the objective results reported thus far with outplacement indicates that its potential value is more in helping professionals adjust to job loss and sustaining or restoring their self-confidence than in actually placing them in jobs" (39, p. 263).

What exactly is outplacement? There is no single definition; the word itself is newly coined. Different people focus on different aspects when discussing outplacement. Definitions vary from the humanistic—terminating employees in a way that preserves their dignity, recognizes their past contributions, and enables them to find a new job quickly and relatively painlessly (17, p. 35)—to the hard-nosed—the removal of redundant or marginal personnel with minimum disruption and cost to the company (22, p. 86). Both perspectives are important—the organization attempts to minimize short-term separation costs and long-term "opportunity losses." The latter might be characterized by the internal employee relations environment and the external public relations perception of the organization, both of which might influence the organization's ability to attract and retain valuable contributors. The organization's reputation as a good employer is one thing that is at stake when separations are inevitable. In fact, the efficient use of human resources dictates the need for a proactive outplacement service. Both the organization and the individual suffer if a minimally effective employee is retained. If an organization decides *not* to act, and thus to allow "deadwood," the decision "has an impact on employee morale, customer relations, shareholder attitude, and company image" (16). In this sense, outplacement is simply a good business decision.

An outplacement program might consist of these steps:

1. *Individual Self-Assessment*—thinking through one's own knowledge, skills and abilities, individual accomplishments, personal strengths, preferences.
2. *Targeted Strategy*—the development of specific objectives and a job-hunting strategy.
3. *Preparation of the Résumé*—résumés are tailored

to the objectives, strategy, and the person's strengths.
4. *Interview Training*—coaching on questions to expect, role playing, feedback on self-presentation.
5. *Locating Jobs*—generating job leads through personal contacts, networking, referral sources, the organization's recruiting contacts, and job listings.
6. *Deciding among Alternatives*—providing the opportunity to talk through job offers and determine the best move.

Throughout this process, individuals may be provided with a new office from which to direct the job search. Secretarial and administrative support might also be provided. Financial arrangements vary but would generally involve severance pay and other benefits, such as personal financial counseling.

Because of the central role that the professional's work plays in his or her self-image, the complete outplacement program must also address the psychological impact of job loss. This is best done by mental health professionals who are trained to deal specifically with this issue. Numerous private consulting firms offer such services; some organizations have similar expertise in staff positions. There are some major reasons why mental health practitioners have a role in outplacement.

Because of the fact that professionals receive greater intrinsic satisfaction from their work than other occupational groups, their self-image, identity, and feelings of personal efficacy tend to be inextricably tied to their work role. Kaufman has pointed this out convincingly (39), citing research findings from several sources:

- Eighty percent of professionals derive ego satisfaction from their work compared to 39 percent of clerical and 29 percent of unskilled workers (32).
- Professionals see their work as a greater "central life interest" than other groups (61).
- Professionals see their work as more important then their leisure pursuits; the opposite is true for nonprofessionals (72).
- The intrinsic nature of the work is important to professionals, but not necessarily to other workers (28,81).
- Among college-educated professionals, satisfaction with the job is more strongly related to overall life satisfaction than for other groups (52,60).

As these findings suggest, job loss deals a much greater psychological blow to professionals than to other types of workers. Kaufman concludes his review of this area by stating, "The research examined thus far clearly implies that joblessness can have a severe impact on the psychological well-being of many professionals" (39, p. 25). To summarize some of these findings:

- Unemployed professionals consistently score lower in self-esteem and higher in anxiety than their working colleagues (24,37).
- Loss of self-esteem can interfere with the professional's career development (73).
- Loss of self-esteem can result in ineffective job searches and poor employment decisions (42).
- Self-perceived failure in the work role has been strongly associated with suicide (9).
- Unemployed professionals have a greater feeling of detachment and apathy (51).
- Unemployed professionals experience higher levels of depression than their employed counterparts (51).
- Professionals are more likely than others to experience shame, feel stigmatized, and avoid social contacts due to job loss (11,23,24).
- For unemployed professionals, lowered self-esteem results in greater hostility and aggression toward others (24,37,43).

The organization must determine the degree to which it is committed to blunting these individual impacts and develop a plan accordingly. The mental health professional might be involved in:

1. Meeting with the supervisor to discuss how the person to be outplaced is likely to respond; coach the supervisor with script and role-play.
2. Overseeing the interchange with the exit interview specialists, since this is the typical "ventilation" period when anger and resentment are likely to surface.
3. Meeting directly with the professional in the process of outplacement to talk through the experience and the normality of certain concerns, stresses, and anxieties.
4. Providing psychological assessment of intelligence, aptitude, interest, and personality and engaging in one-on-one discussions to help rebuild the person's self-esteem; involving the person in a dialogue to understand the results.
5. Conducting ongoing group counseling and peer support groups.
6. Overseeing the psychological impact of the entire outplacement process.

Summarizing what we know about the psychological impact of adjusting to unemployment, Kaufman (39, pp. 297–98) suggests that organizations:

1. Consider all alternatives to termination, for example: natural attrition; early retirement; cutbacks on salary increases, pay, or benefits; shorter work schedules; internal transfers; and retraining.

2. Consider the individual's likely reaction to the termination and attempt to minimize unemployment stress.
3. Notify affected employees as soon as possible after the decision has been made and choose the appropriate person to communicate the news.
4. Initiate outplacement activities to help the person through the transitions to unemployment and job search immediately upon notification of termination.
5. Address the emotional as well as instrumental concerns of the person.

RETIREMENT

The testimonial dinner and gold watch after years of faithful service followed by a life of retirement ease comprise the traditional image that, for professionals, is only rarely borne out in reality. Retirement, in actuality, is a very personal experience with different meanings and consequences for different people. Because professionals tend to identify with their profession, "retirement" from the local organization will very likely be experienced differently that a nonprofessional employee whose entire role identification is with the organization, of which he or she is no longer a part. The professional still has the profession and, indeed, will often continue professional practice through consulting, teaching, independent practice, or lecturing. The trauma of separation need not be as severe *if* the professional:

- Plans ahead for financial needs.
- Plans ahead for independent working options.
- Keeps up to date as a respected technical expert and consultant.
- Maintains ties to the professional society and its activities.
- Identifies opportunities to use valued talents outside the organizational context.

What can the organization do to facilitate the transition into retirement for its professionally affiliated work force? Walker presents the realistic viewpoint that the organization's incentives to influence retirement decisions and transitions will vary depending on the value placed on the work (76, p. 271). With superior performers the organization's challenge is to:

- Use their talents fully
- Keep them motivated
- Maintain up-to-date skills and knowledge
- Provide superior opportunities and compensation

However, for average to poor performers the choices are simpler: terminate or tolerate.

This latter decision is complicated by the legal requirements of the Age Discrimination in Employment Act, which protects workers over the age of forty years from employment-related decisions made on the basis of age. The burden is clearly on the organization to provide the appropriate documentation of job-related performance problems over a reasonable period of time as justification for the termination decision. Often organizations will bypass this unpleasant and unpopular action by offering early retirement incentives that address:

- Financial retirement benefits
- Personal counseling or assistance
- Social issues by establishing a norm that early retirement is perfectly acceptable

The "catch" is that early retirement inducements may attract the superior performer. For this reason, the organization must use existing systems to identify potential retirees who require individual attention and make sure they receive the communication and actions necessary to know where they stand. Three programs have already been described that could contribute to this process:

- Human resource review systems, to define who has the skills and knowledge needed by the organization
- Performance assessment and feedback systems to communicate to the professional how the organization views them; to establish performance documentation against established standards
- Organizational career management systems, to provide the personal assistance and experiences that will help lead the professional to a good retirement decision

Three programs will be described in chapter 6:

- Learning from the job itself, to provide the valued opportunities to keep professionals motivated and excited about their expert role
- Training and education systems to ensure that the skills and knowledge of the older professional is kept current
- Individual development planning, to ensure that the person is being developed to meet the organization's needs and to ensure that the organization is providing resources and opportunities that are meaningful to the professional

Organizations should be aware that professional societies are becoming more interested in protecting the employment rights of their members. Most organizations strive to manage the retirement or outplacement process according to established guidelines so as not to damage their image with the public and reputation with professionals who are potential employees. One professional society, the American Chemical Society, has established guidelines that relate to termination *and* involuntary retirement (1), which they audit for compliance:

- Placement assistance through internal transfer, retraining, or external referral
- Four weeks' advance notice of termination
- Employees with ten years of service should only be terminated for cause or incompetence
- Employees with ten years of service should receive full pension-plan vesting
- Severance pay should be provided at the rate of two weeks' salary for every year of service
- Life insurance and medical benefits should continue for up to two months following termination
- Those terminated due to economic cutbacks should be rehired before similarly qualified new employees
- Anybody who involuntarily retires should be treated as well as someone let go for economic reasons

Employees may want to audit the extent to which the organization's policies reflect the values represented by these guidelines. Economic downturn is one of the concerns in the guidelines and one which organizations may well need to face in reference to the use of its professional work force. Because professionals tend to be intrinsically attached to the work they do, they often resist inducements to early retirement. Kaufman described other options (39); these can be considered by the organization:

- Postpone increases in pay and benefits
- Encourage employees to take their vacations during slow business periods
- Schedule shorter work weeks with reductions in pay
- Consider work-sharing options, supplemented by unemployment insurance benefits
- Schedule employees for alternating periods of work
- Instigate lay-off rotation
- "Lend" employees to other companies
- Transfer ownership to employees or consider stock ownership alternatives
- Reshuffle people through retraining and internal transfers

Another step that organizations can take to address the retirement needs of professional employees is to provide retirement workshops, counseling, or self-help aids. Numerous organizations, including professional associations, currently provide retirement workshops (26) or retirement counseling and planning services (41). In a classic self-help book, *The Three Boxes of Life,* Bolles confronts the individual with the issues and concerns that would be relevant at retirement (7). Finally, the organization can help ensure that the professional employee makes the most of the activities (such as placement services) available through professional associations.

SUMMARY

Chapter 5 dealt with the professional who is progressing in a career and then, finally, leaves through outplacement or retirement. It answers the question, What organizational programs can be put in place to get professionals involved in their own personal development and career movement? Much of it was relevant to the professional's supervisor because of the emphasis on appropriate feedback and performance discussions.

The reader should now be able to answer the following questions:

> What objectives can be met by a well-designed performance feedback system?
> What are the characteristics of an effective performance appraisal discussion?
> Why separate the formal performance appraisal (used for salary administration) from a professional development discussion?
> How might I make the case for a career management system within my organization?
> What are the key ingredients for a career management system?
> What are the points at which a professional is likely to be required to make significant career decisions?
> What are my options beyond a straight-up career path?
> What does an outplacement program look like? What are its pros and cons?
> What is the impact of job loss?
> What are the options to retirement that the organization should consider?

The reader is now better prepared for the kinds of decision processes that will occur through the tenure within an organization, including the difficult job loss situation. It is contingent upon the organization to develop the performance and promotability information described in chapter 4 so that it can be used effectively when outplacement decisions must be made.

REFERENCES

1. American Chemical Society, 1975. *Professional employment guidelines.* Washington, DC.
2. Badawy, M. K. 1975. Organizational designs for scientists and engineers: some research findings and their implications for managers. *IEEE Transactions on Engineering Management* 22(4):134–38.

3. Badawy, M. K. 1983. Managing career transitions. *Research Management* (July-August):28–31.
4. Bailyn, L. 1979. Taking off for the top . . . how much acceleration for career success? *Management Review* (January):18–23.
5. Bassett, G. A., and Meyer, H. H. 1968. Performance appraisal based on self-review. *Personnel Psychology* 21:421–30.
6. Berack, J. A. 1982. Termination made easier: is outplacement really the answer? *Personnel Administrator* 27:63–71.
7. Bolles, R. N. 1978a. *The three boxes of life.* Berkeley, CA: Ten Speed Press.
8. ———. 1978b. *What color is your parachute?* Berkeley, CA: Ten Speed Press.
9. Breed, W. 1972. Five components of a basic suicide syndrome. *Life-Threatening Behavior* 2(1):3–18.
10. Brenner, S. O., and Bartell, R. 1983. The psychological impact of unemployment: a structural analysis. *Journal of Occupational Psychology* 56:129–36.
11. Briar, K. H. 1976. The effect of long-term unemployment on workers and their families. Ph.D. Dissertation, University of California, Berkeley.
12. Burack, E. H., and Mathys, N. J. 1980. *Career management in organizations: a practical human resource planning approach.* Lake Forest, IL: Brace-Park Press.
13. Burke, R. J. 1984. Disengagement from organizations: job loss through termination, permanent lay-off, and retirement. In *Human Resource Management in Canada,* ed. K. Srinvas. Toronto: McGraw-Hill.
14. Burke, R. J., et al. 1972. An examination of important contexts and components of individual quality of life. *ABRP working paper no. 21.* Faculty of Administrative Studies, York University, Toronto.
15. Burke, R. J., Weitzel, W., and Weir, T. 1978. Characteristics of effective employee performance review and development interviews. *Personnel Psychology* 31:903–19.
16. Camden, T. M. 1980. Outplacement: a good business decision. *Commerce Magazine* (Oct.):12–16.
17. ———. 1982. Using outplacement as a career development tool. *Personnel Administrator* 27(1).
18. Campbell, D. P. 1974. *If you don't know where you're going you'll probably end up somewhere else.* Niles, IL: Argus Communications.
19. Cohen, S., and Meyer, H. H. 1979. Toward a more comprehensive career-planning program. *Personnel Journal* (Sept.):611–15.
20. Crystal, J., and Bolles, R. N. 1978. *Where do I go from here with my life? The crystal life planning manual.* New York: Seabury Press.
21. Dalton, G. W., Thompson, P. H., and Price, R. L. 1977. The four stages of professional careers: a new look at performance by professionals. *Organizational Dynamics* (Summer):19–42.
22. Driessnack, C. H. 1980. Outplacement—the new personnel practice. *The Personnel Administrator* (Oct.):84–93.
23. Elder, G. H. 1974. *Children of the great depression: social change in life experience.* Chicago: University of Chicago Press, 1974.
24. Estes, R. J. 1973. Emotional consequences of job loss. Ph.D. dissertation, University of Pennsylvania, School of Social Work.
25. Faber, H. 1975. Corning, New York: hometown absorbs the shock. *The New York Times,* 14 Sept. 1975:4.
26. Ferrini, P., and Parker, L. A. 1978. *Career change.* Cambridge, MA: Technical Education Research Centers, 1978.
27. Fineman, S. 1983. *White collar unemployment, impact and stress.* Bath, Avon: Pitman Press.
28. Friedlander, F. 1966. Importance of work versus non-work among socially and occupationally stratified groups. *Journal of Applied Psychology* 50:437–41.
29. Gerstenfeld, A. 1964. *Effective management research and development.* Reading, MA: Addison Wesley.
30. Giblin, E. J. 1978. Professional organizations need professional management. *Organizational Dynamics* (Winter):41–57.
31. Grass, D. 1979. A guide to R&D career pathing. *Personnel Journal* (April):227–31.
32. Gurin, G., Veroff, J., and Feld, S. 1960. *Americans view their mental health.* New York: Basic Books.
33. Hall, D. T., and Hall, F. S. 1976. What's new in career management? *Organizational Dynamics* (Summer):17–33.
34. Holland, J. L. 1973. *Making vocational choices: a theory of careers.* Englewood Cliffs, NJ: Prentice-Hall.
35. Hymowitz, C. 1985. No more meekly shuffling away: fired workers bargain for benefits. *Wall Street Journal,* 14 February.
36. Jacobson, B., and Kaye, B. 1986. Career development and performance appraisal: it takes two to tango. *Personnel* (January):26–32.
37. Kaufman, H. G. 1973. Relations between unemployment—reemployment experience and self-esteem among professionals. *Proceedings of the American Psychological Association, 81st Annual Convention,* pp. 601–2, Montreal, Canada, August.
38. ———. 1974. *Obsolescence and professional career development.* New York: AMACOM.
39. ———. 1982. *Professionals in search of work.* New York: John Wiley.
40. Kaye, B. 1980. Up is not the only way. *Supervisory Management* (February):2–9.
41. Knowdell, R. L. 1978. The implementation of a career/life-planning program in an industrial setting. *Proceedings of the 86th Annual Conference of the American Society for Engineering Education,* pp. 17–23. Washington, DC: ASEE.
42. Korman, A. K. 1967. Self-esteem as a moderator of the relationship between self-perceived abilities and vocational choice. *Journal of Applied Psychology* 51:65–67.
43. ———. 1974. *The psychology of motivation.* Englewood Cliffs, NJ: Prentice-Hall.
44. Kornhauser, W. 1962. *Scientists in industry: conflict and accommodation.* Berkeley: Univ. of Cal. Press.
45. Kraut, A. I. 1975. Predicting turnover of employees from measured job attitudes. *Organizational Behavior and Human Performance* 13:233–43.
46. Langley, M. 1984. White collar layoffs: many middle managers fight back as more firms trim work forces. *Wall Street Journal,* 29 November.
47. Latack, J. C. 1984a. Career transitions within organizations: an exploratory study of work, nonwork, and coping strategies. *Organizational Behavior and Human Performance* 34:296–322.
48. ———. 1984b. *Pilot study of job loss among managers and professionals.* Columbus: Ohio State University, College of Administrative Science.
49. Lehner, G. 1971. How to manage the victims of a cutback. *Innovation* 21:42–47.
50. Liang, T. T. 1982. *Attrition and promotion of scientific and engineering personnel in navy laboratories under high-grade*

51. Little, C. B. 1973. Stress responses among unemployed technical-professionals. Ph.D. dissertation. Univ. of N.H.
52. London, M., Crandal, R., and Seals, G. W. 1977. The contribution of job and leisure satisfaction to quality of life. *Journal of Applied Psychology,* 62:328-34.
53. Lyons, T. 1971. Role clarity, need for clarity, satisfaction and withdrawal. *Organizational Behavior and Human Performance* 6:99-110.
54. Mainero, L. A., and Upham, P. 1986. Repairing the dual ladder program. *Training and Development Journal* 40 (5): 100-104.
55. McIntosh, S. S. 1973. Outplacement—the new responsibility in termination. *Personnel Administrator* (Mar./Apr.):10-13.
56. Mendleson, J. L. 1974. What's "fair" treatment for terminated employees? *Supervisory Management* 19(11):25-34.
57. Moravec, M. 1982. A cost-effective career-planning program requires a strategy. *Personnel Administrator* 27(1):28-32.
58. Morse, N. C., and Weiss, R. S. 1955. The function and meaning of work. *American Sociological Review* 20:191-98.
59. Northrup, H. R., and Malin, M. E. 1985. *Personnel policies for engineers and scientists.* Philadelphia, PA: Industrial Research Unit, The Wharton School, University of Pennsylvania.
60. Orpen, C. 1978. Work and nonwork satisfaction: a causal-correlational analysis. *Journal of Applied Psychology* 63: 530-32.
61. Orzack, L. H. 1959. Work as a central life interest of professionals. *Social Problems* 7:125-32.
62. Roe, A., and Baruch, R. 1967. Occupational changes in the adult years. *Personnel Administration* 30:26-32.
63. Rosow, J. M. 1974. *The worker and the job.* Englewood Cliffs, NJ: Prentice-Hall.
64. Roth, L. M. 1984. *A critical examination of the dual ladder approach to career advancement.* New York: Columbia University Center for Research in Career Development.
65. Schaffer, H. R. 1971. *The growth of sociability.* Baltimore, MD: Penguin Books.
66. Scherba, J. 1973. Outplacement as a personnel responsibility. *Personnel* 50(3):40-44.
67. Schmidt, P. 1985. Promotions: when to say no. *Computer Decisions* 9 (April):76.
68. Seibert, E. H., and Seibert, J. 1986. Retirement: crisis or opportunity. *Personnel Administrator* (August):43-49.
69. Shepard, H. A. 1958. The dual hierarchy in research. *Research Management* 1:177-87.
70. Sofer, C. 1970. *Men in mid-career.* London: Cambridge Univ. Press.
71. Spruell, G. 1985. Say so long to promotions. *Training and Development Journal* (May):70-75.
72. Staines, G. L., and O'Connor, P. 1979. The relationship between work and leisure. Ann Arbor Univ. of Mich. Survey Research Center.
73. Super, D. E. 1970. Career development. In *Psychology in the Educational Process,* eds. J. Davitz and S. Ball, pp. 428-75. New York: McGraw-Hill.
74. Van Maanen, J. 1977. *Organizational careers: Some new perspectives.* London: John Wiley and Sons, Ltd.
75. Vosburgh, R. M. 1980. The annual human resource review: A career-planning system. *Personnel Journal* (October): 830-37.
76. Walker, J. W. 1980. *Human resource planning.* New York: McGraw-Hill.
77. Walker, J. W., and Gutteridge, T. G. 1979. *Career-planning practices: an AMA survey report.* New York: AMACOM.
78. Warr, P. 1984. Job loss, unemployment, and psychological well-being. In *Role transitions: Explorations and explanation,* eds. V. L. Allen and E. Van de Vliet. New York: Plenum Press.
79. Weitz, J. 1956. Job expectancy and survival. *Journal of Applied Psychology* 40:245-47.
80. Welles, C. 1978. Is outplacement a corporate guilt trip? *Esquire* (August):56-59.
81. White, B. J. 1977. The criteria for job satisfaction: Is interesting work most important? *Monthly Labor Review* 100 (5): 30-35.
82. White, R. W. 1959. Motivation reconsidered: the concept of competence. *Psychological Review* 66:297-333.
83. Zahniser, G., Ashley, W. L., and Inks, L. 1985. *Helping the dislocated worker: adjusting to occupational change.* Columbus: Ohio State University, National Center for Research on Vocational Education.

Chapter 6

Professional Development on the Job

A main theme running through this book is a strong belief that development of technical and managerial skills occurs largely through on-the-job activities and the challenges they bring. The ongoing challenge and responsibility inherent in any job can be made more of a developmental experience. This chapter discusses the systems that will enhance development.

LEARNING FROM THE JOB ITSELF

The Adult Learner

Every organization wants to achieve the best use of its human resources, but the means to this end are anything but singular. Perhaps the most common thread is simply that of work. Education has historically been seen as supporting work and is defined in terms of general university degree programs. Training also supports work but is defined as job-specific and readily translatable back to the job. Business training has been broadly defined as "the formal procedures which a company utilizes to facilitate learning so that the resultant behavior contributes to the attainment of the company's goals and objectives" (22, p. 3). Abolish from your mind that image of a classroom and a blackboard—our definition of training goes well beyond that methodology. Development connotes the entire process of personal and professional growth which expands the definition even further.

What, then, is the key concept? Learning is at the heart of all systems—the acquisition of new abilities, skills, and knowledges. From the organization's perspective there is also one other key concept—relevance to organizational goals. Behavioral change is usually the criterion, even when attitude or knowledge is being addressed in the training. Learning is a process that is inferred from changes in a person's behavior. It is not directly observed, but there are observable behavioral criteria of effectiveness that can be attributed to a given training or development experience.

Learning from the organization's perspective is defined in terms of the degree to which an experience produced a change that furthered the organization's goals. From the individual's perspective, there are times when the individual's personal or professional goals may be in conflict with the organization's goals or the goals of "management." A 1983 research study reported that computer professionals rated "learn new skills" as the number one factor in taking their first job with their current employer, while general managers rated it fourth (7). "Responsibility" was rated highest by general managers and fourth by the computer professionals. Management cannot assume that goals are compatible. The issue becomes magnified as the proportion of professionals within an organization increases and can force the management of these organizations to look at the issue of education and training in a different perspective.

Education and training occur as a natural part of the job and do not necessarily require some separate, distinct location or curriculum. Especially with professionals and scientists, job-oriented learning occurs as part of the process of developing technical expertise. The most relevant learning is that which can be directly applied back to the job. But remember that the work of professionals is not nearly as structured as that of "nonknowledge workers," nor nearly as reactive as that of managers. Therefore, job-oriented learning is critical, or nothing unique will be done by the professional to help solve the organization's problems. In this case, the organization's education and training funds are wasted when they could be better spent on technicians.

The learning process does not occur in a vacuum; the adult learner brings a well-formed set of values, attitudes, behavioral habits, and so on. For adult training to be effective, it must be responsive to the adult learner in a way that conventional education practices are not. As early as 1926, Lindeman wrote about the nature of adult education (18); it took the training profession some fifty years to discover Lindeman's work, and then it was only through Knowles's mid-1970s book, *The Adult*

Learner: A Neglected Species (16). Linderman made several assumptions about adult learners (18, p. 31):

1. Adults are motivated to learn as they experience needs and develop interests that learning will satisfy; therefore, these are the appropriate starting points for organizing adult education.
2. Adults' orientation to learning is life-centered; therefore, the appropriate units for organizing adult education are life situations, not subjects.
3. Experience is the richest resource for adult learning; therefore, the core methodology of adult education is the analysis of experience.
4. Adults have a deep need to be self-directing; therefore, the role of the teacher is to engage in a process of mutual inquiry with them rather than to transmit his or her knowledge to them and then evaluate their conformity to it.
5. Individual differences among people increase with age; therefore, adult education must make optimal provision for differences in style, time, place, and pace of learning.

A similar orientation was described by McGehee in 1958 (21) when he asked, "Are we using what we know about training?" The question is equally applicable today. McGehee also defined the learning process:

1. The learner has certain goals—he wants something.
2. The learner takes actions—he does things to attain what he wants.
3. The actions to attain goals are limited by ability, understanding of the situation, and the degree of feedback on previous actions to attain goals.
4. When the person achieves his goals through newly acquired actions, he has learned.

Inherent in these treatments of adult education is the need to examine the needs and goals of the adult learner. It might even be possible to identify some values and goals that are held in common by the professional audience. For example, Bailyn has recently argued that "continuing education often fails as a solution because it ignores the fact that most engineers learn best by doing." She cites an interview with an engineer: "Asking questions [on the job] is the only way to learn. What I need to know can't be learned by means of a textbook. It is based on experience, on trying out . . . I have taken some courses, but I find that I can do as well on my own when it is something I need to learn" (2, p. 2). This process usually involves watching others, trying out new techniques, and talking to others who are more knowledgeable. In sum, all elements of the learning process may be present on the job:

1. *Motivation*—the person *wants* to learn; the job has presented a challenge.
2. *Role models*—observation of others provides useful information.
3. *Practice*—opportunities to try out the new behavior exist on the job.
4. *Feedback*—from valued experts.

The career management implications appear straightforward: place professionals into positions and situations that challenge their current ability, knowledge, or skill base and, therefore, require them to learn. Provide the necessary elements within the job to foster new learning. Reward the attainment of new abilities, skills, and knowledges. If this cycle can be set in motion, technical obsolescence will be much less likely to become an issue. Professional conferences and paper presentations will still be necessary as an adjunct to the learning that occurs through challenging job assignments—and even as a motivating reward to the professional for having attained new expertise. Another implication is that a supervisor's approach to work assignments should be as systematic and rational as that for education or training. This is largely because, for the professional, the work assignment is often the path to development. Therefore, it can be used as a natural part of the job and can have a greater benefit than other, more formal training.

Assignments

Exactly what opportunities does the organization make available to people? Perhaps it would help to categorize positions according to type, comprised of one category in column A, and one in column B:

A	B
• Scientist	• Individual contributor
• Engineer	• Supervisor
• Manager	• Staff support

This simple categorization shows that there are numerous combinations of roles possible. It is in the organization's interest to recognize the motivating power of the job itself and attempt to match a person with the job which best suits that person's current and future needs. In this example, a scientist who is an individual contributor is unlikely to move into an engineer's staff support role. However, moving into a manager's role or staying in the scientist role and taking on supervisory responsibilities are more likely alternatives.

Cross-functional Moves. Functionally, what different types of positions does the organization have available? A frequent reason for job changes by professionals is a desire to change the direction of their careers (10). If the organization can meet these needs, then retention of valued employees is much more likely. If the scientist or engineer grows weary of pure research, what would renew his or her enthusiasm? Consider:

- Applied research
- Training
- Patent work
- Pure research in a new area
- Following the pure research through to product development
- Supervisory or managerial roles
- Manufacturing
- Quality control
- Purchasing
- Sales
- Personnel and industrial relations

The idea is not to create a "deadwood" position or department in which people who could not perform are put out to pasture. The scientist or engineer has a unique perspective to offer many of these functional areas such that a planned series of short-term assignments or a matrix organization approach could be used. In the latter case, the person might be part of several project teams that report to different functional coordinators. These types of moves can serve a significant motivational purpose if planned as part of an overall career strategy. If cross-functional moves are to be effective, they must be part of a larger plan. Otherwise the person will most likely get the feeling of being jerked around. Identification with the organization might be strengthened by a planned approach, but movement away from the pure research model might threaten the professional identification which is so important for many scientists. If cross-functional moves are used, the issue of professional/scientific community affiliation and identification must be addressed. The pure scientist who moves into a new role may well end up feeling alienated. This issue should be talked through with the person before definite plans are made.

Temporary Assignments. Much of the work of scientists and engineers is of a project nature. That structure can also facilitate their continued professional development. The problem often is that a given project may outlive its usefulness as a developmental assignment long before the project team is disbanded. Or, the project may linger on and on without serving additional useful purposes on the strength of precommitted grants. In fact, the disbanding of existing project teams can be a difficult but necessary issue to address.

Careful job rotation and the use of temporary developmental assignments can fulfill some of the career needs of scientists and engineers. This is true whether it be an initial orientation program for new employees or a planned rotation among more senior employees.

French warns against the practice of assigning an experienced employee to a project requiring existing technology and a new employee to a project requiring new technology (9). Sometimes this is a reasonable practice, when for example short-term goals are paramount. Often, however, it will have a "negative impact on the older engineers' motivation and willingness to learn new approaches and, in the long run, on performance ratings and salary" (9, p. 412).

As project assignments come up, both short- and long-range business goals must be examined. Once specific objectives have been set, personnel can be assigned which meet those objectives. These individuals should see how the temporary assignment will contribute to (or detract from) their career objectives, and be given some negotiation room for project assignment. Particularly desirable project assignments can even be made a reward for previous outstanding performance, costing the organization nothing for a very meaningful reward.

Some assignments should be clearly identified as temporary and developmental in nature. These special projects should really challenge the person's most valued skills and abilities and be used to stretch the person, perhaps into completely new areas. The expected outcome and duration of the assignment should be specified. The issue of when and how to disband a project team should be discussed at the time it is being set up.

Downward Transfer. In addition to lateral or promotional development, there may be times when a downward transfer might be appropriate as part of an overall career plan. This is not a poor performer's demotion; rather, it is a way to further the career of a professional who has worked himself or herself up to a level where it is very difficult to transfer into another functional area without taking what would technically be a demotion.

Whether this option will be a viable positive solution will depend heavily on the way the move is positioned and the person treated. Salary should generally be maintained to reflect the previous level's salary structure. In this way, the person is not penalized for taking a developmental move that in the long run improves the person's options and increases the person's worth to the organization. It is particularly important that the first few people who take such an option are monitored to ensure that the other key steps in an overall career plan take place. Again, the idea is to broaden and challenge the person. Any hint of failure associated with a downward transfer must be carefully and deliberately counteracted if the move is to serve the purpose described here.

Lateral Moves. Lateral moves are simply not used enough by organizations nor respected enough by employees. All too often if the move is not a promotion, it is "tainted" and questions are raised about the person's standing in the organization. In some cases lateral moves are part of well-established career paths upward, a concept that eliminates some of the negativism associated with accepting a lateral move. The releasing department may often have serious questions or even refuse to release a valued employee on a lateral basis. Because of the position of the lateral job, the employee may not understand the career message such a move communicates.

Nonetheless, when handled correctly, the lateral move is one of the most cost-effective tools that organizations have for the development of people. The lateral move should be part of a long-range career plan. It should provide new opportunities, greater challenges, and extended knowledge of the organization. The lateral move should offer a chance to use and develop new skills and abilities. All of these factors should be specified for the person . . . or rather *with* the person. This discussion is a great opportunity to excite the person about the new assignment.

Lateral moves combat the natural limits that a pyramidal organizational structure imposes on career movement upward—but only for a while! Shuffling a person around because there is nowhere to go is not an advisable solution. However, a carefully planned upward route using lateral moves to establish breadth is wholly advised. For professionals who are individual contributors this approach allows the *knowledge* base to be expanded into new technical areas. It allows the professional moving into management an opportunity to work with or supervise many different groups.

Another benefit of lateral moves is that they can be planned as a slate of moves without having to wait for an opening to occur. The timing can coincide with major project completions. The movement can be planned in a proactive manner prior to the move to ensure a smooth transition. In chapter 4 we described human resource review systems that enable organizations to plan this type of movement.

Task Force Assignments. Task force assignments have the potential for providing all the qualitative benefits of a well-planned lateral move, but in a more intense or condensed fashion. They can be powerful motivators, but only when used in appropriate situations and for predetermined periods of time. Task forces are most useful:

- When no organizational position or unit has clear and sole responsibility for the project.
- When different groups have conflicting interests that need to be balanced or confronted.
- When individuals from different units have needed expertise or experience.
- When wide-range organizational acceptance of the task force's outcomes are needed, by providing wide-range membership opportunities on the task force.
- When there is time to explore the issues in some depth prior to arriving at a solution.
- When people development is a priority.

Cohen and Stein have argued that task force assignments are temporary, flexible mechanisms (5), and they can provide people with two things they want and often do not have enough of in their daily jobs:

Opportunity: challenge, growth, development; the opportunity to influence others and progress upward.

Power: authority and its formal trappings, capacity to get the work done, access to resources and decision-makers, credibility.

Specifically, they state:

Task forces, after all, first and foremost permit people who aren't normally involved in a given activity to contribute to it. If it's important and highly relevant to the organization's present needs (a key to access to power in general), task forces give more people access to power and greater contribution. If people are low in opportunity in their normal assignment, a task force can provide increased challenge, a way to grow and develop, recognition for special skills and new connections within the organization. All this can help them be seen as more valuable.

Moreover, task forces provide learning opportunities; they offer the chance for people to learn not only about other organizational issues and tasks, but to meet new people, develop important relationships, see how their own work contributes, and develop the skills that enable them to make new contributions in many areas (5, p. 216).

The task force assignment provides a means of visibility for people. It can be used to build new relationships, develop support from colleagues in high-level positions, and display talents. In particular, analytical skills, strategic thinking ability, and people-influencing skills can be showcased.

Clearly the role *can* provide both opportunity and power to the person who gets involved and uses the role to his or her best advantage. Both the organization and the individual can gain by this approach.

JOB DESIGN

Not all individuals are willing to become systematic career planners nor are all organizations willing to embrace a humanistic philosophy of career management. Notwithstanding, the symbiotic relationship that exists between the individual and the organization is unmistakable. The close association and reciprocal advantage of both is clear. The object is to advance this mutual dependency so that both the individual and the organization gain.

To do this, the individual must better understand the "organizational climate" associated with different positions. Similarly, the organization must better understand the individual and his or her motivational needs. Different types of jobs influence people in different ways, but there are some commonalities. To characterize your organization, department, or position refer to figure 6-1 which describes twenty-seven scales that have been used to measure "job characteristics" or "organizational climate." As a diagnostic aid, the factors have been dichotomized to show low and high characteristics. The descriptions have been revised somewhat, focusing on individual jobs and work groups rather than entire organizations. Figure 6-2 groups the twenty-seven scales under five general dimensions (19).

6-1. Job description scales.

SCALE	LOW	HIGH
1. Engagement	A job that does not lead anywhere; a group that does not mesh and involves going through the motions.	A job that leads to important outcomes; a group that "clicks"; a clear sense of working together.
2. Work facilitation	Job contains routine duties and busywork; peers are burdened with repetitive work; situation hinders involvement or effectiveness.	Job is very nonroutine and, judging from the degree to which others facilitate it, it must be important.
3. Esprit de corps	Job does not satisfy social needs; completing a task does not lead to a sense of accomplishment; low morale within the group.	Job directly and consistently satisfies social needs and provides a sense of accomplishment; high morale within the group.
4. Social	Job does not allow the development of friendly social relationships.	Job easily and naturally leads to the development of friendly social relationships.
5. Supervision	Supervisors present a formal, impersonal front; there is a large "emotional" distance between a manager and the subordinates; supervisors are aloof.	Supervisors do not act any differently from anyone else; they are personal and informal and create a short "emotional" distance.
6. Nondirectiveness	Job is very closely supervised and assignments are given by directive; a strong production emphasis exists; communication and feedback are minimized.	Job is loosely supervised and assignments are usually discussed when given; a concern for people *and* production exists; supervision listens to and provides feedback.
7. Thrust	On-the-job behavior gets bogged down with a lack of any meaningful direction; the group may have a sense of working hard and getting nowhere.	On-the-job behavior is task-oriented and viewed favorably by peers; members of the group motivate by example and keep the group going.
8. Consideration	"People concerns" are low in the group; members show a disregard for others' feelings and desires.	"People concerns" are high in the group; members are thoughtful of each other's feelings and desires.
9. Structure	Job has many rules, regulations, procedures that must be followed; lots of concern about going through the right channels.	Job has few constraints and little red tape; there is a loose, informal atmosphere.
10. Responsibility	Job requires that virtually everything be double-checked; very little independent work.	Job gives a feeling of being one's own boss; it allows you to set your own course and make decisions.
11. Reward	Job rarely results in rewards; most feedback is negative or punishment; people are not treated fairly.	Job gives rewards when work is done well; feedback is positive, specific, and meaningful.

(continued)

6-1. (*Continued*)

SCALE	LOW	HIGH
12. Risk	Job requires that a person "play it safe," which results in little challenge or initiative.	Job supports calculated risks and emphasizes challenge and initiative.
13. Warmth	Work atmosphere is rather cold with little interaction; no sense of togetherness has developed.	Work atmosphere shows good fellowship; plenty of friendly, informal social groups.
14. Support	Job is relatively isolated and receives little support from employees, peers, or managers.	Job receives friendly helpfulness from others in the group (peers), from managers, and from other employees.
15. Standards	Job's goals and performance standards are unclear; there appears to be little emphasis on doing an outstanding job.	Job has clear, explicit goals and performance standards; personal and group goals are used to present challenge.
16. Conflict	Conflict is ignored, smoothed over, or overreacted to; there is a general feeling that differing opinions should not be expressed.	Conflict is used productively as evidence that something is wrong; the group encourages discussion of differing opinions.
17. Identity	Job discourages personal identity, does not make a person feel like a valuable contributor or member of a team.	Job really allows a person to identify with it; the group views it as important, and the incumbent feels a part of the team.
18. Consistency	Policies, procedures, standards of performance, and directions are inconsistently applied to this job.	Policies, procedures, standards of performance, and directions are consistently applied to this job.
19. Formalization	Practices, policies, and job requirements are *not* explicit, standardized, or formalized.	Practices, policies, and job responsibilities are explicit, standardized, and formalized.
20. Planning	Planning for the job and the group never really happens; actions are reactive.	Planning for the job and group is an ongoing process by which job objectives are reached; actions are proactive.
21. Selection	People are selected for this job or this group based on politics or personality rather than job-related criteria.	People are selected for this job or into this group based on ability and performance; objective job-related criteria are used.
22. Tolerance	Errors are dealt with strictly; threats and punitive blame is evident; errors are taken as evidence of inability.	Errors are dealt with in a supportive, learning manner; they are taken as opportunities for improvement.
23. Variety	Job does not demand a variety of valued skills and abilities.	Job involves the use of a wide variety of personally valued skills and abilities.
24. Task identity	Job is fragmented and allows only portions of a process to be completed, resulting in no visible final outcome.	Job requires the completion of an identifiable "whole"; gives the opportunity to work through a process from beginning to end product.
25. Significance	Job does not really have any impact on anyone else; low meaningfulness.	Job has a substantial impact on the lives or work of other people; high meaningfulness.
26. Autonomy	Job is totally dictated; every action is nondiscretionary; work pace and strategy are set.	Job provides substantial freedom, independence, and discretion to schedule work and determine how it will be done.
27. Feedback	Job itself provides no direct feedback to the person regarding quality/quantity of performance.	Job itself provides direct, clear, and accurate information on the effectiveness of performance.

6-2. Job description dimensions and scales.

DIMENSION	SCALES
Structure	Supervision
	Nondirectiveness
	Structure
	Consistency
	Formalization
	Planning
	Selection
	Autonomy
Challenge	Engagement
	Thrust
	Responsibility
	Risk
	Standards
Supportiveness	Reward
	Support
	Conflict
	Feedback
Sociality	Esprit de corps
	Social
	Consideration
	Warmth
	Identity
	Tolerance
Meaningfulness	Work facilitation
	Variety
	Task identity
	Significance

Technical/professional and supervisory/managerial jobs in general can be characterized using these concepts. From the organization's perspective it is helpful to study positions using the dimensions and scales presented here. Especially consider positions exhibiting any of these characteristics:

- High turnover
- High "burn-out"
- Low inherent motivation
- Low productivity

Using the lists in figure 6-1, identify job characteristics that may be contributing to any personnel/productivity problem. For other positions, identify areas in which improvements could be made. Next, consider how the job could be changed to encourage the characteristics that are desired. No value judgments are intended here; organizationally it might be desirable to decrease a position's standing on some of the scales with the understanding that such a job change need not be made until after the incumbent leaves the position.

Given the importance of a realistic job preview, these job description scales can be very useful in a personal decision to leave. That is, if a professional needs and expects a job that is "high" in challenge and sociality and finds out ahead of time that the position does not exhibit these characteristics, then both individual and organization are spared later disappointment. However, if the individual needs structure without all the social hoopla, then the same job would look very attractive.

The point is that jobs can be characterized in many ways, with direct implications for organizational job design and individual motivation. The organization can choose to create jobs that are inherently motivating and can give realistic job previews to potential candidates. The individual can orient toward jobs that exhibit the desired characteristics.

In describing their jobs, most individuals touch on only a few of the characteristics discussed in this section. Those are likely to be the ones that the individual considers most important. The decision to change jobs should incorporate the types of factors discussed in this section. Professional positions generally differ a great deal from managerial/administrative positions in many of these dimensions. Part of the problem with transitions between the two types of jobs may well be due to a tendency to overlook the more ill-defined qualities of a position and focus career decisions on easily quantified and well-defined qualities such as hierarchical position or salary. The "other" characteristics are important, too.

In addition, professionals and scientists often define and design critical elements of their own jobs. Being experts, they have simply more freedom and autonomy to do this. An awareness of the job characteristics that are personally meaningful to the individual can certainly improve that person's ability to influence the way the organization defines the job.

AVOIDING OBSOLESCENCE

What exactly do we mean by professional obsolescence? Kaufman defines it as "the degree to which professionals lack the up-to-date knowledge or skills necessary to maintain effective performance in their current or future work roles" (14, pp. 39-40). Others have presented checklists to assess both individual and organizational tendencies toward obsolescence (24). Obsolescence is a concern for the individual professional and also for the organization, but from a different point of view. The organization has a need for up-to-date skills relevant to the planning and execution of the organization's current and future mission. It therefore needs effectively performing professionals with the skills, knowledge, attitude, and motivation to meet current and future performance demands.

How can the organization ensure that their professional group does *not* become obsolete, thereby threatening their mission and survival? Several key elements are involved, the first of which is effective strategic planning by the organization. The strategic plan should define the organization's mission and objectives based on an analysis of the competitive environment and internal resources. The second key element is to extrapolate from that plan to the professional skills, knowledges, and activities that will be required to support the mission, and in what quantity. The third key element is to translate all this into a staffing and development plan designed to meet the current and future needs of the organization. All of the programs in chapters 3, 4, and 5 will contribute to the organization's ability to follow these steps:

- Formulate a strategic business plan to define mission and objectives
- Identify the professional/technical skills, knowledges, and activities needed
- Consolidate into a staffing and development plan

The organization's policies, procedures, and climate are going to directly affect perceived incentives to remain current in one's technical field. By knowing what technical areas are needed in the future, the organization can directly shape the skills that will be available in the future. The burden then falls on the organization to monitor changes in the environment which might influence the skills needed. Organizational influences include:

- Technical advances
- Legislation
- Economic fluctuations
- Social pressures
- Competitors' actions
- Productivity improvements

One recommendation for addressing this issue has been made by Burack and Mathys (4, p. 375). They suggest that various bodies of technical, managerial, or administrative knowledge and information be coded into a computer program. Individuals would then provide self-assessments in the same areas, and these would also be fed into the computer. "Matching" programs could be used to determine the degree to which current organizational skills will meet a variety of scenarios. This approach would allow periodic needs assessments, in which the differences between needed and current knowledge would generate appropriate training and education responses by the organization.

In order to make such a program work, several problems must be anticipated and dealt with:

- What independent validation of the self-assessments will be required? Can a person claim competence in a specific technical area based on a talking knowledge rather than the expert knowledge needed to meet organizational requirements?
- Will the self-assessments be required, and if so, how will full participation be ensured?
- How will these lists of skills/knowledges be updated? The effectiveness of the system rests on the currency of the information. Establishing and *maintaining* such a skills/knowledge data base becomes a Herculean task that may not be worth the effort.

Another option for the organization is to use the recruiting and placement functions (see chapter 3) to target those areas that the organization needs. Human resource review systems, as described in chapter 4, can be designed to "look for" key skills or knowledges. Assessment systems, described in chapter 5, can be used to ensure the level of skill/knowledge needed. Training and education (see below) can be used to support current employees in their endeavors to remain at "state of the art." In fact, the best strategy for the organization interested in avoiding professional obsolescence is its own ongoing emphasis on professional development.

Policies and procedures must in reality, not just in words, support and even motivate professionals to remain current in their field. In particular, the jobs of professionals within the organization should exhibit the job design characteristics and on-the-job activities described above. This will help motivate the professional to stay current, thereby providing the talent needed by the organization to meet current and future needs. Similar issues exist for the "plateaued" professionals (3,15,27,29) who may be in need of career counseling to avoid "burn-out" (26) or managerial failure (1).

TRAINING AND EDUCATION SYSTEMS

Adult learning is most effective when the focus is on situations rather than subjects. For example, in the management skills area, *leadership* has been a subject that has been pursued for years as a training topic with limited success, partly because the concept is so ill-defined. Recent efforts are centered around situations—for example, employee-counseling situations, task force leadership, holding effective meetings—that is, those situations required by the job and in total defining the leadership demands of the position. The situations can be well-defined, and therefore, the learning objectives can be specified in behavioral terms.

Role of the "Needs Study" in Training

Training resources within most organizations represent a scarce commodity. Because of the finite nature of these resources, the organization should adopt some system of review that results in maximum benefit to the organization. Others have emphasized management self-development and low cost, shared approaches to training (13). Large organizations with training programs must effectively allocate their limited resources. GTE's *Systematic Guide to Curriculum Development* describes the "needs study" and task analysis that precede the production of training materials (28). Patterned after Mager's work (20), the GTE *Guide* is very helpful when thinking about adult training needs; its major points will be summarized here.

A "needs study" is called for when there is a performance discrepancy between what people are doing and what they should be doing. The first question to address is whether the consequences of an action have a greater cost than the resources required to address the problem. Phase 1 is *identification* in which the organization should have some system for employees to identify performance discrepancies. For example, a form entitled "Request for Training Assistance" might be used to elicit the following information:

1. Description of the training need or problem
2. Number of employees involved
3. Job classifications or position levels of employees involved
4. Work location of employees involved
5. Observable effects of the problem
6. Information on the requestor

The problem may be either well-defined or a vague feeling based on the on-the-job presence of outdated technology or knowledge. After following up with clarifying discussions between the originator and others involved, the group moves on to Phase 2—*quantification* of the performance discrepancy. Various impacts should be examined here:

1. *Productivity*—if the discrepancy is removed, will there be a decrease in the time required to complete the project?
2. *Profitability*—will there be a reduction in wasted materials or damaged equipment if the discrepancy is removed?
3. *Knowledge level*—will there be an increase in relevant knowledge if the discrepancy is removed?
4. *Cost/benefit*—if the discrepancy is removed will it produce more in benefits than it costs to remove it?
5. *Safety*—will removing the discrepancy reduce the probability of accidents?
6. *Strategic positioning*—will there be a desirable increase in the organization's relationship with other organizations or in the standing in the market if the discrepancy is removed?

Sometimes the most cost-effective solution is to allow the performance discrepancy to continue. If this is not the case, the needs study continues to Phase 3, *definition* of the performance discrepancy in much greater detail than before. The key here is to describe clearly the difference between desired and actual performance. This is done in conjunction with experts on the subject from within the organization. These are people who work in the area being studied, supervise the area, or have staff responsibility for setting standards and guidelines. The definition of a performance discrepancy is facilitated to the degree that the steps in performing a task have been specified. For example, in the area of problem solving, the steps might be identified as:

1. Identify operating problem
2. Determine problem cause
3. Generate alternative solutions
4. Identify probable outcomes of alternatives
5. Rank order alternatives by probability of success
6. Select best alternative
7. Implement solutions on a trial basis
8. Establish feedback and monitor success of the solution

If a person or group is experiencing difficulty in problem solving, then the key diagnostic question is, At which of the eight steps does the problem exist? These eight steps establish the "performance model" to compare against the employee's actual performance. The performance discrepancy can then be defined in some detail and training can be designed to intervene at the correct step in the process.

In Phase 4, *classification,* the underlying cause of the performance discrepancy is identified. The GTE system identifies the main classifications:

1. *Skill discrepancy*—when the primary cause of the performance discrepancy is lack of general or specific knowledge or skills required to perform effectively.
2. *Environmental discrepancy*—when effective performance is blocked by conditions in the work environment. Subcategories include:
   - *Procedural obstacles*—due to a policy, procedure, practice, philosophy

- *Physical obstacles*—for example, lack of necessary tools or materials, unsuitable work location
- *Human obstacles*—due to peer pressure, managerial or supervisory actions

3. *Motivational discrepancy*—due to an unwillingness on the part of the employee to perform as desired, even though he or she is otherwise capable of it. In this case, training would not be effective because the reward system is simply out of whack. General subcategories include:
   - *Performance is punished*—effective performance results in negative social or physical consequences. For example, in one lab, scientists were punished for exhausting a fire extinguisher, so they began to fight fires with water or other inappropriate material.
   - *Nonperformance is rewarded*—the employee is rewarded in some way for *not* performing.
   - *Performance does not matter*—the consequences of effective and ineffective performance are equally desirable.

This classification phase is an important part of the needs study because the values, needs, and particular situation of the adult learner are critical considerations in the choice of an appropriate intervention. If we commit training resources to address a performance discrepancy caused by an environmental or motivational discrepancy, then we will be wasting our time. In fact, this is what many "Training Departments" do—since they are in the training business, all too often training is determined to be the answer when it may only be addressing symptoms rather than the root causes. In career management this is not at all unusual—we are just beginning to realize the incredibly strong influence that company policies and incentives play in shaping the employee's career actions.

Because of this, there may well be a need in larger organizations for a formally trained study group composed of a behavioral scientist (such as an industrial/organizational psychologist), a training professional, and at least one expert on the relevant subject. This group would study the area in which some training might be needed and then recommend solutions. Because the professional/scientific groups tend to do much of their own support work, the behavioral scientist or training professional will usually serve as a consultant or aide to a chief scientist or chief engineer on a project such as this, rather than provide direct leadership.

Phase 5 of the needs study is *generating alternative solutions,* predicated upon the classification of the performance discrepancy. This is followed by Phase 6, *cost identification* of each alternative solution: exactly what organizational resources would be required to implement each solution? Phase 7 is *benefit identification:* exactly what are the tangible and intangible benefits that would be expected if there were no performance discrepancy? Tangible benefits might include:

- Initiation of promising research
- Greater number of patent applications
- Productivity increases
- Waste/damage reduction
- Profitability increases
- Accident decreases
- Absenteeism decreases
- Turnover decreases

Intangible benefits might also be considered depending on the philosophy or practice of the organization, for example:

- Enhanced competence of lab
- Increased knowledge
- Improved corporate image
- Enhanced job satisfaction
- Increased employee motivation
- Better organizational communication

In Phase 8, *cost/benefit analysis,* a comparison of the costs and benefits for the alternative solutions is made.

Why give this detail on a needs study in a book on career management? Simply stated, the role of training in career development must be defined by the organization in a rational, systematic way. Employees infer from the organization paying for their training that they are being developed and their careers are on track. A series of false assumptions pervades that logic. However all too often organizations use training cosmetically as the path of highest visibility and least resistance. Such training may not be addressing the primary cause of a performance discrepancy. The GTE system has recognized these issues ahead of its time and has developed the system identified here. (For further information, also see *An Ounce of Analysis* by Harless [12].)

The Variety of Methodology

After the needs study has determined that there exists a skill discrepancy solvable through in-house training, the next logical question is, "What type of training?" Training comes in many forms (see Appendix 1). For each possible method of training the following considerations are made:

- Description
- Trainees
- Speed demands
- Complexity
- Time off the job
- Cost

- Individual differences
- Ethical considerations
- Career management considerations

Some of the methods are more likely to be used within the professional/scientific community than others. Regardless of the methodology chosen, the training (especially interpersonal and managerial skills) must be consistent with the organization's culture, policy, and ways of doing business. If it is not, the trainer is only asking for trouble.

For every method, transfer of learning must be addressed. It is critical for the new skill to be used and practiced in the real life situation as soon after the training as possible. Newly acquired skills are quickly forgotten unless used, and the motivation to try to change behavior is lost. Many of the techniques require a relatively sophisticated coach to help translate the training material into job performance. This occurs through the evaluation of individual behavior and feedback on performance—in much the same way as behavior modeling recommends (see Appendix 1).

Training and Education Options

The training and education of professionals are not a concern solely to the organization; they are also a central concern of the profession. Most, if not all, professions have a system of continuing education and of "policing" the adequacy of programs offered to its members. The professional society may offer certification opportunities or requirements to ensure current knowledge. Some organizations have established strong working relationships with university programs, for example the Institute that IBM and Columbia University have established to further the educational needs of employees (6).

Organizations may offer many different types of development opportunities in order to meet organization demands. The classic methods are: educational programs, training programs, and on-the-job activities. Organizations vary in their philosophy regarding which one of these methods is most effective. This will have direct implications for the availability of organizationally sponsored programs in each category. In surveying the programs used by organizations consisting of professionals and scientists, *Peterson's Guide to Engineering, Science, and Computer Jobs* was consulted (25). A representative sampling of the type of training available in the organizations described was detailed according to the three categories. These are presented here to make the following points:

- Programs are more similar than they are different.
- Professional associations are considered an integral part of continuing formal training.
- Orientation is considered an important part of training, and much of it is accomplished on the job.
- On-the-job activities and challenges are by far the most widely used and respected means of development.
- The importance of quickly getting the new employee into a group task as a contributing member is repeated over and over again.

These are organizational programs and policies borne of the reality and experience of what actually works. Following are representative features of the training programs surveyed.

EDUCATIONAL PROGRAMS
- Requirement to take at least forty hours of continuing education offerings each year.
- Graduate programs as part of an individually developed plan.
- Educational assistance program.
- Tuition reimbursement program.
- Graduates at the bachelor's level will begin work on a master's degree on a full- or part-time basis while earning a salary—successful completion is a requirement for continued employment.
- Educational leaves of absence for extended studies.
- Undergraduate and graduate courses offered on-site during evening hours.
- Many technical courses that may lead to the award of a proficiency certificate.
- A special three-year program consisting of continuing formal education leading to a master's degree.
- In-plant, live television classes in technical areas.
- Two employees a year undertake two years of graduate study, receiving a stipend and full benefits.

FORMAL TRAINING
- In-house seminars.
- Professional associations.
- Employee training programs to improve technical expertise, communication, and management skills.
- Professional, personal, and management development courses.
- Encouragement of participation in related professional groups and associations.
- New supervisory training—a forty-hour "transition" program.
- In-house experts share their knowledge and experience in seminar programs emphasizing state-of-the-art information.
- Inclusion in the entry-level program of a series of lectures given by representatives of various disci-

plines, designed to show how all the functions interrelate.
- Participation in industry associations.
- Encouragement of participation in seminars and workshops as well as technical meetings and symposiums.
- In-house training center; during 1981, 32,000 hours of training per month were conducted in one.
- Company-sponsored seminars, workshops, symposiums, and lectures that keep employees abreast of the latest developments in their field.
- Technical career programs that combine on-the-job assignments with formal classroom training.
- In-house training programs designed to supplement, not replace, on-the-job experience.
- First-day induction program for new employees, followed by on-the-job training and, *later*, a more comprehensive orientation program.
- Four-week program designed to provide a smooth transition from college to the work environment.
- A technical and law library available for employees' personal use.

ON-THE-JOB TRAINING
- Coaching from supervisors and experienced co-workers.
- Rotation through a variety of cross-divisional assignments.
- Six-week to twenty-four-month training program.
- Initial work assignments planned to involve the new graduate immediately in a project team or other technical work group.
- Work with peers on a real project involving team effort and producing practical solutions that can cause real satisfaction.
- Seven-week formal orientation program for entry-level employees.
- Use of challenging, real assignments to accelerate skill development in identified skill areas.
- Selection of assignments based on chosen career paths.
- Informal orientation is concurrent with work assignments.
- Encouragement to move from one research group to another to widen perspective and experience.
- Specialized technical training programs designed to meet the needs of each individual.
- On-the-job feedback from the supervisor and other senior members of the department.
- Employees are urged to develop their competence in areas that are beneficial to both the employee and the company.
- Direct, close supervision diminishes as each assignment is successfully completed.
- The new graduate is placed in a functional area and works in a one-to-one relationship with a senior professional.
- New graduates are placed in task forces where they receive on-the-job training.
- Qualified graduates are given broad experience in manufacturing, technical, or business operations before they receive their initial assignments.
- Responsibility, with an opportunity to fail, is a vital part of each assignment. Doing, not simply observing, is the key to career development.
- All training is on-the-job. A series of job assignments is tailored for each individual to diversify experience.
- Experienced employees share knowledge with newcomers to promote strong working relationships and ensure the quality of continuing operations.
- Experienced professionals are encouraged to serve as mentors to newer professionals and provide tutoring on highly specific systems or problems.
- Each new employee is assigned to a team, one member of which will be a personal coach—a seasoned professional who will provide on-the-job counseling and guidance to help the new employee apply academic knowledge and skill in specialized ways.
- Most development occurs on-the-job, with employees applying their skills, innovating, producing results, and learning from mistakes.
- Involvement of the new professional in assignments under the tutelage of an experienced employee as soon as possible after employment.
- Practical on-the-job work experience to provide the new professional with the greatest opportunity to learn, and more importantly, to contribute to his or her chosen field almost immediately.
- Wherever possible, new employees are assigned individual projects to analyze, plan, implement, manage, and successfully complete.
- As part of career development, the new professional rotates through a series of six-month assignments.

The Professional Development Audit

The degree to which an organization provides professional development opportunities may affect its ability to attract and retain professional talent. Remember, the professional orients toward the profession and its values over any one organization. One central value is guaranteed to be one of ongoing, current professional knowledge and training. Because the best professional talent will be asking the questions listed in this section, it makes sense for the organizations themselves to ask those questions and address the issues first. Consider the questions as part of a professional development audit:

What educational assistance or tuition reimbursement is available?

What in-house courses are provided?

Do you offer leaves of absence for professional study?

What policies do you have that encourage professional development?

How many people participate in professional development programs?

Do you provide support to employees for their participation in the activities and conferences of professional societies?

How widely do employees actually participate in professional society activities?

What assistance and encouragement is provided for the publication of professional papers?

How many people have published and how extensively?

Do you encourage registration or certification by the profession or the state or federal governing body?

Do you allow time off to take registration or certification exams?

Do you sponsor refresher courses or pay for outside study courses?

Do you give special recognition to those who have achieved registration or certification within their profession?

Do you have a program to ensure that on-the-job activities are used to develop the technical skills of your people?

Is administrative support (typing, word processing, copying, mailing) made available for the writing of professional articles or books?

Is there a separate professional development department within the organization?

Are assistants or interns available to do the "legwork" for research?

INDIVIDUAL DEVELOPMENT PLANNING

In both Learning from the Job Itself and Training and Education Systems, above, programs were described that can generate important information about an individual's developmental needs. This then must be used in an effective manner. A program that makes use of organizationally available information to address individual developmental needs will be described here.

Development is by nature an individualized issue—given *this* person's knowledge, skills, and attitudes, and the knowledge, skills, and attitudes required by the job, where are the developmental needs and what resources can be pitched against those needs? Development efforts must be relevant to the individual to be effective. One such program, described here, involves:

1. Completion of a form by both the supervisor and the subordinate, independently, asking both to assess the degree to which the subordinate has shown effectiveness in technical and managerial skills. Rather than focusing on the specific accountabilities of the job, this form would address the more generic knowledge, skills, and abilities required in current or future positions.
2. Discussion of differences by the supervisor and subordinate. This discussion should be characterized by mutuality and dialogue—the ratings are negotiable rather than dictated by the supervisor. This is, therefore, a very different situation from a performance appraisal designed for salary administration purposes. The two should be kept quite distinct. The objective of the discussion is to identify two or three areas in which the individual could benefit from development.
3. Preparation of an individual development plan (IDP) that commits resources to address the two or three most pressing developmental needs. This plan must have the full commitment of both the supervisor and subordinate.

The following is an example of the direction which should be given to supervisors preparing to conduct an IDP discussion.

Analyze the Need. Developing employees involves determining where they are now and constructing a plan to ensure that they get where they should be. To identify where the employee is now, each employee selected should complete an evaluation of his or her own strengths and opportunities for improvement by completing the IDP rating form. In giving this assignment to the employee, the supervisor must keep the following points in mind:

- The form is not a performance appraisal. It will not be retained in the employee's personnel file. It will be used only to help the employee and supervisor discuss the employee's developmental needs and formulate a development plan.
- The same form will be used to evaluate the employee, and together employee and supervisor will resolve differences in the ratings and identify development needs in a later meeting.
- This follow-up meeting should be scheduled before the employee begins to work on the form. Setting aside a specific time for this specific purpose shows that the supervisor is serious about developing the employee. Prior to the second meeting, the supervisor should rate the employee on the various skills listed on the form.

The purpose of the second meeting is to determine two areas that employee and supervisor feel should be developed by means of a formal development plan.

There are many factors to consider in selecting these two areas, and there are many methods that could be used. One method of selecting the key development areas is to rely on pure numbers—the numerical ratings made on the IDP form. However, reliance on pure numbers is seldom the best approach. Numbers tempered by sound managerial judgment is a better approach for determining the developmental areas. Consider whether some skills are critical job requirements for the individual. If opportunities exist for improving skills in these areas, perhaps these development areas should be selected. The time frame during which development would have the greatest impact also should be anticipated. If two equally important skills cannot be developed during the same time frame, then the skill that can be developed earliest should be selected. Supervisor and employee should keep the following points in mind when selecting development areas:

- A combination of pure numbers tempered with sound managerial judgment based on the employee's needs is best.
- It is better to select only a few issues and complete the development program than to select too many areas of opportunity and complete none.
- Involving the employee in the selection of development areas and construction of the development plan is an ideal means of obtaining the employee's commitment to his or her own development.

Identify the Development Need. For any individual at least two key opportunities for improvement should be selected, and the developmental need listed and described in the first column of the development plan. Each development need should be one of the major categories on the IDP form; for example:

1. Organizational Knowledge
2. Technical Knowledge
3. Verbal Skills
4. Quantitative Skills
5. Problem-Solving or Decision-Making Skills
6. Results Orientation
7. Self-Management Skills
8. Interpersonal Skills
9. Leadership Skills
10. People Development Skills

Following the general name of the skill being addressed by the plan, describe the specific area that is an issue.

Example: Technical Knowledge: Does not have knowledge in the electron pulse switching area.

The employee and supervisor (with the help of the personnel manager) should determine why a performance deficiency exists in an area. If the problem is personally oriented—for example, lack of assertiveness or self-confidence—are there tangible actions suggesting that the employee lacks confidence? Does the employee speak without conviction about projects? Does the employee accept policies and decisions without fully understanding them? The description should be in terms of observable behavior and specific incidents—*not* psychological traits.

In describing the development need, the supervisor should keep in mind the employee's current job or an immediate future job and identify the problem specifically in terms of that job. For example, instead of indicating "problem in handling people," isolate the problem area:

- Problem with orienting new employees
- Problem with teaching the job
- Problem with motivating the poor performer
- Problem with conducting performance reviews
- Problem with giving recognition to the average employee
- Problem with providing appropriate positive and negative comments regarding performance

The illustrative phrases in each of the areas of the IDP should be written in terms of tangible actions, using these phrases as models to construct the reasons for the deficiency.

Desired Outcomes. Development means getting from one point to another. If supervisor and employee have determined the source of the problem and have listed the activities necessary to get to the point where the development need is met, then the only missing ingredient is how to know that development has occurred. The employee must fulfill three conditions to show that each desired goal has been met.

First, the outcome must be observable, with a quantifiable measure as in figure 6–3 if possible (although this is sometimes difficult in professional skill areas). For example, if the development activity is a review of printed training materials or a counseling session with the supervisor, there should be a measure to assure that learning took place. These outcomes are termed "hard" measures since they are directly observable and quantifiable.

Second, if the development activity involves a problem that is due to a personality trait or an intangible (for example, the employee is not aggressive enough), look for both hard *and* "soft" measures, as in figure 6–4, instead of just one or the other. In the professional area, soft measures are often necessary. In these cases the outcome must be carefully described. "Soft" measures are subjective, but nonetheless important criteria.

Third, if the measure is subjective, make sure that it reflects a consensus of opinion rather than yours alone.

6-3. Example of observable, "hard" outcomes.

DEVELOPMENT NEED	DESIRED OUTCOME*	DEVELOPMENT PLAN
Lack of administrative knowledge—subordinates go around rather than to the employee.	No more than one subordinate per week with a pay or policy question that cannot be answered by the supervisor.	Review procedures booklet and materials describing employee benefits. Meet with subordinates as necessary to clarify issues.
Understanding and interpreting computer reports and operating documents—does not show a complete grasp of the data interrelationship or implications.	Analysis of reports will contain a list of problems, exceptions, and recommendations for action.	Conduct weekly written analysis of computer reports, specifically: (identify reports)

*How we know the activity made a difference.

6-4. Examples of "hard" and "soft" outcomes.

DEVELOPMENT NEED	DESIRED OUTCOME*	DEVELOPMENT PLAN
Does not do a good job answering questions from subordinates, resulting in discomfort by him and complaints by the subordinates.	Fewer complaints from subordinates (hard) and greater ease in answering questions (soft).	Work with the employee to ensure follow-up on questions and answers to subordinates.
Does not present ideas effectively in formal situations.	Willingness to prepare and make effective presentations during progress review meetings (hard) and increased confidence in making presentations to the group (soft).	Have employee prepare analysis of departmental results prior to progress review meeting, outlining key points.

*How we know the activity made a difference.

The most common form of consensus is for the employee and supervisor to agree that the objective has been met. However, a more useful approach would be for the supervisor to identify a neutral party (peer, coworker), to work with the employee and determine whether there has been an improvement in performance in the developmental area.

Identify the Development Plan. The next step is to select the specific activities that both the employee and supervisor believe will promote learning. Sound managerial judgment and ingenuity will be required to construct a set of activities that is practical in both the supervisor's and employee's opinion.

The most effective individual development plans do not rely solely on attendance of a course, whether provided by the organization, a university, or professional societies. Developing skills requires coaching from the boss and on-the-job practice. Many of the examples of activities are on-the-job activities that require coaching and practice. Wherever possible such activities should be used as elements of the development plan. Job assignments themselves are often the key to development. When outside education is warranted, the organization's professional training-and-education person should be consulted.

Set a Timetable for the Development Plan. The parts of the development plan cannot be completed at the same time. The supervisor is limited in the amount of available time, as is the employee. Use sound managerial judgment to evaluate limitations and establish realistic timetables for completing each element of the development plan.

This timetable should be agreed on jointly by supervisor and employee, particularly if there must be some delay on activities the employee especially desires. The development plan is, to some extent, a business contract between the employee and supervisor. It is therefore best to set realistic expectations of when activities can occur and to follow up on each IDP written.

How often should the IDP process occur? Many organizations prescribe an annual one, but that is often unrealistic. Once done initially, an annual review and update might be done with quarterly follow-up. In many cases, the long-term training or special assignments to develop new technologies or areas of professional competence will take more than a year to accomplish. People in professional and scientific roles who rely on complex knowledge areas should not be managed in the highly structured, short-term manner that industry and government usually attempt. The IDP process should be initiated or reinitiated when either the individual *or* the organization feels there is a need to do so.

Follow Up on Results. The start and end dates on the timetable should be the key to tracking results. Supervisor and employee should schedule review meetings ahead of time—get them on both the supervisor's and subordinate's calendar and clarify what will be tracked between the date of the IDP and the follow-up meeting. Clearly identify who will bring what to that follow-up meeting. Then, when it occurs, document the results. Revise the plan as needed and schedule the next follow-up meeting. These should occur *at least* quarterly.

General—Goal Development and Tracking. In summary, a checklist for the development process:

1. Clear definitions are critical to accurate measurement.
   - Specific, behavioral, observable.
   - *Not* generalities or unsupported conclusions.
   - Others unfamiliar with the person need to grasp the development need, desired outcome, development plan, and results.
2. Like any objective, good goals exhibit certain qualities:
   - Specific, measurable, and relevant to the job.
   - Quantitative where possible (exactly *what* will be measured and how?).
   - Qualitative (exactly what will be done?).
   - Actionable (what *actions* will be taken?).
   - Realistic and attainable, but challenging.
   - Clearly assigned responsibility for actions.
   - Reasonable timetable review dates, known to those responsible for execution.
   - Flexibility in adjusting to changing external conditions or priorities.
3. Follow-up is critical to success.
   - Observe performance (what actions were taken, by whom, with what results?).
   - Document performance by describing results.
   - Follow up by the people involved, so everyone stays informed (ensure that measures are realistic and priorities have not changed).

SUMMARY

As the chapter title accurately states, chapter 6 deals with the professional's on-the-job development. This is a key chapter because it focuses on the ever-present issue of professional obsolescence. Equal emphasis is placed on off-job and on-the-job activities that can be used to keep the person growing and learning and motivated.

After reading this chapter, the reader should be able to answer the following questions:

- What are the characteristics of the adult learner?
- What is the difference between training and development?
- How can job assignments be used to develop people?
- When should task force assignments be used?
- How can jobs be *designed* to be developmental?
- How can the organization protect against obsolescence?
- What is a training needs study? How would you do one?
- What training methodology should be used for what training issue?
- How can you "audit" the quality and completeness of your organization's professional development efforts?
- What process should be used to create an individually tailored development plan with the full commitment of the person?

An important theme throughout the chapter is that organizations all too often use training cosmetically as the path of highest visibility and least resistance. To be effective, both short-term training and long-term development issues must be addressed. Professional associations play a key role here. By also playing a role, the organization signals the professional community that this is the type of organization that is willing to make an investment in people.

REFERENCES

1. Badawy, M. K. 1983. Why managers fail. *Research Management* (May–June):26–31.
2. Bailyn, L. 1982. Problems and opportunities for the maturing engineer. *Interim Technical Report*, Office of Naval Research.
3. Bardwick, J. M. 1986. The plateauing trap. Part I: Getting caught. *Personnel* 63 (10):48–52.
4. Burack, E., and Mathys, N. 1980. *Career management in organizations.* Lake Forest, IL: Brace-Park Press.
5. Cohen, A. R., and Stein, B. A. 1980. *Task forces in management: a key development tool.* Cambridge, MA: Goodmeasure, Inc.
6. Columbia University. 1986. A partnership in education. *The Career Center Bulletin* 5 (3):2.
7. Devanna, M. A., and Warren, E. K. 1983. Managing the middle: implications for human resource managers. *Career Development Bulletin* 3 (4):8–12.
8. Dougherty, D. E. 1985. *From technical professional to corporate manager: A guide to career transition.* New York: John Wiley.
9. French, W. L. 1982. *The personnel management process.* Boston: Houghton Mifflin.

10. Gerstenfeld, A., and Rosica, G. 1970. Why engineers transfer. *Business Horizons* 13:43-48.
11. Given, W. B. 1955. The engineer goes into management. *Harvard Business Review* 33 (1):120-23.
12. Harless, J. H. 1975. *An ounce of analysis (is worth a pound of objectives)*. Newnan, GA: Harless Performance Guild.
13. Johnson, S. 1986. Staff development: A low cost shared approach. *Personnel* (January):57-9.
14. Kaufman, H. G. 1982. *Professionals in search of work*. New York: John Wiley.
15. Kelly, J. F. 1985. Coping with the career plateau. *Personnel Administrator* (October):65-76.
16. Knowles, M. 1973. *The adult learner: a neglected species*. Houston, TX: Gulf Publishing Co.
17. Koplow, R. A. 1967. From engineer to manager and back again. *IEEE Transactions on Engineering Management:* EM-14 (2):88-92.
18. Lindeman, E. C. 1926. *The meaning of adult education*. New York: New Republic.
19. Litwin, G. H., and Stringer, R. A. 1968. *Motivation and organizational climate*. Boston: Division of Research, Harvard Business School.
20. Mager, R. F. 1977. *Instructional module development*. Los Altos Hills, CA: Mager Associates.
21. McGehee, W. 1958. Are we using what we know about training? *Personnel Psychology* 11:1-12.
22. McGehee, W., and Thayer, P. W. 1961. *Training in business and industry*. New York: John Wiley.
23. Medcoff, J. W. 1985. Training technologists to become managers. *Research Management* 28 (1):18-21.
24. Northrup, H. R., and Malin, M. E. 1985. *Personnel policies for engineers and scientists*. Philadelphia, PA: Industrial Research Unit, The Wharton School, University of Pennsylvania.
25. *Peterson's guide to engineering, science, and computer jobs*. 1983. Princeton, NJ: Peterson's Guides.
26. Rice, B. 1985. Why am I in this job? *Psychology Today* 19 (1):54-59.
27. Slocum, J. W., Cron, W. L., Hansen, R. W., and Rawlings, S. 1985. Business strategy and the management of plateaued employees. *Academy of Management Journal* (March):133-54.
28. *Systematic guide to curriculum development*. 1976. Stamford, CT: GTE Service Corporation.
29. What to do about plateaued employees. 1986. *Supervisory Sense* (April):1-22.

Chapter 7

Career Program Implementation Issues

Organizations consistently strive for that delicate integration of human resource programs and processes that will guarantee their success in the marketplace. There is no easy solution to the problem of integration because of the vast differences that exist between organizations. Even within a single organization, the solution is elusive. As we address one need with one program, the solution itself can create additional needs. The classic example is the institution of an individual career-planning program that creates the need for a selection system to make use of the information, a training program to address deficiencies, and so on.

The overall model, the integrated, systems approach, is the ultimate objective. Successive approximations to the goal may be the best that can be attained—and that can be a lot. These programs, procedures, policies, processes, and systems can be very powerful individual motivators and organizational change mechanisms. Some programs may even challenge the way things have been or the way people traditionally think, such that resistance to change needs to be addressed. Implementation is bound to occur in phased stages rather than "grand systems" as the organization gradually defines its needs and develops programs to address those needs.

IMPLEMENTING A CAREER MANAGEMENT SYSTEM

Most career-planning programs are internally developed. The AMA study of 225 companies showed that only 2 percent of the programs were developed by external consultants (39). However, 11 percent were purchased as prepackaged materials and 24 percent were developed internally with external assistance. In only 3 percent of the companies was there a separate staff unit for career-planning purposes. In most cases, the program was the full- (24 percent) or part-time (39 percent) responsibility of the personnel staff.

These statistics underline the necessity for line and staff to be involved in the design and execution of the program. People who are knowledgeable about the informal characteristics of the organization should be involved in tailoring the program to fit the organization's social and informal climate, norms, and expectations. People from other departments who are well-respected "shakers and movers" should be directly involved, perhaps as departmental career-planning facilitators.

A career-planning program strikes at the heart of informal power within the organization. Career advancement may have historically been viewed as the result, at least partially, of the favoritism system. A career-planning program is somewhat akin to a "government-in-the-sunshine" bill—job advancement is not determined in smoke-filled backroom caucuses but as the result of an objective, open, public process. Expect some skepticism or resistance to this transition. Try to foresee where these issues are likely to arise and take steps to counteract the possibility of resistance by involving the key players and creating some ownership on their part. A career management system has less chance of being effective when developed in a social/historical vacuum or when purchased "off the shelf" than when it evolves from within.

Policies. Career management systems require strong, supportive policies. They must go beyond the rote recital of "our people are our most important asset" to policies that specify accountabilities and ensure fairness. The following examples describe organizational policies that relate to philosophy, accountabilities, and fairness.

PHILOSOPHY
- The company believes in the planned, proactive use of human resources such that all employees are actively encouraged to grow to the limits of their capability, interest, and motivation.
- The success of the business in this company depends on the quality and effectiveness of the work force. The development of people by every member of the management team requires the same

thoughtful foresight and planning as in any other phase of the business.
- This company believes that overall organizational performance can be significantly improved by encouraging all employees to participate fully in their own growth and development.

ACCOUNTABILITY

- Although each individual is primarily responsible for his or her own development, the company will facilitate growth opportunities. Annually each supervisor/subordinate pair will submit the individual development plan form to the director of human resource development. This will specify activities that support personal growth objectives.
- Each supervisor will provide the constructive feedback necessary for their subordinates to develop realistic and attainable career plans. The second-level supervisor will track the number of realistic versus "wild" career plans submitted by each supervisor's employees.
- Each supervisor will hold a performance review discussion with each subordinate at least every year, during which time career aspirations and developmental activities are discussed. The extent and nature of this discussion will vary depending on the employee's job tenure, nearness to retirement, and similar considerations. A career-planning discussion log will be kept by each supervisor.
- Supervisors will be evaluated on their efforts to develop their people. Supervisors will be required to submit a description of all activities in which they have engaged that facilitated the development of their people. This will be discussed during the supervisor's performance appraisal.
- The company will continue to follow a policy of "promotion from within." Statistics regarding internal/external selections and rationale for all external selections will be maintained by the staffing section and reviewed quarterly with the director of professional development and senior professional staff.

FAIRNESS

- When a lateral or downward move is specifically designated as part of an employee's career plan, that employee should receive salary treatment consistent with the performance rating received in the previous assignment.
- When an employee accepts a developmental assignment in another department or vice-presidential area and is not successful, every reasonable effort will be made to place that employee in a more suitable position while retaining the original salary level.
- When the company initiates organizational changes that result in surplus personnel, every reasonable effort will be made to prepare the individuals affected to enter the company's career management system.
- In those situations where there appears to be a poor "person-to-job match" but no attitude or motivational problem, the human resource department will facilitate the search for a better match. Only after all reasonable efforts are exhausted will demotion, termination, or outplacement be considered.

Procedures. Standardized procedures are particularly important for a career management system, largely because of its interface with the selection and placement system. The program can be a significant opportunity to improve employees' perceptions of the selection and placement system. Procedures are definitely needed to ensure fair and equitable treatment and to guard against potential abuse to the new system. Procedures must clearly define objectives, assign responsibilities, describe the review and approval process, and establish linkages with auxiliary personnel programs. In particular, the flow of documents (such as the career plan) should be spelled out. Sufficient flexibility should be maintained, especially in the pilot stages, for revisions to these procedures in order to meet specific problems or more closely tailor the program to the organization.

Materials. The requirements for materials and forms will of course be a function of the program parameters. Essentials will generally include:

- A set of organizational procedures that define the program
- A career-planning workbook, to be used as a guide by interested employees
- Training materials to support the new career counselor role of the supervisor
- Control and follow-up mechanisms to ensure that supervisors take on these new responsibilities
- A career plan form

Other forms might be required to ensure effective program execution or interface with existing programs; these include logs, development check-off forms, and training request forms.

Introducing the Program. Professional employees differ a great deal in their feelings about programs such as career planning. Many are likely to be skeptical of the organization's motivation. Organizational survival and success in the past may have meant "don't rock the boat or make waves, the company will take care of us." Undertaking a program that confronts the individual with supervisory and higher-up feedback on his or her potential within the organization may be seen as a risky and perhaps frightening experience. Employees may be concerned about what their supervisor or others will think about their career aspirations when they include po-

sitions outside the immediate department or reporting relationship. Fears of "mutiny" may exist. Whether these concerns or fears are realistic is only part of the issue. There is likely to be some truth to such concerns, and these should be anticipated and plans made to counteract them. Even if the fears are not grounded in reality, the perception is likely to raise problems that are just as difficult to address.

When introducing a career management system, have a credible answer to the question, "What does the company get out of this?" Communicate the company's expectations *and* the benefits and risks for the individual. Establish career planning as the visible, working evidence of a "new and improved" human resource system—show how it ties to training, selection, and other programs. Highlight early career-planning successes. Begin implementation at the top and make sure each functional area buys into it. If a subordinate's boss is in the program and speaks highly of it, then the subordinate is more likely to try it. If the supporting policies are shown to be effective, the individual is more likely to risk involvement. Most people will get involved and spend the time necessary *if* they believe that they have more to gain than to lose by entering the program. Training key, respected people in each department as career-planning facilitators can help a great deal to reduce initial reservations about the program.

Introducing a career-planning program to groups of professional people forces the dual career ladder question. In many professional career ladders, the sequence is restricted and the next logical move apparent. However, the individual who wishes to break out of that pattern by gaining broader experience in another functional area or by entering into a more managerial or administrative role must also be served by the career management system. Considerable thought should be given ahead of time to the organization's willingness to support nontraditional career movement. Obviously the program will identify people interested in making such transitions—will this be encouraged or discouraged? If supervisors/managers/administrators with a strong technical base are *needed* by the organization, then the program should be slanted in that direction and "sold" to employees as their opportunity to plan this transition. If, on the other hand, the organization wishes to discourage such movement, additional opportunities, challenge, and incentives should be considered within the professional career track. In either case, the benefits to the employee must be clearly spelled out when introducing the program.

Training. Training requirements will obviously depend on the type of career-planning program that is implemented. If the supervisor is centrally involved—for example, through the career-planning discussion outlined here—then supervisory training is a major necessity (as elaborated in chapter 9). Many supervisors have *never* received training in any type of performance discussion, much less in a specific type such as a career-planning discussion. Technically oriented supervisors may be particularly lacking in such expertise, and thus require even more attention to ensure constructive discussions.

Supervisory training may take a considerable amount of time in the overall program implementation. The skills that are being trained do much more than support the career management system. The skills also make the supervisor a better supervisor and should be considered an important part of management training. The development of expertise in this area also instills a certain amount of commitment to the program. If a from-the-top-down implementation plan is undertaken, the supervisor gains from the experience of going through the program with his or her manager prior to execution with his or her subordinates. This can give added confidence by building familiarity with the process.

Responsibility for supervisory training may be given to an existing training staff. An alternative, one that also makes the program attractive to staff, is to train key people in each department as career-planning facilitators and provide them with all the materials needed to train supervisors in their respective departments. This process must be monitored to ensure quality control, but it can be very effective in transferring "ownership" and expertise to each department.

Although not specifically training, informational presentations should be made to upper management throughout the organization as the first step in implementation. Every effort should be made, beginning with program development, to involve these key "movers and shakers" in the organization. Divest the program of "personnel" trappings and make it something that each functional area can really buy into and support.

Commitment. Much of the previous discussion touched on actions that are necessary to build commitment for the career management system. Additionally, it must be made exceedingly clear that the career management system is "safe"—it will not hurt participants. It should also be clear that the program results in concrete plans, not airy promises with regard to career advancement.

The ultimate commitment is to use the career plans within the training and selection systems. Developmental needs must be addressed by developmental resources, and realistic plans should be brought to fruition. This is not easy to accomplish. The systems must exist to handle these linkages; the human tendency to move toward subjective selection criteria must be guarded against. The career management system should result in a pool of prescreened, qualified candidates for every position that is predicted to open. The organization must be committed to drawing first from this pool of candidates before hiring from outside. The human resource review systems described in chapter 4 represent this integrative effort.

A commitment is also being made to the individual through his or her developmental plan to make organizational resources available for his or her betterment. Systems are needed to follow up on these commitments and ensure their availability and completion.

Schedule. The program may be phased in by a department over a period of up to a year or may be "blitzed in" within one month. There are pros and cons to each approach, but either will work if the essential program pieces, as described in this chapter, are developed and the key linkages are established prior to organization-wide implementation. As with any new program, it is a good idea to give it a pilot phase designed to shake out the bugs and to streamline procedures.

Once implemented, how often should the process be repeated? Annual revisions to career plans are suggested, only partly because this corresponds well with an annual review of human resources. One year assumes a certain amount of change in the person and/or the organization, such that an update of the career plan would be in order.

Traditional Programs. The two main traditional programs to which the career management system must be linked are training (and education) and selection. With regard to training and education, a career plan will pinpoint significant holes in a person's experience and organizational resources must be made available to address these needs. The individual will naturally bear responsibility in this matter also, but in many cases he or she cannot control the availability of certain types of experiences that might be required by the plan. Many needs may be shared by a number of employees. In this way, the career management system can generate an ongoing analysis of training needs, a valuable side benefit.

For the career plan to amount to anything more than a "dream sheet," it must be directly entered into the selection and placement system. Career-planning participants must be given direct consideration for positions that are approved on their career plans. Approval of the career plan must be based on a realistic appraisal of the plan's matching of individual and organizational goals (as elaborated in the human resource review section of chapter 4). If this is the case, then the most likely source of candidates would logically be the career management system. A danger sign for the success of a career management system is that it is not considered the major search factor for internally filled openings.

The career-planning discussion should *not* be tied in any way to the employee's performance appraisal or salary review discussion. These are three very different discussions which must be handled in three very different ways.

Innovative Auxiliary Programs. A career management system designed for professional employees can be a key factor in easing the transition from a professional/technical role to a managerial/administrative role. This may very well be defined as a key purpose of the program, in which case support systems must be attached to the career management system. Following are some example auxiliary pieces that might be added.

Transition Positions. As part of the human resource review, the organization should identify key positions in which the mix of technical and managerial skills is such that it would facilitate movement from a purely technical to a purely administrative position. Approval of a career plan could be tied to passage through these transition positions.

Mentoring Sponsorships. Under normal circumstances, mentors or sponsors are never *assigned;* they develop as a normal part of one's career. However, key transitions beg for the guidance of someone who has been through that life passage. If the organization approves an individual's career plan, it has a responsibility to support that plan. The technical-to-managerial transition forces self- and group-identification issues which can be very disorienting to an individual with no one to talk to about such adjustment issues. A sponsor who has been through it can help define the potential problems and guide progress through the passage.

The mentoring relationship has received a great deal of attention lately, including program design (20,34,42), role of the peer (23), and innovative techniques (22,30). However, skepticism regarding the impact of a mentor has been expressed, as evidenced by articles presenting caveats (29), questioning the necessity (8), presenting "both sides" of the pro-con argument (33), and exemplified by the article "Mentor can be a Millstone" (24). Much more research is required to adequately define the key elements of an effective mentoring relationship.

Transition Support Groups. In like manner, other people experiencing the same life changes can help each other if given the legitimate forum in which to even talk about the changes. Too often, it is considered a weakness to talk about such adjustment issues—that is, the norm is to "tough it out" and act as though the transition is simple. The problem with this approach is that it can break good people and hurt the organization in deep ways. Employees will be less willing to risk the transition even though they are not happy or productive staying with the technical job for an entire career. Internal talent pools "dry up," and even the most brilliantly conceived and implemented career management system will fail because it is perceived as too risky. Attention must be given to the social and psychological changes created by changed organizational roles.

Skills Building. Critical activities are very different in technical jobs and in managerial jobs. Individual development programs should be put in place that train the basics of effective management and supervision. As much as possible, these should be tied to actual on-

the-job activities. For example, if a "coaching-and-counseling" program is offered to the group, it should be grounded in the organization's related systems—performance appraisal, management by objectives, and the like.

The career management program can be the core around which a career development system is built. This book explores innovative programs which can be tied to career development. Organizations will differ greatly in the auxiliary programs needed or wanted. People in general, and professionals in particular, are demanding more involvement in determining their own future. Individual input within the organization's career management system must be encouraged.

Control Point. Two control points should be established. The central point should be in personnel where linkages to other human resource programs can be ensured. Within each department the departmental career-planning facilitators must control the process.

Follow-up Authority. The vice-president of human resources is most often responsible for overseeing the program. Potential for abuse or neglect of the program should be monitored closely and steps taken to address local problems as they crop up. Putting a program in place and ignoring it is tantamount to burying it. Top-level follow-up is needed.

Information Collection. The individual participant in the program supplies the information needed to make the program work. This information must then be consolidated in a form usable to the organization.

Information Storage and Retrieval. A manual or automated system must be designed ahead of time to handle the information that is collected. If job knowledge or job activities are listed in addition to job choices, these should be coded in a way to facilitate searches. This is most easily accomplished in an automated system but is not required for smaller organizations or restricted-entry career management programs where each individual can receive specialized attention.

Evaluation. The effectiveness of the career management system must constantly be monitored against its objectives, which should be clearly stated in measurable terms prior to implementation. Objective measures might include:

- Internal versus external candidate advancements
- Percent of participation by employees
- Number of career-planning employees appearing on selection lists
- Number of development plans completed
- Employee satisfaction with career-planning and advancement systems
- Number of career-planning "successes" (people attaining listed career objectives)

In addition to this informal monitoring, standard techniques of program evaluation should also be applied (5, 40,41), especially if demonstrating the viability or cost-effectiveness of the program.

Revisions. When either informal or formal monitoring identifies areas that could be changed, revisions must be considered in light of their total system impact. The effect on established links with allied programs should be considered. The program must remain accessible, fair, and equitable for all employees before, during, and after revisions. No one should be hurt by program changes. In many cases, additional program pieces might be called for, rather than a change in the existing program.

Additional Linkage. As new programs are enacted, they should be linked to the existing career management system. The review process makes the program ideal for organizational nomination of employees to participate in special or unique opportunities. An especially critical linkage for this group of employees is between the activities of professional societies (seminars, conventions, symposiums) and development plans. Since the employee's personal commitment, loyalty, and motivation are directed toward this professional membership, they must be central pieces in the development plan for the individual.

Maintaining Visibility. Career plan status must be instituted as a legitimate and accepted topic at the executive level. The organization's strategic plan and business objectives should include a career management criterion, and every review should consider it, if only briefly. Top-level support is necessary to the ongoing effectiveness of this type of program—if the program is being monitored at the executive level, it is important by fiat. A few key career-planning "successes" can do wonders to generate interest in the program. Special events could be sponsored through the career management program (speakers, seminars, workshops). Organizational publications should be used consistently to present articles and special features relating to career management. Career-planning facilitators should receive special attention, with their efforts rewarded through recognition. An interdepartmental career-planning committee can be very helpful in planning between-department moves *and* in keeping the program alive as a viable, necessary, and important program.

Feedback to Employees. Employees deserve to know where they stand. If their career aspirations are clearly out of line with organizational realities, they need to get that feedback. Organizational evaluations can be very sensitive pieces of information to communicate to employees. Employees get a sense of how the boss views them, but it is very rare to receive feedback from levels any higher than the immediate supervisor. Depending on how this feedback is handled, an employee could end up feeling either comfortable with his or her role and motivated to perform or bitter and demotivated. The supervisor's role in this is all-important and should be an important part of his or her training. In cases where the individual's and organization's evaluations are really far apart, the career-planning facilitator should participate in the feedback process.

Another question that deserves attention is whether or not the individual should receive any feedback on those occasions when he or she is considered but not chosen for a position. There are pros and cons for either side, but they should be thought through. For example, giving the information helps the person determine the job-related characteristics (knowledge, activities, or the like) that are needed to become a more competitive candidate. This presupposes an objective selection system based on job-related qualifications. Given these conditions, feedback can be immensely valuable. However, in many cases, such feedback can be much more burdensome than the benefits warrant. Instead, the employee should be encouraged to develop in job-related areas without reference to being rejected for the job.

IMPLEMENTING A HUMAN RESOURCE REVIEW

Program Parameters

Complexity and Formality. Human resource programs such as those presented in chapter 4 can be so complex in their informational requirements that they are rejected out of hand or eventually sink under their own weight. Information gathering is important but can be addressed through systems that vary a great deal in complexity or formality. At the simplest, most informal level is the inevitable discussion between supervisors over lunch: "What do you think about Harry for that position in two months, then we can move Judy into Harry's position?" The fact is that the planning of people and positions occurs *anyway;* the challenge is for the organization to do it in a way that best serves the people and the organization. Not all organizations require the complexity or formality of the program that has been described here. To a large degree, the probability of losing highly talented professionals is heightened when they do not know where they stand—the consequences of this outward flow of talent to the organization needs to be weighed. The greater the consequences, the more formal the program should be. As with any program, the complexity of the review should be kept to the barest minimum necessary to meet organizational requirements.

Cost. Cost will vary with the complexity of the program and will be based mainly on the costs for development and the time required to gather and review the detailed information. Very little direct outlay of monies is required. Clerical processes and information storage incurs some cost, but if a detailed skills inventory is developed and computerized, maintenance at the requisite level of accuracy can be quite expensive.

Short- and Long-term Needs. Both short- and long-term needs can be met by a human resource review. With regard to short-term needs, career moves may be approved for the next twelve-month period. These moves should meet individual developmental needs and further the attainment of organizational objectives. Long-range plans could also be considered in broader terms—for example, in defining the skills and abilities that will be needed in the organization in three to five years. These are often critical considerations given professional talent and the need to keep pace with technological advancements. The criticality of making use of the organization's strategic plan is relevant here.

Vertical/Horizontal Emphasis. A human resource review is an ideal forum in which to plan the benefits of horizontal movement for both the organization and the individual. Both lateral and promotional career moves should be considered, as well as demotion or outplacement. Lateral, or horizontal, movement is viewed in very different ways by different organizations. In some, it is a sign that the employee has failed and been "shuffled aside"; in others it is an indication that the employee is being groomed for bigger and better things. In professional/scientific work, lateral movement is very often the norm as projects are completed, modified, or curtailed. There may be many opportunities to move from "research" to "development" and back again. These moves can be planned.

With a formal review mechanism, top-level management can approve lateral movement as part of a well-designed plan to broaden expertise before moving up. If this policy is made clear and supported, lateral movement (with appropriate salary action) can become a valuable training and motivational tool. This policy may also contribute to widening the exposure of the professional within the organization and the scientific peer field, a definite motivator. For example, consider the sequence: research . . . development . . . test . . . evaluation . . . application/introduction in order to develop technical depth *and* breadth.

Voluntary/Involuntary. Employees who are directly discussed in review meetings are usually defined by level and/or performance such that "participation" is involuntary. The individual career-planning component may be a voluntary method by which an employee not meeting the level/performance criteria could be brought to the attention of top management. Such self-initiated visibility may have beneficial effects if coupled with a clear record of competence and potential; or detrimental if not supported by performance.

Participants. In a large organization, the review process should move from bottom to top, such that one set of people would be reviewed at the director or senior director level, another higher level set at the vice-president level, and so on. Cutoffs would have to be established depending on the size and structure of the organization. Reviews could also be structured for unique groups, such as high-potential women and minorities, highly technical research and development people, fledgling scientists, broad-scoped generalists, or project managers; thereby linking the human resource review to special needs and affirmative action commitments.

Preimplementation Issues

Pros and Cons. Enough has been said on the positive side. What about the drawbacks of a professionally oriented human resource review? Few would argue that the objectives of a human resource review are not worthwhile—the issues are usually the more pragmatic ones such as: who prepares the forms, where is the information kept, how long will the review take, why is it necessary in the first place?

Many benefits of the review are not immediate and cannot easily be attributed to immediate profit. Therefore, support and use of the program can generally only be assured if it is required by the highest executives. If the chief executive officer (CEO) wants it and values it, you can be sure the program will work well. If support from the top is lacking, the information most likely will not even be collected. To be successful, the annual review must be a continuing process of information collection, culminating in the meeting. If it is just an annual meeting with little preparation and no follow-up, it will not work.

Developers. The human resource review program should be developed by a professional who has previous human-resources-planning experience and who is familiar with employee record-keeping systems. It is often advisable also to retain the services of a competent human resource consultant who is willing to work closely with the functional representative to tailor a program to that organization's needs and informational capabilities. The internal people from the human resource or personnel department must be involved in order to make the system compatible with the corporate system, while maintaining the uniqueness required in the functional area. Employee record-keeping systems were mentioned because of the heavy informational requirements of a program such as this. Enhancements to the existing system should be attempted if they improve the tracking capability of the system. The top-level initiator of the program must provide prudent counsel on the scope and depth appropriate to the organization. Organizations currently using similar programs should be investigated for workable ideas; resource books, such as this one, should be studied. The program developers must be ready to revise their program to make it workable: pull out the dead weight and focus on areas where results are seen.

Policies. Because plans are made to move people for developmental reasons, movement may be up, down, or sideways. Plans may allow or require the employee to pursue certain training or experiences outside of work. As Grass states, "Organizational practices must be developed which facilitate growth and recognition in the scientific professions. Encouragement should be given to peer discussions and technical exchanges inside and outside the organization, to the publishing of research results, and to participation in decisions on research initiatives and directions" (17, p. 231).

Organizational policies should ensure equitable compensation and benefit packages. For example, required training should be covered under an educational reimbursement policy. Examples of other developmental policies that relate to job assignments or reassignments are:

Professional Development. This policy encourages the professional development of employees through career planning and the annual review of human resources. This may involve lateral or promotional moves, transfers, temporary rotations, short-term job assignments, and/or project teams.

Developmental Lateral Movement. Where lateral movement is designated as developmental, the employee will receive salary treatment through the next appraisal period consistent with the performance rating received in the previous assignment.

Developmental Demotion. Employees moved to a lower salary-level position as a developmental move will retain their current salary level during the term of the assignment, which should not exceed twenty-four months. Salary treatment through the next appraisal period will be consistent with the performance rating received in the previous assignment.

Developmental Reassignments. When an employee has accepted a developmental assignment in another discipline or vice-presidential area and is not successful, every reasonable effort will be made to place him or her in a more suitable position while retaining the original salary level.

Performance Problems. In those situations where there appears to be a poor person-to-job match, but no disciplinary problem exists, the personnel department will facilitate the search for a better match within the department or organization. If there is no resolution, the employee may have to consider demotion, termination, or outplacement.

Procedures. It is recommended that a handbook be prepared that describes the review program in a usable way. Initial reactions to a program such as this will vary to the extent that the packaging of it clearly answers the following questions:

- Why is this being done?
- Who wants it done?

- What do I have to do?
- What do I need to have for the meeting?
- What will we talk about in the meeting?
- What will come out of the meeting?

Essentially, these questions deal with motivation, preparedness, and follow-up. The program and procedures must be packaged for the eye of a professional or manager with little human resources expertise. A standard structure is essential, but the procedures must not be bogged down in too much detail. Again, organizations differ a great deal in the extent to which forms and procedures are formalized.

Materials and Forms. The organizational review of human resources presented in chapter 4 is one example of a structured outline for such a review program. A preliminary description of this program originally appeared in the *Personnel Journal* (38). Again, content is likely to vary depending on the needs of the organization. Other personnel areas that might be included are salary/performance review, reorganization review, affirmative action review, productivity review, turnover review. Technical areas of review might relate to new projects staffing, professional development activities, scientific publishing, or professional/management career tracks.

Program Implementation

Introducing the Program. The overworked expression that "top-level management commitment is critical to success" is quite true with regard to this program. It takes work and discipline to develop the materials necessary and spend the time required to prepare for the review. For some, the objectives may appear ill-defined, vague, or unnecessary. One thing is guaranteed to make it work—the CEO and respected professionals saying they expect to see it initiated and see it work. The program must be sold by the CEO and the functional professionals to senior management and the professional/scientific groups. The functional area's management will play a strong central role in the introduction and administration of the program and, therefore, must make the time and give thought to the most workable implementation plan. The program must obtain the support of top-level management and then use organizational channels to communicate the program to all employees. In this way, the top-levels are able systematically to communicate downward their overall plans, goals, and human resources philosophy.

Training. Beyond explicit descriptions of the purposes and procedures, training in the formal sense will not be required. The program developer should sit through the reviews, both to serve as a consultant and to develop first hand ideas for constructive revisions to the program.

Commitment. As previously mentioned, a program such as this will exist and succeed to the degree that the CEO and respected professionals make it a priority. If everyone accepts its importance, it will be important. Preparing for and conducting the review is a time-consuming chore, and if it can be avoided by managers or professionals, it will be. Commitment on the front end must precede implementation.

Schedule. A human resource review program will generally look ahead one year (short-term needs), then ahead two to five years (long-term needs). Given the time it takes to develop and implement such a program, which can be three to four months for one person, the investment can be quite worthwhile.

Linkage with Current Programs. Every organization has some system by which people are selected or placed into jobs. The organization knows when a job becomes available—but does not often know when a person "becomes available." The human resource review systems identify people within the organization who will be ready to move when the job is available. Review systems also identify the skills and abilities of those people, creating a "talent pool" of available talent within the organization. The linkage to the selection and placement system is the main one to be established, but there are many more.

Virtually every personnel function can be linked to the annual review: compensation (salary projections); recruiting (realistic, proven career paths); equal employment opportunities (affirmative action review); records (streamlined procedures); training (identification of individual and organization-wide needs).

Linkage with Planned Programs. If the organization has not yet developed a career-planning program, it should already be clear that the human resource review can provide an important stepping-stone. Potential for advancement and interests in professional/managerial positions could be described either by the person or by his or her supervisor. In any case, the program should review both people and positions. Vosburgh noted the importance of this linkage in an earlier work:

> ... the annual review of human resources provides the linking pin mechanism by which the organization officially sanctions individuals' career plans and ties them to its own human resources needs. The resulting plans are guaranteed to be more realistic (since a level-by-level review occurs) and more attainable (since organizational needs are considered) than unilaterally developed plans based only on an employee's self-analysis. The systems approach demands that effective career planning be tied to the organization's identified human resources needs, to its training and development program, and to its selection and placement system. Without these factors, it won't take employees long to see that career planning amounts to little more than a useless and time-consuming exercise. However, if a systems approach is used and the

critical linking pin function of the annual review is not overlooked, then the career planning program can be a valuable motivational tool and serve both individual and organizational needs effectively (38, p. 837).

Program Administration. The vice-president of human resources (or similar position) and the equivalent executive over the professional function should be responsible for overseeing the program. Essentially, this involves coordinating the collection of information and the integration of the review's output into other programs. The vice-president of human resources would be responsible for ensuring that the procedures are followed in an accurate and timely manner. Furthermore, involving other executive-level decision-makers in the program is a critical role for the personnel executive.

The collection of information is probably the single biggest task confronting the administrator of a review program. To the degree that the personnel department is justifiably responsible for maintaining some of the records needed in the meeting, personnel should be directly required to produce them (even if this is a time-consuming chore). On the other hand, some information should be developed or maintained by the functional director or vice-president. It is critical at the outset to identify clearly *who* in the review system is responsible for *what*. This will often be largely determined by historical precedents regarding the level at which decisions are made and the degree to which personnel is centralized and influential.

Information Storage and Retrieval. Virtually every modern organization should consider placing the type of data that is required in the review on an automated system. The tracking of this type of information (changes in personnel, job status, and so on) should occur throughout the year to avoid the big scramble just before the review. In lieu of an automated system, simple logging procedures should be developed and integrated into the normal flow of records.

Evaluation. The success of the human resource review is oftentimes more in the eye of the beholder than it is a quantifiable dimension. Key decision-makers will recognize the human resources side of their strategic business planning—or they may just appreciate its impact to a greater degree than prior to the initiation of the review system. The fact that an organization develops and uses such a program often means the accrual of some tangential benefits, such as the goodwill and positive public relations generated by being the type of organization that cares about its people and its future enough to conduct a review of human resources.

Revisions. With a complex program such as this, it is rare to achieve perfection at the beginning. The program administrator must treat the first year's process as a pilot and remain flexible for needed changes that do not destroy the integrity or worth of the program. This latter caveat is included because there will always be those who would try to undercut and destroy this type of program for any number of reasons (it threatens their power; "too much paperwork"; "not my problem, not my job").

Additional Linkage. Throughout the first year's implementation, consider other functions that can be attached to the review. For example, if salary planning is done once a year in October, why not hold the review at that time and accomplish both purposes?

Maintaining Visibility. Keep track of, and document, human resource review "success stories." Make sure everyone knows how important the top people think this program to be. Retain a willingness to revise where necessary. Redesign the records procedures to incorporate ongoing data collection. Promote the program in the organization-sponsored media (newsletters, bulletin boards, and the like).

Feedback to Employees. Much of this section has been written under the assumption that some of the information about a person and his or her career ambitions would be fed back to the person, with additional recommendations for training or education. This is not *necessarily* the case. In fact, employees below director level need not even know the program exists! However, the organization loses many of the positive attitudinal benefits of the review by taking such a secretive stance.

BARRIERS TO IMPLEMENTATION

Career-planning practitioners, consultants, theorists, teachers, and people from many backgrounds write about career planning. Much of the work makes career planning sound better than apple pie or chocolate chip cookies (a personal bias), and just as easy to "bake" and "pass out" to others. However, all the proselytizing in the world cannot remove the negative experience that many organizations have had with "career planning" or "career management" programs. All too often, these are marketed as the panacea for a multitude of organizational problems.

Some often mentioned reasons for failure can be characterized from the middle manager's perspective, for example:

"You should have seen all the forms!"
"I heard how much that garbage cost the company!"
"I just never felt comfortable with the program—no one ever really trained me to use it."
"I've had a good record getting my employees advanced—I don't need this program."
"Those personnel people must think I don't have enough to do. Well, they will just have to wait."
"The first I heard of this program was when I got

these six booklets in the mail—now what am I supposed to do?"

"I never heard my boss or the vice-president mention this program—it must not be very important."

"What do *I* gain by spending my time on this?"

"It seemed like a really good program, but it never really fit into the company."

"People were excited about it at first, but I haven't heard anything about it for months."

An AMA study of 225 companies revealed a less-than-exciting track record regarding the effectiveness of career planning programs: 3 percent very effective, 29 percent moderately effective, 54 percent partially effective, and 14 percent very ineffective (39). The least successful programs were not linked to other personnel programs, did not have clear top management support, and did not train or motivate (reward) supervisors and managers to act as career counselors. An interesting juxtapositioning of the following results from the same AMA survey paints a revealing picture:

88 percent believed career planning was not a fad.
86 percent of managers believed career planning was needed.
85 percent of senior management believed career planning was an important part of employee development.
87 percent believed few supervisors are equipped to do individual career planning.
58 percent of supervisors believed that career planning was not part of their job.

The last two percentages show a clear disparity between the organizational need and the ability and attitude of the supervisor to support the program. The statements, "No one ever showed me how" and "Not my problem, not my job" appear to describe the situation.

Some of the results of the AMA study were more optimistic:

94 percent believed that career planning did not disrupt the organization.
97 percent believed that career planning improved the use of employee talent.
92 percent felt the programs helped employees use other personnel systems more effectively.
91 percent felt career planning enhances current job performance.
89 percent reported turnover does not increase as a result of career planning.

This last percentage contradicts one often mentioned reason for not engaging in career management activities.

The upshot of this analysis is that career management programs sound great and, in the last decade, have been slickly packaged and marketed as discrete individual modules or programs. Too often, an organization will simply buy into a given program without laying the groundwork for more comprehensive solutions that address the issues within that organization. Even the most well designed program will fail unless there are support systems to tie it to the existing personnel and human resource program.

Concern that is expressed by employees regarding career issues is often a signal that much more is wrong with the organization than simply a lack of a career management system. Leach argues that what he calls the organization development (OD) climate largely determines the success of a new career development program: "When career development programs fail (career-planning modules, open posting, assessment centers, etc.), the first place to begin the critique is not with the career development procedure, but the OD context in which these programs are embedded. Even the most sophisticated and costly career development programs cannot flourish in impoverished work climates and cultures" (26, p. 31). In this context, the term *organization development* is used in a very broad sense to indicate the situation into which a career development program is thrust. The point is that this situation must be considered as a major implementation issue.

An equally important consideration in the implementation of a career management system would necessarily be the training required in the organization. Many programs require a level of supervisory sophistication that does not exist in the work force. Simply announcing a program and expecting immediate commitment and ability from supervisors is unrealistic. Attitudes within the organization might also be a stumbling block. Unless a case is made regarding the needs that the program is addressing, it is very likely that the majority of people in the organization will perceive the career management system to be "just another personnel program." In this case, the commitment to the program is not there, nor is the ability to carry it out; therefore, the program fails. The organizational programs that are described in this book face these potential pitfalls also, and strategies for avoiding them are addressed.

Threats to the Organization. Career management activities may challenge existing power structures—that is, if objective, job-related, standardized selection procedures are instituted, the existing informal system may be threatened. Although informal power systems will always be present, career management systems tend to reduce the subjective, discretionary power of some people by increasing the available information on which to make high-quality decisions. For example, an organizational review of human resources (see chapter 4) provides a shared explicit description of the current organization and a plan for the future organization. The statement, "Information about new projects, plans, and jobs will be shared with all employees," is an example of a *policy* that would support career management objectives. A career-planning system might then yield identifiable groups of talent to meet the organization's needs. The selection system matches job requirements and individual qualifications. This type of integrated system makes it much more difficult for a few so-called king-makers to emerge, or for a "political" or "buddy" system to thrive. Those currently holding such power may be extremely skeptical of alternative systems. The human social system will always have an important interplay with whatever system exists. The trick is to involve the key "power people" in the planning stage of the new career management system. Give them an opportunity to work *for* the program, rather than alienate them and ensure resistance and perhaps efforts to undermine the process.

In short, career management is not an apolitical process—it challenges the status quo and tends to democratize the selection process. Sensitivity to this fact is necessary throughout the planning, implementation, and administration of new programs.

At some point in their career, all employees will receive some type of organizational feedback on their potential. Some will decide on their own that they are at the proper level and in the correct role, for example, the scientist who does not want to be a manager. How does this decision on the part of the individual become accepted by the organization? Is there a means by which both the individual and the organization are equal partners in these career management decisions? Is there a role for the "irreplaceable pro" who wants to remain in a professional role?

Threats to the Individual. Although we have been quick to extol the beneficial aspects of career planning from both the individual's and the organization's points of view, in all fairness the potential negative aspects should also be explored. Involvement in career-planning activities usually results in some type of feedback regarding one's job performance and career potential. This is a rare opportunity for organizational feedback over and above that which is received from one's immediate supervisor. When this is positive, it can have a strong motivational effect. However, there will also be cases where the feedback essentially says the person is "at the proper level and should be held in position," or even more devastating, "performance improvement plan required immediately for retention."

If such a program of organizational feedback occurs and it is voluntary, then the individual may undergo considerable anxiety over whether to enter the program and risk negative feedback. If everyone receives feedback, the manner in which the negative comments are handled is very important to the integrity and motivational benefit of the program. In any case, the program will be threatening to some people, creating a "stressful situation."

A related issue is that of the supervisor's power and role in career management activities. If the supervisor-subordinate relationship is good, then the career management process can be very beneficial. However, if the supervisor-subordinate relationship is poor, the individual is likely to conclude that "the boss not only makes this job miserable but has also bad-mouthed me such that my career chances are ruined." This conclusion might be reached regardless of the formality of the career management system. The supervisor holds considerable fate control *anyway;* the addition of career management responsibilities may be perceived as threatening by the individual. In these cases, an independent career-planning facilitator within one's department or a neutral career counselor within the personnel department may be able to modify the supervisor's influence in the process.

The individual may also perceive subtle pressures either to participate or not to participate in a voluntary career-planning program. Going against the grain could then have real or imagined consequences, creating considerable anxiety. For example, the individual might be very interested in moving into another functional or technical area and thus be perceived as committing mutiny. Cross-functional moves for developmental purposes might be a goal of the career-planning program, but the strong departmental norm may work against this ever occurring. Policies can never fully protect the individual against these exigencies, but the issues must surely be surfaced and confronted if the program is to have its full impact.

For the scientist or engineer, career management programs may appear to be yet another paper game by the management people. The scientist might prefer to be left alone with his or her technical work, letting others worry about administrative paperwork. Scientists tend to prefer "scientific competence" as the means of authority, rather than the traditional organizational trappings of power, title, and policies (2). They are unlikely to be easily impressed or become involved in yet another administrative program. Benefits based on *their* value system should be advanced, such as opportunities for greater professional visibility or autonomy. This can be accomplished through policies that set up reward systems based on what is important to the professional rather than what managers assume to be important.

Overcoming Resistance to Change

The fact that people and groups within organizations often resist change is "one of the most ubiquitous organizational phenomenons" (36, p. 122).

Career management programs often unwittingly and

in an unplanned way ask people to go along with a large measure of change. For example, making people a corporate rather than a departmental asset takes away a good deal of managerial control and autonomy. Many R&D managers may have developed the habit of allowing only managerial employees to leave. Losing a top scientist and acquiring a *potentially* top scientist means productivity will drop and, realistically, that the manager will have to pick up a lot of the slack and do much of the work that used to be delegated. The system must reward recruiting and developing good people and provide a mechanism that allows them to be *replaced* with good or potentially good people. This requires *change*.

Even though people do resist change, a compelling but often overlooked counterargument must be faced: people and groups within organizations also *accept* change. This suggests that *change* per se is not being resisted and that the problem should be reformulated in terms of the interplay between the strategy for effecting change and the social/psychological/structural factors present in the groups being affected by the change. In addition, it would be wise to assume that resistance to change is by itself neither good nor bad. Rather, it is always a warning signal that something is amiss and requires attention (25).

Organizations differ in their structure and their reaction to change. Tannenbaum differentiates a mechanistic and an organic model with fairly predictable impacts on reaction to change (37). The *mechanistic* organization is structured in a strict hierarchy with tight controls and closed systems and communication channels. In response to environmental or technological change this organization would most likely create a special group as part of the hierarchy with the purpose of insulating and protecting the whole organization from external or internal influences to change. This characterization is drastic, but suggests an organization that would reject career management techniques as a threat to the status quo. Almost as an antithesis, the *organic* organization is much more flexible and adaptive to change. Controls tend to be more situational and flexible, and systems or communication channels more open. The extreme example is a highly interdependent and integrative system in which members respond mutually and attack problems holistically.

This way of looking at organizational structure and reaction to change may in reality have limited applicability. This is because every reader in management will probably come to the conclusion that theirs is a truly "organic" organization, regardless of evidence to the contrary. This perceptual error may be especially evident at the *top* of the professional management ladder, where the person is characteristically very bright but much better with "things" than with people.

In addition to structural considerations, human social processes must be considered in the implementation of new programs. The idea of getting people involved in planning changes that affect them was historically a very popular conception, but there has been increasing realization that participation may lead to more problems than it solves (25). Coch and French's famous study (9) which extolled the virtues and effectiveness of participation generated considerable research as well as do-it-yourself recipes for managers. We are reminded by others that participation is based on respect (16), and it cannot be bought like a typewriter, conjured up, or created artificially. Lawrence also emphasizes that "participation is a feeling on the part of people, not just the mechanical act of being called in to take part in discussion" (25, p. 222).

It is true that research has provided numerous illustrations of the positive aspects of involving employees in planning for change and that this process "can help bring about their adjustment to changing conditions. People tend to support what they create" (16, p. 273). The trend, however, has been to view participation not as a panacea for effecting change, but in a more limited role (to be described). The tragedy of this bit of history is that participation came to be used as a coercive gimmick to get people to do what you wanted them to do in the first place. People resent being treated this way.

One aspect of the complex problem of resistance to change is that change agents are often overly eager in their promotion of the external technology of change while remaining oblivious to the people and the social arrangements involved. Lawrence terms this "self-preoccupation" resulting in "blind-spots" and an inability to understand the sources of resistance (25). He differentiates the types of change: "The *technical* aspect of the change is the making of a measurable modification in the physical routines of the job. The *social* aspect of the change refers to the way those affected by it think it will alter their established relationships in the organization" (25, p. 223). The main argument is basically that people resist social change, not technical change.

Work groups have explicit tasks to perform; they evolve specific ways of working together, generate binding interpersonal relationships, common values, and group norms. As a subgroup within the organization, it shares the coping and survival concerns of the organization as a whole. The unilateral imposition of a requirement to change may be viewed as threatening to the existent social structure. To the workers, the present system may seem satisfactory, and the purpose of the change unclear. Communication and information flow within the organization appear critical in this regard. If the workers do not understand the situation that prompted the change at the time management demands it, both resentment and resistance tend to be generated.

Although the basis of the authority to initiate change may or may not be viewed as legitimate, the method that is used and the attitude of those presenting the change are very important. As Flory and MacKenzie point out, people do not resist change out of perversity, but will to protest against the methods used to bring about the change (12).

It is also important to realize that in the professional and scientific community, "legitimate" authority is not the be-all, end-all, as it is in classical production or manufacturing concerns. Authority based on "expertise" and respect for one's colleagues is usually more important. This is the informal system of which many managers are not aware.

Devising Implementation Strategies

Negative Strategies. Based on a wide variety of implementation attempts, it is possible to generate a set of strategies that are virtually guaranteed to result in negative outcomes and resistance to change. It is surprising how often these failures occur. Numerous sources are cited below, especially Lawrence (25). Although the original source did not present these in this negative fashion, the ridiculousness of these often unplanned strategies is highlighted when presented in this manner. Following this list of tips will only ensure resistance to program implementation and failure.

STRATEGIES TO AVOID
- Ignore your professional, scientific, individual contributors in plans you make; since they lack management experience, their feelings, experience, awareness of practical problems, and insight into social consequences cannot possibly have any relevance.
- Confront people directly and accuse them of resisting change; do not consider that it takes time to provide coaching and training needed to develop the skills to carry out the new program.
- When planning the program, concentrate only on the concrete details of the procedures and the forms; do not consider how the people involved will receive it.
- Expect that people will automatically resist the proposed change and treat this attitude as a self-fulfilling prophecy.
- Treat resistance as something to be *overcome,* not as a signal that something is wrong.
- Explain the program in highly technical/behavioral/psychological terms so it does not generate questions; cause confusion rather than informed judgment.
- If you must use participation, use it as a gimmick to coerce people to do what you wanted them to do in the first place.
- Make sure your program description carries the implication of a criticism of the people currently making the decisions.
- Impose the program as impersonally and unilaterally as possible through directives, commands, and demands; assume your power to be legitimate and unquestioned.
- Underestimate, neglect, and abuse your people; they will not remember when it comes time to enlist their support.
- Make the program appear to move toward a "more efficient, less personal, more highly specialized type of activity that will disturb the personal and social adjustment the individual has made" (10, p. 227).
- Once the program decision has been made, do not involve the group that is affected in planning the implementation (36, p. 123).
- When giving reasons for the program (and try to avoid this), emphasize your personal goals and do not mention what the organization hopes to accomplish (12, p. 61).
- Ignore the group habit patterns that have developed and put excessive pressure on the professional staff so they fear failure in the new roles expected of them (12, p. 61).
- Make the cost and effort appear too high and the reward too low (12, p. 61).
- Never notify people of the program until it must be implemented immediately (7).
- Make sure the advantages to the individual are never mentioned or considered.

Positive Strategies. Although the inverse of the above suggestions could be used as tips on good strategy, a number of investigators have proposed steps on planning change so that resistance is minimized. The following represent an abstraction and synthesis of suggestions made by Carvell (6) and Lippitt (27).

STRATEGIES TO FOLLOW
- Build a trusting work climate in which people feel free to identify needs for change.
- Communicate the reasons and goals of the change; clarify the need and what the change will achieve.
- Establish broad guidelines for meeting the stated objectives.
- Allow the details to be filled in by the group being affected by the change; involve the employees in planning the change at this stage.
- Encourage airing of fears and resentment, and encourage feedback of any type in order to relieve anxieties about the change. Specifically, ask the questions:

  What would make the professional balk at participation?

What would make the supervisor balk at participation?
Often the answer is "paperwork for personnel"—the individual never sees the direct benefit to him or her.
- Give consideration to group norms and habits.
- State the rewards and benefits attendant on the change for the employee, and keep these promises.

Resistance to change is a very complex phenomenon, yet ever-present in organizations that *must* change in order to survive and compete. Looking back on the issues, it does not seem appropriate to conclude that people "naturally" resist change or do not understand that change is necessary in a changing world and competitive market. It is clear that people resent being treated as pawns or fools and are not sheep to be directed blindly. *Human* resources are some of the most valuable in organizations, and signs of resistance are best viewed from a social, psychological perspective as warning signals that the method of change—not necessarily the change itself—is inappropriate for the existing system. There is no golden solution to the phenomenon of resistance to change, largely because the solution does not lie in stifling or overcoming resistance, but in its creative use.

Synergy and Entropy in Systems Development

One of the most frustrating and perplexing problems facing all new career management programs is the degenerative nature of their impact. A few people can create a lot of excitement about a program, it can be implemented with a lot of fanfare, and it will most likely die a natural death within two to three years, not with a bang but a whimper. Why does this happen and how can such cyclical attempts at systemwide coordination of human resources be avoided? Two interesting concepts will be used to explore this situation: synergy and entropy.

Synergy occurs when individuals or groups work together to produce something that is greater than the sum of their independent contributions. The synergistic effect represents the epitome of optimism, that anything can be conquered, won, or discovered if we work together. Entropy, on the other hand, represents the epitome of pessimism. The entropic effect originates from a principle of thermodynamics which posits that matter, energy, physical resources, and the like can only be transformed in one direction—from useful to useless, from ordered to disordered—in other words, the natural state of the world is degenerative. Anything put into place will wear down; the greater the accumulation of energy and resources, the greater the influence of entropy.

How do these concepts relate to career management system implementation? The concept of entropy implies certain counterbalancing solutions, which are explored by Rifkin and Howard (35). Although their treatment of the subject might be considered somewhat overzealous, we can glean some useful prescriptions from their book:

- *Slow down.* We might speculate that with less expenditure of high-charged energy, there is less opportunity for major erosions in resources and systems. Take the time to develop a system that fits the organization.
- *Decentralize.* The smaller the operating unit, the less decay. The closer the system to the needs and rewards of the person, the less likely it is to be dropped.
- *Conserve.* Make the most of the energy and resources available, because the theory states that it is finite and slipping away. Integrate your career management system with ongoing systems—let it "ride" on them.
- *Participate.* The more participatory the process, the less the energy flow through the system, which reduces the accumulation of disorder. Get *people* to contribute to and sustain the system.

These four principles, whether arrived at through the second law of thermodynamics or not, ring true as a caveat regarding program features that help resist decay and erosion.

Turning to the most optimistic world view of synergism, we can also draw some helpful conclusions. The concept assumes that individuals and/or groups are working together with a common purpose toward a common goal. The concept also assumes a level of efficiency that uses individual input in a manner maximizing the group output. These are two big assumptions. How can we ensure them so that we can gain from the synergistic effect?

A major first step is for the administration to discuss openly the expectations and needs regarding career management systems with the potential users. Rather than design a system or buy a package and then "sell" it to the users, listen to the issues they raise. Clarify expectations and draft a statement of purpose and the goals to which the whole group can strive. Then identify how individuals within the group can contribute to the shared goals. For example, in the career management area, some individuals are probably at a stage where they would gain dramatically from the attention of a well-respected sponsor. Others are likely to be at a stage where they can provide a mentorlike role model for younger employees. This type of situation might lead to a locally developed and operated mentoring system that will outlive the personnel department's forms by many years.

The key to unleashing the positive power of synergy is to define common concerns and goals and then provide a unified direction channeling the energy in beneficial ways. The key to protecting against the negative drain of entropy is to apply the minimum resources at the lowest level necessary to achieve the purpose. Human resource programs, and career management systems in particular, would benefit from the application of these principles.

GATEWAYS FOR IMPLEMENTATION

Identifying the Needs

Career management programs are not usually developed for professionals in the absence of perceived needs relating to securing, developing, and retaining talent. Sometimes these produce internal pressure for action and the need is obvious. More often, lots of little symptoms will exist which, taken together, indicate a problem with career management, or needs that career management programs might address. These needs are summarized below in five categories:

- Recruiting
- Retention
- Knowledge
- Technology development
- Scientific excellence

In each of these cases, the issue of shared commitment should be raised, that is, what exactly is the fundamental concern over each issue? What is the priority? These five categories were explored in depth by Morrison in research related to discretionary funding of laboratory projects (28).

Recruiting. Organizations develop reputations regarding their human resource emphasis that definitely affect their ability to recruit talented people. Within the best academic programs, the visibility and desirability of some organizations over others is clear. More and more companies pitch a "career path" line to young, ambitious scientists and engineers. If the organization is not involved in recruiting, how is new talent brought in? How successful are recruiting efforts? Does the description of the position and the organization incorporate career and long-range concerns? An effectively functioning recruiting program is a key component of a career management system, but it must be supported by visible programs that are in place within the organization. The recruiting program simply allows you to advertise the other more functional pieces.

Retention. Hiring a good person and retaining that person are two ends of the same continuum. Expectations that are aroused on the recruiting end must be met on the job. The organization undoubtedly loses people—the question is how this process is managed, if at all. Are the best people leaving in attempts to stay on the leading edge of technology in their fields? Are there common factors involved in *when* people leave, for example, three years after joining? Do realistic career opportunities exist and have they been communicated?

Knowledge. Is there "knowledge deterioration" within your organization? Kaufman contends that challenging, responsible work stimulates the mature scientist to remain current, and that this occurs only secondarily through continuing education courses or formal education (19). In addition, people who are stimulated by their work to keep current are not as likely to become obsolete as people who are not (32). If the job itself is so important, why isn't more attention directed toward the motivating qualities of the job? "Job enrichment" per se is not the ultimate answer here, partly because of the static approach usually taken. In reality, today's enriched job may become tomorrow's mundane job because the incumbent *learns*. As the incumbent learns, performance is better, and the boss gradually becomes dependent on that level of performance. This leads to a natural reluctance to release that employee to another job. In a few years the "enriched" employee then becomes obsolete or used up.

Technology Development. What new technologies will serve the organization years down the road? How will the organization secure and advance this technology to ensure organizational viability? For example, consider the tax specialist as laws change or the pharmacist as new drugs are introduced or, most conspicuously, the computer science specialist as both hardware and software change. This issue is critical from a career management viewpoint because sponsors of applied work look for the application of known and perfected technologies or processes, and for professional groups that can deliver a known quantity. Numerous noted authorities all stress the importance of discretionary laboratory-based funds that can be used to proceed beyond the limits of contracted, programmed applications (13,28,32). This helps the organization serve the dual needs of providing end-products that are managed against time, manpower, and budgetary constraints while at the same time remaining innovative and ahead of the competition. Discretionary funds also help the professionals within the organization meet their driving needs for scientific excellence unfettered by contractual limitations. Both organizational and individual career management issues related to technological development are addressed effectively through the use of discretionary funds.

Scientific Excellence. As an analogy to genetic inbreeding, there are inbred effects of a scientific pursuit carried on by a group of professionals over a period of years *without* any external examination or comment by others. Professionals within the larger scientific community may have a fresh perspective to offer which advances the state of the art. It is important to realize that much of this scientific-base augmentation is "free" because critiques and discussions occur informally through professional contacts, workshops, and conferences. Dewhirst, Arvey, and Brown demonstrated how important this type of professional interchange was to the performance and satisfaction of research personnel in a large federally funded laboratory (11, pp. 56–63).

The issue is well recognized in the professional field, but there are competing management-dictated demands that may work against a climate of "free interchange." Management is partially defined as a control process designed to focus individual abilities, motivations, and aspirations on organizationally sanctioned and defined group pursuits. To allow total freedom would result in no coordination and no concerted effort toward agreed-upon goals. The fear of management is loss of control. Yet, management also is very utilitarian in its bottom-line concerns such that a measure of scientific review and professional interchange will be accepted if it results in demonstrable outcomes that move the organization forward. The critical point is that this is another area in which both individual and organizational career management needs are met by a very simple process. How does this issue translate to your organization? Where are the opportunities to expand the professional base *and* move the business forward? You may want to try to fit your organization on a continuum of total freedom to publish, exchange information, attend professional society meetings versus restricted access versus no access. Then consider the continuum of total company support versus pay your own way.

In each of these areas (recruiting, retention, knowledge, technology development, and scientific excellence) both individual and organizational concerns have been raised. New programs must not be perceived as either the power-driven desire of management to control or the selfish desire of professionals to extend their reputation. The issues go much deeper in that the fates of the organization and of the individuals comprising it are intertwined. Needs that are identified must evidence this interdependency and thereby gain the support of both the managerial controllers and the professional contributors.

Acknowledgment of this interdependency is also critical from another angle—that is, the distinction between the managerial controller role and the professional contributor role is often blurred. Management dabbles with hands-on work, and professionals often have supervisory and managerial responsibility. These facts should be recognized and false dichotomies challenged. Shared perception of issues and involvement in identifying needs will generally also lead to wide-based support for programs.

Clarifying Roles: Who Does What?

Career management sounds as though it is the concern of the personnel department, yet this is not really so. Career management is also clearly the concern of individuals whose lives are directly affected. To succeed, career management requires departmental commitment and support; if a "personnel program," a straw man, is all that is set up, career management is tantamount to "forms without substance." The program is defined by the process, not the forms or procedures that drive it. The process will be controlled by the department and not by "personnel," so its success will depend on involvement at the local functional group's level.

In many organizations, the personnel department clearly has an important and central role in the development, management, use, and evaluation of career management systems. In these organizations, personnel elucidates issues and involves others in defining solutions. Personnel may facilitate communication, consolidate recommendations, coordinate organization-wide strategies, train users, centralize information, and oversee administration of a career management system. In that case, "personnel" becomes the central clearinghouse for career-related information as well as for business strategy and position information.

The professional or the scientist in a research-and-development (R&D) organization is less likely to experience these roles from someone down in the "personnel office." Morrison conducted a study of personnel departments in the navy's six large R&D labs (28). Contrary to expectations, the results showed that R&D functions required about 10–20 percent *less* personnel support than non-R&D functions. Upon further investigation, it was discovered that the R&D groups were doing a large portion of their own personnel work (recruiting, writing job descriptions, teaching in-house technical courses). When these hours were added to those provided by the personnel department, it was shown that the highly professional/scientific R&D functions did in fact require 10–20 percent *more* personnel support than non-R&D functions. The most successful personnel functions in these labs were those staffed by people who were excellent facilitators, working closely with the functions they supported.

In the absence of the personnel department's involvement in these issues, or due to a limited power base, separate departments often develop mini-systems on their own and run them independent of any organization-wide system. This gives some of the benefits of career management, but the single-department approach is very limited with regard to the two main objectives of such programs: to move the organization foward and to move people forward. The larger the base of career management within an organization, the better these objectives are met. For professionals or scientists who have the opportunity to grow within technical specialties, the system can be much more decentralized in its operations, but policy must continue to be centralized for consistency.

Who then should do what? There is no *one* answer for that, but as a reader of this book, you hold one key to the answer, and it's you. Whether you are reading it from the manager's viewpoint or the professional's viewpoint, there are concrete suggestions throughout this book of actions which can be taken at both the organizational and individual level. Apart from your involvement, the involvement of other individuals and organizational units should be clearly identified. You might want to do this right now. That is, who will be responsible in your current situation for:

- Identifying issues
- Facilitating communication
- Examining alternative solutions
- Consolidating recommendations
- Selecting the best solution
- Developing relevant materials
- Coordinating organization-wide strategies
- Training users
- Collecting information
- Centralizing information
- Using information
- Administering the system
- Evaluating the system's usefulness
- Revising the system

Aiming for Comprehensiveness

With a little revision of French and Bell's taxonomy related to the implementation of organizational intervention (14), we can propose the following components of any new program design:

- Diagnosis and planning
- Action and evaluation
- Process maintenance

Diagnosis and Planning. Diagnosis will reveal the current state of the organization and the processes that maintain its viability. It may also focus on the individual in order to ask questions of performance and potential. Typical diagnostic methods used at this stage of implementation include:

- Direct observation
- Interviews
- Questionnaires
- Surveys
- Task forces
- Panel discussions
- Review of policies and procedures
- Review of organizational records
- Observation of group meetings and departmental dynamics and similar situations

During the diagnostic stage these methods could be used to determine the organization's readiness to accept and use career management programs. The following topics might be investigated.

- Individual attitudes and opinions
- Organizational climate and culture
- Historical management practices
- Degree of participation in goal-setting and decision-making processes
- Relative distribution of power
- Effectiveness of a team approach to work
- Valued skills, abilities, traits
- Commonality of individual and organizational goals
- Competitive versus cooperative norms
- Constraints (external and internal)
- Collaborative climate between groups

Diagnosis might also target the individual, for example:

- Performance in the current position
- Potential for future positions
- Managerial skill strengths and needs
- Match with organization's norms and values
- Match with position's ability and skill requirements
- Future expectations
- Constraints (external and internal)
- Motivational dynamics or deficiencies

The first set of issues relate to human resource planning (as dealt with in chapter 4) and the second set to career planning (as described in chapters 9 to 11). The two processes co-mingle, as do the diagnostic components. The *process* of diagnosis is considered as important as the *results:* the communicative process is either "opened up" or "shut down" by the method of diagnosis. The extent of active collaboration between the user departments and the coordinating department or consultant will have a great impact on the efficacy of the program's execution. This diagnosis could occur as part of an annual organizational review, such as that described in chapter 4.

Planning naturally follows from diagnosis as the information collectors become information analyzers. The question, "What does it all mean and where do we go from here?" occurs at this stage. The level of sophistication, the cost, and the program components should derive from the diagnosis stage. Everyone involved in the diagnosis should continue to be involved in the planning stage. If the personnel department blocks the involvement of local management or if the local management disenfranchises the professional, then the program is unlikely to succeed.

Action and Evaluation. According to this model, the action component is next, which involves execution against the plan. The plan should translate general goals into observable, measurable actions or behavior. The actions must then be relevant and instrumental to goal attainment. Evaluation, therefore, becomes a natural, ongoing extension of the actions because actions are consistently linked to the measurable plan.

Process Maintenance. The process maintenance component of program design is particularly important for career management systems. Initial excitement and expectations or initial passivity and concern might easily change to a stable, positive reaction, especially if the following skills are exercised (14):

- Detect and cope with problems, that is, turn problems into opportunities
- Test the relevance of the program to the organization's needs
- Test for the timeliness and accuracy of previous interventions
- Check for intended and unintended consequences of the program
- Take steps to ensure continued viability and success

Not only is program maintenance an issue, but so is the setting of realistic expectations regarding the length of time required to get the system or program started up and running well. The length of time required to produce top-notch, unequivocally clear output from a career management system can be quite long compared to most organizational programs. Professional and scientific people can usually accept this longer time orientation, but managers are usually oriented toward short-term goals, and this could easily become an issue.

The message is that with career management programs, the initial positioning of a new system is critical but in itself does not ensure continued viability. Continuing maintenance of the process, procedures, policies, and outcomes must occur. This conclusion cannot be overstated. For some reason, people expect magic from systems such as those discussed in this book. Part of the fault may rest with the overselling of program benefits, and part with the lack of process maintenance when the novelty wears off. French and Bell's conclusion is that the extent of follow-up and maintenance explains the numerous short-term failures and the few long-term successes (14).

Summarizing the Program Implementation

A large segment of the organization development (OD) literature is devoted to the examination of variables that appear to influence the success of new program implementation. These discussions are especially relevant to career management systems—they strike at the heart of both the individual *and* the organization. Summarizing the contributions of numerous OD professionals (3,4, 15,21), there are several significant influences on program success:

PREIMPLEMENTATION
- Key people see the problem and recognize the relevance of career management techniques.
- There are both internal *and* external pressures to change.
- There is commitment to a long-term process of change.
- Top management provides support and involvement throughout the process.

IMPLEMENTATION
- An external consultant or top-level company practitioner begins at the top and involves all levels.
- An accurate diagnosis and choice of new programs or processes is made.
- Use is made of collaborative fact finding, problem solving, and decision making.
- A new model of the organization and its processes is generated to guide changes.
- Small, early successes are highlighted and expanded upon.
- Positive changes occur in the organization's climate.
- The resource (external consultant or internal pro) conducts prework and follow-up.

POSTIMPLEMENTATION
- Program processes are checked for congruence with existing organizational structure and policies.
- Internal resources to maintain the program are developed.
- Expectations raised by the program are met.

This list should reinforce the fact that a program cannot be simply taken off the shelf and inserted into an organization without some concern and attention to the human factors and structural and historical context of the intervention. This is particularly critical with organizations composed of professionals, such as R&D labs, where there are clear idiosyncrasies that make it a very different kind of place from the typical manufacturing plant or service organization!

The ability to *effect internal change* in a functioning organization appears to be a necessary ingredient for career management system implementation. Indeed, reaction to change may also be the test of organizational success and survival, regardless of the program or the goals of the organization. The pressing external facts of modernization, technological advancement, and rapid obsolescence create a situation in which organizations must be flexible enough to readjust to changing conditions. Individuals responsible for planning and carrying out new career management programs have found that such rational considerations will rarely counteract the tendency of many to resist change.

POLICY IMPLICATIONS

The dictionary defines a management policy as any governing principle, plan, or course of action, but policies are really much more than that. The organization's policies form a network of rules and statements that say something to employees about what is important and valued by the organization. Policies become translated into operation through procedures, programs, and training, and through informal means whereby members of the organization protect the values and customs that the policies represent.

Human Resource Policy versus Reality

Formal versus Normative. All organizations have human resource policies. Some are formal and written, others are unwritten yet normative (that is, understood, accepted, and enforced by the group to which the policy applies). Many policies attempt to push the responsibility for career coaching onto the supervisor, who may be ill-equipped to handle this role. It is one thing to have executive policy statements such as, "People are our most important asset," but it is quite another thing to have that philosophy put into action. Too often, policy statements are "fluff"—vague statements devoid of supporting systems. Norms will often develop to the effect that the really task-oriented managers do not have the time for such empty proselytizing. The organization must make human resource planning and employee development a real part of the supervisor's job.

All employees determine quickly what is important on the job. We learn through observation what is valued and make decisions as to the "fit" with our own personal value system. If the organization makes no conscious choice with regard to its human resource policy, that certainly does not mean there is none. The implied philosophy that each employee is responsible for his or her own development is really an abdication of responsibility by the organization. What effect does such a policy have? For the short term, employees will tend to persist in and gravitate toward things they do well *now*. This can have drastic long-term implications. The employee becomes more limited by a specific set of skills and knowledge and becomes "stuck" in place with the likely probability that eventually those skills will no longer be needed.

This can be a major problem for professionals, because if they become mired in the work they were educated to do and are good at, then in a few years, they will become obsolete, "used up" by the organization. This approach suits the short-term needs of the immediate supervisor but *not* the long-term needs of the individual or the organization.

The organization also becomes stuck in place by its inability to respond to changing conditions or requirements. As Otte states:

> Career development literature strongly endorses the concept of individual responsibility. If an organization, however, fails to develop employees to fill future organizational needs . . . the organization will suffer as will individuals who find themselves with no place in it. Providing incentives and services that encourage individuals to be personally responsible benefits everyone (31, p. 35).

The organization may have one formal written policy statement, yet in the absence of a strong, central personnel function it may go unnoticed or unheeded. One department may make money available for continuing education or professional association meetings, while another department may not. One department head may conduct a career-pathing system within his or her department, while the next department head may know nothing about it. One department head verbalizes support for "people development;" the next one does not. Clearly, departmental norms for movement and expectations of supervisors will differ in these departments. People will be treated in different ways. The organization loses the consistency necessary for effective coordination of functions when human resource norms are allowed to grow unchecked. The organization requires a formal policy that is clearly supported by specific programs and visible activities.

For example, the ABC Research and Development Laboratory, an imaginary company, has begun to have a history of very little movement between research positions. It appears that supervisors are protecting, screening, and holding on to the research scientists on their team or task force. This has caused some recent problems because exciting new task force assignments have gone unfilled, resulting in the cancellation of two recent contracts, a real concern to the managers. The supervisors, however, do not really have any incentives to let go of their regular team. Instead, there are "disincentives" leading them to hold on to their staff. Consider the impact upon this situation of a policy reading something like this:

> Each employee of the ABC R&D Lab is employed directly by the Lab and is not to be considered the property of an individual supervisor. Supervisors will be evaluated on the degree to which they develop their people—as evidenced through job rotation among depart-

ments or projects. The employee's performance appraisal will be based on the observations of the direct supervisor and each project leader.

There are obviously some pros and cons to making a statement such as this. For one thing, can and will it be enforced? Changing people and their habits and what they have learned takes time, and there must be evidence that the new behavior reaps more rewards than the old. Proper execution of this policy would require a supporting procedure by which all performance appraisals and salary actions are reviewed by a person who is committed to the new approach and has the legitimate authority to approve or disapprove a salary increase. It takes time to develop new norms within a group, and this policy statement serves as a visible signpost at the beginning of the journey.

Supportive versus Antagonistic. Organizations clearly differ in the value they place on their internal human resources. The American automobile industry used to be characterized by attempts to "dehumanize" work and make one person's contribution infinitesimal. The person is seen as easily replaceable. As a result, the absence of feeling a meaningful part of the production led to poor quality products. Recently the industry has begun to initiate programs and manufacturing changes to get the workers *involved* again. When people feel involved and feel that their contribution is important and valued, they are more likely not only to be more productive but to feel better about their jobs as well. Both productivity and job satisfaction are positively affected.

Most people can think of industries and companies that are considered good places to work and others that are seen as not caring about their employees. Some of these images can be traced back to organizational policies and practices that influence career orientation. Some organizations are considered as lifetime employers; others have a record of a more transient work force.

For example, in one organization, above a certain level, most hiring is done externally. This may not be a written policy but it is a well-recognized fact that may have a negative motivational effect on current employees because it appears that hard work and personal sacrifice do not lead to professional or promotional opportunity. At the same time, this policy is likely to increase the probability of current employees leaving to another organization. The vicious circle of more openings and more external hires lessens the commitment to the organization's goals and reduces employee identification with it. Although commitment to the organization is not of paramount concern to the professional, it *is* an issue from the organization's perspective inasmuch as it affects tenure. On the other hand, the policy would ensure that new professional talent is infused into the organization on a regular basis: the individual may be "used up" but the organization does not suffer. A possible negative impact is that the organization may acquire such a poor reputation among professionals that it becomes impossible to attract and retain the best people.

It does no good to have a policy stating that internal candidates will always be considered first if the perception or the reality is that, above a certain level, "outsiders" are brought in. Sometimes the perception is incorrect and simply releasing statistics on the percentage of openings filled internally will counteract inaccurate or unrepresentative observations.

In another example, the organization promotes or assigns new projects almost solely from within but in a "sink-or-swim" fashion. No support is provided by the organization to help the person learn the new technology or to prepare, orient, or train the person for the new role. Failure may mean disgraced demotion or a coerced resignation. It only takes a few such cases for an employee to wonder whether advancement is worth the risk and whether the organization is worth the personal investment in time and energy.

It could be a helpful exercise to identify the different perspectives of the individual and the organization, then to analyze human resource policies as to the degree to which they address *both* concerns. Figure 7-1 presents some of these career concerns. The issues are basically the same, but the perspective is quite different. For example, the individual is wondering whether he or she can handle the job while the company is wondering whether the job is beyond the employee's ability. Clear accountabilities, a planned orientation, and a development plan that addresses potential problem areas would be a programmatic plan of attack to quell anxieties on both sides and facilitate movement into the new job. A lack of concern for the social and technical implications of employee movement can result in human resource policies that are either neutral or antagonistic to individual career aspirations and organizational strategic business plans.

Cliché versus Budgetary. How much money is budgeted this year in your department's education and training line on the budget? Is there an education and training line on your budget? How is that money divided up and used? Is it the "slack" category used to offset unexpected expenses in other categories? Is it the first to disappear from your budget in a crunch? Are training and education dollars really spent to address job and career development needs or are they considered a reward for good performance? How is the money *really* spent—for planned individual development or for once-a-year rest and relaxation (R&R), meaning a weekend outing to a vacation resort for golf, tennis, and fun in the sun? It probably is not practical in the real world to eliminate all R&R from training. In fact, this is one area in which the organization can provide some perquisites. However, the guts of the education and training should

7-1. Individual and organizational career concerns.

INDIVIDUAL	ORGANIZATIONAL
What performance does the company expect of me?	Can the employee perform up to our standards?
Should I risk the move?	Should we risk the offer?
What would the new people be like?	What is the employee really like?
Can I handle the job?	Is it too great a "stretch"?
How well accepted would I be in the new position?	Will others support the employee in the new position?
What are the rewards for doing a good job?	How important is financial reward?
Will I personally gain more than I give up?	Will the company gain more than it gives up?
What are the informal expectations of me?	Will he/she understand and abide by the informal rules?
Will I still feel like I am an important contributor?	Will he/she still be an important contributor?

be without R&R. Exactly what controls are there on "education" expenditures? Apart from education and training, are there other funds available for special opportunities that contribute to an employee's development?

These are tough but penetrating questions to answer. An organization that emphasizes how important its people are yet spends no money on its development is echoing hollow clichés. The manner in which budgeted money is spent also tells a revealing story. The hardnosed manager looks at the bottom line for the story. Specific budgets used in a planned way for employee development help ensure action and graphically illustrate the organization's developmental policies in an indisputable way.

Sometimes this budget is best handled through a central management or professional development function, although not necessarily. For example, IBM makes its managers responsible for developing and acting upon development requests similar to those listed below. A central control point can, however, establish clear criteria for educational funds that are consistent across the organization. An employee development request form could be required; in it the supervisor is asked to provide the following information:

- *Developmental opportunity:* A description of the general area of weakness.
- *Goal:* A behavioral description of what improved performance would look like.
- *Resource:* The proposed method of addressing the deficiency or improving the developmental need.
- *Action plan:* The on-the-job actions that will help translate off-job learning into on-the-job behavior.
- *Cost:* The cost of the program, seminar, activity.

These issues relate not only to policy but also to organizational structure—if the organization is highly centralized with a strong human resource function, then a management or professional development department can be the central clearinghouse to help identify resources and build in action plans. If the structure permits, this can be a significant resource for supervisors who may have no idea of what is available in developmental programs. In this way, the management or professional development department would maintain control over the purse strings and provide a double check on the degree to which a program meets an individual development need. However, in many decentralized laboratory-type situations, this approach might not be possible.

Salary Administration Implications. How important is career management and human resource development to your organization? The answer lies largely in the degree to which career management considerations are reflected in salary administration policies and procedures. Employees pay attention to areas of job accountability that will be measured and will influence their pay. Career management will not become a part of the supervisor's role until there is clear evidence that the organization values these behaviors. This evidence comes through organizational policy statements and performance accountabilities. Extrinsic rewards for career management accomplishments might also take the form of bonus money, special awards, or invitations to conventions. In this way, the existing reward systems are used to reinforce desired behaviors.

Salary administration is a particularly thorny problem with some groups of scientists and engineers. Dual or parallel ladder programs allow some degree of advancement within the professional role with corresponding salary treatment. There are bound to be equity disputes *between* ladders, however, since the administrative/managerial branch is often considered the road to greater power, organizational prestige, and higher salary than the professional branch of the organization. Scientists and engineers strive as hard as administrators to do the best they can in their personal lives and for their families. Although autonomy and special status can be very motivating to professionals, they are unlikely to be pacified by glorious titles (senior research fellow) that carry strong professional reward but very little monetary reward. Success may be measured in very different ways, but one factor will always be salary. Career management policy must recognize this and attempt equitable resolutions of differences in the professional and managerial career tracks.

Who Communicates Policy? Both the organization's management *and* esteemed professionals need to show ownership of career management programs. Although such programs generally originate within personnel departments, they should not be perceived as exclusively personnel programs. Departmental and informal professional leadership must clearly, visibly, and repeatedly express support for the philosophy and practice of career management. This includes verbal support backed up by observable behavior and reinforced by decisions that are made. Top departmental and professional representatives should be involved in the development of the program so they are better able to support the methodology chosen. The chief executive officer should announce the program and express a sincere desire that career management become a high-priority item among all employees at every level. The CEO should translate career management objectives into trackable goals and have these goals listed as part of the performance/incentive goals of the management team.

Doing versus Supervising. Just as in our personal lives, a certain amount of stress on the job is natural, expected, and perhaps even conducive to obtaining a competitive edge, creative impulse, alert response, or the like. However, all too often the job situation becomes overly stressful, leading to inappropriate or maladaptive behaviors, performance decrements, avoidance, and "high anxiety." Major life changes (changing jobs or organizations, geographical relocation, family crises) can trigger these responses but can also occur as a response to the everyday "small" issues that wear us down. Given the importance of one's job, occupation, and career to a personal sense of worth, self-esteem, and success, career management is clearly an area in which stress is a likely component. It should be noted that *some* stress is necessary to produce activity—it is the perceived inordinate amount of stress that may lead to maladaptive behavior. People vary greatly in their tolerance of ambiguity and their reaction to stress.

How can the organization and individual recognize and, indeed, capitalize in a positive manner on these stress-invoking situations? Recognizing sources of anxiety is a first step. Most jobs are composed of both familiar, routine, repetitive tasks *and* novel, innovative, ill-defined activities. Although professionals have a higher tolerance for ambiguity than nonprofessionals, there are certainly instances in which job-induced anxiety will cause avoidance mechanisms to be triggered, resulting in the repetition of familiar patterns of behavior to the exclusion of innovative tasks. This affects both the individual contributor *and* the supervisor. An article in the *Harvard Business Review* described this situation, identifying "one of the most prevalent and costly of these escape mechanisms [as] what we call busyness: the escape into time-consuming activities that managers find less threatening to perform (though much less productive) than the tough aspects of their jobs" (1, p. 99).

The situation becomes exaggerated to the degree that the person has been educated and socialized as a *doer* (scientist, engineer, professional) rather than a manager. Then the comfortable niche into which he or she regresses when managerial problems occur is the *doer* role. Every support mechanism should be looked at from the point of view of reducing stress and anxiety on the job. The transition from professional to manager is not an easy one. A career management policy and program that confronts this problem and challenges participants to break out of that natural reaction would be a tremendous contribution. The organization's policies and procedures should support this transition in key areas:

- Salary treatment
- Support groups or "mentoring" programs
- Managerial training
- "Buy-back" agreements (ability to return to previous job)

The "doer" role created meaningful work for the person. Now, in a management position, it is contingent upon the organization to structure managerial jobs to create meaningful work for the professional. Managerial jobs (as well as professional jobs) should exhibit certain characteristics:

- Obvious, urgent, and compelling needs are addressed by the work group.
- Accountability for action is clear.
- Results are predictable, based on actions.
- Immediate feedback on the effect of the action is received.

The organization's structure, policies, and procedures should support these critical elements. All too often goals are vague, accountabilities are ambiguous, results are unsure, and feedback or reinforcement is untimely. No wonder the new manager has problems—he or she is no longer receiving the satisfaction of personal hands-on accomplishment and is unable to experience the exciting quality of managerial jobs.

Holding the Supervisor Accountable

The main issue with regard to holding the supervisor accountable for career management activities is the fact that generalized expectations become important when transformed into accountabilities that are measured for results and affect performance appraisals and salary reviews. "People development" will receive lip service and little more until evidence of it is required at review time. This really translates into two related sets of behavior: those behaviors aimed at developing the person to handle the demands of his or her current job better than they have been and those behaviors aimed at developing the person for more challenging or higher level positions within the organization than he or she currently holds. The first might be termed job training; the second, career development. Both are essential parts of the supervisor's job and help the employee master current requirements and stretch into broader roles.

This does not necessarily mean "upward and onward" in the traditional management sense. In reference to professionals, the breadth and/or depth of scientific competence are key variables. For example, when Morrison visited a lab and asked scientists what they did and to describe promotions, the discussion indicated that most were doing essentially the same thing that they had done when they entered, but that it was much more complex now and required a greater degree of technical expertise. The formal records showed promotions and salary increases, but these were not referred to at all. In this sense, job training might be thought of as immediate (static or current) and career development as long range (dynamic, future-oriented, and longitudinal).

The supervisory career management roles presented in chapter 11 would be an excellent "checklist" for the supervisor being reviewed. What evidence is there that the supervisor played these roles through the year? Exactly what activities supported job training and career development? Require these answers at review time, making them 20 percent of the review, and in this way the supervisor recognizes a new priority for the year. Naturally, the organization must help by providing the supervisor with the information and skills needed to perform these functions.

SUMMARY

Chapter 7 addressed program implementation issues. It is not always easy to sell, implement, and maintain the programs described in this book. This chapter addressed those issues squarely. Recommendations for avoiding resistance to change and for creating an integrated career management model were presented. The implementations of two specific programs were traced through.

The reader should now be able to answer the following questions:

What procedures and policies are needed to support career management programs? What materials and forms?

How should a career management program be introduced to the organization?
What supervisory and management training is required to support a career management program?
What are the predictable barriers to implementation, and how can they be avoided or minimized?
What should be the role of the personnel department?
What steps should be used when designing an organizational intervention?
What will influence the effectiveness of a program's execution?
How should I deal with resistance to change?
How can the concepts of synergy and entropy be applied to the career management process?
What policy statement and actions are required to support an active career management process?

It is true that the best-laid plans often go awry. The best-designed and most elegant, integrated program may not work due to some of the issues raised in this chapter. It is hoped that knowledge of the potential pitfalls will facilitate the anxious reader's attempt to "try out" some of the recommendations from the previous chapters.

REFERENCES

1. Ashkenas, R. N., and Schaffer, R. H. 1982. Managers can avoid wasting time. *Harvard Business Review* 60 (3):98-104.
2. Badawy, M. K. 1973. Bureaucracy in research: A study of role conflict of scientists. *Human Organizations* 32:123-33.
3. Bennis, W. G. 1965. Theory and method in applying behavioral science to planned organizational change. *Journal of Applied Behavioral Science* 1 (4):337-60.
4. Buchanan, P. C. 1967. Crucial issues in organization development. In *Change in School Systems,* ed. G. Watson. Washington, DC: National Training Laboratories.
5. Campbell, D. T., and Stanley, J. C. 1963. *Experimental and quasi-experimental designs for research.* Chicago, IL: Rand McNally.
6. Carvell, F. J. 1970. *Human relations in business.* London, England: Macmillan.
7. Champion, D. J. 1975. *The sociology of organizations.* New York: McGraw-Hill.
8. Clawson, J. G. 1985. Is mentoring necessary? *Training and Development Journal* (April):36-39.
9. Coch, L., and French, J. R. P. 1948. Overcoming resistance to change. *Human Relations* 1:512-32.
10. Costello, T., and Zalkind, S. 1963. *Psychology in administration.* Englewood Cliffs, NJ: Prentice-Hall.
11. Dewhirst, H. D., Arvey, R. D., and Brown, E. M. 1978. Satisfaction and performance in research and development tasks as related to information accessibility. *IEEE Transactions in Engineering Management* 3:56-63.
12. Flory, C., and MacKenzie, R. A. 1971. *The credibility gap in management.* New York: Van Nostrand Reinhold.
13. Francis, P. H. 1977. *Principles of R&D management.* New York: AMACOM.

14. French, W. L., and Bell, C. H., Jr. 1973. *Organization development.* Englewood Cliffs, NJ: Prentice-Hall.
15. Friedlander, F., and Brown, L. D. 1974. Organization development. *Annual Review of Psychology* 25:313-42.
16. Gilmer, B. H. 1966. *Industrial psychology.* New York: McGraw-Hill.
17. Grass, D. 1979. A guide to R&D career pathing. *Personnel Journal* (April).
18. Greiner, L. E. 1967. Patterns of organization change. *Harvard Business Review* 45 (May-June):119-30.
19. Kaufman, H. G. 1974. *Obsolescence and professional career development.* New York: AMACOM.
20. Klimoski, R. 1985. Designing and implementing a formal mentor program. Paper presented at the Academy of Management, 11 August, San Diego.
21. Kolb, D. A., Winter, S. K., and Berlew, D. E. 1968. Self-directed change: two studies. *Journal of Applied Behavioral Science* 4 (4):453-71.
22. Kram, K. E. 1985. Improving the mentoring process. *Training and Development Journal* (April):40-43.
23. Kram, K. E., and Isabella, L. A. 1985. Mentoring alternatives: Role of peer relationships in career development. *Academy of Management Journal* (March):110-132.
24. Lasden, M. 1985. Mentor can be a millstone. *Computer Decisions* 26 (March):74-81.
25. Lawrence, P. R. 1969. How to deal with resistance to change. *Harvard Business Review,* 47 (1):4-12, 166-76.
26. Leach, J. J. 1980. Career development: some questions and tentative answers. *Personnel Administrator* (Oct.): 31-34.
27. Lippitt, G. L. 1966. Managing change: six ways to turn resistance into acceptance. *Supervisory Management* (August): 48-53.
28. Morrison, R. F. 1981. Utilizing discretionary research funds to support an applied laboratory's goals: a preliminary investigation. Paper read at the annual meeting of the Academy of Management, 2-5 August, San Diego.
29. Myers, D. W., and Humphreys, N. J. 1985. Caveats in mentorship. *Business Horizons* (July/August):9-14.
30. Odiorne, G. S. 1985. Mentoring: an American management innovation. *Personnel Administrator* (May):63-70.
31. Otte, F. L. 1982. Creating successful career development programs. *Training and Development Journal* (February):30-37.
32. Rantfl, R. M., ed. 1978. *R&D productivity: study report.* Culver City, CA: Hughes Aircraft Company.
33. Reich, M. H. 1985. Executive views from both sides of mentoring. *Personnel* (March):42-46.
34. ———. 1986. The mentor connection. *Personnel* (February):50-56.
35. Rifkin, J., and Howard, T. 1982. *Entropy: a new world view.* New York: Bantam.
36. Schein, E. H. 1970. *Organizational psychology.* Englewood Cliffs, NJ: Prentice-Hall.
37. Tannenbaum, A. S. 1968. *Control in organizations.* New York: McGraw-Hill.
38. Vosburgh, R. M. 1980. The annual human resource review: a career-planning system. *Personnel Journal* (October):830-37.
39. Walker, J. W., and Gutteridge, T. G. 1979. *Career-planning practices: an AMA survey report.* New York: AMACOM.
40. Weiss, C. H. 1972a. *Evaluating action programs.* Boston, MA: Allyn and Bacon.
41. ———. 1972b. *Evaluation research.* Englewood Cliffs, NJ: Prentice-Hall.
42. Zey, M. G. 1985. Mentor programs: making the right moves. *Personnel Journal* (February):53-57.

PART 2
INDIVIDUAL CHOICES: WHAT YOU CAN DO

Chapter 8
The Individual's Career Transitions

The typical professional, along with other white-collar Americans, has received information about his or her career from popular literature such as the best-seller *Passages* (41) or *Reader's Digest, Redbook,* or United Airlines' *United*. Most of the articles in these periodicals are based on a myopic, stereotyped view of the adult at work with sufficient exaggeration of aspects to make the material appealing. Not many readers graduated with engineering degrees from MIT, obtained a Harvard MBA, founded their own company, and are worth ten million dollars by age thirty. This chapter is intended to provide a more realistic, research-based perspective about adults and their careers with as much emphasis as available on the unique aspects of being professionals.

First, who are the "true" professionals as referred to in theoretical literature and basic research (2)? In the popular literature everyone appears to fit into that category. True professionals, who are similar to scientists, are not tied to a single employer but view their primary association as one with their colleagues regardless of where they work. They belong to an organization of their colleagues that aids in the administration of a code of ethics, high standards of conduct and ability, and probably a means to remain current within their field. The performance of people in the profession will probably be controlled not only by a review of their peers, but also by licensure or certification by a government body if the work is conducted as a service to the public. The members of the profession are expected to have had extensive academic training in a specific body of knowledge and a significant amount of supervised job experience before being eligible to be called a member of the profession and to affiliate with colleagues. This is required because professionals work in a field that requires complex relationships with people or the application of data in a complex way. You and your colleagues will be in a high-prestige field of work and probably have relatively high incomes. At one time, the majority of the members of a profession were self-employed, but that is less true at this time as our society changes dramatically.

The purest examples of the professional are physicians and lawyers. Two other groups that come very close are university faculty members and basic research scientists. Many fields of work are not as easily classified because the field does not have the formal, legalized structure of medicine or law or the unique, consistent working style and environment of academia or the basic research situation. Without a formal, legal structure (as in law) or a consistent, long-standing informal set of norms (as in the military) that prescribe the behavior of incumbents, individuals become the primary determinants of whether they behave like professionals or not. For example, an individual graduates from an academically respected university with a bachelor's degree in electrical engineering. Knowledge in a specific field has been obtained, but it is not "extensive." Professionally oriented persons would have two primary choices, to obtain an advanced degree in electrical engineering or to go to work in their fields. Such persons, however, would only seek employment with the intent to obtain more education, training, or work that would be specifically in their fields and to increase their knowledge in it to a level that would classify them as experts. Less professionally oriented individuals would have the same two choices. In their case, the additional education might be in a different field, such as business administration, and the reason for going to work might be to escape further education and to start applying what has been learned to the solution of daily problems.

When entering an organization, the two types of individuals will go through similar initiations, but their purposes and concentrations will be very different. Professionally oriented persons will become apprentices in the use of their skills, if possible, to highly respected colleagues in basic electrical engineering research. There will be a primary emphasis on doing high-quality work, honing technical skills to the ultimate degree, and increasing the level of expertise within a specific portion of the field. To a large extent, it can be said that professionals' hearts and minds will be with their tasks, technology, and colleagues, not their organizations. However, professionally oriented persons will also attempt to learn the organizational policies and practices that allow them to acquire as much autonomy in the work situation as possible, to add to their own technical knowledge and skill, and to develop a strong relationship with similar, highly trained colleagues and professional societies both within and outside the organization (13). Thus, effective professionally oriented individuals work at becoming a liaison on technology between the organization and the outside centers of expertise.

Less professionally oriented persons will also try to become established quickly, but it will be within the organization rather than within the field of electrical engineers. Such individuals will probably identify several individuals who are perceived to be successful or unsuccessful in the organization and will model their behavior on the effective behaviors of someone while avoiding the ineffective behavior of others. Less professionally oriented persons will become immersed in the organization and committed to its activities and mission or goals. The organization's policies, practices, and functions become paramount to less professionally oriented persons because the rewards that are most highly valued are offered by the firm (13). Such rewards include promotion (especially into management), salary increases, stability, and security. Such persons will work on learning the organization and becoming liaisons between the work group and other work groups or functions within the organization.

These introductory remarks are not aimed at a high school or college student who is involved in making the initial major career decision. Our assumption is that the initial decision has already been made—at least for the time being, and we are addressing the working adult who is somewhere between college and retirement, who is seeking first employment or is already employed in an organization as a professional but not ready to retire. The emphasis in chapters 9 through 11 will be on the major career decisions that you face during your working life. To place these decisions in perspective, this chapter provides an introduction to the theory that has been developed to aid us in understanding the process that individuals go through when they are maturing in a work setting. Not all theories will be covered, just those that have the most supporting research and/or are deemed to be most applicable to the professional. You will be introduced to how theorists propose that you should ideally go about making your career decisions. Then a brief look will be made at how people actually make their decisions, and why they do it that way. This will be followed by some ideas about what makes a good decision and what you can do to make yours better if you desire to do so.

MAJOR CAREER DECISIONS OF A PROFESSIONAL

Careers are unique to each of us and develop and change at different rates and sequences for each individual. You may or may not be involved in the same career decisions, planning, and development as your peers at any single point in your life. Although decisions and theories are presented here in a sequence, the order may not apply to every individual. Therefore, we have attempted to describe different situations in which decision opportunities arise and discuss how the decisions might be approached differently under various circumstances.

Once you are committed to a specific field, the major decisions you will face at one time or another are:

1. For what organization should I work—government, private industry, small company, self-employed?
2. In what kind of job should I work—should I be a research scientist concentrating on producing a new technology or theory, should I emphasize the translation of such theory into application (development), should I zero in on immediate application and problem solving?
3. How do I plan my career?
4. How do I become familiar enough with the organization (people, products, processes) or clients so that I can focus my work in essential areas or apply my knowledge optimally?
5. Should I be an individual contributor who concentrates on the development and use of my technical or professional knowledge, be a manager of individual contributors in my field, be a general manager of many functions, or be my own boss?
6. How can I keep ahead of or at least current with the knowledge that is constantly being produced in my specialty?
7. How specialized should I be within my field?
8. How do I learn about other specialties within my field and how far should I go in learning them?
9. Should I take an offered promotion, transfer, reassignment, relocation? How do I cope with it?
10. Am I in the right field of work or should I change fields—not just my specialization within my field but the entire occupation?
11. What do I do if I am facing demotion, lay-off, termination?
12. When and how do I go about retiring?

There are many minor career decisions that are faced nearly every day and certainly every year, but most of them can be classified within the purview of one of the above. Before you can become involved in career decisions, you need to have the term "career" placed in the right perspective.

Defining a Career

The definition of a career was provided in very general terms in chapter 1 as a series of work-related experiences that have a common thread such as a core body of knowledge or employer running through them. A career is defined differently for different people (30). If the field of work (occupation) is inextricably linked to the organization because the occupation is unique to the organization, then career, organization, and occupation are realistically perceived by the members of the organization as one and the same. This occurs in many military occupations. If the individual is totally committed to the organization and its career rewards and requirements, then the occupation loses its salience, and career and organization become synonyms to that person. To the "pure" professional, the occupation is synonymous with career and the organization is unimportant, because the individual's primary focus is on the technology and collegial relationships, values, and rewards provided by the occupation and its professional association, not the organization. Any link to the organization is tenuous, and the professional will tend to leave for greener pastures if the organization does not provide the opportunity to reach for technical challenges, to relate to colleagues, and to strive for the rewards of the occupational society. Therefore, it appears that people define a career differently depending upon the central focus in their work life. Some see it as their occupation ("I'm a lawyer"), others interpret it as their organization ("I work for IBM"), while a large proportion probably combine them ("I'm a research agronomist in the Department of Agriculture"). People do not consider location as a major factor in their career decisions. It is tenuously linked to the organization, because most organizations are located in a limited number of geographic areas. However, the location appears to be primarily a component of lifestyle decisions, not career decisions. Therefore, as career decision making is discussed, both your field of work and the organization you work for will be integral parts of the decision. Where you live will be discussed separately.

MAKING CAREER DECISIONS

Most of the decisions that are made every day are highly programmed, that is, made according to rules—cost estimation, budgeting, scheduling. The career decisions that you must make are normally unprogrammed so that you have to establish your own decision rules. To add to the complexity, most of your career decisions are not required ones. There is no finite time period in which a specific decision must be made. Some exceptions to this are deciding on the first job upon graduation and, in the military, choosing the next job you want when your programmed date to leave the present one arises. Even the decision to retire is not as time-bound as it once was. Today many people never completely retire, while others do so in their forties and fifties.

The best-known career decisions involve deciding the course of study to take in school, the field of work to enter, the first employer, and when to retire. However, there is a whole stream of decisions that are being made periodically. Each builds upon or is determined by the previous one. The most critical ones that you will face as professionals were covered in the list of questions above. As you ponder those questions, you will be led in the direction of more and more detailed ones that you have now or will face throughout your working life. You never get away from making career decisions.

As a professional, you learned to pursue a rational, systematic approach to the problem solving involved in both research and application. You have probably carried this with you into your work but may not have applied it to your career decisions. The research on career decision making has been done on high school and college students by counseling psychologists who are interested in helping individuals make decisions about their occupation (1,17,20,22,24,27,28,31,33,35,44,48) and on college students by management faculty who are interested in how students decide for which organization they will work (12,23,26,34,40,43,49,51).

The primary theory that considers how a career decision should be made is not the "rational man" theory of the economist, in which it is assumed that all possible alternatives are known and there is complete knowledge about each alternative so that the single best one can be chosen. The ideal approach is a behaviorial one referred to as the expected utility (EU) theory or multiattribute utility theory (MAUT) (35). Because most training courses and career counseling sessions are designed with many of the characteristics of EU theory embedded in them, they attempt to get the participant to use this approach. An individual may use an approximation of EU theory for some decisions—probably those that seem most critical such as finding a job—but not others—minor decisions such as considering attendance at a company training course. To describe EU theory and its use (35), a key career decision serves as an example: finding a new job in your present field after being released during the acquisition of your company by another.

First, you determine the *objectives* that you desire from your next job. There will be a whole set of these, such as: maximizing your take-home pay, assuring that you will never lose a job again, obtaining a given amount of personal freedom in the job, raising the level or status of your initial job, working without supervising people, maximizing the benefits (such as retirement) that are available, working with high-quality technical or professional colleagues. Next you set up a means to measure each of your objectives (*attributes*). An obvious attribute is the salary and associated income, such as bonuses, that may be available as part of your income. The quality of colleagues can be assessed by their reputations in their fields and how much they publish. Job challenge could be evaluated by the technical/professional complexity of the initial assignment and the past work done in the organization. These qualitative attributes could be placed on a five-point scale from low (1) to high (5).

Now a set of alternative *choices* needs to be established, a difficult task. The choices are under your control, for example, joining a self-help organization such as Forty Plus, mailing résumés to a wide variety of potential employers, visiting personnel offices, interviewing at professional/scientific societies, advertising in professional periodicals, contacting friends within your field, or evaluating going in to your own consulting business.

Each choice will have one or more *outcomes* associated with it describing a future event that may or may not occur. Since the outcomes are not under your complete control, you need to establish probabilities that each outcome may or may not occur for each alternate choice. For example, what is the probability that you will obtain a response when you mail out résumés to personnel offices of potentially relevant employers? Following that outcome, what is the probability that such a response will lead to a second outcome, a job offer? Once the possible outcomes associated with each choice have been established, each outcome is evaluated with respect to every attribute. These valuations are referred to as *utilities* and indicate the utility of each choice in the achievement of your career objectives. This is complex, but you can apply the major elements of EU theory to your own situation if you so desire.

A very similar approach to career decision making is valence-instrumentality-expectancy (VIE) theory which has been studied by Vroom (51). In his study of MBA students at Carnegie-Mellon University searching for their first job, he found that 59 percent chose the organization that they believed would be most instrumental in the achievement of their most highly valued (valent) personal career goals. When he added in the factor of expectancy and considered only the students being offered employment, he found that 79 percent chose the organization that made them an offer and would be most instrumental in helping them obtain their goals. However, 21 percent did not choose that organization even though they had been trained to do so in the Carnegie-Mellon program.

This approach may conflict with your own style. Research indicates that many of us use different methods to make our career decisions. Another approach to career decision making (43) has been referred to as the validator (12). In this instance, graduate students from a technical setting (MIT) were found to use the VIE (scientific) approach up to a point and then to deviate from it. They initially set up a list of expectations about the "ideal" organization that they would like to work for—similar to the objectives and attributes of EU theory. Then they searched for a set of alternatives (organizations) and evaluated them but did not compare them on the attributes. They did not weigh the factors but chose the most satisfactory one using one or two primary goal attributes. Early in the process, these individuals had identified a favorite choice but did not appear to be aware of it. They kept searching and evaluating until a second acceptable choice was found to become a "confirming" candidate. Search stopped and the favorite choice was compared to the confirming alternative on several goal attributes. When the favorite choice did not come out on top on a goal attribute such as income, perceptual and interpretational distortion took place to the detriment of the confirming alternative. Either the weights given to goal attributes were changed to fit—income became less important—or the definition of the goal attribute was changed—income was redefined to include future bonus possibilities, pension income, time off from work. When the desired choice had been rationalized, then the final decision was made to take that offer of employment.

However, there are still more ways that career decisions are made. Glueck (12) found that some of his MBAs and engineers followed the pattern described by Simon (42). This group of "satisficers" used their previous experience to set up goals and levels of attributes that would be *satisfactory* rather than optimal. The search for alternative choices was done one at a time until an alternative was found that was considered acceptable (satisfactory) or too much time passed. If a satisfactory alternative was found, it was accepted and further search ceased. However, if a satisfactory choice was not found within a reasonable time, the levels of the goal attributes were reduced and the choices reassessed. If a satisfactory alternative was identified, it was chosen. If one was not present, the process was started over. No rationalization of the decision occurred, nor were alternatives compared to each other.

All of the above can be classified as different *planning* styles of decision making in which the individual takes responsibility for decision making and goes about it in a rational means-to-end fashion (24). However, not everyone fits into that general category, as vocational counselors have found. In Harren's model of career decision making, the *intuitive* and *dependent* styles have also been observed (17). The intuitive individual takes personal responsibility for career decisions but uses fantasy, feelings, and emotions in the process. Such decisions "feel" right and the individual cannot state how they were made. The dependent-style decision-maker does not take personal responsibility for decision making but projects it outside the self to the environment and is heavily influenced by the counselor, interest test, peers, parents, spouse, children. Such an individual is impulsive, fatalistic, compliant, agonizing, paralyzed, or delaying. Krumboltz found intuitive, impulsive, fatalistic, and dependent decision-making styles in his college samples but not any rational ones (22). Although there is partial support for Harren's categories, the absence of the planning decision style poses problems. It may be real or it may be an artifice of the sample or research approach that Krumboltz used. The goal of all career decision making is to obtain as good a match as possible between the individual and the career situation, present and future. The number of techniques that are available to help with career decision making appears at times to be endless.

THE REASONS WHY YOU MAKE DECISIONS THE WAY THAT YOU DO

The approach taken is a major factor in making decisions, but what are some of its determinants and how are alternatives considered? Why are some goals and attributes important to you at this time in your life and not to others at the same time? The approach to answering these questions is based upon the same one used by an organization that wants to do long-range planning. It determines its current state by assessing its resources, assets, and liabilities. You will need to do the same for yourself by establishing a clear sense of your identity, including what your needs/values/priorities are, what your strengths and weaknesses are, where you are heading, and what life goals are important to you now. In 1957, Super proposed in the first comprehensive theory of adult career development that work in the American culture is a primary means of expressing an individual's self-image (44). The self-image that is pertinent to this book consists of your personal impressions of your abilities, interests, personality, values, needs, aspirations, and experiences that are vocationally relevant. Your self-image heavily influences your career decisions and behavior and, in turn, is influenced by the success you achieve in your career endeavors. Because your work is so intertwined with your self-image, your sense of satisfaction with yourself, self-esteem, is very dependent upon the level of success you perceive that you are achieving in your career.

Most techniques designed to aid in career decision making and planning are built to assist in developing an accurate picture of the self, consistent with the individual's true set of characteristics. This requires accuracy in self-insight to produce a clearly differentiated image of strengths and weaknesses, needs/desires, values/opinions, consistent with your capabilities and how others see you. For example, if you find that all of your scores on an interest test fall in the middle range and you do not have any strong likes or dislikes, then you do not have a clearly differentiated self-image. It will be difficult for you to make career decisions. In addition to being differentiated, it must be well integrated, that is, internally consistent. For example, a high degree of interest in and desire to work on tasks that require systematic, logical reasoning and intense concentration on concepts for long periods of time—as required in computer programming—would not be consistent with a need for a wide variety of different tasks and a lot of social stimulation—as represented in general management.

The third requirement of a self-image so that career decision making and planning can be done effectively is stability. Self-image cannot be changed materially within short periods of time; it cannot change dramatically as you move from one situation to another.

Finally, the self-image must be accurate enough to represent your capabilities in your career decisions. It should not reflect the desires of those around you or depend heavily upon what is socially desirable within your peer group, family, or society. It needs to represent the true you.

Interests and Personality

In assessing your self-image, probably the first thing that comes to mind are your interests. Interest tests have been a part of vocational counseling since the 1920s and the work of E. K. Strong and of D. G. Paterson. The Strong Vocational Interest Blank has been widely used in school settings for many years. It is a very simple test based on hundreds of items covering likes, dislikes, and preferences regarding occupations, school subjects, amusements, activities, and types of people as well as self-descriptions of abilities, characteristics, and behaviors. Originally, the items were administered to thousands of men in many occupations, from accountants to YMCA secretaries. The average for the entire group became the base for establishing unique occupational group scores. Each occupational group was then compared item by item with the general sample. When the difference between the average score for the occupational group (accountants, for example) was statistically different from the average score for men in general, the item was scored for the occupational group. This way specific interests for architects can be said to be significantly different from men in general; someone who scored high on the architect scale is said to have similar interests to those of architects, nothing more. Such an approach is very empirical and atheoretical. Interests can predict the occupational field someone will enter (22 percent accuracy rate) but occupational aspirations are better (41 percent accuracy rate) measures if the two are not congruent. If interests are congruent with aspirations, the accuracy rate rises dramatically to 70 percent (19), but it seems reasonable that the major influence is environmental. The latter is especially strong in childhood but continues until the middle twenties when interests tend to stabilize.

Holland has proposed a theory-oriented approach that can be used to link individuals to occupations (18). His first assumption is that, in our culture, most people can be classified as one of six types: realistic, investigative, artistic, social, enterprising, or conventional. Each type is a product of the interaction between a variety of cultural and personal forces. From this interaction in early life, preferences for some activities over others develop, leading to strong interests in those activities that in turn result in a special group of competencies. Those interests and competencies create a personal disposition to think, perceive, and act in certain ways. For example, if you resemble the investigative type, you would be more likely to seek out investigative occupations or situations such as surgeon, chemist, economist, mathematician, or psychologist. You would be expected to see yourself as scholarly, intellectually self-confident, having mathematical and scientific ability, and lacking in leadership ability. You would be expected to have more investigative competencies to solve problems at work and in other settings than enterprising competencies such as leadership, interpersonal, and persuasive abilities.

By comparing your attributes with those of each model type, the type that you resemble most can be determined—that is your personality type. Then you can determine what other types you also resemble. Holland proposes that the three personality types that you resemble most form your personality pattern. For example, you may be primarily an investigative personality type, followed by a realistic type and then an artistic type. Initially Holland proposed that a six-category system would be adequate to match people and occupations. However, the personality of people proved to be too complex for such a simplistic approach, and he developed the more complex system that effectively provides 120 different personality patterns. Considerable research has been done on Holland's personality types, and the classification of people by type can be successfully done by several vocational preference measures that will be covered in later chapters.

The second assumption that Holland makes is that there are six kinds of environments, the same six represented as his personality types. He assumes that an environment is created by the people congregating in it. Since different personality types have different interests, competencies, and dispositions, they tend to surround themselves with special people and materials and to seek out problems congruent with their interests, competencies, and outlook. Therefore, the environment can be assessed in the same terms that individuals are assessed. The task is accomplished by counting the number of people of different types in the environment and classifying the environment by the three major personality types present, in the same fashion as was done with individuals.

Holland's third assumption is that "people search for environments that will let them exercise their skills and abilities, express their attitudes and values, and take on agreeable problems and roles" (18, p. 4). Thus, investigative types seek investigative environments, enterprising types seek enterprising environments, and so on.

The fourth key assumption is that "a person's behavior is determined by an interaction between his personality and the characteristics of his environment" (18, p. 4). Therefore, if individuals' personality patterns and the patterns of their environments are known, then some of the outcomes of the pairing can be forecasted. Some of those outcomes are choice of vocation, job change, vocational achievement, and social behavior. While the measurement of personality and environmental patterns has been successfully accomplished in considerable research, the interactions of the two patterns have not been as fruitfully explained (19).

To relate his four key assumptions, Holland has developed a hexagonal model of his proposition in which the distances between the type of environments are inversely proportional to the theoretical relationships between them. This spatial arrangement allows him to develop explicit definitions of internal consistency and the congruence between the personality pattern of the individual and the pattern of the environment. For example, highly consistent personality patterns are realistic-investigative (RI) and artistic-social (AS) because they are directly adjacent to each other in the hexagonal model (fig. 8-1). Low consistency that would lead to dissatisfaction with career choices would be represented by conventional-artistic (CA) and enterprising-investigative (EI) personality patterns because each member of the pair is separated from the other by two personality types. Congruence is assessed by how close the personality pattern of the individual matches the pattern of the environment. Holland can assess the differentiation of the personality pattern by comparing individuals' scale scores for each of the six personality types. The absolute differences between the scores of the highest and lowest scale provide measures of how clearly the individuals differentiate among the personality attributes as represented in their self-images.

Some examples of the combination of personality types, personality characteristics, and professional occupations represented in Holland's theory of vocational choice are shown in figure 8-2. The detail that can be represented increases markedly as personality patterns replace personality types. Using his theory of career

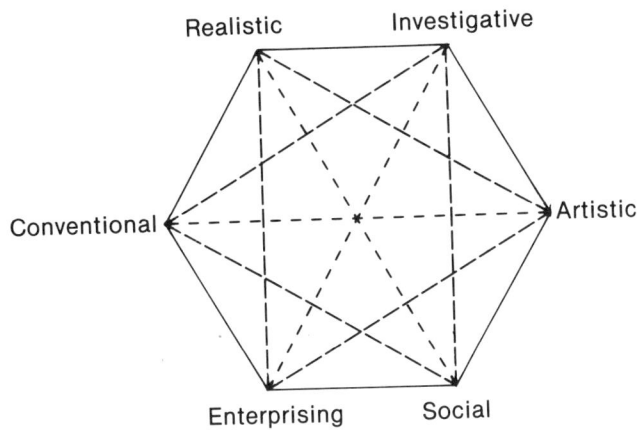

8-1. A hexagonal model for defining the psychological resemblances among types and environments and their interactions.

Adapted from Holland, J. L. 1984. *Making vocational choices: a theory of careers.* 2nd ed. Englewood Cliffs, NJ: Prentice-Hall, p. 23.

choice, Holland has developed a self-administered, self-scored paper-and-pencil questionnaire called the Self-Directed Search, that can be used for career guidance. The questionnaire is available from Consulting Psychologists Press, 577 College Avenue, Palo Alto, CA 94306.

Career Style

One theoretical approach that may be of assistance in identifying your self-image has integrated work on decision making with individual motives, career behavior, and compatible organizational environments. The work started in the 1960s when Driver and his colleagues were involved in studying individual cognitive styles in decision making (39). In the 1970s he started applying the earlier work to career decision making. Although the work has problems because the measures need further development and the supporting research is limited, his approach is intriguing and may provide you with some insights about yourself. Driver has added personality and behavior factors to his ideas of decision style to produce career concepts (9,10). Career concepts are different ways that different individuals look at their careers. For example, some people choose a profession that entails very little opportunity for upward promotion, while others strive very hard to move upward. Neither can empathize well with the other.

The basis for Driver's work is cognitive decision style derived from two primary sources, the search and processing of an amount of information to generate one or more alternatives. Figure 8-3 shows the four cognitive styles proposed by Driver. The *decisive* individual considers a limited quantity of information to develop the single alternative that is chosen. The manager within a production facility may use this style to cope with the

8-2. Examples of personality attributes and occupations matched in Holland's theory of vocational choice (18).

| PERSONALITY TYPE | Personality Factors |||| PROFESSIONAL AND QUASI-PROFESSIONAL OCCUPATION |
	PREFERENCES	COMPETENCIES	VALUES	CHARACTERISTICS	
Realistic	Manipulation of objects, tools, etc.	Manual, agricultural, technical	Money, power, status	Shy, conforming, masculine	Mechanical engineer, civil engineer
Investigative	Investigate phenomena to understand and control	Scientific, mathematical	Science	Analytical, cautious, reserved	Psychologist, physicist, surgeon
Artistic	Free activities to create art forms	Language, art, music	Aesthetic qualities	Disorderly, impulsive, imaginative	Architect, writer
Social	Manipulate others to inform, train, etc.	Interpersonal, educational	Social and ethical problems	Ascendant, helpful, idealistic	College professor, nurse, sociologist
Enterprising	Manipulate others to attain economic gain	Leadership, interpersonal, persuasive	Political and economic achievement	Acquisitive, domineering, impulsive	Lawyer, industrial engineer
Conventional	Systematic manipulation of data	Clerical, computational, business systems	Business and economic achievement	Conscientious, efficient, inflexible	Certified Public Accountant

8-3. Cognitive decision styles (39).

	Amount of Information Used	
NUMBER OF ALTERNATIVES CONSIDERED	LITTLE	A LOT
Few	Decisive	Hierarchic
Several	Flexible	Integrative

myraid of decisions that are faced constantly. The *flexible* person uses a limited amount of information to construct several alternatives. An operating-site staff individual may use this style to provide alternatives from which a line manager makes a choice. The *hierarchic* approach to decision making considers a vast array of information and focuses on the single best possible alternative. The staff operations research analyst would be an individual who approaches a problem situation this way. The most complex decision style is the *integrative* one. In this instance, there is a major search for considerable information, and the individual processes it in a complex fashion to establish several viable alternatives. Such behavior is characteristic of a research scientist.

Driver proposes that the individual's cognitive style will be applied in career decision making and development as a career concept. He assumes that such career concepts are learned early in life and reflect cultural and family influences. Therefore, such concepts can change with life experiences and developmental stages. Career concepts, that is, approaches to career, express deep personal concepts that have different motivations underlying them and provide a framework that the person uses to make career decisions and to implement them. The career concept can be expressed in career behavior such as the frequency of movement across fields, the direction of movement in jobs, and the duration of time in a field. The decisive cognitive style is expressed as a *steady-state* career concept that Driver proposes is typical of professionals and skilled trades (fig. 8-4). The motives behind this concept are not clear at this stage in Driver's work but are hypothesized to come from one of two sources (9). The career style may come from a need for security or, as is characteristic of creative professionals, from a need to be competent and strive for excellence. This latter motive is internal to the individual and not determined by an external source. The choice of an occupation or field of work is made when the steady-state person is young and is maintained for life. Someone who uses such a career concept can be threatened by obsolescence. The steady-state person thrives in an organization that has such characteristics as a set of rewards for competence, an emphasis on product quality, a flat, pyramidal structure with many specialized departments (11).

The career concept that is most frequently written about is the *linear* one. The individuals who follow this approach to their careers require constant upward movement or they become very frustrated. They are driven by a need for power—influence over others—and a need for achievement as measured by the organization or culture within which they work. The cognitive style of such people is hypothesized by Driver to be hierarchic (10) with a possibility of some decisive characteristics as reflected in other research (29). The linear person is conjectured to make a career choice during youth or the late twenties and does not change that approach throughout

8-4. Career concept characteristics (10).

CAREER CONCEPT	DECISION STYLE	MOTIVES	TIME OF CHOICE	Occupational Change	
				FREQUENCY	DIRECTION
Steady State	Decisive	Competence, security	Youth	None	None
Transitory	Flexible	Identity, challenge	Never	Every 1 to 2 years	Lateral
Linear	Hierarchic	Power, achievement	Youth or late twenties	None	Upward
Spiral	Integrative	Growth, nurturance	Cyclic	Every 5 to 10 years	Lateral

life. Any changes within the work setting are upward in the hierarchy. As you may have surmised by now, the fields that are represented by this career concept are mostly managerial, with some political and professional ones.

While the steady-state and linear career concepts may not be especially new to you, Driver's other two may be. He has observed a *spiral* career concept in which the individual changes occupations every five to ten years. These changes are typically lateral and do not appear to be the result of a desire to progress upward as in the instance of the linear person. The spiral career concept appears to be typical of the arts style—creative occupations that use the very complex integrative-decision style and are motivated by growth and nurturance needs.

The fourth basic career concept is the *transitory* one. This individual never makes a choice of a field of work and moves laterally from one to another every one or two years. Such a person appears to be directionless, and the motives behind such behavior are unclear. There may be a search for identity that would be reflected in low income or a desire for challenge or variety that could lead to a financially successful life. Driver conjectures that this transitory career concept is characteristic of the flexible decision style.

If you see yourself using one of the above career concepts when making decisions about the field in which you work or the employer for whom you work, you might also see whether the motives that Driver presents as the driving force behind that career concept are also characteristic of you.

Driver's career theory is based on very limited research at this point in its evolution. It requires much more work before it can be used by individuals to identify their career styles or by the organization to develop a career management program. The measures of career style are not well developed, reliable, and available for general or research use.

Career Anchors

Another major career theorist who bases his work on major differences among individuals' self-concepts is Schein (37). He proposes that your self-concept is tied to your occupation and has three components: self-perceived talents and abilities; attitudes and values; and motives and needs, which combine to form your "career anchor." In contrast to the previous theorists, Schein puts little emphasis on the individual's life prior to his or her first job. He feels that the first few years of the early career are a time of mutual discovery between the individual as a new employee and the employer—a testing time for congruence between self and organization. Through successive trials and new job challenges, each learns more about the other. During this early interaction, the career anchor evolves, develops, and is discovered through actual experience rather than in school. As a result, a test cannot be used to assess your career anchor. It is inside you, functioning as a set of driving and constraining forces on your career decisions and choices. Because it is developed by experience rather than present as latent characteristics, your career anchor changes as you mature in experience. The interaction among your abilities, motives, and values while you work causes change, because you want and value what you are good at; therefore, you increase your talents in what you desire and value. The development of your self-concept (career anchor) becomes increasingly stable with more and more experience, but Schein feels that it never ceases to change and grow. Because the career anchor is based on perceptions of self, it can change in the following ways:

- Perceptions of talents and abilities can change as you gain experience in a variety of work settings, moving from clinic A to clinic B or field operations to headquarters, for example.
- Perceptions of attitude and values can evolve as you gain experience with the norms and values of different organizations such as marketing versus manufacturing or accounting.
- Perceptions of motives and needs are modified by new experience in different situations and by feedback from a wide variety of others.

The career anchor serves to guide, constrain, stabilize, and integrate your career. It is a way of organizing your experience, identifying your area of contribution in the long run, generating criteria for determining the kinds of work settings in which you want to function, and identifying patterns of ambition and criteria for success by which you will measure yourself. It has some stability over your life and is composed of central concerns or values that will not be given up.

Do not expect to identify your own career anchor right away. If you are typical, you have made arbitrary, short-run adjustments in your life and will not be able to see the consistency in the adjustments that give a pattern to your behavior. You will probably need trained guidance to help you isolate your career anchor.

Schein developed his career-anchor-based theory by interviewing forty-four male MIT Sloan School MBAs several years after graduation. Nearly half were identified with a *technical/functional competence* career anchor. These men were not interested in general management per se but accepted management within their technical or functional field. Their work excited them, and their self-image was connected to feelings of competence within their area. Their roots were in analytical work. This group had a lot of conflict because they disdained and feared general management—the traditional career path in American organizations. They could not reveal to their bosses their desire to remain a functional manager and probably would not have had the courage to turn down a general management job if offered one. They placed a high value on getting a job done and doing it right, as did one group of people who used Driver's steady-state career style. Some examples of the jobs represented in Schein's group of interviewees were manager of engineering, high school teacher and department head, company treasurer, and operations research professor.

The remaining four career anchors were nearly equally represented. One of these was the *managerial competence* career anchor. These individuals perceived themselves as having three major competencies:

- *Analytical*—the ability to identify, analyze, and solve problems under conditions of incomplete information and uncertainty.
- *Interpersonal*—the ability to influence, supervise, lead, manipulate, and control people at all levels of the organization toward the more effective achievement of organizational goals.
- *Emotional*—the capacity to be stimulated by emotional and interpersonal crises rather than exhausted or debilitated by them, able to bear high levels of responsibility without becoming paralyzed, and able to exercise power without guilt or shame.

To these individuals, functional management was a stop along the path to general management. Driver's linear career style might be typical of these people.

Schein interpreted a third group of his interviewees as having a *security-and-stability* career anchor. He felt that these individuals tied their careers to certain organizations or types of organizations that provided long-run stability, a good program of benefits/income/retirement, and basic job security. To maintain this, they tended to do what was required of them by the organization, accepting its definition of their careers and trusting it to treat them right. They appeared to yield their own autonomy, conform, and become dependent. From this description, this group of interviewees would appear to fit the stability portion of Driver's steady-state career style. However, when Schein described the behavior of people in this category of interviewees, they appeared to move from one employer to another to maintain geographical stability around family and other nonwork factors. They did not appear to be work- or career-centered in their values. It is possible that such individuals might use Driver's transitory career style.

Schein called his fourth career anchor *creativity* and described the characteristics and behavior of entrepreneurs rather than scientists, inventors, artists, and so on. These men had a need to build or create something that was entirely their own product. They sought to create an extension of themselves through the creation of a product or process bearing their own name, a company of their own, or a personal fortune that was a measure of their accomplishment. Their values and motives overlapped with other anchors and included autonomy, the opportunity to exercise their special talents, the desire to be managerially competent, and the need to build a fortune in order to be secure. They kept entering new ventures but were always very central and visible. Such entrepreneurs can never settle into a total managerial role. They may start an organization and turn it over to others after it grows or attempt to run it and get forced out or develop a unique role to be able to work on research or play a senior executive role and work on special projects periodically. General management and the entrepreneur are very different types of careers. The entrepreneur behaves like those with Driver's spiral career concept do except that the organization, rather than the occupation, is developed and changed.

A fifth career anchor identified by Schein is *autonomy and independence.* These men sought work situations that were maximally free of organizational constraints to pursue professional or technical/functional competence. They felt that organizational life was restrictive, irrational, and/or intrusive into their private lives and were working as a professor, writer, consultant in a small firm, owner of a small retail firm. With autonomy as a key concern, these individuals had no guilt about missed promotions or not aspiring to higher levels. They were not preoccupied with building something but wanted to be on their own and set their own pace, schedule, lifestyle, and work habits.

Do the five career anchors cover all types of people? Schein has partially repeated his work on two other groups attending Sloan courses and found that the classifications worked again for him (37). However, he conjectures that there may be other career anchors, for example:

1. *Basic identity*—in this career anchor, an individual would identify with a uniform, a powerful employer such as IBM, or other external symbols.
2. *Service to others*—these individuals would express their career anchor (basic needs, talents, and values) by helping others. To them interpersonal competence becomes an end in itself, not a means to an end as it is for the person with a managerial competence career anchor. Social work and nursing may be professions that provide the opportunity to express this career anchor.
3. *Power, influence, and control*—someone with this proposed career anchor would need to exert control or influence over others as in teaching, politics, the ministry, and medicine.
4. *Variety*—some people, such as professors, consultants, and journeymen, may have needs and

values to express a broad range of talents. To them flexibility of response is a major value and boredom a fear. Driver's spiral or transitory career styles may be represented here: although the occupation or employer may not change constantly, the task, project, or work would.

Schein's very comprehensive career theory is the major theory that attempts to integrate the individual with the organization (37). However, it requires much more research before it can be accepted as one to which the practitioner can turn for unquestioned guidance in assessing a personal career anchor or developing an organizational career development program. Others have not been able to replicate Schein's work in other settings because the measures of career anchors have not been submitted to sufficient research to establish their validity and reliability under conditions of individual usage (5). The publisher has not made them readily available for such research (38).

A core ingredient in nearly every major theory of career decision making and development is obtaining information about self. The only problem with this is that we know very little about how accurate adults are at making self-evaluations. High school (25) and college students (7) appear to be very poor at estimating their abilities, aptitudes, and interests without including sexual stereotyping and over- and under estimates. The limited information that is available on an adult's accuracy in self-appraisal concerns job performance. In this instance, there is widespread inflation of self-ratings, indicating that working adults are very lenient with themselves. However, adults differentiate one performance factor from others more clearly than their supervisors do. In addition, if the self-appraisal is shared with others, it tends to become more accurate. It appears that the more you search for information about yourself and possible career roles, the better the fit will be between the two (14). Good analysis requires accurate information about yourself, both good and bad. From the very limited research available on adults, it appears that the following may hold true:

1. Well-standardized measures of important characteristics provide much more accurate information than typical open-ended forms or simple checklists.
2. Sharing your self-appraisal with others whom you can trust to give you feedback may help the accuracy of your self-assessment.
3. If your self-esteem (that is, your general feelings about yourself) is low, obtain assistance. The higher your self-esteem, the less you will feel threatened by negative self-discoveries. Thus the higher your self-esteem, the more self-aware and the better your career selection (14).

DOES DEVELOPMENT MEAN CHANGE THROUGHOUT LIFE?

There is a dynamic interaction that goes on continuously between the developing individual and the constantly changing environment (50). At each point in your life you bring previous experiences with you that affect your development. Many of these came from your early family, community, and school situations, including ethnic background, the family's socioeconomic position, parental occupation, relationships with parents, school climate, and community size. Past economic conditions, social/cultural conditions, community structure, and work environment have influenced you, just as those same factors influence you at the present time. In addition, you influence them.

Career Stages and Development

The most comprehensive and best-researched career theory spanning the entire life of an individual was proposed by Super in 1957 (44). In that early statement of his theory, Super proposed that an individual would go through five sequential career-development stages that consisted of specific tasks and were defined by fixed age periods. As research has accumulated, Super has made his theory more flexible and has placed increasing emphasis on the impact of the external situation and participation in life roles on individual career development.

Super's *growth stage*, which covers the period from birth to age fourteen, is important to an adult, because it includes the first awareness of the impending career decisions concerning education and field of work (47). The identification with key people in the family, community, and school takes place along with fantasizing and role-playing about work. Career aspirations, interests, and abilities develop and are carried into the next stage, *exploration*. Exploration was initially proposed as occurring between the ages of fifteen and twenty-four, but research has shown exploration taking place in the mid-thirties and forties respectively (29,32). It appears that self-examination, role tryouts, and occupational exploration do not take place solely in the schooling, leisure activities, and part-time work of adolescents and young adults as originally proposed, but also in the family, work, community, educational, and social settings of many adults. The early exploratory behaviors were originally categorized as tentative (ages fifteen to seventeen), transitional (ages eighteen to twenty-one), and trial (ages twenty-two to twenty-four). In the tentative phase, needs, interests, capacities, values, and opportunities are all considered. Tentative choices are made and tried out in fantasy, discussion, courses, work, and the like. During transition, reality considerations are given more weight as the labor market or advanced training is entered and an attempt is made to implement a self-concept. During the trial period, an appropriate field is located and a beginning job found, and they are tried out as life work.

The next stage, *establishment,* was initially proposed to cover ages twenty-four to forty-four. The first five years of this stage are considered to comprise a trial period in which one or two changes in the field of work would be made before a life work would be found or it became clear that life work would be a series of unrelated jobs. The last fifteen years in this stage are classified as a stabilization period in which the individual acknowledges commitment to the life's work and to the organization by becoming socialized, progressing, and making a secure place in the field or organization. Super proposes that an adult may recycle to the growth stage during the establishment phase by becoming dissatisfied and aware of an impending decision about the career—life work or organization (45). Progress is then made through exploration and into establishment again. The time periods representing the stages are no longer fixed in Super's modification. The time that someone is in a stage can vary widely from one month in exploration to many years in growth before action is taken to move into exploration and formulate a career question.

Originally Super postulated that the individual moved into the *maintenance* stage at age forty-five and continued therein until sixty-five. In this stage the primary concern is to hold onto the place achieved in the world of work. Little new ground is broken, but the individual continues along established patterns. This stage is entered at a point in the career when the individual has become committed to a field of work or organization and established in it. Now it appears that the maintenance stage can be entered early in life or quite late, and it can carry on beyond age sixty-five or terminate many years earlier in the final stage. Super has observed mature individuals who are involved in exploration and maintenance career concerns simultaneously but have solved establishment tasks (46).

The final stage is referred to as *disengagement.* As physical and mental powers decline, activities at work change and eventually stop. Intense activity may change to become selective participation and then observation. Finally, participation in the work role ceases entirely, and other life roles such as that of spouse or leisurite become prominent. Since the 1950s when the time period for this stage was established, life in America has been altered. Early retirement became very common in the 1970s as a surplus of workers was present. However, now the costs to society are catching up, and a push is on to keep people working longer. If you read career theory in the mid-seventies or read today's popular career literature, you would have the impression that questioning your choice of an occupation at age thirty-five or neglecting to start planning your retirement at age fifty-five is maladaptive. Actually it is typical. Therefore, an older individual may be involved with both exploration and disengagement career stage concerns simultaneously because retirement is imminent, yet there is a need or desire to keep working (46).

Stages of Growth in the Organization

Schein also uses the idea of career stages (37). However, he starts out with a variety of common issues and tasks that everyone might face in one form or another at some time, and he does not restrict these to age groups. He acknowledges an initial period of growth and exploration prior to entering the world of work and describes the key process as obtaining valid information about self and various fields of work. Then one decides upon a match between the two that will best use one's talents and provide a chance to achieve success and satisfaction. He indicates that this period typically spans the first twenty-one years of life.

Entry into the world of work may start at age sixteen for some occupations or at age thirty or so for others. These are early- or late-entry occupations respectively. During this stage (ages sixteen to twenty-five), the individual looks for and chooses the first job and adjusts to the daily routine of work. Learning about balancing being a subordinate (dependence) with developing a skill and showing assertiveness (independence) occurs as part of the entry and basic training period.

The entry stage blends into the stage of full membership in the early career (ages seventeen to thirty). The period of making a unique contribution and functioning without close supervision starts. Promotions and lateral moves may occur, but the primary task is for the individual and the organization to test whether or not they can meet each other's needs in the long run. This stage ends symbolically with the granting of "permanent" membership. The symbol of permanent membership is expressed in many ways. Direct ones are securing tenure as in academia or obtaining a satisfactory performance record for three years in civil service. Indirect indicants in business and industry may be entry into a profit-sharing plan or becoming vested in a corporate pension plan.

At age twenty-five or somewhat later, the individual achieves full membership in the organization and enters mid-career. At this time the issues of using one's wisdom and experience beyond one's technical/specialist skills and fulfilling one's need to be helpful and guide and support more junior members are faced. The decision about a specialty must be resolved along with the consideration of remaining a specialist, becoming more of a generalist, or moving toward management. A clear identity in the organization is established and sufficient experience is gained to allow long-range career plans and ambitions to be made, progress to be sought, and targets for measuring progress to be established. Becoming a productive person in the organization should occur in this stage, and the issue of accepting responsibility for one's own and others' work should be resolved. Many remain in this stage until the late career stage that starts at age forty or thereafter.

However, Schein proposes that many face the mid-career crisis between ages thirty-five and forty-five. Now the career and life are questioned, and one's progress relative to ambitions is reassessed, forcing decisions about the importance of work compared to family or personal roles, about leveling off, changing fields of work or employer, or striving onward and upward. For the professional, a key aspect of the mid-career crisis is the problem of staying current in the presence of rapidly changing knowledge, competition from younger, better-trained people, and a declining energy level.

Late career is described as starting after age forty. Many people stay in a nonleadership role until retirement. They may informally influence others but concentrate on either deepening their skills if the decision is to be a technical/functional specialist, broadening their skills and responsibility if later leadership roles are to be assumed, or accepting reduced influence and challenge if the decision is to level off and seek rewards outside of work. In a late-career, senior leadership role, several management issues become paramount: using skills for the long-range welfare of the organization rather than the profession; learning to integrate and influence the efforts of many others rather than one-to-one; and developing broad-perspective, long-range time horizons and an idea of the role of the organization in society. At some time in this career period, nearly all individuals start to decline and face disengagement. Some start very early. The issues of declining competence and motivation, accepting reduced responsibility and influence, and reducing the dominance of work in one's life must be confronted.

Schein's final stage is *retirement,* that is, leaving the organization or occupation. This can occur as early as age thirty-nine or forty for military, police, firefighters, or a few others in unique fields of work, or as late as the eighties for others such as medical practitioners or lawyers. The issues of prime importance in this career stage are confronting the need or requirement to retire and then adjusting to the drastic change in lifestyle, role, and probably standard of living.

The age ranges for Schein's career stages are very broad because of two factors. People in different occupations and organizations move through the stages at different rates, and differences among the personal characteristics of individuals influence the rate of movement as well. Schein feels one should view career stages "as broad sets of common issues and tasks that everyone faces in some form or another rather than [trying] to attempt to link them systematically to particular ages or other life stages'' (37, p. 48). Because of the interaction of career concerns with personal and family concerns, career patterns will be present only within occupations, socioeconomic levels, and/or organizations (37). You should also view your career as a mutually influential relationship between the organization/profession and the person; not only does the profession/organization influence the individual as typically proposed, but the individual influences the profession/organization (37). This is a key point, because it divides the responsibility between the individual and the organization for the adaptation and renewal of your profession/organization and yourself (14).

Building upon Schein's career theory, Derr proposes five career success orientations that motivate today's workers (6): getting-ahead, getting-secure, getting-free, getting-high, and getting-balanced. For the getting-ahead careerist, the job is of central importance. There is intense desire to be promoted, and success is clearly dependent upon having an effective sponsor and going through the right jobs.

The careerists that are motivated by a need for security desire that their work life, pay, and promotions be predictable. In exchange, the employee provides loyalty and a lot of dedicated work.

The getting-free careerist does not want to be managed, so selecting a place to work is critical. Work is important to such an individual but the work environment must provide a maximum amount of autonomy. Freedom to determine their own dress, hours, work pace, operational approaches, and even tasks are of paramount importance to such people. Exciting work is not as important as the freedom surrounding doing it.

The getting-high careerist is turned on by the work itself. Many scientists and artists become fascinated by what they do and work constantly to perfect their expertise. The entrepreneur becomes involved with conquering the risk present in a new product, project, or process. Another type of getting-high careerist is the ideologue who gets caught up in a mission such as social betterment, saving animals, or improving the environment.

The getting-balanced careerists are unique because they balance their careers with their social and personal lives. These careerists are usually much more aware of their life options and carefully work at keeping each aspect in balance with the other two. In this instance, the career is not the principal driving force behind the individual's motivations (6).

If Derr's theory is applied, it means professionals must very carefully select the organization and the environment within which they work. On the other side, organizations must be careful to select professionals that have a career success orientation that is consistent with the environment that is present within them, or the organizations must be willing to adapt to the needs of their professional employees. It may be difficult for the organization to be all things to all people.

Four Stages of Professionals

Of specific interest to professionals is the career stage theory of Dalton and Thompson (4). They describe how each one of four successive career stages—apprentice, colleague, mentor, and sponsor—involves different tasks, different types of relationships, and different psychological adjustments for professionals (3). Their theory was developed as a result of their work with research-and-development scientists and engineers, accountants, and college professors. In the entry stage, the new professional serves as an apprentice and learns to be an effective subordinate who demonstrates willingness to do routine assignments yet aggressively searches out new and more challenging tasks. By leaving this stage too soon, the individual does not learn from the experience of others. If too much sole responsibility is assumed too early, a reputation for mediocre performance that is hard to overcome will be acquired. At this stage each person learns to learn from others and must adjust to the role of a dependent subordinate and to the constant demands of routine work.

The young professional earns the way into the second, colleagual stage by building a reputation as a technically competent individual. Technical skills are developed to a high level by specializing within an area so that strong competence in a critical organizational task can be demonstrated. This earns the independence to control the specific methods required to get a job done. At this stage the professional is still a subordinate but starts to develop the skill to influence others. The individual becomes less dependent and starts to contribute personal ideas about what to do in a given situation. Many professionals stay in this stage for the rest of their careers and have a reasonably successful career although their value to the organization dwindles over time. Only 20 percent of those over forty years of age who are in this stage are considered above-average performers by their organizations.

Movement into stage 3, mentor, takes place because the individual is able to take increased responsibility for influencing, guiding, directing, and developing other people. The competent specialists from stage 2 now broaden their interests and capabilities and consider wider applications of their knowledge and skill. In addition, they may start to deal with others outside the organization for the benefit of those inside. For example, they may acquire clients or contracts, recruit personnel, obtain resources and funds, or help others obtain a promotion. The individual in this stage may serve within one or a combination of three roles: an informal mentor, a manager, or the "idea person." In the first, those in stage 1 become apprentices and learn the ropes. As a manager, professional competence is still important since the role is not far from the specific tasks. The idea person sells innovative ideas and professional/technical expertise. People come to the idea person for help with problems. At this stage, the professional learns to take care of others and assume responsibility for their work. Interpersonal skills become important as well as sufcient confidence in one's ability to produce results and to help others do the same. Eighty percent of those who make it to this stage were perceived by the organization to be above-average performers after age forty.

Stage 4, sponsor, requires that the individual move up from influencing groups of individuals to affecting the direction of the organization or a major segment of it. Here Dalton and Thompson are not referring only to vice-presidents or above, but to key people who reside in many different positions such as the chief geologist of an oil company. These people can play one or more of three roles: manager, internal entrepreneur, or idea innovator. These upper-level managers are not close to the daily detailed work but establish policy and introduce broad programs. This individual is not involved with apprentice-stage personnel but with those in stage 3 who are preparing for stage 4. The internal entrepreneur originates and implements ideas for new products and programs—often in spite of obstacles that deter progress. Such an individual can be considered a maverick and must be constantly successful to maintain status. The third role a stage 4 person might play is that of an idea innovator, the individual, professional contributor. Such an individual becomes the senior professional person in a field and thereby influences the direction of the organization.

All three roles at stage 4 influence the development of key people and are heavily involved in key contacts outside the organization. They bring in new ideas, sell products, establish relations with clients. These outside relationships, including publications, must be structured and focused in areas of major concern to the organization or they will not be viewed favorably. Those aspiring to move into stage 4 must be willing to give up personal control over the daily work and broaden their time horizons and perspective of the world surrounding the organization. Finally, the person in stage 4 must become accustomed to using power; influence over others is a major ingredient of the tasks that are faced.

You do not have to move through the first three stages into the fourth to be successful, and there are no specific ages that define the limits of the stages (4). In fact the duration of each stage appears to vary according to the individual and the situation. To maintain a high performance rating throughout a career, one should try to achieve at least stage 3. Still, every organization requires people who work in all four stages.

Dalton and Thompson also found instances in which professionals had moved backward from stage 4 to stage 3. It may be possible to do so successfully depending upon the climate of the organization and the capability of the individual.

The three career-stage theories described above can be considered to be representative of those that emanate from a broad base of current research and from different disciplines. One or more of them may be of value to you in reviewing your own career, determining what career concerns and issues are of prime importance to you, and establishing those that you should be involved in and, therefore, need to resolve. In other words, one or more of these theories can provide a structure or frame of reference for your own career decision making and planning. All are more flexible than what was proposed from the 1950s into the mid-1970s. The adaptive, changing nature of the individual and the environment and their interaction is becoming the key to career development, not just the fixed, overall controlling effect of heredity and age (15,21,36,46). The latter influences are still present but do not completely dominate as previously thought. In 1980s thinking, you can have some control over your career destiny via your decisions and behavior. In addition, your career destiny is not totally fixed once you have completed—or not completed—your education, in contrast to the impression obtained in the 1960s and 1970s.

SOCIAL LEARNING THEORY OF CAREER DECISION MAKING

In 1979, Krumboltz published his social learning theory of career decision making (21). Although his theory concentrates on educational and occupational decisions and is built around experience with adolescents and young adults, it is directly relevant to the career decision making and development of adults, and that extension will be emphasized here. It omits career stages and provides a simplified way to look at your current situation. Krumboltz proposes that the interaction of genetic factors, environmental conditions, learning experiences, cognitive and emotional responses, and performance skills produce movement along one career path or another via various decisions and development.

At each decision point in your career, you have one or more options available. You and your environment shape the number and type of alternatives available and the way you will respond. Sometimes you face a glut of options while at other times you feel as though there is no choice. Some choices increase your future alternatives while others limit them. Some consequences are irreversible. Every decision becomes a part of you and your situation, part of your experience and next decision.

Influences

Krumboltz proposes that there are four categories of factors that influence you: genetic endowment and special abilities; environmental conditions and events; learning experiences; and task approach skills. *Genetic endowment and special abilities* consist of personal characteristics that have been fraught with controversy. Few people question the fact that sex, race, and physical appearance and characteristics are inherited. However, such agreement is not the case regarding intelligence, musical ability, artistic ability, and muscular coordination as described by Krumboltz, or emotionality (neuroticism), extroversion/introversion, and spatial ability as described by other authors. (See Hamner and Organ [16] and Dixon and Johnson [8] for a discussion of this debate.) While the possibility exists that some people are born with greater or lesser predispositions than you are to take advantage of learning experiences, solve problems, react to stress, nevertheless, the degree of genetic contribution may vary across these specific abilities. Personality and the environment then affect the development of such abilities differently. In these instances, there is an interaction and environment plays a significant role.

Environmental conditions and events that are man-made or natural form the second category of influences on career decision making and development. Krumboltz acknowledges factors that many adults face but that have not been clearly acknowledged in past theories. One of the ways to look at these factors is to consider them as increasing or decreasing career opportunities. For example, science and technology have not been emphasized in public policy for many years, so the number of jobs available in those professions is limited. Those that are present are concentrated in specific areas such as Boston, southern and central California, and Houston, limiting the chance for a high-technology job if you want to live in Grinnell, Iowa. In another example, commercial airlines hired many pilots in 1979 but not in 1982. In the medical profession, there has been a glut of graduates, forcing medical practitioners to locate in rural areas to find sufficient employment rather than in the traditionally more desirable cities.

Education and training opportunities vary in such factors as accessibility by location, the availability of government loans, the use of the GI Bill, and organization policy. A correspondence course cannot provide advanced scientific training to someone in remote Prudhoe Bay, Alaska, away from a relevant graduate school.

Social policies for selecting trainees and new workers have been modified over the last twenty years, altering the techniques used for selection and the requirements that can be stated for employment. The Equal Employment Opportunity legislation has had a dramatic effect on job and occupational opportunities for the handicapped, women, and various racial and ethnic groups.

Tax laws can make different occupations, locations, and types of organizational settings attractive or not. Institutional, professional, organizational, or governmental action can make it difficult or easy to enter a field, can increase or decrease the amount of time required to prepare for entry, and can influence the amount and type of compensation. Even though the income may be high, as in medicine, the cost in time, money, and effort may be too great for the thirty-eight-year-old engineer to embark on a career in medicine.

Labor laws establish who can work in certain jobs, how long someone can work, and the conditions of employment. As the associated costs increase, automation becomes economically feasible, and the number of available jobs and occupations drops. Labor unions and professional societies set rules that restrict entry to their associated fields of work or support legislation that does so. Licensing is required for fields from blacksmithing to dispensing pharmaceuticals.

Nature increases the risk of failure in many occupations, such as farming and mining, and can be very destructive, as in the eruption of Mount St. Helens in Washington which destroyed tourism and logging. As the demand for natural resources rises and falls, so do opportunities in the fields associated with those industries. For example, the 1983 surplus of oil set back the growth of the synthetic fuels industry; the low fixed price of gold drastically reduced opportunities in gold mining until the 1970s. New technical developments such as the airplane, computer, and biogenetics revolutionized the opportunities for different occupations and organizations tied directly to those products and services and heavily influenced related or competitive fields (railroads and typewriter producers, for example).

Changes in the social system also affect job opportunities. The development of a social conscience has led to a desire to provide for the elderly, poor, sick, dependent children. As a result, government employment at all levels has grown dramatically, along with such jobs as social workers, recreation counselors, nursing aides, nursing-home administrators.

Your family provided training experiences and resources that will influence you the rest of your life. Certain expectations were made of you, and habits and values were inculcated. Your parents or other significant individuals provided role models that you have followed. All of these influence your educational, occupational, organizational, and geographical preferences, skills, and selection. They will continue to do so when you consider whether to take evening courses or transfer to a different location or not. Closely allied to this are neighborhood and community factors. What occupational models were available for you to consider? There may not have been a basic research scientist if you were raised in a small West Virginia mining town. To a youth, the peers in the community are powerful influences that can strengthen or weaken socially approved values and preferences for different career decisions. The availability of cultural events and part-time work to gain vocational experience are also important variables.

The last category of environmental influences is the organization. While Krumboltz limits his reference to the early education, introduction to vocational options, and the degree to which you strive to achieve success in various endeavors, he overlooks a major source, your work organization (21). One work organization or another has a definite influence. Over a span of forty years or more, it forces you to make career decisions; it supports, neglects, or limits your continuing education/training; it affects your lifestyle at work and away; it provides limited or a variety of work experiences. The organization can provide leave time and income for you to finish an education that you always wanted, or it can keep your nose to the grindstone and discard you when your knowledge and skills are no longer needed. The choice of an organization is an important career one.

Past learning experiences form the third category of Krumboltz's factors that influence career decisions. Although the complexities of learning situations make it impossible to include them totally in any theory, Krumboltz concentrates on two major sources. He refers to the first of these as instrumental learning, but we will refer to it as *direct*. You are directly involved in the learning process by your participation, overtly as well as covertly, through your cognitive and emotional responses. The antecedents of the particular situation, such as the environment (legal, cultural, technological) and the task/problem characteristics, set the stage for your response and the consequences from which you learn. The consequences are broad enough to include not only the direct effects of your action (self-evaluation of the results, feedback from others, the results that you observe, impact on others), but also how you perceive and feel about your experience with the results. An example of a direct learning experience is shown in figure 8-5.

Krumboltz terms the second major source of learning as associative (referred to as *indirect* here). You learn indirectly, from the experiences of others, either by observing, hearing about, or reading about them. Career guidebooks, stereotypes, policy, and career folklore that circulate through the organization are all examples of this. Another is modeling, in which you observe and imitate the behavior of others. This does not mean concentrating on a single person but on the successful skills

8-5. Diagrams representing direct learning experiences.

GENERAL MODEL			SPECIFIC EXAMPLE		
Genetic endowment; special abilities and skills		Direct, observable results of action	Scott, age 35 white, male; average writing skill		Paper is accepted for publication; supervisor comments on goal achieved
Planned and unplanned environmental condition or events	Covert and overt actions	Covert reaction to consequences (cognitive and emotional responses)	Laboratory policy supports technical writing; relevant project design and data available	Scott writes paper and submits it to top journal for publication on time.	Scott feels elated by accomplishment; considers that it took time from family
Task or problem		Impact on significant others	Supervisor and Scott set goal to submit one technical paper to a journal within 6 months		Laboratory management comments on significance of event; spouse comments favorably on achievement

that several persons demonstrate and trying to copy them to build your own repertoire. Conversely, you try to avoid using skills that you have interpreted as unsuccessful.

You may also learn indirectly by associating your experience with one that appears to you to be relatively similar. For example, success in writing a technical paper for publication in a respected journal may be generalized to making a presentation on the same topic to a lay audience of businesspeople. Such consequences are not inevitable, and subsequent learning may lead to the opposite interpretation, that the two experiences are very different from each other.

The last of Krumboltz's four categories of variables influencing your career decision making and development consists of *task approach skills*. As a result of the interactions among the first three categories of influences—learning experiences, genetic endowment and special abilities, and the environment—you bring to each new task or problem a set of skills, performance standards and values, work habits, perceptual and cognitive processes (selecting, evaluating, and the like), mental sets, and emotional responses. These task approach skills affect the results you obtain from each task or problem and, in accordance, are modified as a consequence of the results. For example, waiting until near the end of a term to do all of the work on a project may yield acceptable results in college, but procrastinating on more complex projects that require support from others at work may result in missing deadlines and obtaining reprimands. The new feedback may cause a change in work habits.

Consequences of the Influences

Krumboltz then proposes that there are three types of consequences that result from the interactions among the four categories of variables that influence you. One of these consequences is *self-observation generalizations*. These are personal statements, overt or covert, in which you evaluate your own performance, either actual or vicarious, in comparison with a standard that you have learned. For example, Scott in figure 8-5 might feel that he can write a better technical paper than most of his colleagues in the lab but still feel that he cannot equal the top people in his field. Self-observation generalizations may not be very accurate as a result of limited experience or inaccurate self-perceptions. Interest inventories and other methods for accumulating self-observation generalizations may or may not be accurate reflections of your true self. Self-observation generalizations also vary as a result of the context in which they are made. Young lawyers consider themselves to be experts in the company of nonlawyers and to be neophytes when in the company of senior partners of a prestigious legal firm.

Values are another type of self-observation generalization. You learn them by emulating the values of people you admire and copy and by experiencing conditions and events that are most satisfying or dissatisfying to you. For example, you may have found that you value working with mechanical concepts and objects, by designing and building new machinery at work, more than working with people, by participating in Little League projects in the community. Your values concerning religion may be the result of the example and teachings of your parents.

Your reactions to a learning experience may be remembered long after you have forgotten the experience unless the experience was particularly dramatic or traumatic. As a result, interest inventories become effective measures of the results of learning experiences.

The second set of consequences from the interaction of influences on you are *environmental (task approach) skills*. These are cognitive and performance abilities and emotional predispositions for coping with the environment, interpreting it in relation to self-observation generalizations, and making covert or overt predictions about future events. They include skills in clarifying your values, setting goals, generating alternative choices, seeking information. Different career styles result from your experiences with the strategies that you try. From successful experiences you conclude that you can influence the course of your own life while your self-observation of generalized failure may lead you to conclude that you cannot. You acquire and perform sequentially related skills that build on competencies already in your repertoire.

The third class of consequences from the interaction of influences is *actions*. The generalizations and skills developed as a result of learning experiences lead to behavior, such as applying for and completing advanced education, that is relevant to career decision making and development. These career behaviors and the decisions that precede them do not occur only while you are in an educational institution but throughout your life. They are just as relevant at retirement as they were in your early years, but you have learning experiences upon which you can base your career decisions.

The general picture of career development presented by Krumboltz is "of an individual inheriting a given structure, being placed in an environment which provides a variety of events and conditions that facilitate or limit activities, and being exposed to a set of learning experiences, some provided by the environment and some self-initiated. These learning experiences generate self-observation generalizations and task approach skills which lead to specific career-related actions" (21, p. 38). An example can be used to make Krumboltz's model more meaningful:

> Kim was born into an upper-middle-class home as the second of two children (genetic endowment). Although she demonstrates facility with mathematics early (direct learning experience), her mother (environmental condition), a divorced artist, tells her that girls do not have quantitative abilities (indirect learning experience). Kim then decides she cannot do mathematics (self-observation generalization) and emphasizes the development of skill in artwork. A family acquaintance commissions her to do a sculpture and others comment on the high quality of her sketches (direct learning experience). With limited academic success (direct learning experience) as a result of poor study habits, self-discipline, and deference to authority (task approach skills), she struggles through two years of college, majoring in applied design. She defers further education and gets a job as a display designer for a medium-sized department store, and teaches sculpting to children part-time.

Using the theories introduced in this chapter, Kim could have taken steps to make the most of her career.

SUMMARY

This chapter is an introduction to the many decisions, ideas, and processes that professionals go through in their career decision making and planning. Depending on the individual's feeling about being a professional, a career can be defined as an occupational field or as employment by an organization. The perspective leads to the application of several approaches to career decision making that can be used by an individual—expected utility theory, valence-instrumentality-expectancy theory, validating, satisficing, intuitive, and dependent. When using one of these processes, one applies a self-image consisting of interests, personality, cognitive decision/career style, and career anchors (values).

Professionals face many career decisions during their working lives. They go through multiple career or growth stages consisting of many tasks. Sometimes these stages occur more than once. Although the titles of these stages vary among different career theories, the processes are similar. Individuals explore their careers, enter organizations, become established, settle in and mature, and finally leave.

Career decisions are influenced not only by how the task is approached and what personal characteristics are present, but also by environmental conditions, events, and past learning experiences. These influences interact to produce the generalizations all people make about themselves, the skills used in the task, and the actions that they take in making career decisions.

After reading this chapter, you should be able to answer the following questions:

What are the major career decisions faced by a professional?
What are the two primary facets of a career?
What are five different approaches that professionals use to make their career decisions?
What influences the career decision-making process?
What career stages do professionals go through during their work lives?

REFERENCES

1. Cochran, L. 1983. Conflict and integration in career decision schemes. *Journal of Vocational Behavior* 23:87–97.
2. Cullen, J. B. 1983. An occupational taxonomy by professional characteristics: implications for research. *Journal of Vocational Behavior* 22:257–67.
3. Dalton, G. W., and Thompson, P. H. 1986. *Novations: strategies for career management*. Glenview, IL: Scott, Foresman.
4. Dalton, G. W., Thompson, P. H., and Price, R. L. 1977. The four stages of professional careers—a new look at performance by professionals. *Organizational Dynamics* 6(1):19–42.
5. Derr, C. B. 1980. More about career anchors. In *Work, family, and the career: new frontiers in theory and research,* edited by C. B. Derr, pp. 166–87. New York: Praeger.
6. ———. 1986. *Managing the new careerists*. San Francisco, CA: Jossey-Bass.
7. DiNisi, A. S., and Shaw, J. B. 1977. Investigation of the uses of self-reports of abilities. *Journal of Applied Psychology* 26:641–44.
8. Dixon, L. K., and Johnson, R. C. 1980. *The roots of individuality*. Monterey, CA: Brooks/Cole.
9. Driver, M. J. 1980. Career concept measures. Paper read at the workshop, *Instrumentation in Career Research—a Look at New Measures for Research and Application.* Annual meeting of the Academy of Management, Detroit, 10 Aug.
10. ———. 1980. Career concepts and organizational change. In *Work, family and the career: new frontiers in theory and research,* edited by C. B. Derr, pp. 5–17. New York: Praeger.
11. ———. 1981. Demographic and societal factors affecting the linear career crisis. Paper read at the annual meeting of the Eastern Academy of Management, Binghamton, NY, May.
12. Glueck, W. F. 1974. Decision making: organization choice. *Personnel Psychology* 27:77–93.
13. Goldbert, A. E., and Shenhav, Y. A. 1984. R&D career paths: their relation to work goals and productivity. *IEEE Transactions on Engineering Management,* EM-31, 3:111–17.
14. Hall, D. T. 1971. A theoretical model of career subidentity development in organizational settings. *Organizational Behavior and Human Performance* 6:50–76.
15. Hall, D. T., and Mansfield, R. 1975. Relationships of age and seniority with career variables of engineers and scientists. *Journal of Applied Psychology* 60:201–10.
16. Hamner, W. C., and Organ, D. W. 1978. *Organizational behavior: an applied psychological approach*. Dallas, TX: Business Publications.
17. Harren, V. A. 1979. A model of career decision-making for college students. *Journal of Vocational Behavior* 14:119–35.
18. Holland, J. L. 1984. *Making vocational choices: a theory of careers*. 2nd ed. Englewood Cliffs, NJ: Prentice-Hall.
19. Holland, J. L., Magoon, T. M., and Spokane, A. R. 1981. Counseling psychology: career interventions, research, and theory. *Annual Review of Psychology* 32:279–305.
20. Houser, B. B., and Garvey, C. 1983. The impact of family, peers, and educational personnel upon career decision making. *Journal of Vocational Behavior* 23:35–44.
21. Krumboltz, J. D. 1979. A social learning theory of career decision making. In *Social learning and career decision making,* edited by A. M. Mitchell, G. B. Jones, and J. D. Krumboltz, pp. 19–49. Cranston, RI: Carroll.
22. Krumboltz, J. D., et al. 1982. Behaviors associated with "good" and "poor" outcomes in a simulated career decision. *Journal of Vocational Behavior* 21:349–58.
23. London, M., and Stumpf, S. A. 1982. *Managing careers*. Reading, MA: Addison-Wesley.
24. Lunneborg, C. E. 1982. Systematic biases in brief self-ratings of vocational qualifications. *Journal of Vocational Behavior* 20:255–75.
25. Lunneborg, P. W. 1978. Sex and career decision-making styles. *Journal of counseling psychology* 25:299–305.
26. Markham, S. 1983. I can be a bum: knowledge about abilities and life style in vocational behavior. *Journal of Vocational Behavior* 23:72–86.
27. McArthur, C. C. 1967. Career choice starts at home. *Personnel Administration* 30 (July-August):3–5, 12–15.
28. Moment, D. 1967. Career development: a future-oriented historical approach for research and action. *Personnel Administration* 30:6–12.
29. Morrison, R. F. 1977. Career adaptivity: the effective adaptation of managers to changing role demands. *Journal of Applied Psychology* 62:549–58.
30. Morrison, R. F., and Cook, T. M. 1985. Military officer career development and decision making: a multiple-cohort longitudinal analysis of the first twenty-four years, MPL TN 85-4. San Diego, CA: Navy Personnel Research and Development Center.
31. Nisbet, J. D., and Grant, W. 1965. Vocational intentions and decisions of Aberdeen Arts graduates. *Occupational Psychology* 39:215–19.
32. Phillips, S. D. 1982. Career exploration in adulthood. *Journal of Vocational Behavior* 20:129–40.
33. Phillips, S. D., and Strohmer, D. C. 1983. Vocationally mature coping strategies and progress in the decision making process: a canonical analysis. *Journal of Counseling Psychology* 30:395–402.
34. Pieters, G. R. 1968. Predicting organizational choice: a post hoc analysis. *Proceedings of the 76th annual convention.* Washington, DC: American Psychological Association.
35. Pitz, G. F., and Harren, V. A. 1980. An analysis of career decision making from the point of view of information processing and decision theory. *Journal of Vocational Behavior* 16:320–46.
36. Schaie, K. W. 1983. Beyond calendar definition of age, time, and cohort: the general developmental model revisited. Invited address presented at the 91st annual meeting of the American Psychological Association, Anaheim, CA, 28 Aug.
37. Schein, E. H. 1978. *Career dynamics: matching individual and organizational needs*. Reading, MA: Addison-Wesley.
38. ———. 1985. *Career anchors: discovering your real values*. San Diego, CA: University Assoc.
39. Schroder, H. M., Driver, M. J., and Streufert, S. 1967. *Human information processing*. New York: Holt, Rinehart and Winston.
40. Sheard, J. L. 1970. College student preferences for types of work organizations. *Personnel Journal* 49:299–304.
41. Sheehy, G. 1974. *Passages: predictable crises of adult life*. Des Plaines, IL: Bantam.
42. Simon, H. A. 1957. *Administrative behavior: A study of decision-making processes in administrative organizations.* 2nd ed. New York: Macmillan.
43. Soelberg, P. O. 1967. Unprogrammed decision making. *Industrial Management Review:* 8:119–29.
44. Super, D. E. 1957. *The psychology of careers*. New York: Harper.
45. ———. 1980. A life-span, life-space approach to career development. *Journal of Vocational Behavior* 16:282–98.

46. ———. 1985. Coming of age in Middletown: careers in the making. *American Psychologist* 40 (4):405–14.
47. Super, D. E., and Bohn, M. J., Jr. 1970. *Occupational psychology.* Belmont, CA: Wadsworth.
48. Tiedeman, D., and O'Hara, R. 1963. *Career development: choice and adjustment.* New York: College Entrance Examination Board.
49. Tyler, J. L. 1983. Love 'em or leave 'em? Evaluating job offers. *Business Horizons* 26 (3):7–10.
50. Vondracek, F. W., Lerner, R. M., and Schulenberg, J. E. 1983. The concept of development in vocational theory and intervention. *Journal of Vocational Behavior* 23:179–202.
51. Vroom, V. H. 1966. Organizational choice: a study of pre- and post-decision processes. *Organizational Behavior and Human Performance* 1:212–25.

Chapter 9

Establishing a Career

With chapter 8 providing a broad overview of an individual professional's career issues, it is time to focus on the more specific, personal situation. What do you do when you are faced with basic career questions? This chapter introduces you to possible approaches you might use to enter and get established in your career. There can be a tremendous culture shock if your expectations about a new organization or job are unrealistic (27). You need to make sure that your wants are not transferred directly into expectations without passing through reality. Self-selection is the major mechanism open to you as an applicant, because most organizations do not have effective means for matching individual and organizational expectations. You need to try to match not only your knowledge and skills, but also other personal factors such as interests, needs, personality, and values, with the organization and job to enhance your career satisfaction.

CHOOSING THE ORGANIZATION

The term *organization* has a wide variety of meanings. The discussion will cover location, size (small versus large firms), purpose (client service, research, production), type of employer (government, private industry, professional partnership, defense contractor), self-employment, and staff versus line. Choosing a workplace is nearly as important to career satisfaction for many people as choosing a field of work.

Location. Location is a major factor in career-related decisions even though it is not a direct aspect of the career itself (23). In the past, people often restricted their occupational search to the area in which they were raised so that family ties, friendships, and other familiar social contacts could be maintained. For those who find developing new social relationships to be traumatic, remaining in the same locale to start a job can be very helpful. There are three sources of considerable stress imposed by simultaneously starting a new job, marrying, and moving to a new community and new social situation. While some find such a complex set of circumstances challenging, others minimize the stress by finding employment in a familiar geographical area and, thereby, eliminating one source of stress. However, limiting a job search to a specific geographical area may minimize your chances of finding the right kind of job in the right kind of organization for you. Typical professionals are very demanding concerning their work. If the employment situation does not meet your personal needs, no amount of community and social stability can overcome the lack of career satisfaction until you adjust by diverting your attention away from work or developing your own source of employment.

Remaining in or moving to a specific location may be required for personal or family health reasons or to capitalize on a career opportunity for another family member. The dual-career family is very common, and compromises must be made to maintain family relationships. Even though such factors are a significant portion of individual career decisions, very little is written about their impact. It appears in our research that location becomes more and more important as professionals become well established in careers that do not absolutely demand relocation, or career opportunities become limited and interest is diverted from them to the family, community, or personal life.

Holland's *Self-Directed Search,* one of the most commonly used vocational counseling aids (13), does not even mention location. Bolles's *What Color Is Your Parachute?,* a comprehensive, best-selling self-help aid to career decision making (6), makes limited reference to location and provides a section that lists career-counselor catalogs for a few locales. Yet as soon as you, a professional, limit your job search to a specific geographical area, you markedly reduce your chances of finding the job-and-organization combination that will meet your personal career needs. Because of your long involvement in education, training, and preemployment experience, your commitment to a career and the requirement to meet personal career needs are probably very high. When you restrict your search for employment, the potential limit you have placed on the achievement of a high level of career satisfaction can produce a high level of stress. Considerable adjustment may be required to reduce the stress. Bolles provides a means for couples to make joint decisions about a location in a lesser-known book, *The Three Boxes of Life* (5, pp. 363–68).

Size. Most organizations in the United States are small, but they do not employ the majority of workers. The chances that you can function as a full-time, employed professional and concentrate on your specialty in a typical small organization (approximately five hundred employees or less) are relatively slim, unless the organization is one that specializes in the product of *your* field such as medicine, law, research and development, or accounting. The financial resources and the need are not well enough developed in small organizations to keep a professional fully occupied. This also means that you cannot expect to develop collegual associations, because the organization cannot afford to employ others like you or to support external professional activities. In addition, the resources typically are not sufficient for you to be compensated in salary, benefits, and perquisites as you would be in a large organization. The security of your continuing employment may also be less, along with the freedom to determine your own direction and progress. With less resources available, your immediate, continuing contribution is more critical to the progress and survival of the organization.

However, there are major advantages to working in a small organization. Normally, you will have much more access to the top decision-makers because of propinquity (fewer layers of management and less physical separation than in large organizations) and your cost. Your salary will be expensive in relation to the other employees'. Thus you may be involved quickly in relatively major decisions. You may be able to have considerable influence on what you do because the managers of small organizations may not be familiar with what someone in your field can contribute. You will need to be assertive and willing to work with ambiguity unless the organization is in trouble and requires your efforts on specific tasks to aid in its survival.

If your interests are broad, a small organization may be a good one for you. Because of its limited resources, it may need to use your abilities in many facets of the business. Accountants may find themselves in production, marketing, personnel, and information systems rather than just accounting. With your considerable experience in learning, you may be required to learn totally new areas of the business quickly. This often means that in two to three years you may find yourself falling behind in the technical areas of your field as you concentrate on the multitude of new areas to which you are exposed.

In contrast, the large organization will expect you to specialize and concentrate on your field of expertise. If you are a lawyer, you may work in patent law or labor law or corporate law but probably not in all three. If you are an engineer, you may work in marketing to provide technical service on company products for customers, in manufacturing to provide technical service on process changes and problems, in development to modify current products or processes or test new ones, or in research to produce new technology, products, or processes; you will probably work in one but not all four of these areas. In a large organization, you may expect to have more colleagues with whom to work and possibly more opportunity to develop and maintain professional relationships than in small organizations. However, you may have additional administrative requirements in the form of progress reports, project proposals, financial summaries, and recruiting. Your job security should be greater than if you were working for a small organization in the same industry.

Organization Purpose. The closer your field of expertise is to the primary purpose of the organization, the greater will be your chances of having a satisfying career within the organization. Being a company doctor in a paper mill will probably not be as professionally demanding or provide the opportunity to influence the organization as being a psychiatrist in a psychiatric hospital. The same holds true if you are a mechanical engineer in a refinery where chemical engineers wield the most influence or in a machine tool plant that is heavily dependent upon your area of expertise to produce its products and develop new ones. A congruency between your field and its contribution to the central purpose of the organization means that your language and approaches to problem solving will be similar to those of your colleagues that are already in influential positions. Your professional contacts will be accepted and valued because they will be familiar to management. What you can contribute will be understood and acknowledged.

Type of Employer. There are advantages and disadvantages to working in either of the two main areas: the government or private industry. Twenty years ago you might have considered government employment as very secure but relatively more bureaucratic and low paying. To an extent it may have been perceived as more volatile because the whims of the political world might change what you would be doing from day to day. Private industry was perceived as a less secure place of employment, but it provided an opportunity for higher income and less administrative control. As governmental regulations increase, private industry has had to become more like government in order to respond to the requirements. In fact, if the "private" concern is regulated by government, as in a public utility, the differences have become minimal. If the private concern is heavily dependent upon government contracts as in aerospace, it becomes an extension of government and is affected by the political climate even more dramatically than government itself.

More basic research is done in government-supported laboratories than in private industry. The proportion of the sales dollar put into research by industry has dropped markedly in the last two decades. Think tank members who review the American economy propose that those dollars have been taken from research and given to lawyers and accountants so that government regulations can be coped with and the owners' interests supported. If so, the professions of accountancy and law are more critical in private industry today than professions emphasizing technology. It appears that private industry has become reactive and short-term oriented, like government, rather than proactive and long-term oriented. However, in general, industry still provides higher pay for the professional and requires much less administrative control and paperwork on a daily basis. Meanwhile, government provides more opportunity to do basic research and exploratory development work. In some fields, such as social service and public health, the government is the primary employer so there are few opportunities in private industry. Government also provides a highly structured environment with the detailed articulation of employment requirements, tasks, and duties that appeals to many professionals.

Professional service organizations are other types of employers. It may be difficult to think of a university as providing a professional service as do hospitals, law firms, and accounting organizations, but there are major similarities that can help you in your choice of an employer. Universities and other such organizations are similar to the extent that the larger ones allow the professional to specialize within a relatively narrow area of expertise. In many, individuals are accountable for making specific contributions, but the process and timing for many activities are self-imposed. For example, a professor is accountable for teaching, research, and administrative contributions in most universities. How the teaching is done, where research funds are generated, what research area to work in, and many other choices are left to individuals and their colleagues to decide rather than prescribed by the organization's management. In such a system, little support is provided for new members, and they must develop on their own. Without a high tolerance for the ambiguity of such a situation, a professional should avoid it. The need to develop many of your own techniques and resources makes the situation similar to that of the entrepreneur. The development of relationships with colleagues who are evaluating progress and imposing their values makes it very different. You are required to gain their acceptance before you can become a tenured member of the organization. The choice of colleagues who are already in the institution becomes critical to your career success. It would be advantageous to you to find an organization that has a group of colleagues with an educational background similar to yours. If your field of work or even your approach to the work is unique, there is a probability that you may become socially isolated from the other employees, and your financial and technical support limited.

Self-employment. The best way to obtain one of the major career requirements of the typical professional, autonomy, is to go out on your own. The major problem with doing this as soon as you complete your professional training is that you are very highly trained in your field of specialization after six or more years of college-level education but have had no experience or training in running a business. Small businesses fail for two reasons: insufficient funds to get them past the extended period of time that expenses exceed income; and insufficient skill and experience in marketing to identify, contact, and develop a relationship with the potential buyers of your service or product. If it is a product that you are designing, you will need to be able to price it competitively and to produce, deliver, and service it on time at an acceptable cost and quality. If you are providing a service, you may need to develop relationships with other individuals or organizations to help you provide a complete line of services. For example, physicians need to have access to laboratories and hospitals, and dentists require assistance from qualified dental technicians. Buying an ongoing practice or business would give you a quicker start than doing it on your own, but you may not have the ability required to keep it running smoothly. A few can take this route to being their own boss, but the most effective routes are: to work for someone who already has a very effective operation and learn the business or to obtain partners from fields that complement your own, such as marketing and finance. Learning the business skills required to practice your profession from others is probably the best initial strategy in any case. Observe, participate in *all* aspects of the operation, and be willing to learn. Many professionals who desire to get out eventually on their own denigrate the nonprofessional aspects of their employer's activities. That is the formula for failure when you try it alone.

Staff versus Line. Working for an organization in which the primary product is the expertise of a unique group of specialists such as geologists, medical practitioners, and lawyers places the professional in a line position. Providing support services such as research and development or accounting in an organization that produces a product like an automobile places the professional in a staff position. Line personnel are directly involved in producing the product or service for which the organization exists. Staff personnel are involved only indirectly, that is, through the line. The requirements of the two types of positions are very different. The line professional serves as the primary contact with the customer of the organization. Customer contact skills and getting a job done on time are overriding issues for the line professional. Consulting, contract research, and service organizations are typical organizations that have professionals as line employees. In these organizations, line professionals are considered critical to the organization's profitability and continuance. These same organizations may require internal staff services such as accounting to provide the information needed to manage the operation. Such staff professionals are not as accountable for demanding schedules and direct sales so their positions normally are more secure and less stressful than line jobs.

Evaluating the Choices

This section has discussed aspects of organizations in which you might pursue a successful—or unsuccessful—career. Now you need to gather the information necessary to compare one organization with another. Bolles provides some excellent counsel in this area (6). Although the typical adult prefers to learn from others in a social setting, you should still do a lot of homework. Libraries, case studies from MBA programs and books, corporate public relations and personnel departments, magazines such as *Forbes,* and newspapers such as the *Wall Street Journal* provide information about the organizations that interest you. A company's recruiting material will normally give you excellent examples of the educational fields that it considers most valuable. For example, an oil company that emphasizes refining and marketing will put its primary emphasis in organic chemistry and chemical-engineering backgrounds in research and application. One that concentrates on exploration and oil production will concentrate on geologists and production engineers. An organization's annual report may also provide insight if its products are identified. A laboratory that specializes in complex communications technology may be an excellent place for someone with a doctorate in electronics but may not be for a social scientist.

While you are doing the reading, you should informally seek out friends and acquaintances who work in a wide variety of organization types. Many will be able to introduce you to theirs, and their organization will probably be typical of others in that industry. For example, one consumer products company will resemble another, and one financial institution will have similar employment and management practices as others.

The next step should be to talk to personnel officers and professionals from your field of work about what someone with your background would do in their organization. This should be an information-seeking discussion, not an employment search interview (6). If it develops into the latter or you have any initial intent to use it as a surreptitious means to inquire about employment, you will not acquire the information you need, and you will alienate a potential employer when that organization becomes your goal.

A technique based upon one of the major theories of motivation is available to help a systematic, rational decision-maker choose the optimum organization (27). The following is an adaptation of this approach that you might want to try yourself. You can modify or enlarge it to fit your circumstances. Let us assume that you are a chemical engineer with ten years of experience and have developed a good idea of what is important to you in the work that you do. Before or shortly after you start searching for information about organizations you should identify the outcomes (goals) that an *organization* (not a specific job) can provide and rate the importance of each one to you. For example:

MEASUREMENT SCALE		GOALS
5 = Extremely important	3	1. High income
4 = Very important	5	2. Acceptable location
3 = Important	2	3. Variety of jobs
2 = Somewhat important	2	4. Educational opportunity
1 = Slightly important		
0 = Irrelevant		

Thus, location is most important, and variety of jobs available in the organization and opportunity for additional education are least important.

Now you start gathering information about the ability of specific organizations to contribute to the goals (outcomes) that you have evaluated, and provide employment in a job that is reasonably congruent with the type of work that meets your needs (see below, Choosing the Job). As you go through your search for information on potential sources of employment (note that this does *not* include applying for work), you need to assess two more aspects of specific organizations. First, you need to estimate the probability that an outcome (goal) will be present in an organization. Let us assume that you have become familiar with a large oil company (Rock Oil Co.), a governmental agency (Federal Energy Agency), and a consulting partnership (Martinez, Davenport, & Townsend). You might assess each in the following way:

ESTABLISHING A CAREER

MEASUREMENT SCALE

1.0 = A 100% chance that this is true in this organization.
.9 = A 90% chance that this is true in this organization.
.8 = An 80% chance that this is true in this organization.

. . .

0 = No chance that this is true.

	Organization		
GOAL	ROCK OIL	FEDERAL ENERGY	M, D, & T
High income	.6	.3	.8
Acceptable location	.4	.4	.8
Variety of jobs	.6	.7	.4
Educational opportunity	.5	.8	.3

Now you can combine the evaluations you have made to establish how close each organization comes to meeting the desires or goals you have set. This is shown in figure 9-1.

Notice that the consulting firm, Martinez, Davenport, & Townsend, comes out highest of the three organizations with Rock Oil and Federal Energy considerably lower and very close to each other.

However, now you need to add the final piece of information to the equation—what are the chances of obtaining employment with the organization? You can do this by following the example below:

MEASUREMENT SCALE

1.0 = A 100% chance of employment
.9 = A 90% chance of employment
.8 = An 80% chance of employment

. . .

0 = No chance of employment

RESULTS (GOALS)

.6 Rock Oil
.8 Federal Energy
.4 M, D, & T

To make a final determination of each organization's potential contribution to your career, you combine the results of the additional evaluation above with your previous assessment of the organization's ability to meet your goals. This is shown in figure 9-1. These calculations change the rank order of the three organizations with Federal Energy moving to number one and Martinez, Davenport, & Townsend dropping all the way down to number three.

This approach can be used for any number of goals and organizations you want to assess. It could also be used to evaluate different jobs.

CHOOSING THE JOB

Searching for an organization in which you want to work is not the final answer to your job search. You must also determine the specific type of job that is best

---

9-1. Combining the organizational choice information.

ABILITY OF THE ORGANIZATION TO MEET YOUR GOALS

RESULT (GOAL)	ROCK OIL*	FEDERAL ENERGY*	M, D, & T*
High income	.6 × 3 = 1.8	.3 × 3 = 0.9	.8 × 3 = 2.4
Acceptable location	.4 × 5 = 2.0	.4 × 5 = 2.0	.8 × 5 = 4.0
Variety of jobs	.6 × 2 = 1.2	.7 × 2 = 1.4	.4 × 2 = 0.8
Educational opportunity	.5 × 2 = 1.0	.8 × 2 = 1.6	.3 × 2 = 0.6
Total ability of organization to meet goals	6.0	5.9	7.8

CONTRIBUTIONS ORGANIZATIONS CAN MAKE TO YOUR CAREER

ORGANIZATION	TOTAL ABILITY TO MEET GOALS		CHANCE OF EMPLOYMENT		TOTAL POTENTIAL CAREER CONTRIBUTION
Rock Oil	6.0	×	.6	=	3.60
Federal Energy	5.9	×	.8	=	4.72
M, D, & T	7.8	×	.4	=	3.12

*Opportunity in organization times importance.

From Wanous, J. P. 1980. *Organizational entry.* Reading, MA: Addison-Wesley.

suited to your abilities, interests, and desires. Basic research may provide the ultimate challenge to someone who wants to learn new technologies and explore the unknown. Technical service to production or consulting in a hospital or accounting firm may provide the ultimate challenge to someone who enjoys day-to-day problem solving. The best way to establish what type of job is best for you is to describe what the people are like who work in the jobs and are satisfied with their careers. People tend to surround themselves with people who share their interests, competencies, and outlook on the world. Thus, where people congregate, they create an environment that reflects the types they are (13). You should try to match yourself with the group most similar to you. If you are reaching maturity in your career, it may not be essential to choose an organization that provides alternate types of jobs since you may have a clear idea of what you want. However, if it is early in your career or you are questioning the type of work in which you are interested, keep your options open by choosing a position in an organization that has other types of jobs available.

Research. If you place a high value on the pursuit of truth and knowledge for its own sake and a low one on its application, you are similar to researchers in a laboratory rather than engineers in a production plant (9), or to faculty members in a research-oriented university department rather than one that emphasizes teaching. The search for truth, the lack of current knowledge, and the indeterminant end product and length of time required to complete the work make it essential that a researcher have the ability to differentiate among a wide variety of dimensions and to make complex combinations of them (12). The individual in the applied setting is constrained by time to reach quick decisions using limited amounts of information and minimal alternatives. In order not only to stay current, but also to push ahead in your field, you will need to search constantly for new knowledge about your work. Much of this will come from your work, but the rest will come from constant reading, contacting colleagues, and presenting your ideas to others via teaching advanced students, publishing, and presenting papers. If you do not enjoy these scientific-style activities, research may not be the appropriate place for you.

You are also like researchers rather than appliers if you question the authority of management (21) and defer to the authority of professional colleagues (9). It is difficult for managers to wield typical administrative authority in research because the resources that they control (time, money, people, and facilities) cannot be programmed accurately to produce a result. The ability to work with the researcher realistically to adapt goals and schedules requires administrative and technical competence.

You and the people around you in research need to have a higher tolerance for the ambiguity of a poorly defined, dynamic situation than people employed in more applied work (18,21). Research performance is difficult to project and evaluate because the length of time needed to complete work is indefinite and often long. The end product may never be reached and, if it is, may not be exactly what was initially sought or intended.

In contrast to the applied world, those in research tend to be more individualistic. In the physical, biological, and life sciences, people are attracted to the work because of their interest in objects and things rather than in people (9). Thus, there is no strong preference for being in and working in groups (21).

Application. The professionals who provide a service directly to others need to have different characteristics and to behave differently than the scientist. For those who work in a corporation or government in which fellow professionals do not dominate as they do in a law partnership, there tends to be more deference to traditional, formal, hierarchical authority and a concern with practical results. Your applied colleagues such as production engineers will tend to assimilate the goals of the organization more and be more committed to an internal reference group and a set of specialized skills (9). Many aspire to become managers and therefore are not as committed to their profession as are those in research or those only loosely connected to the organization such as medical practitioners or academics. The applied professional in a large organization needs to have a greater preference for being in and working in groups in contrast to the individualistic researcher.

The job of the practitioner may vary dramatically from one organization to another. In a corporate setting, physicians may emphasize preventive medicine including physical examinations, process and product toxicology, noise abatement, and safety and spend very little time doing the work that they were primarily trained to do—curing illness and repairing injuries. The industrial job requires a heavy concentration on long-range planning, budgeting, and fighting for projects and changes that management considers inimical to the organization's primary purpose. This diversion of energy away from the job of being a professional not only alters the direction of the work from curative to preventative, but can also be extremely stressful if it is not anticipated and prepared for.

Another form of application in which many professionals are employed is administrative support to the professionals and professional activities of the organization. It is very common for professionals that become disenchanted with their field of work and do not want to become managers to move into staff functions such as personnel, public relations, and financial management. Their knowledge of the professional field and high level of learning ability typically make them valuable to the organization in the staff roles. If the professionals who choose such a "second" career are highly interested in their new field, they can perform better than all but the best-trained staff specialists and will enjoy greater acceptance by the professionals whom they serve because of their common backgrounds, knowledge, and language. On the other side of the ledger, staff-support jobs normally do not pay as well as the professional, line positions nor do they enjoy equivalent prestige in the organization hierarchy.

Management is also application but is a special case. In a typical organization, professionals do not start out as managers but are initially employed as practitioners within their fields of expertise. Why waste the extensive education that has been acquired! In addition, opportunities will arise to determine if you want to go the management route or not. (This will be discussed later in this chapter.)

Comparing Specific Jobs

Next, you need to establish whether a potential job is a good match for you or not. If you are not employed in an organization that has opportunities to try out different types of jobs, you can try to gather information using the same steps that were described in the previous section about organizations. In this instance, corporations will probably have little information available about specific jobs, but they may have some about general categories of jobs such as engineering and entry-level positions. A major library will have information such as the *Dictionary of Occupational Titles* that can be useful to you. You will have friends and acquaintances who will be pleased to describe what they do in their work and what others do in associated positions. After those sources of information have been exploited, the information-seeking interview can be used, but you will need to talk to people who are in or in close contact with the jobs that you are investigating. As before, it may be difficult to get such interviews because those who tried it before you exploited the process to obtain employment rather than information. If you are as insincere as they were, you may ruin your chances not only to glean information, but also to obtain future employment with that organization.

When you are collecting information about specific jobs, it may be advisable to focus on what the job will be like a year or two after you enter it. Although many organizations attempt to provide challenge and top-notch supervision for entry positions, the majority do not achieve such goals. It will take a year or two for you to get through the adjustment period, whether you are in your first job or your fifth one (27; see chapter 10). Your initial experience in a new job will not be typical

9-2. Comparing personal and job characteristics (needs and values).

IMPORTANCE OF THIS NEED/VALUE TO YOU	NEED/VALUE	JOB'S ABILITY TO FILL NEED/VALUE
Low — Average — High	Advancement	Low — Average — High
	Status	
	Being expert	
	Security	
	Structure*	
	Knowledge of results	
	Autonomy	
	Social contact	
	Collegial contact	
	Meaningfulness of work	
	Responsibility	
	Technical challenge	
	Variety	
	Doing excellent work	
	Opportunity to learn	

*Clear goals, procedural rules, and reporting relationships.

of what you will be doing once you get beyond the entry or adjustment period. Therefore, when you are collecting information on the compatibility between your knowledge, abilities, skills, interests, needs, and values and the job's characteristics, concentrate on the real job, not what it is like immediately upon entry.

To help you with your assessment of jobs, you can develop a rating scale that can be used to compare your own characteristics (see chapters 1, 10, and 11) with those of a job (see figure 9-2). Note that figure 9-2 may not contain all of the characteristics that are important to you such as "specific work schedule," "limited effect on family," "benefit plans," and others. The ones that are presented are typically important to professionals (see chapter 1) or may be present in jobs that are considered to be enriched. (An enriched job is one that provides the job-holder with the opportunity to increase knowledge and abilities and to learn new skills. It would appeal to someone with a strong growth need. For more information, refer to *Organizational behavior and performance*, 2nd ed., by A. D. Szilagyi, Jr. and M. J. Wallace, Jr. [Santa Monica, CA: Goodyear Publishing Co., 1980], pp. 148-83 on job design.)

THE JOB SEARCH

After you have determined the kind of organization and job that will be best for you, it is time to concentrate on the search itself. If this is your first real job search, you will be learning and practicing for the first time. If it is not the first time, you may need to learn some new approaches, or it may be so long since you last looked that you must learn how to search all over again. Job-search skill requirements change according to your circumstances, and your skills deteriorate rapidly when they are not in use. The job search occurs when you move from school to a job, from one employer to another, from the ranks of the unemployed to the employed, and from one job to another within the same organization.

Searching for a job should never be approached in a cavalier, off-hand manner. Your career has a major impact on your life and what you get out of it. If you are unemployed, make job search a full-time effort. If you are employed—or in school—start early, prepare carefully, and work at it as much of your time as you possibly can. You are at a definite advantage in the job market if you are employed rather than unemployed.

Your job search will be most effective if you use the following three methods to obtain an interview:

- *Commitment:* Devoting eight hours a day, five days a week, to the job hunt.
- *Going face-to-face:* Knocking on the door, personally, at every organization that looks the least bit interesting to you.
- *Using contacts:* When you find a place you like, or are curious about, but you cannot get an interview there, asking every person you know if they know someone who works there who can get you an invitation to an interview (6, p. 194).

Job Search as a Student

You should start your job search long before you are scheduled to graduate. While you are in school, a prospective employer will treat you as though you are employed, and finding a job when you are employed is much easier than finding one when you are not (6,14). You are a more attractive, employable commodity when you are employed than when you are not.

Your job search as a student will probably be easier and more comprehensive than any other you will conduct during your life. Your school tasks are clearly defined, and the work load is readily forecasted. Most schools have a program set up to assist you in learning to obtain employment and in making contact with potential employers. The representatives of potential employers will even visit your campus to make it easy for you to contact them and will provide information about their organization ahead of time. You will have access to a library that has a wealth of information about employment prospects and employers. Most faculty members are good sources of information and employer contacts, and you can share experiences with fellow students who are in exactly the same situation that you are.

Taking the First Steps. The best single method for a college student to use in obtaining employment—and knowledge about employment—is to participate in a "co-op" program (undergraduate) or an "internship" (graduate).* Both programs provide actual work experience, and the student and employer learn each other's capabilities. Some summer positions have the same characteristics but normally they are not structured in the same way that co-op programs or internships are.

With or without a work experience program, you should start your job search about a year and a half prior to graduation with information-seeking interviews during academic breaks and the summer period. You will not only gather valuable information, but also gain confidence and experience in interviewing. You will find out what you have to offer that employers are interested in, what a realistic salary might be, and the type of work

---

*In both programs, the school develops a working relationship with an employer. Graduation is dependent upon successful completion of the employment portion of the academic curriculum. For teachers, the program is referred to as "practice teaching." Typically a year's experience is included along with a standard academic curriculum. The work experience may or may not be split into two terms.

that you want to do so that you can prepare a generic résumé. Complete this before you are more than a month into your final academic year.

Preparing a Résumé. Nearly every guide to job searching proposes that you prepare a résumé, that is, a summary of your personal data, educational background, employment objectives, and other career-related information such as honors and leadership activities. Although the most popular book on the job-search market downplays the résumé drastically (6), it may be an element that you must include in the steps you take in preparation for your job search as a student. The résumé is a traditional tool in college recruiting so recruiters may be expecting that you will have one. Thus, if one is not on hand to be left with the recruiter, you may be perceived as not being well prepared.

The following guidelines can help you prepare a résumé, and there are several books on developing a résumé (2,19), but your campus placement office will probably have materials, samples, and possibly assistance. If you are applying for an academic or research position, the advice concerning length and succinctness of content is not appropriate. You will need to list all of your publications, thesis/dissertation, and other achievements to portray your research and teaching experience.

The best strategy for using a résumé is to prepare a unique one for each employer that you contact. It should be tailored exactly to the organization and specific job for which you are interviewing. Access to a word processor makes such résumés feasible. To develop one, you will need to search your library for information about the organization and study the material that the recruiter provides to your college placement office.

Your résumé should contain information that puts your best foot forward, is relevant to the decision to employ you in a professional role, and is an accurate representation of you. You should not lie in the résumé, but you should omit negative information. For example, omit marital status if you are separated or divorced. Sex, race, age, religious preference, height, weight, marital status, and other personal data are usually unrelated to the decision to employ a professional either by law or organizational requirement. Thus, they can be omitted unless you consider the factor critical to *your* employment decision. For example, marital status may be a key factor if you intend to require your future employer either to employ or aid in finding employment for your spouse.

The length of your résumé should be one or at most two pages. The following questions can help you assess what you prepare (2, p. 201):

1. How will my résumé look to the employer?
2. Is there sufficient "white space" so that it does not look crowded on the page?
3. Have I adequately demonstrated and communicated my abilities, interests, and skill?
4. Is my résumé free of irrelevant material?
5. If I include a career objective, is it clear and accurate?
6. Are my spelling and grammar correct?

The seventh item on the list should ask, If I were an employer, would I be able to say, "This document summarizes the candidate information that is most pertinent to our requirements and stimulates my interest in discussing employment possibilities further"? Check that you include an effective means to contact you quickly.

Make drafts of the résumé and get others to review your work. If a situation appears to require a résumé, as in college recruiting on campus, take one with you but do not send it ahead. If you have found your own job opening and the situation does not appear to require a résumé immediately, prepare a generic one ahead of any interview. After each interview, revise it to make it situationally responsive and send it to your prospective employer along with a thank-you letter.

Locating Potential Employers. As a student, you have direct access to three major sources of assistance in a job search—a placement office, faculty members, and your peers. For undergraduates, the placement office may be more effective than the faculty, while for graduate students, the priority may be reversed. The most efficient method available to unemployed professionals is their college placement service if they desire to be reemployed in the same field of work (14). The placement office can provide information about employers that can then be supplemented at the library. The placement-service staff can set up appointments with recruiters, and the placement office, career-counseling center, or your department may run short courses in preparing for and practicing an interview. Whether that training is or is not available, sign up for as many relevant recruiting interviews as you can squeeze into your schedule. The practice you get in the first few is valuable. The job search cannot be a full-time job, but it should absorb as much of your time as possible. As soon as you get settled into the routine of your last year, start preparing for and conducting your search. Treat your search as though it is critical and the last one you will ever conduct—even though the odds are that this will not be the case.

The faculty should have information about and access to many employers in your field. Recruiters will make contact with them, and alumni will provide feedback and contacts. At the undergraduate level, your school may be so large that the faculty finds it difficult to get involved in the process unless you are a top student. Nevertheless, they are a major source and should be pursued.

Your fellow students can provide social support by

assisting with practice interviewing and can provide information about employers. Although they may be able to provide some insights resulting from their parents' experience, they are even more valuable if you schedule periodic discussions after information-seeking interviews, employment interviews, and recruiting trips. One group of students designed a form that each completed and made available to the others after each employer contact. The form included information such as salary, benefits, location, starting positions, promotional and job change opportunities, education and training programs, travel requirements, number of available jobs—exactly the type of information needed to make good decisions.

During your final academic year you should use semester breaks and long holidays—Thanksgiving, Christmas—to create as many alternative choices for future employment as are manageable. Although recruiters typically visit a campus to contact professionals and scientists, in some instances they do not. Then you will need to develop your own contacts with employers in addition to relying upon the faculty and fellow students. The approaches described in a later portion of this chapter are to develop potential employment opportunities during those periods. However, the spring break should be too late if you have exploited the other opportunities effectively. By that time you should be visiting prospective employers and/or negotiating with them.

Interviewing. For graduating college students, exploring potential occupations* is significantly related to preparing for interviewing which, in turn, is related to the recruiter's rating of interview performance (25). The relationships with the recruiter's rating drop markedly or disappear if only one preparatory activity is conducted. The recruiter's rating of interview performance is highly correlated with both the opportunity for a second interview and the frequency of job offers.

It appears that concentrated preparation ahead of time can make your interview go more smoothly and increase the chance that you will wind up with a job offer if you so desire (15). One form of preparation is generic and can be done regardless of the organization or organization representative you are contacting. This preparation involves outlining what you want to find out in an interview, learning how to participate most effectively in an interview, and then practicing. Your information-seeking interviews will have helped you to gain confidence in an interviewing situation and to determine some of the information that you need to acquire in each employment interview.

First, set down what you want to express about yourself during an employment interview that will help the prospective employer decide that you are or are not the applicant that should be hired. You may be expected to express your technical/professional competence by solving a problem or your ethics by describing how you would handle a situation. Your social skills may be probed to determine if you would be a good colleague to have around. You may be questioned about your motivation toward continued learning in your field, management, dependability, or available compensation.

Next, list in order of priority what you want to find out during the employment interview that will aid you in determining whether that employer or job is for you. These must be ranked according to priority because on-campus recruiting interviews are typically quite short, ten to twenty minutes. If you and the interviewer share the time as should be done, you will have only five to ten minutes to acquire the information you need. Thus, you need to make sure that you obtain the most important material. Frame your questions so that you demonstrate your preparedness and present the type of person you want to portray.

Finally, practice the interview several times, with a friend serving as interviewer. Practice presenting yourself in a positive way and as someone who knows what is wanted. To help you learn to cope with different situations, your friend should change behavior from one practice session to another. One time you may be attacked by very direct, negative questions while in another one you may be faced with open-ended psychological queries. For example, "Your grade-point average isn't very good. Why?" versus "Tell me about yourself."

Oddly enough, the interviewers may be untrained and uncomfortable during the interviews. Those individuals will often be professionals who have been plucked from the corporation and sent recruiting because of their technical knowledge. What they want to determine is whether you know your field, are dependable and diligent, take initiative, and will get along with your boss and other employees. (To provide yourself with some idea about the questions you might be asked, see Bachhuber and Harwood [2] or *The Endicott Report* [7]).

The initial portion of the interview is the most critical (28). The first impression that the interviewer forms of you is the major determinant of whether you will receive further consideration. Preparing ahead of time by becoming familiar with the organization, its products/services, and reputation in the field and by practice-interviewing will help you markedly. As you approach the scheduled time, take care of the following obvious but important items:

---

*Career exploration consisted of: exploring the environment for an occupation via reading brochures and other materials, trying a part-time job, or attending career orientation programs; self-exploration via completing self-assessment tests, comparing self to types of occupations, or developing career goals; and acquiring career information. Interview readiness consisted of: self-ratings of previous interview (practice or real) performance; discussing interviews with relevant others; and a rating of self-confidence in an interview (25).

1. Groom yourself carefully and dress appropriately; for example, a coat and tie are required for men
2. Check the time and place and be there early enough (5–10 minutes) to compose yourself
3. Check the spelling of the organization and interviewer's name and practice pronouncing them
4. Greet the interviewer by name, shake hands, and remain standing until asked to be seated
5. Sit erectly but not rigidly; concentrate and express interest continuously in what is being said and done; smile and retain eye contact with the interviewer

By the close of your discussion, you should have helped the interviewer establish:

1. Why you are interested in the organization
2. The occupational field/jobs you are interested in
3. Your qualifications and experience
4. What makes you unique from other applicants (2)

If you feel that the interview is not going well, concentrate on sustaining a positive, confident demeanor. The interviewer may be testing how well you handle adversity.

Toward the end of the interview, closure should be provided by the interviewer. Typically you will be given a period of time in which the organization will contact you with a response that could be a rejection, a request to visit a location of the organization for additional interviews, or, in a few instances, an offer of employment. If one of the latter two alternatives are brought up at the end of the interview, you are not required to give an immediate answer. A common approach would be to express your interest in the organization and position and your appreciation but say you are not in a position to make an immediate decision. Provide a time period in which you will be able to give an answer and make sure you have the name and address of the interviewer so that you can do so.

Within a short period after the interview, write to thank the interviewer for the opportunity to be considered for employment. Provide additional information about yourself if it had been requested or is appropriate and express your continuing interest in the organization and job unless you have decided against any further consideration. Indicate your withdrawal from consideration if that is your decision, say that you are looking forward to a future contact, reiterate your earlier response to a job offer or organization visit, open discussion about specific issues, or accept the offer or visit invitation.

It is very common for the organization that is serious about employing you to invite you to visit the location in which you may work. This provides you with the opportunity to meet potential colleagues and to become familiar with the location and facilities. You will need to prepare yourself with questions that will express your interest in the work and organization and will aid you to make the decision about where you want to be employed. There will be time for long, comprehensive interviews, so you should prepare answers to complex, difficult questions such as:

1. How would you handle a (technical) problem?
2. How would you design a (scientific) experiment?
3. What would you do if (an ethical situation)?
4. What are your goals in life? In your career? What have you done to prepare yourself to achieve them?
5. What makes you unique? Why should you be hired?
6. How do you plan—what do you need to help you—to stay up-to-date in your field?

After your visit, follow it up with a thank-you note to the individual who arranged it. If your travel expenses are being reimbursed, include an honest accounting of your expenses and copies of your lodging and other receipts. If you visited more than one organization on the trip, split the expenses equitably and explain your reason briefly.

Establishing a Salary. Salary and benefits are two items that should be investigated during your preparation for the interviews. Your college placement office is normally an excellent source and can be supplemented by the library, a request to your professional society, and discussions with other students involved in their job searches. As a result of your information search, you should have a potential salary range in mind. It should overlap the top of the range that you have established the potential employer has in mind (6). If the employer's range is $21,000 to $24,000, then you might propose $23,000 to $26,000. This keeps your minimum at the top of the expected range and proposes a maximum that challenges the employer to go beyond the top of his range or expresses an intent to work for future raises. Without preparation, you would be working in the dark and would have to depend upon your potential employer to make an offer. In either case, discuss potential raises based on performance and tenure. Determine how often raises can occur and how large they are.

As part of your salary comparison among job offers, find out what the cost of living is where you will be living. There are wide variations from one geographical area to another.

Fringe Benefits. In most organizations fringe benefits account for 30 percent or more of your income. This portion of your income is not taxable. These benefits apply to all employees and vary little according to your performance. Still, they are a major factor in your income. Some items you might want to investigate are:

1. How are the pension-plan cost and payout determined? Is the plan funded or not? At what length of service do you become vested in it?
2. Is there a profit-sharing or a stock-purchase program? What is its cost to you and what value is it to you? Can you withdraw funds if required?
3. Are there vacation, life insurance, and medical plans available, and how are they supplemented by the organization?

One item that you should discuss is the willingness of your potential employer to reimburse you for any moving expenses from school to the location of your employment. Most provide this benefit. You might also discuss assistance in searching for housing, and in a few instances financial aid may be available for purchasing a residence. These aids are not very common but can simplify your move and help you concentrate on the new job.

What gets you hired? Several employers who had multiple candidates for jobs indicated that they would choose the individual that met the following criteria in order of importance (6, pp. 226-27):

1. Does this prospective employee fit in with the people who are already here?
2. Does this prospective employee give me the feeling of great enthusiasm for this particular job?
3. Does this prospective employee have an appearance that I like?
4. Does this prospective employee give me the feeling that he or she would give that extra boost of energy to the work that I like to see?
5. Does this prospective employee seem to have a genuine enthusiasm for our organization and what it is trying to do?

In addition to providing positive responses to these five questions, professionals or scientists must be able to convince a prospective employer that they are technically competent to do their job.

Job Search in Another Organization or as an Unemployed Professional

Once you have left school, finding a new job in another organization or as an unemployed professional is more complex and difficult. The academic system will not be present to provide a structure that delineates and schedules your activities and time or provides services to aid you in self-assessment, learning job-search skills, preparing for your search, and making contacts with potential employers. You must develop your own structure for your job search and, if necessary, seek and use the social support that can help you get the job done.

The first step is making the decision to seek other employment. You are on your own for this decision unless you are losing your job (fired, laid off, or retired). If your decision includes a potential change in your profession or occupation, you should involve yourself in self-assessment and occupational evaluation (see chapters 10 and 11).

Another instance that can trigger your interest in changing jobs is to be approached by another organization about potential employment with them. You can use a lot of the counsel that follows to aid you in your decision making under these circumstances. This is a special case of career decision making and job search. Treat it as thoroughly as you would a complete job search that winds up with two employment options. Contact friends, talk to acquaintances who are in your field and work for other organizations, obtain library materials, visit convention placement centers to bring yourself up-to-date as quickly as possible about the status of employment opportunities in your profession. Quickly assess your personal situation and your career plans and goals. Discuss your present employer's plans for you. Then decide how far you want to go in following up on the contact about the employment opportunity in another place.

If you seek alternate employment outside your organization while you are still employed, you have two major advantages over the unemployed. One advantage is that prospective employers will perceive you as successful and desirable. The other is that you will not face the very high level of stress that is imposed upon the unemployed (see chapter 10). If you are losing your job, some stress may be alleviated if your organization provides "outplacement" services. Whether such services are helpful or not, the following section should be useful.

Once you have decided to seek other employment, you have to establish how much effort you are going to put into the search. If you are thirty or forty years of age, you have over 65,000 or 45,000 hours of work ahead of you, and that warrants whatever effort you can put into finding the best job and organization that is available. If you are unemployed, job search should be a full-time job. If you are employed, put every minute you can spare into it.

Job Clubs. Before you get started in the actual job search if you are unemployed, you should decide whether you want to develop a strong social support system. The job club is an excellent way to help you concentrate on making your job search a full-time activity, helping the search to be effective, and providing the social support that can reduce your feelings of stress (14).

One group of job clubs is Forty-Plus, with branches located in several major cities in the United States and Canada. The fees are low because companies often help support them. A base of operations including facilities, telephone, and equipment is provided to you. While requirements for participation vary from club to club, in most, you need to be forty years of age or older and must have been earning an annual income of $20,000 or more. The members donate time (two to two and a half days a week) to help run the club, and they concentrate on their personal job search the rest of the time. The duties include searching the newspaper for job openings, "counseling" other members via listening, conducting interview training, contacting potential employers and supporting firms, instructing in résumé writing. The Forty-Plus Clubs provide a highly structured environment, which experience indicates is essential to the effective functioning of the organization and obtaining employment within a reasonable period of time. The typical period of time required to obtain employment after joining is three to six months. Bolles provides a list of Forty-Plus Club locations (6).

Azrin has conducted a systematic study of the effectiveness of the job-finding club (1) that he designed using behavior modification theory (4). Although his study was based on welfare-eligible clients, the structure of the club and results are very similar to those reported by Forty-Plus Clubs. The club's success rate was markedly greater than either traditional or intensive employment assistance. The principal features of Azrin's job-club program are (1, pp. 24–25):

1. The job-seeker treats finding a job as a full-time job.
2. The job-seeker utilizes friends and relatives to a very great extent in locating job leads.
3. The present method relies very heavily on standard scripts, composed in part by the clients, specifying what they are to say in the various job seeking situations such as making telephone calls, writing letters, and answering interview questions.
4. The program attempts to provide all the material and facility support necessary for a job-seeker in obtaining a job such as a telephone, writing materials, photocopying material, and newspaper ads, so that the job search will not be hindered by the lack of materials or facilities.
5. The program provides the usual notices of published positions such as help-wanted ads, but does so in the office where they can be scrutinized under the counselor's supervision, thereby assuring their availability and examination each day.
6. The job-seeker seeks employment as part of a group that is structured so as to provide mutual assistance such as exchanging job leads and monitoring each other's telephone conversations, giving each other rides, etc., thereby providing additional support as well as the motivation that comes from being part of a group.
7. The program shows a job-seeker how to obtain interviews for positions that have not previously been publicized or that in fact may not even yet exist, thereby avoiding the intense competition which otherwise arises with multiple applicants for a single position.
8. The program communicates with the job applicant's family and attempts to enlist their support and encouragement for the job-seeker's efforts in order to maintain his motivation and avoid interference from other family-oriented activities.
9. The program arranges for all the job-seeking activities to occur within the structured supervision and encouragement of the job club sessions, requiring none of the activities to be carried out outside of the session with the necessary exception of the actual job interview.
10. The program uses the telephone contact as the primary method of obtaining job leads and arranging interviews rather than visits, drop-ins, or letter writing.
11. The job club program emphasizes the personal and social skills of the individual in addition to the job-related skills which are ordinarily emphasized.

You should seek out a program like the job club or possibly work at setting up a similar set of personal circumstances. The keys to an effective job-search program are making the activities full-time, highly scheduled, and structured, and making certain they are supported by a social system, facilities, and equipment.

The Résumé. One of the first things that you may want to do before you approach a prospective employer is to prepare a résumé. As stated earlier in this chapter, the use of the résumé should be markedly limited (6). Bolles reports that only one job offer results from sending 1,470 résumés and letters requesting an interview. Thus, the résumé fails in its primary use. He also claims that the résumé is not as effective as other methods as a self-inventory to prepare you for your job hunt. It also fails in presenting an agenda for an interview because your specific search for information about the organization with which you are interviewing is much more relevant. However, the résumé can contribute to finding a job by serving as a memory-jogger for the employer (6). Rather than taking a résumé with you to the interview, offer to mail one within one day after the interview. Thus, you do not send one ahead of you but always leave one behind.

The advice that Bolles offers is very logical (6) but might be modified to deal with a couple of very common situations that face the professional. The academic and research worlds are used to obtaining a very complete, detailed résumé so the counsel and guidelines presented earlier regarding length and succinct context are not appropriate. The best strategy, if possible, is to construct a résumé tailored to the specific organization and job for which you are interviewing. This means following up the interview with a résumé or doing a lot of preparation or information-gathering ahead of time.

In looking at your situation, consider the following (5):

1. There are many jobs out there—two million or more at any one time.
2. If you cannot find a job, those with jobs to offer do not know about you.
3. Most people do not know how to find a job.
4. You have power in the job-hunt process. Employers need employees.
5. The employer should pass your screen, not just vice versa.
6. The person who gets hired is the one who knows how to do so, not necessarily the best applicant.

Job-Search Tactics. You should use as many different search methods as you can but concentrate on those that are most effective for professionals. Emphasize the face-to-face meeting with your potential employer. The telephone can be used to set up interviews but should not be used to inquire about employment opportunities.

While "direct application to employers" is the most commonly used and most effective technique for general use (see fig. 9-3), it has to share the top of the list for professionals (14). While the major users of "direct applications" were older, R&D professionals, engineers, and teachers, the groups that actually obtained jobs via direct application were younger, female, white, teachers, poorer performing R&D personnel, and not under pressure to find a job. In fact, obtaining help through your "college placement service" as an alumnus is a much more efficient approach, especially for teachers, young professionals, and job-seekers with strong decision-making ability. Yet this approach is not widely used.

The use of "private employment agencies" is high for managers, minorities, engineers, the highly educated, and senior job-seekers. The characteristics of the users that found jobs this way included engineers, managers, males, whites, and those with less initiative, less education, and greater barriers (high previous salary and overqualified) than the average college graduate job-seeker. The jobs that they found were of lower overall quality than those found through any other highly used method except "friends and relatives" and "newspaper ads."

College faculty members are the major users of "professional colleagues" as a source of new jobs. The jobs that are found are good ones, and the people who found them were senior-level people with strong personalities. "Personal contacts" were most heavily used by minorities who, along with engineers and good performers, found good-quality jobs. Relatively low-quality jobs were found through "friends and relatives" by young job-seekers with low self-esteem and poor decision-making ability.

"Newspaper ads" resulted in low-quality positions (subprofessional, temporary, outside the professional's field, low-salaried). The users who found jobs via this source tended to be out-of-date professionals, managers, engineers, who were older, lower performers, with greater barriers, such as overqualification and high previous salary.

The other methods listed in figure 9-3 were not used very much; however, those who used "professional societies" found high-quality positions although they often had to relocate.

9-3. The effectiveness of various job-search methods.

METHOD	Percent of Users Reemployed/Employed	
	PROFESSIONALS[a]	GENERAL PUBLIC[b]
School placement service	41	21
Direct application to employer	26	48
Private employment agency	26	24
Personal contacts		
Professional colleagues	23	12
Friends and relatives	4	±20
Newspaper ads	13	24
State employment service	10	14
Professional societies	8	—
Professional journals	3	7
Civil service test	NA	13
Other	0	1

a. Adapted from Kaufman, H. G. 1982. *Professionals in search of work.* New York: Wiley, p. 152.
b. Adapted from Bolles, R. N. 1981. *The three boxes of life.* Berkeley, CA: Ten Speed Press, p. 248.

It appears that a professional should concentrate on direct application to employers, college placement services, personal contacts, professional colleagues, and professional societies to obtain high-quality jobs. There is a strong informal network ("old-boy" system) that operates within professional fields. If you are changing fields of work, direct application to employers is by far the best method. (For more detail about the applicability and effectiveness of job search methods for professionals, see "Job Search Methods" in *Professionals in Search of Work* by H. G. Kaufman [New York: John Wiley & Sons, 1982], pp. 151–93.) You can also increase your chances for becoming employed in a top-notch new job if you search, are willing to relocate, and enhance your credentials by updated or additional education, especially if it results in a degree.

Preparing for interviews, interviewing, following up with a letter (thank-you and résumé), and negotiating an offer are no different for someone who is not a college student than they are for someone who is. Those steps were covered earlier in this chapter. If it is hard to get interviews, intensify your efforts and add more search methods to the techniques you are using. If difficulties continue, you may have to move outside your field or try to create job opportunities where they do not currently exist. If you get interviews but nothing comes out of them, work on your interview techniques. You may have to improve certain areas: your preparation by reading material and gathering information; your posture, grooming, and personal habits (no smoking, gum chewing, and the like); your approach to the interview process (sharing the time equally with the interviewer, listening, asking questions, being respectful); salary requirements; and the point of contact (seeing the person doing the hiring, not the personnel department) (5).

The New Job within Your Organization

Most organizations prefer to try to fill positions that are beyond the entry level from their internal labor pool, that is, from their present employees. This gives you an advantage over an outsider *as long as you have a good performance record*. You may not only be perceived as having the potential to be able to perform in the new job based on your past performance but also be given credit for knowing the organization.

The search for a new job in your own organization requires the same generic steps that it takes to look for one outside. The keys are to establish: what it is that you can and want to do in both the short and long term; where the organization has the opportunities available that can help you achieve your goals; and how you can go about obtaining those opportunities.

At General Electric, a manual was developed for use by technical personnel helping them to analyze themselves and establish their goals (24). A complementary manual aids supervisors in working with the General Electric subordinates. Security Pacific Bank has similar, but less complex self-help booklets that are supplemented by one that describes positions and opportunities within that organization. Sun Company has a job-posting system that is reported to be effective in helping employees to identify opportunities within the company. However, Hewlett-Packard has found such a posting system was ineffective because too many unqualified people were applying (29). Instead Hewlett-Packard designed a career-planning program around the work of John Kotter and his associates (17). The employee's desires and career plans are fed into the Hewlett-Packard career management system via the immediate supervisor. Esso Chemical Research Laboratory has a program of self-development designed to not only aid the individual in self-assessment for career planning but also provide information about the present and future organization and related career requirements (10). The final outputs of the Esso program are career decisions and a career development plan.

What do you do if your organization does not have a career development system that helps you identify your personal status and goals and then aids you to combine your goals with the organization's requirements? The task is tougher if you are on your own but it can be accomplished if you are willing to dedicate considerable time and effort to it. Aids to helping you identify your career goals are present in chapters 10 and 11 of this book. Other self-help materials can be purchased, for example, Bolles's *What Color Is Your Parachute?* (6), which is a best-selling, general guide to job search that is updated annually, and Storey's *Career Dimensions* (24). A self-help workbook, *Career Dimensions* brings together the Career Action Planning and Career Development Planning programs that Storey designed and tested in the late sixties and early seventies. It is probably the most comprehensive, carefully designed, and thoroughly tested program available. (The bases for Storey's approach are Donald Super's career theory [26], Malcolm Knowles's theory of adult learning [16], and Sidney Fine's technique of functional task analysis [8]).

As you completed your self-help materials, you may not have been able to identify experiences that gave you an opportunity to test your abilities and interests in areas beyond your present professional activities. If you have not had such experiences, you should try to test your plan at a low-risk level before seeking a transfer or promotion into areas with which you are not familiar. If you are considering a move into staff-support functions, you can try out some of those activities by obtaining a temporary, part-time assignment that exposes you to what individuals in such jobs do. For example, a personnel department often borrows professionals to aid in recruiting, conducting training, serving on job evaluation committees, and performing similar assignments. The public relations department will request your help in giving talks outside the firm, writing company newsletter articles, and performing similar tasks. The financial side of the organization may need temporary assistance in costing out a new product or process, developing a department or program budget, and the like.

If you are considering a move from research to a more applied function, you can: try consulting on a part-time basis; volunteer as a liaison between your work group and those who should be applying the results of your work; obtain a temporary appointment, summer sabbatical, or leave of absence to work in an applied setting.

What do you do if you are considering whether you want to move into management in your organization or not? Basically, you can undergo the same type of trial run to test your interest in management that is possible in other areas. You can try to do as complete a job as possible in subbing for your boss when he or she is on an extended leave or vacation. An introduction to management can be made by serving in a key leadership position in a community organization such as your church, Little League, or tennis club.

If your organization does not have a well-defined career development program, you may be on your own in obtaining the information you need to identify potential job opportunities. Learn what goes on in other departments by talking to people in the cafeteria, before or after meetings, at training programs, during social events. Your supervisor may be able to help you but her or his knowledge of the organization will probably be quite limited. Some members of your human resources (personnel) department may be helpful. Staff functions that often include the opportunity to work and learn what is done in every organizational department are personnel, auditing, and information systems. Therefore, members of those departments may be helpful. You have a great advantage in your search for information: nearly everyone likes to talk about what they do.

How do you become an applicant for the job or jobs that you feel are of interest to you and you are qualified for? The first step is to ensure that the organization considers you to be a top performer in your present job. Your immediate supervisor is the primary source of this evaluation.

The second step is to identify and complete the tenure, education, and job experience that are required before you can become a legitimate candidate for the job of interest to you. Your personnel department may have this information available as part of the job-evaluation program. Otherwise you will need to approach people who are already in the job, work with those people, or their supervisors.

The third step is to make yourself known to those who are involved in the search for potential candidates and the selection of finalists. The latter step is partially achieved by your performance record and discussions while you are searching for information about job opportunities. You should add to it by consulting, making presentations of your project work, and using other, informal situations to become personally known to people. Just as an interviewee should practice interviewing ahead of time, you should learn and practice good consulting and presentation styles and should prepare materials beforehand.

MOVING INTO MANAGEMENT

Nearly all professionals must sometime face the question of whether they should leave their work as a specialist and move into management or remain a professional. The two types of jobs require very different emphasis and behavior and appear to be handled successfully by different types of people. Once the professional moves into management and remains for very long, it becomes very difficult to return to a scientific role. The manager's technical knowledge becomes obsolete very quickly, approximately five years, and it is difficult to catch up.

What Is Management?

To place this section in perspective, it is essential to define management. Being in direct charge of professionals/scientists and technicians involved in doing the tasks of specialists is supervision, a portion of the management role. In fact, even the next level up, which has one level of supervision between it and hands-on professional work, will be referred to as supervision. Both are closely involved in the technology of the tasks and require that the supervisors be currently knowledgeable in the field. The immediate supervisor will typically be in charge of small projects—or portions of a project—with a subordinate junior professional and a couple of technicians. The second level of supervision will often be in charge of two or three immediate supervisors with a total staff of eight to ten.

The next step up the "management" ladder is the entry level of management—often referred to as lower middle management. These individuals are normally not involved each day in technical problems and spend much of their time on administration, financial, personnel, client relations, and planning activities. For the individual who wants to remain as a professional, there is still a chance to "escape" back to the supervisory or specialist roles. You are close enough to the work to keep up with current technology but only for a while and only if you work at it very hard. In professional organizations, there are often two levels of lower middle management and two levels of upper middle management followed by executive status. The executive hierarchy will also have two levels. The two levels exist primarily, because each major level in an organization needs an entry status in which the individual is expected to learn the unique requirements and behaviors needed to function at that level and to serve as a testing ground.

Trying out portions of a managerial job is the best way to establish whether management is the correct road for you to take. Taking a management training course for professionals will provide little help because most are poorly designed (22). It will be difficult to estimate your ability and interest in management when you are trying out a portion of a technical management job because it may be difficult for you to be objective about that portion of the job that is managerial in nature in contrast to the much larger portion that is technical. If you are lucky, you may work in an organization that provides an opportunity to participate in an assessment center that evaluates your managerial potential/career motivation (20).

Managers versus Professionals. Just like professionals who concentrate in their fields of expertise, managers require a high level of mental ability (11). Both groups may share a need for occupational status and self-actualization (11), while self-assurance is dependent upon the success of their work or organization (21). The key difference is the ability of managers to supervise—that is, direct the work of others and organize and integrate their work toward a goal—and to assimilate the goals of the organization. One way to look at the manager versus the professional is to consider that managers have changed the direction of their careers. To a large extent they have left their professions and allied themselves with the organization. Contacts with professional colleagues are reduced and managerial ones substituted. Technical knowledge tends to become obsolete because there is no time to stay current in the field, teach advanced courses, or get into the detail of new work and creative ideas that keep a professional up-to-date. Formal, hierarchical authority becomes paramount over collegual, expert authority because managers depend upon the former themselves.

Like applied professionals, managers seldom can search for all of the information that they would like to have before making a decision. But they must make decisions, often within short periods of time. Scientists, on the other hand, often can search for the additional data they desire. However, managers differ from applied professionals because much of the information they seek and many of the decisions they make are not directly associated with their initial technical field. The transition from professional to management is a difficult and stressful one for a dedicated professional. Often it is too difficult to give up the area of expertise that led to the managerial opportunity, and the change cannot be made. The result is not successful. It is very difficult to turn down a promotion into management, but individuals are often better judges of their interest and potential for making a successful transition than is the organization.

However, midcareer MIT engineering graduates with average grades and without an advanced degree were much more satisfied with their jobs and felt more successful in their careers if they had moved out of staff engineering into functional or engineering management (3). Consultants and entrepreneurs were average in their perceptions of their career success while general managers were top. Entrepreneurs were highest in job satisfaction while consultants and general managers were average.

To provide you with a little self-help in your decision, complete the management questionnaire in figure 9-4. The key for scoring it is at the end of the questionnaire. It is based on research conducted in a large corporate research-and-development laboratory.

Add your scores together on scales I, III, and V, and divide by three. This is your management orientation score. Add your scores for scales II and IV, and divide by two. This is your professional/scientific orientation score. Which of these two is higher? This is a single indicant of the orientation that you share with others in their fields. Research managers tend to have a very favorable perception of themselves, be materialistic and socially assertive, and satisfied with early life. The engineers tended to be academically oriented and to be involved in several things at a time.

The choice of whether to move into management is a very important one. It may determine how satisfied you will be with the work that you do. Managers get things done through others and do not do it themselves. It can be very rewarding or very frustrating depending upon your motivations, abilities, interests, knowledge, and personality. Many professionals chose their field of work because they felt that it provided a path into management. Some are reluctant to move into management because of their involvement in the professional aspects of their work. However, once they make the transition, they derive considerable unanticipated satisfaction from managerial work. A third group is wrapped up in their professional work and cannot alter their central interests to coincide with the requirements of management. A fourth group may be attracted to management but just does not have the personality or ability to perform adequately in that type of job. Which of the four categories you fall into is a question that you have to answer. Before deciding, try out the various aspects of the management job in temporary situations, such as task force or voluntary community organization leadership, and obtain help to assess your own characteristics as accurately as possible. A move into management could be a very satisfying or a miserable experience. The more effort you put into making a choice, the greater the opportunity that you will make the correct one.

9-4. Management questionnaire.

Circle the response for each item in the following four scales that most closely resembles you. Do not skip any.

I. Favorable Self-Perception
   A. Where would you belong in a list of 100 typical people in the kind of job you can do best?
      1. In the top 5%
      2. In the upper third (but not in the top 5%)
      3. In the middle third
      4. In the lowest third
      5. Haven't given it much thought
   B. How good do you think you are, or could be, as a supervisor?
      1. In the top 5%
      2. In the upper 20% (but not the top 5%)
      3. In the upper half (but not the top 25%)
      4. In the lower half
      5. Don't know
   C. How fast do you usually work?
      1. Much faster than most people
      2. Somewhat faster than most people
      3. At about the same pace as most people
      4. Somewhat slower than most people
      5. Much slower than most people
      6. Unable to tell
   D. If you could work on what you would consider an ideal job, you would:
      1. Work entirely autonomously
      2. Work under only suggested priorities
      3. Expect to be told what to do, but *not* how to do it
      4. Expect to be told what to do and receive suggestions as to how to do it
      5. Expect to be told what to do and how to do it

II. Inquisitive, Professional Orientation
   A. How far did you go in school?
      1. Had some college work
      2. Graduated from college
      3. Completed some graduate training
      4. Completed masters
      5. Completed Ph.D.
      6. Post-doctoral
   B. To how many professional organizations do you now belong?
      1. 0
      2. 1
      3. 2
      4. 3 or more
   C. Which one of the following most nearly fits your pattern of reading?
      1. Devote considerable time to reading in areas directly related to work, but little time reading other things
      2. Devote much time to reading of all kinds including that related to work
      3. Find that there is little time for reading though read as much as possible
      4. About the only reading is the newspaper and occasionally a few magazines
      5. Always have more important things to do than read
   D. Which *one* of the following do you think is closest to describing your personality?
      1. Difficult to really get to know
      2. Have some really close friends and a number of acquaintances
      3. Friendly and easygoing; have a lot of friends
      4. Very jolly; the "life of the party" type
      5. Find it extremely difficult to describe myself

III. Utilitarian Drive
   A. Which *one* of the following goals would you *most* like to meet during the next five years?
      1. Earn a *large* amount of money
      2. Become an executive

3. Develop new ideas and inventions
4. Be free to work on ideas of interest
B. At what age did you start dating as a fairly regular part of your social life?
1. Before 14
2. 14 or 15
3. 16 or 17
4. 18 or 19
5. 20 or after
C. In what size city would you prefer to live?
1. Rural or country
2. 5,000 or less
3. 5,000 to 50,000
4. 50,000 to 200,000
5. 200,000 or more
D. How do you usually behave in a group session with your associates?
1. I feel free to express my views, and I sway the group considerably
2. I feel free to express my views, but the group doesn't always share them
3. I am reluctant to express my views, but they are usually very well received
4. I am reluctant to express my views and unsure of their reception
5. I don't usually participate

IV. Tolerance for Ambiguity
A. Generally, in your work assignments would you prefer:
1. To work on one thing at a time
2. To work on a couple of things at a time
3. To have many things "on the fire" simultaneously
B. What is your present marital status?
1. Single
2. Married, no children
3. Married, one or more children
4. Widowed
5. Separated or divorced
C. Indicate the extent to which you have participated in soliciting funds for charity:
1. Very frequently
2. Frequently
3. Occasionally
4. Seldom
5. Never
D. Indicate the extent to which you have participated in making speeches:
1. Very frequently
2. Frequently
3. Occasionally
4. Seldom
5. Never

V. General Adjustment
A. Concerning the material that was presented to you in high school and college, did you find that you:
1. Often felt the need for a more thorough explanation
2. Sometimes felt the need for more explanation than was presented
3. Usually felt that the material was adequately explained
B. During most of the time until you were age twenty-one, or until you left home, did you live in a place where:
1. You were well treated and happy
2. You were fairly well treated and satisfied
3. Conditions were tolerable
4. Conditions were somewhat unsatisfactory
5. You wanted to leave as soon as possible
C. Approximately what annual salary do you think you will be earning ten years from now?
1. $40,000 or less
2. $50,000

(continued)

9-4. (*Continued*)

      3. $60,000
      4. $70,000
      5. At least $80,000
      6. Will be retired by then
   D. When your opinions differ from others, do you generally:
      1. Keep them to yourself
      2. Express them only to associates
      3. Express them regardless of the status of the person differing with you

Score your responses as follows:
  I. A: *1* = 3; *4* or *5* = 2; *2* or *3* = 1
     B: *1* = 3; *2, 4,* or *5* = 2; *3* = 1
     C: *2* = 3; *1, 4, 5,* or *6* = 2; *3* = 1
     D: *1* = 3; *2, 4,* or *5* = 2; *3* = 1
 II. A: *5* = 3; *1, 3, 4,* or *6* = 2; *2* = 1
     B: *2, 3, 4,* or *5* = 2; *1* = 1
     C: *2* = 3; *1, 4,* or *5* = 2; *3* = 1
     D: *2* = 3; *1, 4,* or *5* = 2; *3* = 1
III. A: *1, 2,* or *3* = 2; *4* = 1
     B: *1, 2, 3,* or *4* = 2; *5* = 1
     C: *2, 3, 4,* or *5* = 2; *1* = 1
     D: *1* = 3; *2, 3,* or *5* = 2; *4* = 1
IV. A: *3* = 3; *1* = 2; *2* = 1
     B: *2, 3, 4,* or *5* = 2; *1* = 1
     C: *1, 2, 3,* or *4* = 2; *5* = 1
     D: *1, 2, 3,* or *4* = 2; *5* = 1
 V. A: *3* = 3; *1* = 2; *2* = 1
     B: *1* = 3; *3, 4,* or *5* = 2; *2* = 1
     C: *4* or *5* = 3; *3* or *6* = 2; *1* or *2* = 1
     D: *3* = 3; *1* or *2* = 2

Add your scores on the four items within a scale together. You should then have five summary scores—one for each scale. The maximum score you can get on scales I, II, and V is 12, and the maximum score you can get for scales III and IV is 9. The minimum score you can get on scales I through IV is 4, but it is 5 on scale V.

Adapted from R. F. Morrison. 1961. Factored life history antecedents of industrial research performance. Ph.D. dissertation. Purdue University, West Lafayette, Indiana.

SUMMARY

In this chapter you were provided with some background and suggestions to help you consider what organizations you should enter, the jobs you should seek, and whether to make the transition into management or not. The material is useful for searching out new organizations or jobs and positions within your present situation.

After reading this chapter, you should be able to answer the following questions:

  How important is location to me?
  How can I determine what type of organization I should work in?
  How can I establish what kind of job I should work in?
  How do I search for a job if I am just graduating from college?
  How do I search for a new employer after I have worked for a while?
  How do I search for a new job within my present organization?
  How do I decide to make the move into management?

REFERENCES

1. Azrin, N. H. 1978. *The job-finding club as a method for obtaining employment for welfare-eligible clients: demonstration, evaluation, and counselor training,* final report, 28 July. Anna, IL: Anna Mental Health and Development Center (NTIS No. 287332).

2. Bachhuber, T. D., and Harwood, R. K. 1978. *Directions: A guide to career planning.* Boston, MA: Houghton Mifflin.
3. Bailyn, L. 1982. Trained as engineers: issues for the management of technical personnel in mid career. In *Career issues in human resource management,* ed. R. Katz, pp. 35-49. Englewood Cliffs, NJ: Prentice-Hall.
4. Bandura, A. 1969. *Principles of behavior modification.* New York: Holt, Rinehart and Winston.
5. Bolles, R. N. 1981. *The three boxes of life.* Berkeley, CA: Ten Speed Press.
6. ———. 1984. *What color is your parachute?* Berkeley, CA: Ten Speed Press.
7. Endicott, F. S. 1975. *The Endicott report.* Evanston, IL: Northwestern Univ.
8. Fine, S. A. 1970. Three kinds of skills: An approach to understanding the nature of human performance. Unpublished manuscript, May. Washington, DC: W. E. Upjohn Institute for Employment Research.
9. French, W. 1982. *The personnel management process.* 5th ed. Boston, MA: Houghton Mifflin.
10. Germain, C., and Burgoyne, J. 1984. Self-development and career planning. *Personal Management* (April):21-24.
11. Ghiselli, E. E. 1971. *Explorations in managerial talent.* Pacific Palisades, CA: Goodyear Publishing.
12. Goldberg, A. I., and Shenhav, Y. A. 1984. R&D career paths: their relation to work goals and productivity. *IEEE Transactions on Engineering Management,* EM-31(3):111-17.
13. Holland, J. L. 1979. *The self-directed search.* 1979 ed. Palo Alto, CA: Consulting Psychologists.
14. Kaufman, H. G. 1982. *Professionals in search of work.* New York: John Wiley.
15. Keenan, A., and Scott, R. S. 1985. Employment success of graduates: relationships to biographical factors and job-seeking behaviors. *Journal of Occupational Behavior* 6:305-11.
16. Knowles, M. S. 1984. *The adult learner: a neglected species.* 3d ed. Houston, TX: Gulf.
17. Kotter, J. P., Faux, V. A., and McArthur, C. 1978. *Self-assessment and career development.* Englewood Cliffs, NJ: Prentice-Hall.
18. Kozlowski, S. W. J., and Hults, B. M. 1986. Joint moderation of the relation between task complexity and job performance for engineers. *Journal of Applied Psychology* 71 (3): 196-202.
19. Lathrop, R. C. 1977. Who's hiring who? Berkeley, CA: Ten Speed Press.
20. London, M., and Bray, D. W. 1983. An assessment center to study career motivation. *Career Center Bulletin* 4 (1):8-13.
21. Lorsch, J. W., and Morse, J. J. 1974. *Organizations and their members: a contingency approach.* New York: Harper & Row.
22. Medcaf, J. W. 1985. Training technologists to become managers. *Research Management* 28 (1):18-21.
23. Morrison, R. F., and Cook, T. M. 1985. *Military officer career development and decision making: a multiple-cohort longitudinal analysis of the first twenty-four years,* MPL TN85-4. San Diego, CA: Navy Personnel Research and Development Center.
24. Storey, W. D. 1976. *Career dimensions.* Crotonville-on-Hudson, NY: General Electric.
25. Stumpf, S. A., Austin, E. J., and Hartman, K. 1984. The impact of career exploration and interview readiness on interview performance and outcomes. *Journal of Vocational Behavior* 24:221-35.
26. Super, D. E. 1985. Coming of age in Middletown: careers in the making. *American Psychologist* 40 (4):405-14.
27. Wanous, J. P. 1980. *Organizational entry.* Reading, MA: Addison-Wesley.
28. Webster, E. C. 1964. *Decision making in the employment interview.* Montreal, Canada: Industrial Relations Centre, McGill Univ.
29. Wilhelm, W. R. 1983. Helping workers to self-manage their careers. *Personnel Administrator* (Aug.):83-89.

Chapter 10

Individual Career Processes and Outputs

Once in the organization, the professional must deal with a number of predictable issues. Initially, the newcomer needs to learn how the organization defines the work content and role of professionals. After this early socialization experience, the professional might be satisfied with the "match" or conclude that it is not right and decide to leave the function or the organization. Regardless of whether the decision is to stay or leave the organization, professional obsolescence is an issue which must be faced. And, if the professional decided to stay but the organization decided otherwise, involuntary termination may occur. Later in the career, retirement planning is an activity that all must engage in.

LEARNING ABOUT THE ORGANIZATION

When a professional enters an organization for the first time, a period of socialization to the organization occurs. When this process works effectively, the professional develops:

- A feeling of competence, of really understanding and contributing to the objectives of the group
- A feeling of acceptance by the work group, both professionally and personally
- A comfort level with the day-to-day activities and interactions with others that leads to a sense of security

Not all of the factors that affect this socialization to the organization (the organization's perspective) or personalization of the organization (the person's perspective) are well understood or completely defined. However, there has been a good deal of research and theorizing, and there is a consistency in the stages proposed to describe this process, even though the labels and descriptions differ somewhat from author to author. For example, Feldman presents a three-stage entry model (13,14):

- *Anticipatory socialization* or "getting in"—the testing of the realism of one's expectations
- *Accommodation* or "breaking in"—learning the job, the people, the role, the performance expectations
- *Role management* or "settling in"—handling role conflicts and work/home life conflicts

Buchanan's three-stage early career model (7) is similar:

- *Basic training and initiation*—clarifying one's role, acceptance by the work group, and the testing of one's expectations about the job and organization
- *Performance*—personal impact and contribution issues are resolved; commitment and loyalty develop
- *Organizational dependability*—issues are resolved and the person settles in as a contributor

Porter, Lawler, and Hackman have also introduced a three-stage model (30):

- *Prearrival*—the influence of one's personal expectations and values; the degree to which one was actively recruited versus actively attempting to convince the organization to hire them
- *Encounter*—the degree to which the values and expectations brought by the person are reinforced, ignored, or punished by the organization
- *Change and acquisition*—the organization's impact on the person's self-image, relationships, values, and behaviors

Schein also presents a three-stage model (34):

- *Entry*—learning the organization and expectations
- *Socialization*—learning how to work with others, how to get ideas accepted, how to do the assigned job, how the reward system works; development of an identity within the organization

- *Mutual acceptance*—transition from newcomer to insider; signals from the employee to the organization and vice versa that the relationship is mutually beneficial and rewarding

Finally, Lewin's classic theory of behavioral and attitudinal change shows three stages (27):

- *Unfreezing*—the person is placed in a situation or confronted with data which challenges the accuracy or adequacy of currently held beliefs or attitudes
- *New data*—the dissonance created by unfreezing creates an openness to new data, concepts, behaviors, and an increased observation of other successful models in the environment
- *Refreezing*—the new attitude or behavior is internalized, reinforced, and assimilated into the person's behavioral or attitudinal repertoire

The first few days, weeks, months that a professional spends on a new job can lead to unfreezing, the first step in change. This openness to the environmental cues might be likened to the phenomenon known as "imprinting" in the development of baby chicks—that is, there is a certain critical period of time during which the newly hatched chick is so open to the environment that the first thing to move is perceived as the mother chicken and is followed immediately by the baby chick. This extreme openness to environmental cues can also occur when people are thrown into situations which are so new or different that they have no habitual response or way of thinking about the experience. With professionals, an accommodation needs to occur with the demands not only of the particular organization, but also of the professional community. The individual's need to understand the situation leads to a variety of information-seeking and coping mechanisms. In stage two of Lewin's theory, this new data can lead to changes in behavior or attitude which are then "refrozen" in stage three as they prove productive. The importance of the boss, peers, and subordinates in this process cannot be overstated. The new person is learning many things and establishing many new relationships with people. There is a tremendous amount of observation occurring while the new person is forming hypotheses about what it takes to be successful in this environment. Given this type of analysis it becomes obvious why a natural mentor-seeking behavior occurs during these stages as the newcomer attempts to achieve a successful socialization without all the trial and error that might occur without a successful role model to emulate.

Perhaps the most integrative model is presented by Wanous in his book *Organizational Entry* (37). The stages he presents are:

1. *Confronting and accepting organizational reality.* A number of things will happen in this stage. Personal expectations are either confirmed or disconfirmed. Conflicts are identified between personal values and the organizational environment. The person is very open to which aspects of behavior and performance are reinforced, ignored, or punished.
2. *Achieving role clarity.* The new person is initiated to the tasks of the job and the standards of performance on the job. Accepted behaviors toward one's peers and boss are learned. The reality that "not all my ideas will be accepted as great ones" occurs. The person learns the degree of structure/ambiguity to expect.
3. *Locating oneself in the organizational context.* Resolution of the issues presented in stage two occurs here. The learning of which behaviors will "work" in the organization and the acceptance of these values is the issue. A positive resolution will mean a personal commitment to the work and the establishment of an altered self-image, interpersonal relationships, and personal values.
4. *Detecting signposts of successful socialization.* "Signals" are sent between the person and the organization to indicate a mutual acceptance. The person looks to the performance-appraisal process, the informal feedback, salary increases, being in on shared secrets, the provision of special privileges, or actual promotions to signal acceptance. The organization also looks for signals of commitment from the person: enthusiasm, long hours, "over and above" duty.

The role clarity issue can be particularly difficult for the professional within the organization. Pelz and Andrews found that scientists tend to have an internal motivation to use their valued skills, to make a scientific contribution, and to have the freedom to follow their own ideas (29, p. 100). If the organization is perceived as stifling their ability to express this creativity during the early socialization, then the role clarity and commitment are never achieved. The person gets "stuck" in stage one and never really makes the contribution that he or she might be capable of making. Eiduson points out that the scientist's self-definition is very heavily tied to work and work contributions (10, p. 95). Relationships outside of work are not as central to their personal identity and feelings of self-worth. Because of this, we can infer the even more critical impact of the socialization process on the new scientist in the organization.

In *Professional Education*, Schein describes some mechanisms that are applicable to the early professional career (33, pp. 123–27): apprenticeships, career halfway houses, and workshops. With an apprenticeship the professional works under senior professionals immedi-

ately after graduation. This timing clearly has important implications for the learning of professional norms and career paths. The early career experience will shape the degree of conceptual innovativeness and creativity that is expected on the job. Often the first job appears overly constricting after a more "wide-open" graduate program environment. In the licensed sciences, the apprenticeship is widely used as a necessary part of the professional career path. Putting the novice under the senior professional tends to reinforce the traditional values of the discipline and is an important means of "passing along" the norms of the discipline. Consider the first jobs in the legal, accounting, or medical professions. All tend very quickly to test the idealism of the newcomer with the pragmatics of the business. The way in which the person comes to terms with the expectation versus the reality is part of the professional's socialization to the world of work. One way to diverge from the traditional model of apprenticeship is through alternative paths, such as Schein's "career halfway house" concept. This is his description:

> The role-innovative professional must have in the early part of his career a kind of "career halfway house" where the new conceptions gained in school continue to be supported in an actual job situation until the graduate gains enough self-confidence to pursue his innovative role on his own. . . . Certain kinds of postdoctoral fellowships serve a similar purpose if the project on which the person is working facilitates his learning a new kind of professional role through providing contact with innovative professionals. As community centers in medicine, law, and architecture spring up under the auspices of local professional schools, work in such centers will also serve as a halfway house for postgraduate students. The essence of these various activities is that the young professional retains some link to his teachers while actually pursuing his job or apprenticeship. This link can serve as a counterweight to the traditional norms of professional practice unless, of course, the professional school itself is traditionally oriented. In our view, for role innovation to occur, there must be both a more flexible school and a more flexible set of early career paths. Neither element by itself will be sufficient (33, pp. 124-25).

Professional education can only introduce the person to some of the issues which will be faced on the job. Schein correctly points to the need for continuing education supported by the professional group itself. When you consider the more complex aspects of the professional job, as evidenced in questions posed by incumbents, this need becomes clear:

> What is my appropriate role in the organization?
> How do I plan and manage projects?
> How can I best manage a task force?
> How do I juggle the managerial and professional roles?

After the person has some experience with the organization, the treatment of these issues will be more meaningful and realistic. An example might be the general human relations workshops offered by the National Training Laboratories. These are specifically focused on helping professional groups come to terms with specific issues in their jobs. For example, there is an NTL program for juvenile court judges, probation officers, and social workers to help them deliver a better integrated service to the community. Here, the teamwork aspect was the focus. This is not an unusual need for the individually oriented and educated professional.

Organizations tend to use a mixture of five basic socialization strategies when a newcomer enters the organization. These facts are never really taught in graduate school; it may be helpful to be aware of the activities most likely to occur as you enter a new organization. The basic strategies are:

1. *Training*—the imparting of job-specific knowledge and skills that are directly relevant to the performance on the job.
2. *Education*—the providing of organizational policies, procedures, norms, expectations that are not directly relevant to performance on the job.
3. *Apprenticeship*—the establishment of a one-on-one relationship between the newcomer and an "old-timer" so that both training and education can occur.
4. *Debasement experiences*—the little-discussed practice of doing things designed to unhinge the person from previously held values or beliefs and to so humble the person that he or she is ready and willing to change in the direction of the organizational norms. The newcomer is placed in a difficult, ill-defined, or menial task situation which has the effect of shaking the confidence of the person sufficiently so he or she is open to new ways of thinking.
5. *Cooptation or seduction*—a racy term to describe a subtle process by which newcomers are given illusory choices by committing to a particular view that the organization holds, when in reality the alternative is much less attractive. The newcomer then rationalizes after the choice that the choice was a wise one. For example, the organization curtails funds for travel to professional society meetings but provides extra time to write articles which get published under the organization's name. Does the person orient toward the meetings (taking vacation and personal time) or toward the writing? It looks as though there is a real choice

there, but the organization structures the incentives essentially to make the decision for you.

From another point of view, the Management Progress Study at AT&T tracked 274 new managers through their careers and found that the degree of job challenge in the first year was significantly related to job performance and salary increases later in the career (5). High but attainable challenge in the first year led to the adoption of high work standards; early success led to more challenging assignments, more success, and the development of a "success cycle." *Challenge* was defined as the degree to which:

- The boss sets a model for achievement
- The job itself is stimulating
- One has supervisory responsibility
- The job includes unstructured assignments

In fact, a majority of the errors in prediction from the selection device in that study could be traced to the degree to which challenge was or was not an early part of the person's career experience. This makes an important statement with regard to the interaction between selection and socialization.

The impact of selection in this process is linked to another process at work—that of self-selection. The person chooses a particular profession and receives a large amount of socialization to the profession in the formal educational system. Organizational orientation programs sometimes seem to start with the assumption that an antidote needs to be applied in order to get the person to fit into the organization. In reality, professionals tend to self-select into both the organizations and the jobs that match their own needs and values. Consider the Miller and Wager finding that among 390 aerospace engineers, those with doctoral degrees tended toward basic research and those with master's degrees tended toward applied research units (28). This suggests a need on the part of the organization to be very explicit regarding the nature of the organization and of the jobs available to incoming professionals (see chapter 3).

LEAVING THE FUNCTION OR THE ORGANIZATION

All of the "fit" issues discussed above can lead to one of two possible outcomes: the individual either stays in the job in the organization or leaves either the job or the organization. This decision is affected by external forces as well. Adverse economic conditions or varying levels of government funding can prompt the decision to stay or leave. Several studies have shown the effect of the major cutbacks of government spending during the late 1960s and early 1970s on the employment of professionals. For example, Hall and Mansfield showed that as the economic conditions worsened, professionals began to perceive their jobs as being less secure and offering less personal growth opportunities, resulting in lessened job satisfaction (19). Blonder's work indicates that the mass terminations of fellow professional employees had an impact on those who remained, resulting in: higher anxiety, resentment toward the organization, and lower interest in the work itself (3). Another study carried out by Bucher and Reece showed the security needs of scientists and engineers increased during the recession period (8). People cope with such events in different ways. Kaufman argues that "some professionals may seek a job or career change to cope with the stress generated by insecurity" (20, p. 20). Job insecurity under these conditions also leads to drastic changes in career goals among those who kept their job (9). Job changes create stress (38) that career counselors often must help confront and alleviate (15,31).

If you decide (or someone decides for you) that you are going to leave your function or the organization, the alternative employment settings are these (34, pp. 15–16):

1. Full-time self-employed—such as the small town lawyer or doctor, the individual consultant
2. Part-time self-employed and part-time employee of a service organization—such as an internist at the hospital starting a private practice, or a consulting psychologist who teaches part-time at the local university
3. Partner in a group practice—the small architectural firm or the medical group
4. Full-time employee of a service organization devoted to the delivery of the professional service—the professor at the university, the employee of the accounting firm
5. Full-time employee of an organization not primarily devoted to the delivery of the professional service—such as the professional within the business or government organization
6. Full-time professional representing an association—such as the examiner on a licensing board, the president of the American Medical Association

In large part the personal values of the professional will greatly determine in which of the above roles the person feels most comfortable and in which his or her life's work should be spent. As the person grows and develops and as the career proceeds, either a "bad fit" or a success could lead the person to rethink personal and professional goals. There is always the personal option to move on and try something new. Then our recommendation would be to use career and life planning self-analytic techniques (see chapter 11).

CHANGING PROFESSIONAL AREAS

How do you differentiate being unhappy in your professional area from simply being unhappy in a specific job or situation? Unhappiness with the profession is a much tougher conclusion to reach, partly because so much time and effort have already been invested in it. The emotional stress that occurs around loss of one's job can also lead to a dissatisfaction with the totality of one's own career (12) and the timely conclusion that looking for a job in a completely different area is the answer.

Certain conditions aid in making the occupational change decision (20, pp. 78–80):

- Having voluntarily left a previous job
- Having the financial resources to allow a job search
- Having already experienced a major role change—for example, from an individual contributor to a supervisor
- Not keeping totally up-to-date in the field; experiencing some of the tensions around issues of technical obsolescence
- Not achieving a high level of proficiency in your field; not receiving consistent professional recognition
- Having a willingness to try something new, especially if you are in your thirties

One factor that may lead to the decision to leave a professional occupation is what Glaser describes as the *feeling of comparative failure* (18). In science, there are a few highly visible "great men" who have made the extraordinary achievements in their area of expertise. These heroes, or idols, become models that are rarely attained. Couple this with the typical professional need for recognition in the scientific endeavor and the conclusion is that it is surprising that more people do not become significantly disenchanted with their comparative inability to achieve in their profession. The young professional tends to emulate and internalize the "great man," yet never achieves the same greatness. Over time, the budding professional realizes that he or she will never gain the stature of the heroes of the profession, leading to a feeling of comparative failure. Under these conditions, a professional may be prompted to leave the occupation and pursue other forms of career success.

Bailyn measured the concept of occupational success through two self-report items in her questionnaire (2):

> At this point in your professional life, how successful do you think you are in your work?
> How successful do you think you will be at the height of your career?

Her research showed that the highest paid group in her study, the science professors, expressed the lowest degree of feelings of occupational success. She cites the tendency among scientists to measure their degree of success against the giants of the field (23,24), a concept very much akin to the comparative failure concept presented earlier.

When personal expectations and values are not met, the incentives to consider other occupational alternatives are greater. The other end of the continuum should also be considered. The "great men" who do achieve the pinnacle of their profession will occasionally look for another arena in which to make a major personal or professional contribution. The role will sometimes then blur into one of social conscience, public commentator, social engineer, political figure, or business leader. When one is changing occupational pursuits after a major success, often the next contribution is as an entrepreneur or independent consultant.

AVOIDING OBSOLESCENCE

Kaufman defines professional obsolescence as "the degree to which organizational professionals lack the up-to-date knowledge or skills necessary to maintain effective performance in either their current or future work roles" (20, p. 23). To the extent that this is a current problem, it only forebodes a more ominous future problem. It has been estimated that to stay abreast, 20 percent of the professional's working time should be devoted to reading the published literature (17). The reality is that professionals within organizations only rarely are able to invest this amount of time. Reading is usually oriented very specifically toward a job issue, not in an attempt to keep current in the field. Modern times see such terms as *information explosion* and the *knowledge revolution* becoming a way of life. Professionals have only recently begun to grapple with this issue, and the discussion is revealing obsolescence to be a more complex phenomenon than it first appears.

The negative impact of professional obsolescence can be seen in a number of potential outcomes:

- Low job satisfaction and morale
- Turnover, leaving the organization
- Decreased commitment and productivity
- Limited advancement opportunity
- High costs of activities to keep employees current
- Inability to compete in the market

The organization can attempt to develop "early warning" signals for itself through the monitoring of technical, social, economic, legislative, and cultural changes as they affect the organization's strategic mission. Economic and technical forecasting groups exist to provide this type of data. The more relevant issues here relate to the activities that individuals can engage in to avoid or cope with personal obsolescence. The human resource review programs in chapter 4 can be used to track the extent to which these individual efforts are deemed to be successful by the organization (that is, the ratings of current knowledge, skills, or abilities versus a standard of those needed now or in the future). Organizations might also conduct needs analysis studies to discover discrepancies between current levels of knowledge and those needed in the organization to be successful in the future.

From the individual's point of view, Kaufman identifies three "built-in obsolescence" characteristics that predispose a person toward obsolescence before even begining a career (20, p. 67):

- A limited capacity for knowledge acquisition that is determined by the individual's intellectual and cognitive abilities
- A lack or loss of internal motivation to stay up-to-date that is related to the individual's interests, needs, goals, energy, and initiative
- Personality predispositions that involve a weak self-concept and poor adaptability to change

Obsolescence might be thought of as the inability or refusal to respond actively to change. This is a key issue at midcareer (21), deserving of early warning signals to answer the question, "Are you getting stale?" (11). Professionals vary a great deal in their risk-taking versus cautiousness-prone behavior. The environments of the organizations they work within also vary. If you are protectionistic, introverted, and conservative by nature and have successfully found an organization that shares these values, then you are probably quite comfortable today. However, it is likely that the professional will experience obsolescence and that the organization may not survive if it operates in the typical chaotic environment of today's marketplace. Neither professional nor organization will recognize the onset of obsolescence until it is too late.

Obsolescence is the type of phenomenon everyone figures is going to happen to someone else. Yet, for specialists, who are narrowly focused and have lost their intuitive, peripheral vision, the likelihood of obsolescence is greater. The organization may or may not have the vision, resources, and values to support obsolescence-avoidance programs. Each professional must be personally responsible for keeping up-to-date. As with any other form of personal growth, no one can substitute for you in this area.

Consider also the cyclical nature of much of professional work. Much is project-related and relies on government contracts; the research development cycle creates employment "waves" where many scientists or engineers are needed in a specific area and later many are laid off. What you are working on now may seem all-critical for the moment, but your career will far outlast that single project, and the time to plan it is now.

One clear path to counteract the likelihood of obsolescence is to broaden one's focus. Taking the step into management will develop general people-oriented skills that are always in demand. This is one way to keep your options open. There are often opportunities to redefine your current position to include a portion of "management/supervision" and a portion of "individual contributor."

Managerial experience is surely not the only antidote to obsolescence, and in fact does not even directly address the professional obsolescence phenomenon. Moving too quickly into a purely supervisory position can speed up the rate at which professional obsolescence sets in. Given limited time in the day, the supervisor concentrates on supervision and the professional on individual contributions. Who falls behind in the professional literature more quickly? For whom will professional publications be more likely?

The key to avoiding obsolescence from an individual point of view is to *prevent* it by having both the ability and motivation to continue to learn and to change. This is no easy task. The clear implication for our educational systems is that the focus needs to be less on the transfer of known facts (since they are becoming outdated at a faster and faster pace) and more on the skill of learning how to learn and of having an openness to new learning. The very best teachers are those that are still the very best learners. An advanced degree does not mean the end of the learning process.

The clear charge for professional societies must be to encourage continuing education. That role has certainly not been taken by the large majority of organizations employing professionals, nor is it likely that these organizations would even support the professional's efforts to remain current. The charge, then, falls to the individual efforts of individual professionals with the support and direction of the professional society.

Ths last point is critical. With limited direct observational data and from only one organization's vantage point, the individual professional probably will not have the slightest idea where the profession is headed—current thought, future "hot spots," research topics, social needs, economic realities, and so on. It must be the function of the professional group to provide the organized, strategic leadership and communication needed to crystallize the issues. "Continuing education" in this view should be seen as the process that keeps us all open to learning, stimulated, excited, vibrant; not the more limited traditional sense of the direct transfer of specific facts. Professional societies and publications have traditionally played both roles. Professionals need to know the journals that cover strictly empirical topics and those that engage in the point-counterpoint debates on the less well-defined ethical/moral issues of the day. The mature professional has long since given up on finding the expert's *answer;* to the contrary, the continuing education curiosity tends to peak when the interesting *questions* are surfaced.

Professionals find themselves most obsolescence-prone when they do not recognize the scientific, aesthetic, or applied value of their work. An adult must be motivated to learn; and must see how the new knowledge, skill, or behavior might be valuable. There must be some discomfort or some excitement or there is no incentive to invest the time. Too much of what is packaged today as "continuing education" consists solely of the one-way lecture/classroom/test model. There is a place for that in the total "keeping current" strategy, but typical classroom courses are very limited in their ability to directly counteract professional obsolescence.

It has been said before, but not in relation to professional obsolescence: it is the journey, not the destination. No one ever gets to the point where they are obsolescence-proof. Taking courses might be viewed as one indicator of a more general motivation to remain current. The motivation plays itself out in other ways (reading, writing, talking). As one professional has stated:

> I don't think taking course work in a university is a means of keeping yourself up-to-date. There aren't too many schools teaching courses at the frontiers. Most courses are background and basic. A few are taught from the literature and they are current. There are advanced courses but they're classic, not on the edge of current work. But there are some which are based on the ideas of the past two or three years. These are a small proportion of the curriculum. In general, courses are to bring you to the point where you can pioneer new areas (20, p. 141).

Kaufman's research led him to the conclusion that "participation in graduate courses does reinforce the breadth and depth of knowledge that is indispensable in preventing both professional and job-assignment obsolescence, particularly at midcareer. The discipline and comprehensiveness of graduate-level courses help professionals diversify their in-depth knowledge about new fields actually or potentially related to their work. Such courses allow them to acquire the fundamentals of a subject so they can continue learning about new developments in their area by self-instruction" (20, p. 141). However, he also warns that "it is those who have the weakest knowledge in their field to begin with, and are consequently most obsolescence-prone, who tend not to participate in graduate-level courses. Therefore, it would appear that graduate courses are effective in fighting obsolescence, but primarily among professionals who have the ability and motivation to stay up-to-date in their field" (20, p. 142).

The best prescription is to use the challenge of the job itself to motivate yourself to remain current. Rather than viewing learning as something that happens off-site, a pleasant diversion, look for opportunities in the job itself to learn and grow. In developing their staff members, many leading organizations use on-the-job activities, responsibility, and challenge to "grow" their people. This is less a philosophical statement than it is a tried-and-true method of what seems to work. This strategy clearly puts pressure on the supervisor to define the job in a challenging way and to provide the observational feedback to make the experience a learning one. (Individual skills assessment was dealt with in chapter 3; supervisory feedback skills are treated in chapter 11.)

LOSING YOUR JOB

Professionals out of work present unique problems and opportunities (26). If you have been employed for some time as a scientist/professional, it is often not easy to find another job. The techniques discussed in chapter 9 are appropriate, but the circumstances are different and create a unique problem. You may have quit your job voluntarily for any number of reasons, such as relocating with your spouse, boredom, personality differences. Or you may have been involuntarily terminated in one of several ways:

1. You were fired. The primary reason for this occurring is a personality clash with your boss. Some examples of other reasons are the obsolescence of your professional knowledge and skill, poor work habits or attitude, incompetence, and physical or mental disability such as drug and alcohol abuse.
2. You were displaced as a consequence of a merger or acquisition.
3. You were laid off as a result of funding cuts, project completion, recession, reduced demand for your services resulting from your unique business, or disruption of the economy.
4. You were let go because of poor management of your organization. Some examples are overhiring, overcompensation, inability to compete in the market that requires your services, and bankruptcy.
5. Your services were no longer needed as a result of a shift in corporate direction or emphasis.

A typical professional is involved in a unique personal situation and change when unemployed. Kaufman has investigated this subject in *Professionals in Search of Work* (22), a portion of which is abstracted here. Because of the limited amount of research available, Kaufman broadens the definition of a professional to individuals with a college degree. However, his research and supporting material indicate that the results he describes are even more dramatic when applied to professionals and scientists with advanced degrees.

Psychological Impact

Job loss may place an inordinate amount of stress upon individuals over a long period of time. Recent reviews of the literature on unemployment focus specifically on the psychological impact of job loss (16) and career transitions (25). As discussed in chapter 8, the job and career are central elements in professionals' feelings of self-worth in our culture. Therefore, the loss of a job—or even the feeling that a job might be lost—may dramatically reduce self-esteem. The results are magnified for scientists and professionals because work is more central in their life's interests than it is for nonprofessionals.

As self-esteem, the feeling of adequacy and worthiness, drops, professionals may respond in inappropriate ways. Without an adequate social support system, the loss in self-esteem may lead to the wrong type of job search or to a poor reemployment decision. Typically, people with low self-esteem do a poor job of matching their values, interests, personality, and abilities, with an appropriate job, occupation, and employer. This increases the probability that a second "failure" will be produced. It almost becomes a self-fulfilling prophecy in which unemployed people teach themselves a lesson because they feel that they are not deserving of success and happiness.

As self-esteem declines, feelings of anxiety increase. The increased level of insecurity associated with job loss may be translated into a feeling of powerlessness or helplessness to cope with the situation. The professional may feel aimless and isolated from others because a central source of status in our society—the job—has been lost. Concurrently, the source of income dries up, and the person's role as an economic contributor to the family is lost. Depression may set in. If the depression is marked, professional mental-health assistance should be obtained.

When the job is so important as a measure of self-worth, the loss of a job can cause professionals to withdraw from social contacts to protect their self-esteem. Just at a time when assistance is required from others, less is sought. Social support can help maintain satisfaction from life, but it may be difficult to maintain contact with acquaintances who are not very close. A shift could be made to people who are in similar circumstances, for example, through a job club (see chapter 9).

Contact with others may also be difficult because the unemployed professional feels helpless and may respond with increasing anger. This irritation and hostility are focused not only on the past employer, but also on others, including family and close friends. The inordinately high level of stress can increase anxiety and create physical symptoms such as hypertension, peptic ulcers, heart attacks, arthritis, and even loss of hair. Alcoholism, suicide, and child abuse are extreme responses.

Unemployment is associated with withdrawal not only from social contact but also from work itself. The desire to work and achieve drops. It becomes more and more difficult to search for a job. At these times, social support is critical to maintaining the desire to work and seek employment.

Unemployment is often a time in which professionals start to question how current their expertise is and whether they want to stay in their field of work. This takes place at a time when self-esteem is low and the ability to do an accurate self-assessment is poor. Self-deprecation is a typical companion of the lowered self-image and depression commonly associated with the situational shock of unemployment. Social support and possibly professional assistance are key items to have available when a self-evaluation is undertaken at such a time. Materials that can be used in self-evaluation are included in chapter 9. Becoming involved in professional updating may bolster self-confidence and the incentive to search for a new job.

Factors Affecting Unemployment's Impact

Age. Kaufman reports that it is not the older unemployed individual who is prone to the greatest stress, but the thirty-to-forty-year-old professional who is just becoming established in a field and may have a growing family that creates major financial responsibilities (22).

Sex and Marital Status. Professional men, regardless of their marital status, face high stress associated with unemployment. Married, separated, or divorced professional women have reported significantly less stress under the same circumstances. In fact, stress levels actually appeared to decrease for married professional women if the alternate roles of mother or traditional wife were available and she was not strongly career oriented. Kaufman reports that the individual who has primary financial responsibility for others is subjected to high stress when unemployed, but adequate financial resources reduce the stress materially (22).

A common means of obtaining financial support is for a spouse to obtain work. If the marriage is healthy prior to unemployment and roles are not rigidly defined, this role reversal may work out well. If the roles are rigidly defined, the marriage may deteriorate, and stress may increase for the unemployed professional. The research of Ross and her colleagues indicates that if an unemployed professional's wife becomes employed to increase the family finances over the strong objections of her husband, the chances are great that he will become quite depressed (32). However, if he encourages it, both partners will improve their psychological state. And if he not only approves but shares in the housework, the chances for depression are lowest.

Education. The more time invested in education, the greater the stress imposed by unemployment. Professionals with doctoral degrees, especially from research-and-development departments, were most heavily effected, followed by those with master's degrees. Specialization, intense socialization during the long training period, and identification with their field appear to lead to the deep commitment to their work that causes a high level of stress from unemployment. In contrast, when employed, these same professionals exhibited the least amount of stress in Kaufman's research (22).

Occupation. Professionals from technical fields demonstrated the highest level of stress in Kaufman's work (22). This appears to occur because individuals in technical fields are drawn to the work as a result of their interest in "things" rather than people, and effective coping with unemployment requires social systems of support. Applied engineers are not affected as much as research scientists because the former are required to develop more contact with people in their daily work. If unhappy with their field of work, unemployed professionals are faced with an additional source of stress. They must not only find a new job but also determine if they should change fields.

Social Support. Individuals with access to social support systems coped with stress most effectively. Some examples that Kaufman observed were religious affiliations, healthy family relationships, cultural links within second-generation immigrants, professional societies, and community organizations. Ties to the latter two groups provide not only emotional support but also access to job markets. However, Brittain indicates that close social support via a counselor may be detrimental to the person with a high energy level, strong accomplishments, quick learning skills, and high self-esteem (7). For others, the counselor's role in listening, probing, cajoling, and working together on writing and strategies may be essential.

Unemployment Stages

Kaufman has observed four stages that the typical unemployed professional appears to go through: shock, relief, and relaxation; concerted effort; vacillation, self-doubt, and anger; and resignation and withdrawal (22).

Stage 1—Shock, Relief, and Relaxation. If the job market is bad, this stage may be skipped. Otherwise, it lasts for one to two months. The response to unemployment appears to be positive, and stress is low. The family maintains social contacts, may take a vacation and possibly go on a spending spree. Concerns are not aired with family and friends, and resources are not conserved.

Stage 2—Concerted Effort. During the next three months, the individual concentrates on finding a job. The spouse often provides strong assistance and emotional support. It is common to see the family maintain its previous lifestyle—or even begin splurging—rather than conserve its financial resources. Stress is manifested, but the activity level keeps it manageable.

Stage 3—Vacillation, Self-Doubt, and Anger. If the job search is unsuccessful, cycles of depression and optimism occur. There is a feeling of being a burden to the family. Anger is expressed via aggression and irritation across a broad range of incidents. Anxiety can become extreme. The individual becomes immobilized and fails to seek help from appropriate sources such as creditors. (Creditors will typically provide help by stretching out and consolidating debt payments; they normally do not want to foreclose on a mortgage or repossess goods.) Feelings of technical obsolescence may increase, and the motivation to become reemployed or the level of job that is set as a goal may drop. Since a typical period of unemployment is six months (6), many unemployed approach or enter stage 3.

Stage 4—Resignation and Withdrawal. In this final unemployment stage, the motivation to find work drops dramatically as the failure to find work increases. The person withdraws and stays at home. To cope with rejection by employers, individuals become narrow and rigid in their job search, seeking only those that fit their experience and training closely. Anxiety and desperation are replaced by helplessness and quiescence. Social relations improve but are limited to a few close friends and relatives. Satisfaction with life improves if social support is received, but is low if not received.

Barriers to Reemployment

In Kaufman's study of 137 unemployed professionals, he found that "lack of jobs" was the primary factor limiting reemployment opportunities (22). The effect of the lower demand for labor associated with a recession is exaggerated for professionals because of their more rigid job requirements. In Kaufman's work, "age" was a distant sixth in his list of barriers. However, his sample included only a few older workers. Other research has placed age as the number two barrier for those forty to fifty years old. The effect of the age barrier becomes exaggerated when the professional is a woman or has attained status without requisite education.

Kaufman's second, third, and seventh barriers to reemployment were all related to the ability of the professional to do the job (22). The second was "inappropriate experience," followed by "overqualified" and "inappropriate education." Professionals with doctoral degrees had a tougher time finding reemployment because of their higher salaries and specific training, although a recent doctoral degree improved the chances. People with technical backgrounds, such as civil engineering, and computer specialists had an easier time finding jobs than did those with master's degrees in social science or business. It appears that the labor market is a secondary factor that contributes to the effect of the three "ability" barriers.

The fourth barrier identified by Kaufman's sample was "reluctance to relocate." This barrier interacts with the lack of jobs, because it suggests that it is possible to find a job, but in another locale. Relocation becomes a means to compensate for rigid job requirements, but the desire to move wanes with increasing age.

Barrier number five on Kaufman's list is "previous salary too high." The obvious reemployment strategy to use in overcoming this problem is to lower salary aspirations. However, employers become wary when this is done, because they feel that the professional will leave for greener pastures as soon as a higher salary becomes available.

Number eight and last on Kaufman's list is "unemployed for too long." The obvious strategy to use in surmounting this obstacle is to begin looking for work early, preferably before termination.

Searching for a Job

The methods to use in searching for a new job were covered in the fourth section of chapter 9. However, there is one characteristic of the unemployed situation that should be considered when reviewing that material. When unemployed, the need for social support may be very high. Therefore, self-help groups such as job-hunting clubs like Forty Plus (4) and those proposed by Azrin and Besalel (1) can provide social support, job-search assistance, vocational advice and counsel, as well as handle psychological needs. They combine work-related and non-work-related coping behaviors to aid in reemployment and individual adjustment at the same time. The intensity of job search (the level of job search activity and number of search methods used) is not necessarily related to finding an appropriate job. Effort should be focused on effective methods, because high intensity of search by itself may demonstrate only an intense need to be reemployed and result in underemployment.

Enhancing Employability

As mentioned earlier, geographic relocation is one strategy to use in obtaining a job with better salary, job security, and skill utilization. Highly educated and skilled professionals often find it appealing to move because of their strong need to use their professional knowledge and skill. If unemployed professionals are reluctant to move and local job opportunities are limited, then it may be necessary to accept a pay cut, underemployment, or less job security as a trade-off to avoid uprooting themselves or their families.

Another change strategy that unemployed professionals can use to enhance their employability is additional education. Enrolling in formal university degree courses can provide professional updating within a field, a complementary degree (for example, adding an MBA to a technical background), or a career change to a different field. While a complementary degree such as the MBA diverts the individual away from a professional orientation, it can enhance employability, especially if the person is more management- than profession-oriented. Updating their knowledge in their professional field can help maintain self-esteem as well as minimize the obsolescence of their technical knowledge. The effectiveness of the additional education is increased if the courses are part of an accredited university degree program that has been acknowledged by the profession. In most universities it is also advantageous to attend the day program rather than the evening, continuing education program because of the perceived higher educational standards of the former.

Retraining programs are typically designed to aid the unemployed to change their fields of work. The attractiveness of retraining is dependent upon factors such as financial support, relevance of the training to the existing knowledge and skill of both the participant and potential employers, the assurance of work after the program is complete, and the desire to change occupations. The older unemployed professional appears to find retraining more attractive than relocation or formal education. Many have been waiting for the chance to change fields. The willingness to retrain is based on the belief of individuals that they are able to effect change. This belief deteriorates with the onset of stage 4—resignation and withdrawal—in the unemployment cycle. Therefore, retraining should be initiated prior to that time. The few retraining programs in the United States that are aimed at professionals appear to have been successful; the development of jobs for the participants is a key ingredient.

The fourth technique for enhancing reemployability is job counseling. Hunting competitively for a new job is a skill that many professionals have not used for many years, and they have lost their skill in doing so. In addition, job hunting as an experienced individual is not the same as hunting while in college. Since unemployed professionals who get rejected in several job interviews begin to lose their confidence, a counseling approach should be started soon after losing employment. Counseling can aid individuals to feel that they still have some control over their life and, thereby, help them to combat unemployment stress. While individual counseling has been found to be helpful in improving the employability of even hard-to-place professionals, group counseling may be a better approach because it provides the social support needed to maintain self-esteem and the motivation to work (22). During career assessment in preparation for or support of the job hunt, the concentration should be on past success (6). Identifying specific elements, situations, or factors that are clearly reinforcing to the individual can maintain both effective job-finding behavior and reinforced career targets. A counselor can review the person's history of positive reinforcement, and thereby help maintain a positive psychological state.

PLANNING FOR RETIREMENT

The term *retirement* often carries a negative connotation which reflects a "no-longer-productive-to-society" flavor. It may also carry loss of status, lowered self-esteem, and financial hardship. If you plan correctly, retirement need not be defined in these ways. Retirement does not necessarily mean "out of action." It is interesting that there is no specific word in the Chinese language for retirement; the closest is the word *death*—an interesting and potentially informative comparison. While the subject of retirement planning has been sufficiently covered in the literature, there are aspects of it that are unique to the professional.

Chapter 2 described the central role that work plays in the life, self-concept, and self-esteem of the professional. This fact shows itself in many ways. One indicator is that professionals tend to reject early retirement. Kaufman summarizes: "Studies indicate that almost nine out of ten professionals of preretirement age would prefer to work even if they were made financially secure by receiving money not to work. Despite this fact, some four out of five professionals are retired involuntarily" (22, p. 84). Even if we do not want to retire or do not plan to retire, the organization will likely make the decision for you; therefore, better to prepare yourself according to your own timetable rather than wait to be told that you are through. Planning retirement is another way in which you can take charge of your own career.

More than any other group, professionals have a multitude of options available upon formal retirement. Consider consulting: age is an advantage. Consider teaching, writing the book you have never had the time for, volunteering or doing community work, or getting involved in your professional society.

During the working lives of most professionals, they are specialists rather than generalists. They tend to have selected intensive involvement in narrowly focused areas and to like regular, methodical, precise, predictable activity. The professional life helps structure involvement with other people. Given that there is relative safety in the known and a relative fear of the unknown, it is understandable that retirement planning is often neglected by professionals in the preretirement years.

The greatest retirement fears appear to be around three issues: financial, physical, and psychological. Financial planning receives by far the most attention in organization-sponsored preretirement counseling (36). Kaufman presents a revealing analysis of the impact of obsolescence on preretirement security which realistically reflects the viewpoint of most organizations:

> Professionals who are approaching a mandatory retirement age will often not receive promotions even though deserved, will have limited opportunities to learn about new developments in their fields even if they have the necessary abilities, and may be shunted to dead-end jobs where any self-motivation to avoid obsolescence will soon become nonexistent. . . . As a result of the anxiety generated by such limitations on their career development, professionals in their preretirement period will concentrate their efforts on satisfying their security rather than their growth needs. In fact, managers in their preretirement period derive their job satisfaction primarily from attaining security goals, whereas previously that satisfaction came from goals that gratified growth needs. Since organizations generally do not give older professionals the opportunity to gratify their growth needs, those individuals have no choice but to limit their self-development and concentrate on protecting their positions in the organization until they retire. The image of older professionals sitting back and waiting for retirement further reinforces the organization's argument in favor of an earlier mandatory retirement age (20, p. 84).

Age-specific retirement policies, because they are not based on ability, do not always contribute to either personal or organizational objectives. This is a reality that cannot be ignored and must be planned. Organizations are responding by presenting attractive early retirement packages. This allows a certain amount of discretion in "cleaning out the deadwood" and infusing the organization with younger, more up-to-date professionals.

If your organization does not have an early retirement policy, you might want to suggest an alternative which fits your specific situation. For example, you make $60,000 a year and your retirement pension in five years is $20,000. Suggest that you work four days a week next year for $40,000; three days a week for $35,000 the following year; $30,000 for two days in year three; and $25,000 for one day a week in the fourth year. This allows the organization to save $130,000 over four years and be able to phase out your role during this period (35, p. 81). The limited days per week could force you into different roles befitting your experience: training or consulting, for example. Reduced work periods can be a useful strategy in managing the transition to a different lifestyle.

Full or partial pension payments are currently offered by more than half of the U.S. corporations (20, p. 87). Kaufman argues the need to use "portable pension vesting" to more easily encourage older professionals to leave the organization (20, p. 87). This allows the individual to move on to something more rewarding and allows the organization to encourage greater turnover among less-valued employees.

An interesting social phenomenon is the fact that there is now a more highly educated elderly group in this country than there has ever been. This "graying of America" means no doubt that service organizations will spring up to meet the physical and psychological needs of the elderly professional. Today a number of volunteer organizations exist which provide services to the communities or small businesses that they serve, for example:

- Service Corps of Retired Executives (SCORE)
- Senior Opportunities and Services (SOS)
- Retired Senior Volunteer Program (RSVP)
- Volunteers in Service to America (VISTA)

Thus far, the financial issues have received most of the attention of such groups; as these issues are resolved, the "higher" growth needs will become more of a concern. For now, professional societies provide a useful outlet for professional energies; they should be challenged to more adequately address the issue of contributions by their more elderly members.

SUMMARY

Chapter 10 described individual career processes from early socialization to retirement. It dealt with a number of difficult decisions: occupational change, job change, organization change, job loss, and retirement.

The reader should be able to answer the following questions:

> What are the predictable stages of early socialization to a new organization? What different models exist to explain it?
> How do professionals cope with the stress of imminent or actual unemployment?
> What are the conditions under which a professional is most likely to consider an occupational change?
> What is the concept of "comparative failure"?
> How can I avoid professional obsolescence?
> What impact does job loss have on self-esteem?
> Who is affected most by job loss?
> What psychological stages does the unemployed professional go through?
> What are the "barriers to reemployment"? The strategies for reemployment?
> How is retirement likely to be experienced differently by the professional?

The processes described in this chapter are almost guaranteed to have a strong and potentially negative impact on the person. To the extent that the tips in this chapter help alleviate the more stressful career decision points, it will have achieved its goal.

REFERENCES

1. Azrin, N. H., and Besalel, V. A. 1982. *Finding a job.* Berkeley, CA: Ten Speed Press.
2. Bailyn, L. 1980. *Living with technology: issues at mid-career.* Cambridge, MA: MIT Press.
3. Blonder, M. D. 1976. Organizational repercussions of personnel cutbacks. Ph.D. dissertation, City Univ. of N.Y.
4. Bolles, R. N. 1984. *What color is your parachute?* Berkeley, CA: Ten Speed Press.
5. Bray, D. W., Campbell, R. J., and Grant, D. L. 1974. *Formative years in business.* New York: John Wiley.
6. Brittain, W. P. 1982. Outplacement revisited: the new old personnel function. In *Industrial Behavior Modification,* ed. R. M. O'Brien, A. M. Dickinson, and M. P. Rosow, pp. 286-97. New York: Pergamon.
7. Buchanan, B. 1974. Building organizational commitment: the socialization of managers in work organizations. *Administrative Science Quarterly* 19:533-46.
8. Bucher, G. C., and Reece, J. E. 1972. What motivates researchers in times of economic uncertainty? *Research Management* 15:19-32.
9. Dewhirst, H. D., and Holland, W. E. 1975. Effect of organizational change on career goals of scientists and engineers. *IEEE Transactions of Engineering Management,* EM-22: 114-19.
10. Eiduson, B. T. 1962. *Scientists: their psychological world.* New York: Basic Books.
11. Engel, P. G. 1985. Are you getting stale? *Industry Week* 16 (September):29-30.
12. Estes, R. J. 1973. Emotional consequences of job loss. Ph.D. dissertation, Univ. of Pennsylvania, School of Social Work.
13. Feldman, D. C. 1976a. A contingency theory of socialization. *Administrative Science Quarterly* 21:433-52.
14. ———. 1976b. A practical program for employee socialization. *Organizational Dynamics* (Autumn):64-80.
15. Foxman, L. D., and Polsky, W. L. 1986. Career counselor: The unknown variables in the job changing process. *Personnel Journal,* May, 22-25.
16. Fryer, D., and Payne, R. 1986. Being unemployed: A review of the literature on psychological experiences of unemployment. In *International Review of Industrial and Organizational Psychology,* eds. C. L. Cooper and I. Robertson, pp. 235-78. New York: John Wiley.
17. George, J. L., and Dubin, S. S. 1972. *Continuing education needs of natural resource managers and scientists.* University Park, PA: Pennsylvania State Univ.

18. Glaser, B. G. 1964. *Organizational scientists: their professional careers*. New York: Bobbs-Merrill.
19. Hall, D. T., and Mansfield, R. 1971. Organizational and individual response to external stress. *Administrative Science Quarterly* 16:533-47.
20. Kaufman, H. G. 1974. *Obsolescence and professional career development*. New York: AMACOM.
21. ———. 1982a. Continuing professional development at mid-career. In *College-Industry Educational Conference Proceedings*, 88-97. San Diego, CA.
22. ———. 1982b. *Professionals in search of work*. New York: John Wiley.
23. Kubie, L. 1953. Some unsolved problems of the scientific career. *American Scientist* 41:596-613.
24. ———. 1954. Psychoneurotic problems of the American scientist. *Chicago Review* 8:65-80.
25. Latack, J. C., and Dozier, J. B. 1986. After the axe falls: Job loss as a career transition. *Academy of Management Review* 11 (2):375-92.
26. Leventman, P. G. 1981. *Professionals out of work*. New York: The Free Press.
27. Lewin, K. 1952. Group decision and social change. In *Readings in Social Psychology* 2d ed., eds. G. E. Swanson, T. M. Newcomb, and E. L. Hartley, pp. 459-73. New York: Henry Holt and Company.
28. Miller, G. A., and Wager, L. W. 1971. Adult socialization, organizational structure, and role orientations. *Administrative Science Quarterly* 16:151-63.
29. Pelz, D. C., and Andrews, F. M. 1966. *Scientists in organizations: productive climates for research and development*. New York: John Wiley.
30. Porter, L. W., Lawler, E. E., and Hackman, J. R. 1975. *Behavior in organizations*. New York: McGraw-Hill.
31. Rice, B. 1985. Why am I in this job? *Psychology Today* 19 (1):54-59.
32. Ross, C. E., Minowsky, J., and Huber, J. 1983. Dividing work, sharing work, and in-between: marriage patterns and depression. *American Sociological Review* 48 (6):809-23.
33. Schein, E. H. 1972. *Professional education: some new directions*. New York: McGraw-Hill.
34. ———. 1978. *Career dynamics: matching individual and organizational needs*. Reading, MA: Addison-Wesley.
35. Schwartz, J. 1979. *Don't ever retire but do it early and often*. Rockville Center, NY: Farnsworth.
36. Smith, B. G. 1973. *Aging in America*. Boston: Beacon.
37. Wanous, J. P. 1980. *Organizational entry: recruitment, selection, and socialization of newcomers*. Reading, MA: Addison-Wesley.
38. Werbel, J. D. 1983. Job change: A study of an acute job stressor. *Journal of Vocational Behavior* 23:242-50.

Chapter 11

Programs the Individual Can Implement

It takes time and hard work to become a professional. Once educational goals have been realized and you have made your initial job selection, there is the day-to-day challenge of the job, but beyond that for what *now* are you striving? Are the activities in which you are now engaging going to help you get to where you want to be professionally and personally one, two, five, ten years from now?

Career and life planning is really a goal-setting process. Decisions are made about your life and career with or without your active participation. However, if you take a planned approach, you will be more likely to end up where you would really like to be than if you allow decisions to be made for you by default, simply by failing to make a decision. The message is simple and not new: take control of your own life.

The measure of the success of organizational career-planning programs is largely in the degree to which they make the individual employee responsible for his or her own career development, then provide the resources that allow realistic goals to be attained (3). If your organization does not have a formal career-planning program, you can go through the same steps independently and accomplish the same objectives as you would in such a program. That is what this chapter is all about. Chapters 8 and 9 considered issues related to establishing your career, managing the career process, and exiting the career. All that remains is to *assess* where you are in your career, to set *goals* relevant to where you would like to be, and to establish an *action plan* to get there. Some of these activities can be instituted as organizational programs, but they can also be engaged in independently. Then it is up to you to interest your supervisor in the process for the real career benefit comes when you take the initiative to involve your supervisor. If you are a supervisor, consider making some sections of this chapter available to your people, especially the "supervisory skills training" section. If you are not currently a supervisor, try to interest your supervisor in taking on some of the supervisory career management roles spelled out here. Career management is an ongoing, natural process that occurs as part of a healthy supervisor-to-subordinate relationship. Regardless of whether you are supervisor or subordinate, you need to manage this relationship actively.

INDIVIDUAL CAREER PLANNING

How does a person know when the time has come for career management activities? One easy answer is that career management is a lifelong activity in which one is always engaged. This is true only if career management is defined in its broadest sense, in which all activity is seen as contributing in some sense to your life's direction. The more critical issue here is relative to the individual's involvement in activities over and above those required by the current job and designed to better the individual's opportunity for movement that satisfies career goals. As an individual, how do you know you are ready? What does your organization do to get people started? An organization may become interested in career planning when it realizes that its entire board of directors will retire in six years (as Sun Oil Company did in 1968).

For the individual, the clear but somewhat evasive answer is that each person knows when the moment has arrived. We all have internalized notions of success and some measure of career ambition. We make actual-to-ideal comparisons all the time—that is, we tend to compare where we are now with our (often unverbalized) internal yardstick of where we wanted to be. This is a constantly evolving comparison and is anchored by age, significant life events (marriage), and other significant factors. Concepts of success (the yardstick) vary, but often include:

- Salary
- Title
- Prestige of the organization
- Professional esteem
- Individual accomplishment

- Movement into management
- Achieving a professionally respected position

An internal stream-of-consciousness monologue might run something like this: "I am pretty happy with my job. I make more money than most people my age in my profession, but I don't really work for a very prestigious company and my job title makes me sound like a glorified clerk. This job is okay, but it just doesn't give me the opportunity to use many of my valued abilities and skills and *show* what I can do."

Without a specific career management program, this person might never properly understand his or her personal career issues. People are not their own best diagnosticians. Only the poorest doctors treat themselves. There are many symptoms of career dissatisfaction or crises. The important factor is to have someone identified in the organization who is available to help define the issues with the person.

A person need not feel an impending crisis to be ready for career management activities. Highly motivated professionals will latch onto any activity that might increase their likelihood for advancement (a managerial orientation) or professional visibility and esteem (a scientific orientation). The general cycle of setting and attaining goals, experiencing psychological success and increased self-esteem, followed by greater job satisfaction and job involvement, higher motivation, and stronger goal commitment, is the natural catalyst that throws a person into career management activities. The quest for more challenging, attainable, self-defined, and important work becomes a natural part of the "success cycle," as elucidated by Hall (6).

Just as employers must understand what professionals look for in a career (1) individual professionals would be well advised to develop a strong personal career package (8). Examine your own organization and define for yourself where you would begin to trigger career management activities. Is it by going to your supervisor and requesting a career-planning discussion? Is it by making an appointment with someone in personnel to talk about your career aspirations? Is it by filling out a position-bidding or self-nomination form?

Organizations with formal career management programs also need to define the starting point. If the program involves a once-a-year inventory of interests, when will it occur? How does the organization execute plans such that all information is current, reliable, and valid? The first time a program is used there are bound to be problems with it from a technical point of view. In succeeding years different problems may emerge. There must be clear statements and understandings of when and how individuals can enter the program. A process of updating existing information is also necessary.

From the individual viewpoint, how do you know how well your career is progressing according to plan? We all have some sort of internalized, subjective career plan against which our real-life accomplishments are measured. There are numerous models by which these sometimes ill-defined needs and values can be examined and thereby externalized and objectified. The "plan" might consist of very general stages of life through which you see yourself passing, or the "plan" might be very specific with regard to attaining exact positions, having your work published, earning awards, and so on. In either case, your challenge is to specify your expectations and aspirations so that they can be shared with and acted on by others. In this sense, "checkpoints" are for the individual so that he or she can get into the success cycle and be able to gauge accomplishments.

Checkpoints are also useful from the organization's point of view. These checkpoints differ from those of the individual. The organization may well be concerned about the human resources implications of the following types of situations:

- Increased turnover of professionals
- Reduced productivity levels
- Lack of career movement
- Poor quality of supervision
- End of an important contract
- New breakthroughs by competitors
- Quick movement in some areas, resulting in a lack of successors
- Outdated promotability information
- Unknown mobility of employees
- An unanticipated opening in a critical position
- Trends toward hiring or promoting less-qualified people

Clearly these checkpoints will differ based on each situation and based on the individual or organizational viewpoint. Given your situation, identify your individual checkpoints and your organization's useful checkpoints. (To understand where you are and where you are going in your career, use the career-planning workbook in appendix 2.)

CAREER MANAGEMENT BY OBJECTIVES (MBO)

The most widely used of all management practices is management by objectives (MBO). Just as the organization attempts to manage its business through systematic methods, so too the individual must manage his or her own career through systematic methods. To a large extent the individual's business is his or her career. This is especially true with professionals who identify so closely with their work. The organization has a stake in how well you manage your own career, and you can also learn something from organizational programs that have proven successful. Regardless of whether your organization has a formal MBO program, you can be sure that it is strategically managed against a set of well-specified goals. As an individual, you owe yourselves the same strategic advantage through self-management against a set of well-specified career goals.

Odiorne has presented ten clear reasons why organizations should manage by objectives (11). Although he alludes to the usefulness of this approach when thinking about careers, he does not develop the point. Odiorne's reasons for using MBO can be viewed from an individual career management perspective:

1. *Human beings are purposeful; they live to attain goals.* By nature people strive to reach self-set goals; this is nurtured by our culture in which achievement goals and rewards attainment are set at an early age. Given such a centrally natural/learned process, it only makes sense to use it to attain career goals.
2. *Organizations have a tendency to disperse internally motivated goal-oriented behavior.* The division of labor in organizations often catches you in an "activity trap" in which you are constantly busy but have lost sight of the reason for the activity. Similarly, many day-to-day activities may or may not be advancing your career. Without clear objectives how do you know? It is all too easy to become bored, frustrated, or demotivated by existing conditions and by the vague feeling of going nowhere. It is also easy to fall into the "activity trap" relative to your career.
3. *Managers lose sight of subordinate's goals.* This is perhaps more true when we think about individual career goals versus organizational business goals. Because there is not a clear agreement on goals, the subordinate is wasting some percentage of productive time for activity that is neither useful to the organization, nor useful for the career. The person ends up working harder rather than more productively.
4. *People tend to define their self-worth in terms of the degree to which they have set and achieved meaningful goals.* Without goals, there is only meaningless activity—and often even failure at these activities—producing apathy, lowered self-esteem, and the like. The career is a personal yet public guidepost to achievement; it can be used to enhance self-esteem, or passively be ignored to your detriment.
5. *Knowing what is expected is a characteristic of well-run organizations.* Similarly, knowing what you expect of yourself is a characteristic of a well-run career.
6. *Failure can be caused by failing to achieve goals, but it can also be caused by never knowing what the goals were.* You do not avoid failure by not setting goals, yet you might question the degree to which fear of failure undermines your willingness to set specific goals. A fear of failure may lead many professionals to ignore career management by objectives.
7. *When people know what their goals are, their performance improves.* This is equally true with regard to career goals; information about what is expected can lead to clear changes in behavior and the acquisition of new skills as a natural part of orienting toward the goal. Only in retrospect is this defined as "change" or "growth," but it is one way in which to grow into new roles and to improve.
8. *The solid business is more likely to be one in which goals are being attained.* Only in the failing business is there a tendency to cut corners or cheat customers. Similarly with your career, if you do not have a strong sense of purpose, you are more likely to become dissuaded from your best career course.
9. *The systems and processes of management rest on the clarity of the organization's goals.* Overall career goals are similarly implicated in one's ability to make small career-related decisions in a purposeful manner. Goals help bring order out of chaos.
10. *Goal setting is so vital that it is virtually a necessary condition for effective management.* The use of objectives is not overlaid on the manager's job; it *is* the manager's job. What about career management? It could be similarly argued that career management could not exist apart from goal setting—that objectives are the means by which we manage our careers.

Odiorne also outlines many guidelines to successful goal setting in the organization. We have shortened his list, and the following points are presented from a *career* management by objectives viewpoint:

1. A career goal should be a statement of an end product. It should go well beyond the *activity* required to reach the goal.
2. A career goal must be so explicitly defined that there can be no doubt as to whether it was achieved.
3. A career goal should be anchored by a specific time interval.
4. Career goals should be structured in an ascending order of difficulty—make sure you have some early successes.
5. Set both long- and short-range career goals—strategic *and* operating goals.
6. Look closely at past career goal achievements and set future career goals in this realistic context.

7. Recognize that the act of setting a specific career goal means that you are rejecting other possible goals.
8. Set high but attainable career goals; doing so will help excite action to a greater extent than a routinely expected career goal.

The lesson to be learned in this treatment of career goal setting is that tried-and-true methods of organizational management can also be very helpful to professionals interested in managing their own careers. Solid career management by objectives is followed by the specification of the activities designed to contribute to the attainment of the career goal.

The setting of long-range goals should be in general terms, not so specific that a single job is the goal. If the plan is toward a single job, the probability of achievement is very low, and failure is almost guaranteed. A class, type, or level of career position should be identified to provide direction. The goal can then become more specific as the attainment gets closer.

A PAIRED-COMPARISON APPROACH TO ESTABLISHING PRIORITIES

Individual career planning will ultimately involve personal choices based on preferences, values, and priorities. The process of establishing priorities is often done subjectively when choosing between alternatives A, B, or C. What happens when priorities must be chosen among a much larger range of alternatives? The process of ranking a large number of items as to preference can be simplified with the *paired-comparison* process. For example, suppose you have determined a need to list and establish priorities for any one of the following:

- On-the-job activities I really enjoy
- Off-the-job activities I really enjoy
- Job knowledges I have
- Job knowledges I want to learn
- Working conditions I prefer
- "Corporate culture" I am looking for
- Personal motivators
- Personal frustrations
- Geographical locations I prefer
- Organizations I prefer
- Professional activities/memberships I prefer
- Importance of work/family/leisure activities in my life

Regardless of the subject matter, first make a simple list of the items that are relevant to each category. For example, with the category "geographical locations I prefer," list the locations being considered:

1. New York City
2. Boston
3. Washington, D.C.
4. Atlanta
5. Tampa
6. Dallas
7. St. Louis
8. Kansas City
9. Denver
10. Los Angeles

Next, prepare columns of numbers, one less than the number of items you have listed, and pairing the numbers: 1-1, 1-2, 1-3, and so on. In this case:

A	B	C	D	E	F	G	H	I
1-2	—	—	—	—	—	—	—	—
1-3	2-3	—	—	—	—	—	—	—
1-4	2-4	3-4	—	—	—	—	—	—
1-5	2-5	3-5	4-5	—	—	—	—	—
1-6	2-6	3-6	4-6	5-6	—	—	—	—
1-7	2-7	3-7	4-7	5-7	6-7	—	—	—
1-8	2-8	3-8	4-8	5-8	6-8	7-8	—	—
1-9	2-9	3-9	4-9	5-9	6-9	7-9	8-9	—
1-10	2-10	3-10	4-10	5-10	6-10	7-10	8-10	9-10

To calculate your priorities, start with the first column and ask, Do I prefer 1 or 2, in other words, do I prefer New York City or Boston? Circle the number representing the city you prefer, then move down to the next paired comparison and ask the same question, this time choosing between New York City and Washington, D.C. Circle your response and proceed down each column until you have made choices from each set of paired comparisons.

Next, total your choices by counting the number of times each item number was chosen. Suppose the totals were as follows:

ITEM	TIMES CHOSEN
1	3
2	5
3	4
4	9
5	8
6	8
7	0
8	1
9	2
10	6

Finally, list the choices, beginning with the city chosen the most number of times, ending with that least often chosen:

PRIORITY NUMBER	CITY
1	Atlanta
2	Tampa
3	Dallas
4	Los Angeles
5	Boston
6	Washington, D.C.
7	New York City
8	Denver
9	Kansas City
10	St. Louis

A city or location in the Sun Belt would be the obvious choice. After you make this listing, look at it critically one more time to determine whether the final result really makes sense to you. If there are ties in the total; for example had you chosen Tampa and Dallas the same number of times, check the grid and see which one you circled the first time they were paired, in this case 5-6, and that is the one to put first.

This paired-comparison method of identifying priorities can be used effectively in group workshops also—collapsing the numbers to get a group total allows individuals to view their priorities in the context of group priorities, which is guaranteed to generate some good discussion.

LIFE PLANNING

Much of this and other career-related books focus on the person interacting with a profession and an organization. What is too often neglected are the personal interests that also influence your career decisions. Career planning needs to be put in its proper, and larger, context of life planning (10,14). Individuals differ greatly in the extent to which they impose a structure on life. Some people prefer not to prepare but to let the "chips fall where they may." Sometimes this approach works, sometimes not. It has been said that luck is a crossroad where preparation and opportunity meet. Bolles provides a realistic perspective on this issue:

> There is always the random unpredictable event that comes crashing in, to upset the "best-laid plans of mice and men." What is true of society, is true also of our own individual lives. Consequently, most of us simply cannot plan in any detailed or far-reaching sense, down the corridor of our years. The best that we can hope to do is to organize our luck. Or (to put it more accurately) the best we can do is to organize ourselves and our knowledge or picture of what we are looking for, in such a way that we will be prepared to take advantage of whatever may come along—by accident, luck, circumstance, serendipity, fate, Providence, or an act of God (2, p. 33).

This advice is given in the context of overall *life* planning. His view is that people make decisions among alternatives throughout life, and that the act of *not deciding* is in itself a choice that is made for rather than by the person. The advice predicated on this analysis is to develop a contingency plan ("Plan B") for every decision. Make Plan B thinking a *habit* so that you do in fact have alternatives and do not find yourself at a dead end. Bolles develops this point by defining the powerless, victim mentality illustrated by the following attitude:

> My life is essentially at the mercy of vast powerful forces (or a vast powerful force) out there and beyond my control. Therefore I am the victim of, and at the mercy of:
> [Usually at least four are selected]
>
> - My history, my upbringing, my genes, or my heritage.
> - My social class, my education (or lack of it), or my I.Q. (or lack of it).
> - My parents, my teachers, or an invalid relative.
> - My mate, my partner, my husband, or my wife.
> - My boss, my supervisor, my manager, or my co-workers.
> - The economy, the times we live in, the social structure, or our form of government.
> - The politicians, the large corporations, or the rich.
> - Some particular enemy, who is out to get me, and who has great power: an irate creditor, an ex-boyfriend or ex-girlfriend, a combine, or the Devil.
>
> ... As a consequence, it makes little difference what I want out of life; I have had to learn to settle for whatever I can get, since I am relatively powerless (2, p. 49).

Emotionally and psychologically, the "take charge" attitude is the opposite of this "learned helplessness" type of attitude. What methods might we use to learn how to take charge? Virtually the entire text of Bolles's *Three Boxes of Life* is devoted to answering this question through a series of simple exercises (2).

Bolles heavily develops the point that there are three major endeavors ("boxes") in life in which we all participate: education, work, and retirement. People go through these phases at different rates, and people spend overlapping times in each box. For example, more and more senior citizens are returning to formal educational institutions during their retirement years. Professionals often continue their educational efforts during their predominantly work-centered period. Many professionals also work during their retirement period. There are cultural expectations around how long you should spend in each box. When in the education box you are expected to learn. When in the work box you are expected to hold down a job and to work. When in the retirement box you are expected to play. Therefore, the three "periods" of life translate into the three overlapping functions of learn, work, and play. Because of cultural expectations, you may often be out of balance with regard to the amount of time spent on each of these functions at any one point in your life.

It is impossible to determine the optimal distribution of our time for each of these three functions unless you have made some conscious decisions regarding your "meaning" or mission. What will satisfy you? What makes you feel fulfilled? What is your goal? Your target, purpose, objective, ambition, or design? As you ask these questions you begin to impose some order and direction to your activities. Bolles presents the following theoretical structure which he argues "overlays" the issues relevant in each of the three boxes.

1. *What's happening.* This is an awareness of the environment around us. Unless you know where you are and that your basic needs can be met, you are most likely to spend time on this one.
2. *Survival.* This is a concern for (on different levels) physical and financial survival, emotional survival, and spiritual survival. Any of these can capture our entire attention at given times and in different kinds of situations.
3. *Meaning or mission.* As previously stated, these are the goals and plans that help us structure our world and our time.
4. *Effectiveness.* There is a basic human need to be effective. However, people differ greatly in the degree to which they are self-critical, self-directed, and self-actuated or able to evaluate how well they are doing and try to improve.

In learning, in work, in play, if you are preoccupied with issues related to "what's happening" or "survival," it is predictable that the issues of "meaning or mission" will not receive much attention. If you are able to deal with the "meaning or mission" kinds of issues, then you are much more likely to focus on the "effectiveness" issues. The task is even greater when you realize that we must grapple with the issues in each box. Survival and meaning issues often receive different treatment in the education, work, and retirement boxes.

The message is that we can very easily get stuck in any of Bolles's three boxes of life. It is our direct and personal challenge to work ourselves out of the three boxes. Do not expect someone to do that for you; the sooner you take charge of your own destiny, the more fulfilled you will be. The reality is often that it takes a crisis to force us into the introspection necessary to do a credible job of so imposing-sounding a task as "life planning."

The balance of Bolles's book provides self-assessment instruments and exercises that support the personal awareness and choice components of life and work planning. The objective largely becomes a better balance between the amount of time devoted to the learning, working, and playing components of life.

SUPERVISORY SKILLS TRAINING

The Supervisor's Role

A supervisor needs to know a great deal and be a role model of some basic interpersonal skills (13) in order to deliver a total career management system. Good supervisors play many roles when it comes to the development of their people. Identified by Leibowitz and Schlossberg (9), the following roles clearly affect a subordinate's development:

1. Communicator
    - Holds formal and informal discussions with employees
    - Listens to and understands an employee's real concern
    - Clearly and effectively interacts with an employee
    - Establishes environment for open interaction
    - Structures uninterrupted time to meet with employees
2. Counselor
    - Helps employee identify career-related skills, interests, values
    - Helps an employee identify a variety of career options
    - Helps employee evaluate appropriateness of various options
    - Helps employee design/plan strategy to achieve an agreed-upon career goal
3. Appraiser
    - Identifies critical job elements
    - Negotiates with employee a set of goals and objectives to evaluate performance
    - Assesses employee performance related to goals and objectives
    - Communicates performance evaluation and assessment to employee
    - Designs a development plan around future job goals and objectives
    - Reinforces effective job performance
    - Reviews an established development plan on an ongoing basis
4. Coach
    - Teaches specific job-related or technical skills
    - Reinforces effective performance
    - Suggests specific behaviors for improvement
    - Clarifies and communicates goals and objectives of work group and organization

5. Mentor
   - Arranges for an employee to participate in a high-visibility activity either inside or outside the organization
   - Serves as a role model in an employee's career development by demonstrating successful career behaviors
   - Supports employee by communicating to others both in and out of the organization the employee's effectiveness
6. Advisor
   - Communicates the informal and formal realities of progression in the organization
   - Suggests appropriate training activities that could benefit employee
   - Suggests appropriate strategies for career advancement
7. Broker
   - Assists in bringing employees together who might mutually help each other in their careers
   - Assists in linking employees with appropriate educational or employment opportunities
   - Helps employee identify obstacles to changing present situation
   - Helps employee identify resources enabling a career development change
8. Referral Agent
   - Identifies employees with problems (career, personal, health)
   - Identifies resources appropriate to an employee experiencing a problem
   - Bridges and supports employee with referral agents
   - Follows up on effectiveness of suggested referrals
9. Advocate
   - Works with employee in designing a plan for redress of a specific issue for higher levels of management
   - Works with employee in planning alternative strategies if a redress to management is not successful
   - Represents employee's concern to higher-level management for redress on specific issues

Amazingly, these roles are rarely the target of supervisory development efforts. The roles are not theoretical; they are behavioral, and one of the most potent training techniques could easily be applied to them—that of behavior modeling.* Behavior modeling is a fancy psychological term for a simple age-old concept: a picture is worth a thousand words. Rather than having things explained, you are shown how to do something, allowed to do it, evaluated, and allowed to do it again. The steps in behavior modeling are:

- The supervisor makes a clear statement of the desired behavior and *demonstrates* excellent performance in a real-life situation.
- The supervisor puts together a *guide* in skeleton outline form which provides step-by-step tips.
- The subordinate *practices,* in a safe environment, exactly those behaviors expected on the job.
- The supervisor gives *feedback* and social reinforcement in the practice session in specific, constructive, behavioral terms.
- The subordinate engages in additional *practice* and planning on how to transfer the skills back to the job.

The nine supervisory roles can be "taught" through a series of behavior-modeling modules. In addition, the roles are clearly enough identified to incorporate them into the performance appraisal of each supervisor in the organization. This notion is consistent with our discussion in the organizational section regarding the need to hold supervisors accountable for career management activities.

An important fact stressed by Leibowitz and Schlossberg is that the supervisor-to-subordinate relationship is the natural unit for attacking the career management process (9). The supervisor has the opportunity to observe the subordinate's behavior in a variety of situations, usually on a daily basis. If the supervisor is a well-trained observer, he or she can develop a rich pool of behavioral "evidence" from which to work with the subordinate. The supervisor also has a different, often broader perspective than the subordinate. This can help round out the subordinate's perspective, making a more realistic career plan likely. This discussion should *not,* however, occur as part of a performance-appraisal process—the role demands in the two situations are so different that combining them just does not work.

There is the practical reality that one's boss has considerable "fate control" over one's life and career. It simply makes sense to develop organizational systems that orient both the supervisor and subordinate toward working together as a team in a common career management effort. Effective supervisory performance of the career management roles will help the subordinate (in his or her development) *and* the supervisor (through sharing expertise and increasing advancement potential). The *team* perspective needs to be built into the process.

Another reason the supervisor-subordinate pair is the natural team for career management actions is that if recommended organizational policies are enacted, then the development of subordinates is inextricably linked

---

*Although there are many excellent treatments of this topic, a good introduction to behavior modeling can be found in: *Changing Supervisor Behavior* by Goldstein and Sorcher (4).

to the ultimate goals and rewards of the supervisor. This link is often ignored in the short-term pressure for instant results. If the organization values employee development, managers should be taught to see this link and should be rewarded for career management activities. That is, "people development" should be a part of the supervisor's performance appraisal and individual development plans should be required where they make sense.

Career management is an ongoing natural part of the supervisor-to-subordinate relationship. A good supervisor does these things, usually without calling them career management activities. Unfortunately, they are rarely taught. What is clear is that career management is a process that amounts to much more than the once-a-year career-planning discussion required by some systems. A formal career-planning program may well require a specific career-planning meeting (see chapter 5), but the supervisor should not be allowed to think that such a meeting is the extent of his or her commitment to subordinate development.

If the supervisor is to fill the career management roles (even *with* training), the organization must provide him or her with the information needed to establish and maintain credibility in the eyes of the subordinate. A few examples drawn from the list of roles may portray this concern clearly:

ITEM	INFORMATIONAL NEED
As counselor, "helps employee identify a variety of career options."	Complete and accurate description of each position within the organization.
As mentor, "arranges for an employee to participate in a high-visibility activity."	Ongoing method of knowing what planned projects, activities, and the like are available.
As advisor, "suggests appropriate training activities that could benefit employee."	Training courses, both external and internal, that are available.

In particular, information about jobs in an organization is critical, and must go well beyond the usual "job specifications" that are usually written for job-evaluation purposes. The information must be relevant to employees' career-planning concerns. This type of information can be very valuable to the supervisor who will probably not have the broad-based knowledge needed for effective career counseling, yet would probably not wish to "lose face" or credibility by admitting this. (The section on internal selection and placement systems in chapter 3 describes position profiles as one way of making this type of information more readily available.)

Career counseling is an important function that might be handled in many ways. It certainly does not do any good to have a "career counselor" in the personnel department who helps you develop a "dream sheet," files it in the career-planning files, and never looks at it again. Although there is a legitimate training and coordinating role for a career counselor in many organizations, the ongoing coaching and counseling role is rightfully a part of the supervisor's responsibilities. The supervisor needs to know this is an important part of his or her job or it will get lost in the short-term pressures to produce. The supervisor needs to have the information about the organization and specific jobs that will enable him or her to perform effectively, to have the responsibility clearly assigned, and to have the required skills to help.

Providing Skills to the Supervisor

Career counseling can be viewed either as a scary new assignment to be avoided or as a natural extension of the supervisory relationship. The organization's actions will greatly determine this positioning. Training may even be perceived differently depending on whether it is marketed as a career-counseling seminar or an advanced management development workshop. "People development" is one set of managerial skills that does not exist in isolation from other managerial skills. Thompson and his associates clearly demarcate the separate roles of the professional employee and the manager in assuming responsibility, obtaining information, planning a career path, and follow-through (15). These roles must be clearly defined and communicated to maximize the effectiveness of the program and of the supervisor.

Using a behavior-modeling approach to training and based on the career management roles listed earlier, a training program can be designed, focusing on the specific behaviors necessary for a supervisor to carry out the career management roles. In the following sample Guide to Effective Career Management a supervisor at an imaginary company, Olson's, works with a subordinate named Lee and assumes the nine career management roles.

COMMUNICATOR
- Consistently questioned Lee to obtain involvement.
    "How do you think you're getting along with others in the project group?"
    "What effect do you think that would have on someone?"
- Involved Lee in defining the issues.
    "In meetings, who in the group does the most talking?"
    "Has anyone in any of your project groups ever asked you out for a beer after work?"

- Listened for the real meaning behind Lee's words.

    "You say you demand perfection, but do you really mean that working with others frustrates you—that you could do the job better and faster than they could?"

    "Aren't you saying that you really would like to be more accepted by the people you work with?"

- Established a free environment for a frank interchange.

    "I want you to know you can feel free to say anything in this meeting."

    "Let me be totally open and candid with you . . ."

COUNSELOR

- Helped identify career-related interests and values.

    "Do you see your future at Olson's within the scientific field or upward within management?"

    "How would you define a 'successful' person?"

- Helped identify career options.

    "Okay, Lee, within Olson's what do you see as your career options?"

    "Describe to me what you would consider the perfect job for you."

- Helped evaluate appropriateness of options.

    "Let's talk a little bit about how reasonable those goals are in terms of your preparation . . ."

    "I can tell you now that leaving Olson's may be something that you would regret in six months."

- Helped design a strategy to meet career goals.

    "Let's work together on a plan to get you from where you are now to where you'd like to be . . ."

    "If you want to progress in management, I would recommend that you consider the following steps . . ."

APPRAISER

- Identified critical job elements.

    "Lee, a project *team* is just that—you need to work *with* people, not overpower them."

    "Sure the technical aspect is important on this project, and we *do* need the special equipment."

- Communicated performance expectations.

    "In the next month I expect to see better working relationships between all members of the group . . ."

    "You will abide by equipment checkout procedures."

- Reinforced effective job performance.

    "Lee, you've impressed me and others by your technical ability and your energetic attack on problems."

    "I have full confidence in your ability to accomplish everything we've laid out."

- Established follow-up expectations of Lee.

    "These are the objectives I would like for you to attain by the next time we meet . . ."

    "By the time we meet in a week I expect to see the following . . ."

COACH

- Suggested specific behaviors for improvement.

    "Why don't you ask Sarah and Lloyd out to lunch this week, and try letting *them* do the talking!"

    "Try going in a little slower, work on listening to the other guy."

- Taught specific job-related skills.

    "Let's work together in the next week on listening skills."

    "Here, let me show you what Jean was trying to explain to you about the valve."

- Clarified the goals of the organization.

    "Olson's has been successful based on its small project teams working together with precise teamwork."

    "The small project team is the key to our success and we're committed to making it work."

- Inspired Lee to resolve obvious problems.

    "I'm counting on you and your experience . . ."

    "I really expect you to give this your best shot . . ."

MENTOR

- Arranged for employee to participate in a high-visibility activity.

    "All I need to see is motivation on your part to improve and I will nominate you for the president's special project team."

    "I intend to nominate you for one of the president's special project teams."

- Served as a role model by demonstrating successful career behaviors.

    Maintained a very person-oriented style throughout the discussion.

    "Let me tell you about Dr. Kellum and Dr. Smythe and their careers . . ."

- Supported employee to others in the organization.

    "I intend to speak to George Kelton about those checkout procedures and what you told me."

    "I'll talk to Harry about that and make sure he gets both sides of the story."

ADVISOR

- Communicated the realities of progression in the organization.

    "Lee, I know of no one who has risen above project supervisor in this organization who didn't have very effective group management skills."

    "If you really want to get ahead you need to start learning how to work with others more effectively."

- Suggested appropriate training activities that could benefit the employee.

  "Lee, I know of an excellent university executive development program that focuses specifically on project membership and leadership."

  "Perhaps you would be interested in a listening skills program."

- Suggested appropriate strategies for career advancement.

  "Continue to use your technical skills, but begin to think about improving your managerial skills."

  "Make a good impression on the people you work with on the president's team, and your career will be helped by it."

BROKER

- Assisted in bringing employees together to mutually help each other.

  "I think you and Jake ought to get together and talk . . ."

  "We have a new employee that is going through orientation next week, I'd like you to spend a few hours with him."

- Assisted in linking employee to appropriate educational opportunities.

  "I'm setting up an appointment for you with our training director."

  "Here's the telephone number for continuing education . . ."

- Helped identify obstacles to changing the present situation.

  "Let's talk about things that might keep you from attaining your objectives."

  "Frankly, you've begun to develop a reputation for 'taking over' and no one wants to work with you. Something has to change here."

REFERRAL AGENT

- Identified personal problems.

  "Have you considered professional counseling or help with this problem?"

  "Has your wife's health always been so poor?"

- Identified resources for an employee with a personal problem.

  "You do realize our company has a confidential referral service?"

  "The counseling center down at the university might be able to help you with that."

- Bridged and supported employee with the referral agent.

  In report, stated he would "follow up weekly to determine progress."

  "Lee, let me know how I can help you with this."

ADVOCATE

- Worked with employee to address a specific problem with upper-level management.

  "Let me help you with a plan to change my boss's perception of you."

- Worked with employee to plan alternative strategies.

  "If that doesn't work, we'll talk again and see what we can come up with."

- Represented employee's concern to higher-level management.

  "Let me take your side of the story to my boss and we'll see what we can do about it."

  "On *that* one, I'll support you all the way."

HANDLING THE CAREER-PLANNING DISCUSSION

The supervisor is extremely important in the career-planning process. If *you* are a supervisor of professional, scientific, or technically oriented people, you are likely to spend a great deal of time on technical issues. You also need to consider the professional and management development part of your role. Within a career-planning program, your role as supervisor goes through a series of steps. First, you need to *prepare* for the career-planning discussion:

- Your goal is to assist the employee in formulating a realistic, attainable career plan. You are not fulfilling your responsibility unless the plan is both realistic (given the employee's strengths and weaknesses) and attainable (given the company's constraints).
- When your subordinate asks to schedule a career-planning discussion, request that he or she first furnish you with a copy of his or her career plan and/or a self-assessment of key technical and managerial skills so that you will have a common reference from which to begin.
- Meet with your own supervisor regarding the feasibility and future availability of the positions listed on your subordinate's career plan.
- Set a specific date and time for the meeting with your employee, instructing him or her to bring a completed copy of the career-planning worksheet and plan (see Employee's Career Planning Worksheet in appendix 2).
- Review the job record of the employee (personnel file and other documents) and analyze strengths and weaknesses.

Second, as a supervisor you need to review some background information regarding what to expect in the career-planning discussion:

- Your role is to discuss, suggest, draw out, clarify, and act as an advisor or counselor; the employee

must retain the primary initiative and feel that it is truly his or her plan.
- Do not assume a directive or authoritarian role; you may at times need to persuade or negotiate in order to get your views understood and to reach a mutually acceptable plan.
- The goal is to find out how the employee views his or her situation; you should not assume you know already.
- Probe the scientific-professional versus organizational orientation of the employee and, without inserting value judgments, explore how those feelings might affect the employee's career planning.
- People strive to maintain a favorable self-image so their view of their own performance may be somewhat different from yours, leading to what you consider an overly optimistic plan; for example, they may minimize the importance of liabilities, enhance their view of accomplishments, or "gloss over" their weak areas.
- Listening skill is critical. Encourage your subordinate to state his or her position—"This is *your* plan; I'm only here to *help,* so why don't you begin by reviewing your self-assessment and proposed career plan with me." Use probing questions to keep the discussion moving—"*Why* is it you feel that's a good choice?" or "What led you to decide on that?" "What was your thinking here?"
- Make reference to your different perspective as supervisor and suggest that it might help "round out" the employee's perspective.
- Adjourn the meeting if the employee becomes over-emotional or hostile, if the meeting "stalls," or if it becomes unconstructive. Suggest that you both give the issue more thought and try to understand each other's views.
- Establish a specific time and date for a follow-up meeting if needed.

Third, there are two likely possibilities for how the subordinate might view his or her career potential. An employee may be aiming too high, in which case the following hints for the supervisor apply:

- Question the basis for this aspiration—"Why do you feel you might be qualified for this position?" or "What led you to choose this position?"
- Present information that might allow the person to revise his or her estimate "gracefully" without "losing face." It is important to the employee's motivation to maintain his or her self-esteem.
- Do not use such words as "ridiculous," or "impossible."
- Honestly and sincerely present *your* views.
- Stress importance of developing a *realistic* career plan that can be approved at the vice-presidential level.
- Use a constructive, positive approach.
- Avoid talking about personal traits, about which little can be done, for example, instead of saying, "you're undependable," say "remember when you didn't meet the deadline on that project I assigned you so I didn't have the information I needed for the meeting with my boss"; instead of "you don't use good judgment," say "remember when you suggested that we . . . and you neglected to consider . . ."
- Focus on short-range, not long-range plans. What can be done in the present job to improve performance and develop needed skills or knowledge? Assign responsibility for resolving any performance problems to the employee.

Conversely, an employee might be underaspiring and *not* setting his or her sights as high as might be realistic. The following hints should be considered:

- Question reason for not wishing to progress higher.
- Address any misconceptions regarding the demands, stress, and other facets of the higher-level positions.
- Encourage the employee to speculate about actually staying in the same position.

Finally, you will actually conduct the career-planning discussion. The first discussion with an employee will take the most preparation time for both the supervisor and the employee. Remember that he or she has often already invested a great deal of time and thought in completing a workbook (see appendix 2). Your investment in the process may involve preparation of the worksheet (also see appendix 2), which will be compared to the same document prepared independently by the employee in order to reach a common perspective. It is very important that this initial contact be a positive and constructive experience for both of you.

The purpose of this career-planning discussion is to discuss specific lateral and promotional career choices as they relate to the employee's demonstrated strengths and weaknesses. Essentially, you as supervisor will be asked to review a person's knowledges, training, experience, assets, liabilities, and achievements (summarized on the worksheet) and develop a workable career plan that matches the person's particular background. The final plan should be one that you believe is realistic and can honestly support when representing the plan to your own immediate superior. Position descriptions should be consulted for information about any position that is considered. A comparison of the person's past experience with the requirements of the position should give some indication of the developmental activities that would be appropriate for that person.

At the end of the first discussion, which will probably last between one and two hours, the two of you should have identified key developmental needs and a set of several lateral and promotional jobs which might be acceptable. It is quite likely that there may be some disagreements or disillusionments that surface in the first meeting, so unless it comes easily, do not try to reach mutual agreement in the first meeting. A second meeting will usually be required to finalize a career plan. For the first meeting, aim for a full and honest discussion, making sure to get the employee's point of view. As the supervisor, you might also:

- State that you hope your viewpoint has given him or her some helpful information to think about—which should result in a better Career Plan.
- Express an appreciation for the time and effort put into the career planning program.
- State agenda for next meeting: to identify activities that support a development plan, to narrow down lateral and promotional alternatives, and to finalize a Career Plan.
- Set specific date and time for follow-up meeting.

At the follow-up meeting the plan is finalized and these last steps are taken:

- Review completed Development Plan and Career Plan.
- Go over each section.
- Agree on the "route" of greatest interest—that is, does the person have the skills and motivation to pursue a professional or a managerial track, to remain a specialist, or to broaden into a generalist?
- Agree on two lateral positions (at most) the employee is ready for *now* and two lateral positions requiring development (this is a maximum; if the employee is only ready for or interested in one, then list only one)—and list the agreed-upon developmental activities.
- Agree on two promotional positions (at most) the employee is ready for now, two promotional positions requiring development, and two lateral moves from the promotional moves listed previously (again, this is a *maximum* intended to give flexibility; if the employee is only ready for or interested in one, then list only one)—and list the agreed-upon developmental activities.
- Agree on a maximum of two long-range career goals (three to five years from now).
- Ask if there is any other information he or she could add.
- Make sure all information is complete and accurate.
- Signatures indicate agreement on the drafted career plan; *make sure the employee realizes that the plan will now be reviewed up through the levels and final approval will be made by the vice-president of the area.* This process will take time and may require revisions for the plan to be acceptable to the company's human resources needs.

Before ending the follow-up meeting, express an appreciation for the time and effort the employee has put into career planning, and list the follow-up actions you will take:

- Will have Career Plan typed up for signatures.
- Will look into opportunities to accomplish developmental activities.
- Will forward Career Plan to your own supervisor for review up through the levels to the vice-president.

If all of these steps are followed by the supervisor (with modifications for local program content), the discussion is much more likely to be a constructive one.

WORKSHOP CAREER-COUNSELING APPROACHES

The self-directed workbook in appendix 2 structures a self-paced appraisal. For many individuals, this process does not come easily. Often it is preferable to seek out a group workshop or individual counseling that focuses on career issues. In general, a workshop should allow participants to learn a career-planning process, understand what resources are available, assess themselves, set goals, write action plans, and, in some cases, define how to involve the supervisor in the plans. Workshops are often a key portion of an organization's career management program. Sometimes this is a natural outgrowth of the training department's bias toward workshops; sometimes it is a result of a well-thought-out strategy that respects the power of group interaction and discussion to clarify attitudes.

Training delivered in organizations can be a powerful force in career development. Internally delivered workshops have broadened their focus from specific, job-related information and skills to more complex areas such as self-assessment and career planning (12). If such programs can capture but a fraction of the $60 billion spent per year by organizations on education and training programs (12, p. 63), then the need for external programs of varying quality is lessened.

Many professional societies offer programs designed to clarify the career alternatives of people within their profession. Other organizations specifically address career issues, for example, the careers division of the Academy of Management. Outside consulting firms and training seminar houses have recognized the need for this type of offering, and vocational counselors and psychologists offer individual testing and group workshops to help clarify a person's thinking on alternatives.

Workshops will generally consist of two types of activities: *self-analysis* (similar to the type of data often found in structured workbooks) and *role-playing* (to clarify attitudes and improve interaction skills in specific situations). A sometimes unstated objective is to improve the self-esteem and confidence of the person participating in the session. To be motivated to attend, people are often experiencing some personal tension in their lives which might lead them to downgrade themselves or their abilities. The group situation allows people to see that others share similar concerns or problems and allows them to "depersonalize" some of the issues. The skilled group leader will recognize these dynamics and use the group to model supportive behaviors and to maintain or enhance the self-esteem of the participants.

The Career Development Division of the American Society for Training and Development has published a list of resources (5, pp. 62–63), which are relevant here:

WORKSHOPS AND SEMINARS
1. *Career Planning in Organizations.* This is a three-day workshop offered quarterly by the Division of Management Education at the University of Michigan (1735 Washtenaw Avenue, Ann Arbor, MI 48109).
2. *Career Development: A Framework for Managing Human Resources.* This is a two-day workshop offered periodically by the NTL Institute (P.O. Box 9155, Rosslyn Station, Arlington, VA 22209).
3. *Designing Career Development Programs for Organizations.* This is a two-day workshop offered on a regular basis by Career Research and Testing, Inc. (1190 South Bascom Avenue, Suite 211, San Jose, CA 95128).
4. *Designing Effective Career Development Systems: The Pieces and Where They Fit.* This is a two-day workshop offered periodically by the Career Development Research Project staff at Georgia State University (Department of Vocational and Career Development, Georgia State University, University Plaza, Atlanta, GA 30303).

NEWSLETTERS AND BULLETINS
1. *Career Development Bulletin.* This is a quarterly bulletin published by the Center for Research in Career Development at Columbia University. The center also publishes a career development bibliography as well as a working-paper series (814 Uris Hall, Columbia University, New York, NY 10027).
2. *Career Planning and Adult Development Newsletter.* This is a monthly newsletter published by the Career Planning and Adult Development Network (1190 South Bascom Avenue, Suite 211, San Jose, CA 95128).
3. *Career Development Division of ASTD.* This is a membership organization which American Society of Training and Development (ASTD) members can join. It publishes a newsletter, working papers, and monographs, including an annotated bibliography (ASTD, Suite 305, 600 Maryland Avenue, S.W., Washington, DC 20024).
4. *Career Development Review.* This quarterly publication features a variety of career-related article abstracts (P.O. Box 376, New York, NY 10024).
5. *Human Resource Planning Newsletter.* This monthly newsletter includes articles regarding a broad array of human resource issues, including career development (Advanced Personnel Systems, 756 Lois Avenue, Sunnyvale, CA 94087).
6. *Human Resource Planning.* This is a quarterly journal published by the Human Resource Planning Society, a membership organization that holds an annual conference (Society: P.O. Box 1080, Marshfield, MA 02050; journal only: P.O. Box 2553, Grand Central Station, New York, NY 10163).

BOOKS
1. Bolles, R. 1981. *What Color Is Your Parachute?* Berkeley, Calif.: Ten Speed Press. This manual is revised and reprinted annually.
2. Burack, E., and Mathys, N. 1980. *Career Management in Organizations: A Practical Human-Resource–Planning Approach.* Lake Forest, Ill.: Brace-Park Press.
3. Hall, D. T. 1976. *Careers in Organizations.* Pacific Palisades, Calif.: Goodyear Publishing, Inc.
4. Jelinek, M. 1979. *Career Management: For the Individual and the Organization.* Chicago, Ill.: St. Clair Press. This is a book of readings.
5. Kaye, B. 1982. *Up is Not the Only Way: A Guide for Career Development Practitioners.* Englewood Cliffs, N.J.: Prentice-Hall.
6. London, M., and Stumpf, S. A. 1982. *Managing Careers.* Reading, Mass.: Addison-Wesley.
7. Miller, D. B. 1980. *Career 80/81.* Saratoga, Calif.: Donald Miller. This is a bibliographic reference which is periodically updated.
8. Morgan, M. A. 1980. *Managing Career Development.* New York: D. Van Nostrand. This is a book of readings.
9. Schein, E. H. 1978. *Career Dynamics: Matching Individual and Organizational Needs.* Reading, Mass.: Addison-Wesley.
10. Storey, W. D., ed. 1979. *A Guide for Career Development Inquiry: State-of-the-art Report on Career Development,* ASTD research series, Pa-

per No. 2. Madison, Wisc.: American Society for Training and Development.
11. Walker, J. W., and Gutteridge, T. G. 1979. *Career Planning Practices: AMA Survey Report.* New York: AMACOM, 1979.

The resources just listed are some of the *external* sources that provide another perspective for you in managing your own career. There are numerous *internal* resources that will also be helpful. Key among them is the concept of taking control of your own career. Take responsibility *yourself* for knowing where you are and where you want to be in your career. As in any good business decision, the challenge is to have all the relevant information on which to make a high-quality decision. You need the information in a timely manner and you need to consider alternatives before deciding on a course of action.

In chapter 3 there is information that the *organization* should make available to employees to help their career decision making, and there is information that *you* currently have available (see above, "Individual Career Planning"). Where else is career information available? Other people in the organization can prove very valuable; key people carry not only the "historical memory" of how and why people have moved in the past but also the "future awareness" of the direction and needs of the organization. Technically oriented jobs can often lead to tunnel-vision regarding opportunities throughout the organization. Seek out those key people with broader perspective and find ways to broach the subject of career options and opportunities (see chapter 9, "The Job Search").

Different departments are likely to have relevant information in different areas. For example, the internal auditing staff know the financial issues, and they also may travel to the company's other offices so they have a broader perspective of options at different geographical locations. The professional corporate personnel staff should have realistic information about people needs and position needs. Find the aggressive, sharp person within a few of these functions and you will receive some valuable input regarding the direction of the organization and the career tracks that might be available and valued.

SUMMARY

Chapter 11 addressed the very real issue of what you can do to support your own career even if the organization is doing nothing. It recommended different techniques for involving your boss in the process. The central message was that you must take control of your own destiny and manage your own career; no one else is going to do that for you.

The reader should now be able to answer the following questions:

When do you need to begin "career planning"?
What self-assessments need to occur in career planning?
What personal or organizational barriers to accomplishing your career goals can you anticipate?
What does "management by objectives" have in common with career planning?
How should you choose between competing priorities?
How does career planning fit into the broader issue of life planning?
What are the supervisor's career management roles? If you are a supervisor, how can you do them better? How can your own supervisor do them better?
How would an effective career-planning discussion be conducted between supervisor and subordinate?
What workshop or counseling about career-planning options are available, and how can you contact them?

There are numerous things that professionals can do to manage their own careers. This chapter has dealt with many and has provided the sources for further outside help in career planning.

REFERENCES

1. Bewayo, E. D. 1986. What employees look for in first and subsequent employers. *Personnel* (April):49–54.
2. Bolles, R. N. 1978. *The three boxes of life.* Berkeley, CA: Ten Speed Press.
3. Dalton, G. W., and Thompson, P. H. 1986. *Novations: strategies for career management.* New York: Scott, Foresman.
4. Goldstein, A. P., and Sorcher, M. 1974. *Changing supervisor behavior.* New York: Pergamon.
5. Gutteridge, T. G., and Otte, F. L. 1983. *Organizational career development.* Washington, DC: ASTD Press.
6. Hall, D. T. 1976. *Careers in organizations.* Pacific Palisades, CA: Goodyear Publishing Co.
7. Hill, N. C. 1985. Career counseling: what employees should do—and expect. *Personnel* (August):41–46.
8. Jomaoas, D. B. 1985. Developing a personal career package. *Supervisory Management* (January):14–15.
9. Leibowitz, Z. B., and Schlossberg, N. K. 1981. Training managers for their role in a career development system. *Training and Development Journal* (July):72–79.
10. Montana, P. J., and Higginson, M. V. 1978. *Career life planning for Americans: agenda for organizations and individuals.* New York: AMACOM.
11. Odiorne, G. S. 1980. *Guide to successful goal setting.* Westfield, MA: MBO, Inc.

12. Sonnenfeld, J. A., and Ingol, C. A. 1986. Working knowledge: charting a new course for training. *Organization Dynamics* (Autumn):63-79.
13. Souerwine, A. H. 1978. *Career strategies: planning for personal achievement*. New York: AMACOM.
14. Super, D. E. 1980. A life-span, life-space approach to career development. *Journal of Vocational Behavior* 16:282-98.
15. Thompson, P. H., Baker, R. Z., and Smallwood, N. 1986. Improving professional development by applying the four-stage career model. *Organization Dynamics* (Autumn):49-62.

PART 3
CONCLUSIONS

Chapter 12

Delving into the Unknown

Throughout this book we have attempted to maintain a balanced relationship between the organization and the individual professional or scientist. We assume that one does not perform effectively without the active participation of the other, although at times either may lose awareness of this interdependency and concentrate entirely on self-interest. The overriding issue is how to establish and sustain this balanced, interdependent relationship over a long period of time. Both the organization and its members—the individual professionals, scientists, managers, and support staff—must keep changing and developing. Key issues and research requirements can be viewed from four different perspectives: the organization, the individual, the integration of the two, and career research itself.

CAREER MANAGEMENT: THE ORGANIZATIONAL PERSPECTIVE

Key Issues

One key issue that must be considered by the designers and managers of any career development system is how to integrate all of the system's components so that it functions smoothly and achieves its goals. How far out of synchronization programs can become when they are not integrated became apparent in one large aerospace corporation. One location's training and education department spent millions training engineers and technicians in the organization's current business activities. However, the corporate strategy initiated several years earlier was designed to change that location's goals, products, and activities. As the strategical plans moved into final implementation, the engineers and technicians who had been trained were laid off because their skills were no longer relevant. New employees with applicable knowledge and skill were employed. Because the education and training program was not consistent with corporate plans, not only were millions of dollars in the corporation's investment in human capital lost, but there were also major disruptions in the individuals' commitment to the organization, in careers, and in family lives.

To make a career development system work, the requirements of the organization must be specified in sufficient detail for effective actions to be designed and taken. For example, manpower planning will not be useful if the results are left only in aggregate, labor-cost terms; they must be translated into projections of the number of future personnel required at different organizational levels, and the types of knowledge and skills that will be needed.

A second key issue is how adequately the organization considers the individual in the design and implementation of the career development system. To make the system work, all organization members, from the individual professional to the managers and human resource support staff, must be able and willing to participate. For example, if the organization has not done an adequate job of manpower planning or has not appropriately shared the information with its members, individuals cannot include the organization in an effective way in their career plans. Therefore, the ability of the organization's members to participate in a career development system is not solely dependent upon psychological abilities such as intelligence and cognitive skills, but heavily upon the ability provided via well-designed system components, appropriate shared information and other resources, effective support staff and management, and adequately trained individuals. The willingness of professionals to participate emanates from two primary sources: the consistency between the rewards provided by the organization and those valued by the individual members during the course of their careers, and the clear linkage of career activities and performance with the rewards that are available at any period in the careers of professionals and scientists. Possibly another way to express this key issue is to propose that the career development system be internally consistent. There must be incentives for professionals and scientists to work on career activities that are congruent with the organization's requirements, and there must not be organizational barriers or punishments present to deter such performance.

Research and Practice Requirements

Manpower Planning. The technologies that can be used for projecting the manpower requirements of an organization several years into the future are evolving, and this research needs to continue. The quantitative methods that are used are based on historical data, and management's responses to surveys of manpower needs are based upon their short-term plans. If the organization does not change (rate of growth, product mix, and so on), such techniques can provide quite accurate forecasts of its requirements. As the organization maintains its stability, it becomes possible to estimate adequately not only aggregate manpower requirements, but also the requirements of major segments such as occupational fields or operating departments. However, better techniques need to be developed so that requirements can be projected under more dynamic circumstances in which turnover rates, growth rates, product mixes, and corporate strategy, change. For example, what would the impact be on staffing requirements if a hospital changed its strategy from the provision of a broad spectrum of services in a single location to one in which out patient services provided in many satellite locations throughout a community would be emphasized?

While aggregate levels of manpower requirements can currently be usefully projected, the technology for dividing those gross numbers into smaller levels of knowledge and skill demands has not been developed. If a work force does not need to change, there is no problem. The organization just hires and develops more of the same. However, if a change in technology is forecasted, career developmental processes should be used to change the available knowledge and skill of the current employees, and a new mix of professionals should be hired. Without adequate methods for estimating new future needs, the transition of the work force to meet organization objectives becomes very inefficient if not wholly inadequate.

Improved ways of incorporating environmental issues such as labor market expectations, birth rates, and demographic changes, need to be made. These would provide better estimates of the problems the organization might face in meeting not only its overall manpower requirements, but also its needs in specific scientific/professional fields.

It is not possible to set and evaluate progress toward goals in the career development system without making improvements in the means of projecting the organization's manpower requirements and its chances of obtaining an adequate supply externally. The career development system will lose its credibility with the members of the organization if they cannot depend on the career information that they receive to be accurate enough for their career planning or on the programs to be adequate for their career development.

Another ingredient essential to effective manpower planning is the ability to predict the effect of changing technology on the way that the organization conducts its business. There is no research to establish how technically competent a professional, supervisor, manager, or executive must be to do an effective job. It has been assumed that professionals and scientists must stay current with the technology and avoid obsolescence. However, the training and development of managers have varied from emphasis on being a broad, nontechnical generalist during the 1960s and early 1970s to the current concentration on a modicum of expertise through all managerial levels up to executive. There has not been adequate research on the effect of new technology on an organization and its people. Thus the practitioner cannot base career development programs on the needs of managerial personnel for competency in new technology.

Organization Planning and Career Structures. As the organization changes its strategy, improves its ability to accomplish its goals, and influences or adapts to its environment, it traditionally changes its structure. While organization design is important, it is outside the scope of this book. Suffice it to say that a change in design and how it functions has a major impact on the people in the organization. Projecting such changes and preparing people to adapt to the changing organization and to function effectively under new policies, procedures, and norms are functions of the career development system. Research has not yet been done to provide the guidelines necessary to prepare people for major changes. We do not know the conditions that "force" executives to redesign the organization so that we can project the need for reorganization and can start the development of personnel well in advance.

Even if the organization structure remains static, how the career structures should be defined and managed for a technical/professional organization is not well researched. Many organizations have initiated dual, triple, and even quadruple career ladders that recognize the differences among professionals and scientists, managers of professionals, staff support for professionals, and managers of nonprofessionals. There are many opinions on what is required to make such parallel ladders work, but there has not been any systematic evaluation to prove the real effectiveness of such approaches. Until such research provides guidelines, it will continue to be difficult to provide optimal career development and career rewards for professionals.

Most organizations have very little definition of a career structure for their employees. What is provided is generic in nature and may or may not be shared with em-

PART 3
CONCLUSIONS

ployees. The military is one organization that has a considerable amount of detail available about various career paths and has attempted to share it with its officers. The structured career policies and practices force the officers to make career decisions at specific times and provide guidelines to career planning. However, it is still not known whether such detailed career information is good or bad. How structured should career patterns be for the good of the organization and the professionals employed by it? High structure normally is related to a limited ability for the organization to adapt to its environment and may produce inappropriate career performance from its members. The solutions to these problems are not known.

Succession Planning. A unique organization chart can depict not only the current incumbents in each management position, but also potential replacements according to their present status. This system has been in use for many years. Current status is typically represented by such evaluations of each individual as "immediately promotable," "promotable in two years," "never promotable," or "should be replaced." While methods for assessing managerial potential and evaluating current performance have been developed via considerable research and have been applied individually in many organizations, little is known about their application in a highly professional setting. As noted earlier, it is not known how much technical knowledge and skill is required at different levels to manage an organization that specializes in the development of new knowledge or the application of state-of-the-art technology. Current methods for assessing management potential do not include this factor.

While there are many descriptions of succession planning, there has been little research on its effectiveness in aiding the organization to meet manpower requirements over the long term. Questions that remain to be answered are: how accurate are the current estimates of managerial and professional potential and, if some miss the mark, why do they do so; how do you establish a succession plan for an organization that does not exist now but will in the future, assuming that succession plans need to be as dynamic as the organization; should a succession plan be translated into a career development plan for each individual in the organization and, if so, how is it accomplished and managed over time; and how much information about the succession plan should be shared with individual members of the organization? The answers to such questions may vary for professional succession versus managerial succession.

Effective succession planning depends upon the organization's ability to acquire accurate data about the past, present, and future (potential) performance of the organization's professionals. The Early Identification of Management Potential Research (36,76) and the Career Pattern Study (4), conducted at Exxon and AT&T respectively, indicate that it is possible to predict managerial potential. However, there does not appear to be any similar research that predicts the potential of professionals as well. What has been done does not appear to be applied in any organization (24,56). At Rensselaer Polytechnic Institute in the 1970s, preliminary research was conducted on the selection of research and development managers (44), but considerable additional work involving larger and more representative samples than at Rensselaer, in longitudinal designs, needs to be done before the results are ready for conclusive application. More research needs to be done in both the early identification of the potential professional and the application of that knowledge.

Performance appraisal is an area in which a large amount of research has been done. Nearly all of the research has concentrated upon the design of the instrument and the dyadic relationship between the appraiser and the appraisee. It seems that the problem of providing accurate information about current performance to management for its use in succession planning, reassignment, and other decision making has seldom been considered and certainly not solved. Changing the form or developing expensive, complex measuring scales is not the answer. The perspective is that performance appraisal by a supervisor is imbedded within a much larger system that needs and uses the information; this must be considered in research before any breakthroughs can be made (33).

Rewards and Barriers in Development. To our knowledge, there has been little consideration given, by either the researcher or the practitioner, to the incentive properties of various rewards or punishments present in the career management system. Because the career management process takes place over a long period of time (a thirty-to-forty-year career span from the individual's perspective), what is perceived by the individual as a punishment (relocation, for example) at one stage may be overlooked by the organization that is focusing on a reward (potential promotion) a few years later. Management must become more aware of the fact that an immediate relocation has a probability of occurring at the rate of 100 percent while a 25-to-75-percent probability of future promotion is much lower and a lot more ambiguous. If relocation is considered desirable by the employee, the conflict may be resolved. If the organization provides an optimal level of relocation support, the deterrents that individuals perceive within the move may be alleviated enough for the individual to accept the change and focus on the more distant opportunity for a promotion. Current research has little to offer practitioners when they need to design or manage incentives within their career programs.

There is considerable research on the generic categories of potential rewards that are valued by scientists and professionals as noted in chapters 1 and 8, but this research has not been extended to the applied level so that the practitioner can use the information. The issue has been acknowledged in studies of managers who are productive in their current jobs, but no longer promotable because of lack of opportunity or potential to perform at a more senior level. The same situation is present among professionals and their managers, but we know very little from any research into maintaining or increasing motivation and the level of productivity. Little is known about the employee in the mid- and late-career periods (17). If commitment to the work is a key ingredient in the productivity of a professional or scientist, the organization needs to know more than is currently known about encouraging commitment early and maintaining it over the long thirty-to-forty-year period of the career. A major deficiency in the work environment of midcareer professionals is recognition. Midcareer professionals require as much feedback and "equitable" compensation as younger employees so that they do not feel taken for granted (17). Exactly the same treatment may not be required for more mature personnel, but at this stage, the term *equitable* is not clearly defined.

Probably the toughest problem for an organization to solve is how to provide all employees *equal opportunity* to prove themselves. Under ideal conditions, whether they are eligible for the organization's rewards—challenging assignments, recognition, visibility, promotions, raises—would be dependent upon their own performance and potential. Even in the military, where career policies, structures, and practices are specified in great detail, it is very difficult to provide equal opportunity to officers in initial assignments. The circumstances vary widely because of supervisory practices, operational requirements, and immediate needs of the services. Nevertheless, there is not any research to provide the guidance necessary to designing policy, practices, and information systems so that individual capability is not overlooked or suppressed as a result of inequitable treatment or opportunity.

Although the organization can work on minimizing the internal barriers that interfere with motivation and performance, a recent, external phenomenon has arisen that affects careers markedly. This is the "dual-career" couple. The problem of transfer and relocation has been recognized, but little is known about the effect on family life of odd, variable working hours, travel, and other factors. These factors would appear to become even more crucial when both marital partners are involved in careers.

Another factor that is alluded to but not resolved in human resources texts is whether there should be rewards provided to individuals, supervisors and managers, and supporting staff for their participation in career development. If it is decided that they should, then how should such rewards be provided without diverting individuals from the primary goals of the organization? Little is yet known about avoiding goal displacement.

Learning Processes. Organizations seem to have decided that learning only occurs in the classroom except when the work is relatively simplistic as on the assembly line. Starting in the 1970s, that assumption has been challenged. In fact, as much as 80 percent of the learning of professionals and scientists may take place not in a classroom but in the work situation (55). Therefore, education and training should be designed to support the learning that takes place during work. If this approach is used, how should education and training programs be designed and implemented, and how should work be shaped to provide the best combination and opportunity for learning?

Education and Training. Formalized education and training are most effective when directly linked to specific job-related needs and are immediately applied (17). However, much more research needs to be conducted before we will be able to assess adequately the complex requirements of senior-level professionals, scientists, and managers. In fact there may be different training needs present at different phases of a career (18). In addition, it is apparent that teaching people how to manage and to learn similar complex skills requires considerable research and development to make that education and training task most effective (75). Instructional designs may need to vary according to the career phase, age, or experience of the individual. For middle-aged and older professionals, there is a need to determine the best methods to use in training and retraining so that they avoid technical/professional obsolescence (47,75).

Research needs to be done not only to develop better instructional technologies but also to identify different approaches that individuals take to learning. Then these learning styles should be matched with the appropriate training method. While one theory of differences in learning styles has been proposed, the associated research has been too controversial for the theory to gain wide acceptance (14,26,27,70). How do learning styles vary among highly educated professionals, and which styles are most effective? Can individuals with poor learning styles be taught to use the better ones?

Work Experience. Since the late 1960s, Kaufman, at the Polytechnic Institute of New York, and Dubin and Farr, at Pennsylvania State University, have investigated the methods that appear to be most effective in helping professionals and scientists avoid technical obsolescence. Their results appear to show that there is not yet an effective link between formal training in technology and its immediate application at work. However, those methods that initiate or build upon individual initiative seem to work best. The locus of such an approach is the work itself. A professional will learn something new if it is required to get the work done. Therefore, the best learning strategy would seem to be the management of work and work assignments. Education and training should become flexible enough to support this strategy on an almost individual basis.

To effect such a strategy, more research is needed. How do people go about optimally learning on the job? How much of a learning challenge can different people absorb at work? What means will determine the present status and the learning/performance potential of individual professionals? A means to establish the current and evolving knowledge and skill requirements of a position needs to be developed. Then techniques need to be designed to help in determining if there is an effective match between the job as a learning vehicle and the capability of the individual who should be assigned to it. If the match appears to be unrealistic because the individual is not at a high enough current status to make the transition effectively, then it must be determined if some directly relevant training can aid the individual sufficiently so that a change becomes practical.

For most well-defined positions, including research and development, it is apparent that the work can become routinized so that learning for the incumbent becomes minimal. At the present time, little, if anything, is known about how to determine when this occurs. There is not yet an answer to the question about what a reasonable time is to leave someone in the job after the job has been mastered so that the organization receives a reasonable return on its investment during the learning process. Until those questions are resolved, it will be impossible to determine when transfers or job rotation should take place to be most effective from both individual and organizational perspectives.

Up to this point, a relatively short-term, nearly static model of individual-to-job matching has been described. The issue is actually very complex. There is no technology allowing the design of sequences of assignments, over a thirty-year career, to develop the complex set of knowledge, skills, and attitudes required of senior professionals, scientists, and managers. Thus, optimal career patterns, including alternate sequences and jobs cannot be defined in any systematic way that is not primarily dependent upon personal opinion or experience and past organization practices.

To provide a wide exposure to organization practices, organizations have often followed a frantic pattern of transfers from project to project, function to function, and location to location. As Glueck stated over a decade ago (15), this may not only be expensive but also dysfunctional to the performance of the organization and the effectiveness of the individual. Research should be conducted to establish how much mobility and relocation is optimal, and how they should be designed to provide the desired results.

A basic component of the learning that takes place in a work setting seems to be social or interpersonal. Professionals use informal networks to learn how to get work done in the organization, to solve problems, to determine the priorities of work. The work of Berlew and Hall has identified how critical initial socialization is for the new employee (2). "Getting off on the right foot" is extremely important (18). London acknowledges this fact in the development of a model of career motivation (39) and in the applications at AT&T that he has described (41). While Hall has proposed that socialization at midcareer is primarily internal and less dependent upon the surrounding role senders (17), more research is required to establish this proposition as fact. Hall's premise may be true when the change in roles occurs in small increments, but it may be false when there is a dramatic change such as: a reversal in policy or corporate strategy; transferring from one functional or product area to another; altering technologies (73); job loss (23,35), organization alteration such as restructuring, merging with or acquiring another company, or going into bankruptcy (73); demotion, career plateauing, or retirement. A more formalized support system may be required for professionals to learn their new roles effectively.

It has been proposed that mentors and sponsors may be valuable roles that support employees while they learn new jobs and social roles in the organization (25,31). If mentorship includes a heavy component of emotional linkage between the mentor and protégé, it may be difficult for the organization to prescribe such a relationship. Research should be conducted to establish how a mentor-protégé relationship evolves and if such a role set or situation can be formalized. If sponsorship can be assumed to be similar to mentorship, except with the omission of the emotional linkage, it may be more feasible to establish sponsorships at initial entry and under conditions of major changes. However, research is required to see if such roles and relationships can be designed, what programs are required to implement them, and, if they can be developed, if they are effective in assisting with the change process.

A key learning/adaptation situation that is not well understood is the transition from specialist as a professional to manager. Nothing is known about the process whereby the allegiance shifts from science or the profession to the organization or if such a transition is even necessary. Very little is known about how the individual changes his or her focus from specific personal task performance behaviors to the general performance behaviors and outcomes of others. Until more is known about this transition process and how to manage, support, and evaluate it, organizations will continue to ruin many good professionals by promoting them to create mediocre or poor managers.

Adaptability. The ability of people to adapt to change appears to be a combination of the learning ability, personality (52), and the desire to change. The need to adapt continuously to small increments of change in the environment is represented in the problem of obsolescence in technical/professional knowledge and skill. Dramatic changes have been outlined above. Before we can design and apply support systems to develop and maintain the adaptability of employees, more must be learned about individual adaptability. Is adaptability a skill or characteristic that is already present when an individual enters the world of work as an adult and never changes thereafter? Or is it something that can be developed, maintained, or relearned by individuals? If the ability of individuals to adapt deteriorates over time, what causes it to do so? Many employees in midcareer continue to grow, others reach a plateau, and still others stagnate and decline. The personal, organizational, and other factors that contribute to the different reactions are not known and require research (73). A developing area of research, the career transition process, should throw some significant light into this dark void in our knowledge (5,35,58).

Career-Planning Assistance. The majority of adult working Americans do not do any career planning. As a result, the consequences of a career decision are usually formulated in immediate terms, not long-range career terms. Today's intuitive response to a problem may have very positive immediate results but be counterproductive to future career outcomes. In research on the careers of Navy officers (54), there were many examples of this. How much is the responsibility of the organization? To a great extent, this is a moral question, but it would appear that the organization is accountable for providing a reasonable amount of support so that the individual has the opportunity to make an informed decision and career plan. If professionals are to be accountable for their own careers, what is the best way for the organization to help them to initiate their career planning?

One method of providing support is through a career-counseling program. Considerable research has been done on the career decision-making and planning process that might be used by youths in high school and college, but little on adults. Self-help workbooks are available in some organizations, many conduct career-planning work groups, and others provide a formal career counselor. It is not known if any of them are effective, and, if so, which is best. Nor is it known how to adapt such programs to the characteristics of different participants. For example, one military research-and-development laboratory found that a three-and-a-half-day career-planning course for nonprofessionals could be condensed into two days for technical and scientific personnel and include the same processes and material.

Self-analysis and career-planning workbooks generate questionable data since self-analysis is notoriously inaccurate, and most participants never complete the process. Such materials are available in only 15 percent of the companies participating in one survey. Workshops appear to attract only 10 to 15 percent of the employees of an organization and after the first year or two are used primarily by new employees. People do not bother to put in the time or effort. Is it necessary? If it is, research is needed to see how participation can be increased and how the results can be improved. To help in this research requires the definition of a good career plan. Only then could different methods for helping individuals to produce career plans be designed and evaluated.

Many organizations require their employees to produce a development plan every year. For some employees this may be counterproductive and create resentment. If career planning is a skill and can be developed, it is also one that can deteriorate if not used. However, it may not need to be repeated every year after the skill has been developed and used over a fifteen-to-twenty-year period. It is not known how often career-planning skills need to be refreshed and used at different points in the career. Nor is it known how often an individual should do career planning, and how detailed the individual should be. What circumstances should cause the organization to influence an employee to initiate a career plan, to update a career plan, or to completely reassess and possibly revise one? Those research questions have not been answered to date and are important ones for the designing of an organization's career development program and policies.

While techniques and timing are important, so is the process that is used to develop an operational career plan and to integrate it with the career and career development opportunities present in the organization. The principal participants in this process are typically considered to be the individual, the supervisor—or levels of supervision—and the human resources development staff. Defining their roles is not easy, because they may have conflicting roles. For example, the supervisor's role as a "career advisor" conflicts with that of a "performance evaluator." The human resources specialist's role of serving the individual in a detached, objective manner conflicts with the one in which serving the needs of the organization is dominant. At the present time, it has not been determined how far the organization should go in supporting individuals' career-planning process without providing inappropriate influence. London has described the problem in an anecdote from a "fast-track" manager who said that his most successful career decisions were made by his firm (40). When he made his own decisions, they typically turned out to be the wrong ones. The role of each participant in the process needs to be defined but there is no research to guide us in designing the roles so that they are optimum and are well-coordinated.

Once the roles of the participants are well defined, then it must be determined how much and what type of training is required before the participants can perform effectively in their roles. In addition, the best methods to use in conducting the training must be established. Neither category of research is currently available.

The Career Information System. The advent of computers has made it possible for the organization to store, process, and retrieve huge quantities of information. However, it is not practical for the organization to collect, store, and make readily available everything that everyone might want to know about its employees (50). The cost is too high to collect and prepare such a vast quantity of data and to ensure its quality. While the cutoff point for accumulating data is a pragmatic, cost decision, it is difficult to place a value on the ability to keep track of all facets of employees' records so that optimal use can be made of the information to ensure that they develop. However, those judgments can be made by the management of the organization. The questions about who should have access to the various categories of information are not as easily answered. How much information should be shared with an employee and with an employee's supervisor? Should information about whether or not employees are considered "fast track" or "promotable," marginal and undesirable performers, or available for reassignment—be shared? Not enough is known about the differential effects of positive and negative information on employees and their supervisors to answer this question. Should the organization develop and maintain information about all of its jobs—the duties and requirements—and share it with employees? Should job openings be shared with employees? Rae reports very good results from a job-posting system at Holiday Inns while a program at Hewlett-Packard did not work at all (62). What is the difference between an effective and ineffective program? What would be the best method to use in sharing the information? Should computer terminal access, paper files, supervisors, or human resource specialists be made available? Each source has advantages and disadvantages regarding credibility and the ability to provide social support, counseling, and interpretation.

The credibility of any information system is dependent upon the accuracy of the information, its timeliness or availability, its relevance to the user's need, how it is presented, and how readily and correctly it can be interpreted. Career information is very personal to the individual professional, and any error, misinterpretation, or negative connotation develops a strong reaction. The supervisor or human resource specialist will probably bear the brunt of such a response. During 1984, IBM tested and installed a computerized career-counseling system in one of its divisions (49), but the Army has found such a system for officers to be very expensive (57). The Navy has found that catalogs of job descriptions and a general career guidebook for officers are not used by its officers, but a bimonthly career newsletter is. Human resource specialists who participate in making reassignments are not considered credible if contact is made via letter or telephone, but their acceptance increases markedly if contact is face-to-face. It appears that the key to much of the utilization and acceptance of the Navy's career information is the advice provided by the untrained, immediate superior and the ability of the organization to acquire, make available, and correct errors in the computerized personnel record data. At this stage research is needed to determine how accurate career information must be, how much should be shared with employees, how the information sharing should occur, and how much training is needed to make the system work for its participants.

Integrating and Evaluating the System. As proposed above, one of the key issues in career management is the integration of the subsystems of manpower planning, organization and career structure design, and the like (67). Most subsystems, policies, or programs are developed to solve a specific, ad hoc problem, and sufficient time, money, or interest is not available to look at the interaction of the new program with the other elements of the system. The subsystem's impact may distort that of others and nullify, divert, or even reverse their direction. For example, extreme emphasis on a program of upward mobility for a select group of employees may create resentment on the part of nonparticipants who have worked hard to earn special assignments or promotions. An emphasis on being credited with assignment to a specific type of job may divert people from immediately applying training or concentrating on optimum performance while in the job. Research is required to determine how the elements of a career management system interact, and how such interaction can be made synergistic rather than independent or conflicting.

Once a program has been put into place, it is very seldom evaluated to determine its usefulness or to look for improvements (19). While an organization may feel that such evaluation should center on whether the program has been effective in solving its problem, the evaluation should be theory-based as well. If it is not based on a generic model of a career management system and theory-based, the results will neither contribute to learning in the field nor generalize to other situations. Thus, the organization and society in general are not capable of determining what factors within the new program will and will not work effectively in different situations and organizations. For example, performance-appraisal programs have seldom been designed to meet continuing needs: of employees for feedback and personal planning information; of supervisors for motivational aids to maintain or improve performance; of management to make decisions regarding promotion, demotion, reassignment, and compensation; of human resource staffs for program design inputs; and of executives for information about the current effectiveness and future potential of its work force (10). Research on the design of the appraisal-form format and the supervisor-subordinate interview process results in a very limited perspective of the appraisal program. The designers of appraisal subsystems, therefore, have little to aid them in the development of an optimal program and related policies.

The evaluation of a program is not possible without determining its goals. Then the goals need to be translated into a comprehensive set of criteria at both the organization and individual levels (73). Since most programs continue over time, the evaluation should not be conducted just once, but must keep pace with other changes. Otherwise the change in its effects cannot be observed as the environment, other programs in the system, and individuals in the organization change. For example, governmental and organizational retraining programs have often been ineffective because they are keyed neither to the continuing needs of the local labor market and organization nor to the interests of individuals and are not adapted as those change.

Establishing a single measure of the effectiveness of a specific program or system, while perhaps easier, is not a realistic approach. Managers and staff may be able to discern a single problem—and its resulting performance criterion—as salient at the time a program or policy is designed, but this will not hold true for very long. For example, performance-appraisal research has concentrated on immediate criterion problems, such as whether the results provided by immediate supervisors are sufficient for executives to determine which are the best employees in the organization. However, some appraisal programs that solved the immediate problem of separating high- from low-performing employees were discontinued because they did not meet other criteria such as acceptance (the participants did not feel that the method or process was acceptable to them), practicality (completion of the process was too time consuming), or discrimination over time (the spread among employees disappeared after three or four years). Multiple criteria are required to assess adequately the effectiveness of any career development system program. Research is required to determine what is an adequate set of such criteria and how these criteria can be measured and combined to provide the information that management requires for practical program evaluation.

CAREER PLANNING: THE INDIVIDUAL PERSPECTIVE

The organization and the individual become so intertwined in the career development process that it is difficult to distinguish between them.

Key Issues

A large proportion of the literature that concentrates on individuals and their careers has come from the field of vocational counseling and counseling psychology. Those fields have concentrated on helping students who are in high school or the early years of college choose their occupational fields. Most of the research coming out of those disciplines has been done on youth of twenty years of age or less. Researchers from the field of gerontology have focused primarily on only one career issue, retirement or preparing for it. Their work typically starts with adults who are fifty-five years of age or older. Thus, the career questions, attitudes, concerns, and behaviors of adults in the key working ages of twenty-two through sixty-five years have been significantly overlooked. In the American culture, work is a central life issue, yet the majority of research has emphasized only the initial choice of a field of work and adjusting to retirement from that field. It would appear that much more needs to be done to increase the knowledge of the dynamics of individuals' careers between the ages of twenty-two and sixty-two, which represents 53 percent of the normal life cycle.

The second key issue is a derivative of this myopic view of adults and their careers. Professionals do not just choose an occupational field as a teenager or college sophomore, choose an employer as a graduating senior or graduate student, and then work away in that field and organization until retirement without changing. They make a myriad of constantly evolving career decisions and encounter many different situations during the course of their careers. What causes these changing situations and concerns and what are the best ways to resolve them are key issues that continue throughout life. A life-span, longitudinal approach must be taken before we can develop useful insights into career issues.

The third key issue is that the career of a professional is imbedded within a personal lifestyle and cultural system. The interaction of the individual, career, organization, family, and society must be included in research paradigms before we can establish what factors are the most critical influence on career development. Such research becomes very complex, time consuming, and expensive but will provide the major breakthrough required to help the designer of career development systems.

Research and Practice Requirements

Individual Differences. Abilities, personality, interests, and values of individuals and groups of individuals, and their relationship in the choice of and continuance in occupations, have been studied for many years. This research has centered on individuals in the high school and early college age groups. In several studies reported over the last fifteen years, Krumboltz and his colleagues at Stanford University and Harren and his colleagues at Southern Illinois University have identified different styles used by college students in making career decisions (see chapter 8). The research needs to be improved, replicated, and extended to cover a larger span of career ages and occupational experiences before it can be used effectively in the design of career-decision support programs. Driver and his associates at the University of Southern California have presented a theory based on decision-making styles that proposes that several different styles of behavior are used by people in the self-management of their careers (see chapter 8). However, the latter theory is in its embryonic stage and needs to be more adequately articulated, to have measures more carefully designed and tested, and to be replicated by other researchers on different populations before it can be used in organizational settings as an aid to career development system design.

The amount of available research on sex differences in managerial positions has increased markedly in the last few years. Now it needs to be extended to professionals to help define differences in progress, if they exist, within professional careers and to determine whether possible differences can be attributed to sex. Then it must be established how the environment can be changed most effectively so that discrimination as a result of the environment is eliminated (68).

The disproportionate representation of the different races in scientific and professional careers in America is so blatant that its presence hardly needs to be stated. Still we do not have the research that provides answers that can help society equalize the differences (68). The problem of increasing the value placed upon, interest in, and motivation for completing the intensive education required in scientific and professional fields among blacks, Spanish-speaking Americans, and American Indians has not been resolved. The research in the area has been very weak and limited dramatically because of its political ramifications.

Career Decision Making. There are three primary issues that need to be resolved via research before additional progress can be made in helping professionals to improve their career decision making. The most obvious of these is defining a *good* career decision, so the effectiveness with which the decision was made can be assessed. There is no definition of "successful" versus an "unsuccessful" career decision. Unless an effective means of considering personal and contextual, and short- and long-term factors can be developed to identify a good career decision, there will always be uncertainty about the appropriateness of a career decision and the effectiveness of the process by which it was made. For example, in both a military setting (53) and a business environment (40), it was noted that, several years after the fact, many senior managers felt that they had received—and often rejected—better counsel about appropriate earlier career options from representatives of the organization than the alternatives they had ultimately chosen. Thus a decision to do something at one point in time, such as obtaining a promotion, escaping a miserable boss, or avoiding travel, might have immediate satisfactory consequences, but detrimental ones later. Some research has been done using the assumption that a "successful" career decision is one in which the consequences of the decision are consistent with the values of the decision-maker (32). It is not known how well this immediate criterion holds up over an entire career.

Some other criteria that might be used to evaluate the quality of a career decision are:

1. Rapid promotion (upward mobility) and potential for advancement.
2. High income.
3. The decision-making process is carefully completed, and the scientific method is followed to a rational choice.
4. Life quality such as family, personal, and community concerns is considered as well as work.
5. Career satisfaction (occupational and organizational).
6. Job satisfaction.
7. Career commitment (occupational and organizational).
8. Job involvement.
9. Career adaptability.
10. Growth and development of abilities.
11. Vocational maturity.
12. Job performance.

At this stage, it is not known how to determine the best criterion to use for an individual professional at a point in time. To add to the complexity, the salience of criteria at one point in time may shift over the career. It is also not known why that occurs and what can be done to make the changes acceptable and go smoothly (47).

To help in the development of a useful approach to identifying "successful" career decisions, we need to determine how often and for what period of time deviations or "side excursions" from an optimal career sequence can be made without being detrimental to career progression. Can someone go into "limbo" on a project or job that does not have visibility, relevant learning experience, professional challenge, or other career-contributing characteristics for a week, a year, two years, five years, one, two, or three times, without losing the opportunity for organizational rewards?

The second primary decision-making issue is the problem of when the professional should go through a comprehensive career decision-making and planning process and when a short, quick-fix approach is adequate. An obvious moment in which a major effort must be made is during the initial choice of an occupation during high school or early college years, and another is during the employment-seeking period as you approach graduation. If you lose a job or approach mandatory retirement, it is clear that a careful career decision-making and planning procedure should be carried out. However, other times are not as clearly determined by circumstances. Is a quick review sufficient as you plan your yearly or periodic development activities, receive an offer of promotion or transfer, become annoyed with your boss, are given an outstanding or unsatisfactory performance appraisal, or are involved in a myriad of other less dramatic situations?

It is obvious from discussions with individuals that the annual requirement by human resources departments to complete a career plan is typically seen as an obnoxious paper requirement rather than an opportunity to plan a career. The need to make career decisions and to plan activities may creep up on the individual and not be significant enough to be recognized. As yet, it is not known how to trigger the process before a crisis hits. It would appear that an emphasis on problem awareness and identification, not just problem solving, is needed.

The third primary decision-making issue is the problem in determining what the best process is for a professional to use in making career decisions and plans. Something is known about how college students make their career decisions, that is, establish their decision-making style, but what the optimal method is and if the method should change according to the situation, experience, and characteristics of the individual are questions yet to be answered. Once an optimal method is agreed upon, can it be taught or aided? Much of this research is dependent upon determining what a *good* career decision is.

The Career Decision-Making Process. As discussed in chapter 8, several early career theories assume that people go through career stages in a lock step process delineated by specific ages. The period of ages seventeen to twenty-two is referred to as exploration and involves career decision making. Recent theory and research indicates that this activity continues through much of life and into traditional retirement ages. We have assumed that career decision making and planning are skills that can be taught and learned by youths and adults. Research needs to be done to demonstrate that this is true and whether it is applicable to everyone. If it is not applicable to all (73), are there characteristics of individuals and situations in which career decision making and planning can be learned? If it is learned, how is it best taught and how often should training or experience be repeated so that the skill is retained?

What are the factors that impede or facilitate career exploration by individuals of all ages under different circumstances? Is it intended or fortuitous, systematic or random, self-oriented or environment-oriented, self-initiated or externally initiated? The minimal research available indicates that self-initiated career decision making is not as successful at producing appropriate exploration and planning behavior as externally initiated (73).

The methods that are used to aid career decision making and planning have received very little research except for that focused on group-counseling approaches. The decision-making style of the individual may be a critical factor in determining which method is the best one to use in aiding individual career decision making (66). There are many handbooks available to aid individuals who desire to work on their own. It is not known if this method is of value and if it is universally useful, and if so, under what conditions. Bowen and Hall have compared do-it-yourself approaches, counseling or coaching options, and career planning workshops (3). They favor the workshops such as those used at the Lawrence Livermore Laboratory (20).

Self-analysis and planning workbooks are available in few organizations, and workshops appear to attract a minimum number of the employees in an organization. Not even students participate voluntarily—only 10 to 15 percent at MIT, for example. The efficacy of psychological counseling by a vocational counselor has been questioned by many participants but may be applicable to some individuals who are under extreme stress such as job loss (23). People do not appear to be willing to put in the time and effort required to do career decision making and planning. Is it really necessary that they do so? If it is, how can participation be increased and the quality of results improved?

Nearly every comprehensive approach to career decision making starts off with a self-evaluation to establish a personal base for comparing alternative decisions. Some, such as those developed by Kotter and his associates (28), are very comprehensive and time consuming and others, as in Holland's approach (21), are more parsimonious and less time consuming. Holland's methods have received extensive research and been refined until they show useful consistency and accuracy over time. (For example, young male investigative types (highly represented by scientists) did an effective job of predicting actual job entry, graduate major, and ideal and projected plans seven years after it was administered [59].) Tests, inventories, autobiographies, may be useful, but the results are not readily translated as an input into the decision-making process except in an extensive system such as Holland's. Tests and inventories have sex and racial biases in them, and little is known about their effect. What is the effect of low scores on individual self-esteem or willingness to use the information? In general, self-assessment is not very accurate, and means need to be found to make it better if it is an integral part of career planning (69).

Counseling. An aid to career decision making and planning that is frequently sought is the vocational counselor, school psychologist, or counseling psychologist (63). Such individuals have a strong background of training and experience in psychotherapy plus some vocational counseling. With the overlap in two diverse fields, the question arises as to whether the mix is too complex for a single individual to work with. Most college and secondary school students where the efforts of most vocational counselors are centered feel that career counseling is poorly done. Why is this true? If mental health counseling was separated from vocational counseling, as is done in Canada, how does one counselor establish when the client should be referred to a colleague in the other field? Is vocational counseling more effective with adults who usually have a clearer concept of the world of work even though the academic training of counselors is focused on youth? Adult career counseling that covers questions about adjustment to work, occupational change, job search, development planning, adaptability, transfer/relocation, retirement, and so on appears to be too different from the initial occupational-choice situation of youth to be learned via the same training. What should the training be, how should the counseling take place, and who should receive such counseling if it is to be effective? Counseling is normally handled as though it involves a single decision at one point in time. What is required to help it be learned as a continuing developmental series of decisions instead?

Computer Aids. The computer is evolving as an aid to career decision making. Minor has developed computer-based programs to aid IBM personnel in their career decisions (48,50). However, only a few years earlier, Myers and his colleagues found that computer aids for providing career information to Army captains were too expensive in contrast to more traditional methods (57). Is the computer an effective means of providing career information? Will people use it? These research questions need to be answered.

Implementing Decisions. While there has been considerable research covering how people go about making career decisions and some on how they can be helped to do so, there is very little on how to implement career plans. The problems of implementation by individual professionals are magnified if they do not work for a sophisticated firm such as IBM that puts considerable effort into many career development programs, for example, education and training. There has been conjecture that some individuals choose a more senior individual as a role model and try to emulate that person. Other opinions are that individuals select what they perceive as the best behaviors of several role models and pattern themselves after those. At the same time they identify poor behaviors of others and try to avoid those behaviors or concentrate on alternate behaviors. There is no research yet upon which to base advice to professionals or development of organizational programs.

Another implementation aspect that is present in the popular literature is mentoring or sponsorship. Very little is known about the differences between mentors and sponsors and how they function. Are they really effective and, if so, are they more appropriate for some organizations, such as academia, than others or do they work better for some types of people than others? How do such relationships develop and how would individuals establish them on their own? There is little guidance from the research literature to use in the design of a sponsor program that would aid in the development of individual professionals. While the immediate supervisor is an obvious candidate for the role of a sponsor, how can an individual get the supervisor to serve in such a role if the organization does not prescribe and reward it?

Adaptability. The same comments that were made under this heading in the section above on organizational research requirements hold true for research on the individual. However, the criteria for the individual are personal ones such as feelings of competence, career and job satisfaction, technical and professional knowledge and skill, job performance, or promotability. Under these circumstances, very little is known about people and their capacity to adapt to major changes in their environment. Is this an inherent characteristic of the individual or one that is learned at an early age and programmed never to change? If so, research is required to help the organization to react by identifying personnel with the ability to adapt, placing them in the situations that require such behavior, and protecting nonadaptable employees from major changes if "productivity" is to be maintained. If the aptitude for adaptation is present in all professionals and adaptability can be developed, research is needed to help teach professionals how to adapt and how to maintain that ability (18). If the ability is learned, how is it learned or, after it is once learned, how long is the ability retained before a "refresher course" is required?

One of the times individuals need to know most about their capacity to adapt is when they are contemplating a change in career. In this instance, new professional knowledge and skills must be learned as you would expect. However, your ability to adapt will be stretched much further. The techniques, attitudes, and values used to set priorities and the associated products or services produced and delivered will probably be very different, requiring you to change your work life and habits markedly. In addition, the environmental context (regulations, taxes, professional contacts, work associations) will vary, and new interfaces will need to be developed. Little research is available to help you determine if you have the ability to adapt under these circumstances, and, if you do, what approaches would be most helpful to you. Kaufman's research on job loss (see chapter 10) provides some insight into the adaptability of individuals (23) but is focused on too specific a situation for the results to be applied to others. The separate works of Brett (5) and Nicholson (58) provide excellent starting points for future research.

Avoiding Obsolescence. The successful professional faces a unique situation that requires constant adaptation, that is, the ability to keep up-to-date or ahead in a field in which there is a constant infusion of new knowledge. Although the research required to provide the guidance to help individuals keep abreast of their field is developing, many gaps are present (13). Traditional continuing education and training do not appear to be especially effective in contrast to work experience. The latter places major demands on professional knowledge and skill, includes a significant level of technical uncertainty, and provides for a major level of individual discretion (29,30). Participating in an advanced degree program and professional activities also contributes to professional updating. However, it is not known how to translate this research into application via the design and implementation of policy and programs.

The research that is being conducted appears to be heading away from traditional education and training and toward experience-based learning at work as the best method the professional can use to enhance, broaden, or maintain technical proficiency (55). This appears to be the common thread in the work of Rothman and Perrucci (65), Kaufman (22), and Kozlowski and Farr (30). If the organization does not provide the opportunity, the individual must volunteer for special assignments and, on personal time, read directly applicable literature, teach courses, and take challenging, degree-oriented courses. However, the dynamics of how the process works is not understood, especially for the individual who is stuck in the same job for several years.

Job Transitions. Recently Brett has provided an excellent summary of the salient research and theory covering job changes such as organizational entry, geographic relocation, promotion, demotion, and lateral transfer (5). As she indicates, there is little empirical research that focuses directly on personal and role development. The measures must be taken at least twice, once when the individual is in the "old" job and then when the "new" job has been mastered, to be able to measure if development has occurred. Her model predicts that the more the job context changes, the more development occurs. However, the material that was reviewed involved managerial personnel who deal heavily with job context. The research needs to be done to see if job content can be changed in similar ways to produce professional development. It is apparent that some individuals adapt well to changes in job content and others do not (52), but the reasons for this are not known. As Brett proposes (5), it is not known how to link a sequence of job transitions together to form a career development plan that will help both the growth needs of the individual and the distant objectives of the organization for mature, skilled personnel (55). How much change can specific individuals handle? Can this level and type of change be increased by the providing of support systems such as training, financial support, or sponsorship? What are the best methods for an individual to use in adapting to job transitions?

Changing Careers. There are many kinds of descriptive, anecdotal material and "how-to" publications about changing careers, but very little research. There have been few guidelines developed out of research to help you to determine if you should change, when it should be done, what to change to, or how to go about doing it. One possible explanation for this phenomenon is the presence of career stage theory that postulates that career exploration occurs only between the ages of seventeen and twenty-one. It is becoming obvious in the study of adult careers that exploration continues throughout life although decisions made early in the career tend to be more exploratory in nature while those occurring in midcareer tend to be more terminal (60).

Entering Management. Every professional who is successful in a field will be faced with the problem of remaining as a professional or moving into management. The research that was described in chapter 9 may help you make some comparisons between yourself and those that make a successful transition, but the information is very sketchy. Simple rules for determining whether a professional should leave the organization or remain and look toward advancement are available (51), but such research-based models are few and far between. It appears from considerable research that professionals contrast materially with managers in their interests, personalities, behavior, needs/motivations, and skills/abilities. To date, it is not known which of these can be changed during a transition to management and which are inherited or learned once and for all as a child.

We will probably be unable to resolve the problems associated with making an effective change from professional to manager until we know more about what and how people learn or fail to learn from their work experience. Brousseau (6) and Morrison and Hoch (55) have taken very different approaches to studying the problem but provide some initial insights into it.

Occupational Field. While Roe and Baruch (64) found that their thirty subjects had not done much career planning when they changed fields of work as adults, others describe a much more systematic process (74). The success of the procedure appears to be dependent upon the presence of careful planning, adequate resources, and a social support system in concert with a switch to an occupation and environment that is much more compatible with the characteristics of the person involved. All of that blasé statement appears to be logical and is supported by small fragments of research. Still there is not much empirical, theory-based research to test the thesis or fill in the gaps that make it difficult to move from general statement into personal application. Holland's work is an excellent start (21); it provides a means of self-assessment to match personal characteristics with congruent sets of occupations. His model depicts compatible environments but does not provide a directly applicable means for the individual to collect the data from the relevant organization or work situation. That gap needs to be filled. In addition research should be done into how the transition should be made to minimize the stress to the professionals and their families and to maximize the opportunity for it to be successful.

Organizations and Locations. There are many books describing job search (which can be interpreted as searching for a job in a different organization), but none could be found that were based upon theory or a comprehensive set of research. There is considerable information available from surveys that compile the most frequent activities or approaches that are used (16). However, such studies do not say how much of the search activity is based upon the folklore about how to do it, and how much is based upon the most effective way to search for an individual professional with specific characteristics, from a specialized field, and going from one unique setting to another.

Most advice on geographical location has focused upon the economic problems of moving, selling one's residence, and purchasing a new one. While these factors are key ones, there are others that also appear to be significant. These are the social adjustments that occur for all family members both in the situation that they leave and in the new one that they approach. Most organizations not only overlook social readjustment but also the work-resocialization process that is present for mature new employees as well as those who are entering the world of work for the first time. Brett has provided an excellent summary of the little that is known about career transition (5), and Louis provides a very good theoretical perspective (42,43). However, both authors correctly indicate how little we know about a relatively simple job transfer within the same site, about relocation, promotion, and organization change.

The unique situation involving job loss has been approached by Dyer (11) and in a seminal book by Kaufman (23). While many of the recommendations that Kaufman presents for further research are common to the field of career research, two are especially applicable to those who lose their jobs involuntarily because of their unique situations. One of his proposals is the evaluation of coping responses to unemployment stress. In this instance not only the individual who has lost the job is of concern, but also the entire family. Longitudinal studies are required to monitor different coping strategies from their inception to their completion. A second recommendation of Kaufman's is to focus on the identification of high-risk groups (23). Initial, small-scale studies indicate that professionals are affected by job loss more than other job families, but more needs to be done so that the problem can be ameliorated when it arrives.

Retirement. As Minor has found in his recent review of the literature (49), there is very little research on retirement as a phase in career planning and development. The void is even greater for professionals. There are many programs present in corporations and the government that propose to help employees plan, but they are not based on any research. Anecdotal evidence indicates that professionals can phase out of full-time employment into full-time retirement by working less and less. The period can be as short as six months or as long as twenty years depending upon employment status, the ability to initiate their own work, personal desires, and careful planning. It appears that irregular work is common among older physicians and realistic retirement plans are affected by the physicians' values (61). Research is required to establish when retirement planning should be started for different people, how people should be aided in their preparation for retirement—including financial planning and support—and how the organization should support and remain in contact with the retiree after employment is terminated. Because of the intense involvement of professionals in their work, the issue of retirement is especially critical.

Life-Span Career Development. Although there is theoretical acknowledgement of life-span career development (71), there is no present research that follows the individual professional from childhood, when occupational interests are spawned and abilities are honed, to full-time retirement when work is no longer an issue. With the intense commitment to their work that professionals develop early in life, demonstrate in a long, complex educational process, express in self-initiated work efforts, and reflect in the difficult withdrawal symptoms shown in retirement, unique life-span career research is required. Unless it is used by society to force career decisions and behaviors, such as retirement, on professionals, age does not appear to be a determining factor in a career. More research is required to establish what causes career decisions to be made and career behaviors to occur without reference to the stultifying perspective of chronological age. If age then appears as the primary causal factor, then so be it, but research should not start out with arbitrary career stages formed by age limits. Research that is not based upon age groupings appears to find career concerns that are supposed to terminate at age twenty-four still present at age forty-five (52,72) and probably at age sixty. Career stage theories that are defined by chronological age groupings do not appear to provide the ultimate answer to the question of career issues.

CAREER DEVELOPMENT: THE INTEGRATION OF MANAGEMENT AND PLANNING

The need to integrate the programs that make up a career management system was identified in 1966, and a means was proposed to do so (12). Nearly twenty years later there are only glimpses of what was recommended being done. A more complete job of describing the requirements and specifying unique programs that need to be developed to integrate career management and career planning has been made, but no current examples of what was proposed could be pointed out (37). One possible answer to the dilemma of why so little progress has been made is represented in an article by Meahea and Duffy (45). Their "integrated" model focuses on training in a classroom as the key ingredient to development with little emphasis on the job behavior where most learning occurs and none on macro issues such as manpower planning. Myopia can be the Achille's heel of progress in career development.

Key Issues

The first key issue in career development is the level of adaptation that is required by the organization and its members for the requirements of both parties to be optimally met. In a recent incident in a research-and-development laboratory, a nationally recognized scientist resigned shortly after accepting a promotion to middle management that removed the scientist from daily involvement in his field of specialization. The organization provided the principal highly valued reward it could offer, managerial promotion, but it removed the opportunity for the individual to obtain the rewards that he desired, recognition as a scientist and autonomy over his own activities. The organization did not appear to be flexible enough to provide the individual with a promotion that recognized the individual's needs and rewarded him in a manner consistent with them. By accepting the promotion, the scientist indicated that he was not aware of how important it was to him to remain a professional. It became apparent that the promotion required him to give up his primary commitment to his profession and transfer his allegiance to the organization. Neither the scientist nor the organization appeared to be aware of this requirement or, if they were, to consider negotiating a compromise that was acceptable to both.

A second key issue in the integration of career management and career planning is the sharing of relevant information between the organization and its members. Sharing too much information may be just as ineffective as sharing too little. There are many techniques that can be used to share information but we need to use those that are best in the context of an organization comprised of adults who are professionals. For example, in one small corporation of three hundred employees, a highly valued technician resigned shortly after a management position had been filled from outside. The job requirements had not been shared with employees, and the personnel department had not searched its records for any current employees with relevant experience. The technician had had very appropriate previous experience and should have been considered an excellent candidate for the vacancy. Both parties were major losers in this instance because information was not shared by the corporation and the firm had not set up a mechanism for acquiring information about its employees' interests, abilities, and experiences. Possibly another way to express this issue is to say that the professional should be considered as an active participant in the career development system rather than as an impersonal object to be managed by the organization.

Research Requirements

Before the organization and its individual members can work at making an optimum match of their requirements, each party must determine what its requirements are and how much flexibility it has in their achievement. At the organizational level the requirements for specific fields of technical expertise and their application to customers/clients, services, products, or processes must project far enough in the future for a career development system to function effectively. This appears to be at least five years. However, research is required to establish the best techniques to use for such forecasting and to determine the minimum time span that must be covered. Projecting managerial requirements and an aggregate of nonmanagerial personnel, as currently practiced, is not adequate for a career development system involving the high levels of specialized knowledge present in professionals.

A corollary to the organization's problem in specifying its requirements is the analysis individual professionals must make of their own needs and the determination of where adaptation to the requirements of the organization can be made. As noted earlier in this chapter, the techniques available are not as accurate as they should be, and further research is required to improve them.

While Bruni and his colleagues have identified some of the sources of career information and the characteristics that appear to be related to their use or nonuse (1,7,8), more research needs to be done. For instance, Bruni's work was done in a single environment and describes general data covering the first twenty years of life at work. The research needs to be made more definitive by establishing if the same sources and characteristics are salient for professionals in their initial career entry, during midcareer, and at the time they are leaving. We need to determine those organizational and individual factors that are related to the use of each information source.

The next facet of information sharing that requires research is determining how much and what kind of information should be shared and when. Some organizations post nearly all job openings so that any employee can apply and feel that the procedure works very well. Others have tried such a program and terminated it because it produced more problems than successes. Why were the results different in different organizations? Some organizations inform all employees about those who are on a "fast track" (expected to be promotable much faster than average) while other firms keep such lists very secret. Which should it be?

To make the integration of career management and career planning work as effectively as possible, research should be conducted to identify the roles that various individuals should play and how they should be introduced to those roles. For example, the career information-sharing research indicates that the immediate supervisor is the key individual with human resource personnel secondary even in a highly centralized organization (1,7,8). However, the roles that each should play were not clearly delineated, and none was trained in any structured way to play his or her role. In the conduct of such research it should be kept in mind that individuals, except at the lowest entry point, play two roles. They are both individuals as members of the professional staff, management, or the support staff and a representative of the organization. The vice-president of research and development and the chief surgeon of a hospital not only set direction for the myriad of subordinate professionals and managers but also react as individuals in the organization.

The last area of research that will be introduced under the topic of integration seems to require not only research, but also the determination of moral responsibilities. The question is to what extent should the organization accept responsibility for the career of its individual members? Should organizations make available to their employees both career-planning aids and individual and group life-planning experiences as some propose (38)? How far should the organization go? Organizations demote, lay off, plateau, retire early, or fire long-term employees that become technically obsolete. Their rationale is that career development was the employee's own responsibility and that he or she did not keep up. However, very few organizations clearly spell out such accountability and consequences to their employees even though the success of the organizations themselves is dependent upon the continuing growth and development of their professional personnel. To what extent should the responsibility for career decisions, planning, development, and support be shared? If responsibility is to be shared, is research needed to establish how the shared responsibility should evolve and what is required to make it work?

SPECIAL ISSUES IN CAREER RESEARCH

There are issues that are either beyond the scope of an individual organization or permeate all facets of the career development system.

Unique Topics

Career research has focused primarily upon childhood, adolescence, and young adult age groups. Work on middle-age is slowly developing, but there is a major void on those in the forty-five-to-seventy-year age range outside of the geriatric literature (19). We need to know much more about career development throughout the working life (18,68,73).

Professionals do not develop their career-related life in isolation from the rest of their life cycle dimensions such as education, social, childhood environment, interests, personality, mental faculties, or physiological factors (71). Thus progress in career development research will be partially dependent upon the concurrent change that occurs in those characteristics. Research in developmental psychology has demonstrated that the differences in mental abilities that are present in a group of engineering students in their early twenties not only were present fifty years later but also had increased significantly. It can be assumed that such changes would have had a material effect on the individuals' career behavior, development, and outcomes, but research is required to establish the magnitude and direction of the interaction between career and mental ability development. The same question arises when social, physiological, and other life cycle factors are brought up (68).

Some research has been conducted on sex and racial differences among individuals in their work settings, but much more needs to be done (18). Much is needed to be known about cultural, racial, and sex differences in career values, aspirations, and attitudes so that appropriate policies and programs can be designed and practices modified to overcome discriminatory barriers.

The interaction between the individual's career and the nonwork environment requires much more research. As more and more women have entered the job market, family issues have come to the forefront as an area of interest. The conflict between career roles and other life roles such as that of spouse or parent has become apparent (18), and there has not been sufficient research to enable us to provide means to resolve such conflict. The conflict can become a major factor in the life of a professional in which commitment to work is so strong.

In American society, where upward mobility has formed much of the basis for the lifestyle for so many years, the family couple in which both have careers appears to provide a dilemma. While research such as Yogev and Brett's (77) provides some insight, much more must be learned about the effect of "dual career" couples on their aspirations toward upward mobility. How much, if any, is the desire to put in the extra personal time and effort required of a high-performing professional dampened by the presence of a partner who also has a career? In the same instance, we need to do careful research to establish means by which dual career couples in collaboration with their employers can resolve the problems present in moving from one geographic location to another.

Our society is becoming over educated (9). There is a glut of Ph.D.'s in science and engineering, lawyers, medical practitioners, and others. Research should be conducted to determine how the problem can be alleviated including better use of those who already hold advanced degrees and the reduction of the number who are to come.

The Research Process

Research on any career development system or subsystem requires a dynamic, not static design. The time frames in most "career" research are too short to look at change over a career. In most instances a four-year study is considered longitudinal, but it does not come close to covering or simulating the span of an entire career (68).

There is little research on *planned* career development programs in the work setting, and this should be done (73). Usually career research takes advantage of naturally occurring events; however, it is possible to study planned changes under experimental conditions and to do *comparative* studies of different types of change. For example, multiple methods of self-directed career planning could be compared, and random assignment to challenging jobs could be studied in contrast to lateral transfer.

A basic problem of those involved in career research is the lack of adequate measures of many variables that we wish to study (18). While Super (72) and Holland (21) have worked diligently on the construction of many of their instruments and have made them available to other researchers and practitioners, others have not done so. Measures of adaptability, obsolescence, career anchors, career style, career satisfaction, and many others have not gone through careful development so that they can be widely used in a consistent manner. Much more effort should be placed on this aspect, which is so important to making research useful.

The samples that are involved in the research must be broadened so that the experience can be generalized (68). Different types of occupations need to be represented as in Holland's work. Different types of organizations should be sampled so that we can learn how to modify applications from one to another. Different cultures should be involved so that our practices can be modified within multinational organizations to meet the cultural requirements of their employees.

Research in career development requires multiple levels of analysis, ranging from approaches across cultures and organizations to individual considerations (23). Improvements in research methods now make it possible to assess environmental factors outside the organization such as societal change, laws, and labor markets. Complex sets of internal environmental variables, such as different policies, programs, practices, and work group norms, can be handled to consider the effects of the organization on the career development of its work force. Groups of employees can be studied by carefully defining members who are clearly different from each other (54). For example, the early career development of a group of engineers who entered the organization in one period of time can be compared with that of a group entering at a different period in time. The obsolescence of one employee defined by a common life or career history could be compared with the obsolescence of another employee with a different, but also common life or career history. It is now possible to tease out the effects of age or individual development factors such as abilities, social maturity, and physiological change on career development in adults. In the past we have seldom considered these multiple levels of analysis.

A key to broadening any research findings to apply from one organization, situation, or individual to another is replication. Present and future research must be repeated by different researchers as well as in different settings before it can be considered robust enough to be translated into wide application. Human resource departments are filled with histories of programs that have fallen by the wayside at a huge loss of money, time, and effort because there was no research behind them or what was done was inadequate (46).

With the complexity of the research that has been described throughout this chapter, it should be apparent that one answer to getting it done is to do it cooperatively (23). The resources to conduct such research are just too limited for any single source to conduct it all. Employers, professional societies, academic institutions, and government must join hands to make a significant dent in what is required.

SUMMARY

This chapter has emphasized the dearth in research on adult career development and the even greater void regarding professionals and scientists. The biggest gap is at the organizational level in career management. Little has been done in an experimental or research way to analyze manpower planning, organization planning, and other large issues. Such research should be conducted in conjunction with studies of the issues faced by supervisors and human resources specialists in the administration of specific programs.

While considerably more research has been conducted at the individual level, still more is required to clarify answers to the unique problems of professionals and scientists. Adaptability is a primary area to concentrate on, emphasizing the development and maintenance of professional competence and assistance with the transition to management.

Career research also must be designed and conducted to cover a wide range of variables over long periods of time. It appears that the change aspect of the developmental process has not been emphasized to the extent that it must be.

After reading this chapter, you should be able to answer the following questions:

What is known and what is not known about career development?
What research is required to provide an adequate base of knowledge for the design of better career management systems and career planning systems, and of processes to integrate the two into an overall career development system?
Why has so little career research been done?

REFERENCES

1. Backman, T. W. H., Bruni, J. R., and Randolph, P. L. 1984. Interrelations among career counseling, organizational commitment and career satisfaction. Paper read at the 9th Psychology in the DOD Symposium, Colorado Springs, Apr.
2. Berlew, D. E., and Hall, D. T. 1966. The socialization of managers: effects of expectations on performance. *Administrative Science Quarterly* 2:207-23.
3. Bowen, D. D., and Hall, D. T. 1977. Career planning for employee development. *California Management Review* 20 (2):23-35.
4. Bray, D. W., Campbell, R. J., and Grant, D. L. 1974. *Formative years in business*. New York: John Wiley.
5. Brett, J. M. 1984. Job transitions and personal and role development. *Research in Personnel and Human Resources Management*, Vol. 2:155-85.
6. Brousseau, K. R. 1984. Job-person dynamics and career development. *Research in Personnel and Human Resources Management* 2:125-54.
7. Bruni, J. R., Backman, T. W. H., and Randolph, P. L. 1984. The impact of information quality on career decision making. Paper read at the 9th Psychology in the DOD Symposium, Colorado Springs, Apr.
8. Bruni, J. R., Randolph, P. L., and Butler, M. C. 1984. Implementing career decisions: information acquisition and career uncertainty. Paper read at symposium, *Implementing career decisions: Preparing for and negotiating assignments*. Annual meeting of the Academy of Management, Boston, Aug. 15.
9. Chubin, D. E. 1983. Career patterns of scientists and engineers. In *Scientists, engineers, and organizations,* edited by T. Connolly, pp. 310-27. Belmont, CA: Brooks/Cole.
10. Cleveland, J. N., Morrison, R. F., and Bjerke, D. J. 1986. Rater intentions in appraisal ratings. Paper read at symposium, *Purpose of performance evaluation: Rater intentions vs. organizational uses*. First annual meeting of the Society for Industrial and Organizational Psychology, Chicago, April 10-11.
11. Dyer, L. D. 1973. Job search success of middle-aged managers and engineers. *Industrial and Labor Relations Review* 26 (3):969-79.
12. Ferguson, L. 1966. Better management of manager's careers. *Harvard Business Review* 44 (2):139-52.
13. Fossum, J. A., Arvey, R. D., Paradise, C. A., and Robbins, N. E. 1986. Modelling the skills obsolescence process: a psychological/economic integration. *Academy of Management Review* 11 (2):362-74.
14. Freedman, R. D., and Stumpf, S. A. 1980. Learning style theory: less than meets the eye. *Academy of Management Review* 5 (3):445-47.
15. Glueck, W. F. 1974. Managers, mobility, and morale. *Business Horizons* 17 (6):65-70.
16. Granovetter, M. S. 1974. *Getting a job: a study of contacts and careers*. Cambridge, MA: Harvard Univ. Press.
17. Hall, D. T. 1980. Career development of established employees. Paper read at symposium, *The late career stage of employee participation in organizations*. Annual meeting of the Academy of Management, Detroit, Aug. 11.
18. Hall, D. T., and Hall, F. 1976. Research on organizational career development: where are we and where do we go from here? Unpublished manuscript.
19. Hall, D. T., and Richter, J. 1984. The baby boom in mid-career. *Career Center Bulletin* 4 (3):15-16.
20. Hanson, M. C. 1981. Career counseling in organizational groups. In *Career development in the 1980s,* edited by D. H. Montross and C. J. Shinkman, pp. 379-92. Springfield, IL: Charles C. Thomas.
21. Holland, J. L. 1984. *Making vocational choices: a theory of careers,* 2nd ed. Englewood Cliffs, NJ: Prentice-Hall.
22. Kaufman, H. G. 1974. *Obsolescence and professional career development*. New York: AMACOM.
23. ———. 1982. *Professionals in search of work*. New York: John Wiley.
24. Keller, R. T. 1980. Profile of a technical innovator. Paper read at the annual meeting of the Academy of Management, Detroit, Aug. 11.
25. Klimoski, R., and Jacobs, T. 1985. Structural considerations in a public utility's program for mentors and management trainees. Paper read at career workshop, 45th annual meeting of the Academy of Management, San Diego, Aug. 11.
26. Kolb, D. A. 1981. Experiential learning and the learning style inventory: a reply to Freedman and Stumpf. *Academy of Management Review* 6 (2):289-96.
27. Kolb, D. A., and Plovnick, M. S. 1977. The experiential learning theory of career development. In *Organizational careers: some new perspectives,* edited by J. Van Maanen, pp. 65-87. New York: John Wiley.

28. Kotter, J. P., Faux, V. A., and McArthur, C. 1978. *Self and career development.* Englewood Cliffs, NJ: Prentice-Hall.
29. Kozlowski, S. W. J. 1984. Technology and structure: contexts for engineer technical performance and updating. Paper read in symposium, *Strategies for adapting professional skills to changing technologies.* Annual meeting of the American Psychological Association, Toronto, Aug. 28.
30. Kozlowski, S. W. J., and Farr, J. L. 1984. Individual, organizational, and perceptual contributions to engineer technical performance and updating. Unpublished manuscript.
31. Kram, K. E. 1986. Mentoring in the workplace. In *Career development in organizations,* edited by D. T. Hall, pp. 160-201. San Francisco, CA: Jossey-Bass.
32. Krumboltz, J. D., Hamel, D. A., and Scherba, D. S. 1982. Measuring the quality of career decisions. In *Assessing career development,* edited by J. D. Krumboltz and D. A. Hamel, pp. 159-71. Palo Alto, CA: Mayfield.
33. Landy, F. J., and Farr, J. L. 1983. *The measurement of work performance.* New York: Academic.
34. Landy, F. J., Zedeck, S., and Cleveland, J., eds. 1983. *Performance measurement and theory.* Hillsdale, NJ: Erlbaum Assoc.
35. Latack, J. C., and Dozier, J. B. 1986. After the axe falls: job loss as a career transition. *Academy of Management Review* 11 (2):375-92.
36. Laurent, H. 1968. Research on the identification of management potential. In *Predicting managerial success,* edited by J. A. Myers, Jr., pp. 1-34. Ann Arbor, MI: Foundation for Research on Human Behavior.
37. Leibowitz, Z., and Schlossberg, N. 1981. Designing career development programs in organizations: a systems approach. In *Career development in the 1980s,* edited by D. H. Montross and C. J. Shinkman, pp. 277-91. Springfield, IL: Charles C. Thomas.
38. Lippitt, G. L. 1979. Developing life plans. *Training and Development Journal* 33 (6):102-8.
39. London, M. 1984. Toward a theory of career motivation. *Academy of Management Review* 8 (4):620-30.
40. ———. 7 Aug. 1984. Personal communication.
41. ———. 1984. Theory- and research-based applications for early career development. Paper read in symposium, *New Approaches to Early Career Development: Solutions for Declining Motivation.* Annual meeting of the American Psychological Association, Toronto, Canada, Aug. 28.
42. Louis, M. R. 1980. Career transitions: varieties and commonalities. *Academy of Management Review* 5 (3):329-40.
43. ———. 1982. Managing career transitions: a missing link in career development. *Organization Dynamics,* 10 (4):68-77.
44. Manners, G. E., Jr., and Steger, J. A. Undated. Selection guidelines for research and development managers. General Electric Report No. 5.
45. Meahea, L. W., and Duffy, J. F. 1980. An integrated model for training and development: how to build on what you already have. *Public Personnel Management* 9 (4):336-43.
46. Medcof, J. W. 1985. Training technologists to become managers. *Research Management* 28 (1):18-21.
47. *Mid-career perspectives: the middle-aged and older population.* 1978. Scarsdale, NY: Work in America Institute.
48. Minor, F. J. 1984. A computer-based information system to support employee development planning. Paper read at the annual meeting of the Academy of Management, Boston, Aug.
49. ———. 24 October 1984. Personal communication.
50. ———. 1986. Computer applications in career development planning. In *Career development in organizations,* edited by D. T. Hall, pp. 202-35. San Francisco, CA: Jossey-Bass.
51. Morrison, D. G., and Schmittlein, D. C. 1981. Model of careers in a simple hierarchy: generalizing the junior professional's decision rule. *Bell Journal of Economics* 12 (1):310-20.
52. Morrison, R. F. 1977. Career adaptivity: the effective adaptation of managers to changing roles. *Journal of Applied Psychology* 62:549-58.
53. ———. 1983. *Officer career development: surface warfare officer interviews,* NPRDC TN 83-11. San Diego, CA: Navy Personnel Research and Development Center.
54. Morrison, R. F., and Cook, T. M. 1985. *Military officer career development and decision making: A multiple-cohort longitudinal analysis of the first twenty-four years,* MPL TN85-4. San Diego, CA: Navy Personnel Research and Development Center.
55. Morrison, R. F., and Hoch, R. R. 1986. Career building: Learning from cumulative work experience. In *Organizational careers,* edited by D. T. Hall, pp. 236-73. San Francisco, CA: Jossey-Bass.
56. Morrison, R. F., et al. 1962. Factored life history antecedents of industrial research performance. *Journal of Applied Psychology* 46 (4):281-84.
57. Myers, R. A., Cairo, P. C., Turner, J. A., and Ginzberg, M. 1980. *Cost-benefit analysis of the officer career information and planning system* (Research Report 1256). Alexandria, VA: U.S. Army Research Institute, August.
58. Nicholson, N. 1984. A theory of work role transition. *Administrative Science Quarterly* 29:172-91.
59. O'Neill, J. M., Magoon, T. M., and Tracey, T. J. 1978. Status of Holland's investigative personality types and their consistency levels seven years later. *Journal of Counseling Psychology* 25 (6):530-35.
60. Phillips, S. D. 1981. Career exploration in adulthood. *Journal of Vocational Behavior* 20 (2):129-40.
61. Quadagno, J. S. 1978. Career continuity and retirement plans of men and women physicians: the meaning of disorderly careers. *Sociology of Work and Occupations* 5 (1):55-74.
62. Rae, J. H., Jr. 1984. Job opportunities system of Holiday Inns, Inc. *Career Center Bulletin* 4 (3):15-16.
63. Rice, B. 1985. Why am I in this job? *Psychology Today* 19 (1):54-59.
64. Roe, A., and Baruch, R. 1967. Occupational changes in the adult years. *Personnel Administration* 30 (4):27-32.
65. Rothman, R. A., and Perrucci, R. 1970. Organizational careers and professional expertise. *Administrative Science Quarterly* 15 (3):282-93.
66. Rubinton, N. 1980. Instruction in career decision making and decision-making styles. *Journal of Counseling Psychology* 27 (6):581-88.
67. Schein, E. H. 1986. A critical look at current career development theory and research. In *Career development in organizations,* edited by D. T. Hall and Associates, pp. 310-31. San Francisco, CA: Jossey-Bass.
68. Sonnenfeld, J., and Kotter, J. P. 1982. The maturation of career theory. *Human Relations* 35 (1):19-46.
69. Srebalus, D. J., Marinelli, R. P., and Messing, J. K. 1982. *Career development concepts and procedures.* Monterey, CA: Brooks/Cole.

70. Stumpf, S. A., and Freedman, R. D. 1981. The learning style inventory: still less than meets the eye. *Academy of Management Review* 6 (2):297-99.
71. Super, D. E. 1980. A life-span, life-space approach to career development. *Journal of Vocational Behavior* 16 (3):282-98.
72. ———. 1985. Coming of age in Middletown: careers in the making. *American Psychologist* 40 (4):405-14.
73. Super, D. E., and Hall, D. T. 1978. Career development: exploration and planning. *Annual Review of Psychology* 29:333-72.
74. Swenson, A. A. 1978. *Starting over: how to recharge your life-style and career—with firsthand accounts of the new pioneers who have done it.* New York: A and W.
75. Wexley, K. N. 1984. Personnel training. *Annual Review of Psychology* 35:519-51.
76. Wunder, S. 6 September 1984. Personal communication.
77. Yogev, S., and Brett, J. 1985. Patterns of work and family involvement among single- and dual-earner couples. *Journal of Applied Psychology* 70 (4):754-68.

Appendix 1

A Comparison of Training Methods

ON-THE-JOB METHODS

- Orientation/job-instruction training
- Apprentice training
- Coaching
- Job rotation

OFF-THE-JOB METHODS

- Vestibule training
- Business games/simulations
- Case study
- Role playing
- Behavior modeling
- Lab/T-group/sensitivity training
- Lecture
- Videotape, films, television
- Conference/discussion
- Team training
- Programmed instruction

ON-THE-JOB METHODS

ORIENTATION/JOB-INSTRUCTION TRAINING

Description: Overall orientation to the organization and specific step-by-step demonstration of job operation.
Trainees: Employees can be run in groups of any size for the overall orientation—this could even be done by videotape; if a large multiincumbent job, the job demonstration would also have no constraints on the size of the group. Often one-on-one is required for either of these approaches.
Speed demands: Requires a limited, prescribed period of time—occurs only once.
Complexity: Simple overview; can often be handled via one-way communication, such as videotape.
Time off job: Slight; usually done prior to beginning the job. With the exception of task- or group-specific information, many elements of orientation should be delayed about six months so the new employee can learn the organization and its culture and language.
Cost: Very low.
Individual differences: The presentation could be slanted for special groups (minority, women, handicapped); ignores tailoring to individual needs when done in groups.
Ethical considerations: May paint too rosy a picture; may neglect certain areas; problem of updating.
Career management considerations: Opportunity to get the new employee "on board"; give a feel for the organization and positions within it; provide knowledge of policies and procedures regarding selection, training. The organization as a career employer can be stressed within the presentation.

APPRENTICE TRAINING

Description: The employee is "apprenticed" to a "master" at the job to learn specific skills in a one-on-one situation; more intense and structured than coaching.
Trainees: One-on-one, or approximately that figure.
Speed demands: Takes a long period of time, with the option of recycling slower learners; open-ended.
Complexity: Involves complex, specific skills.
Time off job: Usually on-the-job training with the employee contributing at higher levels over time; sometimes involves simulations.
Cost: Minimal, with the employees making on-the-job contributions.
Individual differences: Often used with trade groups; some job-related problems with involving handicapped groups; excellent opportunity for one-on-one individual tailoring.
Ethical considerations: Sometimes there is informal peer group pressure to pass the apprentice; degree of structure and rigor varies with the "master."
Career management considerations: Benefits from the potential mentor relationship with the master; in-

formal discussions regarding career possibilities generally occur.

COACHING

Description: The supervisor/manager provides on-the-job coaching with the employee; generally done at the management level through feedback and suggestions for improvement; less intense or well-structured than apprentice training.

Trainees: One-on-one; a good supervisor provides coaching to all of his or her people.

Speed demands: None; occurs over several years.

Complexity: Can be as complex as the job itself.

Time off job: None

Cost: Very low; only requires the supervisor's time.

Individual differences: The good supervisor handles this; method relies on the supervisor's ability; great opportunity for individual tailoring to the specific person and the specific job.

Ethical considerations: "Coaching" may be an easy way out for the supervisor who may not do anything; depends on the supervisor's ability in this area; evaluation of efficiency is sometimes based solely on the quality of the subjective relationship.

Career management considerations: Effectiveness of coaching depends on supervisor's ability and interest; when done well the supervisor can be a key resource for career management.

JOB ROTATION

Description: Movement through several related jobs within the same general area to provide orientation to the total operation and insight into interrelationship of functions.

Trainees: Limited, because the organization does not want too many unseasoned, untrained people moving around.

Speed demands: May rush the trainee through too many jobs too quickly; need time standards. If it occurs *too* quickly, and is *too* prescribed, this may appear to create "ticket-punching" behavior and a low-risk approach to the job so that performance becomes standardized at a low level.

Complexity: Often used with upper-level management positions where some prior expertise is expected.

Time off job: Negligible, but minimal contributions while on the job.

Cost: Minimal—some waste in tying up organizational resources with someone who is not fully contributing.

Individual differences: Generally targeted at upper-level management positions; individual tailoring can be high because specific proficiency requirements are not set; much individual attention.

Ethical considerations: The organization must put up with poor proficiency in order to broaden the person; resentment by other employees due to special treatment; issue of individual desire to rotate versus forced compliance.

Career management considerations: Can be a valuable means of exposure and broadening.

OFF-THE-JOB METHODS

VESTIBULE TRAINING

Description: Off-the-job training using simulated equipment which maximizes transfer back to the job; usually used with lower-level blue-collar tasks but may also be used with highly technical equipment. For example, military pilots are trained, tested, and retrained on simulators, and military tactics are taught using computer-simulated war games.

Trainees: Equipment restricts the number of trainees at any one time; cost of simulators generally precludes large numbers of trainees.

Speed demands: Method may require specific speed requirements, can even be used as a selection device.

Complexity: Used with complex equipment where the consequence of errror is high; therefore practice on simulators occurs until the trainee masters the task to a near-zero error rate.

Time off job: High requirements for both the trainee *and* the trainer.

Cost: Very high; equipment and time costs. *But* in comparison to the expense or risk of learning on real equipment, might be considered low.

Individual differences: Sometimes used with blue-collar hard-core unemployed to teach basic job skills; individual work on the simulator provides immediate feedback and reinforcement even with the higher-skill-level jobs.

Ethical considerations: The degree to which the simulator is an accurate representation of the demands of the job (physical fidelity); trainees may fail the simulator yet be able to perform on the job.

Career management considerations: Generally only involves motor skills training, but may also be used to teach interaction; cause and effect, and problem solving.

BUSINESS GAMES/SIMULATIONS

Description: Participants are placed in situations that reflect the activities in which they are expected to perform effectively either in current or future jobs. These are *situational* simulations that do *not* involve the use of computer or machine simulators.

Trainees: Individual or small groups.

Speed demands: These situations are generally *timed* so that each participant has equal opportunities to show his or her skills.

Complexity: The activities can be highly technical or demand strong management skills.

Time off job: Requires time off the job.

Cost: Depends on the activity being simulated, the need for special equipment and so on. If videotaped for feedback or self-analysis purposes, add equipment and set-up charges.

Individual differences: The technique is open ended in that different people may handle the situation in very different ways.

Ethical considerations: Can be an anxiety-producing situation for the participant. Participants may vary in their intrinsic motivation to perform. The validity of the situation may be questioned.

Career management considerations: Can be useful to provide a "realistic preview" of management activities—this can be helpful to nonmanagement employees in determining their ability and interest in management.

CASE STUDY

Description: Harvard's renowned method of business education—read and discuss specific situations and answer a series of "What-would-you-do-if"-type questions within groups. Allows self-learning and develops independent thought. Widely used with doctors and lawyers; good way to learn problem solving.

Trainees: Small- to medium-size groups under a discussion leader.

Speed demands: Varies somewhat, but the case study can *compress* time and work through lengthy real-life problem situations in a short time.

Complexity: Handles a broad range of situations varying in complexity; focus is on problem solving and decision making.

Time off job: Requires time off the job.

Cost: Minimal—need facility, case material, discussion leader.

Individual differences: This method has a recognized individual orientation, although some may hide by not talking. Requires reading comprehension and analytical abilities.

Ethical considerations: Comfort level within the group may affect participation; how well an individual performs depends largely on verbal fluency. Sometimes it is difficult to conceal the people or company in the case study. Method can break down because it is seldom supported by the material required to apply the learning to situations that may not be very similar.

Career management considerations: Case studies can be developed specifically to address career management issues in order to get people thinking through choices and considering pros and cons.

ROLE PLAYING

Description: Participants try out new behaviors in structured role-playing situations; involves action—the doing and practice of theory.

Trainees: Small number; requires practice, feedback, and more practice.

Speed demands: Allows immediate transfer of learning into practice in a "safe" situation.

Complexity: Addresses complex behavioral, social, interpersonal interactions; less effective for specific skills training.

Time off job: Requires some time off the job.

Cost: Minimal, often used within the design of a larger curriculum.

Individual differences: For some, may be a threatening situation, be perceived as unrealistic (play acting), or be seen as too abstract to be helpful.

Ethical considerations: Can be manipulative when the trainer's personal orientation biases the model of effectiveness used. Can be too abstract an approach all by itself to produce real behavior change. Participant anxiety over being forced to role-play in front of the group.

Career management considerations: Can be very helpful to develop the empathy and awareness that comes through putting yourself in someone else's shoes. Critical supervisor-to-subordinate discussions can be effectively demonstrated.

BEHAVIOR MODELING

Description: Begins with a clear statement of the desired behavior and a *demonstration* and *guide* to follow; followed by *practice* in a realistic situation; *feedback* and social *reinforcement;* finally, transfer to the actual situation is planned.

Trainees: Best in very small groups, or even one-on-one.

Speed demands: Relatively open-ended; the extent to which the trainee requires repetition of practice and feedback will vary.

Complexity: For use with a wide variety of specific motor skills, as well as complex behavioral/interpersonal skills such as performance counseling.

Time off job: Time off the job will vary with the complexity of the topic and the individuality of the training.

Cost: Relatively low for the change in behavior that can result.

Individual differences: Can be easily tailored to individual needs. Often there is no one "right" way, just a general structure that allows for individual differences in style.

Ethical considerations: Degree to which feedback in front of a group is constructive, manipulative, or confrontational; participant anxiety over "performing," as in role playing.

Career management considerations: A *very* effective means of producing positive behavioral change; can be especially useful in training supervisors to conduct an effective career-planning discussion with subordinates.

LAB/T-GROUP/SENSITIVITY TRAINING

Description: Small group training, usually in interpersonal skills or group dynamics. Generally conducted off-site with trained process facilitators.

Trainees: Small groups.

Speed demands: The basic interpersonal behavior pattern that these programs address generally require a one to three week program.

Complexity: Method addresses intepersonal skills not technical skills.

Time off job: Can be extensive.

Cost: Often quite high, especially if held at an off-site resort.

Individual differences: Designed to work with individuals, generally best for emotionally/psychologically stable people.

Ethical considerations: The methodology with perhaps the greatest ethical considerations. The process can be highly traumatic and anxiety producing. The issue of forced or coerced participation is therefore highly relevant. The efficacy of the method rests entirely on the capability of the trainer (group facilitator). Finally, there is a major transfer-of-learning problem when the changed person reenters the unchanged organization. This is a *very* touchy process—without a very competent trainer and detailed, clinical follow-up, the technique can creates more problems than it solves.

Career management considerations: May be useful in some instances, for example, for the new supervisor or manager who does not realize the impact of his or her actions on the group. This method is rarely used with professionals/scientists, but is more likely to be used with their managers.

LECTURE

Description: One person talking in order to transfer information from his/her notebook into your notebook; one-way communication with limited opportunities for clarifying questions.

Trainees: No limit; class can be as large as physical facilities allow.

Speed demands: Quick transfer of *knowledge,* no opportunity for *skill* development; as fast as instructor can talk and you can write.

Complexity: Transfer of information provides the first step for learning complex tasks—theory; can be complex theory.

Time off job: Requires class time.

Cost: Can be very cheap when class is large; partly depends on amount of time off the job.

Individual differences: Absolutely no acknowledgement of individual differences; everyone treated equally, no individual tailoring.

Ethical considerations: In large classes, passing incompetents; criteria for "passing"; very poor for many purposes, such as skill development of attitude/behavior change.

Career management considerations. Accomplishes little more than exposure to new ideas or concepts.

VIDEOTAPE, FILMS, TELEVISION

Description: Use of audiovisual techniques and learning principles with best instructor.

Trainees: Unlimited number.

Speed demands: Very fast transmission of information; may be repeated.

Complexity: Large variations from simple to complex; may be highly technical and utilize sophisticated audiovisual aids in the presentation.

Time off job: Requires some time off the job; often offered after work hours.

Cost: Initial setup and production can be very expensive; ongoing use relatively inexpensive.

Individual differences: Absolutely no consideration for individual differences nor opportunity for clarifying questions.

Ethical considerations: Attention and motivation issues; no trainer-trainee relationship; no feedback or reinforcement; questionable criteria for successful completion.

Career management considerations: May be used to impart information—for example, tapes on different on-the-job activities to be used for career planning; personal planning needs to supplement this method. A personal tool increasingly being used, especially in the medical community, is the use of professional cassette tapes that are played on the car stereo to update knowledge.

CONFERENCE/DISCUSSION

Description: A planned meeting with a specific purpose and goal; a participative method which allows ideas to be pooled.

Trainees: Limited to small groups.

Speed demands: Can be used to quickly disseminate information; speed of incorporation depends on the group.

Complexity: Can be very successful in dealing with complex, conceptual data and for the development or modification of cognitive attitudes.

Time off job: Time demands vary, may depend on the composition of the group (such as the proper grouping of employee levels).

Cost: Moderate, requires an appropriate conference room and time of participants (usually at higher pay levels).

Individual differences: Although verbal skills and the ability to interact effectively are preconditions, the process is very responsive to individual perspectives.

Ethical considerations: Efficacy often rests on the discussion leader's ability to draw participants out.

Career management considerations: This method can work well to address directly career management issues within groups that are composed of employees in like circumstances. It can also serve career management purposes by composing "vertical slice" groups so that potential mentors have an opportunity to observe and get to know younger participants. The discussion format allows issues of common concern to be surfaced.

TEAM TRAINING

Description: Groups undergo training designed to improve their ability to function effectively as a team. For team-building purposes, intact work groups are trained.

Trainees: Small groups.

Speed demands: Varies.

Complexity: Addresses task-completion and resource-utilization issues; addresses group issues.

Time off job: Minimal time if on the job; more time if an off-the-job conference.

Cost: Varies depending on consultant, on-the-job, or off-the-job design.

Individual differences: May have the effect of "leveling" individual differences for the good of the group.

Ethical considerations: In group's natural pressure to conform and lessen deviance, may stifle individuality; question of most correct normative values for the group.

Career management considerations: Increasing one's skills to work effectively within a team may meaningfully contribute to an individual's career decisions; especially if that person has historically been an individual contributor who, perhaps, has shied away from groups.

PROGRAMMED INSTRUCTION

Description: A method of written instruction, sometimes delivered by computer, that subdivides sequential tasks and walks the learner through a self-paced program of instruction. It uses learning principles and directs the learner to the difficulty level that the person can handle.

Trainees: Unlimited numbers when booklets are used; if computer terminals are used, some limits are imposed.

Speed demands: Self-paced, depends on the person and the complexity of the task.

Complexity: Can handle complex tasks—of either information or skills.

Time off job: Requires time off the job.

Cost: Initial investment can be moderate to high.

Individual differences: Designed to handle this; participants can vary widely in ability or skill level.

Ethical considerations: Motivation or interest may affect learning; retention is more likely to be poor.

Career management considerations: Great method for learning basic and complex information in new technical or functional areas. It is self-initiated and self-taught. However, programmed instruction is rarely used with professionals/scientists because their tasks are difficult to separate into clear steps and they tend to become impatient with the slow, structured pace.

Appendix 2

A Career-planning Workbook

CONTENTS

Introduction

1. *Personal Work History Analysis*—to help you structure your thinking about where you have been and how you feel about it.
2. *Activity Analysis*—to help you examine valued or enjoyed activities both off and on the job and list needed developmental activities.
3. *Technical and Professional Position Knowledge Analysis*—to help you summarize critical job knowledge acquired through training, experience, or education and list knowledge needed for future jobs.
4. *Managerial Skills Analysis*—to help you become familiar with critical managerial skills and to appraise your current ability and strongest skills.
5. *Position Analysis*—to enable you to go through an objective matching process with the activities, knowledges, and managerial skills of jobs. For each job, overlap and needed development are identified.
6. *Reality Testing*—to help you examine personal barriers (motivation, loyalty, and commitment) and organizational barriers (structure, norms, job availability) to your career plan.
7. *Follow-up*—to help you identify the next steps in the career-planning program (completion of the career-planning worksheet and a request for a career-planning discussion).

The subjects here are much more job-related and streamlined than many career planning workbooks currently on the market. The focus is toward available jobs within the organization rather than a broader job market envisioned by the popular "life-planning" workbooks. This workbook can be completed in three to four hours compared to the twenty hours and more required by some others, and it results in the specific information needed to conduct an intelligent job matching process.

INTRODUCTION

How important is work and your career to you? For most people, work takes up 35 to 50 percent of their waking lives and helps define self-image. For example, when asked to describe themselves, people invariably mention their occupation. The effect is even more pronounced with professionals who, as a group, are more involved in their work. Some of your most valued skills, abilities, and knowledges are used in your jobs. The work role permits you to use those abilities and provides the opportunity to have an effect, to make a difference. The feeling of joyousness when you perform effectively might only be matched by the emptiness or despair when you have failed at some task. In either case, the work role affects your feelings about yourself, your self-esteem. Work is important far beyond the monetary compensation you receive. In fact, studies show that most people would work even if they no longer needed money. Studies also show that people's careers are a major determinant of overall life satisfaction and perceptions of quality of life.

Why, then, do careers sometimes unfold haphazardly? Is it possible to plan your career actively or must you just sit back and let it happen? Your personal policy can be to encourage your development of professional and managerial talents through active participation in career planning. It is a benefit that may not be provided by your organization but that you can pursue nonetheless. Career planning involves a two-way commitment. Your organization has a stake in the development and proper use of its human resources; you have a stake in the success of your organization.

Basically, this workbook provides a means for you to prepare a formal career plan that will assist you, through a planned sequence of developmental assignments, in realizing your career aspirations. The program represents a planned approach to human resources management. It reflects a need for you to match your own talent, potential, and career desires to the objective requirements of available positions within your professional field.

When you have finished the worksheets that follow, you will be in a much better position to plan your professional career. You will be able to describe where you have been and where you would like to be in the future.

The career plan should be developed in discussion with your immediate supervisor and then reviewed through the reporting levels as appropriate. This review process gives your organization an opportunity to provide feedback to you that makes your ultimate career plan both realistic and attainable. When a position becomes open, the selecting manager will logically consider the following factors in the decision-making process: job-related activities, job-related/professional knowledges, managerial skills, past accomplishments, and career-planning information. This workbook will help you analyze all of these factors in relation to your experience and will make a case for your own suitability for desired positions.

By taking these steps, you will be able to plan your own future and become more involved in your own professional development.

Completing the Career-Planning Workbook

Career planning is a serious venture, but it is also an exciting adventure. The experience of completing this workbook should provide you with important insights. It is a structured guide that will help you address some very difficult questions. The workbook is solely for your own use, so you should be as honest and candid as possible. Each section culminates with information that is directly transferrable to your career plan. If you do a complete job on the workbook, the first draft of your career plan will essentially be written. The responses to your employee's career-planning worksheet, which is used in the discussion with your supervisor, will also be generated through completion of the workbook.

In preparing and submitting your career plan, you may wish to check off the following steps as they are completed.

1. *Complete this workbook.* Its purpose is to analyze individual work history and future aspirations. Completing it may also assist you in making a decision whether or not to proceed by involving your supervisor. Once completed, you need not necessarily share the information in it with your supervisor or anyone else, unless you specifically wish to do so.
2. *Decide whether to proceed with a written career plan.* This is a personal decision on your part.

After completing this workbook you may feel that you are not yet ready to initiate a career plan. This is a reasonable option that will not have any negative consequences for you.

3. *Complete the employee's career-planning worksheet.* It is at the end of the workbook; its purpose is to summarize your self-analysis from the workbook and relate it to specific professional or management career choices and relevant developmental activities. Ask your supervisor to complete a similar worksheet, and these will be the basis for your career-planning discussion. The worksheets provide a common frame of reference and are intended to facilitate an open, honest discussion between you and your supervisor.
4. *Complete a proposed career plan.* Note that this plan may be revised, to make it more realistic and attainable, either during the career-planning discussion with your supervisor or later in the review process.
5. *Request a career-planning discussion with your supervisor.* Provide him or her with a copy of your proposed career plan. Your supervisor will schedule the meeting, then do some detailed work to prepare for it (completing the supervisor's career planning worksheet, for example). Your supervisor may not have been trained in how to conduct this type of discussion, so you may need to provide some of the information in this section.
6. *Meet with your supervisor for the career-planning discussion.* Both of you will be expected to share information from your worksheets. Your supervisor will contribute a useful independent perspective which may provide additional information that will improve your career plan. The plan agreed on must be one that you are committed to and your supervisor can support.
7. *Obtain feedback.* Following the review process, your career plan will be returned to you for your approval. Changes may either be recommended or required. This feedback should help you develop a career plan that is realistic and attainable.

1. PERSONAL WORK HISTORY ANALYSIS

Purpose: This section will help you structure your thinking about where you have been in your work history, why you work, what elements of the job you like and dislike, and what accomplishments and disappointments you have had in the past. This information will prepare you for examining your future course.

(continued)

Job History

List the major full-time jobs you have held, beginning with your current position.

	POSITION TITLE	DEPARTMENT/COMPANY	Month/Year BEGIN	Month/Year END
A				
B				
C				
D				
E				
F				

When completing the remaining worksheets, use *A–F* to refer to each of these jobs.

Reasons to Work

In column 1 check off reasons why most people work; in columns 3, 4, and 6 check off your own reasons to work; and in column 5 rank the top ten of these.

1	2	3	4	5	6
MOST PEOPLE WORK FOR THESE REASONS	REASON TO WORK	I WORK FOR THESE REASONS	WHICH JOB ALLOWED THE MOST OF THESE?	RANK-ORDER THE IMPORTANCE OF THE REASONS	I MIGHT LEAVE MY JOB TO FIND ONE THAT WILL ALLOW ME
	Financial security				
	Self-respect				
	Community respect				
	Independence				
	Recognition/approval				
	Help others				
	Exert influence				
	To be challenged				

(*Continued*)

1	2	3	4	5	6
MOST PEOPLE WORK FOR THESE REASONS	REASON TO WORK	I WORK FOR THESE REASONS	WHICH JOB ALLOWED THE MOST OF THESE?	RANK-ORDER THE IMPORTANCE OF THE REASONS	I MIGHT LEAVE MY JOB TO FIND ONE THAT WILL ALLOW ME
_____	To advance self	_____	_____	_____	_____
_____	Sense of accomplishment	_____	_____	_____	_____
_____	Family security	_____	_____	_____	_____
_____	Prestige	_____	_____	_____	_____
_____	Increase skills	_____	_____	_____	_____
_____	Increase knowledge	_____	_____	_____	_____
_____	Exert leadership	_____	_____	_____	_____
_____	Allows off-job fun	_____	_____	_____	_____
_____	To be important	_____	_____	_____	_____
_____	To fill up time	_____	_____	_____	_____
_____	Personal growth	_____	_____	_____	_____
_____	Interaction with others	_____	_____	_____	_____
_____	Exert power	_____	_____	_____	_____
_____	(Continue this list with your own reasons)	_____	_____	_____	_____
_____		_____	_____	_____	_____
_____		_____	_____	_____	_____
_____		_____	_____	_____	_____
_____		_____	_____	_____	_____

Job Likes and Dislikes

List your jobs from the earliest to the current position, and consider each job's variety, autonomy, responsibility, challenge, physical surroundings, co-workers, geography, commuting distance, type of work, supervision, pressure, hours, and any other facet of the job. Then look over the lists and identify likes and dislikes that are common to more than one job.

JOB TITLE	THINGS I LIKED ABOUT THE JOB	THINGS I DISLIKED ABOUT THE JOB
(current position)		

COMMON LIKES: COMMON DISLIKES:

Personal Assets and Liabilities

List your jobs from earliest to current position, and consider motivation, naivete, intelligence, sensitivity, technical knowledge, abrasiveness, independence, education, youth, experience, perseverance, originality, enthusiasm, objectivity, and others. Then look over the lists and identify assets and liabilities that are common to more than one job.

JOB TITLE	ASSETS (STRENGTHS) I BROUGHT TO THE JOB	LIABILITIES (SHORTCOMINGS) I BROUGHT TO THE JOB
(current position)		

COMMON ASSETS:

COMMON LIABILITIES:

Job Accomplishments and Disappointments

List your jobs from earliest to current position, and consider specific routine duties, special assignments, projects, or any task on which you did exceedingly well or poorly. Then look over the lists and determine tasks that you perform best and tasks that have led to disappointment.

JOB TITLE	MAJOR ACCOMPLISHMENTS	MAJOR DISAPPOINTMENTS	HOW DID THIS MOVE COME ABOUT?
_____	_____	_____	_____
_____	_____	_____	_____
_____	_____	_____	_____
_____	_____	_____	_____
_____	_____	_____	_____
_____	_____	_____	_____
_____	_____	_____	_____
_____ (current position)	_____	_____	_____

WHAT TASKS DO YOU PERFORM BEST?	WHAT TASKS DO YOU PERFORM LEAST WELL?	IS THERE A PATTERN ABOVE?

2. ACTIVITY ANALYSIS

Purpose: You perform many activities, both on and off the job, and ideally these should be things you enjoy doing and are not conflicting. Sometimes this is not possible, so it is helpful to consider the relative importance of various activities. In this section you will consider on-the-job activities that you will need in future jobs and in the last exercise in this section, you will define developmental activities you could perform in these areas.

Example Developmental Activities. In each case, the developmental activity must be very specific, and satisfactory completion of it must be measurable. This may require some research on your part to find the most relevant set of books, classes, and the like.

OFF-JOB

- Professional society activities
- Publication in peer-reviewed journals
- College seminars
- Continuing education classes
- Professional licensure
- Professional certification
- Civic activities
- Speakers' bureau
- Study of specific books
- Research in specific areas
- Company practices/procedures
- General and executive instruction
- Correspondence courses
- Professional journals
- Outside training
- Teaching in university programs

ON-JOB

- Teaching in-house professional courses
- Review of technical reports
- Training courses
- On-job training
- Sitting in for supervisor
- MBO/stretch goals
- Assessment center
- Visiting other departments
- Special projects
- Serving as assessor
- Career-planning facilitator
- Task force
- Matrix team
- Temporary swap
- Cross-training
- Committees

Off-the-Job Activity Analysis

List all the things you do off the job, whether important or trivial, in the left-hand column. (Examples are listed; fill in your own.) Then mark checks in the next two columns where appropriate. Finally, indicate in the right-hand columns how you would feel if your job interfered with the activity.

OFF-THE-JOB ACTIVITIES	AN ACTIVITY I REALLY ENJOY	I WISH I HAD MORE TIME FOR THIS	My Feeling if This Activity Was Not Allowed or Was Interrupted by Job Demands		
			UPSET	NEUTRAL	GOOD
Driving					
Watching television					
Listening to music					
Entertaining					
Dancing					
Cooking					
Eating					
Sex					
Teaching					
Drinking					
Dining out					
Sailing					
Swimming					
Tennis					
Racquetball					
Softball					
Backgammon					
Chess					
Car repair					
Woodworking					
Travel					
Religion					
Reading					
Writing					
Classes					
Personal business					
Community clubs					
Volunteer work					
Vacation					

On-the-Job Activity Analysis

Consider general activities such as supervising, computing, coordinating, teaching, organizing, evaluating, analyzing, persuading, writing, talking, training, advising, working independently, working with others, designing, implementing, planning. Fill in the key activities in current or future jobs.

ACTIVITY	STRENGTH?	NEEDS DEVELOPMENT?	NECESSARY IN A FUTURE JOB?	POSSIBLE DEVELOPMENT ACTIVITY

3. TECHNICAL AND PROFESSIONAL KNOWLEDGE ANALYSIS

Purpose: In addition to activities, any job also requires certain specific types of knowledge. Such technical and professional knowledge might be learned in any number of different ways, for example, training, education, and experience. In this section, you will examine knowledge you possess and knowledge you do not currently possess but that would help you in your career.

Known Areas

List current professional and technical knowledge that you have in column 1 and explain how and when you acquired it and how you have applied it in column 2.

CURRENT KNOWLEDGE	HOW DEVELOPED?

Developmental Areas

List professional and technical knowledge you do not have but think you need in column 1 and list how you might acquire this knowledge in column 2. After completing the lists, go back to the previous table, Known Areas, and place an asterisk by the five areas in which you are *most knowledgeable*. Place an asterisk next to the three developmental activities in the following table that are *most important* to you.

NEEDED KNOWLEDGE	DEVELOPMENTAL ACTIVITY

4. MANAGERIAL SKILLS ANALYSIS

Purpose: In addition to the technical competence required to perform a job, there are also important managerial skills that are required. Naturally, different jobs require different "proportions" of these managerial skills; however, all of the ten managerial skills below have been shown to be critical for effective performance within the *management team* of a company. In this section, you will analyze your performance with regard to each of these ten skills to decide whether you are interested in professional or managerial positions.

Managerial Skill Definitions

Leadership: Ability to direct and coordinate the activities of others, to provide instructions to others, to involve others actively in problem solving, to take charge when appropriate, to influence decision making in groups, to provide direction and structure to a task, to explain task requirements and identified goals clearly, to choose and assign tasks in accordance with the development needs of subordinates, and to offer and solicit information relevant to solving a problem.

Control and follow-up: Ability to monitor the accomplishment of prescribed goals and targets, to summarize progress, to set up systems to determine the impact of decisions, to check, test, or verify that assigned actions are being carried out, and to provide the necessary facts and details when delegating assignments to others.

Organizing and planning: Ability to structure information and activities systematically to meet task requirements, to classify and categorize related information, to organize data provided by others, to be well prepared for meetings and presentations, to have necessary information readily accessible when needed, to set realistic goals within time constraints, and to establish appropriate priorities.

Perceptual and analytical: Ability to comprehend, identify, and assimilate the critical elements of a situation, to separate a large task into component parts, to attend to details of a problem, to interpret implications of various courses of action, to perceive how information relates or is related, to recognize priority issues, to manipulate data, to perceive differences in people, and to draw conclusions regarding both data and people-related issues.

Decision making: Ability to use logical and sound judgment in choosing a particular course of action, to make high-quality decisions, to generate workable alternative courses of action, to incorporate and make logical use of facts, and to integrate and use all available information effectively.

Decisiveness: Ability to take action promptly and firmly when called upon to do so, to make decisions based on incomplete information, to make all decisions necessary in a given situation, to demonstrate initiative and courage to act, to take a firm stand when challenged, to defend one's actions resolutely, to take action in the face of conflicting or contradictory information, and to make unpopular but necessary decisions.

Interpersonal: Ability to be sensitive to the needs and feelings of others, to establish and maintain harmonious relations with others, to create and maintain a congenial, supportive work environment, to be receptive to and accepting of individual differences, to reconcile effectively differences of opinion, and to deal effectively with others regardless of level, status, background, or competence.

Flexibility: Ability to change approaches to problems or tasks with the presentation of new information, to be receptive and adaptive to changes in the situation, to acknowledge and incorporate alternative points of view, to reconsider and modify one's approach in response to the progress being made on the task, to maintain constructive behavior under pressure, and to incorporate others' information into one's own decisions.

Oral communication: Ability to present information clearly, concisely, and effectively, to explain decisions orally, to persuade, influence, or argue convincingly through oral presentation, to respond effectively to questions without hesitation, to use correct grammar, and to highlight points with body gestures or voice inflection.

Written communication: Ability to present information clearly and effectively through written means, to provide clear, concise instructions to others via memos or other written correspondence, to write reports and memos that are easy to follow and understand, to persuade or influence others through written presentation, to use correct sentence structure, paragraphs, and punctuation, and to make effective use of outlines, headings, and subheadings when presenting reports.

Managerial Skills Analysis

In the worksheet that follows, place a rating next to each managerial skill using the following scale:

- 8 = Outstanding
- 7 = Well above satisfactory
- 6 = Above satisfactory
- 5 = Satisfactory (does *not* mean "average," but "effective")
- 4 = Below satisfactory
- 3 = Well below satisfactory
- 2 = Weak
- 1 = Not observed (have not had the opportunity to use this skill)

In the right-hand column, defend your strong ratings and list possible developmental activities for weak ratings.

MANAGERIAL SKILL	RATING	EXPLANATION
Leadership		
Control and Follow-up		
Organizing and Planning		
Perceptual and Analytical		
Decision Making		
Decisiveness		
Interpersonal		
Flexibility		
Oral Communication		
Written Communication		

MY FOUR STRONGEST MANAGERIAL SKILLS ARE:

1.
2.
3.
4.

MY TWO WEAKEST MANAGERIAL SKILLS ARE:

1.
2.

5. POSITION ANALYSIS

Purpose: This is a critical point in career planning; you have done quite a bit of preparation and are now ready to examine specific positions. The rationale behind the career-planning program and the entire personnel system is to match the company's human resources talent better with the objective requirements of positions that need to be filled. The *Position Guide* contains a position profile that describes each professional and managerial position in the company in terms of activities, knowledges, demands and restrictions, characteristics, and managerial skills (see example in figure 5-4). You will need to work with these profiles in detail to complete the next set of worksheets.

For each position in which you are interested as a career move (either lateral or promotional), you will analyze your strengths and weaknesses.

Position Guide

Position Title: _____ **Position Title No.** _____

STRENGTHS	DEVELOPMENTAL NEEDS
Activities in which I am proficient:	Activities I have not performed:
Technical/professional knowledge that I have:	Technical/professional knowledge that I would have to learn:
Demands, restrictions, or characteristics that excite me:	Demands, restrictions, or characteristics that concern me:
Managerial skills in which I am strong:	Managerial skills I need to develop:

Developmental activities (what could I do to better prepare myself for this position?):

Position Guide

Position Title: _____ **Position Title No.** _____

STRENGTHS	DEVELOPMENTAL NEEDS
Activities in which I am proficient:	Activities I have not performed:
Technical/professional knowledge that I have:	Technical/professional knowledge that I would have to learn:
Demands, restrictions, or characteristics that excite me:	Demands, restrictions, or characteristics that concern me:
Managerial skills in which I am strong:	Managerial skills I need to develop:

Developmental activities (what could I do to better prepare myself for this position?):

Position Guide

Position Title: _____ **Position Title No.** _____

STRENGTHS	DEVELOPMENTAL NEEDS
Activities in which I am proficient:	Activities I have not performed:
Technical/professional knowledge that I have:	Technical/professional knowledge that I would have to learn:
Demands, restrictions, or characteristics that excite me:	Demands, restrictions, or characteristics that concern me:
Managerial skills in which I am strong:	Managerial skills I need to develop:

Developmental activities (what could I do to better prepare myself for this position?):

Position Guide

Position Title: _____   **Position Title No.** _____

STRENGTHS	DEVELOPMENTAL NEEDS
Activities in which I am proficient:	Activities I have not performed:
Technical/professional knowledge that I have:	Technical/professional knowledge that I would have to learn:
Demands, restrictions, or characteristics that excite me:	Demands, restrictions, or characteristics that concern me:
Managerial skills in which I am strong:	Managerial skills I need to develop:

Developmental activities (what could I do to better prepare myself for this position?):

6. REALITY TESTING

Purpose: A career plan that is both realistic and attainable requires asking yourself difficult questions. This section involves reality testing, the process of examining anything that might be a barrier to the fulfillment of your career plans. Your challenge is both to become aware of potential barriers *and* to determine how these barriers might be overcome or turned into gateways.

Barriers might be categorized as: personal barriers that involve your own motivation and commitment to making your career plan a reality, and organizational barriers that involve departmental structure and size, availability of positions, and unwritten norms regarding qualifications you are expected to have.

Personal Barriers

Why are you planning your career now?

How committed are you to your long-range goals?

How willing are you to sacrifice valued off-the-job activities to accomplish on-the-job tasks? (See previous section on Activity Analysis.)

Do you have the necessary technical and professional knowledge and the desire to perform as an individual contributor (committed to the professional ladder), or do you have the necessary managerial skills and interest to move into a managerial role?

What are the major personal deficiencies that may hinder your movement upward?

Have your personal values ever conflicted with your job role or career expectations? Explain. Might this type of thing continue to be a problem?

How many hours a week are you willing to devote to your job?

How willing are you to work extra hours?

Do you leave work immediately at quitting time?

Would you be willing to work weekends or nights if job requirements demanded it?

How mobile are you? Are you willing to put geographical location ahead of your career? Why?

How do family and off-the-job commitments affect your career plans? Is this acceptable to you?

Do you see any other personal barriers that might hinder your movement upward? Describe them. How might they be overcome?

Organization Barriers

Have you considered the structure and size of the departments in which you have a career interest? (Refer to your organization's functional charts in those departments in which you have made a career choice, and write down potential bottlenecks or positions where the numbers are limited. For example, perhaps the Liquid Polymers Department has been a popular career choice in the past, but it consists of only six people and is therefore very limited with regard to availability.)

Have you received feedback through either formal or informal channels as to how you are perceived at higher levels in the company? Might any of these perceptions serve to block your movement? How might these be overcome?

Do you have reason to believe that your supervisor would attempt to block your movement? Would your supervisor let you make a lateral move that is part of your career plan and contributes to your development?

If you have considered looking for a position outside of the company, what about the company or your circumstances has led you to consider this course of action? Are these issues still relevant? Can they be overcome?

(continued)

Often there are unwritten but perfectly reasonable norms regarding movement into certain positions. It is in your best interest to seek out information regarding these norms. Write down the result of your inquiry in each of the departments you contact.

Do you foresee any other organizational barriers that might hinder your movement upward? Describe them. How might they be overcome?

What concerns do you have about career planning?

Seek independent confirmation of your self-analysis with a peer who knows you well. Ask for confirming *and* contradicting data. Objective input to self-assessments are very important to keeping them realistic. What are the differences in views between how you see yourself and how others see you?

7. FOLLOW-UP

Once the worksheets are completed ask yourself whether you feel prepared and committed enough to submit your career plan for review and approval by management. Along with the decision to proceed, there is some risk. For example, you may receive unexpected negative feedback (*but* this is information that you need to know and you might never have received it); or you may be offered a lateral move rather than a promotional move (*but* this widens your experience and will make you more qualified at higher levels).

Following completion of the career-planning worksheet below, your next step is to request a career-planning discussion with your supervisor. Essentially, the two of you will develop a career plan to which both of you are committed. You should be ready to accept any position you have listed on your career plan. Your supervisor should feel committed to supporting the career plan through the levels of review, and then later to provide you with the opportunities you need to accomplish your developmental activities.

Employee's Career-Planning Worksheet

Used to summarize your workbook thinking, this can be very helpful in preparing for your meeting with your supervisor, should you choose to request one. Provide a copy to your supervisor prior to the meeting. The categories of information correspond to sections in the workbook; the entries are numbered consecutively to facilitate point-by-point discussion with your supervisor. Following the meeting you will submit a career plan identifying positions of interest to you.

Employee's Name: _____ **Date:** _____

PERSONAL WORK HISTORY

1. The things I have liked most about the jobs I have held are:

2. The things I have disliked most about these jobs are:

3. The major assets or strengths I have brought to jobs are:

4. The major liabilities or shortcomings I have brought to jobs are:

5. Some of my major accomplishments, or significant achievements, are:

6. Some of my major disappointments, or failures, are:

ACTIVITIES

7. The types of tasks, or activities, I perform best are:

8. The types of tasks, or activities, I perform least well are:

9. The developmental activities I could perform to become better qualified are:

POSITION KNOWLEDGE

10. The five most knowledgeable areas I have are:

11. Other types of knowledge I have are:

12. The types of knowledge I most need are:

13. The developmental activities I could perform to learn these knowledge areas are:

MANAGERIAL SKILLS

14. The four managerial skills in which I am strongest are:

15. The managerial skills in which I am weak are:

16. The developmental activities I could perform to practice and develop these managerial skills are:

BARRIERS

17. The personal barriers that concern me are:

18. The organizational barriers that concern me are:

Index

Academy of Management, 235
Accommodation, 209
Accountability, 142
Actual movement, 70
Adaptability, 245–46, 251–52
The Adult Learner: A Neglected Species, 123–24
Age bulge, 21
Age Discrimination in Employment Act, 118
Aging, 118
AMA, 103, 104, 141, 150
American Chemical Society, 118
American Indians, 249
American Society for Training and Development, 235
American Society of Personnel Administration, 22
American Telephone and Telegraph (AT&T), 53, 55, 62, 212, 243
Andrews, F. M., 210
Annual development plans, 246
Anticipatory socialization, 209
Anxiety, 216
Apprenticeships, 180, 210–11, 261
Archambeau, Dennis, 47
Army, U.S., 247
Arvey, R. D., 156
Assessment
  approaches to, 64, 95–96
  effectiveness in, 96
  employee participation in, 96
  errors in, 96
  feedback systems, 95
  individual development discussions, 98–99
  lectures as, 63
  for merit salary review, 95, 98
  by organizations, 18, 25–27
  performance, 95
  for personal development, 19, 95
  for promotional opportunity, 95
  use of videotapes in, 58
Assessment centers, 52–63
  development of, 53, 57
  development use of, 62
  ethics and, 62–63
  job selection and, 62
  minorities and, 55
  nominations, 73
  participant feedback, 57, 58
  problems with, 53–54
  supervisory review, 60
  team meetings, 58
  utility of, 56
  validity of, 55–56
Assignment procedures, 19
Assignments, 124–26
Automation, 70
Autonomy, 4, 129, 161, 176
Azrin, N. H., 199, 218

Bachhuber, T. D., 196
Badawy, M. K., 55, 67
Bailyn, L., 124, 213
Baruch, R., 252
Basic research, 189, 192
Basic training, 209
Basset, G. A., 96
Behavioral documentation, 58
Behavior modeling, 133, 229, 263
Behavior modification theory, 199
Behavior Observation Scales, 27
Behaviors, career, 184
Bell, C. H., 157
Bell Labs, 5
Bench strength, 31
Benefits, 36
Berlew, D. E., 33, 245
Besalel, V. A., 218
Blacks, 55, 249
Blender, M. D., 212

Bolles, R. N., 119, 187, 188, 190, 199, 200, 201, 227–28
Bowen, D. D., 250
Brett, J. M., 252, 253, 256
British War Office Selection Board, 53
Brittain, W. P., 217
Brousseau, K. R., 252
Brown, E. M., 156
Bruni, J. R., 254
Buchanan, B., 209
Bucher, G. C., 212
Burack, E., 130
Burn-out, 130
Business games, 262
Business goal summary, 84
Business-plan-based (BPB) reviews, 69, 74–76, 82–83
  business issues, 75, 83
  demographic mix profiles, 82–83
  functional excellence, 83
  level of, 89–90
  organizational structure, 75
  personnel actions, 75, 83
  promotability mix summaries, 76
  technologies covered, 76

Canadian Civil Service, 25
Career Action Planning program, 201
Career anchors, 175–77
Career assessment. *See* Assessment
Career changes, 212
  occupational field, 252
  professional to manager, 252
Career counseling, 230
  self-help workbooks, 246
  workshop approaches, 234–35, 246
Career decisions, 6, 168–77, 249–51
  aids for, 19

289

Career decisions (cont.)
  choice of job, 191-94
  government vs. private industry, 188-89
  location, 187-88
  process in, 250
  professional service employment, 189
  purpose of organizations, 188
  research vs. application, 192-93, 202
  self-employment, 189
  size of organization, 188
  staff vs. line, 189-90
Career development
  definition of, 7
  key issues in, 254
  research on, 254-56
  systems, 241-42
Career Development Planning program, 201
Career Development Position Guides, 105, 107
Career Dimensions, 201
Career exploration, 196
Career management
  definition of, 6
  equal opportunity provisions, 244
  incentives in, 243-44
  informal, 68
  information systems in, 247
  practices, 21
  systems integration in, 247
  systems models, 13-16
Career management programs, 99
  approval procedures, 104-5
  complexity of, 102
  costs of, 102
  degree of formality of, 102
  goals for, 100-101
  individual information, 108
  individual needs, 102
  jobs information, 105, 107-8
  lateral movement and, 103
  level-by-level review, 104-5
  long-term needs, 102-3
  optimal characteristics of, 100
  organizational needs, 101-2
  problems with, 100, 104
  professional vs. bureaucratic needs, 100
  savings in, 101
  short-term needs, 102-3
  supervisory role, 108
  targets for participation, 103-4
  voluntary participation in, 103
Career management systems
  commitment to success of, 143-44, 148
  consultants and, 141
  corporate management information, 17
  current practices, 22-28
  evaluation of, 21, 145, 149, 158
  external inputs, 13
  feedback to employees, 145-46, 149
  implementation of, 20-21
  internal inputs, 13-14
  linkage with other programs, 145, 148-49
  materials, 142
  occupational classification, 17
  organizational commitment to, 143-44, 148
  outputs, 16
  personnel staff and, 141
  policies, 141-42, 159-63
  prepackaged, 141
  procedures, 142
  processes, 14-16
  revisions, 145, 149
  rewards, 17
  scheduling for, 144, 148
  supervisory roles, 162-63
  training for, 143, 144, 148
  visibility of, 145, 149
Career paths, 86, 102, 114
  dual career ladders, 114-16
  lattice, 114
  management ladder, 114
  matrix, 114
  shoestring, 114
Career patterns, 114
Career Pattern Study, 243
Career planning, 6-7
  books, 235-36
  discussions, 230-34
  disincentives to participation in, 99
  individual, 223-24
  individual differences and, 248-49
  key issues in, 248
  management by objectives (MBO), 224-26
  newsletters and bulletins, 235
  organizational role in, 19
  paired-comparison process, 226-27
  passivity in, 102
  review of plan, 73
  supervisory skills training, 228-32
  workbooks, 40, 267-89
  workshops for, 234-35, 246
Careers
  definition of, 169
  linear, 174-75
  spiral, 175
  steady-state, 174
  style, 173-75
  transitory, 175
Career stages, 177-81
  late-career, 179, 244
  mid-career, 178-79, 214, 244
Career structures, 242-43
Career success orientations, 179
Carnegie-Mellon University, 170
Carvell, F. J., 153
Cascio, W., 56
Case studies, 263
Challenge, 212
Change, 151-53, 154, 177, 209
  social, 182
  technological, 69-70, 182
Changing Supervisor Behavior, 229
Choices
  evaluation of, 190-91
  of jobs, 191-94
  managers vs. professionals, 202-3
  of organizations, 187-90
Coaching, 262
Coch, L., 152
Cognitive decision styles, 173
Cohen, R., 126
Cohen, S. L., 101
Colleagues, 180
College placement services, 200
Color-coding, 75-76, 82-83
Columbia University, 133
Comparative failure, 213
Compensation, 36, 40
Competence, 5
  managerial, 176
  requirements for, 84
  technical/functional, 175
Computers, 246
  as aids, 251
  and professional obsolescence, 130
Consulting, 192
Content validity, 57
Control points, 145
Co-op program, 194
Cooptation, 211
Cost/benefit analyses, 131, 132
Creativity, 176
Cross-functional moves, 124-25

Dalton, G. W., 180-81
Debasement experiences, 211
Decision Analysis Chart (DAC), 35, 47
Decision implementation, 251
Decision-making. *See also* Career decisions
  cognitive styles in, 173-75
  dependent, 170-71
  intuitive, 170
  reasons for, 171-77
  social learning theory, 181-84
Demographic mix profiles, 82
Demotions, 16, 124, 147
Departmental meetings, 38-40
Derr, C. B., 179
Developmental opportunities, 73
Developmental positions, 33
Development of professionals. *See* Professional development
Development plans
  individual, 74
  special project, 74
  work group, 74
Dewhirst, H. D., 156
Dictionary of Occupational Titles, 193
Disengagement, 178
Dixon, R. C., 181
Drexel University, 24
Driver, M. J., 173-75, 176, 249
Dual-career families, 187, 244, 255-56
Dual-career ladders, 114-16
Duffy, J. F., 254
Dyer, L. D., 253

Early Identification of Management Potential Research, 243
Economic downturns, 119
Education
  adult, 123-24, 130
  for career management, 244
  continuing, 20, 211, 214-15
  formal, 133-34
  in-house training, 20, 26
  levels of, 26
  long-term, 15-16, 20
  managerial, 86
  methodology, 132-33
  on-the-job training, 133, 245, 261-62
  professional, 86, 211
  programs, 133
  systems, 130-35

for unemployed professionals, 218
Eiduson, B. T., 210
Employee inventories, 74
Employee relations, 37
Employees
  annual reports to, 38
  first jobs of, 33-35
  stability of, 82
  terminated, 116
Employee training programs, 13-14
Employers
  access to, by job-seekers, 195-96
  types of, 188-89
Encounter, 209
The Endicott Report, 196
Engineers, role expectations of, 67
Entropy, 154
Entry-level positions, 32-33
Environmental conditions, 181
Equal employment opportunity, 47, 102, 182
Equitable compensation, 244
Esso Chemical Research Laboratory, 201
Establishment, 178
Ethical issues, 62
Ethics, 2, 3
Excellence, standards of, 3, 5
Expected utility (EU) theory, 169
Expertise, 2
Exploration, 177
Exxon, 243

Family ties, 187
Farr, J. L., 252
Federal Bureau of Investigation (FBI), 55
Federal personnel career program, 24
Feedback, 58, 59, 69, 87, 145-46, 244, 247
  informal systems for, 95
Feeder positions, 72
Feldman, D. C., 209
Figgins, R., 35
Financial counseling, 117
Fine, Sidney, 201
Finkle, R. B., 54
Florida Power and Light, 25
Flory, C., 153
Follow-up, 145
Forty Plus, 198, 218
French, J. R. P., 152
French, L., 125
French, W. L., 35, 157

Friendships, 187
Fringe benefits, 197-98

General Electric, 24, 53, 55, 96, 201
General Telephone Company of Florida (GTF), 46, 47-48
Genetic endowment, 181
Geographical location, 253
Geographic relocation, 218
Glaser, B. G., 213
Glueck, W. F., 170, 245
Goal displacement, 244
Goals
  individual, 225-26
  management vs. professional, 156
  organizational, 225
Goldstein, A. P., 229
Government, 188
Grass, D., 67, 147
Growth, 177
GTE, 46, 55, 131
Gutteridge, T. G., 23

Hackman, J. R., 209
Hall, D. T., 33, 212, 224, 245, 250
Hamner, W. C., 181
Handbook for Analyzing Jobs, 40
Harless, J. H., 132
Harren, V. A., 170-71, 248
Harvard Business Review, 162
Harwood, R. K., 196
Hewlett-Packard, 201, 247
Hierarchical ladders, 114
Hiring, 13
Hoch, R. R., 252
Holiday Inns, 247
Holland, J. L., 172-73, 187, 250, 253, 256
Holzbach, R. I., 7
Howard, T., 154
Huck, J. R., 56
Human resource policies, 159-62
Human resource programs
  administration of, 149
  complexity of, 146
  comprehensiveness, 157-58
  cost of, 146
  development of, 147, 154-55, 157-59
  failures in, 153
  implementation, 148-59
  lateral movement, 146, 147
  procedures, 147-48
  selection for, 146-47
  short-term and long-term needs, 146

Human resource programs (*cont.*)
  threats to the individual, 151
  threats to the organization, 150-51
  voluntary participation, 146
Human resource reviews
  business-plan-based, 69, 74-76, 82-83
  individual needs and, 68-69
  "knowledge-area"-by-person matrix, 92
  organizational, 69-74
  organizational needs and, 68
  position-to-person matrix, 91, 92
  for project terms, 93
  purpose of, 67-68
  tactical work-group, 69, 83-87
  technical/scientific careers and, 67, 87
Human resources inventories, 45
Human resource system, 7

Identification, professional, 2-3, 5
Imprinting, 36, 210
Individual development discussions, 98
Individual development planning
  desired outcomes, 136-37
  follow up, 138
  need identification, 136
  needs analysis, 135-36
  plan identification, 137
  timetable, 137-38
Individual development plan (IDP), 68, 135, 136, 138
Information
  collection of, 145
  on individuals, 108
  storage and retrieval of, 145, 149
  systems in career management, 247
Integrated Personnel System, 47-48
Internal résumés, 76
International Business Machines (IBM), 53, 55, 133, 161, 247
  Federal Systems Division, 24
Internships, 18, 24, 194
Interviewing, 196-98
Intuition, 170-71
Inventories, skill, 18

Job clubs, 198-99, 216
Job counseling, 218
Job-match, 35, 108
Job misalliance, 47
Job performance, 14

Job satisfaction, 101
Job searches, 194-202
  establishing a salary, 197
  fringe benefits, 197-98
  from another organization, 198-201
  internal, 201
  interviewing, 196-97
  locating potential employers, 195-96
  résumés, 195
  students and, 194-98
  tactics, 200-201
  unemployed professionals and, 198-201
Jobs
  analysis of, 40
  bidding for, 111
  changing, 124, 252
  characteristics of, 127
  comparison of, 193-94
  loss of, 116, 216
  posting of, 47, 111
  previews of, 18, 24
  rotation of, 262
  types, 191-93
Johnson, L. K., 181

Kaufman, H. G., 116, 117, 119, 129, 155, 200, 201, 212, 213-20, 251, 252, 253
Key positions, 70, 72
Knowledge, 155
  search for, 192
  specialized, 2
  and training systems, 131
"Knowledge-area"-by-person matrix, 92
Knowles, Malcolm, 123, 201
Kotter, John P., 201, 250
Kozlowski, S. W. J., 252
Kraut, A. I., 56
Krumboltz, J. D., 171, 181-84, 248

Labor laws, 182
Lateral movement, 103, 125, 146, 147
Lawler, E. E., 209
Lawrence Livermore Laboratory, 250
Lawrence, P. R., 152, 153
Leach, J. J., 23, 150
Leadership, 130
Learning
  direct, 182

  indirect, 182
  processes, 244-45
Leibowitz, Z. B., 228-29
Lewin, K., 210
Lewin's field theory, 33
Liang, T. T., 114
Licensing, 182
Life insurance, 198
Life planning, 19, 227-28
Life-span career development, 253
Lindeman, E. C., 123
Line personnel, 189-90
Lippitt, G. L., 153
London, M., 245, 246
Louis, M. R., 253
Loyalty
  employee, 22
  professional, 2-3

McCormick, E. J., 43
McGehee, W., 124
MacKenzie, R. A., 153
Mager, R. F., 131
Maintenance, 178
Management
  abilities, 40-43
  definition of, 202-3
  professionals in, 6, 16
Management by Objectives (MEO), 224-26
Management Progress Study, 55, 212
Management trainee programs, 72
Managerial nominations, 52
Managerial positions, 33-34
Manager vs. professional, 203, 252
Manpower planning, 67, 242
Mansfield, R., 212
Marcson, S., 35
Martin Marietta, 24
Matching, person-to-position, 34, 43, 46-47
Mathys, N., 130
Matrix configurations, 114
Matrix management roles, 92
Mead Corporation, 24
Meahea, L. W., 254
Meaning, 228
Medcof, J. W., 67
Medical plans, 198
Mental health, 117-18
Mental-health assistance, 216
Mentors, 144, 180, 245, 251
Methodology, 132-33
Meyer, H. H., 96, 101
Mid-career crisis, 179

Miller, G. A., 212
Minor, F. J., 251, 253
Minorities, 182, 249, 255
Minority groups, 55
MIT, 203
Mix distribution, 82
Monsanto, 26
Moravec, M., 103, 104
Morrison, R. F., 7, 155, 156, 163, 206, 252
Motivation, 132, 214
Moving expenses, 198. *See also* Geographical relocation
Multiattribute utility theory (MAUT), 169
Mutual acceptance, 210

National Training Laboratories, 211
Navy, Department of the, 114, 156, 247
Needs studies, 131
New data, 210
Newspaper ads, 200
Nicholson, N., 252
Norms, 159
North Carolina State University, 24

Obsolescence, 202
    avoidance of, 16, 26, 213-15, 252
    in organizations, 1-2, 130
    professional, 22, 129-30
Odiorne, G. S., 225
Office of Strategic Services (O.S.S.), 53
Openness, 92
Organ, D. W., 181
Organization
    mechanistic, 152
    organic, 152
Organizational appraisal, 95-97. *See also* Assessment
Organizational behavior and performance, 194
Organizational climate, 127
Organizational dependability, 209
Organizational development (OD), 150, 158
Organizational Entry, 191, 210
Organizational planning, 242
Organizational reality, 210
Organizations
    accountability in, 142
    change in, 151-53
    choice of, 187-91
    diagnoses, 157
    fairness, 142
    government, 188-89
    information requirements, 38-40
    location of, 187-88
    obsolescence in, 1-2, 130
    on-the-job learning, 123-26, 134
    paternalistic, 102
    philosophy, 141-42
    planning in, 157-58
    private, 188-89
    professional service, 189
    professionals in, 167-68
    purpose in, 188
    size of, 188
    slow-growth periods in, 68
    structure of, 75
Orientation, 18, 24, 261
    systems, 31, 36-38
Otte, F. L., 159
An Ounce of Analysis, 132
Outplacement, 16, 20, 27-28, 116-18, 198
    definition of, 116

Parallel ladder programs, 161
Passages, 167
Past learning experiences, 182
Paterson, D. G., 171
Pearson, Joan M., 38
Peer review, 52
Pelz, D. C., 210
Pensions, 198, 219-20
People calls, 86
People development, 230
People reviews, 76
Performance, 209
    annual reviews of, 95
    assessment of, 51, 95
    department review, 69-70
    measurement of, 57
    problems, 147
    records, 201
Perrucci, R., 252
Personal contacts, 200
Personal development, 5
Personality types, 172
Personnel
    automatic search system for, 46
    movement of, 75-76
    selection of, 47
Personnel Journal, 148
Personnel staffs
    actions of, 75
    role in career management, 141, 157
Peterson's Guide to Engineering, Science, and Computer Jobs, 133
Placement, 18
    career management systems and, 144
    internal systems, 40
    strategies for, 92
Policies
    cliche vs. budgetary, 160-61
    doing vs. supervising, 162
    formal vs. normative, 159-60
    salary administration, 161-62
    supportive vs. antagonistic, 160
Porter, L. W., 209
Position analysis questionnaire, 43
Position fill requirements, 44
Position information, 45-47
Position profiles, 46
Position-to-person matrix, 91, 92
Potential assessment, 51-52
Power, 176
Prearrival, 209
Private employment agencies, 200
Private industry, 188
Productivity, 131
Professional development, 123
    audit, 134-35
    educational systems, 130-35
    individual planning, 135-38
    on-the-job learning, 123-26
Professional Education, 210
Professionals
    in administrative support, 192-93
    career decisions of, 168-77
    career stages of, 180-81
    characteristics of, 3-6
    colleagual associations, 188, 200
    definition of, 2-3, 167-68
    development of, 147
    disengagement of, 16
    job changes as, 213
    management by, 192, 202-3, 252
    needs of, 1
    outplacement of, 117
    personality characteristics of, 4
    plateaued, 131
    retirement of, 118-19
    scientists as, 3
    self image, 117
    unemployed, 198-201, 215-19
Professional service organizations, 189
Professionals in Search of Work, 200, 201, 215
Profitability, 131
Profit-sharing, 198

Programmed instruction, 265
Project assignments, 125
Projected movement, 70
Project staffing, 70
Promotability, 31, 76
Promotability mix summaries, 76
Promotion, 14
　barriers to, 102
　technical-to-managerial, 114
Promotional moves, 103
Publishing, 20

Racial differences, 255
Rae, J. H., Jr., 247
Ranftl, R. M., 26
Ready placements, 70, 72
Reassignments, 14
Recognition, 2, 67, 68, 244
Recruitment, 18, 31, 155, 196–97
　external, 72
　filling the pipeline, 34
　first job placement, 34–36
　internal/external mix, 34
　person–position match, 34, 43
　plans, 75
Reece, J. E., 212
Reemployment barriers, 217–18
Refreezing, 210
Rensselaer Polytechnic Institute, 243
Research, 192
　independent, 16
Résumés, 195, 199–200
　in human resource reviews, 76
　internal, 47
Retention, 155
Retired Senior Volunteer Program (RSVP), 200
Retirement, 27–28, 118–19, 179, 253
　early, 118
　planning for, 20, 219
Retraining programs, 218
Review-and-challenge procedures, 90
Rifken, J., 154
Risk, 4
Roe, A., 252
Role clarity, 210
Role expectations, 67
Role management, 209
Role-playing, 235, 263
Roth, L. M., 115
Rothman, R. A., 252

Safety, 37, 131
St. John, W. D., 37
Salaries, 197

Salary reviews, 68
Schein, E. H., 5, 175–77, 178–79, 209, 210–11
Schlossberg, N. K., 228–29
Scientific competence, 151
Scientific excellence, 155–56
Scientists, 67
Sears Roebuck, 53, 55
Security Pacific Bank, 201
Seduction, 211
Selection, 18
Self-analysis, 235, 246
Self-Directed Search, 173, 187
Self-employment, 189
Self-esteem, 216, 235
Self-evaluation, 177
Self-image, 171
Self-observation generalizations, 183
Self-selection, 212
Senior Opportunities and Services (SOS), 220
Sensitivity training, 264
Service Corps of Retired Executives (SCORE), 220
Service to others, 176
Severance pay, 117
Sex differences, 249, 255
Sexual stereotyping, 177
Simon, H. A., 170
Skill classifications, 40
Skills
　administrative, 41
　building of, 144–45
　decision-making, 41–42
　managerial, 56–58
　performance, 131
　supervisory, 42–43, 228–32
　technical, 43–45, 52–53, 111
Small organizations, 188
Socialization, 209, 210
Social learning theory, 181
Sorcher, M., 229
Spanish-speaking Americans, 249
Special projects, 20
Sponsors, 180, 245, 251
Stability, 82, 171, 176
Staffing
　plans, 72, 75, 86–87
　quality, 76
　quantity, 76
　succession, 70, 72
　technological change and, 69–70
Staff personnel, 189–90
Standard Oil of Ohio (SOHIO), 53, 55
Stein, B. A., 126

Stock-purchase programs, 198
Storey, W. D., 201
Strategic retention needs, 87
Stress, 187
Strong, E. K., 171
Strong Vocational Interest Blank, 171
Students, 194–98
Succession planning, 19, 243
Succession staffing, 70
Sun Oil Company, 201, 223
Super, D. E., 171, 177–78, 201, 256
Supervisors
　accountability of, 163
　counseling training for, 230–32
　handling career-planning discussions, 232–34
　relationship with subordinates, 229–30
　role of, 228–29
Supervisory evaluations, 52
Supervisory skills, 108
　training in, 228
Support groups, 114
Survival, 228
Synergy, 154
Systematic Guide to Curriculum Development, 131
Systems in career management. *See* Career management systems
Szilagyi, A. D., Jr., 194

Tactical work-group reviews, 83
　business goal summary, 84
　career path issues, 86
　closing of, 87
　competency requirements, 84–85
　issues identification, 87
　people calls, 86
　staffing plans, 86–87
Talent, 31
Talent pools, 68, 69
Tannenbaum, A. S., 152
Task approach skills, 182, 183
Task force assignments, 126
Task Force on Assessment Center Standards, 53, 55
Tax laws, 182
Team training, 265
Technical positions, 33–34
Technical services, 192
Technical-to-managerial moves, 110–11
Technology development, 155
Temporary assignments, 125
Tenure review, 63
Tests, 63

Thompson, P. H., 180-81
The Three Boxes of Life, 119, 188, 200, 227
Training, 130-35
   needs assessment, 75
   supervisory, 143
Transfers
   downward, 124
   lateral, 125-26
Transition positions, 144
Transition support groups, 144
TRW, 116
Turnover, 47
Two-career families, 187, 244, 255-56

Unemployment, 215-19
   age and, 216
   educational level and, 216-17
   occupation and, 217
   psychological impact of, 216
   sex and, 216
   social support and, 217
   stages of, 217
Unfreezing, 210
University of Cincinnati, 24
Upward mobility, 102

Vacations, 198
Valence-instrumentality-expectancy (VIE) theory, 170
Validators, 170
Values, 183
Variety, 176
Vestibule training, 262
Volunteers in Service to America (VISTA), 220
Vosburgh, Richard, 46, 56, 69, 103, 104, 105, 148
Vroom, V. H., 170

Wager, L. W., 212
Walker, J. W., 23, 118
Wallace, M. J., Jr., 194
Wanous, J. P., 191, 210
Washington University, 26
Weyerhaueser, 27
What Color Is Your Parachute?, 187, 201
Whipple, Dennis, 47
Women, 21, 55
Work experience, 14, 244-45

Xerox, 56

Yogev, S., 256